# THE ROUTLEDGE HANDBOOK OF AUSTRALIAN INDIGENOUS PEOPLES AND FUTURES

Providing an international reference work written solely by Aboriginal and Torres Strait Islander authors, this book offers a powerful overview of emergent and topical research in the field of global Indigenous studies. It addresses current concerns of Australian Indigenous peoples of today, and explores opportunities to develop, and support the development of, Indigenous resilience and solidarity to create a fairer, safer, more inclusive future.

Divided into three sections, this book explores:

- What futures for Aboriginal and/or Torres Strait Islander peoples might look like, and how institutions, structures and systems can be transformed to such a future;
- The complexity of Aboriginal and Torres Strait Island life and identity, and the possibilities for Australian Indigenous futures; and
- The many and varied ways in which Aboriginal and Torres Strait Islander peoples use technology, and how it is transforming their lives.

This book documents a turning point in global Indigenous history: the disintermediation of Indigenous voices and the promotion of opportunities for Indigenous peoples to map their own futures. It is a valuable resource for students and scholars of Indigenous studies, as well as gender and sexuality studies, education studies, ethnicity and identity studies, and decolonising development studies.

**Bronwyn Carlson** is Head of the Indigenous Studies Department, Faculty of Arts, Macquarie University, Australia.

**Madi Day** is a Lecturer in the Department of Indigenous Studies at Macquarie University, Australia.

**Sandy O'Sullivan** is a Professor of Indigenous Studies at Macquarie University, Australia.

**Tristan Kennedy** is Pro Vice-Chancellor (Indigenous) at Monash University, Australia.

# ROUTLEDGE ANTHROPOLOGY HANDBOOKS

www.routledge.com/Routledge-Anthropology-Handbooks/book-series/RANTHBK

# THE ROUTLEDGE HANDBOOK OF AUSTRALIAN INDIGENOUS PEOPLES AND FUTURES

*Edited by Bronwyn Carlson, Madi Day,
Sandy O'Sullivan and Tristan Kennedy*

LONDON AND NEW YORK

Designed cover image: Kevin Butler, *Stairway to Kevin*, 2022. Acrylic polymer paint and enamel spray paint on canvas, 75cm x 75cm. Courtesy of the artist. Photography: Heather Froome

First published 2024
by Routledge
4 Park Square, Milton Park, Abingdon, Oxon OX14 4RN

and by Routledge
605 Third Avenue, New York, NY 10158

*Routledge is an imprint of the Taylor & Francis Group, an informa business*

*British Library Cataloguing-in-Publication Data*
A catalogue record for this book is available from the British Library

ISBN: 9781032222530 (hbk)
ISBN: 9781032222547 (pbk)
ISBN: 9781003271802 (ebk)

DOI: 10.4324/9781003271802

Typeset in Sabon
by Newgen Publishing UK

*We thank the Wallumattagal clan of the Dharug-speaking peoples for the privilege of working on their homelands where Macquarie University is located. This collection includes contributions from numerous Indigenous peoples and we respect and honour our respective ancestors and the Elders who continue to guide us.*

*The editors, who are all members of The Centre for Global Indigenous Futures, would like to dedicate this collection to Indigenous peoples worldwide. We particularly want to pay tribute to the 'Big Playas'— those Indigenous scholars who came before us and who paved the way for us to be in the academy. You have provided us with an intellectual genealogy and we are grateful for it.*

# CONTENTS

Contents

Contents

Contents

# FIGURES

# WARNING

Aboriginal and Torres Strait Islander readers are advised that this book may contain images, names and descriptions of deceased persons, as well as their artwork.

# TERMINOLOGY

Please note, there is no universally agreed-upon terminology for referring to the many diverse groups that comprise the Aboriginal and Torres Strait Islander peoples of this continent and surrounding islands. Aboriginal peoples, who, together with Torres Strait Islander peoples, are the Indigenous peoples of this place colonially referred to as Australia. Throughout the collection, many authors refer to 'so-called Australia' to make the point that this is a continent, not a country. 'Australia' as it is now referred to was built on a legal fiction of terra nullius (nobody's land) and claimed for the British Crown, despite being home to hundreds of self-identifying nations.

In many cases, authors identify and describe people by their Country names (for example, Dharug) if appropriate. Although attempts have been made to ensure these are correct, the editors acknowledge that terms and spellings may differ, and we apologise for any offence this may cause.

Country with a capital 'C' refers to the culturally defined homelands of Aboriginal and Torres Strait Islander people, for whom 'Country' is a complex term, encompassing cultural practices, customs, law, place, language, spiritual beliefs, material sustenance, family and identity all in relation to the lands, waterways and seas to which people are connected.

# CONTRIBUTORS

**Kaiya Aboagye** is a lecturer at University Western Sydney. She teaches Indigenous Social Sciences and is a PhD candidate within the School of Sociology and Social Policy at the University of Sydney. Kaiya's writing and research centres on Afro-Indigenous history, relations and experiences in the Global South. Her work offers philosophical developments in Afro-Indigenous theory, praxis and methodology. Kaiya seeks to build critical theory that is in service to Bla(c)k communities, in ways that might engender a praxis of liberation and an Afro-Indigenous language for transgression beyond the carceral dynamic of state politics over black bodies. Kaiya's ancestral lineages connect her to Zenadth Kes (Erub Island in the Torres Straits), Kuku Yalanji Nation in far north Queensland, Ni Vanuatu, and the Ashante from Ghana.

**Arlie Alizzi** is a Yugambeh postdoctoral fellow of the University of Melbourne. He is a writer, researcher and editor, and lives and works between Wurundjeri Country (Melbourne) and Yawuru Country (Broome). His research areas include Indigenous Education and queer and trans theory.

**Julie Ballangarry** is a proud Gumbaynggirr/Dunghutti woman and PhD candidate at the School of Government and International Relations at Griffith University, Brisbane.

**Dylan Barnes** is a Wiradjuri person with cultural connections to the Ngardi People of East Arnhem Land and the Darkinjung Peoples of the Central Coast, and is a research assistant and Masters of Research student at the Department of Indigenous Studies, Macquarie University.

**Rose Barrowcliffe** is Butchulla and a postdoctoral research fellow at Macquarie University. Rose's research has led her to work with libraries and archives around the country. In 2021, Rose was appointed the inaugural First Nations Archives Advisor to the Queensland State Archives (QSA). This appointment coincided with the Queensland Government's Path to Treaty. Rose's work is helping to guide QSA to promote the use of records for

Indigenous self-determination to support the Treaty process and beyond. Recognition for Rose's writing includes the 2020 Mander Jones Award and the 2021 Sigrid McCausland Emerging Writer's Award.

**Bindi Bennett** is a Gamilaraay woman, mother and social worker. She is committed to improving and growing cultural responsiveness; re-Indigenising Western spaces, understanding and exploring Indigenous Knowledge Systems and exploring the human–animal bond.

**James Blackwell** is a proud Wiradyuri man and research fellow at the Coral Bell School of Asia Pacific Affairs at the Australian National University, Canberra.

**Gawaian Bodkin-Andrews** is a member of the Bidigal clan within the D'harawal Nation, and is Professor and Director of Indigenous Research in the Office of the Deputy Vice-Chancellor Indigenous Leadership.

**Tracey Bunda** is a Ngugi/Wakka Wakka woman and grew up on the lands of the Jagera/Jugera/Yugarapul peoples. Tracey is currently the academic director of the Aboriginal and Torres Strait Islander Studies Unit, University of Queensland, and leads the whole of university Indigenisation of the curriculum and convenes the Critical Aboriginal and Torres Strait Islander Studies major in the Bachelor of Arts and Social Sciences. She is a national education leader.

**Bronwyn Carlson** is an Aboriginal woman who was born on and lives on D'harawal Country in NSW, Australia, and is the head of the Department of Indigenous Studies, Macquarie University. She is the recipient of several Australian Research Council grants, and is widely published on the topics of Indigenous cultural, social, intimate and political engagements on social media, and on colonial monuments and truth-telling. Bronwyn is the author of *The Politics of Identity: Who Counts as Aboriginal Today?* (Aboriginal Studies Press, 2016), the co-author of the book *Monumental Disruptions: Aboriginal People and Colonial Commemorations in So-Called Australia* (Aboriginal Studies Press, 2023), and is co-editor on a number of edited collections focusing on Indigenous activism on social media, and Indigenous futures. She is the founding and managing editor of the *Journal of Global Indigeneity* and is the director of the Centre for Global Indigenous Futures. In 2020, she was elected as a Fellow of the Australian Academy of the Humanities.

**Lynda-June Coe** (she/her) is a proud Wiradjuri and Badu Island woman from Erambie, Cowra NSW. She is an educator, activist and PhD student at Macquarie University where her research focus explores Indigenous resurgence in settler-colonial 'Australia'. Lynda-June is currently the Family Wellbeing and Campaign Manager for the Dhadjowa Foundation, supporting First Nations families who have been impacted by deaths in custody.

Over the past 20 years, she has engaged in community-led activism co-organising and supporting various campaigns such as 'Water is Life' climate action, Black Lives Matter, stopping Aboriginal deaths in custody and stopping the forced removal of Aboriginal children. She stems from a family and community steeped in Wiradjuri love and resistance—that legacy continues today.

**Madi Day** specialises in research concerning the relationship between settler colonialism and gendered violence, and resistance from Aboriginal and Torres Strait Islander LGBTQI+ communities. They are a lecturer and PhD candidate in the Department of Indigenous Studies at Macquarie University.

**Travis De Vries** is a Gamilaroi, Darug and Dutch concept artist, and producer. He is the host of the podcast *Broriginals*, producer of *Fear of a Black Planet*, and the founder and director of *Awesome Black*.

**Jodi Edwards** is a proud Yuin women with Dharawal kinship connections. She was awarded the inaugural Vice Chancellors postdoctoral Indigenous research fellowship at RMIT University in Melbourne in 2022. Jodi completed her doctorate at Macquarie University in 2021, entitled 'Weaving the Past into the Future: Continuity of Aboriginal Cultural Practices in the Dharawal and Yuin Nations'. Jodi is deeply interested in the continuity of cultural knowledges and practices, and her research is community centred and driven. She established the Illawarra Flame Trees in 2013 and mentored many young people, teaching language and other cultural practices. She has recently published *Dharawal Words, Phrases and Activities* (2022) and is currently researching ancient songlines along the south coast of New South Wales.

**Andrew Farrell** is a lecturer in the Department for Indigenous Studies at Macquarie University. Andrew is from Jerrinja Aboriginal community on the South Coast of NSW. Their current published research is multidisciplinary with a focus on Aboriginal LGBTIQ+ gender and sexualities, media and online studies, and drag. They are also a board member of the Aboriginal and Torres Strait Islander LGBTIQ+ community organisation Black Rainbow.

**Bronwyn Fredericks** (Aboriginal woman from SE Queensland) has over 30 years of experience working in and with the tertiary sector, state and federal governments, and Aboriginal and Torres Strait Islander community-based organisations. Bronwyn is currently Pro-Vice Chancellor (Indigenous Engagement) at The University of Queensland.

**Stephanie Gilbert** (TubbaGah Wiradjuri/Kamilaroi) is the coordinator for Aboriginal Researcher Development in the Aboriginal and Torres Strait Islander Studies Unit, University of Queensland. Stephanie has worked in higher education since the 1990s, bringing a high level of expertise to leadership, research and education with a key focus on Indigenous higher education.

**Emma Johnstone** is a First Nations Dunghutti woman, living in Dharawal Country. She is an undergraduate university student, currently studying Ancient History and Ancient Languages at Macquarie University. Emma has also studied modern history and Indigenous studies, with a focus on Indigenous oral histories. She is currently working on a project which examines the way that neurodivergent people experience academia, and hopes to further explore this field.

**Tristan Kennedy** is Pro Vice-Chancellor (Indigenous) at Monash University. He is currently working on individual and collaborative research projects that investigate Indigenous peoples' use of digital and social media. His most recent research, sponsored by Facebook Australia, culminated in an industry report titled *Indigenous Peoples Experiences of Harmful Content on Social Media*, which addresses the identification of negative and harmful content as well as survival strategies and the creation of digital counter-narratives by Indigenous peoples. Tristan is an editor of the *Journal of Global Indigeneity* and a member of the Centre for Global Indigenous Futures.

**Ambelin Kwaymullina** belongs to the Palyku people of the eastern Pilbara region of Western Australia, and is a writer, illustrator and law academic with the University of Western Australia.

**Sharlene Leroy-Dyer** is a Saltwater woman, with family ties to Darug, Garigal, Awabakal and Wiradyuri peoples. Sharlene is Associate PRME Director–Indigenous Engagement for the University of Queensland Business School and Senior Lecturer in Employment Relations. Sharlene's expertise centres around Closing the Gap on Aboriginal and Torres Strait Islander disadvantage in education and employment, focusing on the empowerment and self-determination of Aboriginal and Torres Strait Islander peoples in education, employment, entrepreneurship, leadership and governance. Sharlene contributes towards improving Indigenous employment programmes at a policy and business level, supporting Indigenous entrepreneurship and Indigenous governance.

**Noeleen Lumby** is an Aboriginal woman born on the ancestral land of the Dharawal people and a PhD candidate at Macquarie University. She has had a career in Aboriginal education and has completed a Masters of Indigenous Language Education (USYD) and a Masters of Research (MQ). Her research focus is returning language to Country, and Noeleen has supported communities in language revitalisation projects.

**Ash Markstone** is First Nations Dunghutti woman, currently living on Dharawal Country. She is an interdisciplinary academic, based in the Faculty of the Arts, Social Sciences and Humanities at the University of Wollongong. Her research areas extend across Indigenous Studies, environmental sustainability, sovereignty, domestic violence, neurodivergence, futurisms, history, education, advocacy and justice.

**Kelly Menzel** is a proud Ngadjuri woman with ancestral connections to Bundjalung Nation, and is Associate Dean (Education), Gnibi College of Indigenous Australian Peoples at Southern Cross University. She seeks to expose the causative factors of institutional racism, which, despite policies of diversity and inclusion, continue to exacerbate the socio-economic, educational and health gaps between Australia's Aboriginal and Torres Strait Islander and non-Indigenous populations, and to explore the possibilities of reforms that may facilitate Aboriginal and Torres Strait Islander peoples' social mobility through professional advancement and achievement.

**Meryn Murray** is First Nations Dunghutti woman, living on Wodi Wodi land in Dharawal Country. She is an experienced primary school teacher who has worked in South-West Sydney for the last 15 years where she has led numerous Aboriginal education initiatives within and across schools. Meryn advocates for high expectations, truth-telling, community engagement and evidence-informed practice to support Indigenous students.

**L. Wilo Muwadda** recently commenced a PhD course in Public Health at the University of Central Queensland. This is part of his journey to build his academic skills on Indigenous knowledge systems by analysing Australian Aboriginal health programmes. Wilo has spent 20 years as a health promotion officer in the field of sexual health. This includes work he has done internationally in Papua New Guinea and work he has done as a former member of the International Indigenous Working Group for HIV/AIDS under the Canadian Aboriginal AIDS Network. Wilo has a master's degree in Social Sciences (Indigenous Studies). His master's thesis is a systematic mapping review of Indigenous health research conducted by the University of Sydney. Wilo has developed an analytical framework based on the lore of reciprocity to study the processes of reciprocity in Indigenous community health research. He received an International Golden Key Award for his undergraduate degree in Indigenous Community Management and Development. Wilo focused on the Dr Cornell and Dr Begay method of 'cultural match' to develop a methodology of 'Indigenous Cultural Coherence' and apply this framework to Indigenous sexual health promotion practices in northern Queensland and Papua New Guinea. Implemented, these culturally appropriate programmes maintain Indigenous ways of disease mitigation and prevention programmes. His PhD supports the voice of Aboriginal men on sexual health, focusing on the crossroads of cultural pathways where Aboriginal men navigate sex, drug use and sexual health services in North Queensland, Australia.

**Lou Netana-Glover** is of Ngāti Whātua, Ngāpuhi and Tainui descent and belongs to the Yuin people of the south-east coast of so-called Australia. Her research interests are the relationalities of Oceanic connections, identity, and original law of place and hence settler lawlessness on place.

**Sandy O'Sullivan** is a Wiradjuri transgender/non-binary person and professor of Indigenous Studies at Macquarie University. They are a 2020–2024 ARC Future Fellow, with a project titled Saving Lives: Mapping the Influence of Indigenous LGBTIQ+ Creative Artists. The project will explore the unique contribution and influence of queer artists to understand how modelling complex identities contributes to the well-being of all First Nations' peoples. Since 1991, they have taught and researched across gender and sexuality, museums, the body, performance, design and First Nations' identity. Sandy was the inaugural director of the Centre for Collaborative First Nations' Research at Batchelor Institute in the Northern Territory and was recently Deputy Head of School of Creative Industries at the University of the Sunshine Coast. They recently completed an internationally focused Australian Research Council programme examining the representation and engagement of First Nations' Peoples across 470 museums and Keeping Places, and they continue to engage with the Museum Queeries collective in Canada. They also recently completed an ARC Linkage project mapping creative practice across the Barkly Region of the Northern Territory (Creative Barkly). Sandy's work is often across both industry and the academy, and recently they completed a national review of Aboriginal and Torres Strait Islander dance and theatre makers for the Australia Council for the Arts. In addition to their academic work, Sandy has been a musician, performer and sound artist since 1982 and has held national and international arts residencies and performed and exhibited in a range of venues.

**Jo Anne Rey** is a Dharug Aboriginal community member, through her Dharug-Randall lineage. In 2019, Jo completed her doctoral thesis: 'Country Tracking Voices: Dharug Women's Perspectives on Presences, Places, and Practices' at Macquarie University. Based on her research, in 2018 she was invited to develop a first-year undergraduate unit within the Macquarie University Indigenous Studies department. This local Aboriginal community focus was a first in Australia. In 2020, Jo became a research fellow with Macquarie University's Indigenous and Geography departments, weaving post-doctoral Dharug research across three Dharug sites: Shaw's Creek Aboriginal site, Blacktown Native Institution and Brown's Waterhole, in the Lane Cove National Park.

**Zac Roberts** is a Yuin scholar from the South Coast of New South Wales. His research interests centre on Indigenous histories, with a particular interest in interrogating the unspoken space of Indigenous narratives within the broader national history of Australia. Zac is currently a PhD candidate in the Department of Indigenous Studies at Macquarie University, where he is researching the relationship between Indigenous and Jewish communities in Australia since 1788.

**Lynette Russell** AM is an award-winning historian and Indigenous Studies scholar. She is currently a Kathleen Fitzpatrick Laureate Fellow at Monash University. She is also Deputy Director of the Australian Research Council's Centre of Excellence in Biodiversity and Heritage, and Director of the Monash Indigenous Centre. Her new research, Global Encounters & First Nations Peoples: 1000 Years of Australian History, focuses on the past 1,000 years of Australian history, documenting explorer encounters with Indigenous people prior to the arrival of the British in 1788. She has a PhD in history from the University of Melbourne and has taught and researched in the area of historical and anthropological studies for over twenty years. Lynette has supported many families through the process of ancestry research in the archives and has authored her memoir, *A Little Bird Told Me: Family Secrets, Necessary Lies*, published in 2002.

**Mykaela Saunders** is a Koori/Goori and Lebanese writer and teacher, and the editor of *This All Come Back Now*, the world's first anthology of Blackfella speculative fiction (UQP, 2022). Mykaela won the 2022 David Unaipon Award for her manuscript *Always Will Be: Stories of Goori Sovereignty from the Future(s) of the Tweed*, forthcoming with UQP in 2024. Her novel *Last Rites of Spring* was also shortlisted for the Unaipon Award in 2020, and received a Next Chapter Fellowship in 2021. Mykaela has won prizes for short fiction, poetry, life writing and research, including the Elizabeth Jolley Short Story Prize and the Oodgeroo Noonuccal Indigenous Poetry Prize.

**r e a Saunders** (Regina Saunders) is an artist, curator, activist, academic, cultural educator and creative thinker who is engaged in an arts-led, research-based practice. r e a is a descendant from the Gamilaraay/Wailwan people from the Central West New South Wales and Biripi people from the mid-North Coast of New South Wales. Their current research is located within the area of innovative research-creation, exploring how the senses both influence and shape the Indigenous experiences of the colonial archive. r e a is a lecturer in the Aboriginal and Torres Strait Islander Unit, The University of Queensland.

**Ros Sawtell** is a PhD candidate. She is an Aboriginal woman who does not know her traditional connections to Country, although she now has a connection, albeit by respectful choice, not bloodlines, where she is supported, cared for and accepted by many of the community members living on Yugambeh Language Country.

**Corrinne T. Sullivan** is an Aboriginal scholar from the Wiradjuri Nation in central-west New South Wales and an associate professor of Geography at Western Sydney University. Her multidisciplinary research interests focus on experiences and effects of body and identity in relation to Aboriginal and Torres Strait Islander peoples. Her current work explores Indigenous Australian sexuality and gender diversity through the perspectives of youth, older people and sex workers.

**Jacinta Walsh** identifies as a Jaru woman and proud mother to three boys. Jacinta is a PhD Candidate and a research officer with the Monash Indigenous Studies Centre in the Faculty of Arts at Monash University. Jacinta was adopted and raised in a non-Indigenous, multicultural family in the outer Eastern suburbs of Melbourne. She has two siblings who are of Sri Lankan descent and one brother of English descent. In 1998, Jacinta approached Link-Up and began a 20-year journey of reconnection with her Aboriginal birth father and his family in Western Australia. Jacinta's research interests lie in Aboriginal family history, narrative and identity formation and reformation, and stories of intergenerational family knowledge repatriation and reconnection.

**Tamika Worrell** is from Gamilaroi Country and has been grown up by Dharug Country Western Sydney. She is currently undertaking her PhD in the School of Education at Macquarie University. Professionally, she is a lecturer in the Department of Indigenous Studies, Macquarie University. Tamika is a contributing author to *Growing Up Aboriginal in Australia Anthology*, edited by Dr Anita Heiss.

**Frances Wyld** is a Martu woman (Aboriginal People of the Pilbara region of Australia) living on Kaurna land, a lecturer in communications, and a lecturer at the University of South Australia. She teaches Indigenous Knowledges, methodologies and cultural studies. Her doctorate used autoethnography, storywork and mythography to centre Indigenous Knowledges within an academic environment to establish an Indigenous voice for ethical research and teaching. She has an ongoing collaboration with Sámi academics in Sweden that has produced a project on climate change and Indigenous perspectives. Her publications include both scholarly and creative writing elements.

# ACKNOWLEDGEMENTS

Everyone whom we've worked with throughout the years, who have informed our research in productive ways; the Forum for Indigenous Research Excellence (FIRE), now the Centre for Global Indigenous Futures[1] (CGIF); the global symposia that have come out of FIRE and CGIF; and everyone who participated in them: Cultured queer / queering culture: Indigenous perspectives on queerness (2015); Reterritorialising social media: Indigenous people rise up (2015); Decolonising criminal justice: Indigenous perspectives on social harm (2016); Indigenous peoples rise up: An international symposium on the global ascendancy of social media activism (2019); Indigenous futurisms (2019); Digital intimacies (2022) and many more to come. To all the members of the Centre for Global Indigenous Futures who share the vision of a world in which Indigenous people are thriving. We are looking forward to all the possibilities and collaborations this global network will bring.

We would also like to acknowledge and thank our colleague Dr Terri Farrelly who supported the editors in bringing this collection into being. From chasing us to complete what was needed to keeping track of authors and compiling all that was necessary to submit to the publisher—your organisational skills are impressive.

*Bronwyn:* I want to thank my colleagues in the Department of Indigenous Studies, who are truly the best mob that someone could ever hope to work with. When you get to work with such inspirational people, work becomes productive and enjoyable. A bunch of big dreamers, schemers and networkers who I am thankful to know. For being so supportive of all that I do and who never fail to make me a lovely cup of tea, I would like to thank my partner in all things in life, Mike. I am lucky to have two supportive sisters, Noe and Deb. I would also like to acknowledge my Mum, Sandy King, and my children, Anastasia, Jason, Rebecca and Connor. I am thankful for the distractions my grannies provide me, Scarlet, Jack, Aurora, Evie, Phoenix, Isaac and Grace—you are the future.

*Madi:* Foremost, I want to thank my siblings Ellie and Cassi Day, who are my home and my greatest supporters. Thank you to my mentors, Professor Bronwyn Carlson and Professor Sandy O'Sullivan. Thank you to my community, friends and colleagues. Special thank you to A/Professor Corrinne Sullivan and Dr Jo Rey. Thank you, Karina, SG, Cass, Aims and Tetei for taking care of me and my chihuahua. Finally, thank you to the queer and trans mob who came before us, who burned this path with love, rage and tenacity.

*Sandy:* Mandaang Guwu first and foremost to Madi Day. Through their actions they provide ongoing assurance that our future is in very good hands. Mandaang Guwu to my colleague, boss and wrangler, Bronwyn Carlson, who has modelled what it is to be an Aboriginal professor in this continent. Mandaang Guwu to everyone I work with … you make my world better. As an Australian Research Council Future Fellow, my role is to expound on the complexity of who we are as Indigenous people. This anti-colonial work is only possible because of the insistence from our community, our families and all Indigenous peoples that we cannot be reduced. This Handbook represents that expansive view, and for that I am grateful. Mandaang Guwu.

*Tristan:* I want to thank my friends and colleagues in the Department of Indigenous Studies at Macquarie University who have provided a most enjoyable space to write, research and develop ideas. Working with such future-focused Indigenous scholars is a great privilege. Thanks to Evie and Audrey, Jo and Mark, you keep me grounded and offer endless support for my work. Thanks also to our amazing network of Indigenous scholars and allies across the globe. Indigenous research continues to face challenges, but thanks to the groundbreaking work and the immeasurable generosity of Indigenous peoples, the future is immensely promising.

## Note

1  See www.globalindigenousfutures.com

# INDIGENIST FUTURISMS

*Ambelin Kwaymullina*

Indigenist Futurisms
are stories
grounded in Indigenous ways of knowing
being and doing
and in our deep knowledge
of injustice
Like all our stories
our futurist narratives
are informed by the tales of our Ancestors
which tell of realities
that are holistic
non-linear
pluralist
and in which everything lives
and is related to each other

Indigenist Futurisms
can only be articulated
by Indigenous peoples
speaking across and through many knowledges
including those the West calls
literature
art
design
science
health
humanities
But in our interconnected systems
we do not divide knowledge
into these boxes

Our learning-ways
flow in circles
cycles
and connections

Indigenist Futurisms
cross what would be thought of
in a linear sense
as past
present
future
and reject the notion
that progress necessarily entails
things such as
species extinction
pollution
exploitation
inequality
We question the colonial systems
of thought and governance
that have brought these things
into Indigenous homelands
and draw on our cultural literacies
including our scientific literacies
to create futures
born of connection
between all life

Indigenist Futurisms
are hope

*Dr Ambelin Kwaymullina belongs to the Palyku people of the eastern Pilbara region of Western Australia, and is a writer, illustrator and law academic with the University of Western Australia.*

# INTRODUCTION

*Bronwyn Carlson and Madi Day*

The genesis of this book came on 24 May 2021, when Bronwyn Carlson received an email from Goenpul scholar, Distinguished Professor Aileen Moreton-Robinson that simply stated, "I forgot to mention I have nominated you as lead editor for the Routledge Handbook of Indigenous People ☺". Bronwyn was subsequently contacted by Routledge and invited to submit a proposal. Professor Aileen Moreton-Robinson is one of our 'Big Playas'—a person who is considered one of the seminal thinkers in Indigenous Studies and who is highly respected for their contribution to the academy. Moreton-Robinson and others have gifted us an intellectual genealogy that provides a foundation for us to stand upon.

Bronwyn began her university career in 1999 as an undergraduate. This was an exciting time. Jackie Huggins' influential feminist text *Sister Girl: Reflecting on Tiddaism, Identity and Reconciliation* (1998; 2022) had just been published the year before followed by two other foundational texts. The first was Moreton-Robinson's *Talking Up to the White Woman: Indigenous Women and Feminism* (1999) and the second was Māori scholar, Professor Linda Tuhiwai Smith's *Decolonizing Methodologies: Research and Indigenous Peoples* (1999). The enduring importance of both of these texts is demonstrated by the fact that both have been reprinted a number of times and in 2021, a special twentieth anniversary edition of *Talking Up to the White Woman* was released and in that same year, a third edition of *Decolonising Methodologies* was released. Both of these texts changed the landscape for Indigenous students in Indigenous Studies and provided a critique and challenge to settlers and their studies of Indigenous peoples.

Sixteen years after Bronwyn, Madi was fortunate to come through Indigenous Studies as it expanded to include a considerable canon. Nurungga academic Lester Irabinna Rigney prompted an important shift towards Indigenist research practices and an anti-colonial critique of knowledge and sciences (1999; 2001). Bronwyn's PhD supervisor, Torres Strait Islander scholar, Professor Martin Nakata, published *Disciplining the Savages, Savaging the Disciplines* (2007) enabling us to articulate our lives under settler colonialism with more agency, nuance and complexity. Nakata wrote, "one of the goals of this book is to persuade the reader that understandings of the Indigenous position must be 'complicated'

DOI: 10.4324/9781003271802-1

rather than simplified though any theoretical framing" (2007, p. 12). Similarly, Palawa scholar, Distinguished Professor Maggie Walter introduced a groundbreaking agenda challenging colonial statistics and inaugurating Indigenous data sovereignty. Edited by one of the few Indigenous sociologists in so-called Australia, Walter's edited collection *Social Research Methods* on to the fourth edition (2006; 2009; 2010; 2019) and the recent edited collection *The Oxford Handbook of Indigenous Sociology* (2021) challenged the discipline of sociology to reconsider its relationship to Indigenous lands and peoples.

Murri scholar, Professor Bronwyn Fredericks' research on urban identity, health and education applied a new vein of critical theory to the impact of knowledge, discourse and policy on everyday Indigenous lives (2006; 2009; 2013). Tanganekald, Meintangk Boandik scholar, Professor Irene Watson was the first ever Aboriginal person to graduate with a law degree in South Australia in 1985 and has profoundly influenced legal thinking on this continent ever since. Watson's 2015 book, *Aboriginal Peoples, Colonialism and International Law: Raw Law*, draws on Aboriginal law to investigate the legality and impact of colonialism from our perspectives. Like other Big Playas, Watson has an archive of publications that have given us the intellectual genealogy we need to continue the work and carve out new agendas.

In 2016, Professor Bronwyn Carlson published *The Politics of Identity: Who Counts as Aboriginal Today?* (2016) and it was immediately introduced to Indigenous Studies classrooms and curricula. Madi remembers reading this book cover to cover at their kitchen table, immersed in it even as family cooked and cleared plates and chattered around them. These canonical texts forged what we now know as Indigenous Studies. Bronwyn's work then expanded into the digital space, exploring Aboriginal and Torres Strait Islander people's social, cultural, political and intimate engagements online on social media. In 2021, she co-authored *Indigenous Digital Life: The Practices and Politics of Being Indigenous on Social Media*. Settler societies habitually frame Indigenous people as a people of the past with cultures frozen in time and our identities tied to some static notions of 'authenticity'. However, Indigenous people are actively engaged in future-oriented practice, including through new technologies. Bronwyn's work has informed a move across Indigenous Studies that now includes digital life. Noongar Professor Tristan Kennedy (2019) drew on this work in his own doctorate which focused on hypermasculinity in the online metal scene. Both Bronwyn and Madi have published on settler violence across digital platforms and particularly social media and dating sites (Carlson & Day, 2021; 2022).

The discipline continues to expand to include other interdisciplinary, anti-colonial works including those influenced by Professor Sandy O'Sullivan's diverse oeuvre of thinking on museums, creative practice, gender and queerness (2008; 2013; 2021). In 2020, the Department of Indigenous Studies at Macquarie University established the first Indigenous queer studies units extending Indigenous Studies' existing critique of coloniality and gender (O'Sullivan 2021; Day, 2021; 2020; Carlson et al., 2022; Farrell, 2022). The tree of Indigenous scholarship branches ever outwards, sprouting new and exciting branches and even seedlings of subdisciplines like Indigenous queer studies, Indigenous criminology, transnational and translocal Indigenous Studies and many more.

Many of the 'Big Playas' were the first on many levels—first in family to attend university, first to graduate and first to pursue postgraduate studies and higher degree research. While the notion of 'first' brings some celebrity, each has, however, demonstrated a generosity to those of us who have come after them. Many, if not all, of these scholars contributed to significant institutional reforms and success programmes that improved the lives and experiences of Aboriginal and Torres Strait Islander university students, and many continue this work in leadership roles to this day. Being a part of Indigenous Studies is more than joining an intellectual community, it also entails contributing to a legacy of generosity and support for future Indigenous scholars. As Black Latina scholar, Professor Lorgia García Peña writes in her book *Community as Rebellion* (2022), this is "how we survive in the face of white supremacy, and how we grow and thrive as scholars" (pp. 22–23).

There are several 'Big Playas' not mentioned here due to the confines of space who have contributed to a legacy of intellectual and practical knowledge. Those of us in the field of research from our various disciplinary perspectives know who they are as do they themselves. Collectively, the work of many Aboriginal and Torres Strait Islander thinkers and scholars has shown us a way to make sense of the world, how to navigate it, to challenge it and to survive it. The work of these scholars and practitioners has gifted us the means to critique the systems and structures that try to contain and reduce us—and at times attempt to eliminate us. They have also shown us the power in living and thinking beyond these systems. This legacy of rigorous scholarship and activism enables us to challenge, demolish constraints and imagine a world after them in which we are thriving.

This collection pays homage to the Big Playas of Indigenous Studies on this continent and is replete with contributions from Aboriginal and Torres Strait Islander peoples who are the beneficiaries of prior scholarship. While we acknowledge those who made a significant contribution in the academy, we also need to acknowledge those who provide an equally important contribution through their art activism, their creative works and community efforts outside of the academy, those who offer practical solutions to the vicissitudes of colonisation. This collection includes contributions from established scholars and early career researchers and graduate students. It includes work from creative writers including those who write on speculative fiction and the field of knowledge known as Indigenous Futurisms—a term coined by Anishinaabe scholar, Professor Grace Dillon (Dillon, 2012) to denote the manifold ways in which Indigenous peoples can explore possibilities for change, future directions and the continuity of survival. Some authors are also Elders and knowledge holders in our communities. This compilation is therefore scholastic, artistic, practical and eclectic.

The book is divided into three themes, *Future Worlds*, *Intimacies*, and *Digital Futures*. These themes are the focus of the Centre for Global Indigenous Futures (CGIF), a collective of scholars whose members include the editors and many contributors. CGIF explores the complexities of Indigenous life, ingenuity and identity in order to imagine futures in which Indigenous people are thriving. As a collective, we consider Indigenous love, joy, intimacy, sexuality, identity, care, relationality, representation and digital life, and how these might emerge and evolve to facilitate and secure futures where we flourish and grow. Global Indigenous research conducted through CGIF opens up possibilities and opportunities for Indigenous futures. CGIF aims to:

- Explore how Indigenous peoples and communities are imagining their futures
- Centre Indigenous peoples, knowledges and practices
- Challenge dominant research paradigms
- Build world-leading collaborative research capacity that is Indigenous-led and sustainable
- Ensure a continuity of research training, development and investment in Indigenous peoples and communities.

This collection meets these objectives and presents an assemblage of 30 chapters divided into three themes. The cover by Aboriginal artist Kevin Butler, titled *Stairway to Kevin* (2022), pays homage to the past but clearly articulates that we are already imagining ourselves in the future. As Tuhiwai Smith (2012, p. 255) reminds us:

> One of the strategies that indigenous peoples have employed effectively to bind people together politically, asks that people imagine a future, that they rise above present-day situations which are generally depressing, dream a new dream and set a new vision.

In a similar vein, Palyku scholar and author Ambelin Kwaymullina's prose poem 'Indigenist Futurisms' featured at the start of the collection, reminds us that "Indigenist Futurisms can only be articulated by Indigenous peoples" and that "Indigenous Futurisms are hope".

The first theme, *Future Worlds*, explores how institutions, structures and systems can be transformed towards a just future. This theme comprises 11 chapters. The second theme, *Intimacies,* explores the complexity of Indigenous life and identity and applies this research to explore future possibilities for Indigenous peoples. This section comprises 13 chapters. The final theme, *Digital Futures*, explores the many and varied ways in which Indigenous people use and fashion technology to their own needs. This third and final section includes six chapters

The chapters throughout this collection provide insights into the way in which Aboriginal and Torres Strait Islander peoples are working towards a more just future for us all. This is an original compilation whose objective is to provide a more vigorous and comprehensive understanding of what it means to be Indigenous while contemplating the possibilities of what it could mean in the future. All contributions are authored by Aboriginal and/or Torres Strait Islander people. The works are underpinned by knowledge of the past and hope for futures where we will continue to survive and flourish.

## References

Carlson, B. (2016). *The politics of identity: Who counts as Aboriginal today?* Aboriginal Studies Press.

Carlson, B., & Day, M. (2021). 'Love, hate and sovereign bodies: The exigencies of online dating'. In A. Powell, A. Flynn, & L. Sugiura, L. (Eds.), *The Palgrave handbook on gender, violence and technology* (pp. 181–202). Palgrave Macmillan.

Carlson, B., & Day, M. (2022). Colonial violence on dating apps. In H. Arden, A. Briers, & N. Carah (Eds.), *Conflict in my outlook*. University of Queensland Press.

Carlson, B., & Frazer, R. (2021). *Indigenous digital life: The practices and politics of being Indigenous on social media*. Palgrave Macmillan.

Carlson, B., Kennedy, T., & Farrell, A. (2022). Indigenous gender intersubjectivities: Political bodies. In M. Walter, T. Kukutai, A. Gonzales, & R. Henry (Eds.), *The Oxford handbook of indigenous sociology* (pp. 1–21). Oxford University Press.

Day, M. (2020). Indigenist origins: Institutionalizing Indigenous Queer and Trans Studies in Australia. *Trans Studies Quarterly, 7*(3), 367–373.

Day, M. (2021). Remembering Lugones: The critical potential of heterosexualism for studies of so-called Australia. *Genealogy, 5*(3), 1–11.

Dillon, G. L. (2012). *Walking the clouds An anthology of Indigenous science fiction*. University of Arizona Press.

Farrell, A. (2022). *Indigenous LGBTIQ+ community online* [Unpublished PhD dissertation]. Macquarie University.

Fredericks, B. (2006). Which way? educating for nursing Aboriginal and Torres Strait Islander peoples. *Contemporary Nurse, 23*(1), 87–99.

Fredericks, B. (2009). The epistemology that maintains white race privilege, power and control of Indigenous Studies and Indigenous peoples' participation in universities. *Critical Race and Whiteness Studies, 5*(1), 1–12.

Fredericks, B. (2013). 'We don't leave our identities at the city limits': Aboriginal and Torres Strait Islander people living in urban localities. *Australian Aboriginal Studies, 1,* 4–16.

Huggins, J. (1998/2022). *Sister Girl: Reflecting on Tiddaism, identity and reconciliation.* Queensland University Press.

Kennedy, T. (2019). *Writing on the wall: Hypermasculinity in the online heavy mental scene* [Unpublished PhD dissertation]. Flinders University.

Moreton-Robinson, A. (1999; 2021). *Talkin'up to the white woman: Indigenous women and feminism.* University of Minnesota Press.

Nakata, M. (2007). *Savaging the disciplines: Disciplining the savages.* Aboriginal Studies Press.

O'Sullivan, S. (2008). Indigenous imprint: multimedia/intermedia strategies as an Indigenous dissemination tool for practice-based research. *Ngoonjook, 32,* 51–55.

O'Sullivan, S. (2013) Reversing the gaze: Considering Indigenous perspectives on museums, cultural representation and the equivocal digital remnant. In L. Ormond-Parker, A. Corn, C. Fforde, K. Obata, & S. O'Sullivan (Eds.), *Information technology and indigenous communities* (pp. 139–150). IGI Global.

O'Sullivan, S. (2021). The colonial project of gender (and everything else). *Genealogy, 5*(3), 67.

Peña, L. G. (2022). *Community as rebellion: A syllabus for surviving academia as a woman of color.* Haymarket Books.

Rigney, L. I. (1999). Internationalization of an Indigenous anticolonial cultural critique of research methodologies: A guide to Indigenist research methodology and its principles. *Wicazo sa review, 14*(2), 109–121.

Rigney, L. I. (2001). A first perspective of Indigenous Australian participation in science: Framing Indigenous research towards Indigenous Australian intellectual sovereignty. Lecture. Flinders University, Adelaide.

Smith, T. L. (1999/2012). *Decolonising methodologies: Research and Indigenous peoples,* University of Otago Press.

Walter, M. (Ed.) (2006; 2009; 2010; 2019). *Social research methods.* Oxford University Press.

Walter, M., Kukutai, T., Gonzales, A. A., & Henry, R. (Eds.) (2021). *The Oxford handbook of Indigenous sociology.* Oxford University Press.

Watson, I. (2015). *Aboriginal peoples, colonialism and international law: Raw law.* Routledge.

# PART I

# Future worlds

This section explores what futures for Australian Indigenous people might look like, and how institutions, structures and systems can be transformed towards a just future, such as:

- What a sustainable future might look like for Australian Indigenous people
- Country and climate change
- What future work, housing, home, health and well-being, social life, sovereignty and justice might look like for Australian Indigenous people
- The future of global Indigenous networks

DOI: 10.4324/9781003271802-2

# 1

# THE FUTURE IS INDIGENOUS

*Bronwyn Carlson*

### Introduction

One of the strategies that indigenous peoples have employed effectively to bind people together politically, asks that people imagine a future, that they rise above present-day situations which are generally depressing, dream a new dream and set a new vision.

*(Linda Tuhiwai Smith, 2012, p. 255)*

As I write this chapter, the world is still in the grip of the Covid-19 pandemic, with new strains challenging health professionals in terms of vaccinations and keeping people safe. Across this continent now colonially referred to as Australia,[1] floods and bushfires are becoming regular features of the evening news. Only recently we saw the devastation of the horror summer of bushfires across the homelands of peoples on the east coast and other parts of the continent. The bushfires were unprecedented in this area and ravaged 5.8 million hectares and killed an estimated billion more-than-human ancestors. The communities on the mid-north coast have experienced constant flooding to levels that have not been seen before.

Indigenous people have for a long time called for our knowledges to be respected and to be operationalised to help combat the damage that settlers have done and continue to do to our homelands. We have largely been ignored unless it has been in the interests of the settlers. Although we have been written out of most future thinking and planning across settler colonial nations, we continue to imagine futures in which Indigenous peoples are thriving. It all begins with 'imagining otherwise' as noted by Cherokee scholar Daniel Heath Justice (2012). This chapter proposes that the future is Indigenous—settlers have strived for our elimination but we are still here. This chapter will first outline colonisers' efforts to eliminate us to claim our homelands as their own. I will also draw attention to how this continues in contemporary times through policy and practice including state-sanctioned killings (Allam & Evershed, 2019). Maintaining colonial narratives about discovery assists settlers to imagine they have right to our homelands due to our failings as peoples with no futures. Demonstrating how colonialism limits the ability to even imagine

DOI: 10.4324/9781003271802-3

otherwise, I discuss hope as a strength that drives our determination. Discussing radical hopeful imaginaries, I turn to Indigenous Futurisms as a field that provides not only hope but guides us to imagine otherwise as an act of visioning that plants the seeds of the future which is not yet here.

## Our imminent disappearance

From the moment the colonisers arrived, Indigenous people were seen as only a temporary people, soon to be left behind by the unstoppable forward march of modernity. As explained by Kanaka Maoli scholar Noelani Goodyear-Ka'ōpua, Indigenous people were posited as "mere vestiges of a quickly fading and increasingly irrelevant past" (2017, p. 184). For the first two centuries of settlement across this continent, popular ideas from race science dominated settler thinking, which straightforwardly envisioned a future that did not include Indigenous peoples (Carlson, 2016b; Carlson & Frazer, 2021). Through the establishment of public policy and discourse, settlers actively sought to bring about a vision of a 'new country' that did not include Indigenous people. Policies of segregation, separation, absorption and assimilation variously but directly sought to hasten our disappearance (see Carlson, 2016b). For example, one of the first pieces of legislation to be passed following Federation, the White Australia Policy passed in 1901, highlighted how racial purity was essential to building of the new nation. Then-Attorney General Alfred Deakin stated:

> We have the power to deal with people of any and every race within our borders, except the aboriginal [sic] inhabitants of the continent, who remain under the custody of the States. There is that single exception of a dying race; and if they be a dying race, let us hope that in the last hours they will be able to recognize not simply the justice, but the generosity of the treatment which the white race, who are dispossessing them and entering into their heritage, are according them.[2]

This extraordinary claim which speaks not only to the 'right' of dispossession but also the plan for racial purity, lays the foundation for the reinvented nation as it summons the gratitude Indigenous people are expected to demonstrate in their dying days. Additionally, in the newly established constitution, Section 127 provided that, "Aboriginal natives were not to be counted for the purposes of calculating population numbers" (Arcioni, 2012, p. 288). Clearly, in the new look for the future of a federated country, Indigenous people would not exist. It was fully expected that we would not be here to bear witness to the atrocities committed against us and our homelands.

Imagining our demise was a preoccupation of settlers and was deeply embedded in their knowledge production and taught through their institutions. Anthropology, for example, is a discipline that has been particularly complicit with this thinking. Much anthropological research has only considered Indigenous peoples in the past (Deloria, 2020; Carlson, 2016b; Gray, 2007). Indeed, research in this field can be viewed as both predicting and aiding the total, imminent disappearance of us. Anthropologists have contributed to the volume of research that has deemed us biologically inferior, on the brink of extinction, and it was used to rationalise, justify, develop and hone policies of Indigenous elimination (Nakata, 2007; Deloria Jr, 1988). Anthropologists were agents of the colonial government focused on our demise. Research that supported these views built the careers, wealth and reputation of many anthropologists. Anthropologists wrote of Indigenous people as somehow 'stuck' in a static past, incapable of cultural change. Any evidence of cultural change only became understood as further proof of the disappearance of supposedly 'authentic' Indigenous people (Carlson, 2016b). Native American scholar Vine Deloria Jr (1988, p. 78) captured the sentiment that many Indigenous peoples hold when thinking about how anthropologists have infiltrated our communities and built long and lasting careers writing about what we lack. Deloria Jr argues: "Into each life, it is said, some rain must fall, some people have bad horoscopes, others take tips on the stock market […] But Indians have been cursed above all other people in history. Indians have anthropologists" (1988, p. 78).

As objects of scientific enquiry, then, Indigenous peoples were given no opportunity for alternative futures: we could either die out biologically and culturally, as predicted; or we could become like the settler, and lose our Indigenous identities. This complete foreclosure of Indigenous futures is no accident; it is central to the logic of settler futurity. Settler colonialism, as a political structure as we now know (see Wolfe, 2006), and explained by Unangax̂ scholar Eve Tuck and colleague Rubén Gaztambide-Fernández (2013, p. 73) "aims to vanish Indigenous peoples and replace them with settlers, who see themselves as the rightful claimants to land, and indeed, as indigenous". A particularly public example is that of Senator Pauline Hanson, leader of the Australian One Nation political party, who has made numerous claims that she is Indigenous because she was born in Australia. In 2019, Hanson was filmed confronting a group of young Indigenous people, telling them, "I'm Indigenous, I was born here, I'm native to the land. So, you know, I'm Australian as well, and I'm Indigenous" (cited in Carlson & Kennedy, 2021, p. 5). Tuck and Yang (2021) identify the widespread settler desire to 'become Indigenous', and thereby claim a legitimate connection to the stolen land they occupy. Hanson continued to pester the young people. "Do you know the word Indigenous? It means native to the land, I was born here", she said. In what quickly became a laughable moment for Indigenous people across social media platforms, Hanson then asked, "Where's my land if not Australia?", to which one of the young people responded by telling Hanson that her land was, "um, England".[3] Despite the hilarity this evoked in many Indigenous people, we understand how powerful this kind of belief can be, how it can take hold and assume authority. After all, the original claim to our land is based on the assumption of rightful ownership.

I have previously written extensively about the politics of identity (see Carlson, 2016b), which is arguably another tool of settler colonialism that works to eliminate Indigenous peoples by constantly engaging in arguments about who or what counts as an 'authentic' Indigenous identity. Of course these arguments do not consider the settler policies and practices which aimed to eliminate us and that have left deep scars that many are still struggling to heal from. Criteria for who or what counts is often shifting and is generally based on settler ideas of what it means to be Indigenous and not our own ideas of ourselves or our relationships with each other. As Deloria Jr (1988, p. 82) asserts, "not even Indians can relate themselves to this type of creature who, to anthropologists, is the 'real Indian'. Indian people begin to feel that that they are merely shadows of a mythical super-Indian". Similarly, Torres Strait Islander scholar Martin Nakata weighs in regarding the 1898 Cambridge Anthropological Expedition that went to the Torres Strait Islands. The expedition involved a group of eminent scholars, scientists and anthropologists who built their careers on measuring and recording details of Torres Strait Islander peoples' physical and mental capacities measured against Western scientific knowledge of 'normality':

Ethnology and early anthropological theory once again informed practices in a way that not only framed the snapshot but also provided a background against which Islander society itself became in reality little more than an offstage presence imagined into being by a scientific audience.

(Nakata, 2007, p. 102)

Today we hear the old arguments that colonial violence is in the past as if such practices and policies have no bearing on the present. Beginning with massacres, settlers attempted to rid the lands of our ancestors (Reynolds, 2006). Scholars have mapped some of the massacres and this information is becoming more available as these horrific stories are revealed (see Elder, 1998; Ryan, 2020). Through policy and practice, every aspect of Indigenous lives was regulated and controlled. As settler colonial scholar Patrick Wolfe (2011) argues, through policy and practice the work of elimination continues:

This end is pursued by means of strategies which, though varied and versatile, exhibit a high degree of cross-cultural consistency. Apart from the relatively straight-forward procedure of frontier homicide, these strategies typically include territorial removal and/or confinement, the imposition of regimes of private property (whereby ancestral patrimonies are broken down into private allocations that can be individually transferred into settler hands), discourses of miscegenation (whereby Natives produce settler offspring), Native citizenship, child abduction, total-institutional surveillance (reserves, prisons, boarding schools), intensive educational programmes, religious conversion and related assimilationist interventions. These procedures continue the invasion beyond the frontier, demographically eroding the Native constituency.

(Wolfe, 2011, pp. 272–273)

Wolfe also argues that settler colonialism has both negative and positive dimensions, "replacing as well as destroying".

The Native child is not only taken away. In train with his or her disappearance, the child is domesticated, individualized, reprogrammed, bred White. Through the alchemy of assimilation, the social death of the Native becomes the birth of the settler. In its positive aspect, therefore, the logic of elimination marks a return whereby the Native repressed continues to shape settler social institutions.

(Wolfe, 2011, p. 273)

Across this continent, after the immediate devastation of massacres, a new process was enacted. This involved forcibly containing those deemed 'full-blood' to government confinement camps known as 'reserves' where Indigenous people could 'naturally die out'. This sentiment is expressed clearly in Deakin's 1901 speech mentioned above. 'Full-blood' Indigenous people were assumed to be a 'dying race', as expressed by Turner, "the wandering savage [...] doomed to extinction by the progress of that type of humanity with which it was impossible to assimilate him" (Turner, 1904 cited in Attwood and Markus, 1997, p. 1). The position of those of mixed descent with an admixture of colonisers' blood was a source for official concern, however, especially with the growth of this population in the 'contact zones' during and following frontier expansion, violence and dispossession

(Bleakley, 1961). It was thought the presence of colonisers' blood indicated a genetic inheritance that embodied the capacity to progress culturally.

These ideas were based on pseudo-scientific thinking that imagined a hierarchy of humans where Indigenous peoples were positioned as 'primitive natives' and understood in terms of our distance from the 'civilised' Europeans who stood at the top of a global human racial and cultural hierarchy (Carlson, 2016b, p. 24). This hierarchy was predicated on the concept of European cultural progress as the indicator of superior intelligence—and as measured via the meanings constructed through Enlightenment knowledge (Gascoigne, 1994). This strand of European intellectual thought theorised a hierarchy of the progress of different human cultures in direct relation to biological and racial determinants. So, on the one hand, 'full-blooded' Indigenous people were seen as archaic survivors of the past, soon to die out completely, while on the other, those of mixed descent were understood as in the process of being absorbed and assimilated into the mainstream population (Blyton, 2022). Here, their claims and connections to their Indigenous heritage would soon be erased and forgotten. In both cases, there was no future for Indigenous people, imagined or otherwise.

### State-sanctioned killings

Settler colonialism continues its mission of our erasure. Indigenous women and non-binary people are particularly targeted. The continued killings are a settler colonial practice where our lives are deemed worthless (Carlson, 2021). I draw attention here to the missing and murdered Indigenous women across Turtle Island, now referred to as North America (Moeke-Pickering et al., 2021). Publicly we know that thousands of Indigenous women, girls and Two-Spirit people are missing and/or presumed murdered (Lezard et al., 2021; NIMMIWG, 2019). If thousands of settler women were missing and murdered in any location or specific province, there would be outrage in the world.

The killing of Aboriginal women has a long history, a long-revered history, where the colonial perpetrators of this violence are often sanctioned in their actions (Carlson, 2021; Carlson & Day, 2021; Day & Carlson, 2022). In national news, we are informed almost every week that another Aboriginal and/or Torres Strait Islander person has died while in police or state custody. Settler colonial institutions are literally killing us. As I write, Indigenous people are watching the inquest into the death of Ms Nelson,[4] who died in custody in Victoria. Ms Nelson was not convicted of any alleged crime. She was being held on remand. She was 37 years old. Lying on the floor of a cell, Ms Nelson cried out for help over nine times. A prison nurse suggested Ms Nelson be taken to hospital; however, a doctor disagreed. Staff gave her paracetamol, anti-nausea medication, and a blanket, all passed through a flap in the cell door. The lack of human care has not gone unnoticed. Three hours after guards last checked on her, Ms Nelson was found dead on the floor. This was the third time Ms Nelson had been held in custody for shoplifting, an offence that does not carry any jail time. She is one of over 500 Indigenous people who have died in custody since findings from the 1991 Royal Commission into Aboriginal Deaths in Custody[5] were handed down. Our survival in this word is truly miraculous.

The disappearance of Indigenous people, their absence from the future, is absolutely necessary for settler futures. As argued by Tuck and Gaztambide-Fernández (2013, p. 79), "settler futurity is ensured through an understanding of Native-European relations as a thing of the past". Much like here across this continent Tuck and Gaztambide-Fernández

(2013) reflect on the way in which Native American peoples have been written out of the future of a 'promised land' now referred to as the United States of America. They write:

> The future of the white race [...] require[s] the elimination of lesser humans and the refinement of the cultural attributes that define the white subject, whose manifest destiny it is to take the place of the savage in the promised land.
>
> (Tuck & Gaztambide-Fernández, 2013, p. 79).

Settlers not only imagine a 'promised land', but they also literally invent a narrative that supports this idea. In both locations this relies on the notion that a 'brave explorer' discovered the lands: the story of Columbus there and Cook here. In relation to this continent, the fairy tale also includes the concept of terra nullius—the doctrine that upheld the idea that these lands were unoccupied.

## Settler narratives: Captain Cook

While settler imaginings of Indigenous elimination may no longer be quite as explicit in political and popular discourse as they were for the first two centuries of colonisation, Indigenous futures are still tightly constrained by settler narratives. One such narrative is that James Cook discovered Australia and that it was a peaceful process of claiming lands that belonged to nobody—vacant lands. Such is the power of this narrative that settlers invest time, energy and a significant amount of money to ensure its longevity.

As an example, former prime minister Scott Morrison announced he would dedicate more than $12 million to 'rediscover' Cook.[6] The plan was to allocate $6 million to fund a replica of Cook's ship, the *Endeavour*, to circumnavigate Australia. Across social media platforms, Morrison known publicly as 'Scomo', was called out for his lack of knowledge on Cook's travels and was quickly informed that Cook never circumnavigated Australia (see Carlson & Farrelly, 2023). Whether or not Scomo was misinformed or ignorant of the facts doesn't matter; he was the most powerful political individual in the country. As Carlson and Farrelly (2023) argue, the lie is not important—the narrative is. And when told by the incumbent prime minister, particularly so!

I do not have to go far from my home to be reminded of colonisers who have benefited from the lie. I leave my home and drive along the Princes Highway. I pay for things with currency dedicated to the Crown. The mall down the road from me is called Crown Street Mall. I drive up Macquarie Pass; I pass Endeavour Park; I work at Macquarie University, not far from Cook's river. Cook and everything that myth stands for is all around us—embedded into our lives in such a way it appears normal. Statues and other colonial monuments are regularly the topic of heated debate (Carlson & Farrelly, 2023). They have become targeted by Indigenous rights groups and supporters of the Black Lives Matter movement who protest against Indigenous/Black deaths in custody, incarceration rates and police brutality. They are targeted for what they stand for. And also preserved for what they stand for.

In 2020, busts of former prime ministers Tony Abbott and John Howard on Wadawurrung and Dja Dja Wurrung peoples' lands known now as Ballarat, were vandalised and sprayed with red paint.[7] Howard's bust was spray-painted with the word 'homophobe', while Abbott's was covered with words including 'fascist' and 'pig'. Similarly, on the lands of the Nyoongar peoples now known as Perth, a statue of Captain James Stirling had its neck and hands painted red, and an Aboriginal flag painted over the inscription on the base.[8] In Warrane (Sydney), during expected Black Lives Matter protests in 2020, dozens of police were deployed to guard the Cook statue in Hyde Park[9] for fear it might be targeted by protesters. Several members of the public joined forces with police to protect the statue. In this bizarre scene of state-sanctioned protection of a statue and public fear of their founding father's demise, the hypocrisy was visible—while Black Lives Matter protesters were being threatened with arrest if they were to attend rallies because they were risking spreading the coronavirus, those who were in support of the statue were able to congregate there freely alongside police (Carlson & Farrelly, 2023). The Betoota Advocate, a satirical news website, responded with a story posted on Instagram entitled "Police Urged to Treat Indigenous People in Custody as Carefully as They Treat the Statues" (@betootaadvocate June 15, 2020).[10] Despite such police presence, two people still managed to vandalise the statue, spray-painting the phrases "sovereignty never ceded" and "no pride in genocide".

## The foreclosure of Indigenous futures

Anishinaabe scholar Grace Dillon (2016, cited in Muzyka, 2019, para. 5) reminds us, "So often, so many of us are viewed as the last of the race, or the lost race, or the vanishing race", and arguably this is deliberate. The last of our kind is a narrative that sees some sort of empathy with Indigenous people who were destined to disappear. These stories get re-enacted in popular culture precisely because they produce a hero/heroine figure who can be noted as 'the last', for example, in films like *The Last of the Mohicans* (1992). In this example, even the 'last of' was played by a white man. In these tales white people are positioned as superior and the death of the Indigenous peoples is always inevitable. We are often portrayed as nameless people, with no agency, no humanity and always less than human. Histories are rewritten and our humanity is erased. 'The last' is a symbol of what was, what has passed; a 'last' can be memorialised as heroic, noble, an emblem of white history's 'progression'.

Indigenous people are always understood by what we supposedly lack: education, employment, good health, good morals, a work ethic, capacity for change (Nakata, 2012; Carlson, 2020). Popular discourse constantly distinguishes between so-called 'authentic' Indigenous people—who, in the settler mind, live in the remote outback, barefoot on red earth—and so-called 'urban' Indigenous people—who have lost all connection to 'real' Indigenous life (Fredericks, 2013; Carlson, 2016b). In this sense, the widespread 'deficit discourse' also extends forward in time: Indigenous people supposedly even lack a future. 'The last' is a useful commemoration of our extinguishment as Indigenous people and a 'lack' is a reminder of the price we pay for not acquiescing to the master settler narratives which ironically demand our 'authenticity'. Such is the ambiguity of the settler project!

Thus, settler futures, as expressed through political, cultural and national narratives, invariably foreclose Indigenous futures. As Barker and Lowman (2016, p. 198) argue, "the structures, systems, and stories of settler colonialism, then, guide what future settler societies can look like". In a more recent example, the new television series *1883* (Sheridan, 2021) follows the life of Yellowstone's John Dutton's ancestry and provides a backstory to the series *Yellowstone* (Sheridan & Linson, 2018) and how the family came to 'own' most of the land. In this series the main character 'Elsa Dutton' is white, and is played by Isabel May. Eliza rejects society's norms and expectations and 'becomes Native' by proximity and is gifted the name Lightning Yellow Hair. This provides an element of nobility to the Yellowstone story where settlers claim ownership of the land by way of intergenerational occupation. In one scene the 'new Native'—Lightning Yellow Hair—rides up to a massacre site. The site shows the killings of Native women who appear to have been raped and then slaughtered. Lightning Yellow Hair pays no attention to this site of Native deaths—even though she is now supposedly Native. As she rides up to the site, she merely informs her father that one of the other settlers has been bitten by a snake. While she plays at being Indian (Deloria, 1998), there is no connection to this identity other than dressing up and calling herself Lightning Yellow Hair. There is no relationality, no obligation, no reciprocity. However, even Lightning Yellow Hair dies. Maybe pretending to be Indian has its repercussions!

## Indigenous Futurisms: a people of the future

Settler futures are astonishingly myopic. Actions justified in the name of 'progress' are, in fact, often radically short-sighted. The wealthiest settler states—including those now referred to as the US, Canada, New Zealand and Australia—all seem to be working towards a future that is limited in depth, scope and imagination. Wholesale ecological collapse, devastating wars and famines, rapid deforestation, the poisoning of vital water sources by pipelines cutting across Country,[11] the extinction of entire species, the acidification of oceans, the aridification of once-lush plains, the leaking of oil into oceans, bushfires scorching tens of millions of hectares of bushland, the rapid heating of the entire planet, all constitute the ecological demise of a future for all. It would seem, at this point in history, that settler futures, while foreclosing Indigenous futures, are working towards the collapse of human and planetary futures altogether.

But what if this were not a forgone conclusion? What if the settler logics of elimination, possession and domination were not the prevailing logics of society, and what if settlers managed to rethink their self-appointed assessment as a people who are forward thinking, enlightened, progressive and advanced? What if they understood wholly the lies in which their entire belief system was formed? If this were to happen, a paradigm shift would be possible where we might begin to envision more hopeful futures, one that Cree scholar Dallas Hunt imagines, "wherein Indigenous futurities are not subjected to the processes of settler colonialism?" (2018, p. 84). Would settlers have the capacity to rethink their standpoint that Indigenous peoples are of the past and finally see Indigenous people as peoples of the future, the way we have always imagined ourselves to be? These are questions ingrained with hope, and it is perhaps the potential demise of the planet and the recognition of this that argues the need for that hope.

The politics of 'hope' has long attracted the attention of radical thinkers, such as Marxist philosopher Ernst Bloch (1986), postcolonial educator Paulo Freire (1996), and feminist and anti-colonial scholar Sara Ahmed (2013) among others. Far from constituting a form of naive or politically impotent optimism, these scholars have instead conceptualised hope as constituting new horizons of the possible. For many Indigenous peoples, to hope is to keep the future open to difference, to what Bloch describes as the not-yet become (see Anderson, 2006). Hopeful imaginaries are not just reactions to current power structures, but radical expressions of creative love and desire (Carlson & Frazer, 2021). Hope does not rely on settler benevolence because if it did, our ancestors would have given up hope, yet they never did. Our families continue to hope for a future for their children, families and ancestors to come. In hoping for a future where we thrive, Indigenous people action their desire for hope through acts of defiance and refusal (Simpson, 2007). Hope is a precursor to critical consciousness, to the evaluation of old ideas and the development of new ways of conceiving a future; it is a powerful tool for change.

Over the last 20 years, an identifiable Indigenous movement has been merging around this kind of radical hopeful imaginaries, unconstrained by settler logics. First described by Dillon (2012), 'Indigenous Futurisms' encompasses distinctively Indigenous perspectives on the past, present and futures, often expressed through the forms of science fiction, speculative fiction, comics and visual art, and often incorporating Indigenous knowledges, ontologies and cultures. The movement closely parallels that of 'Afrofuturism', which plays at the intersection of the African diaspora with technologies both current and fantastic, and as embodied in the novels of Octavia Butler, who was said to have written in a way that imagined an alternative life to the one that was envisioned for her as a Black woman. Butler wrote several novels including *Parable of the Sower*, which was first published in 1993, then again in 2012. The novel offers a dystopian warning that if we, the human race, continue along our current path, then unimaginable horrors await us. In Butler's dystopian world, a strongman has risen to power in the United States, and climate change is decimating the environment. The economy is falling apart. Income inequality is out of control. Resources are scarce, and violence has forced people to isolate. The year is 2024. Thinking about Butler's work as only dystopian misses the invitation to embrace the essential message of Butler's work—that the only constant life has ever offered us is change and it offers hope. As Butler articulates: "The world is full of painful stories. Sometimes it seems as though there aren't any other kind and yet I found myself thinking how beautiful that glint of water was through the trees" (2012, p. 263).

Afrofuturism offers the same sense of hope, which is identifiable in the Marvel film *Black Panther* (2018). In a 2019 article entitled, 'Redefining the Colonial: An Afrofuturist Analysis of the Wakanda and Speculative Fiction', African American scholar Ricardo Guthrie questions how can Black speculative fiction refashions a de-colonial space beyond Wakanda, in the current nation states and community places within which Afro-diasporic peoples struggle daily for sustenance, power and joy. Guthrie also asks how an imaginary realm of the African world untouched by colonialism affirms Black genius and futurity to enable current generations to deprogramme ourselves and combat anti-Black racism (2019, p. 15). These are similar questions posed in Indigenous Futurisms. However, for us it is also about our relationship to Country—to place.

It is true that colonisation severely limits the imagination of the colonised. Like Black people around the world, Indigenous people are often historicised and placed in the past without imagining what the future might look like. Indeed, the future is not where we were intended to be. The colonial project is dedicated to our elimination. The importance of Indigenous Futurisms is that it restores Indigeneity as a political force that has, and continues to survive all efforts to extinguish threats to its existence. Indigenous Futurisms is a political form of storytelling and imaginings which uses the future as a means of engaging with issues faced in the present and the past. It is a force for activism, a mode of storytelling that reignites a precolonial past with possibility. As Māori scholar Tāwhanga Nopera argues, "stories remind us of who we are and the places we belong" (2016, p. 28). Similarly, Cherokee author and literary critic Daniel Heath Justice suggests Indigenous writers can produce work that demonstrates potential for transformative change when they are their best imaginative selves. They argue, "we can't possibly live otherwise until we first imagine otherwise".[12] Such imaginings and contemplations include a world filled with possibility and free of the oppressive forces of colonialism. Contrary to colonial regimes that position Indigenous peoples and cultures as embedded in a precolonial past with no place in the present or future, Indigenous Futurisms threatens ongoing colonial fantasies of a world where Indigenous peoples have vanished or have assimilated through imaginings of future possibilities and the practicalities required to bring these to fruition.

Indigenous Futurisms emerged partly as a response to concerns from Indigenous scholars around current academic framings of both Indigeneity and settler colonialism. Indigenous Studies, historically, has tended to reproduce colonial ideas of Indigenous precarity, often unwittingly, by understanding Indigenous peoples as culturally static and threatened with imminent extinction. According to this thinking, then, the urgent task is to 'salvage' this knowledge before it is lost for all time. Indigenous Studies historically has been dominated by settlers. It is only recently that Indigenous Studies has become the field of Indigenous scholars. This has had significant implications for the ways that our knowledge is produced, circulated, reproduced and stored, and also for the validation of Indigenous identities.

Settler Colonial Studies, on the other hand, centres on understanding colonialism as a continuing force in the present, but here there is a concern that seeing colonialism as a 'structure' precludes possibilities of creative action and hopeful becomings (Davis et al., 2017). For me, Indigenous Futurisms bypasses both these issues by seeing Indigenous people as always-already imagining and building other futures. This is why in all that I teach, Indigenous Futurisms is at the core of my thinking. I am always inspired by my colleagues and global relatives such as Grace Dillon, who reminds us: "Indigenous Futurisms are not the product of a victimized people's wishful amelioration of their past, but instead a continuation of a spiritual and cultural path that remains unbroken by genocide and war" (2016, p. 2).

### The Department of Indigenous Studies: Indigenous Futurisms Symposium

I am fortunate to work in a Department of Indigenous Studies that is home to fabulous Indigenous scholars. We always consider Indigenous Futurisms. We see futurist scholarship as important to our discipline so that we don't just privilege settler colonialism by framing ourselves as victims with no agency or capacity to imagine something different. In 2019, just before the global Covid-19 pandemic swept across the world and back, when travel and gatherings were a regular thing, we were fortunate to have Grace Dillon attend our Indigenous Futurism event along with:

- Noongar writer Claire Coleman who is best known for their award-winning books *Terra Nullius* and *The Old Lie*;
- Palyku legal and literary scholar Ambelin Kwaymullina, whose poem features in this volume;
- Yugambeh freelance writer, editor, curator Arlie Alizzie, whose research focuses on Indigenous Futurist literatures;
- Māori artist and scholar Tāwhanga Nopera and Mexicana scholar Rafael/a Luna Pizano;
- Gomeroi scholar and poet Alison Whittaker; and
- Professor of Indigenous Studies and Wiradjuri scholar Sandy O'Sullivan.

There are some who produce work that aligns with the genre of Indigenous Futurisms like Claire Coleman and Ambelin Kwaymullina, but there is yet a real paucity of scholarly work that looks at the genre itself. This is an embryonic and exciting field of study whereby ideas can flourish in a scholarly environment, itself imagined into being by scholars whose activism is constantly regenerated by collegiality in the field. Arlie Alizzi's chapter in this volume is an example of this activism and the emergence of this field of study as an important aspect in imaging our futures.

This was the first of its kind in Australia, and arguably the focus on Indigenous Queer Futurisms may have been the first gathering like this in the world. Heath Justice, on their website, poses the question "What would fantasy fiction look like with women, Indigenous people, queer folk, and other stereotyped or marginalised communities at the centre rather than the margins?".[13] We take Heath Justice's inquiry to heart in the work we do in the Department of Indigenous Studies and we are very committed to ensuring Indigenous women's and queer participation in all that we do. The persistence of queer Indigenous identities is arguably one of the most enduring forms of resistance to settler colonialism (Day, 2021). Settler colonialism combined with Christianisation has targeted queer peoples and continues the violence towards them (Carlson et al., 2022; Day, 2021; Wilson, 2015; Farrell, 2017). Most Indigenous societies pre-colonisation were not limited to the colonial gender binary which is enforced as part of the colonial project. Since colonisation and the impact of Christianisation, we have seen severe discrimination from settlers and, sadly, within our own communities (Carlson et al., 2022; O'Sullivan 2021; Keovorabouth, 2021).

Queer Indigenous Futurisms is an extension of Indigenous Futurisms and expands the terrain of inherited possibilities for imagining and (re)imagining our past, present and future to include imaginings of the future that do not sit comfortably with settler colonial narratives. Our imaginings will include the retelling of erased pasts with a myriad of diverse expressions of gender and sexualities. At the symposium, we explored the commitment, care and innovations of queer Indigenous peoples who have carried our communities forward, even in the face of severe discrimination from settlers (Carlson et al., 2022). Indigenous Futurisms allows us to reimagine a world or worlds where discrimination does not exist, or where we are so strong and certain of our place as sovereign beings that its force carries no impact .

## Sci-fi and Indigenous futures

While only recently formalising and becoming more visible, the work of Indigenous Futurisms has a long history—even if these works have generally been described as science fiction or fantasy (Hunt, 2018). Sci-fi features prominently in discussions of Indigenous Futurisms. Supposedly unfettered by the old structures of the 'actual', science fiction is meant to make possible radical alternatives, future worlds, previously unimaginable utopias. But as a genre, even in the most fanciful sci-fi stories, settler narratives of Indigenous elimination are often perpetuated. For instance, science fiction narratives often centre on eco-activists saving worlds from ecological collapse and achieving more sustainable futures. But as Hunt (2018, p. 71) argues, "who is accorded space in these futures and who is not?" The 2009 blockbuster film *Avatar*, for instance, draws liberally on Indigenous narratives and symbolism, but notably it is still the white 'hero' who saves the day, and it is through his 'becoming Indigenous' that this happens. Hunt (2018) situates this narrative within what Fee (1987) describes as 'totem transfers', where an identifiably Indigenous character suddenly appears in the narrative, gifts a particular, always significant, item or piece of knowledge to a settler, which in turn 'Indigenises' them, and then just as suddenly, disappears.

This narrative constitutes a form of a key figure in settler storytelling that has been referred to as 'the vanishing Indian'. Ultimately Indigenous people are still eliminated.

While always concerned with futures yet-to-come, sci-fi narratives have rarely afforded a future for Indigenous peoples. Instead, when they do appear, it is only as what Byrd (cited in Hunt, 2018) describes as 'past tense presences'. Despite these ongoing issues, and against the dominant trope of Indigenous peoples as somehow backward-looking, sci-fi has long been an important art form for Indigenous peoples globally. It has constituted a vital outlet for expression of Indigenous desire, hope, longing and imagination. Indeed, it's no accident that the first film dubbed into Diné (Navajo) language was *Star Wars: A New Hope* (Fricke, 2019).

Palyku scholar Ambelin Kwaymullina (2014, p. 27) reflects on this and argues:

> I am often told that it is unusual to be both Indigenous and a speculative-fiction writer. But many of the ideas that populate speculative-fiction books—notions of time travel, astral projection, speaking the languages of animals or trees—are part of Indigenous cultures.

It is the case, therefore, that science fiction as a genre of speculation is drawn from the stories of Indigenous peoples whose cosmologies have always engaged in speculative storytelling about space, time and inventiveness. In contemporary times, Indigenous engagement with sci-fi and experimental film is not just about aesthetic enjoyment, but has much broader implications, as Gómez-Barris (2017, p. 87) explains, "where Indigenous cultural activists make room for perceiving and making life otherwise". "Making life otherwise" inspired Aboriginal writer Ryan Griffen who developed the television series *Cleverman*. Griffen stated that for as long as he could remember, he loved film and television (Griffen, 2016, para. 1). He loved the storytelling and saw it as a way to take him out of his reality and show him possibility. He grew up faced with limitations around his identity, fuelled by racism. He wrote the story for his son in an attempt to reimagine what might be possible and stated:

> I wanted to create an Aboriginal superhero that he could connect with, no matter what others said. I wanted a character that would empower him to stand and fight when presented with racism. Just like the old dreaming stories, Cleverman would be able to teach moral lessons; not only for my son, not only for Aboriginal people, but for many more out there as well.
>
> (Griffen, 2016, para. 8)

And as Kwaymullina explains, the imaginatively expansive nature of the genre means it remains open to Indigenous lifeways—particularly its engagement with what Anishinaabe, Métis writer Elizabeth Le LaPensée calls "the hyper present now" where "we look seven generations before, and seven generations ahead" (Le LaPensée cited in Fricke, 2019, p. 119).

## The futures in Indigenous activism

Aboriginal and Torres Strait Islander people have long expressed distinctively Indigenous futures through myriad forms of political expression. In 1963, for instance, the Yolngu people at Yirrkala sent petitions to the Australian Parliament's House of Representatives, written in both English and their own language on tree bark, in protest of the excision of 300 square kilometres of their land for a bauxite mining project (Marawili, 2016). In 1972, four Aboriginal activists set up a beach umbrella on the lawns of Parliament House and established the Aboriginal Tent Embassy in protest of the Commonwealth's approach to land rights (Carlson & Coe, 2022). More recently, in 2015, the #SOSBlakAustralia campaign digitally connected Indigenous and non-Indigenous people globally, opposing policy that would see the closure of hundreds of small, remotely located Indigenous communities across Western Australia, and bringing major Australian cities to a standstill (Carlson & Frazer, 2016).

Indigenous activism is often framed as only 'standing in the way of progress': the #SOSBlakAustralia protesters, for instance, were framed by mainstream media as 'selfish rabble' who were inconveniencing upstanding citizens trying to get to work (Carlson & Frazer, 2016); and the protesters at Mauna a Wākea in Hawai'i were widely understood as "obstructions on a march to 'the future'" (Goodyear-Ka'opua, 2017, p. 186). While these kinds of political expressions might be understood as purely reactionary and entirely entangled within the dualistic battle between the evil of colonialism and the good of Indigenous sovereignty, they contain much more than that. As Indigenous scholar Rachel Flowers (2015, p. 36) asserts, "For Indigenous peoples' struggles, the unified 'no' is also a resounding 'yes' to something different, a yes to a reality 'to-come'". Indigenous political expression is always about other futures as Goodyear-Ka'opua (2017, p. 186) explains that it "is actually protecting the possibilities of multiple futures"—futures generally more expansive and favourable for human and more-than-human flourishing. Indigenous people are concerned with what Goodyear-Ka'opua calls "the deep time of human survival" (2017, p. 192)—not settler time, not extractive time, which will sacrifice almost everything, including future possibilities of human existence, for the myopic vision of a settler future. In this sense, Indigenous activists are, as Goodyear-Ka'opua (2017, p. 187) explains, "Protectors of the future, not protestors of the past".

Indigenous Futurisms is not necessarily utopic or optimistic. Many authors writing within the Indigenous Futurisms genre engage with the realities of ongoing colonialism around the world, and the apocalyptic nature of the present for many Indigenous communities. Revolutionary change can only come when it is firstly imagined. Indigenous Futurisms plays a role in this opportunity for change as it asks the very questions that need to be asked: what can a future look like that is free of settler colonialism and free of oppression? Indigenous Futurisms engages with question marks, ponderings and cogitations that engender theoretical approaches to ways of being and acting, to resistance, possibilities and hope where these were once not on our horizon. In their TedX talk, Kiowa, Tongan artist Jordan Cocker comments that "we, as Indigenous peoples, are the latest version of our ancestors and we are accountable to our future ancestors".[14] This is at the core of Indigenous philosophy as we are relational beings. As Aboriginal political philosopher Mary Graham argues, "the foundation of Law is a complex and refined system of social, moral, spiritual and community obligations that provided an ordered universe for people" (2014, p. 18). Graham asserts: "Aboriginal logic maintains that there is no division between the observing mind and anything else: there is no 'external world' to inhabit. There are distinctions between the physical and the spiritual, but these aspects of existence continually interpenetrate each other" (Graham, 1999, np).

We need to understand our relationship with Country and how this is connected to everything in the universe. We need to view the world as part of us and treat it so. As Cree scholar Alex Wilson (2015) asserts, we need to see ourselves as a relation of land and not just in relation to land. There is much to learn from Indigenous peoples.

Indigenous Futurisms is an act of visioning. This allows us to plant the seeds of the future, which is not yet here. Maybe we can change the narrative—for the benefit of all humanity. Maybe we can challenge colonialism and imagine a world where it no longer has power and control. Indigenous Futurisms starts with visioning—what is possible. Indigenous activist and writer Erica Violet Lee (2016, para. 6) explains in their essay 'Reconciling in the Apocalypse': "In knowing the histories of our relations and of this land, we find the knowledge to recreate all that our worlds would've been, if not for the interruption of colonization".

Indigenous Futurism combines speculative imaginings of the future with Indigenising, and emphasises the interrelationship of past, present and future in Indigenous cultures and thought.

The future is definitely Indigenous. Settlers have told their stories and have shown that they may not have the ability to imagine a world where relationality, or indeed, responsibility, is at the centre of thinking. What we have seen recently in terms of climate change, including floods and wild fires and droughts and rising sea levels, and the pandemic and other emerging strains of illness demonstrates an urgent need for revolutionary change. And we need revolutionary leaders to bring about change. Indigenous Futurisms confronts not only colonial ideology and its insistence on white narratives of origin, but it also refutes settler narratives, unsettles their validity and authority. In so doing, Indigenous Futurisms sets up a field of study whereby Indigenous knowledge can be returned to its precolonial eminence. In this way, Indigenous Futurisms can infiltrate and inform literature, science, cosmology and all modes of scholarship so that the lived realities of Indigenous imaginings may be continually under scrutiny and constantly subject to hope.

## Notes

1 I make the point that this is a continent not a country. 'Australia' as it is now referred was built on a legal fiction of terra nullius (nobody's land) and claimed for the British Crown, despite being home to hundreds of self-identifying nations. Day (2021) uses the term "in so-called Australia" to draw attention to the falsehood of the claim.
2 See http://historichansard.net/hofreps/1901/19010912_REPS_1_4_c1/
3 See www.youtube.com/watch?v=myngWhgRTg4
4 For more information, see www.sbs.com.au/nitv/article/2022/05/14/prison-guard-lied-veronica-nelson-about-getting-help-she-died
5 See www.naa.gov.au/explore-collection/first-australians/royal-commission-aboriginal-deaths-custody
6 See www.perthnow.com.au/politics/federal-politics/prime-minister-scott-morrison-wants-aussies-to-rediscover-captain-james-cook-with-12m-project-ng-b881081256z
7 See www.abc.net.au/news/2020-06-15/busts-of-tony-abbott-john-howard-vandalised/12355190
8 See www.abc.net.au/news/2020-06-12/captain-james-stirling-statue-vandalised-before-blm-rally/12348328
9 See www.pedestrian.tv/news/captain-cook-statue/
10 See www.betootaadvocate.com/uncategorized/police-urged-to-treat-indigenous-people-in-custody-as-carefully-as-they-treat-the-statues/
11 The term 'Country' as I have previously written, "has a deep significance for Aboriginal people. It is through Country that we explain our ancestral connections to place and philosophical views on creation" (Carlson, 2016a, p. 499).

12  See https://danielheathjustice.com
13  See https://danielheathjustice.com
14  Indigenous Futurisms: Cultures of Radical Love, TedX Talk by Jordan Cocker www.ted.com/talks/jordan_cocker_indigenous_futurisms_cultures_of_radical_love

## References

Ahmed, S. (2013). *The cultural politics of emotion*. Routledge.

Allam, L., & Evershed, N. (2019, 3 March). The killing times: the massacres of Aboriginal people Australia must confront. *The Guardian, 3*.

Anderson, B. (2006). 'Transcending without transcendence': Utopianism and an ethos of hope. *Antipode, 38*(4), 691–710.

Arcioni, E. (2012). Excluding Indigenous Australians from 'the people': A reconsideration of sections 25 and 127 of the Constitution. *Federal Law Review, 40*(3), 287–315.

Attwood, B., & Markus, A. (1997). *The 1967 Referendum or when Aborigines didn't get the vote*, Australian Institute of Aboriginal and Torres Strait Islander Studies.

Barker, A. J., & Battell Lowman, E. (2016). The spaces of dangerous freedom: Disrupting settler colonialism. In S. Maddison, T. Clark, & R. De Costa (Eds.), *The limits of settler colonial reconciliation* (pp. 195–212). Springer.

Bleakley, J. W. (1961). *The Aborigines of Australia*. Jacaranda Press.

Bloch, E., Plaice, N., Plaice, S., & Knight, P. (1986). *The principle of hope* (Vol. 3, pp. 1938–1947). MIT Press.

Blyton, G. (2022). Australia: tainted blood—scientific racism, eugenics and sanctimonious treatments of Aboriginal Australians: 1869–2008. In K. Duncan & A. M. Neal (Eds.), *Get your knee off our necks* (pp. 253–273). Springer.

Butler, O. E. (2012). *Parable of the sower*. Open Road Media.

Carlson, B. (2016a). Striking the right cord. *AlterNative: An International Journal of Indigenous Peoples, 12*(5), 498–512.

Carlson, B. (2016b). *The politics of identity: Who counts as Aboriginal today?* Aboriginal Studies Press.

Carlson, B. (2020). Indigenous killjoys negotiating the labyrinth of dis/mistrust. In T. Moeke-ickering, S. Cote-Meek, & A. Pegoaro (Eds.), *Critical reflections and politics on advancing women in the academy* (pp. 105–123). IGI Global.

Carlson, B. (2021). Data silence in the settler archive: Indigenous femicide, deathscapes and social media. In S. Perera & J. Pugleise (Eds.). *Mapping deathscapes: Digital geographies of racial and border violence* (pp. 84–105). Routledge.

Carlson, B., & Coe, L. J. (2022, 12 January). A short history of the Aboriginal Tent Embassy: An indelible reminder of unceded sovereignty. *The Conversation*. https://theconversation.com/a-short-history-of-the-aboriginal-tent-embassy-an-indelible-reminder-of-unceded-sovereignty-174693

Carlson, B., & Day, M. (2021). Love, hate and sovereign bodies: The exigencies of online dating. In A. Powell, A. Flynn, & L. Sugiura (Eds.), *The Palgrave handbook on gender, violence and technology* (pp. 181–202). Palgrave Macmillan.

Carlson, B., & Farrelly, T. (2023). *Monumental disruptions: Colonial commemorations and Aboriginal Australians*. Aboriginal Studies Press.

Carlson, B., & Frazer, R. (2016). Indigenous activism and social media: The global response to #SOSBLAKAUSTRALIA. In A. McCosker, S. Vivienne, & A, Johns (Eds.), *Rethinking digital citizenship: Control, contest and culture* (pp. 115–130). Rowman and Littlefield International.

Carlson, B., & Frazer, R. (2021). *Indigenous digital lives: The practices and politics of being Indigenous on social media*. Palgrave Macmillan.

Carlson, B., & Kennedy, T. (2021). Us mob online: The perils of identifying as indigenous on social media. *Genealogy, 5*(2), 52.

Carlson, B., Kennedy, K., & Farrell, A. (2022). Indigenous gender intersubjectivities: Political bodies. In M. Walter, T. Kukutai, A. Gonzales, & R. Henry (Eds.), *The Oxford handbook of indigenous sociology* (pp. 1–21) Oxford University Press.

Davis, L., Denis, J., & Sinclair, R. (2017). Pathways of settler decolonization. *Settler Colonial Studies, 7*(4), 393–397.

Day, M. (2021). Remembering Lugones: The critical potential of heterosexualism for studies of so-called Australia. *Genealogy, 5*(3), 71.

Day, M., & Carlson, B. (2022). Predators & perpetrators: White settler violence online. In D. Callander, P. Farvid, A. Baradaran, & T. Vance (Eds.) *(Un)Desiring whiteness: (Un)Doing sexual racism* (pp. 1–20). Oxford University Press.

Deloria, P. J. (1998). *Playing Indian*. Yale University Press.

Deloria, V. (1988). *Custer died for your sins: An Indian manifesto*. University of Oklahoma Press.

Deloria, V. (2020). Research, redskins, and reality. In *American nations* (pp. 458–467). Routledge.

Dillon, G. L. (2016). Indigenous futurisms, Bimaashi Biidaas Mose, flying and walking towards You. *Extrapolation, 57*(1/2), 1.

Dillon, G. L. (Ed.). (2012). *Walking the clouds: An anthology of Indigenous science fiction*. University of Arizona Press.

Elder, B. (1998). *Blood on the wattle: Massacres and maltreatment of Aboriginal Australians since 1788*. New Holland.

Farrell, A. (2017). Archiving the Aboriginal rainbow: Building an Aboriginal LGBTIQ portal. *Australasian Journal of Information Systems, 21*, 1–14.

Flowers, R. (2015). Refusal to forgive: Indigenous women's love and rage. *Decolonization: Indigeneity, Education & Society, 4*(2), 32–49.

Fredericks, B. (2013). 'We don't leave our identities at the city limits': Aboriginal and Torres Strait Islander people living in urban localities. *Australian Aboriginal Studies, 1*, 4–16.

Freire, P. (1996). *Pedagogy of the oppressed* (revised). Continuum.

Fricke, S. N. (2019). Introduction: Indigenous futurisms in the hyperpresent now. *World Art, 9*(2), 107–121.

Gascoigne, J. (1994). *Joseph Banks and the English Enlightenment: Useful knowledge and polite culture*. Cambridge University Press.

Gómez-Barris, M. (2017). *The extractive zone: Social ecologies and decolonial perspectives*. Duke University Press.

Goodyear-Ka'ōpua, N. (2017). Protectors of the future, not protestors of the past: Indigenous Pacific activism and Mauna a Wākea. *South Atlantic Quarterly, 116*(1), 184–194.

Graham, M. (1999). Some thoughts about the philosophical underpinnings of Aboriginal worldviews. *Worldviews: Global Religions, Culture, and Ecology, 3*(2), 105–118.

Graham, M. (2014). Aboriginal notions of relationality and positionalism: A reply to Weber. *Global Discourse, 4*(1), 17–22.

Gray, G. G. (2007). *A cautious silence: The politics of Australian anthropology*. Aboriginal Studies Press.

Griffen, R. (2016, 26 May). We need more Aboriginal superheros, so I created Cleverman. The Guardian. www.theguardian.com/tv-and-radio/2016/may/27/i-created-cleverman-for-my-son-because-we-need-more-aboriginal-superheroes?CMP=gu_com

Guthrie, R. (2019). Redefining the colonial: An Afrofuturist analysis of Wakanda and speculative fiction. *Journal of Futures Studies, 24*(2), 15–28.

Hunt, D. (2018). 'In search of our better selves': Totem transfer narratives and Indigenous Futurities. *American Indian Culture and Research Journal, 42*(1), 71–90.

Justice, D. H. (2012). Literature, healing, and the transformational imaginary: Thoughts on Jo-Ann Episkenew's taking back our spirits: Indigenous literature, public policy, and healing. *Canadian Literature, 214*, 101–108.

Keovorabouth, S. T. (2021). Reaching back to traditional teachings: Diné knowledge and gender politics. *Genealogy, 5*(4), 95.

Kwaymullina, A. (2014). Edges, centres and futures: Reflections on being an Indigenous speculative-fiction writer. *Kill Your Darlings, 18*, 22–33.

Lee, E. V. (2016). Reconciling in the Apocalypse. https://policyalternatives.ca/publications/monitor/reconciling-apocalypse

Lezard, P., Prefontaine, N., Cederwall, D. M., Sparrow, C., Maracle, S., Beck, A., & McCleod, A. (2021). 2SLGBTQQIA+ Sub-Working Group MMIWG2SLGBTQQIA+ National Action Plan Final report.

Mann, M. (Director). (1992). *The Last of the Mohicans* [film]. Morgan Creek Productions.

Marawili, D. (2016). A short history of Yolngu activist art. *Artlink, 36*(2), 18–25.

Moeke-Pickering, T., Rowat, J., Cote-Meek, S., & Pegoraro, A. (2021). 7. Indigenous social activism using Twitter: Amplifying voices using# MMIWG. In B. Carson & J. Berglund (Eds.), *Indigenous peoples rise up: The global ascendancy of social media activism* (pp. 112–124). Rutgers University Press.

Muzyka, K. (2019, 8 March). From growing medicine to space rockets: What is Indigenous futurisms? *CBC.* www.cbc.ca/radio/unreserved/looking-towards-the-future-indigenous-futurism-in-literature-music-film-and-fashion-1.5036479/from-growing-medicine-to-space-rockets-what-is-indigenous-futurism-1.5036480

Nakata, M. (2012). 'Better'. In M. Grossman (Ed.), *Blacklines: Contemporary critical writings by Indigenous Australians* (pp. 132–144). Melbourne University Publishing.

Nakata, M. N. (2007). *Disciplining the savages, savaging the disciplines.* Aboriginal Studies Press.

NIMMIWG. (2019). *Reclaiming Power and Place.* The Final Report of the National Inquiry in Missing and Murdered Indigenous Women and Girls. www.mmiwg-ffada.ca/final-report/

Nopera, T. (2016). *Huka can Haka: Taonga performing tino rangatiratanga.* [Unpublished PhD dissertation]. University of Waikato.

O'Sullivan, S. (2021). The colonial project of gender (and everything else). *Genealogy, 5*(3), 67.

Reynolds, H. (2006). *The other side of the frontier: Aboriginal resistance to the European invasion of Australia.* UNSW Press.

Ryan, L. (2020). Digital map of colonial frontier massacres in Australia 1788–1930. *Teaching History, 54*(3), 13–20.

Sheridan, T. (Creator) (2021) *1883* [TV Series]. Linson Entertainment, Bosque Ranch Productions, 101 Studios and MTV Entertainment Studios.

Sheridan, T., & Linson, J. (2018). *Yellowstone* [TV Series]. Linson Entertainment, Bosque Ranch Productions, Treehouse Films, 101 Studios and MTV Entertainment Studios.

Simpson, A. (2007). On ethnographic refusal: Indigeneity, 'voice' and colonial citizenship. *Junctures: The Journal for Thematic Dialogue, 9*, 67–80.

Tuck, E., & Gaztambide-Fernández, R. A. (2013). Curriculum, replacement, and settler futurity. *Journal of Curriculum Theorizing, 29*(1), 72–89.

Tuck, E., & Yang, K. W. (2021). Decolonization is not a metaphor. *Tabula Rasa, 38*, 61–111.

Tuiwai Smith, L. (2012). *Decolonizing methodologies: Research and Indigenous peoples.* Zed Books.

Turner, H. G. (1904). *A history of the colony of Victoria: From its discovery to its absorption into the Commonwealth of Australia* (Vol. 1). Longmans, Green.

Wilson, A. (2015). Our coming in stories: Cree identity, body sovereignty and gender self-determination. *Journal of Global Indigeneity, 1*(1), 4.

Wolfe, P. (2006). Settler colonialism and the elimination of the native. *Journal of Genocide Research, 8*(4), 387–409.

Wolfe, P. (2011). Race and the trace of history: For Henry Reynolds. In F. Bateman & L. Pilkington (Eds.), *Studies in Settler Colonialism* (pp. 272–296). Palgrave Macmillan.

# 2

# FOREIGN POLICY FUTURES

*James Blackwell and Julie Ballangarry*

### Indigenous foreign policy futures: where to from here?

When looking towards the future of foreign policy, First Nations peoples have much to offer. There are many opportunities to contribute to the international system as it exists now, and to freely participate in it as sovereign Indigenous nations, and change the way we view the very nature of the system itself. We as Indigenous peoples possess unique ways of seeing the world, of behaving and interacting, of relationships, and of knowing. There is some contemporary research on Indigenous approaches to international relations. This is evident from Indigenous interactions and advocacy within the United Nations system, and how Indigenous peoples have leveraged such platforms to advance our rights and positions (Davis, 2012). It is also seen in the ways in which Indigenous peoples have undertaken our own specific practices of inter-polity relations before and whilst within the confines of colonial state and international systems. (Graham, Brigg, & Weber, 2021). These specific movements and advancements, especially in regard to Indigenous approaches to international relations, are somewhat present in contemporary literature. However, large gaps remain in the literature as well as in international relations practice with respect to Indigenous political philosophies and approaches to engaging with the international system. Moreover, in the last few years some Western settler-states have begun to incorporate Indigenous values into their work (Blackwell & Ballangarry, 2022; Mahuta, 2021). What this chapter explores is the fundamental questions of Indigenous foreign policy futures. In broad terms, what does this look like, what do we mean when we talk about it, and, most importantly, what questions need asking and work needs doing to achieve a 'Indigenous Foreign Policy' future? Exciting and challenging times await for the international community, and it is (hopefully) one which more greatly includes and recognises Indigenous peoples.

### Indigenous peoples' exclusion from foreign policy: the journey into the twenty-first century

When discussing Indigenous peoples' exclusion from foreign policy, it is important to understand the historical exclusion of Indigenous peoples both in political terms and also

DOI: 10.4324/9781003271802-4

social ones. Colonisation brought forced dispossession, massacres, wars over land, and the removal of our children, among many other injustices (Behrendt, 2001; Logan, 2014; Ryan, 2020). The arrival of colonising powers forcibly removed us from our lands and culture, and violently denied our rights to sovereignty, with often brutal consequences. Even events such as national Federation, or territorial independence from the empire, Indigenous peoples continued to face exclusion and discrimination. This was because "imperialism [...] had a similar end result of marginalising the original peoples through policies and processes of genocide, dispossession, exclusion and discrimination" (Davis & Williams, 2021, pp. 15–33; see also Aanya, 2004; Reid, Cormack, & Paine, 2019). Of course, Indigenous peoples' exclusion from the political system did not mean that we were excluded from its effects. For example, in Australia, close to one in two Indigenous people were either forcibly taken from their families as children, or are a descendant of one of these children (The Healing Foundation, 2021, pp. 17–19). In Canada, well over 150,000 Indigenous children were taken from their families to residential schools. Recently, an untold number of children's remains were located in mass graves on school complexes (Hamilton-Diabo, 2021; Lightfoot, 2015; Office of the Prime Minister (Canada), 2008; Walker, 2009, pp. 1–2). Other policies sought to exclude our involvement in workplaces, politics, and general society.

Whilst there were some advancements made on Indigenous rights throughout the twentieth century, including Australia's 1967 referendum[1] and Aotearoa New Zealand's Treaty of Waitangi Act 1975,[2] these were either not as successful as they were set out to be, as successful as they were made out to be by governments, and were ultimately disappointing to Indigenous peoples. Fundamentally, approaches to Indigenous inclusion were designed with little to no input from Indigenous peoples, with initial policy decisions having detrimental impacts on policy success. Many Indigenous peoples and communities are currently still not afforded rights, to authentically advocate for ourselves or shape our own policy futures through self-determination, including foreign policy. Indigenous women in particular are even more disenfranchised from policy discourse and development, facing systemic "marginalisation and exclusion", minimising the right to self-determination, and serving as an obstacle of "effective representation and participation" which continuously remains "largely unaddressed" (Davis, 2012b, p. 80; Australian Human Rights Commission, 2020, pp. 80–83). The consequence of inadequate policy development sees Indigenous peoples still fighting the same issues decades after some of these first movements for justice, inclusion, and fair treatment began. For example, in 2017, Australian Indigenous peoples presented the broader Australian public with the Uluru Statement from the Heart, calling for an enshrined Indigenous Voice to Parliament (Davis & Williams, 2021, pp. 8–14, 144–156; Referendum Council, 2017). Unsurprisingly, it fell on deaf ears, although elections in 2022 and a new Labor government signal potential progress on this front (Butler, 2022; Turnbull, Brandis, & Scullion, 2017, p. 1). Meanwhile in other nation states, such as Aotearoa and Canada, Indigenous peoples are also equally fighting for their rights and for greater recognition within their societies, despite having signed treaties many centuries ago. In Canada, Indigenous people still regularly have to fight, often violently or financially, for their rights, especially as environmentally damaging projects are built across their lands without consent (Gorelick, 2008, pp. 50–52; Spiegel, 2021; Stacey, 2018). Māori in Aotearoa (New Zealand) also struggle with recognition, rights, and the asserting of culture in the face of marginalisation (Reid, Cormack, & Paine, 2019).

What we see in practice in settler-colonial nation states stems from narratives derived from those with 'authority' to produce knowledge. Within the academy, such narratives were generally told from the colonial point of view, triumphing the 'positive' consequences of colonialism, and providing a 'proud history' of colonised nations. Whilst there has been a shift in this paradigm, with more Indigenous peoples sharing our perspectives, including in this book, many Indigenous peoples, across the globe, would argue the behaviour of colonial powers amounts to the historical, and potentially ongoing, genocide of our peoples. Such a view is articulated by Eualeyai/Kamillaroi scholar Larissa Behrendt (2001):

> [P]olitical posturing and semantic debates do nothing to dispel the feeling Indigenous people have that this is the word that adequately describes our experience as colonised peoples. This description of dispossession and the forced removal of children from the point of view of the victim/survivor of historical and colonial processes is hard to fit into academic and legal discourse.
>
> (p.132)

This has meant two things: that Western understandings of the world have prevailed as legitimate knowledge production in disciplines such as political science and international relations, whilst Indigenous knowledges have been delegitimised through exclusion. Thus, the exclusion of Indigenous peoples at a domestic level parallels the exclusion of Indigenous peoples from foreign policy.

As a result, two key areas of contributions get neglected by mainstream scholars and practitioners: first, our contributions and efforts in shaping the international legal system and human rights frameworks, and second, the unique approaches and ways of being we as Indigenous peoples have, that speak to current trends in global world politics, alongside theories for understanding the world from an international relations framework. This is the ultimate reflection of settler-state colonialism which Indigenous peoples find ourselves subject to. We are often viewed as 'other', as "not constitut[ing] authentic political communities", and thus are not peoples on whom foreign policy and international relations have any effect (Beier, 2009, pp. 11–15; Landriault & Savard, 2019).

However, despite this, Indigenous peoples do have long histories of engaging with the international system. This includes Indigenous peoples taking grievances to European colonial powers during the nineteenth century, and the Council of the Iroquois Confederacy seeking League of Nations arbitration, and ultimately League of Nations membership, in disputes with Canada in the 1920s (Aanya, 2004; Lepage, 1994). Such efforts, although ultimately unsuccessful, pushed forward the notion that Indigenous peoples are not merely domestic constituents of the nations that purportedly represent us, and that international human rights should not face barriers such as domestic jurisdiction or Eurocentric notions of sovereignty (Aanya, 2004). During the 1970s, Indigenous communities began to interact with one another, and learn lessons on the global movement for rights, and how to push for recognition as sovereign communities (Wilmer, 1993). Such global conferences, declarations, and establishment of inter-nation bodies such as the American Indian Parliament and the Nordic Sámi Council, alongside globally significant protest movements such as the Aboriginal Tent Embassy in Canberra, Australia, pushed forward Indigenous assertions about our place within the broader international system of states, and within the structures and international institutions those states had established.

Such work continued with the United Nations Declaration on the Rights of Indigenous Peoples (UNDRIP), where we saw Indigenous peoples interacting within the United Nations system with the clear intent to assert our rights and advance self-determination. Developed over a multi-decade-long process culminating in its ratification in 2007 (notably voted against by the four 'CANZUS' nations of Canada, Australia, Aotearoa New Zealand, and the United States), UNDRIP represents an Indigenous critique of "the Westphalian notion of sovereignty manifest in the narrative of dispossession that underpins the international legal and political system" (Davis, 2007, p. 55). By engaging international systems, often independently of the states purportedly there to represent our interests, Indigenous peoples saw the 'universality' and "commonality of the discrimination and loss of rights we faced at the hands of colonialism" (Davis, 2012a, p. 20). Such sharing of experiences and focusing on shared goals for the future shaped the drafting of UNDRIP standards to extend the "already existing international human rights standards pertaining to the individual to the collective" (Pritchard, 1998). Indigenous peoples advanced an agenda of rights which centred on culture and self-determination, doing so within international structures of power.

## What is an Indigenous foreign policy approach?

Indigenous peoples globally have a wealth of unique ontologies, epistemologies, and cosmologies which possess tremendous potential for international relations and foreign policy. Indigenous peoples possess ongoing cultural practices that have the ability to advance not only Indigenous rights when we act on our own in the international arena, but advance the rights of others through an Indigenous approach to foreign policy and international relations, if adopted by settler states. These, however, are not currently acknowledged, nor treated as legitimate approaches, and Indigenous relational political thinking is largely neglected and overlooked within international scholarship and policymaking (Brigg, Graham, & Weber, 2021; Irwin, 2021; Landriault & Savard, 2019). We are generally not seen as 'authentic political communities' who have serious views on or approaches to foreign policy. To say that First Nation peoples have nothing of value to add to foreign policy or international relations, neglects not just our long histories of diplomatic practice, relational values, and unique ontological approaches, but also neglects a growing field of scholarship exploring such issues.

Within the continent of Australia, there are over 250 Indigenous languages with around 800 dialects, each representing unique cultures, laws, and histories, and each part of complex multipolar systems with relations around and beyond the continent (Australian Institute of Aboriginal and Torres Strait Islander Studies (AIATSIS), nd; Macknight, 1976; Macknight, 2011; Pascoe, 2018). Multi-polity gatherings of Indigenous peoples also occurred across the continent, with Indigenous peoples conducting complex relationships based on shared understandings of cultural practice (Pascoe, 2018). Such ways of being are "different ways of practicing and conceptualising political ordering and inter-polity relations", especially when looking at traditional Western practice, and philosophical underpinning (Brigg, Graham, & Weber, 2021, p. 12). 'Aboriginal Australian' approaches place individuals within the same system as political epistemologies based on relationality to each other, where individuals are autonomous, self-regulating their own relationships to others, country, and law (Brigg, Graham, & Weber, 2021). In the words of Mary Graham, a Kombumerri/Wakka Wakka scholar, everyone "is his or her own law-bearer" (Graham, 1990, in Brigg, Graham, &

Weber, 2021, p. 14). The interconnectedness of 'Aboriginal Australian' ways of being—where individuals share collective but individuated and reciprocal responsibility to law and care for Country—is different to Western inter-polity relations, but possesses an ability to speak to Western ways of knowing and being (Blackwell, 2022b).

The fundamental basis for many Indigenous cultural values revolves around a series of interconnected concepts that are identified in Kirkness and Barnhardt's 4Rs Framework; Respect, Relationships, Reciprocity, and Responsibilities (Kirkness & Barnhardt, 1991). These form the basis of an individual-centric ontology where the relationality of individuals to these four frameworks, as Brigg, Graham, and Weber articulate, forms a strong basis for a unique but integrated approach for foreign policy discussion (Brigg, Graham, & Weber, 2021, pp. 18–19). We can see this at work in theory and practice with Mātauranga Māori, or Māori, knowledge and its potential contributions to foreign policy and international relations. Mātauranga Māori is "the body of knowledge originating from Māori ancestors, including Māori world view and perspectives, Māori creativity and cultural practices", as well as "the unique Māori way of viewing the world, encompassing both traditional knowledge and culture" (Hikuroa, 2017, pp. 5–6). It talks about a relatedness of the world where all things are both related and interconnected, and have responsibility to one another, as well as to the system as a whole (Hikuroa, 2017; Salmond, 2012). Within te ao Māori (the Māori world), such interconnectivity can be expressed through the "all-encompassing networks of kin relations, or whakapapa" (Salmond, 2012, p. 73). As Marshall Sahlins (1985) writes, "The [Māori] universe is a gigantic kin, a genealogy", with such networks and relations "often spoken of as plants, rooted in the soil, branching and sprawling across the land" (p. 195; Salmond, 2012, pp. 73–74). Combined with the concept of Tikanga Māori, the process of living Māori values, people had responsibilities towards knowledge, land, and life, with reciprocal obligations to one's ancestors, and towards "plants and animals, as well as living people" (Salmond, 2012, p. 74; see also Mead, 2016). Tikanga Māori, a "conceptual system" dealing with ideas and beliefs on correct ways of behaviour, moral responsibilities, and cultural process, also contains customary acts of practice, and is an essential part of Mātauranga Māori that "cannot be understood" without the other (Mead, 2016, pp. 7–8, 25–26).

The strong relationship between Tikanga Māori and Mātauranga Māori, and their joint focus on interrelatedness, obligation, and behaviours, shows the strong applicability of both towards political thought and foreign policy and the strong applicability generally of Indigenous approaches. However, when scholars and practitioners focus only on the differences between Indigenous and Western approaches, it contributes to the very notions of colonialism that the Indigenous approach seeks to reject, and enables "scholarly mining of Indigenous philosophy for dominant knowledge's own projects" (Brigg, Graham, & Weber, 2021, p. 19). If one is to position Indigenous and Western inter-polity relations as oppositional forms, this places both frameworks under a Western lens, with its focus on oppositionality and conflict. Thus, Indigenous ways of knowing and doing become an 'escape', instead of ontologies which offer meaningful contributions to Western approaches, and vice versa (Brigg, Graham, & Weber, 2021). Indigenous political thought and diplomatic practice do, and should, exist *in relation with* Western approaches rather than *in opposition to*. And when Indigenous approaches are brought into mainstream thinking, such relationality, rather than oppositionality, is made clear.

## What is the current state of First Nation foreign policy?

Generally, settler-states—including Australia—have historically not engaged with Indigenous peoples on foreign policy discourse, ignoring and neglecting the strong contributions that we have to offer. However, within the last few years we have seen some movement, albeit incrementally, which offers interesting insights into what Indigenous peoples might achieve and contribute to foreign policy, as well as the challenges that remain. The first Western settler-state to promote an 'Indigenous foreign policy' was Aotearoa (New Zealand), which launched its agenda in the early months of 2021. Nanai Mahuta, Aotearoa (New Zealand)'s foreign minister, the first Māori woman to hold that role, has made the embedding of Māori values a cornerstone of her time in office. Centred in tirohanga Māori, or a Māori world view, she looked to use the changing focus on Indigenous foreign policy to reframe Aotearoa (New Zealand)'s identity, and pursue a foreign policy which followed shared core values, including:

- *manaaki*—kindness or the reciprocity of goodwill;
- *whanaunga*—our connectedness or shared sense of humanity;
- *mahi tahi* and *kotahitanga*—collective benefits and shared aspiration;
- *kaitiaki*—protector (Mahuta, 2021, pp. 2–3).

These are values reflected in Māori culture, law, and cosmology, applied to a Western way of operating in the international arena. Further, each of these values, when in relation with each other, gives a sense that everything is 'connected and purposeful' (Mahuta, 2021). The vision shared by Mahuta also looked to recognise and include Indigenous knowledges, economic participation, and broader perspectives, to create a long-lasting impact, as well as to forge stronger connections with Indigenous peoples globally, ensuring Indigenous issues become a feature of foreign policy practice. What we see, then, is attempts to strongly embed tirohanga Māori in the work of the settler-state within its foreign policy, and move discussions of Māori beyond the domestic into the international sphere.

There are definitely flaws within this approach, and issues have remained unaddressed or undeveloped for some time since the policy was launched. In July of 2022, nearly 18 months after the policy was launched, Minister Mahuta, in a pre-recorded speech in Wellington, did not advance these ideas much beyond her original speech in February 2021 (Mahuta, 2022,; Evett, 2022). While again discussing how these values "emphasise meaningful, mutual, enduring relationships where mana and sovereignty are respected", and how they are applicable to "relationships between individuals and peoples, as between countries and governments, large and small", she did not give much in the way of what this means for Aotearoa New Zealand's foreign policy, or what work she or her ministry is doing regarding this agenda (Mahuta, 2022). Indeed, Secretary of Foreign Affairs Chris Seed was unable to give explicit cases of foreign policy being actioned in line with Māori values beyond "proportionate recruitment of staff" (Evett, 2022, para. 7). Indeed, as Evett writes, such approaches in the past have been seen as "brown ethnic icing on a […] white cake", and Aotearoa (New Zealand) risks their Indigenous foreign policy becoming "similarly hollow due to the disconnect between rhetoric and action" (Evett, 2022, para. 5). What is required here is more than work that is achievable by Mahuta or other advocates alone. Mahuta is "pushing against an institution that has ensured unparalleled policy stability for almost 80 years by repeatedly cloning itself", and Māori have for generations pushed to wear down these systems while themselves being worn down in return (Evett,

2022, para. 9). Despite these concerns, and serious they are, Māori values in foreign policy has great potential, and is truly promising, and shows what Aotearoa (New Zealand) is trying to advance in practice in this space. It represents one path countries have taken with Indigenous foreign policy, with its own risks and lessons for others.

Presenting strong contrasts with Aotearoa (New Zealand), before May of 2022, Australia's Indigenous foreign policy approach was much more bureaucratic-minded, as demonstrated by the 2021 Indigenous Diplomacy Agenda (IDA) (Adamson, 2021; Department of Foreign Affairs and Trade, 2021). The Agenda followed on from the 2015 Indigenous Peoples Strategy, which acknowledged that the Australian government needed to engage better with Indigenous peoples. However, the IDA and its terms of reference were developed without any significant levels of consultation with Indigenous peoples and no accountability mechanisms (Blackwell, 2021c). Indigenous peoples who were involved in the consultation process came from within the Department of Foreign Affairs and Trade (DFAT). This raises concerns around the validity of only using Indigenous bureaucrats in consultation processes, as current institutions merely seek to place us within a system that is not designed for us, and without our involvement or recognition of our perspectives. This does not let Indigenous peoples set the agenda for our own destinies, and is instead government dictating the terms of our participation (Moreton-Robinson, 2011). Although the ambitions of this policy were large, it was evident that the agenda focused heavily on bureaucratic changes DFAT could implement in its own interests rather than Indigenous peoples' interests (Blackwell, 2021c). It was also not clear, nor was there any explanation, on what was meant by efforts to 'benefit' Indigenous people; what this looked like, for whom, on what time frame, and who was accountable to Indigenous peoples for said benefit (Department of Foreign Affairs and Trade, 2021). This is not the standard of policy we should apply to Indigenous peoples, but it is the norm when policymakers too often speak for, rather than with, and aid in the 'othering' of Indigenous peoples throughout policy, and foreign policy in particular. The IDA did represent a significant first step, with some calling it at the time 'a strong move in the right direction' for Australian foreign policy, but the policy did not live up to that level of promise (Blackwell, 2021b). It appeared to use Indigenous peoples merely for the advantage in assisting the mainstream, irrespective of what contributions we may have on our own, as part of what Brigg, Graham and Weber term "the scholarly mining of Indigenous philosophy for the dominant knowledge's own projects" (Brigg, Graham, & Weber, 2021, p. 19), or what Evett noted with Aotearoa (New Zealand)'s policy at risk of becoming "an exercise in window-dressing" (Evett, 2022, para. 12).

In 2022, as part of the May federal election campaign, the Australian Labor Party promised to overhaul DFAT's approach and launch a specific 'Indigenous foreign policy' in its place (Australian Labor Party, 2022a; Australian Labor Party, 2022b, p. 16). While the details on this were scant before the election, the policy taken forward was to engage properly and respectfully with Indigenous communities. Alongside the appointment of a 'First Nations Ambassador', there would also be an 'Office of First Nations Engagement', which would seek to understand from Indigenous communities, leaders, and advocates how Indigenous "identities, perspectives and practices" can be incorporated into our overseas engagement, how to "embed First Nations perspectives in Australia's international diplomacy", and how to "support a new model of trade which actively includes and advances First Nations people" (Australian Labor Party, 2022a; Australian Labor Party, 2022b,

p. 16). This work is not attempting to do more than listen, hear, and devise stronger policies going forward, but it represents a fundamental shift for Australia.

DFAT under the former Morrison government[3] suggested that they saw Indigenous peoples as integral parts of developing an authentic Australian foreign service, achieved by building Indigenous peoples into Australia's diplomacy (Adamson, 2021). However, our involvement in foreign policy development and diplomacy, although inclusive of Indigenous peoples within the department, was limited to already existing structures and practices of Australia's foreign policy institutions, and would not extend much beyond this (Adamson, 2021; Blackwell & Ballangarry, 2022). What we see from the current Albanese government instead is a policy that looks to ground its work in UNDRIP, but also to engage with countries such as Aotearoa (New Zealand) and Canada, on shared issues "such as treaty, reconciliation, supporting UNDRIP, and First Nations participation" (Blackwell, 2022a, para. 10). Of course, like Aotearoa (New Zealand), there is a scant amount of detail here, and much will be revealed over the course of successive years, and it is important that the agenda maintain the support it has from senior government members, but also staff, Indigenous and non-Indigenous, within DFAT. For as Blackwell (2022a, para. 12) suggests, "this moment represents a hopeful advancement in the way we not only think about foreign policy, and First Nations policy", but also how we think about the settler-states we live in.

## How could states achieve an Indigenous foreign policy?

What is it that we want to see next? How can foreign policy authentically meet the objectives for Indigenous peoples, to value our unique positions? Current approaches to policy need to be examined to ensure that future policy processes are inclusive of Indigenous peoples, but also in line with the UNDRIP principles of self-determination, to ensure that genuine momentum in this space can be achieved. Since the mid to late 1980s, policymaking processes have come to rely heavily on a centralised 'policy community' model, an inherited feature of the many settler-states' political systems (Ballangarry, 2022, in Blackwell & Ballangarry, 2022). This model relies on relatively closed policy communities to formulate and develop their respective portfolio's suite of polices. The nature of centralised policy-making is exacerbated in foreign policy, as the locus of power is concentrated in the hands of the executive branch of the government, senior bureaucrats within foreign ministries, and ministerial advisers, the latter two having a large influence over foreign policy (Blackwell & Ballangarry, 2022). For many Indigenous peoples, their role in policy communities is generally consultative in capacity. Consultative processes range from non-participation and tokenistic in nature, to genuine engagement, highlighting the influence of power policy actors have to the different levels (Arnstein, 1969, pp. 216–224). They signify the difference between engaging in empty rituals of participation and having the power needed to affect process outcomes (Arnstein, 1969). Despite the fact that Indigenous peoples may be 'involved' in policy processes, Indigenous peoples are continuously articulating that their voices are not being heard. Indigenous peoples hold little power, with consultations being held in a tokenistic manner. Ironically, approaches to Indigenous peoples and policy are often penned as 'working in partnership'; however, the reality of this does not align.

There are two overarching challenges when it comes to Indigenous peoples achieving a foreign policy which is inclusive of Indigenous peoples. The first is the presence of Indigenous peoples within the foreign policy sphere, and the challenge this provides to dominant perspectives. Our mere presence in these spaces, as we can see with Indigenous peoples and the United Nations system, or with UNDRIP, provides a critique of "the Westphalian notion of sovereignty manifest in the narrative of dispossession that underpins the international legal and political system" (Davis, 2007, p. 55). Furthermore, given our unique relational approaches, possessing the ability to speak to Western practice also allows us to inherently challenge it—if given the space to do so. Our presence in international policy will always present challenges, as our sovereignty, and being, challenges the very notion of identity settler-states hold about themselves and their relationship to us. This is part of the problem Evett (2022) has identified with Aotearoa (New Zealand), that institutions of foreign policy have been successful in ensuring unparalleled policy stability by the repeated cloning of itself, and its staff. To repeat a joke about Western foreign ministries, "the only goal of Cybermen[4] is to make more Cybermen" (Goodwillie, 2020, para. 13), and the only goal of foreign affairs departments is to make more foreign affairs staff. Cybermen do not make good foreign policy, but exist purely to grow their own ranks, and to destroy those in their path. This is what happens often to Indigenous peoples in international spaces: conversion or destruction.

The second challenge to achieving Indigenous foreign policy includes the role Indigenous peoples play in the policy design process. For too long, policy development has excluded us at all levels, domestically and internationally. Whether this is by deliberate design, as is the case with many policy areas during the twentieth century, or merely a product of our exclusion from political and social structures of power, the result is the same: Indigenous peoples do not have input or a say over policies which affect us, least of all in the foreign policy space. Both of these challenges centre around the involvement of and input from Indigenous peoples, and enabling us to have a direct impact on how foreign policy is developed and enacted, and the solution to them is clear: structural reform. Indigenous peoples require genuine participation and engagement, which will only be achieved when we have a legitimate seat at the table where our voices are equal to those who sit beside us. This is the exact type of solution that, within Australia, an Indigenous Voice enshrined in the Constitution, as envisioned by the Uluru Statement from the Heart, was designed to facilitate, and that within Canada, the United States, and Aotearoa (New Zealand), historical treaties are meant to set the agenda for (Asch, 1997; Davis & Williams, 2021; Macklem & Sanderson, 2016). Of course, as we see in all of these countries, government is very unwilling to change its approach when it involves weakening what they see as their structures, or their power, and they are also often unwilling. We know all too well the history of government casting a 'blind eye' towards promises made and assurances given, when the price of keeping them becomes too great (*McGirt v. Oklahoma*, 2020).

In the immediate future, what we need at all levels within foreign policy apparatuses is states undertaking proactive actions to genuinely work in partnership with Indigenous peoples. In terms of staffing, recruiting Indigenous peoples brings with it a wealth of lived experience and inherited knowledges. This not only enhances the work of the state internally, but also how states position themselves externally. In the Australian context, Indigenous peoples have the oldest governance structures on the planet, coexisting with neighbouring polities in complex relationships, and managing to preserve these even following colonial invasions and subjugations (Pascoe, 2018). Our practices and values are rooted in our cosmologies, cultures, and most importantly, languages. These practices are something that can be embedded in and be useful to modern settler-states, if done effectively, with Indigenous peoples (Brigg, Graham, & Weber, 2021). These values and structures are also rooted in an approach inclusive of sustainability, and relationality not just to people but also to Country (Brigg, Graham, & Webber, 2021; Russ-Smith, 2021).

Our expertise in caring for Country, waters, and the natural world as a whole is something the global community can and should benefit from in the face of climate change and its related challenges, and represents a strong area of potential inclusion. Second, policy approaches by states need to reflect Indigenous world views and unique cosmologies. These cosmologies and world views challenge traditional policy approaches, and shift our understanding of fundamental issues and principles within foreign policy. To better reframe and reflect our place within world structures, the embedding of our approaches is central to the advancement of our values within foreign policy. Additionally, support by states for principles found in UNDRIP, alongside greater enhancement of treaty rights, implementation of constitutional recognition, and other such structural power supports can play a vital role in this venture. These are the tools that can ensure that governments uphold the rights of Indigenous peoples whilst providing levers to make sure of accountability. These suggested actions aim to create the foundation for structural change within current governments and institutions, so that the development of policy can truly reflect our shared sovereignty and unceded rights.

Of course, what this chapter has not addressed going forward is Indigenous peoples playing roles as independent sovereign entities, acting independently of overarching settler-colonial governments, and asserting themselves in the international arena as independent polities. However, we acknowledge that this has happened and have seen some examples of this, including with the Iroquois attempts to join the League of Nations and undertake arbitration therein, which was, as we know, unsuccessful (Aanya, 2004; Lepage, 1994). On the international stage, Indigenous peoples rarely have a seat at the table as independent polities, instead more often than not relying on their 'representative' states to intercede on their behalf, or appearing at global events as part of their 'representative' states. This does not mean that Indigenous peoples cannot and should not assert themselves as independent polities. It is both how we have existed for millennia, and can bring great potential benefits. One of the tenets of nation-building for Indigenous people is to act as a nation, 'assert decision-making power', and have 'effective governing institutions' which match 'political culture' and values (Cornell & Kalt, 2007). There are also examples of Indigenous peoples establishing inter-nation dialogues and organisations; to work together to solve common problems, compare approaches, and even advocate on the world stage, concrete examples of Indigenous diplomacy in action (Wilmer, 1993). Such methods have had successes, and advance the ideas and values of Indigenous peoples beyond the domestic sphere, a barrier which is extremely hard to break out of. It is likely that alongside settler and colonial states pursuing Indigenous foreign policies, we are likely to see much more independent participation in the global system by Indigenous peoples acting as independent, sovereign polities. And this is something we welcome.

We do not seek to prescribe here whether Indigenous peoples should seek to enter the world stage as independent polities, whether they should seek to push to change the approach of their 'representative states', or both. But to advance Indigenous interests at home and abroad, this will only be possible when Indigenous peoples are fully embraced by the global polity, in an authentic and genuine way (Graham & Brigg, 2020). Furthermore, a state's foreign policy reflects its values and identity on a global stage, so how governments engage with Indigenous peoples and seek to include us in policy, especially on issues of foreign policy, is telling of their democracy, diplomacy, and how they view human rights on a global scale (Devetak & True, 2006). Even more telling is how states react to our presences in the international sphere when it comes to our independent actions, and to us asserting our places as sovereign peoples with unique cultures and approaches to world politics. Governments of all stripes have wonderful opportunities to set global standards when it comes to respecting Indigenous peoples and our rights, and allowing us to assume a greater presence in world politics.

## Notes

1 The 1967 referendum in Australia sought to change the Australian Constitution to grant the federal government the power to make laws regarding Indigenous peoples, as well as to allow Indigenous peoples to be counted in the decennial national census. It was Australia's most successful referendum, with 90.77% of Australians, and every state jurisdiction, voting yes.
2 The Treaty of Waitangi Act 1975 gave the 1840 Treaty of Waitangi legal recognition and force within New Zealand law, and established the Waitangi Tribunal to investigate breaches of the Treaty by the New Zealand government that occurred after 1975, as well as to recommend remedies.
3 The Morrison government (in office 2018–2022) was a period of centre-right Australian government run by the Liberal and National Parties of Australia, from when Scott Morrison took over from Malcolm Turnbull in August 2018, until their defeat at the May 2022 Australian general election. They had been in government under various prime ministers since 2013.
4 Cybermen are a race of human-cyborgs from the British television show *Doctor Who*, whose main goal is to convert humanoid species into more Cybermen, to grow their ranks, enabling them to continue this process exponentially.

## References

Adamson, F. (2021, 20 May). *The contribution of Indigenous Australia to our diplomacy*. Department of Foreign Affairs and Trade.
Anaya, J., & Anaya, S. J. (2004). *Indigenous peoples in international law* (2nd ed.). Oxford University Press.
Arnstein, S. R. (1969). A ladder of citizen participation. *Journal of the American Institute of Planners, 35*(4), 216–224.
Asch, M. (Ed.). (1997). *Aboriginal and treaty rights in Canada: Essays on law, equity, and respect for difference*. UBC Press.
Australian Human Rights Commission. (2020). *Wiyi Yani U Thangani (Women's Voices): Securing Our Rights, Securing Our Future Report*. Australian Human Rights Commission.
Australian Institute of Aboriginal and Torres Strait Islander Studies (AIATSIS). (nd). *Map of Indigenous Australia*. Australian Institute of Aboriginal and Torres Strait Islander Studies (AIATSIS). https://aiatsis.gov.au/explore/map-indigenous-australia
Australian Labor Party. (2022a). *Policies: First Nations*. Australian Labor Party. www.alp.org.au/policies/first-nations
Australian Labor Party. (2022b). *Labor's Commitment to First Nations Peoples*. Australian Labor Party.
Ballangarry, J. (2022). Indigenous issues and policymaking approaches: The centralised nature of policymaking and the implications for Indigenous voices [Unpublished manuscript].
Behrendt, L. (2001). Genocide: The distance between law and life. *Aboriginal History, 25*, 132–147.
Beier, J. M. (2009). Forgetting, remembering, and finding indigenous peoples in international relations. In *Indigenous diplomacies* (pp. 11–27). Palgrave Macmillan.
Blackwell, J. (2021a, 12 February). Foreign policy's 'Indigenous moment' is here. *The Interpreter*. www.lowyinstitute.org/the-interpreter/foreign-policy-s-indigenous-moment-here

Blackwell, J. (2021b, 2 May). Australia is pursuing a more Indigenous-focused foreign policy. But does it miss the bigger picture?. *The Conversation.* https://theconversation.com/australiais-pursu ing-a-more-indigenous-focused-foreign-policy-butdoes-it-miss-the-bigger-picture-161189

Blackwell, J. (2021c, 16 November). Where were First Nations people at COP26?. *Canberra Times.* www.canberratimes.com.au/story/7510913/wherewere-first-nations-people-at-cop26/

Blackwell, J. (2022a, 28 May). Labor's First Nations foreign policy looks like real, substantive change. *Canberra Times.* www.canberratimes.com.au/story/7756003/labors-first-nations-foreign-policy-promises-real-change/

Blackwell, J. (2022b). First Nations and Australia: Walking together or walking alone? In B. Brooklyn, B. T. Jones, & B. Strating (Eds.), *Australia on the world stage* (pp. 1–16). Routledge.

Blackwell, J., & Ballangarry, J. (2022) Indigenous foreign policy: A new way forward? *AFFPC Issues Paper Series 1.* https://iwda.org.au/assets/files/AFFPC-issues-paper-Indigenous-Foreign-Policy-Blackwell-Ballangarry-FINAL.pdf

Brigg, M., Graham, M., & Weber, M. (2021). Relational Indigenous systems: Aboriginal Australian political ordering and reconfiguring IR. *Review of International Studies, 48,* Special Issue 5: Pluriversal Relationality, 891–909.

Butler, D. (2022, 11 April). Yarrabah Affirmation calls for Voice referendum in next parliamentary term. *NITV.* www.sbs.com.au/nitv/article/2022/04/11/yarrabahaffirmation-calls-voice-referen dum-next-parliamentary-term

Cornell, S., & Kalt, J. P. (2007). Two approaches to the development of Native Nations. In M. Jorgensen (Ed.), *Rebuilding Native Nations: Strategies for governance and development* (pp. 3–33). University of Arizona Press.

Davis, M. (2007). The United Nations Declaration on the Rights of Indigenous Peoples. *Australian Indigenous Law Review, 11*(3), 55–63.

Davis, M. (2012a). To bind or not to bind: The United Nations Declaration on the Rights of Indigenous People five years on. *Australian International Law Journal, 19,* 17–48.

Davis, M. (2012b). Aboriginal women: The right to self-determination. *Australian Indigenous Law Review, 16*(1), 78–88.

Davis, M., & Williams, G. (2021). *Everything you need to know about the Uluru Statement from the Heart.* UNSW Press/NewSouth Publishing.

Department of Foreign Affairs and Trade. Australian Government. (2021). *Indigenous diplomacy agenda.* www.dfat.gov.au/sites/default/files/indigenous-diplomacy-agenda.pdf

Devetak, R., & True, J. (2006). Diplomatic divergence in the Antipodes: Globalisation, foreign policy and state identity in Australia and New Zealand. *Australian Journal of Political Science, 41*(2), 241–256.

Evett, J. (2022, 7 October). Does New Zealand's Indigenous diplomacy measure up? Asia & the Pacific Policy Society. Policy Forum. www.policyforum.net/does-new-zealands-indigenous-diplom acy-measure-up/

Goodwillie, I. (2020, 20 May). Doctor Who: 10 things that make no sense about the Cybermen. *Screenrant.* https://screenrant.com/doctor-who-cybermen-no-sense/

Gorelick, M. (2008). Discrimination of aboriginals on native lands in Canada. *UN Chronicle, 44*(3), 50–52.

Graham, M., & Brigg. M. (2020, 9 November). Why we need Aboriginal political philosophy now, more than ever. *ABC Religion and Ethics.* www.abc.net.au/religion/why-we-need-aborigi nal-political-philosophy/12865016#:~:text=Aboriginal%20peoples%20of%20Australia%20h ave,the%20world's%20oldest%20political%20designers.

Hamilton-Diabo, J. (2021, 19 August). Indian Residential School findings: How diverse Indigenous communities deal with grief and healing. *The Conversation.* https://theconversation.com/ind ian-residential-school-findings-how-diverse-indigenous-communities-deal-with-grief-and-healing-163415

Hikuroa, D. (2017). Mātauranga Māori—the ūkaipō of knowledge in New Zealand. *Journal of the Royal Society of New Zealand, 47*(1), 5–10.

Irwin, R. (2021). Rewilding policy futures: Maori whakapapa and the ecology of the subject. *Policy Futures in Education, 19*(3), 307–323.

Kirkness, V. J., & Barnhardt, R. (1991). First Nations and higher education: The four R's—Respect, relevance, reciprocity, responsibility. *Journal of American Indian Education, 30*(3), 1–15.

Landriault, M. (2019). An Indigenous perspective on Canadian Foreign Policy. *Canadian Journal of Native Studies, 39*(1), 65–89.

Lepage, P. (1994). Indigenous peoples and the evolution of international standards: A short history. In M. Léger (Ed.), *Aboriginal peoples: Towards self-government* (pp. 1–24). Black Rose Books.

Lightfoot, S .R. (2015). Settler-state apologies to Indigenous peoples: A normative framework and comparative assessment. *Native American and Indigenous Studies, 2*, 15–39.

Logan, T. (2014). National memory and museums: Remembering settler colonial genocide of Indigenous peoples in Canada. In *Remembering genocide* (pp. 126–144). Routledge.

Macklem, P., & Sanderson, D. (Eds.). (2016). *From recognition to reconciliation: Essays on the constitutional entrenchment of Aboriginal and treaty rights.* University of Toronto Press.

Macknight, C. (2011). The view from Marege: Australian knowledge of Makassar and the impact of the trepang industry across two centuries. *Aboriginal History, 35*, 121–143.

Macknight, C. C. (1976). *The voyage to Marege: Macassan trepangers in northern Australia.* Melbourne University.

Mahuta, N. (2021). A different approach. *New Zealand International Review, 46*(3), 2–5.

Mahuta, N. (2022, 4 July). Diplosphere Conference 2022. New Zealand Government. www.beehive. govt.nz/speech/diplosphere-conference-2022

*McGirt v. Oklahoma.*(2020). Supreme Court of the United States. www.supremecourt.gov/opinions/ 19pdf/18-9526_9okb.pdf

Mead, H. M. (2016). *Tikanga Maori: Living by Maori values* (rev. ed.). Huia Publishers.

Moreton-Robinson, A. (2011). Virtuous racial states: The possessive logic of patriarchal white sovereignty and the United Nations Declaration on the Rights of Indigenous Peoples. *Griffith Law Review, 20*(3), 641–658.

Office of the Prime Minister (Canada). (2008, 11 June). Prime Minister Harper offers a full apology on behalf of Canadians for the Indian Residential Schools system. www.canada.ca/en/news/arch ive/2008/06/prime-minister-harper-offers-full-apology-behalf-canadians-indian-residential-scho ols-system.html

Pritchard, S. (1998). *Setting international standards: An analysis of the United Nations draft declaration on the rights of indigenous peoples.* Aboriginal and Torres Strait Islander Commission.

Referendum Council. (2017) *Final report of the Referendum Council.* Referendum Council, Department of Prime Minister and Cabinet.

Reid, P., Cormack, D., & Paine, S. J. (2019). Colonial histories, racism and health—The experience of Māori and Indigenous peoples. *Public Health, 172*, 119–124.

Russ-Smith, J. (2021). Giyira: Indigenous women's knowing, being and doing as a way to end war on country. In M. MacKenzie & N. Wegner (Eds.), *Feminist solutions for ending war* (pp. 15–28). Pluto Press.

Ryan, L. (2020). Digital map of colonial frontier massacres in Australia 1788–1930. *Teaching History, 54*(3), 13–20.

Sahlins, M. (1985). Hierarchy and humanity in Polynesia. In A. Hooper & J. Huntsman (Eds.), *Transformations of Polynesian culture.* The Polynesian Society.

Salmond, A. (2012). Back to the future: First encounters in Te Tai Rawhiti. *Journal of the Royal Society of New Zealand, 42*(2), 69–77.

Spiegel, S. J. (2021). Fossil fuel violence and visual practices on Indigenous land: Watching, witnessing and resisting settler-colonial injustices. *Energy Research & Social Science, 79*, 102189.

Stacey, R. (2018). The dilemma of indigenous self-government in Canada: Indigenous rights and Canadian federalism. *Federal Law Review, 46*(4), 669–688.

The Healing Foundation. (2021). *Make healing happen: It's time to act.*

Tribunal, N. Z. W. (2011). *Ko Aotearoa tēnei: A Report into Claims Concerning New Zealand Law and Policy Affecting Māori Culture and Identity. Waitangi Tribunal Report 2011.* https://ndhadeli ver.natlib.govt.nz/delivery/DeliveryManagerServlet?dps_pid=IE6295346

Turnbull, M., Brandis, G., & Scullion, N. (2017). *Response to Referendum Council's report on Constitutional Recognition [Joint Media Release].* Prime Minister's Office (Australia).

Waitangi Tribunal. (2011). *Ko Aotearoa Tēnei: A report into claims concerning New Zealand law and policy affecting Māori culture and identity*. Waitangi Tribunal.

Walker, J. (2009). *The Indian Residential Schools Truth and Reconciliation Commission*. Parliamentary Information and Research Service.

Wilmer, F. (1993). *The Indigenous voice in world politics: Since time immemorial*. SAGE.

# 3

# A CERTAIN WISDOM

## 'Living Law' before 'More, More, More'

*Jo Anne Rey*

### Acknowledgements

I pay my respects to my Elders, past, present and emerging, and acknowledge I write from Gayamarigal Ngurrayin (area), one of the 29 areas of Dharug Ngurra (Dharug Country), also known as Sydney, Australia. In this chapter, 'Country' is capitalised to connote the physicality and metaphysical elements of our place of belonging. I acknowledge and recognise my Ancestral obligations to Wallumatta, the Dharug place and people of the Wallumai, the Black Snapper Fish. Macquarie University, where I am a researcher, is on Wallumatta. I acknowledge and pay my respects to all Ancestors, Dharug and other Indigenous Elders and all the scholars who have informed my journey.

Additionally, as a Dharug Aboriginal community member, and a concerned citizen, Indigenous Law as I have been taught, is critical to sustainable well-being, for humans and other-than-humans. As such, it contributes to the global conversations in environmental forums by articulating essential Dharug understandings in response to climate-challenging issues and the need for sustainable futures. One such forum, the Eighth Frontiers Environmental Law Colloquium, in February 2022, through Macquarie University Centre for Environmental Law and Auckland University, became the location for the presentation of the basis of this chapter, so that non-Indigenous audiences receive a broader understanding of the role Indigenous Law has played in sustainability across time.

### Introduction: Country crying out for change

All that has been, has changed.
All that will be, will change.
It's how we manage the change that makes the difference.

(Author unknown)

This chapter considers the practical gap between the dominating approaches of the last 234 years since colonisation on this continent, currently called 'Australia', and

DOI: 10.4324/9781003271802-5

those sustainable approaches of the last 65,000 years, or more. In doing so, I hope to turn perspectives and practices towards sustainable futures as we face climate-changing catastrophes.

The real context of Australia belongs to the multi-millennial wisdom derived from the land, the sea, the sky—knowledges developed by the First Peoples of the continent for the purpose of sustainability—not just for human beings but for all the living presences upon which human beings depend (Watson, 2015).

Since 1788, just 234 years ago, that wisdom—the Living Law—has been denied, outlawed, shamed, desecrated and hidden by the arrival of the British, driven by patriarchal, human-centricity creating unsustainable greed and imbalance. This outcome didn't start here because it was already happening across all the colonised regions of the planet. However, finding solutions that transform the existing problematic practices to global sustainability is possible and can start with this continent's Living Law. Just as Martinez (2018, p. 151) asks, "How can the core sustainable economic—environmental ethics of this [discussed] traditional Indigenous model be adapted to modern environmental and politico—economic changes?", this chapter addresses what that journey can look like if centred in essential relationality.

The structure of the chapter will commence with the context in which we find ourselves today within the continent currently named 'Australia'. However, as will be shown, given that much of the problem has originated from patriarchal human-centricity across the colonised and urbanised domains, the place of urbanised degradation is the centre of focus and presented as critical to finding sustainable solutions globally.

Secondly, I will discuss what I've referred to as Living Law, being the basis of 'Australian' Indigenous cultural practice, relationality and moral and ethical sustainable integrity.

Thirdly, Living Law will then be contrasted with Western consumption narratives and corporate practices, which I call the Law of 'More, More, and More', which is the unsustainable mismanagement of the last 234 years on this continent (Howlett & Lawrence, 2019)

Fourthly, I will offer some ideas for consideration in an effort to overcome the gap between existing problematic practices amounting to serious mismanagement of Country, and how change towards sustainable futures may be considered. Given that my area of belonging, obligation, caring and connection resides within Dharug Ngurra, also known as Sydney 'Australia', examples of alternatives will be drawn from here, with the intention that they may offer approaches that can be applied in some form to other urbanised areas.

## Some context

The problem for European-centric and Western societies that have driven and perpetuated colonisation, is that they had no connection with the lands in which they arrived. Whether it be Australia, America, Canada, South America or India (just to name a few), the intent of colonisation was not to care for Country, but only to take over and develop the place for the benefit of the Western powers participating, and thus reap the profits in the process. For Australia, it was the British Empiricists.

In the 'Australian' context, this started on Dharug Ngurra in 1788, more commonly known today as most of the Sydney metropolitan area, and quickly also impacted the Dharawal and Awabakal peoples to the south and north (Karskens, 2010). Like a rash, the takeover spread across the continent, and with name changes at every step of the way, so-called 'Australia' grew. Along with the name changes, multiple massacres of the human inhabitants resisting this invasion occurred (Reynolds, 1987). Adding to the human demise, the mismanagement of land and water resources, 'heroic' narratives, greedy vested interests and a determination to suck every morsel out of the landscapes, the continent fell victim to the genocidal intent of the colonisers (Tatz, 2017). Country is now gasping for survival—just like the million fish that gasped their last in the Murray-Darling Basin across 2019. Quentin Beresford articulates this history of mismanagement across 233 years in his most recent book, *Wounded Country: A Contested History of the Murray-Darling Basin* (Beresford, 2021).

What becomes extremely clear is that the spiral of blindness, arrogance, greed, ignorance and political shenanigans, which is power-centric rather than Country-centric, continues and is an unsustainable system undermining the vast water system that around one-quarter of the continent relies upon.

However, while Beresford's (2021) work is extremely important because it focuses on the huge Murray-Darling Basin, a food bowl covering more than one million square kilometres that includes and crosses four 'Australian' States: South Australia, Victoria, NSW and Queensland (an area larger than France and Germany together), it is only one part of the story that needs to be considered in the face of pending climatic catastrophes at our doorstep (Beresford, 2021).

## Some statistics

It has been argued (Rey, 2022a) that recent evidence from the Australian Conservation Foundation (ACF) shows the deep link between human presence and other-than-human extinctions. Some statistics, using 2016 figures (Ives et al., 2016), show that:

- nearly 90 per cent of Australia's human population lives in its towns and cities (ACF, 2020, p. 7);
- towns and cities in Australia are where 25 per cent of the nationally listed threatened plants are located; and
- 46 per cent of threatened animals are located (ACF, 2020, p. 2; Ward et al., 2019).

So, these urban statistics position the need for caring for Country *alongside* rural and remote regions, by reinforcing the impact and threat that human-centric systems are having on other-than-humans.

Further statistics from Ward et al. (2019) show that across Australia more than seven million hectares of habitat have been destroyed by human beings (ACF, 2020, p. 9). Pastoralism and land clearing has historically been, and continues to be the culprit (Beresford, 2021).

According to Foley (2020, para. 23), "Government policies have shifted over time but habitat loss from urban development and agriculture have remained mainstay threats. According to the CSIRO, habitat loss from land clearing is a primary driver of biodiversity loss in Australia".

Given urbanisation is not simply an Australian issue, it is reasonable to recognise these imbalances can be globally extended. As the Intergovernmental Panel on Climate Change (IPCC, 2022, p. 7) summary notes:

The assessment of climate change impacts and risks as well as adaptation is set against concurrently unfolding non-climatic global trends e.g., biodiversity loss, overall unsustainable consumption of natural resources, land and ecosystem degradation, rapid urbanisation, human demographic shifts, social and economic inequalities and a pandemic.

In the current climate-challenging context, therefore, recognising humanity's central role in the demise of ecologies demands that we are central to the restitution processes, locally.

Here is a short list of some of catastrophic destructions and extinction events relevant to this continent since 2018:

- The largest living organism on the planet, the Great Barrier Reef, is under threat with frequent coral bleaching events (Lyons, Hill, Deshong, Mooney, & Turpin, 2020).
- The mega-fires of the summer of 2019–2020 wiped out more than 10 million hectares including 'suitable habitat for 69 per cent of all plant species (17,197 species), and 44 per cent of Australia's threatened plants being burnt' (Gallagher et al., 2021, p. 1166).
- Around a million fish died in the Murray-Darling Basin as a result of the condition of the river system (Beresford, 2021).
- The Hawkesbury-Nepean River system (known as the Dyarubbin to Dharug people) is under threat from the NSW State government as they try to raise the Warragamba Dam wall (against their World Heritage obligations, against Dharug and neighbouring custodians' wishes, against renowned archaeological advice) (Gooley, Chung, & Elder, 2022).
- Extensive recent flooding (autumn 2022) has occurred along coastal northern NSW and South-east Queensland through La Niña and warming ocean currents ('A Super Charged Climate', 2022).

This is the context for this continent. And each continent will have its own rendition of the non-climatic global trends simultaneously affecting planetary systems in their context. Combined, futures are looking grim; extinctions are looking inevitable. Given that this demise on our continent has only commenced with colonisation, 234 years ago, it seems logical, and fair, to bring the voice of First Peoples of this continent, our Indigenous ways of knowing, being and doing, that have sustained us for more than 65,000 years, out from the icebox of marginalisation that has nearly extinguished all the Indigene (human and other-than-human) across the continent. As the IPCC (2022, p. 9) has noted: "This report recognises the value of diverse forms of knowledge such as scientific, as well as Indigenous knowledge and local knowledge in understanding and evaluating climate adaptation processes and actions to reduce risks from human-induced climate change".

While the responsibility for the demise of this continent's ecologies, as Beresford (2021) shows, lays squarely at the feet of settler-colonialism, a production underpinned by white, patriarchal empiricism, the context today shouts to the fact that current events are causing land and environmental managers to question the dominant narratives, perspectives and priorities rendered as this continent's 'national identity'. Understanding First Nation's Living Law offers an opportunity to transform practices from perpetuating hierarchical disconnections for the purpose of increasing vested interests' power and wealth, to sustainable systems of Country-connection and a worthy, legitimate national identity (Whyte, 2018).

# What is Living Law?

## Some definitions

It is important to define Living Law in the broader context of 'Aboriginal Law'. The Aboriginal term 'Law' has guided and continues to guide the culture and its practice across this continent for 'ever'. Professor Irene Watson, of the Coorong peoples, uses the term 'Raw Law' (Watson, 2015, p. 1). As she points out, this term for the Aboriginal code of 'social and political conduct' applies to when the formation of Law was 'raw': multi-millennia ago, and was, certainly, the reality at time of invasion, though it was unrecognised and denied, and colonisers constructed a fake narrative that we were without Law—being "uncivilised and without society" (Watson, 2015, p. 1).

However, many have their own ways of expressing Aboriginal Law. Aunty and Dr Mary Graham, a Kombumerri and Wakka Wakka Elder, say "law is the land", cultural practice, and law is "the foundation of relationality" (Graham, 2014, p. 17). Larrakia Elder, from the Northern Territory, and International Grandmothers' Committee representative Bilawarra Lee say Aboriginal Law resides in the foundational understanding that:

> All life found on Mother Earth is entwined in relationships, and all life can be traced back to [...] the forms, and our dependencies, our responsibilities, obligations, connections, caring and together builds our belonging. [...] The land is my Mother [...] Land is the starting point from where it all began, [...] the land is our food, our culture, our spirit, and our identity. Aboriginal law and life originates in, and is governed by, the land. The connection to land gives Aboriginal people their identity and a sense of belonging. We believe everything has a spirit and that life is a continual spiritual, emotional, mental, and physical journey, which is constantly changing [...] and our journey is inseparable from Mother Earth.
>
> (Lee, 2013, pp. 12–14)

Adjunct Professor Deborah Bird Rose adds (1999, p. 178):

> A fundamental proposition in Indigenous law and society is that the living things of a country take care of their own. All living things are held to have an interest in the life of the country because their own life is dependent upon the life of their country. This interdependence leads to another fundamental proposition of Indigenous law: those who destroy their country destroy themselves.

So while many have different ways of expressing Aboriginal Law, I've chosen the term 'Living Law' because it takes the next step and recognises its continuing presence, its place and its practice across aeons, which always has, and always will underpin sustainable social, political and environmental existence. After all, more than 65,000 years of continuing Aboriginal civilisation, surely, defines sustainability. And I use the term 'civilisation' in the true sense of the term, that is, 'having a *civil* society' not a society that boasts its' so-called developments, or progress.

As we know, colonisers in 1788 made a land grab, starting on Dharug and Dharawal Ngurra/Country, known as Sydney, and then through a process of violence, ignorance and greed, stole the continent on behalf of the British Empire. Beresford's (2021) *Wounded*

*Country* gives an insightful account of the process and thinking that underpins the last 234 years since what I call the 'Possessed-Possessors' arrived (Rey, 2022a), following from Professor Aileen Moreton-Robinson's (2015) work *The White Possessive*.

### *Living Law: a web of relationality*

As others noted above, Aboriginal Law is founded in relationality, recognising life is an interweaving, not a hierarchy. Living Law is therefore a living relationality, with presences, with places and with people. Together they make up Ngurra, or Country. I use the term 'presences' for all forms having a presence: human, other-than-human, physical, metaphysical.

My representation of this web of relationality is presented in Figure 3.1.

Accordingly, for me as a Dharug person, Living Law *is* relationship, the purpose of which is sustainable well-being—for humans and other-than-humans. In countries such as Mexico, Indigenous peoples speak of a relationality that Salmon (2000) describes as 'kin-centric ecology'. For well-being to be sustainable in any ecology (including social/human ecologies), it must be agentic, or alive and living; *all* elements in the web of relationality need to be active and agentic. Thus, its web of interaction is the agency of any *living* relationship. The Dharug term 'Ngurra' or 'Nura' for Country (capitalised) expresses the living relationality of kincentric ecology (Salmon, 2000).

I will now explain how this interaction proceeds. While this is common knowledge within a human-centric relational space, framing this through a kin-centric ethics, I suggest is unknown to the majority of non-Indigenous people in the 'Australian' context, based on the hierarchical nature of the settler-colonial, Christian mindset and history of this continent.

Firstly, *recognition* of the Other (human and other-than-human) must be activated for any relationship to proceed. Recognition requires acceptance of the need for the

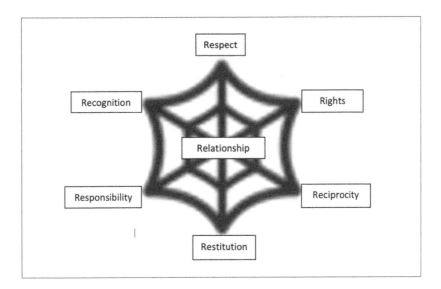

*Figure 3.1* 'Living Law': A web of active relationality (Rey, J., 21.03.2022).

*relationship* to be activated. Secondly, for any relationship to be sustainable, it must be founded in equity, and actively recognise that Others (human and other-than-human) also have *rights*. Thirdly, any sustainable relationship requires *respect* for those rights and this respect must be shown across the interactions of the relationship. Fourthly, for any relationship to be sustainable, it requires taking and holding *responsibility* in word and deed to honour the relationship. Being responsible for the well-being of the land is integral to any custodial relationship, for example. Fifthly, responsible, equitable and respectful relationship requires *reciprocity* in caring for and being cared by and through those relationships for sustainable well-being. Sixthly, when those relationships are contravened, restitution and reparation are required.

Based on this core, therefore, logic dictates that sustainable Country, involving humans and other-than-humans, requires Living Law as the active and collective practice for sustainable custodial relationships. As such, just as happened for tens of thousands of years on this continent and continues (when possible), human collectives must be caring for Country so Country can care for us. Without the human practice of Indigenous custodianship, the well-being of the Indigene (human and other-than-human) falters. Cutting people from Country, as happened in the cities such as Sydney, Australia, established unsustainable practices. Sustainable relationality requires localised, collective custodianship. This is the heart of Indigenous custodial relational obligation and practice, and why on this continent Aboriginal Law has been practiced and maintained for more than 65,000 years.

### Living Law: a web of custodial practice (even when Country is a city)

Whereas the previous section outlined what Living Law is, it is important to look at how it is practised. For this, examples come from Rey's (2019) doctoral research into continuing Dharug custodial practice, even when Dharug Country has been colonised for 234 years and covers most of the Sydney metropolitan area. Today, Sydney's human population is nearly five million inhabitants, reflecting a very diverse, cosmopolitan and globalised culture. Sydney's urban geographical size covers an area of 12,368.2sq km. Through the accounts of seven Dharug women, this research study showed that custodial practice was being continued through formal (tertiary, secondary and primary school) and informal educational programmes, including transgenerational storying, puppetry, the visual arts and dance, all associated with places of cultural significance (Rey, 2019). This custodial practice focuses on relationships and involves connecting, caring and belonging to the Dharug presences (human, other-than-human and ancestral), places and people that is Living Law (see Figure 3.2).

As such it shows that, even when Country is a city, Living Law is being fostered through continuing custodial practice by Dharug community. This localised relational custodianship, what Steele et al. (2021) call "quiet activism", is being undertaken across several Dharug sites, including cultural fire and women's camps (Rey, 2022b).

Integral to this active relational custodianship is perpetuity. However, due to settler-colonialism imposed upon the continent since 1788, and the imposition of current Western law subsuming Living Law, equitable relationship as a caring for Country practice struggles to survive because Western Law fails to acknowledge its own unethical and moral illegality. As such, it dishonours the relationships it requires for sustainability. In this next section I explain why.

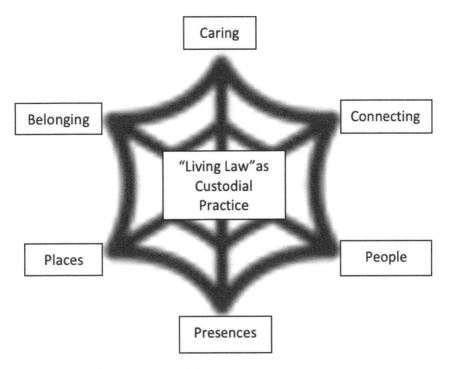

*Figure 3.2* 'Living Law': A web of custodial practice.

Source: Adapted from Rey, J. (2019). *Dharuganura Web of Interrelatedness*. Country Tracking Voices: Dharug women's perspectives on presences, places and practices (Thesis).

## The current law of more, more and more: 'deep colonisation'

In the continent currently called 'Australia', human-centricity involves and is fostered by the Australian dream of possession and 'progress' (Moreton-Robinson, 2015). In the process, it becomes a developer's dream. This is the dream of attaining and possessing more, more and more, originating in the British empirical arrogance for expansion and control of wealth, resources, states and human beings (Moreton-Robinson, 2015; Beresford, 2021).

Today, this ambition sits within economic narratives that promote human consumption and is sustained by the introduced British/Westminster legal system. Rose (1999, p. 182) called this continuing cultural consumption and arrogance 'deep Colonisation'. When examined closely, this obsessive compulsion to possess (things, places, people and spaces—including, most recently, other planets) is underpinned and legitimised through several factors. They include disconnection (Rose, 1999), racism (Brook & Kohen, 1991), patriarchal hierarchies of power (Day, 2021; Plumwood, 1993), and associated agendas enacting and enforcing Christian, empirical and Anglo cultural conversion through education systems, mass media, 'for profits' and marketing networks (Martinez, 2018).

Commenting on the investment in possessing places as integral to settler-colonialism, Kyle Powys Whyte explains:

> Settlers can only make a homeland by creating social institutions that physically carve their origin, religious and cultural narratives, social ways of life and political and economic systems (e.g., property) into the waters, soils, air and other environmental dimensions of territory or landscape. That is, settler ecologies have to be inscribed into Indigenous ecologies.

The correlative of this, he [Whyte] concludes, is that "settler colonialism can be interpreted as a form of environmental injustice that wrongfully interferes with and erases the sociological contexts required for Indigenous populations to experience the world as a place infused with responsibilities to humans, nonhumans and ecosystems" (Whyte, 2017, cited in Pugliese, 2020, p. 84).

Simultaneously, empirical custom was also initially 'inscribed' physically into convict bodies through a British law system that began with a 'night watch' in 1796 and which evolved into a constabulary. Punishments included whipping, the treadmill and being placed in irons by the military overseeing the convicts ('Colonial Police' n.d.). However, as ex-convicts, ex-military and other settlers increased the population, squatting on land and later taking up land grants, inscriptions into the lands, its creatures, forests and water systems soon erupted (Karskens, 2020).

These ecological inscriptions were based on fraudulent land titles, false claims, concepts and narratives that underpinned the enactment and enforcement of empirical custom. To support this, I refer to the work of Professor Gary Lilienthal and Professor Nehaluddin Ahmed (2019, p. 231), who interrogate the legality of colonial seizure of undocumented lands, through British allodial title, which was the functioning basis for land title at the time of colonisation in Australia. They state: "The research question is whether a colonial regime could ever lawfully seize the lands of prior undocumented owners, capriciously and without natural justice and procedural fairness, based on imported legal maxims". Their finding was that:

> In Australia, the crown had tried to introduce English custom in Australia as local law, but they did it by committing serious wrongs. This would nullify introduction of their legal maxims into Australia. Their claims to acquisition of allodial title to Australian lands would thus be sufficiently defective to reduce their holdings to mere colour of title. Their mala fides in their attempts at land acquisition would defeat any claim to convert their colour of title into a successful claim for adverse possession.
>
> (p. 231)

To clarify, in legal terms 'colour of title' means only having the appearance of ownership of personal or real property through the production of some kind of evidence, but actually there is either no title or a vital defect in the title. For example, someone may have a document claiming title, but they have previously deeded it to another. Selling the property without informing the buyer would thus be fraudulent. Claiming to own allodial title on the continent of Australia, with no treaty, denies the reality of the existing Indigenous Law.

Thus, the norms of settler-colonialism became embedded over time, and the injustices perpetuated across the continent were supported by 'progress narratives' for the creation of a national identity and capitalist greed. As Janke (2021, p.2) notes, there was:

> the attempted eradication of it [Aboriginality] by the dominant culture. It was not taught in schools, or spoken about in social circles when I was growing up. The history of dispossession that we were taught ignored the details. I was made to feel ashamed of my culture; it was not valued.

Further, as Moreton-Robinson (2015) and Beresford (2021) have each shown, successive governments have been regularly influenced by vested interests, particularly developers. The whole colonial narrative of the settlement of Australia was founded in the 'heroic' tradition of 'discovery' and exploration. The diaries of white explorers such as Surveyor-General Thomas Mitchell, have been the foundation of the non-Indigenous identity as 'Australian', reinforced through the Anglo education system designed for cultural conversion, and expanded through narratives of the superiority of Western scientific methodologies. What hasn't been alluded to until very recently is that all of these 'heroic' explorations, have culminated in the progressive undermining of the well-being of land and water resources through mismanagement and greed for profit (Beresford, 2021). As Pascoe (2014) shows, those diaries only reflect what the writer was prioritising, and wilfully left out evidence of Aboriginal presence and settlement as the actual intent was to provide a narrative that would encourage development and takeover of those lands for colonisers.

However, it wasn't sufficient to simply take over the lands, destroy sacred sites and perpetuate fake law. From the earliest days of settlement, British colonisers did not accept the cultural norms of the original inhabitants and wanted to 'civilise' the 'primitives'. This involved enforcing British clothing norms, English language literacy and numeracy, and Christian beliefs and practices. There are many accounts of this subjugation, including those that involved kidnapping Bennelong, attempted indoctrination of Boorong through Christian education using the Bible (Lake, 2018), and eventually the establishment of the Parramatta and Blacktown Native Institutions, authorised under Governor Lachlan Macquarie (Brook & Kohen, 1991; Norman-Hill, 2019). This practice of institutionalising children began what is currently called 'The Stolen Generations' (Australia, 1997).

Re-enforcing British cultural norms also involved education practices, systems and values following the West (Martinez, 2018). From a grazing economy to a resources extraction economy, it is no coincidence that capitalism was supported by an educational system promoting STEM (Science, Technology, Engineering and Mathematics) solutions rather than sustainable caring for Country solutions. Urbanisation is supported by more urban planning and development rather than sustainable living solutions; more wealth and consumption agendas are promoted through business, finance and Western economics, underpinned by marketing and 'success' narratives. All of this is underpinned by the current legal system that predominantly supports a 'business as usual' approach (Martinez, 2018).

Together, these forces, these ways of thinking, knowing and doing, saw the establishment of the fiction of rightful sovereignty across this continent (Moreton-Robinson, 2015). This fact *is* a festering wound that denies the Living Law of 65,000 years, which lies at the heart of the destruction and near extinction of the Indigene (both human and other-than-human) since 1788. Well may Beresford speak of the 'Wounded Country' in the title of his

2021 work. As Indigenous scholars write, without healthy Country there can be no healthy people (Maclean et al., 2013).

False legal authority was established through colonising practices that ignored their own British legalities, but worked for the British Empire while denying the existing, established and effective sustainable system of Living Law, being the basis for legal practice for at least 65,000 years. Logic recognises, therefore, that this wounded Country is the existing foundation of any future relationality, which in turn underpins community well-being or its demise. Indigenous demise is totally linked to the lack of relationship with Country that has been practised illegally for 234 years. Relationality therefore underpins the sustainability of ecological systems reliant on Indigenous custodial practices.

## Making the turn towards sustainable futures

Currently, Australia still has not formally adopted the UN Declaration on the Rights of Indigenous People (UNDRIP), which was signed in 2007 by 143 nations, with only four (Australia, New Zealand, Canada and the US) voting against the resolution (UN, 2007). Yet, with climate change events more frequent, whether they be mega-fires, devastating droughts, or floods, all of which are costing billions of dollars to the society, we must ask, what does it take to make the turn towards sustainable futures and what Martinez (2018) calls traditional sustainable ecological–economic ethics? I suggest it takes acceptance of Living Law as the primary basis for sustainable futures, rather than waiting for international treaties to be signed. For human cultural and societal change to happen, I argue those changes must be underpinned by Recognition, Respect, Rights, Responsibility, and appropriate Restitution within localised areas of belonging. Whether the sites for these changes are workplaces, education places or community places, bringing Living Law elements into their contexts can transform for sustainable futures.

### *Living Law turning away from human-centric to relational consciousness*

*Recognition* that human-centred consciousness needs the hierarchies to be flattened both within social structures and across the physical context in which they reside is fundamental. At work, narratives of 'Bosses and Workers' need to change to 'Mentors and Mentees'. Rather than hierarchical roles being differentiated by power, status and income differentiation, workplaces need to have collegial networks, recognising that all roles contribute equitably towards the success of the collective whole. From the security guard to the executive management, collaboration rather than competition brings collective respect and responsibility.

*Respect* for the various roles being undertaken in any human-centred domain underpins the consciousness of equity within the relationships that are providing the nurturing and sustenance for collective well-being, for the individuals within the organisation and for the organisation as a whole. Respecting the relationship with the physical presences and places within which they reside, builds a consciousness of relationships with other-than-humans and opens the individuals and the organisation to its responsibilities to care for the broader context. Designing urban environments with Country in mind establishes alternative frameworks across diverse relationships (Thwaites, 2022).

*Responsibility* as a consciousness to be fostered, not only in terms of the role being undertaken but also for the benefit of the area in which the people and the organisations inhabit, informs a balanced and healthy system that is sustainable. Fostering responsibility develops a sense of accountability, which includes being responsible for the outcomes of the enterprise. Changing the purpose of work from 'for profit' to 'for sustainability' creates a sense of 'lifeworkings' rather than lives working (Mitchell, 2017; J. Rey, 2022b). A sense of meaning and caring for Country strengthens a sense of resilience and well-being. It's no coincidence that in Indigenous cultures there is the saying 'Healthy Country, healthy people' (Maclean, Ross, Cuthill, & Rist, 2013). Changing the mentalities that drive 'power over' to 'assistance for' brings healthy relationships into workplaces that can drive shared opportunities for collective building not individual privilege. Shared opportunities are underpinned and strengthened by the recognition of the rights of others for equitable sustainable outcomes.

*Rights*, as the basis for equitable relationships, go beyond the human sphere. The rights of the river to be healthy, the air to be clean, the earth to not be polluted should be a given, and yet Western law and many governments struggle to accept that these rights are as inalienable as the rights of a child to be more than 'an object belonging to their parents' (UNICEF, 1989). Australia's current failure to endorse the UNDRIP is a standout negligence in accepting the foundational fact that for relationships to be sustainable, they must include equitable rights (UN, 2007).

Happily, some Indigenous groups are leading the way to make this change. In February 2021, in Canada, legal personhood was granted to the Muteshekau Shipu (Magpie River), by the Innu Council of Ekuanitshit and the Minganie Regional County Municipality (Townsend, Bunten, Iorns, & Borrows, 2021).

Recognising rights requires respect and responsibility. For these changes to be made in workplaces, recognising reciprocity and restitution (when necessary) within the relationship is critical for sustainable futures beyond the walls of any enterprise. The work of Terri Janke in educating industry towards protecting the rights of Indigenous knowledges and cultural practices is one example of important workplace relationships (Janke, 2021).

*Reciprocity and Restitution* ground all the other elements of 'Living Law' in the reality that relationships across diverse contexts and involving diverse processes are not always easy. Reciprocity and restitution enact the respect, the responsibility, the integrity and authenticity of the relations: the kin, because it involves the giving and the giving back. Custodial caring for Country recognises, respects and responds to the agentic dimensions of well-being. Wellness cannot be sustainable without mutuality: the giving and the receiving. Practising kin-centric ecologies keeps kin close and honest.

Accepting reciprocity opens pathways to undertake appropriate restitutions. Such acceptance requires governance grounded in relationality between humans, and the presences, places and practices founded in custodianship. It requires relationship with the Indigene. Such custodianship recognises the significance of situated contextual relationships with the localised ecologies of place, building living webs of connecting, caring and belonging across human–other-than-human networks. Such a web returns daily life to a localised, collective of 'quiet activism', though it is recognised that 'loud activism' might initially be required for governments to accept the need for cultural change and restitution to occur (Rey, 2022b). Given the circumstances we are now facing with dramatic climate-changing contingencies, short-term thinking cannot sustain us. Individualistic, competitive, profit-taking mentalities suck from the well-being of the majority of humans, let alone involve any consideration for other-than-humans on which we depend.

In the urban landscapes, such as Dharug Ngurra (Sydney), domination rather than reciprocity has been the active agency of colonisation. Custodianship has come from a minority of the broader human population because traditional custodians have been removed from accessing their sites of significance through land ownership and false titles.

Strengthening custodial presences and practices implemented through Indigenous Living Law opens opportunities to care for and be cared for *by* Ngurra. Work opportunities in national parks, along the rivers, underpinned by Living Law responds to the reciprocity and restitution that are required because of colonisation. Providing housing in cities for Indigenous workers to lead the training of teams of carers from localised communities enacts the reciprocity that is outstanding. Strengthening reciprocity through secure life provisioning (housing, income) changes the pressure for 'profit making success' that drives anxiety and depression undermining mental health outcomes. Keeping competition to sport and replacing it with cooperation strengthens practical problem-solving for mutual well-being. Collective team building strengthens collective continuity. Strong communities support strong families. Strong collectives build strong communities that support strong families. Strong families raise strong and supportive individuals, who are strong in connecting, caring and belonging to presences, places and people. Sustainable production offers trade within sustainable networks that aren't mired in 'hope for the future' but instead, secure in knowing they are working to strengthen 'now'.

## Altogether: remembering a certain wisdom

This chapter first addresses the problematic context of climate-challenging crises, with a focus on human-centric cities and towns, particularly Dharug Ngurra, also known as Sydney, Australia. It is then argued that we need to bring change to our relationship with other-than-humans for the sake of ecologically sustainable futures. Further, it offers Australian Indigenous Living Law, a web of relationality, as the ethical, foundational and logical approach forward and explains how it both underpins custodial practice and offers opportunities for the future. The chapter finally details focused changes that will transform a variety of places when put into practice.

Whether we apply Living Law to workplaces, educational places or communal and governance places, we have a method founded in practices, principles, ethics and epistemologies that have sustained this continent for tens of thousands of years. The fundamental logic woven through the wisdom of relationality as the source of sustainable practices is 'home grown', adapted across this continent called 'Australia' and quietly, persistently, activated by the longest-living civilisation on the planet. Concurrently, it aligns with traditional Indigenous knowledges across the planet. Keeping kin (human and other-than-human) close, collectively caring, and continuing custodianship provide a certain wisdom that can carry the Indigene and broader communities together for sustainable futures. Recognising that urbanisation of Country, such as Dharug Ngurra (Sydney), is a global issue arising from human-centricity, makes 'Living Law' relevant to all the cities and their contexts across the planet. It is clear we have the precedent and the wisdom, but remaining outcomes depends on next steps. Do we have the wherewithal to make it work? Our futures may well depend upon it.

Yanama budyari gumada—Ngurrayin

Walk with good spirit—locally.

## References

Australia, C. o. (1997). *Bringing them home: National Inquiry into the Separation of Aboriginal and Torres Strait Islander Children from Their Families.*

Australian Conservation Foundation (ACF). (2020). *The Extinction crisis in Australia's cities and towns: How weak environmental laws have let urban sprawl destroy the habitat of Australia's threatened species.* www.acf.org.au/reports

Beresford, Q. (2021). *Wounded country: The Murray-Darling Basin—a contested history.* New South.

Brook, J., & Kohen, J. (1991). *The Parramatta Native Institution and the Black Town: a history.* New South Wales University Press.

Day, M. (2021). Remembering Lugones: The critical potential of heterosexualism for studies of so-called Australia. *Genealogy, 5*(3), 71.

Foley, M. (2020, 20 July). Why is Australia a global leader in wildlife extinctions? *Sydney Morning Herald.* www.smh.com.au/politics/federal/why-is-australia-a-global-leader-in-wildlife-extinctions-20200717-p55cyd.html

Gallagher, R. V., Allen, S., Mackenzie, B. D. E., Yates, C. J., Gosper, C. R., Keith, D. A., & Nimmo, D. (2021). High fire frequency and the impact of the 2019–2020 megafires on Australian plant diversity. *Diversity & Distributions, 27*(7), 1166–1179. https://doi.org/10.1111/ddi.13265

Gooley, C., Chung, L., & Elder, B. (2022, 14 January). Global heritage body and floodplain councils slam Warragamba Dam proposal. *Sydney Morning Herald.* www.smh.com.au/politics/nsw/global-heritage-body-and-floodplain-councils-slam-warragamba-dam-proposal-20220114-p59o7f.html

Graham, M. (2014). Aboriginal notions of relationality and positionalism: a reply to Weber. *Global Discourse, 4*(1), 17–22. https://doi.org/10.1080/23269995.2014.895931

Howlett, C., & Lawrence, R. (2019). Accumulating minerals and dispossessing Indigenous Australians: Native title recognition as settler-colonialism. *Antipode, 51*(3), 818–837.

Intergovernmental Panel on Climate Change (IPCC). (2022). *Climate Change 2022 Impacts, Adaptation and Vulnerability Working Group II Contribution to the Sixth Assessment Report of the Intergovernmental Panel on Climate Change: Summary for Policymakers.* www.ipcc.ch/report/ar6/wg2/downloads/report/IPCC_AR6_WGII_SummaryForPolicymakers.pdf

Ives, C. D., Lentini, P. E., Threlfall, C. G., Ikin, K., Shanahan, D. F., Garrard, G. E., & Kendal, D. (2016). Cities are hotspots for threatened species. *Global Ecology and Biogeography, 25*(1), 117–126. https://doi.org/10.1111/geb.12404

Janke, T. (2021). *True tracks.* University of New South Wales Press.

Karskens, G. (2010). *Colony: A history of early Sydney.* Allen & Unwin.

Karskens, G. (2020). *People of the River: Lost worlds of early Australia.* Allen and Unwin.

Lake, M. (2018, 21 November). Why we should remember Boorong, Bennelong's third wife, who is buried beside him. *The Conversation.* https://theconversation.com/why-we-should-remember-boorong-bennelongs-third-wife-who-is-buried-beside-him-107280

Lee, B. (2013). *Healing from the Dilly Bag.* Xlibris.

Lilienthal, G., & Ahmad, N. (2019). Colonial land title in Australia: A meta-legal critical inquiry. *Commonwealth Law Bulletin, 45*(2), 231–256. https://doi.org/10.1080/03050718.2019.1634610

Lyons, I., Hill, R., Deshong, S., Mooney, G., & Turpin, G. (2020). Protecting what is left after colonisation: Embedding climate adaptation planning in traditional owner narratives. *Geographical Research, 58*(1), 34–48. https://doi.org/10.1111/1745-5871.12385

Maclean, K., Ross, H., Cuthill, M., & Rist, P. (2013). Healthy country, healthy people: An Australian Aboriginal organisation's adaptive governance to enhance its social-ecological system.(Report). *Geoforum, 45,* 94.

Martinez, D. (2018). Redefining sustainability through kincentric ecology: Reclaiming Indigenous lands, knowledge, and ethics. In M. Nelson & D. Shilling (Eds.), *Traditional ecological knowledge: Learning from Indigenous practices for environmental sustainability.* (New Directions in Sustainability and Society, pp. 139–174). Cambridge University Press. https://doi.org/10.1017/9781108552998.010

Mitchell, A. (2017). Lifework Part II. https://worldlyir.wordpress.com/2017/04/09/lifework-part-ii/

Moreton-Robinson, A. (2015). *The white possessive: Property, power, and indigenous sovereignty.* University of Minnesota Press.

Norman-Hill, R. (2019). Australia's Residential Schools. In S. J. Minton (Ed.), *Residential Schools and Indigenous Peoples: From genocide via education to the possibilities for processes of truth, restitution, reconciliation, and reclamation* (pp. 1–29). Routledge.

Pascoe, B. (2014). *Dark Emu, Black Seeds: Agriculture or accident?* Magabala Books.

Plumwood, V. (1993). *Feminism and the mastery of nature*. Routledge.

Pugliese, J. (2020). *Biopolitics of the more-than-human: Forensic ecologies of violence*. Duke University Press.

Rey, J. (2019). *Country tracking voices: Dharug women's perspectives on presences, places and practices*. [Unpubished PhD dissertation]. Macquarie University.

Rey, J. (2022a). Quiet activism through Dharug Ngurra: Reporting locally grown—not from the European South. *From the European South, 10*, 25–40.

Rey, J. (2022b). Weaving 'lifeworkings: Goanna walking between humanism and posthumanism, Dharug women's way. In R. Hediger (Ed.), *Reworking labor and leisure in the Anthropocene*, (pp. 220–237). Bucknell Press.

Reynolds, H. (1987). *Frontier*. Allen & Unwin.

Rose, D. B. (1999). Indigenous ecologies and an ethic of connection. In N. Low (Ed.), *Global ethics and environment* (pp. 175–187). Routledge.

Salmón, E. (2000). Kincentric ecology: Indigenous perceptions of the human–nature relationship. *Ecological Applications, 10*(5), 1327–1332. https://doi.org/10.1890/1051-0761(2000)010[1327:KEIPOT]2.0.CO;2

Steele, W., Byrne, J., Hillier, J., Houston, D., & Maccallum, D. (2021). *Quiet activism: Climate action at the local scale*. Palgrave Macmillan.

A Supercharged Climate: Rain bombs, flash flooding and destruction (2022, 18 March). *Reports*. Climate Council. www.climatecouncil.org.au/resources/supercharged-climate-rain-bombs-flash-flooding-destruction/

Tatz, C. (2017). *Australia's unthinkable genocide*. Xlibris.

Thwaites, M. (2022). Small embers of change: Decolonising architecture. *The Commercial Project, 10*, 108–111. https://thelocalproject.com.au/print-publication-articles/issue-no-10/

Townsend, J., Bunten, A., Iorns, C., & Borrows, L. (2021, 3 June). Rights for nature: How granting a river personhood could help protect it. *The Conversation*. https://theconversation.com/rights-for-nature-how-granting-a-river-personhood-could-help-protect-it-157117

UNDRIP. (2007). United Nations Declaration on the Rights of Indigenous Peoples. www.un.org/development/desa/indigenouspeoples/declaration-on-the-rights-of-indigenous-peoples.html

UNICEF. (1989). United Nations Convention on the Rights of the Child. www.unicef.org/child-rights-convention

Ward, M. S., Simmonds, J. S., Reside, A. E., Watson, J. E. M., Rhodes, J. R., Possingham, H., & Taylor, M. (2019). Lots of loss with little scrutiny: The attrition of habitat critical for threatened species in Australia. *Conservation Science and Practice*. https://conbio.onlinelibrary.wiley.com/doi/pdf/10.1111/csp2.117

Watson, I. (2015). *Aboriginal peoples, colonialism and international law: Raw law*. Routledge.

Whyte, K. (2018). Settler colonialism, ecology, and environmental injustice. *Environment and Society, 9* (1), 125–144.

Whyte, K. P. (2017). Is it colonial deja vu? Indigenous Peoples and climate change. In J. A. a. M. Davis (Ed.), *Humanities for the environment: Integrating knowledge, forging new constellations of practice*, (pp. 88–104). Routledge.

# 4

# STAYING WITH THE FIRE

## Sustainable futures using Indigenous Knowledges

*Frances Wyld*

### Prologue

I use a prologue to introduce myself and to bridge into the work to come. I am Martu, living on Kaurna land. I work as a teaching scholar within a university. Storying is my methodology established through my Doctor of Communication thesis. In writing the start of this chapter, I must admit that I have written and erased it a few times. Procrastination has been evident for many months. There are several stories to tell, and I can't seem to find the right words. I am writing about fire in winter, a wild and wet winter of storms where many have experienced the harsher elements of this land. I write about storms elsewhere (Wyld, 2011), storms that I have weathered and some that I have not. Over a cosy winter's lunch with my story work mentor, Dr Karen Martin, we story storm metaphors. Is it a ship that has seen the big storm and turned away to seek safe harbour? Maybe. Or did the ship sail into the storm, leaving me clinging to a life raft waiting for a sighting of land? I will know when I get to the end of this work. Either way, next week I start teaching again and it is the stories of students that will take precedence. For now, I light a fire for guidance, and these yarns with Dr Martin are part of the relatedness and reciprocity of the work we do, as Kovach (2021) documented, storying a yarn with another mentor, leading the way for conversations within Indigenous methodologies. I use autoethnography as writing the self in culture, in a world that tells me stories through its elemental patterns.

### Introduction

Staying with the fire is a story of staying with the work of maintaining Critical Indigenous Knowledges within teaching and research to problematise a sustainable future for all. Fire is both life giving and life taking. Used in our daily lives to heat water, food or ourselves, fire is used to keep Country 'clean' so all species can grow as they should, in the right place. It is used to burn back combustible growth to mitigate out of control wildfires that destroy. Fire is also within us, passion for our knowledges as Aboriginal peoples that have sustained life on this continent for over 60,000 years. This is a fire worth staying with and keeping faith with. I use story work as a methodology, writing in the moment alongside

DOI: 10.4324/9781003271802-6

academic scholarship to give a sense of relatedness, mindfulness and to ground myself within the elemental patterns mentioned in the abstract to this chapter. In the chapter I talk of the world today and how the principles of respect, relatedness and reciprocity are key to maintaining life for kin on this planet. The discussion focuses on my work as an Aboriginal curriculum developer and not necessarily surviving within the academy but using fire to sustain and heal the trauma of the daily burns of working in a colonised system, mindfully, holding onto joy.

### Crisis or critical: the world today

The lead character of a cartoon published in an international newspaper described the world today and declared that we are in crisis (First Dog on The Moon, 2022). I would agree with them but only to say that it is the non-Indigenous world that is in the crisis they describe. Scholars like Kyle Whyte (2020) would warn against working within crisis epistemologies and speak of its direct links to colonisation. With this is mind, I embrace the idea of staying with the trouble and with the kinship of other beings on this earth and consider other creative ways to think about climate change that Donna Haraway stories (2016). Haraway speaks of two repeated stories in the era we live: Firstly, technology will not magically fix us. It is useful, but we need to embrace more than that. Secondly, it is not 'game over' for the earth. Instead, we stay with the trouble and learn to live as communities of more than just people and their desires:

> Staying with the trouble requires making oddkin; that is, we require each other in unexpected collaborations and combinations, in hot compost piles. We become-with each other or not at all. That kind of material semiotics is always situated, someplace and not noplace, entangled and worldly.
>
> (Haraway, 2016, p. 4)

This thought linking to Whyte's (2020) debunking of crisis epistemologies is a recognition of Indigenous relatedness to the earth because of the humanities' need to keep things the way they are, instead of looking for solutions that perhaps are steeped in Indigenous ways of knowing. One of these ways is to think in terms of community, not capitalism, as I story in a section further on.

In the same year as Haraway published *Staying with the Trouble* (2016), Brendan Hokowhitu (2016) challenged our need to be in a place of resistance to decolonise Western methods, theories and pedagogies. He challenged us to speak even if it was unintelligible to the Western academy, and here I must make a confession: I was resistant to naming myself as a critical Indigenous theorist until reading Hokowhitu's chapter while preparing a talk for the Native American and Indigenous Studies conference in Brisbane in 2022. I could see the demarcation for the words 'crisis' and 'critical'.

Crisis and critical share an etymology that points to a turning point in a disease. I take etymologies seriously as they are the stories of words through time. I thought that I could not use the term 'critical' because I was not diseased at the time of working on an Indigenous climate change project. I then came to know that the world was diseased, and the turning point would be embracing Indigenous Knowledges. Taking up Critical Indigenous Studies as described by Hokowhitu (2016) was a way to work with our knowledges in conversations with other Indigenous peoples and a way to decentre whiteness. It is the words that Hokowhitu uses to end his 'monster' chapter that makes this declaration: "As Critical Indigenous Studies turns its gaze away from white guilt, and making whiteness guilty and towards robust self-criticism, insurrections of knowledges will rise, realities will resolve, Indigenous bodies will chant, Indigenous bodies will beat, Indigenous bodies will throb" (Hokowhitu, 2016, p. 101).

For this is not just a way to work with other Indigenous peoples within methods embodied within our beings, but also a way to teach with our content, centred and ready for students to come alongside us and find their own stories within our knowledges, without rancour, and as a way forward. I do this as Haraway describes moving into her words, that she will work:

> with all the unfaithful offspring of the sky gods, with my littermates who find a rich wallow in multispecies muddles, I want to make a critical and joyful fuss about these matters. I want to stay with the trouble, and the only way I know to do that is in generative joy, terror, and collective thinking.
>
> (Haraway, 2016, p. 31)

Imagine that we can work in a way that is critical and joyful, in the moment, storying life.

## Weevils in the oats: decolonising the curriculum

Last night I was aiming to fire up my slow cooker to test a recipe for cooking oats overnight for a comforting winter's morning porridge, but to my dismay, the box of oats was infested with weevils. The box went straight into the bin and out with any other opened packet of oats, wheat and corn product. I cleaned the shelves and then wiped everything again with vinegar. Airtight containers and replacement foods are now on order as I sit and work and make the correlation of the work within Critical Indigenous Studies and decolonising the curriculum also needs to be airtight, staying within the space of knowledges and joy, and free of distractions. The wings of birds become airtight as they thrust down in flight. Sometimes it is about resistance, sometimes it is not, as we allow ourselves to get drawn into a story, adding to our own ways of knowing informed by nature. Outside my window the sky turns golden. I can turn my email off and shut out the world of work, make my wings airtight as I reach into the joy of storying. There was a time when I was working on my doctoral thesis named for my bird, the Rainbow Lorikeet, when I would work at this time of the day with the birds as kin. Since then, the trees that were the roosting places of my kin have been removed around my home because they were a hazard to humans. It was a sad moment, but my joy remains, inked on my skin.

If you can find what you are good at in this world, what brings you joy, cling onto it like a barnacle on the hull of ship in a storm. Joy in these times is important. Chelsea Watego (2021) tells us it is found in being radical, in not going along to get along. Before her, Sara Ahmed (2010) reminded us that happiness is not a given. According to its etymology, it is an outside construct based on luck, whereas joy is created by the individual. What brings you joy? For me, it is curriculum development as it is storytelling with a purpose.

I have been assigned courses in many forms, from development to delivery. If I had learned the firestick farming practices of my Martu heritage, perhaps I would be out on Country using fire; instead, I am here on Kaurna land using fire as a metaphor for curriculum management. There is joy in hitting that delete button that removes the colonising work that has gone on before you, but I will not story it as a violence along the lines of the embers of a Franz Fanon (1963) fire ready to burst into decolonising flames. That is not how we do it. Instead, before deleting, I carefully look over the landscape, noting the wetness in the soil, the direction of the wind, the type of flora and the season, as fire practitioner Victor Steffensen (2020) would do before a cultural burn. The season will tell me how much I can expect to achieve working within the system, for this is how it is done. We work within the Australian Qualifications Framework and within the university's laws, and if we didn't, the work would not be compliant. The academic year is a time frame of seasons with due dates for making changes or creating new courses. If I have a year, then bigger changes can be made, and the fire can be worked through all landscapes. If I have only a number of weeks, then it is a cool burn with flames gently licking through components of readings, topics and assignments, working with what I have, staying within the framework dictated by the university, but even with this cool, gentle burn, the course can align with decolonising principles.

The first step is to privilege Indigenous voices through reading choices (Rigney, 1999). The scholarship of Indigenous writing is well and truly established, publishing within all the disciplines so there are no excuses not to find Indigenous papers, chapters and books to include in the curriculum. For many courses on Indigenous topics, a whole course can be developed using only Indigenous voices. A course should tell a story and even though darker elements need to be told, there is also room for the positive voices that tell of peoples who have survived on this continent for millennia and know how to live within a changing environment, caring for its country and its inhabitants. The course should use an Indigenous pedagogy. For me, that is looking to the guidance of Karen Martin (2008; 2016), Veronica Arbon (2008), and Jo-Ann Archibald (2008) and putting the protocols of respect, relatedness and reciprocity throughout. Students are encouraged to work from the head and the heart, to find their place alongside Indigenous Knowledges, to find a sense of belonging and a willingness to be part of a community.

## A return to community

In researching climate change (Wyld, 2021), I travelled through a region with a Traditional Owner where I walked the land of his ancestors. This region is now used for sugarcane production, part of the all-important capitalism that is meant to bring us the good life, but I was shown a different good life, one sweetened by the kin who had always belonged there. Maria Mies, co-authoring a book (2014) with academic and activist Vandana Shiva, comments on the former definition of the good life and the myth that what is desired is the development strategies of the countries of the global north. Shiva published another book, *Oneness vs the 1%*, in 2018 that further challenged capitalism that only benefits those at the top, stating:

> The business of grabbing and money-making, through a violent extractive economy that the 1% have built, is burdening the earth and humanity with unbearable and non-sustainable costs and has brought us to the brink of extinction. We do not have to escape from the earth; we have to escape from the illusions that enslave our minds and make extinction look inevitable.
>
> (2018, pp. 174–175)

Shiva is calling for the rest of us, the 99 per cent to come together in oneness, or as Indigenous people may say, in relatedness, to speak to the 1 per cent, those high-wealth individuals at the top of the chain, holding on to more than they would ever need in this life while others live in poverty. Some of these individuals, as Shiva would note (2018), hide behind so-called philanthropy. I had the pleasure of seeing Shiva speak at a festival one year. I remember sitting there, messy in my festival chair, ready to listen—messy because I had just been engaged in a crowd participation event based on India's Holi Festival and had been covered in colour only minutes before. Sitting with anticipation and still filled with the joy of moving to the music as canons of colour were fired into the crowd of people and with our own little pouches, we threw colour up into the air and at each other as a sign of oneness. This festival is known for creating a village of music and dance over four days and is a highlight of the calendar.

Shiva also makes an unscripted appearance in a controversial documentary I will not name but instead will quote one of the film-makers who I also connected to through the life of the climate change project. Although non-Indigenous, in reading his work there is a similarity with Haraway (2016) in that we are making kin. Like Haraway, Ozzie Zehner also argues against putting all our faith in technology but rather considering changing the way we live, because

> We've built neighbourhoods deep in forests that are bound to catch on fire, we've built our cities right up to the banks of constricted rivers prone to flooding, we've erected tall buildings atop triggered faults, and so it's really no surprise that we've constructed an energy system pressed right up against the very limits of power production.
>
> (2012, p. 172)

He goes on further to discuss how we live, how we build our houses and create communities. He, like Indigenous and traditional peoples, looks to the wisdom of our ancestors: "The best we can do is to craft a plan based on our ancestral wisdom, ethical bearings, technological capabilities, and historical understandings" (2012, p. 194).

We need a return to community, a return of the protocols of respect, relatedness and reciprocity, or as Whyte puts it, epistemologies of coordination and kinship (2020) for a future not just the present.

## Working with the land: fire mitigation

No chapter on staying with the fire storying a future of sustainability would be complete without a section on fire mitigation, yet I do not have this practical knowledge. One of the leaders in this knowledge is Victor Steffensen and his book on *Fire Country* (2020). In the switch to Zoom and other technologies during the Covid-19 pandemic, a world of evening talks connected us more than ever. I still smile at the thought of listening to a talk by Steffensen where he was parked on the side of the road, speaking to many ears via his mobile phone as he travelled from one training session to another in this big land of ours. I also connect to the wisdom of Kaurna Elder Uncle Lewis O'Brien and his work with Irene Watson on fire mitigation:

When you say, talk about bushfires, this is the way we think about it. We say, "Nature likes bushfires, and we'll help her, we'll light a few fires and assist". We can then say, "We'll assist you and you'll in turn assist us". So we balance the realm. (2014, p. 455)

He later talks about how his people knew when to burn, and in this and further conversations with him, I am now trying to learn about the blooming of the Drosera. I have a long way to go but will keep listening to the knowledge holders and staying with the fire that for me remains just a metaphor, and perhaps that is enough.

## Weathering the storm

In the prologue, I posed a question for myself on whether I survived the storm. What storm is that, you may ask? It is the storm of colonisation that has a desire to keep us trapped in a way of being and knowing that is not our own, asking us to do the work and be strong, be resilient when our knowledges are not recognised and we are sidelined. It is having to manage that storm of fire within as we are talked about, not with. It is being punished for the failure of whiteness to understand our pedagogies and being denied the same support as the non-Indigenous leaders get within curriculum development, and that firestorm within burns us, not the other.

Decolonising the curriculum is the choice to head into the storm, all kinds of storms. It is knowing what is created might be destroyed when the course reverts to the coordination of another. It is fighting for a pedagogy that is based on Indigenous epistemologies and ontologies where whiteness tries to take the helm and put itself back into the centre. I tell myself to be patient, that the change is generational, as I further discuss in the next section. For now, I want to focus on trauma and healing.

Judy Atkinson (2002) is an important scholar when we story trauma. Her ground-breaking book *Trauma Trails: Recreating Songlines* is a reminder that I have other work to do. For now, within the themes, protocols and with a bit of deep listening, I connect to these words about relatedness:

These are the relationships that have been made by, and in turn have characterised, Aboriginal peoples throughout time: enduring connections held across generations with ancestors who have made us what we are, with country which has formed us and has been formed by us in ceremony and ritual; the interconnectedness and inter-dependencies between people in kinship and other affiliations, and with the corporeal and non-corporeal world. These are fundamental considerations in construction a healing process.

(Atkinson, 2002, pp. 215–216)

She goes on to talk about surviving the chaos of "natural disaster and human discord" (2002, p. 216), and I want to stay here because I am really good at creating chaos, but this section is about healing; I must story differently.

Healing, like decolonising, is a process that requires maintenance. I was reminded of this recently while sitting in a dentist surgery waiting room. A song was playing over the room's speakers and was one that I had recently been trying to find the name of to download onto a playlist. And don't you love a playlist? They are like the curated soundtrack of your life. Previous attempts to find the song using keywords had resulted in impulsive downloads of the wrong song. However, as in the way of the storyteller who listens and connects to the words of the world minutes later, while sitting in the waiting room, I open the newspaper app on my phone to read the day's news and there in front of me was an article storying the person who wrote the song. At that moment I realised this was the song, and the universe had heard me when I said, 'I wish I knew its title'. I went back and reread the article (Winship, 2022) and was intrigued further by the story of Keala Settle and her childhood in Hawaii, raised by a Māori mother. Settle is pictured with her arms raised in a muscle pose exposing the cultural ink on her forearm. Her ink and the bearded character she inhabits as she powers on with her anthem make me grateful that, even though she regrets putting her trauma on display, I am glad she did, for she speaks for many of us working on the outside (Lorde, 2007) alongside the trauma to create change. There is more I want to connect to, but that part remains private as I am not as brave as Settle. My own ink is often hidden from the world and even from me.

Healing is a process. Find your joy and stay connected to it. Accept yourself, forgive yourself. Tap out when you need to. I have seen too much death, and it is better to absent yourself for a day, a week, a month, even years than forever. Embrace your difference; it makes you unique; turn it into a superpower. Be mindful; be in the moment. Connect to Country, find your community, and if you can't find it, create one. Keep talking until someone will listen, whether it is with a friend, family, an audience or a professional therapist. Tell your story, because you matter. Wear your scars with pride, like ink on skin. Stay with the fire that burns inside you. It will sustain you in the troubled times to come. Then tell your story.

## Bright sparks, many fires

The saga of the porridge goes on in my home. The texture is right but a smell from the cooker's rubber ring pervades, and it is not tasty. Out comes the vinegar to clean the ring. Perhaps I will give up on oats and adopt a decolonising diet in the same way I moved into Critical Indigenous Studies and stopped putting whiteness in the centre. It is the seeds of oats that are important, that are used for food for both our human and our non-human kin. It is a metaphorical and literal seed that I story here with the mention of youth, our future.

Lighting the fire inside students using Indigenous knowledges is a privilege, but I am not so egotistical to think that young ones doing great things has anything to do with me. Their success is not my story to tell. I am merely trying to amplify voices of young ones. I will say that I did try to connect with Seed Mob for a climate change report (Wyld, 2021) but failed. Well, of course I did. What am I to these young ones but a blind old woman who needs to be challenged like the woman in the 1993 Toni Morrison speech? Fortunately, I did connect with one former member who had graduated out of the working group and was providing Indigenous Knowledges to visitors at a botanic garden as a tour guide, educator and knowledge holder. That connection gives me the ability as a storyteller within the protocol of relatedness to honour their work and celebrate the power of youth for the spark they give to a sustained life.

Shiva (2018, p. 171) writes in *Oneness vs the 1%* about seeding freedom in the title previously mentioned,

> Seeding the future when possible extinction stares us in the face; seeding freedom when all freedoms of all beings are being closed for the limitless freedom of the 1% to exploit the earth and the people, to manipulate life and our minds: this calls for a

quantum leap in our imaginations, our intelligences, our capacity for compassion and love, as well as our courage for creative nonviolent resistance and non-cooperation with a system that is driving us to extinction.

The only option Shiva says is to heal the earth, which many Indigenous people are saying, including Seed Mob, in Australia. There is a lot to admire about Seed Mob, also known as the Seed Indigenous Youth Climate Network.[1] Their commitment is to climate justice, to resistance to fracking in the Northern Territory, and to not just their connection to but also freedom from a larger non-Indigenous youth environmental network. On their website (https://nt.seedmob.org.au/water_is_life) is a film where they document their connection to a youth activist who was a leader in the No Dakota Access Pipeline[2] movement. I recognised this person from following the protest via social media and was delighted to see the connections the young people are making, yet still listening to the wisdom of Elders who remind them that it is about the health of the land.

I am about to start teaching another semester. Some students will be young ones, others not so young. The storytellers and readings will be Indigenous, and the theory will be Critical Indigenous Studies across all courses. I think of the wisdom from Marie Battiste and James Youngblood Henderson published, perhaps before some of the younger students were born, their book on *Protecting Indigenous Knowledge and Heritage* (2000). Their words on sensing the world to know how to listen to and protect the land connects to Hokowhitu (2016) and his claim that Indigenous Knowledges can sometimes be unintelligible to the Western academy. But there are some simple messages that lie with a reminder that the word 'kind' shares an etymology with kin, that within our survival we depend on relatedness alongside reciprocity.

## Conclusion: after the storm there is a rainbow

In the prologue, I spoke of a yarn with esteemed scholar Dr Karen Martin. Within these chats we had also spoken of the colours of fire. Martin (2021) had used the colours to organise a programme. In my research I had found that fire can be equally organised in the colours of the rainbow and had started to story this way, but the mixing of metaphors had complicated the message and I erased that story, bookmarking it as an idea for the future. A rainbow appeared to a lone surviving family of a biblical story telling them they would live. But it is more than a catastrophic flood that humanity faces. All the elements are in flux, and we must learn to live sustainably on this earth. If we do not, the earth will go on even if humanity as a whole does not find a way to live with the troubles using Indigenous Knowledges. It will burn, and all life will cease to be, but the earth will start again as it has done in the past. The earth will go on without us. Meanwhile, I see the rainbow I was seeking in the prologue; land is in focus.

## Notes

1  See www.seedmob.org.au
2  See https://americanindian.si.edu/nk360/plains-treaties/dapl

## References

Ahmed, S. (2010). *The promise of happiness*. Duke University Press.
Arbon, V. (2008). *Arlathirnda ngurkarnda ityirnda: Being-knowing-doing: de-colonising Indigenous tertiary education*. Post Pressed.

Archibald, J. (2008). *Indigenous storywork: Educating the heart, mind, body, and spirit*. UBC Press.

Atkinson, J. (2002). *Trauma trails, recreating song lines: The transgenerational effects of trauma in Indigenous Australia*. Spinifex Press.

Battiste, M., & Henderson, J.Y. (2000). *Protecting indigenous knowledge and heritage: A global challenge*, (pp. 83–101). Purich Publishing.

Fanon, F. (1963). *Concerning violence*. Penguin Books.

First Dog on the Moon (2022, 22 July). Europe is ablaze, Italian glaciers are collapsing. The climate crisis is here! *The Guardian*.

Haraway, D. J. (2016). *Staying with the trouble: Making kin in the chthulucene*. Duke University Press. https://doi.org/10.1515/9780822373780

Hokowhitu, B. (2016). Monster: Post indigenous studies. In A. Moreton-Robinson (Ed.), *Critical Indigenous Studies*. University of Arizona Press.

Kovach, M. (2021). *Indigenous methodologies: Characteristics, conversations and contexts* (2nd ed). University of Toronto Press.

Lorde, A. (2007). *Sister outsider* (2nd ed). Crossing Press.

Martin, K. L. (2008). *Please knock before you enter: Aboriginal regulation of outsiders and the implications for researchers*. Post Pressed.

Martin, K. L. (2016). *Voice and visions: Aboriginal early childhood education in Australia*. Pademelon Press.

Martin, K. L. (2021). Back to the fire: Gamification strategy. Unpublished discussion.

Mies, M., & Shiva, V. (2014). *Ecofeminism* (2nd ed.). Zed Books.

Morrison, T. (1993). *Toni Morrison—Nobel Lecture*. Nobel Prize. www.nobelprize.org/prizes/literature/1993/morrison/lecture/

O'Brien, L., & Watson, I. (2014). In conversation with Uncle Lewis: Bushfires, weather-makers, collective management. *Alternative, 10*(5), 450–460. https://doi.org/10.3316/informit.808382641205953

Rigney, L. I. (1999). Internationalization of an indigenous anticolonial cultural critique of research methodologies: A guide to Indigenist research methodologies and its principles. *Journal of American Native Studies, 14*(2), 109–121.

Seed Mob (2022) *Seed*. Seed Indigenous Youth Climate Network. www.seedmob.org.au/

Shiva, V. (2018). *Oneness vs the 1%: Shattering illusions, seeding freedom*. Spinifex Press.

Steffensen, V. (2020). *Fire country: How indigenous fire management could help save Australia*. Hardie Grant.

Watego, C. (2021). *Another day in the colony*. University of Queensland Press.

Whyte, K. (2020). Against crisis epistemology. In B. Hokowhitu, A. Moreton-Robinson, L. Tuhiwai-Smith, C. Andersen, & S. Larkin (Eds.), *Routledge handbook of critical Indigenous studies*, (pp. 52–64). Taylor & Francis Group.

Winship, L. (2022, 19 July). 'I put my trauma on display'—Keala Settle on hating her signature song. *The Guardian*.

Wyld, F. (2011). Writing the ephemeral of culture. *Social Alternatives, 30*(2), 40–43. https://doi.org/10.3316/ielapa.20110958

Wyld, F. (2021). The land as research participant: A storytelling project on climate change and Indigenous perspectives. *Journal of Australian Indigenous Issues, 24*(1–2), 22–34. https://doi.org/10.3316/informit.046669925438109

Zehner, O. (2012). *Green illusions: The dirty secrets of clean energy and the future of environmentalism*. University of Nebraska Press. https://doi.org/10.2307/j.ctt1d9nqbc

# 5

# SETTLER COLONIALISM, JEWS, AND INDIGENOUS PEOPLES

## Theorising homelands as a point of connection in Indigenous-Jewish relations in so-called Australia

*Zac Roberts*

### Introduction

What does it mean to belong to a homeland? For both Jewish and Indigenous peoples, the notion of connecting to place, to Country, or to a homeland is an important aspect of identity and culture (Aronson et al., 2019; Graham & Markus, 2018; Netana-Glover, 2021). Within Indigenous contexts, this is our connection to and identification with our Countries—the lands, waters, and skies our ancestors fought for and that we continue to fight for under the ongoing settler colonial regime. For Jews, this connection usually emerges within the context of Eretz Yisrael, the 'Promised Land' (Friesel, 2019; Troen & Rabineau, 2014), or the biblical land of the ancestors from which Jews were expelled and to which they were promised to return by God. When asked about any similarities shared between Indigenous and Jewish peoples and communities in so-called Australia,[1] one of the more common examples given is this perceived shared sense of connecting to a homeland. While at first glance a superficial comparison can be drawn, when such a comparison is contextualised with recognition of ongoing settler colonial projects in both so-called Australia and Palestine-Israel, the connection becomes much more constrained.

The first Jews to interact with Indigenous people were those who arrived as convicts on the First Fleet in 1788 (Levi, 2006; Rutland, 1997). Despite the longevity of Jewish existence on this continent, there is still relatively little written regarding Indigenous and Jewish interactions, relations, or encounters. This is particularly evident when compared to the large corpus of scholarship that exists regarding Indigenous people and Christianity (for example: Cruz, 2019; Harris, 1990; McDonald, 2001; McLisky, 2015) and Indigenous people and Islam (Onnudottir et al., 2010; Stephenson, 2009, 2010). Jewish relations with Indigenous communities are characterised by Jewish scholar Colin Tatz (2004) as a

DOI: 10.4324/9781003271802-7

disappointment, though Tatz considers the significance of this relationship comparatively with the civil rights movement in the United States and the anti-Apartheid movement in South Africa. When Jewish-Indigenous relations are considered within the specific context of this continent, a more complex relationship emerges spanning friendship (Cohen, 2021), working relations (Epstein, 2019), activism (Miller, 2012), and situations of violence and oppression (Bartrop, 1999; Ludewig, 2020).

This chapter uses Australian Jewish and Indigenous communities as a case study to explore the notion of—and connection to—Country/homelands. As Jonathan Grossman (2019) notes, the term 'homeland' is undertheorised in scholarship, particularly when used in reference to diasporic communities. I define the term here following the work of Walker Connor, who writes that homelands connote "a spiritual bond between nation and territory" (1994, p. 205), where that real or imagined territory is maintained with material and symbolic ties with that territory. It is also important to acknowledge that the connection between community and homeland exists regardless of whether diaspora members or their ancestors have ever been to that homeland. That is, Indigenous peoples maintain spiritual and cultural ties to their Countries/homelands despite forced relocations and dispossession because of settler colonial doctrines (Netana-Glover, 2021), and diasporic communities maintain ties to their homelands even if they live in the diaspora (Grossman, 2019).

Homelands, then, function as a uniting aspect around which all members of a particular community can gather and find connection, though the question that remains is whether Indigenous connections with Country and Jewish connections with Eretz Yisrael are indeed comparable. I explore this concept in three ways: First by conceptualising homelands in both an Indigenous and a Jewish context, and how these may be understood as a point of connection between Indigenous and Jewish communities. I then explore Jewish positioning within settler colonial frameworks in so-called Australia and occupation of Indigenous homelands. I do this with particular attention to Jewish migration both before and after the Holocaust and increasing theorising of the migrants-as-settlers. Finally, I explore how Jewish participants in my research conceive their situatedness on Indigenous homelands, and how recognition of Australia as a settler colonial enterprise influences understanding of an occupied-Palestine. In doing so, this chapter contributes to the growing body of scholarship regarding non-Christian migrant relations with Indigenous peoples whilst challenging popular accounts of how, or on what grounds, those relations are formed.

The oral history interviews utilised here were conducted as part of my ongoing doctoral research exploring the history of Indigenous and Jewish community relations since 1788. This larger study called for individuals who are Indigenous, Jewish, or both Indigenous and Jewish to participate in a one-hour-long, one-on-one oral history interview. During the interview, each participant was asked about their experiences with and understanding of interactions between Indigenous and Jewish people and communities, their understanding of the similarities and differences between Indigenous and Jewish communities, and any specific examples they wished to share. A guiding set of questions was followed; however, discussion was allowed to flow freely depending on the answers given and the direction each participant took. Each participant was given the option of being identified by their first name or a pseudonym, and all information presented here has been included with explicit and ongoing consent and in accordance with the protocol approved by the Macquarie University Human Research Ethics Committee.

## Conceptualising homelands

I am writing this chapter on D'harawal Country, on the south coast of what is colonially referred to as New South Wales. This is not my Country, but I was grown up here and much of my learning has been shaped by this Country and community. I am a freshwater/saltwater man—a Walbunja Yuin man through my paternal family line. My Country shares a border with D'harawal, and our communities share stories, histories, and learnings. Many of my ancestors lived and died on D'harawal Country, and many others crossed between both during their lifetimes. I am guided by their journeys and their knowledges, just as I am guided by D'harawal ancestors as I tread carefully on this Country.

I begin with this discussion of Country because it is central to my own understanding of the world and is at the heart of how I conduct myself and my work. Country as a term is used by many Aboriginal and Torres Strait Islander people to refer to our connection with land, ancestors, and communities—though it is also much more than that (Carlson, 2016a; O'Brien & Watson, 2014). Country goes beyond the physicality of land, including landscapes, waterscapes, and all living and non-living elements within those lands and waters (Langton, 2006; Rey, 2022; Tynan, 2021). Country also extends beyond the land and waterways to the moon, sun, stars, clouds, and other celestial bodies (Noon & de Napoli, 2022). There is no separation between land, sea, and sky Countries because everything is connected, and everything is relational (Tynan, 2021). Country, then, is a place of origin both literally and also culturally and spiritually.

Quandamooka scholar Aileen Moreton-Robinson (2015) theorises Indigenous connection to land and Country as an ontological belonging. That is, our sense of belonging is derived from an ontological relationship to Country and the kinship systems that connect us as individuals to other members of our communities, and our communities to other nation groups across the continent. Our ways of knowing, doing, and being, are guided by the knowledges of our ancestors passed down in oral traditions since time immemorial (Whap, 2001; Wildcat et al., 2014). Knowledges are held by Country, reflected in Country, and guide how we as Indigenous peoples interact with and care for Country. There is no separation between us and Country, for we are all part of the relational cycle of knowledge (Carlson, 2016a; Wildcat et al., 2014).

Connection with Country does not end when we live elsewhere. I do not feel any less connected to Country when I am living on D'harawal land. I am always connected to land and ancestors, and I am always guided by those knowledges and teachings. My connection to my Country guides how I conduct myself on other peoples' Country. This ontological belonging and connection between Indigenous peoples and our lands thus fulfills Connor's (1994) definition as a spiritual connection between people and land, regardless of whether we are physically present on Country or not.

What, then, of Jewish homelands? The concept of a homeland is perhaps most clearly articulated within the concept of Jewish diasporic communities. Here, Jews living in the diaspora remain oriented towards a particular place to which they maintain spiritual and material ties—Eretz Yisrael (Grossman, 2019). In Jewish thought, the Jewish connection to Eretz Yisrael begins with a covenant between Abraham and God. The Book of Genesis describes how Abraham is instructed by God to "Go out of your native land [...] to the land that I will show you [...] and the Lord appeared to Abram and said I will assign this land to your offspring" (Genesis 12:1–3, 7). The land to which Abraham migrated later takes the name Eretz Yisrael, and Abraham's descendants are referred to as the Israelite people.

The covenant between God and Abraham, and the gift of land, is central in the Torah, the Hebrew Scriptures.[2] When Moses leads the Israelites out of Egypt in the Book of Exodus, God reasserts the covenant when he instructs Moses to "Set out from here, you and the people you have brought up from the land of Egypt to the land of which I swore to Abraham, Isaac, and Jacob" (Exodus 33:1). Both the Book of Numbers and the Book of Deuteronomy detail the Jewish peoples' preparation for entering Eretz Yisrael. While Moses himself was never allowed to enter, it nevertheless remained his most profound wish to the extent that his final words, as recorded in Deuteronomy 31:1–8, are a reminder of the covenant and promise of the land: "Be strong and bold, for you are the one who will go with this people into the land that the Lord has sworn to their ancestors to give them; and you will put them in possession of it".

The story of the covenant between God and Abraham and the biblical story from Abraham to Moses is how Jews understand their religious, cultural, and national origins. It becomes a focal point in Jewish cultural and religious memory. When the Jewish people are later exiled and dispersed throughout other nations, the covenant between Abraham and God regarding Eretz Yisrael, the longing to return to the homeland as handed down in the covenant, becomes a uniting aspect for all Jewish people. Regardless of what other national identities Jews may adopt within the diaspora, Eretz Yisrael remains central to Jewish ideology. It operates, then, as a spiritual bond between the Jewish people and the territory of the covenant.

On a superficial level, both Jewish conceptions of Eretz Yisrael and Indigenous conceptions of Country are certainly similar. Connection to land is grounded in the cultural and spiritual foundations of each community. For Indigenous people, this is through the Dreaming—spiritual and ancestral stories transmitted through songs, ceremonies, or stories that inform and guide cultural law/lore, relationships, and systems of knowing, being, and doing (Robin et al., 2022). For Jews, it is through the Tanakh, the Hebrew scriptures. Following Connor's (1994) definition, then, Indigenous Country and Eretz Yisrael constitute a spiritual connection between the nation (people) and territory (land), and thus can be individually understood as a homeland for those communities. However, does this individual definition as a homeland mean that Indigenous homelands are truly comparable to Jewish homelands?

## Homelands as connection

When asked about points of connection between Indigenous and Jewish communities, Lara (she/her) clearly stated, "Oh, very much connection to land. Connection to land and displacement" (Lara, personal communication, 25 May 2022). Lara is a Canadian-Kiwi Jew currently living on Nyoongar lands in Western Australia. She moved to so-called Australia as a teenager, after having lived in both Canada and Aotearoa (New Zealand). She says that the first time she got to know an Aboriginal person was as an adult while working at a not-for-profit organisation and that "just listening to peoples' stories like, it's been very, very eye opening" (Lara, personal communication, 25 May 2022). Lara identified several points of connection between Indigenous and Jewish experiences, though the one she kept coming back to was connection to land and histories of dispossession. When asked to elaborate on this, she went on to say:

> The last 2,000 years, we've sort of like, been kicked [...] around the globe [...] forced from a place that was hugely, deeply meaningful to us. All of our religious rights, you know, centred on that land and the stories of, you know, wanting that land back. You know, just everything's really centred around that and it is a massive sense of loss. But now also, you know, a sense of regaining. Of, you know, having self-determination and having self-management in particular. Being able to make our own decisions and live freely as we were and as we want to be.
>
> (Lara, personal communication, 25 May 2022)

A similar understanding was articulated by Leah (she/her), a Wiradjuri woman who converted to Orthodox Judaism after meeting her now-husband, a non-religious Canadian Jew. Leah, like Lara, draws on the notion of dispossession, saying:

> there's always been this extraordinary connection that Jews have with our plight [...] and there's always been an extraordinary understanding of what it is to be dispossessed from Country because a lot of that mob yearned for home. Even though they've been here for three generations and call Australia home and they know that this is their home, they still let yearning to be able to go back to the place where their ancestors bones are.
>
> (Leah, personal communication, 1 February 2022)

For both Lara and Leah, this understanding of dispossession or removal from your homeland, and the desire to reconnect operates as a fundamental point of connection between Indigenous and Jewish peoples. This shared understanding of not only what connection to your homeland means for your community, but the desire to get that land back and reconnect with your land or return to where your ancestors lay, is a shared experience.

Leah's use of the term 'Country' in her description of Jewish connection to land is also interesting. She is also not the only person interviewed as part of my doctoral research to use the term in both Jewish and Indigenous contexts. Shoshana (she/her), a Jewish woman living on Gadigal Country, described her connection to both 'Australia' and Eretz Yisrael as "kind of like living off Country, but I'm also living on Country at the same time" (Shoshana, personal communication, 21 December 2021). She also notes that while she identifies as both Australian and Jewish, when she goes to Israel it is "like going home" despite never having lived there (Shoshana, personal communication, 21 December 2021). Another Wiradjuri woman, identified here as Zoe (she/her), began her interview with a clear articulation of how she understands her connection to Wiradjuri Country and community (Zoe, personal communication, 28 February 2022). When discussing connection to homelands as a point of similarity between Jewish and Indigenous peoples, Zoe not only specifically identified connecting with Country as an example, but also noted that it is nice to speak with others who "really understand that connection to Country" (Zoe, personal communication, 28 February 2022).

Zoe is speaking here within the context of conversations she has had with a Jewish colleague at her workplace following a cultural competency course undertaken by all staff members. Part of the course focused on Indigenous connection with Country, and Zoe noted:

> one of our assignments that we did in this course, is to pick a place of significance to you. And it's an interesting exercise, because a lot of Australians who don't [...] identify with, you know, first- or second-generation immigrants or anything like that find it very difficult to think of somewhere that they connect to. And when they reflect upon their identity, it's difficult. Whereas with [my colleague] and myself, I have a place where I'll go with my dad and our animals, and just, it's like a cathartic experience, and then [colleague] had the Jerusalem wall. And that physical touch of being on Country is something that we talked about. And it's very similar in our two cultures.
>
> (Zoe, personal communication, 28 February 2022)

A similar understanding was articulated by Rebecca (she/her), a Koori[3] woman who converted to Judaism in a Reform synagogue[4] as an adult. Rebecca does not use the term 'Country' specifically, but does draw on the notion of Country as kin and the spiritual or religious aspects of Country and connecting with Country:

> There's this similarity, I suppose, between the worldview of ancient Israel and even contemporary Zionism, where the land is key to your identity. And in Aboriginal culture, the land is the heart of [...] of what we know. And, you know, belonging to a distinct people, having a kind of [pause] whether you call it the Dreaming or a broader spiritual orientation that connects you to your kin. So, there are those sort of commonalities...
>
> (Rebecca, personal communication, 7 February 2022)

Zoe speaks from her perspective as a Wiradjuri woman, while Lara and Shoshana speak from their perspectives as Jewish women living on Aboriginal lands. Leah and Rebecca speak from their perspectives as women who are both Jewish and Aboriginal. Each of these conceptualisations of connecting with land and Country are informed by their individual connections with their own homelands and communities. They are each informed by different relations with other groups—work, community organisations, or through participation in both Jewish and Aboriginal community life. As such, any connections they draw between Indigenous and Jewish relations with homelands comes from their own understandings of what that means, and must be taken as a genuine recognition of perceived similarities between Jewish and Indigenous relations with homelands. However, while this may be a commonly held understanding amongst both Indigenous and Jewish peoples, it is by no means universal. Further, the idea that Indigenous Country and Eretz Yisrael are comparable becomes much more constrained when situated within settler colonialist structures—in both so-called Australia and Palestine—and the way Jews are situated within these structures.

## Jews, belonging, and settler colonialism in so-called Australia

Settler colonialism is the process through which colonisers "come to stay" (Wolfe, 2001, p. 96). In this phenomenon, settler colonisers establish their own policies, processes, governances, and institutions, a key component of which is the "logic of elimination" (Wolfe, 2006, p. 387) whereby settler colonisers destroy to replace. This elimination is both physical—the mass murder and attempted genocide of Indigenous peoples—and via policy and procedure that maintain the settler colonial state (Kauanui, 2016; Wolfe, 2006). Australia is indisputably a settler colonial state, and the beginning of this setter colony is founded with the arrival of the First Fleet in January 1788. Here, British colonisers began constructing systems that attempted to eliminate Indigenous peoples from our lands, assimilate us into the settler colonial system, and dispossess us from our people, communities, lands, and histories (Carlson, 2016b). These structures remain intact today, and Indigenous peoples across the continent continue to experience the discrimination and racism that uphold the power structures that legitimise the settler colony (Bargallie, 2020).

In Australian historiography, it is a commonly cited fact that Jews have been here since the beginning of British settlement in 1788 (Bartrop, 1999; Bersten, 2018; Crown, 1990; Rubinstein, 2006; Rutland, 1997). Jews were among the first wave of British settlement, with anywhere between six and twenty-four Jewish convicts present on the First Fleet, though the total number is contested (Bersten, 2018; Levi, 2006; Rutland, 1997). Unique in its position in global histories of Jewry, 'Australia' is the only Jewish diaspora where Jews were present from the beginning of non-Indigenous occupation. This positioning signalled what Paul Bartrop describes as the "normalcy of the Australian Jewish situation" (1999, p. 91) and what John Stratton (1996) describes as a policy of ambivalence towards Jewish migration and settlement. While not Christian, the presence of Jews as part of the British convict fleets meant that they were overwhelmingly seen by other British settlers as British first and Jewish second (Bartrop, 1999). As William Rubinstein writes, Jews were not "considered to be aliens to quite the same extent as elsewhere" (1982, p. 163) because Jews were British by nationality and thus shared the same civil and legal rights as other British settlers. As such, the Jews who arrived at the beginning of British settlement benefited from the emerging structures of the settler colonial state though admittedly without the same religious freedom experienced by their Christian counterparts.

Not all Australian Jews today trace their ancestry to convict settlement, however. Many Jews migrated to the pre-federated colonies in the nineteenth century (Bersten, 1997; Offer, 2019; Price, 1964), and thousands arrived as Holocaust survivors after the Second World War (Corbett et al., 2021; Forrest & Sheskin, 2015). The role of migrants, refugees, and others forced to relocate present an interesting subset of this system that has sparked both debate and insight (Byrd, 2011; Curthoys, 2001; Day, 2016; Indelicato, 2022; Sexton, 2014; Sharma & Wright, 2008; Veracini, 2010). Throughout history, many non-white but non-Indigenous people have found safety on other peoples' land—as refugees, as displaced people, and as part of large-scale forced migration schemes. But are these people, who are racialised by the white majority and experience persecution, racism, and discrimination from white Australians, considered settlers as defined by settler colonial theory? Wolfe argues that regardless of "internal complexities", settler societies "uniformly require the elimination of Native alternatives" (2013, p. 257); however, this is not accepted by all scholars of settler colonialism. Lorenzo Veracini, for example, distinguishes migrants from settlers, arguing that "migrants, by definition, move to *another* country and lead diasporic lives" (2010, p. 3; italics in original). Settlers, however, move "to *their* country" (2010, p. 3; italics in original), suggesting that there is a difference in the type of presence between migrants and settlers. This asserts both Wolfe's claim that settlers "come to stay" (2001, p. 96) and the possessive logic outlined by Aileen Moreton-Robinson (2015).

The colonisation of the continent colonially referred to as Australia was underscored by a logic of elimination and possession and, as Moreton-Robinson reminds us, those who can call Australia 'home' is "inextricably connected to who has possession" (2015, p. 7). Possession is guarded by white Australia, and while Australia now is more multicultural than it used to be (Australian Bureau of Statistics, 2022), the dominant institutions, law, government, and the epistemologies that underscore them all remain anglicised. The right to belong to Australia is measured, legitimised, and sanctioned by these anglicised institutions (Gatwiri & Anderson, 2021; Piperoglou, 2022). As such, a sense of belonging and sense of legitimacy is more easily felt for white and white-passing migrants (Moreton-Robinson, 2015), yet non-white migrants and refugees who do not possess—as possession remains with the white majority—nonetheless share the benefits of Indigenous dispossession.

For some of the Jewish participants I interviewed, the distinction between those who arrived as Holocaust survivors, and those who arrived in other circumstances was important. One such example is from Sophie (she/they),[5] a young Jewish person living on Dharug Country, who stated in our interview:

> there's definitely been Jews who have come as colonisers. And I only say that to differentiate between Jews that came as Holocaust survivors and their families. And that's just to say that that's a different experience.
> (Sophie, personal communication, 21 March 2022)

Sophie is a descendant of Holocaust survivors on their paternal family line, and for them this differentiation is important because the experience of Holocaust survivors and the circumstance of their arrival is significantly different to that of Jews who arrived prior to the Second World War. Indeed, as David Slucki (2019) reminds us, the Jews who arrived in so-called Australia following the Holocaust had direct experiences with systemic discrimination, violence, and oppression in a way that many Jewish migrants prior to the War had never experienced.

For Australian Jews descended from Jewish convicts, or those who came voluntarily prior to the Holocaust, the experience of being Jewish in so-called Australia was vastly different to the experience of being Jewish in other parts of the world. Anti-Semitism was far less prevalent across this continent until the 1930s (Bartrop, 1999; Rutland, 1997) and reached a high in the 1940s and 1950s (Kaiser, 2022), owing partly to the positioning of Australian Jewry within white Australia. Many of the Jews who arrived as Holocaust survivors after the Second World War, however, spoke Yiddish as a primary language and came from Eastern European countries racialised under Australia's restrictive immigration policies (Rubinstein, 2006). This disruption to the social and cultural make-up of Australian Jewry caused a shift in the way Jews were perceived by white Australians broadly. While Jews were still settlers, and thus beneficiaries of ongoing Indigenous dispossession, it became much clearer that Jews were also a cultural and religious minority within Australian settler society.

The different experiences of Jewish settlers highlight difficulties with defining groups as either inside or outside the settler colonial structure. This follows what Iyko Day describes as populations that "exceed the conceptual boundaries that attend 'the immigrant'" (2016, p. 20), while some migrants are initially deemed 'non-white' but eventually assimilate or are otherwise later incorporated into the white population, such as Greek and Irish settlers (McGrath, 2010; Nicolacopoulos & Vassilacopoulos, 2004; Piperoglou, 2022). Others like Jews and Asian indentured workers were enslaved, forcibly removed, or arrived in so-called Australia as a result of traumatic circumstances like the Holocaust (Bartrop, 1994; Indelicato, 2022; Langfield, 2012). Jodi Byrd extends this thinking, conceptualising settler colonialism as "a cacophony of contradictorily hegemonic and horizontal struggles" (2011, p. 53). Additionally, Byrd (2011) argues that a settler colonial setting should not be approached as a static field. Rather, settler colonial settings should be approached as comprising a variety of third spaces "where racialised and colonised peoples, existing in the same geographical space, interact with one another as well as the coloniser" (Byrd, 2011, p. 54). This definition of settler colonialism disrupts the absolute binary between coloniser and colonised encompassed within Wolfe's definition, and the dichotomy of settler/migrant in Veracini's. By allowing for space to explore historical conditions contextualising the circumstances of arrival—and subsequent stay—of diasporic communities, we can better understand Jewish situatedness on Indigenous homelands.

## Jewish situatedness and contested conceptions

The first question asked in each interview was 'how do you see yourself fitting into this story?' The choice to participate in this project was situated wholly with each interviewee following an open call for participants. In practice, as the researcher, I did not communicate with potential interviewees until they reached out with an interest in participating. For this reason, the purpose of this initial question is to situate each interviewee within their own contexts and understand their entry point to this research. In response to this question, one participant, a Jewish woman identified here as Amy (she/her), stated:

> First and foremost, I want to acknowledge [Gadigal Country] and pay respect to [Gadigal Country], because I feel where I fit into the story […] is very much predicated on the fact that I'm conscious that I am on land that is, and always will be Aboriginal land.
>
> (Amy, personal communication, 8 February 2022)

Amy is, as of time of writing, the only Jewish person interviewed to begin with an Acknowledgement to Country during our interview, and noted that she lives and works on sovereign and unceded Indigenous land. I include this not to shame or judge the other interviewees, but to highlight that each of the people included in this chapter have different relationships with homelands and recognise their position on and relationship to Aboriginal and Torres Strait Islander lands in different ways. These differences necessarily result in different discussions, different responses to questions, and ultimately different understandings of Indigenous and Jewish relations across the continent colonially known as Australia.

Amy was born overseas and arrived in Australia as a teenager in 1989 (Amy, personal communication, 8 February 2022). Since arriving here, she has lived primarily on Gadigal land in the vicinity of the Jewish community in Sydney's eastern suburbs. She states that she became aware of Indigenous and Jewish community relations "as soon as I arrived" and that:

> I can't really separate my conduct on this land from the fact that it's, you know, geographically where I sit. So, I'm very conscious of that. And I feel very grateful and respectful of the [...] the wisdom and the traditions and the customs that go along with that.
>
> (Amy, personal communication, 8 February 2022)

She goes on to explain that the recognition and understanding that she is living, working, and raising her children on unceded Gadigal land comes with "a significant weight [...] and a responsibility to conduct myself in a certain way on this land" (Amy, personal communication, 8 February 2022). She draws a direct connection between her understanding of the world and her Western education and upbringing and "my Jewish values", noting that "I've realised that that's the unique lens with which I see the world" (Amy, personal communication, 8 February 2022). For Amy, then, the way she understands and forms relations with other people and communities, and her entry point to this research, is fundamentally underscored by the recognition of Indigenous connection to land, and her own Jewishness.

Amy's understanding of her situatedness is also reflective of her status as a migrant who has connections with a homeland outside of Australia. A dual sense of belonging for migrant communities is well established in academic literature globally (Babar, 2016; Bhabha, 1996; Clary-Lemon, 2010; Dutto, 2016; Gatwiri & Anderson, 2021; Grossberg, 1996; Klingenberg et al., 2021). How identity and belonging should be assessed, particularly in instances where migrant and diasporic communities have dual or multiple connections across borders, continues to be questioned (Klingenberg et al., 2021; Naidoo, 2007). As Lawrence Grossberg (1996) reminds us, the way individuals construct their identities is both continuous, and occurs across different social and cultural contexts. For migrant communities, this occurs in response to both the connection felt or developed to the places and communities they have migrated to, and the ones they have left behind.

This is particularly true for diasporic communities like global Jewish communities. Jewish identities are constantly producing and reproducing themselves in response to both their connection with their physical geographical location and Eretz Yisrael—the homeland to which all Jews are understood as being connected (Grossman & Raviv, 2022; Liwerant, 2021) even if they have never been there. Throughout history, there has been a sense of longing to return to this remembered or imagined homeland. While those in the diaspora may feel a very real sense of identification and belonging to their geographic location, this is necessarily intermingled with the ongoing sense of connection to and identification with the culturally remembered homeland.

It is not surprising that discussion regarding Palestine was often begun with a statement asking that this not be included in the final transcript and edited out of the saved audio recordings. For those who chose to include it in the approved transcript, I was usually asked to confirm that their identity would remain anonymous, and many chose to utilise a pseudonym instead of their first name. For some of the people who were interviewed for this project, the topic of Palestine and the State of Israel was brought up of their own accord because "I feel like it is important to include" (Joe, personal communication, 21 October

2022), though with notable hesitancy. Sophie, for example, brought it up in response to a question regarding whether they saw Indigenous and Jewish relationships as being recip-rocal, stating:

> Um I think it's also without [...] without making this too hotly political I think it's also then complicated by Palestine, and Israel and Zionism and how Jews define antisemitism.
>
> (Sophie, personal communication, 21 March 2022)

The reason for both Joe's and Sophie's hesitancy stems from the growing conflation between anti-Zionism and anti-Semitism. Anti-Semitism—hatred towards Jewish people—can be expressed in many ways. The 2021 *Report on Antisemitism in Australia* states that between 1 October 2020 and 30 September 2021, there were 447 anti-Semitic incidents logged across the continent, including 272 physical assaults, verbal abuse, vandalism, and graffiti, and 175 threats by email, telephone, postal mail, or posters (Nathan, 2021). This was an increase of 35 per cent compared to the previous year in the overall number of reported anti-Semitic incidents, consistent with other reports claiming an increase in anti-Semitism in Australia (Fitzsimmons, 2022; Vergani et al., 2022) and around the world (Groarke & Tamer, 2022). In May 2021, a surge in anti-Semitic acts was seen in Australia following 11 days of intense fighting between Israeli forces and Palestinian armed groups in the Gaza Strip (*Gaza after the May Escalation*, 2021; A full list can be seen in: Nathan, 2021, pp. 30–78). Many of these involved targeting Jewish schools, synagogues, and private houses with swastikas, graffiti, and verbal abuse, and many of these instances referenced Palestine, Zionism, and the ongoing Gaza conflict.

Zionism refers to support for the continued existence of the State of Israel. Anti-Zionism, then, refers to calls for the State of Israel to be disestablished. While some Jews purport Zionism as a central tenet of being Jewish (Lewin, 2020; Shapira, 2009), not all Jews are Zionists (Alreoy, 2016; Benesh, 2021; Friesel, 2019), despite a dominant belief on the part of both non-Jews and Jews alike that Jewish people are—or should be. Thus, when non-Zionist Jews or non-Jews who do not support the State of Israel question, critique, or outwardly state that Israel should be disestablished, it can be interpreted as being anti-Semitic to Jews, who position Zionism as a central element to Jewish identity. However, as Peter Beinart (2019) writes in an article for *The Guardian*, "Anti-Zionism is not inherently antisemitic–and claiming it is uses Jewish suffering to erase the Palestinian experience". This is not to say that all statements again the State of Israel are not anti-Semitic—when Jews are verbally or physically harassed, or Jewish institutions are vandalised in response to the actions of the Israeli state, it is anti-Semitism. Critique of the State of Israel, and in particular the actions taken against Palestinians, is not.

Many Zionist Jews position themselves alongside Indigenous peoples due to a shared connection to homelands (Sarzin & Sarzin, 2010). However, this positioning is not always accepted by Indigenous peoples due to the notion of Zionism and the understanding of the State of Israel as a settler colony (Barakat, 2018; Benesh, 2021; Veracini, 2019). An interesting example of this was reported in *The Australian Jewish News* in 2021, where a Jewish student reported a lecture delivered by the Macquarie University Department of Indigenous Studies to the Anti-Defamation Commission (ADC) for using a map to illustrate settler colonialism on a global scale (Zlatkis, 2021). The map identified Palestine along-side other nations that have experienced or are experiencing settler colonial domination, though the topics of Palestine and Israel were not discussed in the lecture itself. As reported in *The Australian Jewish News*, the ADC claims that it is an "outrageous accusation" that Jewish "return to Israel and the establishment of the Jewish State is a classic example of colonialism" and that such a claim rejects Jewish people "their historic homeland" (Zlatkis, 2021). No such claims were made in the lecture; nonetheless, the situation was included in the 2021 *Report on Antisemitism in Australia* (Nathan, 2021) and highlights the complexity of Indigenous and Jewish relationships.

The analysis of Zionism and Israel/Palestine as a settler colonial regime generates many objections. As Yoav Peled (2017) outlines, one of these is the argument that Zionist intentions were not outwardly colonial. Max Kaiser (2022) refutes this, noting that assessing a process of dispossession and violence from the standpoint of the intention of the dispossessors is problematic. Further, the primary case for an assessment of Zionism in Palestine as settler colonialism "is that it has systematically replaced Palestinians on their land with Jewish settlers" (Kaiser, 2022, p. 15). That is, the State of Israel destroys to replace (Wolfe, 2006). The idea that the State of Israel is a settler colony, however, is not necessarily well recognised by Jewish people—or if it is, it comes with many conflicted feelings. In our interview, Amy stated that one thing she has struggled with over the last few years is the conversations happening around Israel as a settler colonial project. She states:

> When it comes to Israel [...] I find it quite challenging because I find that this idea that, you know, like the idea of dispossession. That Israel dispossessed Palestinians, and that the State of Israel is a sort of white colonialist, Zionist enterprise [...] I find very, very challenging and difficult to sort of understand where it comes from.
> (Amy, personal communication, 8 February 2022)

Amy is very open regarding these concerns, describing the idea of Israel as being stolen land as something that "for me is quite troubling" because "where there was First Nations continuous possession to Australia until it was invaded. That is not the story of Israel. So [...] it's not a comparable situation" (Amy, personal communication, 8 February 2022).

A different perspective is given by Joe (he/him), a young Jewish man who grew up attending a Jewish day school on Gadigal Country. He says he only become "really aware of Indigenous issues and settler colonialism and stuff" when he began university, but when he did begin learning, it:

> made me start, you know, really thinking about what I've been taught my whole life. About, you know, Israel and our *right* to Israel because of the covenant and also just about how like, how all of it has gone about. The violence and war and all that. I don't have a sort of like, clear understanding yet I'm still trying to figure it all out. But I've definitely begun like, questioning things a lot more and I wouldn't say I'm strictly and surely like, Zionist, now even though I was raised that way for a long time.
> (Joe, personal communication, 21 October 2022)

Joe raises an interesting and incredibly important point here. One stark difference between Indigenous conceptions of Country and Jewish attachments to Eretz Yisrael is this sense of entitlement. When the State of Israel was established on Palestinian land in 1948, Israel's Declaration of Independence speaks of the 'right' of the Jewish people to establish their State.

This sense of entitlement does not exist in Indigenous world views. Our understanding of our relationship to Country is not constructed on the 'right' or entitlement to Country. We do not own Country, as Country is not a possession to be owned. If anything, we belong to Country, as we are part of the reciprocal relationships that exist between all living and non-living entities within Country (Rey, 2021). This is the difference between an ontological relationship with the land and a non-ontological relationship. As Lorenzo Veracini (2019) writes, Zionists are not Indigenous to the land—they entertain a historical, non-ontological relationship to it. It is meaningful, and it is spiritual, but it is fundamentally a different type of relationship to that of Indigenous relations with Country.

## Conclusion

The idea of a homeland as a spiritual connection between people and land is applicable to both Indigenous conceptions of Country and Jewish conceptions of the promised land, Eretz Yisrael. In both relationships, land functions as a place of origin historically, culturally, and spiritually in different ways. For this reason, connecting to a homeland is often posited as a point of similarity or connection between Indigenous and Jewish people and communities in so-called Australia. While this may be true on a superficial level, as this chapter has shown, the reality is much more complex.

The role of settler colonialism in both so-called Australia and Palestine, and the hesitancy to engage in those discussions operates as a limiting factor in genuine engagement between Indigenous and Jewish community members. While many Jewish people openly recognise that they live on Indigenous lands and thus benefit from ongoing Indigenous dispossession, this way of thinking is less easily applied to the State of Israel. This partially due to the sense of entitlement to that land—a notion that does not exist in Indigenous conceptions of Country. Where Jews feel that they have the *right* to possession, Indigenous relations to Country operate as an ontological belonging. This difference thus suggests that while Jewish and Indigenous cultures are connected through the notion of a homeland, the way those connections operate is fundamentally different and altogether not comparable.

## Notes

1  I use the term 'so-called Australia' to draw attention to the fact that this continent was claimed under the legal fiction of terra nullius, land belonging to nobody, where in fact this continent is home to hundreds of self-identifying nations of Aboriginal peoples.
2  The first five books of the Christian Old Testament–Genesis, Exodus, Leviticus, Numbers, and Deuteronomy.
3  A general grouping term sometimes used to refer to Aboriginal people from NSW and Victoria.
4  In Australia, Reform Judaism is the most liberal branch of Judaism. The other two are Orthodox and Conservative.
5  Following discussion with Sophie, I only use they/them pronouns when referring to them in this chapter, though I recognise that their personal relationship with gender identity and expression goes beyond a single set of pronouns.

## References

Alreoy, G. (2016). *Zionism without Zion: The Jewish territorial organization and its conflict with the Zionist organization*. Wayne State University Press.

Aronson, J. K., Saxe, L., Kadushin, C., Boxer, M., & Brookner, M. A. (2019). A new approach to understanding contemporary Jewish engagement. *Contemporary Jewry, 39*, 91–113.

Australian Bureau of Statistics. (2022). *Cultural diversity of Australia: Information on country of birth, year of arrival, ancestry, language and religion.* www.abs.gov.au/articles/cultural-diversity-australia

Babar, S. (2016). Burnt shadows: 'Home', 'cosmopolitanism' and 'hybridization'. *Journal of Humanities and Social Sciences, 24*(2), 109–126.

Barakat, R. (2018). Writing/righting Palestine studies: Settler colonialism, indigenous sovereignty and resisting the ghost(s) of history. *Settler Colonial Studies, 8*(3), 349–363.

Bargallie, D. (2020). *Unmasking the racial contract: Indigenous voices on racism in the Australian public service.* Aboriginal Studies Press.

Bartrop, P. (1994). *Australia and the Holocaust, 1933–45.* Australian Scholarly Publishing.

Bartrop, P. (1999). Living within the frontier: Early colonial Australia, Jews, and Aborigines. In S. Gilman & M. Shain (Eds.), *Jewries at the frontier: Accommodation, identity, conflict* (pp. 91–110). University of Illinois Press.

Beinart, P. (2019, 7 March). Debunking the myth that anti-zionism is antisemitic. *The Guardian.* www.theguardian.com/news/2019/mar/07/debunking-myth-that-anti-zionism-is-antisemitic

Benesh, M. (2021, 25 May). Peeling back the mythology of the Australian Jewish left. *New Voices.* https://newvoices.org/2021/05/25/peeling-back-the-mythology-of-the-australian-jewish-left/

Bersten, H. (1997). Jews in rural New South Wales. *Australian Jewish Historical Society Journal, 13*(4), 596–634.

Bersten, H. (2018). Sydney, Australia's early Jewish community. *Western States Jewish History, 50*(3), 105–122.

Bhabha, H. K. (1996). Culture's in-between. In S. Hall & P. du Gay (Eds.), *Questions of cultural identity* (pp. 53–60). SAGE.

Byrd, J. (2011). *The transit of empire: New directions in Indigenous Studies.* University of Minnesota Press.

Carlson, B. (2016a). Striking the right chord: Indigenous people and the love of country. *AlterNative, 12*(5), 489–512.

Carlson, B. (2016b). *The politics of identity.* Aboriginal Studies Press.

Clary-Lemon, J. (2010). We're not ethnic, we're Irish!: Oral histories and the discursive construction of immigrant identity. *Discourse & Sociology, 21*(1), 5–25.

Cohen, H. A. (2021). Purposeful interaction of Jews with Aborigines in the mid-1960s: ANUJSS and the Nulla Nulla Club for Aboriginal children at Wallaga Lake. *Australian Jewish Historical Society Journal, 25*(2), 263–288.

Connor, W. (1994). *Ethnonationalism: The quest for understanding.* Princeton University Press.

Corbett, T., Hödl, K., Kita, C. A., Korbel, S., & Rupnow, D. (2021). Migration, integration, and assimilation: Reassessing key concepts in (Jewish) Austrian history. *Journal of Austrian Studies, 54*(1), 1–28.

Crown, A. (1990). The Jewish press in Australia. *Arts: The Journal of the Sydney University Arts Association, 15*, 87–107.

Cruz, G. T. (2019). Mission tracks in the bush: Theological reflections on two aboriginal missions in nineteenth-century Australia. *Interreligious Studies and Intercultural Theology, 3*(1–2), 103–124.

Curthoys, A. (2001). Immigration and colonisation: New histories. *UTS Review, 7*(1), 170–179.

Day, I. (2016). *Alien capital: Asian racialization and the logic of settler colonial capitalism.* Duke University Press.

Dutto, M. (2016). Land, culture and new ways of belonging: Encounters between Italian migrants and Indigenous Australians in Far Away Is Home. La storia di Clely (Diego Cenetiempo, Australia/Italy, 2012). *Flinders University Language Group Online Review, 5*(1), 63–73.

Epstein, A. (2019). *Melekh Ravitsh: The eccentric outback quest of an urbane Yiddish poet from Poland.* Real Film and Publishing.

Fitzsimmons, C. (2022, 11 September). 'I'll stop your bloodline': Anti-Semitism reports grow across Sydney schools. *Sydney Morning Herald.* www.smh.com.au/national/nsw/i-ll-stop-your-bloodline-anti-semitism-reports-grow-across-sydney-schools-20220909-p5bgrf.html

Forrest, J., & Sheskin, I. M. (2015). Strands of the diaspora: The resettlement experience of Jewish immigrants to Australia. *Journal of International Migration and Integration, 16*, 911–927.

Friesel, E. (2019). Jews against Zionism/Israel: On the ambivalences of contemporary Jewish identity. In A. Lange, K. Mayerhofer, D. Porat, & L. H. Schiffman (Eds.), *Comprehending and confronting antisemitism: A multi-faceted approach* (pp. 427–439). De Gruyter.

Gatwiri, K., & Anderson, L. (2021). Boundaries of belonging: Theorizing Black African migrant experiences in Australia. *International Journal of Environment Research and Public Health, 18*(38), 1–13.

*Gaza after the May escalation.* (2021, 3 November). United Nations Office for the Coordination of Humanitarian Affairs. www.ochaopt.org/content/humanitarian-bulletin-november-2021

Graham, D., & Markus, A. (2018). *Gen17 Australian Jewish Community Survey: Preliminary Findings.* Australian Centre for Jewish Civilisation.

Groarke, D., & Tamer, R. (2022, April 28). Anti-Semitism continues to rise across the world, according to new report. *SBS News.* www.sbs.com.au/news/article/anti-semitism-continues-to-rise-across-the-world-according-to-new-report/k6j2ms97r

Grossberg, L. (1996). Identity and cultural studies—Is that all there is? In S. Hall & P. du Gay (Eds.), *Questions of cultural identity* (pp. 87–107). SAGE.

Grossman, J. (2019). Toward a definition of diaspora. *Ethnic and Racial Studies, 42*(8), 1263–1282.

Grossman, J., & Raviv, O. S. (2022). Israel, the Jewish diaspora, and the Palestinian refugee issue: A mixed relationship. *Journal of Ethnic and Migration Studies,* 1–19. https://doi.org/10.1080/1369183X.2022.2111548

Harris, J. (1990). *One blood: 200 years of Aboriginal encounter with Christianity: A story of hope.* Albatross Books.

Indelicato, M. E. (2022). Beyond whiteness: Violence and belonging in the borderlands of North Queensland. *Postcolonial Studies, 32*(1), 99–115.

Kaiser, M. (2022). *Jewish antifascism and the false promise of settler colonialism.* Palgrave Macmillan.

Kauanui, J. K. (2016). 'A structure, not an event': Settler colonialism and enduring indigeneity. *Lateral, 5*(1), 1–8.

Klingenberg, A., Luetz, J. M., & Crawford, A. (2021). Transnationalism—recognizing the strengths of dual belonging for both migrant and society. *Journal of International Migration and Integration, 22,* 453–470.

Langfield, M. (2012). 'Don't forget you are Jewish': Holocaust survivors, identity formation and sense of belonging in Australia. In A. Hayes & R. Mason (Eds.), *Cultures in refuge: Seeking sanctuary in modern Australia* (pp. 67–78). Ashgate.

Langton, M. (2006). Earth, wind, fire and water: The social and spiritual construction of water in Aboriginal societies. In B. David, B. Barker, & I. J. McNiven (Eds.), *Social archaeology of Australian indigenous societies* (pp. 139–160). Aboriginal Studies Press.

Levi, J. S. (2006). *These are the names: Jewish lives in Australia, 1788–1860.* Melbourne University Publishing.

Lewin, A. D. (2020). Zionism—The integral component of Jewish identity that Jews are historically pressured to shed. *Israel Affairs, 26*(3), 330–347.

Liwerant, J. B. (2021). Globalization, diasporas, and transnationalism: Jews in the Americas. *Contemporary Jewry, 41,* 711–753.

Ludewig, A. (2020). Utopian colonial settlers: Dreaming of Jewish colonies in northern and western Australia. *Settler Colonial Studies, 19*(2), 176–192.

McDonald, H. (2001). *Blood, bones and spirit: Aboriginal Christianity in an East Kimberley town.* Melbourne University Press.

McGrath, A. (2010). Shamrock Aborigines: The Irish, the Aboriginal Australians and their children. *Aboriginal History, 34,* 55–84.

McLisky, C. L. (2015). 'And They'll Know We Are Christians By Our Love': Exploring the role of Christian love on Maloga Mission, 1874–1888. *Journal of Religious History, 39*(3), 333–351.

Miller, B. (2012). *William Cooper—Gentle warrior: Standing up for Australian Aborigines and persecuted Jews.* Xlibris.

Moreton-Robinson, A. (2015). *The white possessive: Property, power, and Indigenous sovereignty.* University of Minnesota Press.

Naidoo, L. (2007). Re-negotiating identity and reconciling cultural ambiguity in the Indian immigrant community in Sydney, Australia. In H. Singh (Ed.), *Indian Diaspora: The 21st Century. Migration, Change, and Adaption* (pp. 53–66). Kamla-Raj Enterprises.

Nathan, J. (2021). *Report on antisemitism in Australia 2021*. Executive Council of Australian Jewry.

Netana-Glover, L. (2021). Complexities of displaced Indigenous identities: A fifty year journey home, to two homes. *Genealogy, 5*(3), 1–7.

Nicolacopoulos, T., & Vassilacopoulos, G. (2004). Racism, foreigner communities and the onto-pathology of white Australian subjectivity. In A. Moreton-Robinson (Ed.), *Whitening race: Essays in social and cultural criticism* (pp. 32–47). Aboriginal Studies Press.

Noon, K., & de Napoli, K. (2022). *Astronomy: Sky country*. Thames and Hudson.

O'Brien, L., & Watson, I. (2014). In conversation with Uncle Lewis: Bushfires, weather-makers, collective management. *AlterNative, 10*(5), 450–461.

Offer, E. (2019). High holidays on the high seas: The voyage experience of Jewish migrants sailing to Australia in the mid-nineteenth century. *Jewish Culture and History, 20*(4), 317–336.

Onnudottir, H., Possamai, A., & Turner, B. (2010). Islam: A new religious vehicle for Aboriginal self-empowerment in Australia? *International Journal for the Study of New Religions, 1*(1), 49–73.

Peled, Y. (2017). Delegitimation of Israel or social-historical analysis? The debate over Zionism as a colonial settler movement. In J. Jacobs (Ed.), *Jews and leftist politics: Judaism, Israel, anti-semitism, and gender* (pp. 103–122). Cambridge University Press.

Piperoglou, A. (2022). Migrant acculturation via naturalisation: Comparing Syrian and Greek applications for naturalisation in white Australia. *Historical Studies in Ethnicity, Migration, and Diaspora, 40*(1–2), 59–78.

Price, C. (1964). Jewish Settlers in Australia, 1788–1961. *Australian Jewish Historical Society Journal, 5*(8), 357–413.

Rey, J. A. (2021). Indigenous identity as country: The "Ing" within connecting, caring, and belonging. *Genealogy, 5*(48), 1–12.

Rey, J. A. (2022). Quiet activism through Dharug Ngurra: Reporting locally grown—not from the European South. *From the European South, 10*, 25–40.

Robin, L., Robin, K., Camerlenghi, E., Ireland, L., & Ryan-Colton, E. (2022). How dreaming and Indigenous ancestral stories are central to nature conservation: Perspectives from Walalkara Indigenous Protected Area, Australia. *Ecological Management and Restoration, 23*(1), 43–52.

Rubinstein, W. D. (1982). *The left, the right, and the Jews*. Croom Helm.

Rubinstein, W. D. (2006). Patterns of Jewish immigration to Australia and their impact upon Australian Jewish identity. *Australian Jewish Historical Society Journal, 18*(2), 231–235.

Rutland, S. D. (1997). *Edge of the diaspora: Two centuries of Jewish settlement in Australia* (2nd rev. ed.). Lynne Rienner.

Sarzin, A., & Sarzin, L. (2010). *Hand in hand: Jewish and Indigenous people working together*. New South Wales Jewish Board of Deputies.

Sexton, J. (2014). The vel of slavery: Tracking the figure of the unsovereign. *Critical Sociology, 42*(2), 1–15.

Shapira, A. (2009). The Jewish-people deniers. *Journal of Israeli History, 28*(1), 63–72.

Sharma, N., & Wright, C. (2008). Decolonizing resistance: Challenging colonial states. *Social Justice, 35*(3), 120–138.

Slucki, D. (2019). 'Black and white': Yiddish writers encounter Indigenous Australia. In S. Gilbert & A. Alba (Eds.), *Holocaust memory and racism in the postwar world* (pp. 121–145). Wayne State University Press.

Stephenson, P. (2009). Keeping it in the family: Partnerships between Indigenous and Muslim communities in Australia. *Aboriginal History, 33*, 97–116.

Stephenson, P. (2010). *Islam dreaming: Indigenous Muslims in Australia*. NewSouth Publishing.

Stratton, J. (1996). The colour of Jews: Jews, Race and the white Australia policy. *Journal of Australian Studies, 20*(50–51), 51–65.

Tatz, C. (2004). An essay in disappointment: The Aboriginal-Jewish relationship. *Aboriginal History, 28*, 100–122.

Troen, I., & Rabineau, S. (2014). Competing concepts of land in Eretz Israel. *Israel Studies, 19*(2), 162–186.

Tynan, L. (2021). What is relationality? Indigenous knowledges, practices and responsibilities with kin. *Cultural Geographies, 28*(4), 597–610.

Veracini, L. (2010). *Settler colonialism: A theoretical overview*. Palgrave Macmillan.

Veracini, L. (2019). Israel-Palestine through a settler-colonial studies lens. *Interventions, 21*(4), 568–581.

Vergani, M., Goodhardt, D., Link, R., Adanczyk, A., Freilich, J. D., & Chermank, S. (2022). When and how does anti-Semitism occur? The different trigger mechanisms associated with different types of criminal and non-criminal hate incidents. *Deviant Behavior, 43*(9), 1135–1152.

Whap, G. (2001). A Torres Strait Islander perspective on the concept of Indigenous Knowledge. *Australian Journal of Indigenous Education, 29*(2), 22–29.

Wildcat, M., McDonald, M., Irlbacher-Fox, S., & Coulthard, G. (2014). Learning from the land: Indigenous land based pedagogy and decolonization. *Decolonization: Indigeneity, Education & Society, 3*(3), 1–15.

Wolfe, P. (2001). Land, labor, and difference: Elementary structures of race. *American Historical Review, 106*(3), 866–905.

Wolfe, P. (2006). Settler colonialism and the elimination of the native. *Journal of Genocide Research, 8*(4), 387–409.

Wolfe, P. (2013). Recuperating binarism: A heretical introduction. *Settler Colonial Studies, 3*(3–4), 257–279.

Zlatkis, E. (2021, 11 March). Macquarie University 'wipes Israel off map'. *Australian Jewish News.* www.australianjewishnews.com/macquarie-university-wipes-israel-off-map/#:~:text=MACQUARIE%20University%20has%20been%20accused,state%20is%20a%20colonial%20territory.

# 6
# ABORIGINAL AND TORRES STRAIT ISLANDER INCLUSION IN THE WORKPLACE

## Challenging racist policy and practice

*Sharlene Leroy-Dyer and Kelly Menzel*

### Protocols in action

The authors of this chapter would like to acknowledge it has been written on the unceded sovereign lands of the Gubbi Gubbi, Turrbal, Yuggera, and Kombumerri peoples and the Bundjalung Nations of Australia. We pay genuine respect to their Elders past and present, and to the Aboriginal peoples for whom these lands are significant. We pay our respects to our Ancestors and Elders who have paved the way and to whom we are accountable.

This chapter uses the four-point Indigenous standpoint theory as articulated by Dennis Foley (2003). Both authors identify as Aboriginal (Darug, Garigal, Awabakal, and Wiradyuri and Ngadjuri with ancestral connections to Bundjalung Nation) and are actively involved in the Indigenisation of tertiary education. Both authors are employed by tertiary educational institutions and have a sound understanding of critical race and critical social theory. Further, this chapter is written to support First Nations peoples globally to continue the Indigenisation of tertiary education and to grow strong curriculum/s and graduates. Where possible, First Nations languages are privileged.

We will predominantly use the term 'Aboriginal and Torres Strait Islander peoples', as opposed to 'Indigenous' or 'First Nations'. When the term 'Indigenous' is used, it largely relates to government policy—except when referring to Indigenisation of curriculum and Indigenous Knowledges—and where 'First Nations' is used, it is in a global context. In addition, we use the term 'peoples' to signify that Aboriginal and Torres Strait Islander peoples are not one people or nation, but a collective of peoples and nations. We frequently refer to whiteness and non-Indigenous peoples as 'whites/white' people. The words 'whites/white' people might be considered inflammatory and cause the white people reading it a fragility response (DiAngelo, 2018). The invisibility of whiteness means that white people often do not like being called white (Moreton-Robinson, 2004; Young, 2004). This invisibility leaves whiteness unnamed but ever present. It is the unspoken norm from which everyone/everything else deviates. We name, and make visible, whiteness in this chapter.

DOI: 10.4324/9781003271802-8

## Introduction

The academy worldwide has traditionally been dominated by an Anglo-centric culture permeated by the staff employed and the students attracted, actively dedvaluing the knowledges and experiences of the 'other'. This structure and system is flawed by a whiteness view, with a regime of power that has material effects (Moreton-Robinson, 2005), especially for staff and students who do not fit this view. As Aboriginal women, we actively strive to dismantle racialised power structures and openly challenge the white privilege that is so prevalent in the academy. The role of privilege in shaping aspirations often remains unmarked, as whites are taught not to recognise white supremacy, white power, and white privilege—just as men are taught not to recognise male privilege. Critical race theory (CRT) is an important tool, which offers critical perspectives on race and inequities, and the dynamics of power and privilege in the academy (Rabaka, 2022). Indigenous feminist theory (Liddle, 2014) focuses on decolonisation, Indigenous sovereignty, and human rights for Indigenous women. Critical race, Indigenous feminist, and decolonising scholars discuss ways that global, political, cultural, economic, and political systems and structures of the past 500 years precipitate racialised contemporary realities (Dar et al., 2021), and despite the vast intellectual history, the academy remains largely devoid of these debates.

## Setting the scene in the academy

White, able-bodied, cisgendered, heterosexual men provide the human norm against which deviation is measured, and equity and diversity policies and principles employed by universities do not interrogate the institutional and systemic whiteness that exists within its structures, practices, and assumptions perpetuated. Institutional and systemic whiteness facilitate race-based, horizontal and lateral violence within the academy (Day, 2020; Frogley, 2018). Horizontal and lateral violence are a product of colonisation (Bailey, 2020) and often described as internalised colonialism (HEROC, 2011). We contend that "institutional racism textures the experience of Aboriginal staff and students alike. Staff in positions of power continue to be predominantly white men and curriculum is unashamedly whitewashed" (Menzel & Cameron, 2021, p. 129).

Arnesen (2001, p. 92) contends:

> Whiteness is, variously, a metaphor for power, a proxy for racially distributed material benefits, a synonym for "white supremacy", an epistemological stance defined by power, a position of invisibility or ignorance, and a set of beliefs about racial "Others" and oneself that can be rejected through "treason" to a racial category.

Grzanka, Frantell, and Fassinger (2019, p. 1) state, "[t]he construct [of] White guilt is typically motivated by the recognition of unearned and unfair racial privileges, the acknowledgement of personal racist attitudes or behaviour, and/or the sense of responsibility for others' racist attitudes or behaviour". White guilt blocks critical reflection because whites end up feeling they are individually to blame for all racism (Leonardo, 2005).

Grosfoguels' (2011) definition of racism refers to a "human line" that divides what is considered superior and what is considered inferior. He further argues (2020, p. 10):

people classified above the line of the human are recognised socially in their humanity as human beings and, thus, enjoy access to rights (human rights, civil rights, women rights and/or labour rights), material resources, and social recognition to their subjectivities, identities, epistemologies and spiritualities. The people below the line of the human are considered subhuman or non-human; that is, their humanity is questioned and, as such, negated.

## Intersectionality: race and gender

As Aboriginal women, we face discrimination along multiple axes—in particular race and gender. Crenshaw (2011) argues that Black women face employment discrimination based on the intersection of oppressions like racism and sexism. The term 'Black women' as originally used by Crenshaw referred to African American women; however, we have re-presented the term in Australia to include Aboriginal and Torres Strait Islander (Blak) women.

The intersectional issues that Aboriginal women experience are often misunderstood and unrecognised in higher education (Suarez et al., 2022). The inadequacy of explaining the experiences and outcomes of Aboriginal women and those of other Black women in gender research continues to hold a prominent position in the diversity field. The under-employment of Aboriginal women in the academy (Department of Education, Skills and Employment, 2020) creates isolating environments and leaves us in search of affirmation and community, and as such, we as sistas foster unique relationships with one another in order to obtain support and encouragement. As Aboriginal women we are trying to survive in educational environments that perceive our knowledges as inferior and thus not worth knowing (Leroy-Dyer, 2018).

Crenshaw used intersectionality to describe the unique oppression Black women face as individuals holding both gendered and racially minoritised identities (Crenshaw, 1989, 1991). Although Crenshaw wrote about the experiences of Black women in America, intersectionality can highlight and explain the "distinct ways power impacts people's lives in accordance with other varied identities" (Suarez et al., 2022, p. 94). Intersectionality has been utilised across a multitude of disciplines and has advanced Indigenous feminist and critical race theory scholarship, and although intersectionality has been explored by many Black women, its relevance here for Aboriginal women scholars in the academy cannot be denied. Intersectionality is a tool that allows us to understand the complicated experiences of the world, of people, and human experience. Intersectionality highlights "inequality, relationality, power, social context, complexity, and social justice. These ideas are neither always present in a particular project, nor do they appear in projects in the same way" (Collins & Bilge, 2016, p. 25). Intersectionality can simultaneously contribute to a common diversity and equity agenda.

Suarez et al. (2022, p. 96) note that intersectionality as "critical inquiry and praxis serves to empower marginalised people and communities". Collins and Bilge (2016, p. 33) assert that intersectional critical inquiry "invokes a broad sense of using intersectional frameworks to study a range of social phenomena", while the praxis, on the other hand, "sees both scholarship and practice as intimately linked and mutually informing each other, rejecting views that see theory as superior to practice" (Collins and Bilge, 2016, p. 33). Through intersectional analysis, scholars may ascertain which identities make a difference based on the analysis of power.

As a concept, intersectionality suggests that the confluence of systems of subordination shape individual experiences in distinct ways (Crenshaw, 1991). As a method, intersectionality in higher education can enable the academy to move beyond being superficial and one-dimensional, and ensure that particular groups are not excluded or marginalised from discussions of diversity and equity in higher education and that the voices of these populations are integrated into this discourse (Museus & Griffin, 2011; Museus & Saelua, 2019). Intersectionality therefore:

> constitutes both a valuable tool for deconstructing complex dominant systems of oppression while also serving as a salient theoretical lens for pursuing new lines of inquiry and illuminating new voices in higher education research—thus challenging the whiteness and the status quo.
>
> (Museus & Saelua, 2019, p. 62)

## Hands up if you are racist

Racism is not discussed nearly enough in academia to describe the subtle or not-so-subtle acts perpetrated in its name. The word is skirted around and watered down. Language like 'discrimination' and 'marginalisation' are furtively used in the public discourse as less-than-veiled synonyms. This watering down dilutes the impact of the perpetration and experience of racism (Berman & Paradies, 2010; Hooks, 1992; Moodie, et al., 2022). Racism can be uncomfortable to discuss and almost everyone can identify extreme acts of racism (Moreton-Robinson, 2013; Rigney, 1999; Smith, 1999). These are the acts that people can see, like physical violence or abuse aimed at someone who is almost always considered to be different (Grieves, 2009; Hage, 2010). However, Grosfoguels' (2020) definition in the above section enables the ability to understand the nuances and forms racism takes and avoids any reductionist definitions of racism.

We are interested in the more covert, subliminal, unconscious acts of racism (Coates, 2011). This is the type of racism we experience every day. Coates (2011, p. 1) states "[c]overt racism may be viewed as racism which is hidden; secret; private; covered; disguised; insidious; or concealed. Covert racism varies by content", and this is also a form of violence (Wilson, 2011). Bobo (1997, p. 464) refers to it as "laissez faire racism". We see covert racism as more powerful and damaging than visible, willingly read, overt racism. These two forms of everyday racism fuel violence and hate, but the former is more potent in its insidiousness. Holroyd, Scaife and Stafford (2017, p. 2) argue "unlike some paradigmatic forms of wrongdoing, discriminatory behaviour resulting from implicit bias is often unintentional, unendorsed, and perpetrated without awareness; and the harms may be particularly damaging because they are cumulative and collectively perpetrated".

Racism is not simply the behaviour or beliefs of one individual (although it can be), but rather it is a systemic concept "which maintains or exacerbates inequality of opportunity among ethnoracial groups" (Bernam & Paradies, 2010, p. 217). Racism is just one manifestation of the broader phenomenon of oppression (along with sexism, ageism, ableism, etc.), which is about prejudice, power, and privilege. Berman and Paradies (2010, p. 217) contend racism can occur at several levels, which co-occur in practice:

Internalised racism occurs when an individual incorporates ideologies within their worldview which serve to maintain or exacerbate the unequal distribution of opportunity across ethnoracial groups. Similarly, interpersonal racism occurs when interactions between people serve to maintain or exacerbate the unequal distribution of opportunity across ethnoracial groups. Finally, systemic (or institutional) racism occurs when the production and control of, and access to, material, informational and symbolic resources within society serve to maintain or exacerbate the unequal distribution of opportunity across ethnoracial groups.

All organisations have embedded inequality in their practices, processes, actions, and meanings that result in and maintain racial inequalities, and each organisation varies in the degree and severity to which racial inequalities are present. Racism also tends to be fluid and ever changing, morphing into different forms, and can be linked to societal, political, and historical influences (Acker, 2006). We experience racism in our everyday work life. When we engage with staff as individuals and as team members, our professional knowledge and methods are frequently challenged, and we are often required to defend our teaching—the approaches that we use and decisions that we make. We are constantly told we are 'special recruits' and made to feel that we do not belong in the academy or that we did not get here on merit. Affirmative action legislation enshrines this in our organisations to the detriment of us.

These experiences also contain elements of lateral violence. Lateral violence, referred to as interpersonal racism in the quoted Berman and Paradies (2010) passage above, is a concept that originated from early theorists such as Fanon (1963) and Friere (1970), and is a phenomenon in the academy, in professions such as nursing, and in the Indigenous community. In nursing, "[a]lso known as horizontal violence, bullying, and incivilities, lateral violence describes behaviours intended to demean, under-mine, and/or belittle a targeted individual working at the same professional level" (Sanner-Stiehe & Ward-Smith, 2017, p. 113). In the Indigenous community, lateral violence "describes how members of an oppressed group direct their dissatisfaction inward" (Clark, Augoustino, & Malin, 2016, p. 43). We (the authors) have been bullied and undermined by colleagues, who have gone around us to management, to discuss what we are doing and their 'concerns' with our approaches, or simply to state that they could do 'better' than us. Management have never, in our experience, questioned or challenged this undermining and we are almost always required to defend the approaches we use.

Many universities have heavy-handed and managerialist processes, and there is a plethora of critiques of the neoliberalisation of universities (Natanel, 2016; Nash, 2019), the bloating of administrators and managers, and the diminished power of academics, such as us, to steer decisions and policy (Regano, 2016). These phenomena intersect with issues such as race, gender, class, ability, and sexuality (The Res-Sisters, 2016) and how such groups are disempowered by institutional processes. The disempowerment we have experienced as Aboriginal academics has taken a significant toll. In one instance, a colleague, who had no management, performance review, or mentoring responsibility, sought out exams marked by an Aboriginal academic, not for cross marking or moderation purposes, or to provide any form of critical feedback, but rather to re-mark all of them. Following this, the Aboriginal academic was sent a lengthy email detailing their failings, explaining how all the grades were changed, and the necessary steps needed to take professionally, to remedy the concerns this colleague had, and how best to address the weaknesses of this Aboriginal academic. The email included the person's line manager and the Head of School, both of whom remained silent on the issue.

There have been issues 'about us' taken directly to the highest levels of university management to discuss, without us, and decisions have been made about us, without us. These decisions have then become known to us, and we have had to defend ourselves against the allegation or criticism. People of colour who are academics, must fight for their knowledge to be considered legitimate (Bernal & Villalpando, 2002). Bernal and Villalpando (2002, p. 171) argue "[a] Eurocentric epistemological perspective can subtly-and not so subtly-ignore and discredit the ways of knowing and understanding the world that faculty of colour often bring to academia". This may also be an example of a heavy-handed university in which senior executive levels go over the heads of people who have expertise and experience from the front line, coupled with institutional and systemic racism (Tate & Bagguley, 2017). Additionally, Lea (2008) argues bureaucrats benefit from generating the idea of Aboriginal dysfunctionality, and Walter (2016) argues Indigenous Peoples are viewed through a lens of disparity, deprivation, disadvantage, dysfunction, and difference (5Ds). Further, Garond (2014) states:

> Within the Australian context, ongoing public debates on socio-economic and health issues within Australian Indigenous communities now commonly feature the term 'dysfunctional' to qualify the various 'problems' which are popularly assumed to be prevalent within Indigenous communities, from high rates of unemployment to alcohol abuse and 'domestic violence'.
>
> (p. 7)

"Dysfunctionality speech", as Garond (2014, p. 8) refers to it, and data that focus on difference, disparity, disadvantage, dysfunction, and deprivation (the 5Ds) (Walters, 2016), characterises much of the rhetoric used in public discourse to discuss Aboriginal Peoples and communities in Australia and "points to the difference of the oppressed as the source of their own oppression, and emphasises, in a contrastive manner, the worth of neoliberal values" (Garond, 2014, p. 8). Garond continues, saying the concept of dysfunctionality is perpetuated "as justification for state intervention, with a strong emphasis on disciplining and reforming behaviours and inducing individual 'responsibilities'" (p. 7). Wildman and Davis (1994) have argued, in similar situations to those that have been discussed, that university executives tend not to listen, and it is often worse for people who are not able-bodied or white men. Universities are historically white spaces, not only in the types of knowledges available but also the cultural practices in which academic staff are required to practise and perform (Trudgett & Franklin, 2012). Organisationally, universities perpetuate systemic and institutional bias that has tacit racist overtones (Trudgett & Franklin, 2012). Barney (2016) suggests this negatively textures the experience of Aboriginal staff and students.

## Structures that shape racism

Meyerson and Scully (1995) consider the conflicting tensions in individuals and how we make sense of often dangerous systemic institutional situations and the identity work required to deal with the violence of dominant oppressive forces. They refer to these individuals undertaking this identity work as 'Tempered Radicals'. Tempered Radicals are "individuals who identify with and are committed to their organisations, and are also committed to a cause, community, or ideology that is fundamentally different from, and possibly at odds with the dominant culture of their organisation" (Meyerson and Scully, 1995, p. 586). Evans and Sinclair (2016) build upon this idea regarding leadership in the Aboriginal and Torres Strait Islander art space. They contend the ongoing effects of colonisation have created dissonance in Aboriginal and Torres Strait Islander communities when the colonisers enforced leadership structures based on Western colonial structures. These structures are then dangerous for the Aboriginal individual and community and perpetuate ongoing models of lateral violence (Evans & Sinclair, 2016).

Most white people in colonial settler states are not educated to see themselves as part of an oppressive system or as perpetrators of oppression (Barter-Godfrey & Taket, 2009). The dominant, white class are taught to see themselves as neutral, and everything else is 'other' (Powell & Menendian, 2016). As De Beauvoir (1949) articulates, *others* are opposed to us. Othering establishes a benchmark that allows humanity to be divided into two (or more) groups (Barter-Godfrey & Taket, 2009). One, that embodies the white middle-class norm, has its identity valued, while the *other* is defined by its faults, devalued, and susceptible to racism, marginalisation, and discrimination (Staszak, 2008). As discussed above, the Australian Aboriginal and Torres Strait Islander communities are seen through the lens of the 5 Ds—difference, disparity, disadvantage, dysfunction, and deprivation (Walter, 2016). This is the ultimate form of othering and is at the heart of race-based violence.

Ong (2006, p. 2) posits "[t]he spectre of the dysfunctional other constitutes a counter-model which serves to celebrate such values, and the rationality of individual responsibility and fate". This is also a form of deficit discourse. Fogarty and colleagues (2018, p. 2) refer to deficit discourse' "as [...] a mode of thinking that frames and represents Aboriginal and Torres Strait Islander identity in a narrative of negativity, deficiency and failure".

It is our contention that racial othering is a form of racial apartheid that is perpetuated in the academy, systems, and other institutions in Australia. As Dodson (1994) notes, the white community, particularly in settler colonial states such as Australia, benefit from this. Whilst othering and racialisation occur at a macro-level, they are reproduced at a micro-level in everyday talk and behaviour (Robus & Macleod, 2006). We, as individuals, therefore have the responsibility to reflect on our own contribution to othering, racism, and racialisation to challenge the dominant paradigm—no matter how uncomfortable. Self-reflection about racism is difficult. It makes people squirm and want to argue about how we are now 'post racism' (Hollinger, 2011). This is unquestionably not true. Attempts to dismiss the realness of racism obfuscates the issue. We are not colour blind or post-racism, and more particularly race still matters (Buchan & Burnett, 2019; Hagerman, 2014; Hooks, 1992). Moreover, this is relevant to dominant, middle-class white men who overwhelmingly benefit from the status quo (Kimmel, 2014; Pierce, 2016; Stanner, 1973), particularly in the academy. McIntosh (1988, p. 6) argues "[t]he dominant white class needs to get truly distressed, even outraged, about unearned race advantage and conferred dominance and think about what to do to lessen them". Considering this brings into focus the concept of whiteness, which is inextricably interconnected with white supremacy, and explains why we are all a little bit racist.

## Why we are all a little (lot) racist

Whiteness is considered neutral (Dyer, 1997), and a point from which everything else deviates. Harris (1993, p. 1709) posits that whiteness as a racial identity, and property are interwoven. This means "whiteness, initially constructed as a form of racial identity, evolved into a form of property, historically and presently acknowledged and protected". Other forms of racial identity are not protected but rather Harris (1993, p. 1709) trace "the origins of whiteness as property in the parallel systems of domination of Black and Native American peoples out of which were created racially contingent forms of property and property rights". Whilst Harris writes from an American perspective, her grounding in law and affirmative action aligns with the idea of the perpetuation of dysfunctionality in marginalised groups. Further, Sue (2006, p. 15) contends "[w]hiteness would not be problematic if it weren't (a) predicated on White supremacy; (b) imposed overtly and covertly on People of Colour; and (c) made invisible to those who benefit from its existence". White supremacy is a global, political, cultural, and economic system. Ansley (1989, p. 1024) argues:

> By "white supremacy" I do not mean to allude only to the self-conscious racism of white supremacist hate groups. I refer instead to a political, economic and cultural system in which whites overwhelmingly control power and material resources, conscious and unconscious ideas of white superiority and entitlement are widespread, and relations of white dominance and non-white subordination are daily reenacted across a broad array of institutions and social settings.

Gibbons (2018, p. 730) adds, "[t]his broader sense of white supremacy as a system of dominance 'daily reenacted' is the starting point here, understood as a continuously developing, violent historical construction, built through multiple stages of colonial conquest, genocide and imperialism".

Historically, there was a belief held that violence perpetrated against people of colour was a legitimate form of 'pre-emptive self-defence', and this has filtered into contemporary life (Dowd-Hall, 1993). Rondini (2018, p. 60) argues, "[t]his is a core principle through which Whiteness has long been constituted". Members of intersectional groups, minority, and marginalised communities, particularly men, have been depicted as perpetrators of violence, both physical and sexual, against the white community, in particular white women (Fanon, 1986). This dangerous narrative has then been the foundation stone built upon to justify acts of violence perpetrated by white men against people of colour (Rondini, 2018). Wade (2015) refers to this as lethal, colonial 'benevolent sexism'. This narrative also supports the notion that white men should rightfully remain in power as protectors and defenders, because clearly men of colour cannot be trusted and women—particularly white women—need protecting (Moreton-Robinson, 2011). Further, Day (2019, p. 370) speaks about Aboriginal LGBTI people experiencing extreme forms of "discrimination [and] existing at the margins of the margins and subject to intersecting oppressions", whilst O'Sullivan (2021, p. 1) notes that "gender roles are reformed through colonial restrictions". This narrative and the racist ideology that underpins it, perpetuate racist stereotypes and fit the rationale and justification in maintaining the white supremacist, patriarchal status quo (Bell, 1980; Nagel, 2013).

Whiteness, white supremacy, and white privilege are fundamentally interwoven, and these three concepts conceal racism, thus allowing the white dominant class to remain in power whilst remaining innocent of racism. Sue (2006, p. 15) argues, "[i]f we are to overcome, or at least minimise the forces of racism, we must make whiteness visible". If whiteness remains invisible, it is equated with normality and superiority, and people of colour will continue to experience oppression and discrimination. Thus, whiteness must be discussed, and much of the onus falls on white people to initiate the conversation and reflect on the structural power imbalance that benefits them.

Our experiences in the academy are quite the opposite: the onus almost always falls on an Aboriginal and/or Torres Strait Islander Person or on People of Colour to initiate the discussion and it is often unilateral. There is a shift in the Australian academy to include Indigenous Knowledges and ways to engage ethically and productively with Aboriginal and Torres Strait Islander Peoples in curriculum development (Australian Government Department of Health, 2016; Universities Australia, 2011). It is understood that Aboriginal and Torres Strait Islander curricula must adhere to the appropriate standards, and the content must meet the same rigorous requirements of other curricula content (Rigney, n.d. cited in Behrendt et al., 2012). This means there has been a sharp increase in requests from non-Indigenous staff and schools to 'assist' in the development of curricula and to guest lecture or run workshops on Aboriginal and Torres Strait Islander specific content (O'Sullivan, 2019). We are frequently approached and aim to accept all invitations to collaborate, co-design, and co-construct, as we believe acts of reciprocity and relationality are essential building blocks for reconciliation (Leroy-Dyer, 2018; Moodie, et al., 2022). However, in our experience this is almost always non-reciprocal. Our knowledge has been appropriated, reproduced without our permission, frequently misconstrued, or misrepresented, and has been colonised in some way. Ultimately, the outcome has been an increased, unpaid workload, with (our) knowledge being appropriated, and no level of collaboration, co-construction, or shared learning between academic staff or schools. Fredericks and White (2018, p. 247) state, "we are acutely aware how gender, class and race intersect to work against us in ways that continue to marginalise and oppress us and maintain the status quo within the higher education sector".

Trudgett, Page, and Coates (2021) state in Australia the number of Aboriginal and Torres Strait Islander Peoples in leadership positions in universities has risen steadily in recent years. However, the number of Aboriginal and Torres Strait Islander teaching staff remains low (CATSINaM, 2017; Department of Health, 2016; Universities Australia, 2011). Further, there is a low number of non-Indigenous teaching staff 'allies' with requisite knowledge and skills to teach into Indigenous Knowledges and ways to engage ethically and productively with Aboriginal and Torres Strait Islander Peoples (CATSINaM, 2017). Therefore, building cultural responsiveness and humility in the workplace, upskilling, and capacity building staff are critical steps for implementing and delivering curriculum. Non-Indigenous academics must be actively engaged and reciprocal in this process, to be appropriately and adequately educated in Aboriginal and Torres Strait Islander cultures, histories, and contemporary realities. Further, it is imperative staff are trained in appropriate pedagogical strategies and philosophical underpinnings so they can safely and effectively educate students in Aboriginal and Torres Strait Islander content (CATSINaM, 2017; Department of Health, 2016; Universities Australia, 2011).

It is recognised in the literature (Taylor, et al., 2014; Taylor, Kickett & Jones, 2014; Universities Australia, 2011) that commitment from leadership and executive is critical to developing a culturally capable academy. However, moving towards this level of commitment requires an evaluation of the attitudes of individuals, as well as an evaluation of the culture of systems and structures across management and the impact of policies and strategies. We contend this is an area that is currently lagging and creating a huge barrier to any real change from occurring.

### Ultimate othering

There is a long-standing rhetoric in anti-multicultural politics that warns of division and tribalism (Bowler, 1999), the belief being, the more diverse the group, the more the group will break up into 'tribal' subgroups and create disharmony (Bowler, 1999). This idea draws heavily on the nationalist, sociobiological belief that community, even nations, can only be wrought in circumstances of cultural sameness (Ardrey, 1967) and assimilation is a foundation stone of this nationalist belief. This taps into the concept of othering discussed above. The fear of the other plays into a xenophobic intolerance. Penrose (1993, p. 45) argues, "as long as the nation is built around social constructions of uniform 'people' and place [...] it will not change the intolerance of difference which leads to the marginalisation of particular individuals and groups". Since the evolution of modern nation states, a central problem has been this promotion of a single identity, composed of a culturally uniform people, bound within a definitive territory (Renan, cited in Bhabha, 1990). This single identity is typified by being a white man, in a uniformly white state.

So, if a nationalist community is uniform and homogeneous (white), what of the 'others'? Hsu (2019, p. 296) introduces what he calls the "paleo-narrative and white atavism". This is a social and racial fiction caused by the romanticising of hunter/gatherer and Indigenous hunter/gatherer ways of life and the noble savage. The paleo-narrative is "an imaginary structure that invokes an idealised version of humanity's past to envision an optimal, implicitly white body defined in terms of purity, instinct, and austere power" (Hsu, 2019, p. 297), and this has racial and national implications. The paleo-narrative is disassociated from cultural and historical contexts, and in doing so "obscur[es] the material determinants of racialised health disparities" (Ng, 1993, p. 297) and racialised sociocultural and political structures. This intertwines with the discussion above that perpetuating racist (and sexist) ideology underpins the justification that we are all safer if power remains in white, men's hands. This further ties into our personal experiences where our Indigenous Knowledge is appropriated and reworked by white people, who think it appropriate to do so. This narrative began at the turn of the nineteenth to the twentieth century, but there was a re-emergence of paleo lifestyles in the 1970s that continues today.

White nationalism is a form of cultural hegemony and imperialism (Bauman, 1992), is dangerous, and is particularly relevant today. Moreover, we contend white Australia has some problems with its past (Boucher, 2009), although there have been recent moves—such as attempts to challenge Australia Day as a day of celebration (Reconciliation Australia, 2018); the spread of Aboriginal and Torres Strait Islander language in classes; lectures on Aboriginal maths, science, and astronomy; the public impact of *Dark Emu* (Pascoe, 2014) that included the generation of a children's book version *Young Dark Emu* (Pascoe, 2019); NAIDOC themes that speak directly to Aboriginal and Torres Strait Islander political issues and are embraced by many non-Aboriginal organisations—and most people support moves to ban climbing on Uluru. This is largely performative and masks ongoing problems that are reflective of a disconnection between popular sentiments and the political elite, conservative intellectual brokers, public policy, and institutional path dependence (Kane, 2014; Kay, 2005). This path dependence means that even if an institution were committed to making change, the sets of decisions faced within institutions, for any given circumstance, are constrained by the decisions that have been made in the past. This is somewhat limiting because past circumstances may no longer be relevant, so progress can be excruciatingly slow.

Institutional path dependence is also reflected in processes at the academy in Australia. The concept of colonialism is frequently taught, but from a perspective of 'hindsight' rather than by addressing the ongoing effects of the invasion and colonisation of Australia, and the enduring trauma experienced by Aboriginal and Torres Strait Islander communities (Burgess et al., 2019). This is reflective in the example we gave above where non-Indigenous staff and faculty are less focused on collaboration and co-constructing curriculum, and more focused on acquisition and appropriation of a resource. There appears to be a disinterest in discussing and respecting contemporary experiences—from a first-hand perspective—but rather in acquiring the knowledge, altering it, and disseminating without the appropriate cultural input or expertise. This is further intersected with the current neoliberal political elite in Australia promulgating the concept of Aboriginal dysfunctionality, whilst at the same time ignoring the "collective oppression attributed to the enduring effects of colonial policies, and to the misrecognition of colonial history, of Aboriginal culture and disadvantage" (Garond, 2014, p. 8). There is no crisp, 'white' solution to this, and change will be slow, but it is certainly achievable with a genuine commitment to strengthening Aboriginal sovereignty, autonomy, and self-determination (Howard-Wagner, 2018).

Further, Hindess (2014, p. 87) states, "[w]hile apparently universalistic, talk of human progress has always been tied to a ranking of societies: while all of humanity is thought to progress, different portions are seen to have done so at different rates and to different degrees". This can be connected to Social Darwinism (Leonard, 2009), the narrative being that African and First Nations Peoples would fail to 'develop' and thus eventually die out (Claeys, 2000), which was perpetuated alongside imperial colonisation and into the early twentieth century. Hindess (2014, p. 87) goes on to say, "[w]hile this unsavoury complex of ideas may have lost much of its earlier appeal, it remains influential both in the West and in international affairs; for example, in contemporary discourses of development and modernisation". Thus, the negative impact of invasion and colonisation of Australia is scarcely discussed in politics, and Aboriginal and Torres Strait Islander voices have been missing or silenced in the narrative (Referendum Council, 2017). In fact, the effect of colonial history and previous colonial policies is significantly downplayed (Lattas & Morris, 2010). This means there has been a lack of 'truth-telling' and a perpetuation of the Great Australian Silence (Anderson, 2003; Attwood, 2005; Stanner, 1969). Telling the truth is a relatively simple concept, as it "brings to light colonial conflict and dispossession, but also acknowledges the strength and resilience of Aboriginal and Torres Strait Islander peoples and cultures" (Reconciliation Australia, 2020). However, Boucher (2009, p. 46) posits, "[i]ndeed, in many ways Indigenous histories represent an historiographic paradox; the category of (Ab)original Australians functions as a constant reminder of the wholesale theft that underpins the Australian nation-state", and apparently this is very uncomfortable to discuss.

As discussed above, whilst Aboriginal and Torres Strait Islander issues are being publicly and actively debated—in a 'one step removed' kind of manner—we assert the political elite, particularly the neoliberal elite, are uncomfortable with a 'truth-telling' process (Mencevska, 2020 Wedesweiler, 2020. Truth-telling is unsettling, perhaps a little too unsettling for the settlers (Regan, 2010). It requires reflexivity (Corntassel, Chaw-win-is, & T'lakwadzi, 2009). A process of truth-telling requires a change of mindset: an honest, full, and frank public discussion and understanding about the invasion and ongoing effects of the colonisation of Australia and its impact on Aboriginal and Torres Strait Islander communities—such as dispossession, trauma, and grief. It is time the neoliberal elite stopped celebrating an imagined, palatable Australia and afforded a rightful remembrance that recognises the humanity of the lived experiences of Aboriginal and Torres Strait Islander Peoples. This is not a sunburnt country of bronzed, white bodies, bushrangers, and Banjo Patterson. Australia is not a white nation founded on white success, or off the sheep's back. We would describe neoliberal Australia as lacking the desire and impetus to reconcile with 60,000 years of Aboriginal and Torres Strait Islander humanity and custodianship.

### Truth-telling: and what keeps happening

The perpetuation of Aboriginal dysfunctionality discussed earlier in this piece propagates the concept that Aboriginal Peoples cannot make critical, thoughtful decisions about our own communities and maintains that the dysfunctionality suggests an absence of moral governance. This "[d]ysfunctionality posits a moral vacuum that needs to be filled by government and the solutions of practical public intellectuals who today rationalise neoliberal forms of governmentality by presenting them as grounded in social science' (Lattas & Morris, 2010, p. 62). It disrespects and infantilises Aboriginal and Torres Strait Islander communities.

This is also reflected in our experiences in the academy in Australia. When we raise issues about experiences of racism or violence, we are frequently disbelieved or simply ignored (Frogley, 2018). This results in us having to repeat our concerns or having to escalate our concerns, which in turn paints us as troublemakers—a term we have both been referred to as. Furthermore, it makes us targets for systemic violence because we deign to raise our voices to publicly identify acts of racism and violence.

Aboriginal and Torres Strait Islander communities have been clearly explaining what is required for a very long time. So, why are we so frequently ignored, dismissed, or derided by leadership, the government, the political elite, and the ruling class? Why are we ignored in our workplaces? Universities are aligned with the current neoliberal political elite, and they have dehistoricised and depoliticised the Aboriginal and Torres Strait Islander experience in Australia (Garond, 2014) and a new historicity has been created. The extensive use of dysfunctionality speech and the narrative around Aboriginal and Torres Strait Islander communities propagates neoliberalist reform (Austin-Broos, 2011) and weakens Aboriginal autonomy and self-determination (Howard-Wagner, 2018).

The endurance of dysfunctionality speech undermines the self-determination of Aboriginal and Torres Strait Islander communities in Australia. The neoliberal vision of 'humanity and social order' (Morris & Lattas, 2010) is, as Garond (2014) states, a:

> functionalist vision of humanity as ordered by the rational responses of self-disciplined, self-helping and self-achieving individuals to the neutral and unavoidable

demands of a market-driven world. 'Dysfunctionality' seems to point towards an ensemble of counter-rules and values which have been allowed (by the 'laissez-faire' of 'governments') to flourish, and must cease to be tolerated.

(p. 16)

We have no desire to become a neoliberalist subject (Garond, 2014). Does this lack of desire make us dysfunctional, irrational, and lacking self-discipline? It must. Moreover, Aboriginal dysfunctionality narrative seeps into our daily life. We have regularly been put in a position where we must defend the academic performance of Aboriginal and Torres Strait Islander students to non-Indigenous teaching staff, leadership, and management (Moodie et al., 2022). There is an assumption amongst non-Indigenous staff that Aboriginal and Torres Strait Islander students underperform; are problematic, difficult and time consuming; and that somehow these students exist in a dysfunctional silo, do not try hard enough, and are separate from the rest of the university body. We have been repeatedly asked to supply all the support mechanisms we have put in place for the students. The onus falls on us alone. We have been asked 'what are *you* doing for *them?*' We have been drawn into meetings to discuss or defend 'issues' about *them.* Not once was support for Aboriginal and Torres Strait Islander students offered from the institution, nor were any suggestions ever proposed on how the institution might systematically invest in Aboriginal and Torres Strait Islander student progression. We have never been asked what we might need or want from the university to support the students (Oliver et al., 2013; Oliver et al., 2015). Many universities have no formalised strategy or plan on how to recruit, support, or retain Aboriginal and Torres Strait Islander students or staff, nor how to embed Indigenous Knowledges or other ways of knowing in the curriculum (Universities Australia, 2022). As such, we are frequently forced to 'Indigenise on the run'. This process is put back on us, as isolated individuals, without the institution taking responsibility for the historical and ongoing role of the system in generating poorer outcomes for Aboriginal and Torres Strait Islander students and staff (Trudgett & Franklin, 2012). Ansley, as cited in Harris (1993 cited in Bernal & Villalpando, 2002, p. 171), states:

[a] political, economic, and cultural system in which whites overwhelmingly control power and material resources, conscious and unconscious ideas of white superiority and entitlement are widespread, and relations of white dominance and non-white subordination are daily reenacted across a broad array of institutions and social settings.

The responsibility being placed back on to us is incredibly frustrating, time consuming, and ultimately an unsustainable approach. Until there is more collective responsibility in universities, the turnover of Aboriginal and Torres Strait Islander staff will remain high, and the retention of Aboriginal and Torres Strait Islander students will remain low (Barney, 2016; Trudgett & Franklin, 2012).

## Future employment equity

The future of work for Aboriginal and Torres Strait Islander Peoples—where employment equity is achieved—involves comprehensive labour market policies and programmes, implemented by both governments and organisations (Leroy-Dyer, 2022). These policies and programmes must be Indigenous-centric, autonomous, proposed, implemented and governed by Aboriginal and Torres Strait Islander Peoples—and not imposed on us. They should not be about us, without us (Leroy-Dyer, 2022).

Below we make some suggestions which will aid in facilitating Aboriginal and Torres Strait Islander Peoples' social mobility through professional advancement and achievement in the academy:

1. Good intentions are not enough. Good intentions give the user a warm, fuzzy feeling from perceptions—but the outcome may have no actual benefit for Aboriginal or Torres Strait Islander Peoples or the community. To be a successful accomplice, educators and leadership must go beyond being well intentioned. What is critical is being conscious of one's values such as respect, humility, and commitment. Being dedicated to creating a world with justice and equity takes doing real, values-based, and behaviour change work, and is more than a performative action.

2. Workplace assessments/reviews must be culturally responsive. Western institutions require us to be assessment driven, and Professional Performance Reviews (PPRs) are what staff are currently held accountable to in the academy. Knowledge of Aboriginal and Torres Strait Islander history and contemporary experiences and cultural responsiveness are currently not part of this process—and we will not do anything unless we are made to—thus Indigenous Knowledges and cultural responsiveness must be included as part of PPR processes for any substantive change to occur.

3. Increased cultural responsiveness training—This training should be aimed at executive and leadership teams. Largely, leadership teams are excluded from having to attend such training and this separates them from any level of accountability to cultural responsiveness principles and practice. Leadership and executive team members must lead and role model cultural responsiveness principles and practice in this space.

4. Whiteness must be discussed and become everyday vernacular in the academy. Addressing racialised forms of exclusion requires that the white academy stop forgetting and instead engage with its past, and most importantly, its present continuities with violence. Engaging with its past requires white academia to recognise how the university continues to serve as an arm of the state, perpetuating and hardening borders that facilitate access, circulation, and the value of white knowledge at the expense of non-white people and our knowledge. Much of the onus falls on white people to initiate this conversation and reflect on the structural power imbalance that benefits them.

5. Non-Indigenous academics must be actively engaged and reciprocal in these processes. To be appropriately and adequately educated in Aboriginal and Torres Strait Islander cultures, histories, and contemporary realities is fundamental. It is imperative staff are capacity built in appropriate pedagogical strategies and philosophical underpinnings so they can safely and effectively educate students in Aboriginal and Torres Strait Islander content.

6. Do not lump us into equity groups. As Sovereign Peoples of this country, Aboriginal and Torres Strait Islander Peoples should have access to education and training that ensures we have self-determination. Affirmative action and Equal Opportunity Employment initiatives, such as identified roles, must be meaningful; however, if implementing these initiatives, the academy must ensure that their workplace is culturally responsive to this; otherwise, we are being set up to fail in these roles.

7. Aboriginal and Torres Strait Islander Peoples are diverse. We are not 'one size fits all', so stop treating us like we are. Listen and learn about the diversity within our culture and do not pigeonhole us into 'Indigenous centres' in the academy. We all have very different lived experiences, and the academy will be more culturally rich when this is acknowledged and embraced. There is no quick fix or single approach that will work.

## Conclusion

Social justice means that Aboriginal peoples have the right to autonomy, sovereignty, and self-determination. Autonomy, sovereignty, and self-determination remain at the core of Aboriginal and Torres Strait Islander civil rights. This means Aboriginal and Torres Strait Islander communities have the right to decide for ourselves how to address issues facing the community. However, we need the white community and systems to acknowledge the ongoing effects of colonisation, recognise their white complicity and privilege within systems, and assume some accountability and responsibility for shifting their values, practices, and behaviours to truly enact the principles of inclusion and diversity.

Australian colonial institutions such as governments and universities remain out of step with the faster moving and more progressive, broad social phenomena occurring. Bureaucratic tendencies and systems continue to be out of step with the wishes of both the Aboriginal and the non-Aboriginal community, which is to have genuine reconciliation, truth-telling, and healing. Further, due to the repetitive nature of the political discussion regarding racism and Aboriginal and Torres Strait Islander issues, Aboriginal and Torres Strait Islander Peoples experience a sense of déjà vu (Moodle et al., 2022). This erodes our trust in institutions, the political process, and the political elite. We have been very clear, for a very long time. It is now time for institutions and the political elite, particularly the neoliberal political elite, to face things head-on. It is time to go through the truth-telling process, to take responsibility for the injustices incurred, the violence perpetrated, and the pain inflicted to undertake a peace-making process. Aboriginal and Torres Strait Islander Peoples are open to this.

## Definition of terms

**Accomplice:** uses their privilege to challenge existing conditions at the risk of their own comfort and well-being.

**Closing the Gap (CTG):** is a strategy that aims to improve the life outcomes of Aboriginal and Torres Strait Islander Peoples.

**Critical Race Theory (CRT):** is a cross-disciplinary intellectual and social movement of civil rights scholars and activists who seek to examine the intersection of race, society, and law and to challenge mainstream liberal approaches to racial justice.

**Decolonising:** the process in which we rethink, reframe, and reconstruct systems that preserve the Europe-centred, colonial lens.

**Dysfunctionality speech:** characterises much of the rhetoric used in public discourse to discuss Aboriginal Peoples and communities in Australia and "points to the difference of the oppressed as the source of their own oppression, and emphasises, in a contrastive manner, the worth of neoliberal values" (Garond, 2014, p. 8)

**Indigenous Feminist Theory:** is an intersectional theory and practice of feminism that focuses on decolonisation, Indigenous sovereignty, and human rights for Indigenous women and their families. The focus is to empower Indigenous women in the context of Indigenous cultural values and priorities, rather than mainstream, white, patriarchal ones (Liddle, 2014).

**Intersectionality:** is a framework that postulates multiple identities or social categories intersect at an individual (micro) level that reflect the macro-level systems which expose the privilege and oppression that occurs in said systems, such as racism, ageism, sexism, and ableism (Crenshaw, 1991).

**Lateral violence:** describes "behaviours intended to demean, under-mine, and/or belittle a targeted individual working at the same professional level" (Sanner-Stiehe & Ward-Smith, 2017, p. 113)

**Neoliberalisation:** Associated with policies of austerity and attempts to cut government spending on social programmes, neoliberalism is a policy model that encompasses both politics and economics and seeks to transfer the control of economic factors from the public sector to the private sector. Many neoliberal policies enhance the workings of free market capitalism and attempt to place limits on government spending, government regulation, and public ownership

**Other:** are opposed to us. Othering establishes a benchmark that allows humanity to be divided into two (or more) groups (Barter-Godfrey & Taket, 2009).

**Path dependence:** the tendency of institutions or technologies to become committed to develop in certain ways as a result of their structural properties or their beliefs and values.

**Self-determination:** At its core, self-determination is concerned with the fundamental right of people to shape their own lives. In a practical sense, self-determination means that we have the freedom to live well, to determine what it means to live well according to our own values and beliefs.

**Sistas:** a relational term used between Aboriginal and Torres Strait Islander women who may or may not be blood related.

**Tempered Radicals:** are "individuals who identify with and are committed to their organisations, and are also committed to a cause, community, or ideology that is funda-mentally different from, and possibly at odds with the dominant culture of their organisation" (Meyerson and Scully, 1995, p. 586).

**Whiteness:** Whiteness is considered neutral (Dyer, 1997), and a point from which everything else deviates. Harris (1993, p. 1709) posits whiteness as a racial identity, and along with property, identity is interwoven, meaning "whiteness, initially constructed as a form of racial identity, evolved into a form of property, historically and presently acknowledged and protected" (p. 1709).

## References

Acker, J. (2006). Inequality regimes: gender, class and race in organisations. *Gender & Society, 20*(4), 441–464.

Anderson, W. (2003). *The cultivation of whiteness: Science, health, and racial destiny in Australia.* Basic Books.

Ansley, F. L. (1989). Stirring the ashes: Race, class and the future of civil rights scholarship. *Cornell Law Review, 74*(6), 993–1077.

Ardrey, R. (1967). *The territorial imperative: A personal inquiry into the animal origins of property and nations.* Collins.

Arnesen, E. (2001). Whiteness and the historians' imagination. *International Labor and Working-Class History, 60,* 3–32.

Attwood, B. (2005). *Telling the truth about Aboriginal history.* Allen & Unwin.

Austin-Broos, D. (2011). *A different inequality: The politics of debate about remote Aboriginal Australia.* Allen & Unwin.

Australian Government. Department of Health. (2016). *Aboriginal and Torres Strait Islander Health Curriculum Framework.* Australian Government. Department of Health.

Bailey, K. A. (2020). Indigenous students: Resilient and empowered in the midst of racism and lateral violence. *Ethnic and Racial Studies, 43*(6), 1032–1051.

Barney, K. (2016). Listening to and learning from the experiences of Aboriginal and Torres Strait Islander students to facilitate success. *Student Success, 7*(1), 1–11. https://doi.org/10.5204/ssj.v7i1.317

Barter-Godfrey, S., & Taket, A. (2009). Othering, marginalisation and pathways to exclusion in health. In A. Taket, B. Crisp, A. Nevill, G. Lamaro, M. Graham & S. Barter-Godfrey (Eds.), *Theorising social exclusion* (pp. 166–172). Routledge.

Bauman, Z. (1992). Soil, blood and identity. *Sociological Review, 40*(4), 675–701. https://doi.org/10.1111/j.1467-954X.1992.tb00407.x

Behrendt, L., Larkin, S., Griew, R., & Kelly, P. (2012). *Review of higher education access and outcomes for Aboriginal and Torres Strait Islander peoples: Final report.* Aboriginal and Torres Strait Islander Higher Education Advisory Council, Department of Industry, Innovation, Science, Research and Tertiary Education. Government of Australia.

Bell, D. A. (1980). Brown v. Board of Education and the Interest-convergence Dilemma. *Harvard Law Review, 93*(5), 518–533.

Berman, G., & Paradies, Y. (2010). Racism, disadvantage and multiculturalism: Towards effective anti-racist praxis. *Ethnic and Racial Studies, 33*(2), 214–232. https://doi.org/10.1080/01419870802302272

Bernal, D. D., & Villalpando, O. (2002). An apartheid of knowledge in academia: The struggle over the "legitimate" knowledge of faculty of color. *Equity & Excellence in Education, 35*(2), 169–180. https://doi.org/10.1080/713845282

Bhabha, H. K. (1990). *Nation and narration.* Routledge.

Bobo, L. D. (1999). Prejudice as group position: Microfoundations of a sociological approach to racism and race relations. *Social Issues: A Journal of the Society for the Psychological Study of Social Issues, 55*(3), 445–472. https://doi.org/10.1111/0022-4537.00127

Boucher, L. (2009). Trans/national history and disciplinary amnesia: Historicising White Australia at two fins de siècles. In J. Carey & C. McLisky (Eds.), *Creating white Australia.* Sydney University Press. https://open.sydneyuniversitypress.com.au/9781920899424/cwa-transnational-history-and-disciplinary-amnesia-historicising-white-australia-at-two-fins-de-sicles.html#Chapter3

Bowler, S. (1999). 'Ethnic nationalism': Authenticity, atavism and international instability. In K. J. Brehony & N. Rassool (Eds.), *Nationalisms old and new: Explorations in sociology* (pp. 35–50). Palgrave Macmillan.

Buchan, B., & Burnett, L. A. (2019). Knowing savagery: Australia and the anatomy of race. *History of the Human Sciences, 32*(4), 15–134. https://doi.org/10.1177/0952695119836587

Burgess, C., Tennent, C., Vass, G., Guenther, J., Lowe, K., & Moodle, N. (2019). A systematic review of pedagogies that support, engage, and improve the educational outcomes of Aboriginal students. *The Australian Educational Researcher, 46,* 297–318.

Claeys, G. (2000). 'Survival of the fittest' and the origins of Social Darwinism. *Journal of the History of Ideas, 61*(2), 223–240.

Clark, Y., Augoustinos, M., & Malin, M. (2016). Lateral violence within the Aboriginal community in Adelaide: It affects our identity and wellbeing. *Journal of Indigenous Wellbeing: Te Mauri-Pimatisiwin, 1*(1), 43–52.

Coates, R. D. (Ed.). (2011). *Covert racism: Theories, institutions, and experiences.* Brill.

Collins, P. H., & Bilge, S. (2016). *Intersectionality.* John Wiley & Sons.

Congress of Aboriginal and Torres Strait Islander Nurses and Midwives (CATSINaM). (2017). *The Nursing and Midwifery Aboriginal and Torres Strait Islander Health Curriculum Framework: An adaptation of and complementary document to the 2014 Aboriginal and Torres Strait Islander Health Curriculum Framework.*

Corntassel, J., Chaw-win-is, & T'lakwadzi. (2009). Indigenous storytelling, truth-telling, and community approaches to reconciliation. *ESC: English Studies in Canada, 35*(1), 137–159. https://doi.org/10.1353/esc.0.0163

Crenshaw, K. (1989). Demarginalizing the intersection of race and sex: A Black feminist critique of antidiscrimination doctrine, feminist theory and antiracist politics. *University of Chicago Legal Forum, 1989*(1), 139–167.

Crenshaw, K. (1991). Mapping the margins: Intersectionality, identity politics, violence against women of color. *Stanford Law Review, 43*(6), 1241–1299.

Crenshaw, K. (2011). Demarginalizing the intersection of race and sex: A Black feminist critique of antidiscrimination doctrine, feminist theory and antiracist politics. In H. Lutz, H. Vivar, & L. Supik (Eds.), *Framing intersectionality: Debates on a multi-faceted concept in gender studies* (pp. 1–18). Taylor & Francis.

Dar, S., Liu, H., Dy, A. M., & Brewis, D. N. (2021). The business school is racist: Act up! *Organization, 28*(4), 695–706.

Day, M. (2020). Indigenist origins: Institutionalizing indigenous queer and trans studies in Australia. *Trans Studies Quarterly, 7*(3), 367–373.

De Beauvoir, S. (1949). *Le deuxième sexe* [The second sex]. *NRF essais (in French). 1, Les faits et les mythes* [Facts and myths]. Gallimard.

Delgardo, R., & Stefancic, J. (2017). *Critical race theory: An introduction* (3rd ed.). NYU Press.

Department of Education, Skills and Employment. (2020). Indigenous Staff Figures in Higher Education. www.education.gov.au/higher-education-statistics/resources/2020-staff-indigenous

DiAngelo, R. (2018). *White fragility: Why it's so hard for white people to talk about racism.* Beacon Press.

Dodson, M. (1994). The end in the beginning: Re(de)finding Aboriginality. The 1994 Wentworth Lecture. https://aiatsis.gov.au/publications/presentations/end-beginning-redefinding-aboriginality

Dowd-Hall, J. (1993). *Revolt against chivalry: Jessie Daniel Ames and the women's campaign against lynching.* Columbia University Press.

Dyer, R. (1997). *White: Essays on race and culture.* Routledge.

Evans, M. M., & Sinclair, A. (2016). Navigating the territories of Indigenous leadership: Exploring the experiences and practices of Australian Indigenous arts leaders. *Leadership, 12*(4), 470–490. https://doi.org/10.1177/1742715015574318

Fanon, F. (1963). *The wretched of the earth.* Grove Weidenfeld.

Fanon, F. (1986). *Black skin, white masks (get political).* Pluto Press.

Fredericks, B., & White, N. (2018). Using bridges made by others as scaffolding and establishing footings for those that follow: Indigenous women in the Academy. *Australian Journal of Education, 62*(3), 243–255.

Frogley, A. (2018). I'm not a racist but… *Advocate: Newsletter of the National Tertiary Education Union, 25*(3), 20.

Garond, L. (2014). The meaningful difference of 'Aboriginal dysfunction' and the neoliberal 'mainstream'. *Etropic: Value, Transvaluation and Globalization Special Issue, 13*(2), 7–19.

Gibbons, A. (2018). The five refusals of white supremacy. *American Journal of Economics and Sociology, 77*(3–4), 729–755.

Grieves, V. (2009). Aboriginal spirituality: Aboriginal philosophy Casuarina: The basis of Aboriginal social and emotional wellbeing. *Discussion Paper Series: No. 9.* Cooperative Research Centre for Aboriginal Health.

Grosfoguel, R. (2011). Decolonizing post-colonial studies and paradigms of political-economy: Transmodernity, decolonial thinking and global coloniality. *Transmodernity: Journal of Peripheral Cultural Production of the Luso-Hispanic World, 1*(1), 1–38.

Grosfoguel, R. (2020) What is racism. *Journal of World-Systems Research, 22*(1), 9–15. http://dx.doi.org/10.5195/jwsr.2016.609

Grzanka, P. R,. Frantell, K. A., & Fassinger, R. (2019). The White Racial Affect Scale (WRAS): A measure of white guilt, shame, and negation. *The Counselling Psychologist, 48*(1), 1–31. https://doi.org/10.1177/0011000019878808

Hage, G. (2010). The affective politics of racial mis-interpellation. *Theory, Culture & Society, 27*(7–8), 112–129.

Hagerman, M. A. (2014). White families and race: Colour-blind and colour-conscious approaches to white racial socialization. *Ethnic and Racial Studies, 37*(14), 2598–2614. https://doi.org/10.1080/01419870.2013.848289

Harris, C. I. (1993). Whiteness as property. *Harvard Law Review, 106*(8), 1707–1791.

Hindess, B. (2014). Unintended rhetoric: The 'Little Children are Sacred' report. In J. Uhr & R. Walter (Eds.), *Studies in Australian political rhetoric* (pp. 1–14). ANU Press.

Hollinger, D. A. (2011). The concept of post-racial: How it's easy dismissal obscures important questions. *Daedalus, 140*(1), 174–182.

Holroyd, J., Scaife, R., & Stafford, T. (2017). What is implicit bias? *Philosophy Compass, 12*(10), 1–18. https://doi.org/10.1111/phc3.12437

hooks, b. (1992). *Black looks: Race and representation*. South End.

Howard-Wagner, D. (2018). Aboriginal organisations, self-determination and the neoliberal age: A case study of how the 'game has changed' for Aboriginal organisations in Newcastle. In D. Howard-Wagner, M. Bargh, & I. Altamirano-Jiménez (Eds.), *The neoliberal state, recognition and Indigenous rights: new paternalism to new imaginings* (pp. 217–237). ANU Press.

Hsu, H. L. (2019). Paleo-narratives and white atavism, 1898–2015. *SLE: Interdisciplinary Studies in Literature and Environment, 26*(2), 296–323. https://doi.org/10.1093/isle/isz01

Kane, J. (2014). What's at stake in Australian political rhetoric? In J. Uhr & R. Walter (Eds.), *Studies in Australian political rhetoric* (pp. 3–16). ANU Press.

Kay, A. (2005). A critique of the use of path dependency in policy studies. *Public Administrations, 83*(3), 553–571. https://doi.org/10.1111/j.0033-3298.2005.00462.x

Kimmel, M. (2014). *Angry white men: American masculinity at the end of an era*. Johns Hopkins University Press.

Lattas, A., & Morris, B. (2010). The politics of suffering and the politics of anthropology. In J. Altman & M. Hinkson (Eds.), *Culture crisis: Anthropology and politics in Aboriginal Australia* (pp. 61–87). UNSW Press.

Lea, T. (2008). *Bureaucrats and bleeding hearts: Indigenous health in Northern Australia*. UNSW Press.

Leonard, T. C. (2009). Origins of the myth of social Darwinism: The ambiguous legacy of Richard Hofstadter's Social Darwinism in American thought. *Journal of Economic Behavior & Organization, 71*, 37–51.

Leonardo, Z. (2005). The color of supremacy: Beyond the discourse of 'white privilege'. In Z. Leonardo (Ed.), *Critical pedagogy and race* (pp. 37–52). John Wiley and Sons.

Leroy-Dyer, S. (2018). Aboriginal enabling pedagogies and approaches in Australia: Centring and decolonising our approaches. *International Studies in Widening Participation, 5*(2), 4–9.

Leroy-Dyer, S. (2022). Closing the gap on Aboriginal and Torres Strait Islander employment disadvantage in Australia, in S. Dhakal, R. Cameron, & J. Burgess (Eds.), *A field guide to managing diversity, equity and inclusion in organisations* (pp. 33–46). Edward Edgar.

Liddle, C. (2014). Intersectionality and Indigenous feminism: An Aboriginal woman's perspective. The Postcolonialist. http://postcolonialist.com/civil-discourse/intersectionality-indigenous-feminism-aboriginal-womans-perspective/

McIntosh, P. (1988). *'White privilege: Unpacking the invisible knapsack'. White privilege and male privilege: A personal account of coming to see correspondences through work in women's studies.* Wellesley College Center for Research on Women.

Mencevska, I. (2020). Truth telling in Australia's historical narrative. *NEW: Emerging Scholars in Australian Indigenous Studies, 5*(1). https://doi.org/10.5130/nesais.v5i1.1552

Menzel, K., & Cameron, L. (2021). A meeting of freshwater and saltwater: Opening the dialogue of Aboriginal concepts of culture within an academic space. In T. McKenna, D. Moodie, & P. Onesta (Eds.), *Indigenous Knowledges: Privileging our voices* (pp. 126–157). Brill Sense.

Meyerson, D. E., & Scully, M. A. (1995). Tempered radicalism and the politics of ambivalence and change. *Organization Science, 6*(5), 585–600. https://doi.org/10.1287/orsc.6.5.585

Moodie (Gomeroi), D., Menzel (Ngadjuri), K., Cameron (Dharug), L., & Moodie (Gomeroi), N. (2022). Blak & salty: Reflections on violence and racism. *Indigenous Women's Voices*, Zed Books. https://doi.org/10.5040/9781350237506.ch-004

Moreton-Robinson, A. (2004). *Whitening race: Essays in social and cultural criticism*, Aboriginal Studies Press.

Moreton-Robinson, A. (2005). Whiteness, epistemology and Indigenous representation. In A. Moreton-Robinson (Ed.), *Whitening race: Essays in social and cultural criticism* (pp. 75–88). Aboriginal Studies Press for the Australian Institute of Aboriginal and Torres Strait Islander Studies.

Moreton-Robinson, A. (2011). The white man's burden: Patriarchal white epistemic violence and Aboriginal women's knowledges within the academy. *Australian Feminist Studies*, 26(70), 413–431.

Moreton-Robinson, A. (2013). Towards an Australian Indigenous women's standpoint theory. *Australian Feminist Studies*, 8(78), 331–347. https://doi.org/ 10.1080/08164649.2013.876664

Museau, S. D., & Saelua, N. A. (2019). Realizing the power of intersectionality research in higher education. In D. J. Mitchell, Jr (Ed.), *Intersectionality in higher education: Theory, research and praxis 2.* (pp. 61–70). Peter Lang.

Museus, S. D., & Griffin, K. A. (2011). Mapping the margins in higher education: On the promise of intersectionality frameworks in research and discourse. In K. A. Griffin & S. D. Museus (Eds.), *Using mixed-methods approaches to study intersectionality in higher education: New directions for institutional research* (No. 151, pp. 15–26). Jossey-Bass.

Nagel, M. E. (2014). *The end of prisons: Reflections from the decarceration movement*. Brill–Rodopi.

Nash, K. (2019). Neo-liberalisation, universities and the values of bureaucracy. *The Sociological Review*, 67(1), 178–193. https://doi.org/10.1177/0038026118754780

Natanel, K. (2016). On becoming 'bad subjects': Teaching to transgress in neoliberal education. In R. Thwaites & A. Pressland (Eds.), *Being an early career feminist academic* (pp. 239–254 ). Palgrave Macmillan.

Ng, R. (1993). A woman out of control: Deconstructing sexism and racism in the university. *Canadian Journal of Education / Revue canadienne de l'éducation*, 18(3), 189–205.

O'Sullivan, S. (2019). First Nations' women in the academy: Disrupting and displacing the white male gaze. In G. Crimmins (Ed.), *Strategies for resisting sexism in the academy* (pp. 115–127). Palgrave Studies in Gender and Education. Palgrave Macmillan. https://doi-org.ezproxy.library.uq.edu.au/ 10.1007/978-3-030-04852-5_7

O'Sullivan, S. (2021). The colonial project of gender (and everything else). *Genealogy*, 5(3), 67. https://doi.org/10.3390/genealogy5030067

Oliver, R., Grote, E., Rochecouste, J., & Dann, T. (2015). Indigenous student perspectives on support and impediments at university. *Australian Journal of Indigenous Education*, 45(1), 23–35.

Oliver, R., Rocheciyste, J., Bennell, D., Anderson, R., Cooper, I., Forrest, S., & Exell, M. (2013). Understanding Australian Aboriginal tertiary student needs. *International Journal of Higher Education*, 2(4), 52–64.

Ong, A. (2006). *Neoliberalism as exception: Mutations in citizenship and sovereignty*. Duke University Press.

Pascoe, B. (2014). *Dark Emu*. Magabala Books.

Pascoe, B. (2019). *Young Dark Emu*. Magabala Books.

Penrose, J. (1993). Reification in the name of change: The impact of nationalism on social constructions of nation, people and place in Scotland and the United Kingdom. In P. Jackson & J. Penrose (Eds.), *Constructions of race, place and nation* (pp. 27–49). University College London Press.

Pierce, J. E. (Ed.). (2016). *Making the White man's West: Whiteness and the creation of the American West*. University Press of Colorado.

Powell, J. A., & Menendian, S. (2016). *The problem of othering: Towards inclusiveness and belonging*. Othering and Belonging: Expanding the Circle of Human Concern. www.otheringandbelonging. org/the-problem-of-othering/

Rabaka, R. (2022). W. E. B. Du Bois's contributions to critical race studies in education: Sociology of education, classical critical race theory, and proto-critical pedagogy. In M. Lynn & A. D. Dixson (Eds.), *Handbook of critical race theory in education 2* (pp. 197–211 ). Routledge.

Reconciliation Australia. (2018). *Let's talk. January 26*. ACT: Reconciliation Australia.

Reconciliation Australia. (2020). *Truth-telling and reconciliation. Five Dimensions, truth-telling.* www.reconciliation.org.au/truth-telling-and-reconciliation/

Referendum Council. (2017). Uluru–National Convention, 23–26 May. www.referendumcouncil. org.au/event/first-nations-regional-dialogue-in-uluru.html

Regan, P. (2010). *Unsettling the settler within: Indian Residential Schools, truth telling, and reconciliation in Canada.* UBC.

Regano, K. (2016). Challenges to feminist solidarity in the era of new public management. In R. Thwaites & A. Pressland (Eds.), *Being an early career feminist academic* (pp. 169–194). Palgrave Macmillan.

Rigney, L. I. (1999). Internationalization of an Indigenous anticolonial cultural critique of research methodologies: A guide to Indigenist research methodology and its principles. *Emergent Ideas in Native American Studies, 14*(2), 109–121.

Robus, D., & Macleod, C. (2006). 'White excellence and black failure': The reproduction of racialized higher education in everyday talk. *South African Journal of Psychology, 36*(3), 463–480.

Rondini, A. C. (2018). White supremacist danger narratives. *Contexts, 17*(3), 60–62.

Sanner-Stiehe, E., & Ward-Smith, P. (2017). Lateral violence in nursing: Implications and strategies for nurse educators. *Journal of Professional Nursing, 33*(2), 113–118.

Smith, L. T. (1999). *Decolonizing methodologies: Research and Indigenous Peoples.* Zed Books.

Stanner, W. E. H. (1969). *The Boyer Lectures 1968—After the Dreaming.* Australian Broadcasting Commission.

Stanner, W. E. H. (1973). *White man got no dreaming: Essays 1938–1973.* ANU Press.

Staszak, J. F. (2008). Other/otherness. *International Encyclopedia of Human Geography.* Elsevier.

Suarez, C. E., Owens, D. R., Hunter, J. D., Menzies, C., & Dixson, A. D. (2022). Intersectionality, mentorship, and women of color in the academy. In M. Lynn & A. D. Dixson. *The handbook of critical race theory in education* (pp. 93–107). (2nd ed.). Routledge.

Sue, D. W. (2006). The invisible whiteness of being: Whiteness, white supremacy, white privilege, and racism. In M. G. Constantine & D. W. Sue (Eds.), *Addressing racism: Facilitating cultural competence in mental health and educational settings* (pp. 15–30). John Wiley & Sons.

Tate, S. A., & Bagguley, P. (2017). Building the anti-racist university: next steps. *Race Ethnicity and Education, 20*(3), 289–299. https://doi.org/10.1080/13613324.2016.1260227

Taylor, K., Durey, A., Mulcock, J., Kickett, M., & Jones, S. (2014). *Developing Aboriginal and Torres Strait Islander cultural capabilities in health graduates: a review of the literature.* HWA.

Taylor, K., Kickett, M., & Jones, S. (2014). *Aboriginal and Torres Strait Islander Health Curriculum Project: Findings from preliminary consultation process.* HWA.

The Res-Sisters. (2016). 'I'm an early career feminist academic: Get me out of here?' Encountering and resisting the neoliberal academy. In R. Thwaites & A. Pressland (Eds.), *Being an early career feminist academic* (pp. 267–284). Palgrave Macmillan.

Trudgett, M., Page, S., & Coates, S. K. (2021). Peak bodies: Indigenous representation in the Australian higher education sector. *Australian Journal of Education, 66*(1), 40–56. https://doi.org/ 10.1177/00049441211011178

Trugett, M., & Franklin, C. (2012). *Not in my backyard: The impact of culture shock on Indigenous Australians in higher education.* 1st International Australasian Conference on Enabling Access to Higher Education, Adelaide, Australia, 5–7 December. https://opus.lib.uts.edu.au/handle/10453/ 115373

Universities Australia. (2011). *National Best Practice Framework for Indigenous Cultural Competency in Australian.* Universities, Department of Education. Canberra; Employment and Workplace Relations.

Universities Australia. (2022). Indigenous Strategy 2022–25. Universities Australia. www.universiti esaustralia.edu.au/wp-content/uploads/2022/03/UA-Indigenous-Strategy-2022-25.pdf

Wade, L. (2015, 15 June). The lethal gentleman: the 'benevolent sexism' behind Dylann Roof's racism. *The Conversation.* https://theconversation.com/the-lethal-gentleman-the-benevolent-sexism-beh ind-dylann-roofs-racism-43534

Walter, M. (2016). Data politics and Indigenous representation in Australian statistics. In T. Kukutai & J. Taylor (Eds.), *Indigenous data sovereignty: Toward an agenda* (pp.79–108 ). ANU Press.

Wedesweiler, M. (2020). Truth-telling: A key to liberating Australia from a deliberate silence. *NEW: Emerging Scholars in Australian Indigenous Studies, 5*(1). https://doi.org/10.5130/nesais. v5i1.1561

Wildman, S. M., & Davis, D. A. (1994). *Language and silence: Making systems of privilege visible.* Faculty Publications, Santa Clara University.

Wilson, W. J. (2011). The impact of racial and non-racial structural forces on poor urban Blacks. In R. D. Coates (Ed.), *Covert fascism: Theories, institutions, and experiences* (pp. 17–40). Brill.

Young, S. (2004). Social work theory and practice: The invisibility of whiteness. In A. Moreton-Robinson (Ed.), *Whitening race: Essays in social and cultural criticism* (pp. 104–118). Aboriginal Studies Press.

# 7

# THERE IS NO SUCH THING AS A BLANK SLATE

## Accountability in decolonising universities

*Kelly Menzel and Bindi Bennett*

### Positioning

The authors of this chapter would like to acknowledge it has been written on the unceded sovereign lands of the Jinibara and the Kombumerri peoples and the Widjabul Wiabul peoples of the Bunjalung Nations of Australia. We pay genuine respect to their Elders past, present and future, and to the First Nations peoples of all Countries whose lands are significant and to our Country, within what is now referred to as Australia. We refer to non-Indigenous peoples as settlers. The word 'settler' might be considered inflammatory and cause white people reading it a fragility response (DiAngelo, 2018). Whether others have come here by choice or by colonisation consequences, our land was never ceded, and we, as First Nations peoples, are the Sovereign peoples. We work from an Australian Indigenous women's standpoint with Indigenous Women's A-colonial Theory (IWAcT) (see Figure 7.1). We identify as cisgendered Aboriginal women and can only speak from our own lived experiences. However, it is our hope IWAcT is non-exclusionary and is transparent, fluid and translatable for those who identify neither as male or female, or identify as non-binary.

### Why I can't hold space for you anymore

Do you really want to know why I can't hold space for you anymore?
Because you see my body
as an extension of your entitlements
Because I have held space for you before
and every time, the same thing happens
You take up all the space
and expect me to use my time,
energy and emotion in service of fulfilling your desires:
to validate you as someone who is good and innocent
to be the appreciative audience for your self-expression
to provide the content of a transformative learning experience
to perform my trauma to affirm your innocence

DOI: 10.4324/9781003271802-9

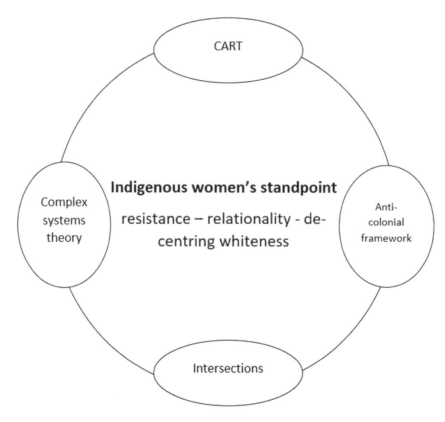

*Figure 7.1*  Indigenous Women's A-colonial Theory (IWAcT) model.
Source: Menzel, 2021, p. 82.

to celebrate your self-image
to center your feelings to absolve you from guilt
to be always generous and generative
to filter what I say in order not to make you feel uncomfortable
to make you feel loved, important, special and safe
and you don't even realize you are doing it…

Excerpt from *Conspicuous Consumption Economies of Virtue and the Commodification of Indigeneity* by Elwood Jimmy and Vanessa de Oliveira Andreotti (2021, p. 5)

## Introduction

As Aboriginal women, our work will always be philosophically aligned with anti-colonial discourses (Dei & Asgharzadeh, 2001), Critical Anti-Racism Theory (CART) (Dei, 1999; Dei & Lordan, 2013) and intersectionality (Crenshaw, 1989). Our Indigenous Knowledges and knowledge systems are holistic and complex. An anti-colonial discourse framework gives us a guiding framework to critique and challenge colonised spaces (Dei & Asgharzadeh, 2001; Dei & Jordan, 2013) and to continue the dismantling of the colonial systemic environment.

Our experience is the basis on which this chapter has evolved. While the story began 250 years ago with the invasion and colonisation of so-called Australia, there is an atom-isation in the experiences shared in this chapter that reinforces the Western imposition of knowledge, creating tangible markers of racism for the Indigenous higher education experi-ence. We examine the extent to which universities are the sites of systemic and structural racism and violence, and do this through a process of exploring the violence perpetrated in the academy. We are interested in exploring shared and personal experiences of race-based systemic violence and what this means in terms of 'survivance' (Vizenor, 1999, p. vii) in the academy: "an active sense of presence, the continuance of native stories, not a mere reaction, or a survivable name. Native survivance stories are renunciations of dominance, tragedy and victimry". Our own direct experience of race-based violence illuminates how other systems and structures can be implemented to reduce the ongoing violent nature of current Western academic systems. We expand on our individual experiences as a compel-ling narrative that weaves through time and place, linking our experiences as Indigenous women's experiences of systemic violence in the academy to privilege our voices and make way for *non-colonialist, a-colonial* approaches.

## The current system

When I criticise a system, they think I criticise them—and that is of course because they fully accept the system and identify themselves with it.

(Merton, 1967, cited in Hand, 2005, n.p.)

Many Western systems are broken and not working, except for those people who are the most privileged (McIntosh, 1988). Our issue with Westernised systems, especially the Australian higher education sector, is that it is full of racial violence, which is largely aimed at Aboriginal peoples (us). Violences perpetrated on Aboriginal peoples in the higher educa-tion space include systemic violence, interpersonal violence, interracial violence, horizontal violence, and epistemic violence (Berman & Paradies, 2010; Moodie et al., 2019). This is further exacerbated by the silence from our peers, which acts as a protagonist enabling continued and ongoing violence. Those around us seem to be disinterested in account-ability and responsibility at the personal level, which then seeps into roles and systems (Bishop, 2020).

Violence includes, but is not limited to: expecting Aboriginal people to do all of the labour including physical labour, and emotional and spiritual labour on everything pertaining to race, colonisation and Aboriginal people (Bodkin-Andrews & Carlson, 2016; Universities Australia, 2022). A classic example of this is expecting us to talk about the ongoing intergenerational traumas of colonisation in Australia—to other staff and students—as cap-acity building exercises. It is our experience that many non-Indigenous academics bow out of the shared responsibilities and accountabilities of this learning by giving excuses such as: we did not learn this in school, I did not/do not know, I am worried I will offend, and I do not feel comfortable teaching this.

Another current issue with universities is their (mis)understanding of Indigenisation. Indigenisation is a multilayered and holistic university-level and university-wide organisa-tional change initiative (Pidgeon, 2016). It is the incorporation of Indigenous perspectives, content and knowledges within the curriculum, including pedagogy, Indigenous facilitators and a shift in values and attitude from wider personnel with overall governance. It is supposed to lead to a more diverse, inclusive and safer environment. For universities to really change, it is vital the organisation experience a 'changing of the guard' with the inclusion of First Nations people placed in positions where they (we) have the power to instigate change. The organisation must value First Nations people hired, their cultures, ways of speaking and respect them and their views—and this must be modelled to the outside world (Universities Australia, 2022). However, many First Nations positions are never envisioned to have power, influence, voice or a seat at any table. Instead, if the university is slightly proactive, there may be one pro-vice chancellor (Indigenous) or an Indigenous professor to lead the way. In Australia, many universities have not started this restructuring and so non-Indigenous peoples still 'lead' in the Indigenous space. Many universities have little or no Elder community governance for, and by, First Nations staff, and so at best the expectation is that course content and curriculum will be co-designed and open for non-Indigenous input, negotiation and development. Often this 'co-developer' is white and privileged—both as a white person but also based on their role and gender—and so can have more power, voice and control than the—often sole—First Nations staff member. Many do not understand pedagogy, let alone Indigenous pedagogy, and this means meaningful development of different and diverse ways of teaching, research and assessment are often missed.

When hiring First Nations staff to Indigenise curricula and workplaces, non-Indigenous staff often do not know that they themselves are being asked to challenge and change their values and to become a safer work colleague, contributing to a more inclusive environment. We have been often told that people are 'blank slates' (personal communication, 2021). In saying this to us, we have the thought they are indicating they have no preconceived ideas, biases about First Nations peoples. Of course, this is incorrect. Everyone holds a world view and their own biases. What they are wielding here is their white privilege (McIntosh, 2018), where they have been allowed to connect when or if they so choose. What this says to us is that they have not been affected by marginalisation or oppression, and so it has not impacted their slates. We posit the reason academics are so culturally unresponsive is due to the large number of international staff (many of whom are people of colour)—who "never knew there were Aboriginal people here (in Australia) and have never spoken to one" (personal communication, 2021). In addition to this, many universities want to hold on to the old ways of doing things that were/are less confrontational but also less of a real learning opportunity. Many are reluctant to do any content or change that will result in anyone (particularly white privileged people) feeling uncomfortable, accountable, responsible or challenged. Indeed, it appears people are resistant to experiencing any form of discomfort. Hence, the way these positions and the Indigenisation of institutions are set up to fail from the beginning, means the positions (and ideas) are set up to fail from the beginning.

The Science in Australia Gender Equity (SAGE) (2015) pathway to the Athena Swan Charter is a framework that aims for good practices in higher education and research institutions by advancing gender equality, representation, progression and success for all. The Athena Swan Charter also speaks to the intersectionality of women. SAGE takes this a step further and includes diversity as a focus. The Athena Swan Charter allows an organisation to benchmark its work in relation to gender equity, diversity and inclusion against international standards, and SAGE is the only organisation that administers the Athena Swan framework in Australia. As such gender equity, diversity and inclusion within universities in Australia are not measured against international standards, and we contend one of the biggest challenges in the Western academic environment is the concept of safety and cultural safety (or lack thereof). 'Safe' can be defined as free from harm or hurt—so feeling safe means you do not anticipate either harm or hurt, emotionally or physically (Preisler, 2013). Trauma can arise from a single or repeated adverse event that threatens to over-whelm a person's ability to cope (Kezelman, 2014). When it is repeated over a period, it can become complex trauma (Kezelman, 2014). We teach that First Nations people will already have complex trauma from repeated colonisation, racism, oppression, social disadvantage and marginalisation. If trauma goes untreated, it creates a stress response in the body. A trigger is an internal or external experience that is a reminder of one or more traumatic events. When a trigger is present, an individual's mind and body respond as if the threat is present (Van der Kolk, 2022; Pickens et al., 2017).

Ways in which we, as Indigenous staff, are often placed in unsafe situations includes the content we are expected to teach/deliver. When we are teaching, we are often teaching trau-matic content that not only affects ourselves but also has larger implications for our com-munities and the peoples around us. We are acutely aware of the intergenerational traumas of colonisation—whereas many of our learners are not (Bodkin-Andrews & Carlson, 2016; Cullen et al., 2022; Gaywsh & Murdoch, 2018). This often places us in precarious situations—where we are at the front of the room, unprotected—having to address racist or harmful comments, statements and questions based on racist assumptions and bias, such as Aboriginal people cannot hold eye contact (often stated after an hour or more of holding eye contact with someone), or you don't look Aboriginal (personal communica-tion, 2021, 2022) and confusion over why Aboriginal people cannot just get over it, as it was a long time ago. Excuses for allies in not assisting in managing these spaces to be safer include that they are not competent, confident, aware or able to teach in the space with us. Alternatively, they will approach us following a racist or harmful incident and apologise that it occurred, but remained silent whilst it was occurring.

Frequently, when we push back against people or situations that are culturally unsafe, we have been and continue to be at risk, being accused of being unhelpful, uncollegial, lazy, angry, stupid, of not upholding faculty standards, or just not interested/disengaged (personal communication, 2020, 2021, 2022). We have had these accusations made about us and to us, about other First Nations colleagues. Many times, when starting. new employ-ment staff speak about other First Nations peoples who have left, using these stereotypical excuses for why they left instead of being honest about the social, spiritual and emotional harm that colonised institutions continue to inflict on the well-being of First Nations peoples. These excuses continue to create a spiritual, emotional and cultural load and work burden on First Nations staff, perpetuating the myth that everything 'Indigenous' should fall to the Aboriginal staff members and that the wider university holds no real responsi-bility, accountability or consequences for the lack of cultural responsiveness of the univer-sity and settler staff and students.

### *Anti-colonial discursive framework*

Away from entitlements, towards accountabilities
Away from cost/benefit calculations, towards honoring gifts
Away from transactions, towards gratitude and reciprocity
Away from projections, towards facing realness (the good, the bad, the broken, and the messed up within and around us)
Away from accumulation, towards decluttering

Away from playing to score, towards renouncing the game
Away from being coddled, towards being coached
Away from seeking drama, towards seeking depth
Away from hope and hopelessness, towards trust in moving together
Away from separability, towards entanglement
Away from centring humanity, towards centring the unbound metabolism of the land.
(Jimmy & de Oliveira Andreotti, 2021, pp.131–132)

We have found that many non-Indigenous people have the privilege of denying the systemic, historical and ongoing violence of colonialism. They deny any complicity in the harm this violence causes; and the fact that comforts, securities, and enjoyments are subsidised by expropriation and exploitation of Australia's resources seems lost to many settlers (McMillan et al., 2018). As well as this, many settlers continue with the myth that they are not part of the land they live on. They see themselves as separate from each other and the land, rather than 'entangled' within a living ecology and wider network of ways of knowing, being and doing (Martin & Mirraboopa, 2003). It is our experience that many settlers deny the magnitude and the complexity of the problems we need to face together, instead looking for performative, quick, easy and simplistic solutions that make them feel and look good.

We challenge the language of decolonisation. 'Decolonise' as a term suggests systems are already colonised—which is true but does not grapple with the fact that the coloniser/settlers are not going to leave any time soon—and that to truly address colonisation, we would have to rip down many of the colonised systems (health, education, law) (Alessandrini, 2022, Fanon, 1961/2004, 1970) and start again, placing Indigenous knowledges at the forefront. As much as it hurts to say this, we believe this is just not going to occur in our lifetime. Instead, we suggest an anti-colonial discursive framework.

Dei and Asgharzadeh (2001) state their "aim [with the anti-colonial discursive framework] is to envision a common zone of resistance in which the oppressed and marginalized groups are enabled to form alliances in resisting various colonial tendencies" (p. 297). Simmons and Sefa Dei (2012) additionally request consideration of "the possibilities of a counter theoretical narrative or conception of the present in ways that make theoretical sense of the everyday world of the colonized, racialized, oppressed and the Indigene" (p. 67). This is very much what we envision, from an Australian Indigenous women's standpoint with Indigenous Women's A-colonial Theory (IWAcT). Dei and Asgharzadeh (2001, p. 298) argue: "the relevance of a theory should be seen in how it allows us to understand the complexity of human society and to offer a social and political corrective—that is, the power of theories and ideas to bring about change and transformation in social life".

This is what we—as Aboriginal Early Career Matriarch (Balla, 2019) researchers—are trying to achieve with our research and practice. IWAcT seeks to privilege Indigenous women's perspectives, creating an Indigenous women's zone, to decentre whiteness and further challenge systemic race-based violence by radically challenging colonial systems and framing a-colonial spaces.

Dei and Asgharzadeh (2001) place an emphasis on the discursive rather than the theoretical, and prefer to work within the principles of a guiding framework that considers the changing nature of academic and political spaces, due to the changing nature of social realities. E. Carlson (2017), a white settler academic, refers to Dei and Asgharzadeh's framework (2001, cited in E. Carlson, 2017) and goes on to demonstrate the "value and practices of the anti-colonial research methodology to academia generally and settler colonial studies specifically" for settler scholars (E. Carlson, 2017, p. 496). This is the embodiment of the framework, which is to "work within a more flexible, transparent, and fluid language" (Carlson, 2019, p. 298) rather than becoming rigid and inflexible. Wintoneak and Blaise (2022, p. 435), two settler scholars, embrace feminist anti-colonial methodology and voice the Derbarl Yerrigan, an important river in Western Australia, through three "river-child stories". They untangle the colonial and ecological legacies of the colonial project and call for new ways of thinking and producing knowledge. Further, Rigney (2003, p. 45) has utilised an anti-colonial approach to expose the "relationship between Australian colonial knowledge and Australian colonial power, in and through sport". O'Sullivan (2019, p. 107) argues,

[i]f asserting our complex identities as Indigenous people in all forms is an anti-colonial act of resistance and remonstrance, then it will only be through our own agency over the presentation of the diversity of our lives that we will truly be free of the shackles of colonial oppression.

These very different scholarly works demonstrate the embodiment of political resistance when utilising an anti-colonial approach, but also the transparent, fluid and flexible nature of utilising an anti-colonial framework. These are paramount to IWAcT. Further, IWAcT is twofold and we want the theory to be freely utilised by both Indigenous and non-Indigenous people, ultimately to challenge, decolonise and deconstruct Western spaces and to create a-colonial spaces that are new and not colonised, from conception.

The anti-colonial discursive framework acknowledges and respects the importance of locally produced knowledge that emanates from deep, cultural, ancient histories. This is very much aligned with an Indigenous approach (Denzin et al., 2008, Kovach, 2015, 2021, Smith et al., 2018). Further, approaches such as the anti-colonial discursive framework see marginalised groups, such as Indigenous communities, "as subjects of their own experiences and histories" (Dei and Asgharzadeh, 2001, p. 300). This is aligned with the principles of self-determination—which is fundamental for First Nations communities and knowledges (United Nations, 2007). These ideas have been explored by Fanon (1963), and fundamentally the aim is to interrogate and challenge institutional power in systems and structures.

Essentially, an anti-colonial stance "fosters the idea that intellectuals should be aware of the historical and institutional structures and contexts which sustain intellectualism" (Menzel and Cameron, 2021, p. 301). Further, we contend that everyone, Indigenous and non-Indigenous, within the academy has a responsibility to challenge the colonial, historical and institutional structures, and contexts within the academy. Our work—as early career matriarch researchers—like the anti-colonial framework, offers an alternative discourse to the existence of Western colonial oppression and brings to light the recolonisation that occurs within the academy through the perpetration of race-based violence and violent processes and practices. We offer a theoretical framework that challenges the colonial discourse, and urge a radical reframing of language that is used in the academy which influences practice and processes.

The anti-colonial discursive framework foregrounds "oral, visual, textual, political, and material resistance of colonized groups" (Menzel & Cameron, 2021, p. 301), and this "entails a shift away from a sole preoccupation with victimization" (p. 302). To utilise the framework is to critique "the wholesale denigration, disparagement, and discard of tradition and culture in the name of modernity and global space" (Menzel & Cameron, 2021, p. 302). This creates a:

> site of/in tradition, orality, visual representation, material and intangible culture, and aboriginality (sic) that is empowering to colonized and marginalized groups. In Australia some disciplines are engaging in this space more than others (Howett et al. 2009; Lee, 2017). The anti-colonial perspective seeks to identify that site and celebrate its strategic significance.
>
> (Menzel & Cameron, 2021, p. 301)

The matter of race-based violence is so complex, and the issues are so interwoven that we contend one theoretical framework is not enough to address decolonising concerns. Therefore, we have entwined these theoretical frameworks, and further celebrated and placed an Australian Indigenous women's standpoint at the centre of the theory.

## Critical anti-racism theory

Dei (2013, p. 3) argues anti-racism is 'read' through an anti-colonial gaze. By 'read', Dei means reasserting the necessity to place race and anti-racism (back) at the centre of debate. He contends there is a great need for a critical and sophisticated understanding of how race and anti-racist practice are placed in contemporary terms. He has framed (2000a, 2000b) and reframed (2013) Critical Anti-Racism Theory (CART). CART is a set of ideas about the "salience and centrality of race" (Dei, 2013, p. 3).

While the term 'race' is used, the theory places emphasis on the recognition of the importance of how identity/ies is/are shaped, and includes "ethnicity, class, gender, sexuality, disability, language and religion, and the situational and contextual variations in intensities of oppressions" (Dei, 2013, p. 3). Race is an integral part of identity. Dei (2013, p. 2) states: "The reality of race emerges from the everydayness of racism and not the other way around. In other words, it is racism that has made race real", and CART further adds to the anti-colonial framework. CART recognises that oppression occurs at multiple sites, and this oppression needs to be contested on an individual level and collectively—this is also a central tenet of intersectionality. We are keen to add to this further, privileging Indigenous women's standpoint, because while the anti-colonial framework and CART acknowledge Indigeneity, they do not privilege Indigenous women's voices. They are viewed from a black male gaze, which excludes us, as Indigenous women and as those who are neither men nor women or identify as non-binary.

## Intersectionality

Intersectionality is a framework (Bowleg, 2012; Crenshaw, 1995) that postulates multiple identities or social categories intersect at an individual (micro) level that reflect the macro-level systems that expose the privilege and oppression that occur in said systems, such as racism, ageism, sexism and ableism (Crenshaw, 1995). Davis, 2020, p. 67) defines intersectionality as "the interaction between gender, race, and other categories of difference in individual lives, social practices, institutional arrangements, and cultural ideologies and the outcomes of these interactions in terms of power". Conceived by Crenshaw (1989), intersectionality is rooted in Black feminist scholarship and was intended to address the experiences of women of colour who have otherwise been excluded from feminist and anti-racism discourse (Crenshaw, 1992). It is now a staple of feminist and women's studies and scholarship. Crenshaw argues that intersectionality requires theorists to address gender and race (and other identities) to demonstrate how these interact to shape the elements and experiences in Black women's lives (Crenshaw, 1991). Intersectionality was originally developed from a US perspective, but it has been applied in Australian contexts (Bastos, Harnois, & Paradies, 2018). Intersectionality has been applied to sectors such as social work (Mattsson, 2014) and public health (Bowleg, 2012; Hankivsky & Cormier, 2011), and we contend intersection(ality) has a place in higher education (Museus & Griffin, 2011). From Crenshaw's perspective, intersectionality compounds disadvantage, and she has been critical of white women repurposing intersectionality to talk about complexity of identity rather than recognising that it is a tool to highlight oppression (2017). We are concerned with the intersection between culture and gender because these are core intersections of Indigenous women's standpoint, but not to the detriment of other intersections that influence Indigenous women's lives. Thus, we see the necessity for an Australian Indigenous theoretical approach that places Indigenous women's experiences at the centre, and that includes the elements of intersection(ality) coming from a place of strength, in the broader setting of the academy. This is the aim of IWAcT.

## Complex systems theory

Complexity theory enables understanding of complex and diverse systems that are only partially understood by traditional scientific methods (Schneider & Somers, 2006). Complexity theory traverses many disciplines, such as the social sciences, ecological sciences and information technology (Berkes & Berkes, 2009), and it has the potential to profoundly influence the way we think, act and experience the world.

Complexity theory emerged in the mid-twentieth century from the study of weather systems (Kauffman, 1993). It was "first noted by Lorenz in his study of weather systems and reflects the non-linearity of such systems" (Schneider & Somers, 2006, p. 354). This is where the concept of the 'butterfly effect' was born. The 'butterfly effect' is the "phenomenon of large, disproportionate change [...] [that] illustrates that initial conditions form unique influences on a non-linear system" (Schneider & Somers, 2006, p. 354). The butterfly effect is relevant to our work because all systems are interconnected, and it is marginalised communities that bear the brunt when things go wrong in systems. An example of this is when banking systems collapse or when monetary systems are debased. The net effect is a massive increase in economic inequality. Economic inequality leads to inequality in other areas of life, such as housing, health and welfare (Doyle & Stiglitz, 2014), hurting those who have less to lose, and those most affected are in marginalised groups (Darity & Nembhard, 2000). Schneider and Somers (2006, p. 362) argue: "Changes in one variable can have large changes in others", and we are considering the effect that proposed changes or recommendations can have on systems and structures such as the academy.

Complexity theory is especially relevant when studying systems, structures, organisations, leadership and change management (Uhl-Bien et al., 2007). Complexity theory can be applied to the study of systems to offer insights on how systems and structures can become more sustainable, accessible and equitable (Schneider, 2002). IWAcT takes components of complexity theory, alongside elements of the anti-colonial discursive framework, CART and intersectionality, and can be applied to critique, expose, challenge, (re)frame and assist with decolonising spaces, along with creating new a-colonial spaces. The anti-colonial discursive framework, CART and intersectionality, complexity theory and IKPs need to be united and applied via IWAcT, to further disrupt systemic processes that position Indigenous Australian peoples and Knowledges as the other within the academy. IWAcT can be applied to decolonise current systems and to establish new systems—a-colonial systems—through collaboration, co-construction and co-development that may facilitate Indigenous social mobility through advancement and achievement and through education for future populations to utilise.

## De-Westernising ourselves as learners

You don't really get it, do you? You don't even know how much harm you have caused or the harm you are causing right now. You don't know that your 'success' as a settler or an immigrant happens at the expense of my body, of my people, and of the land. You don't know that your hope is the hope of the continuity of violence and unsustainability. Your deficit theorization of me cannot even fathom that I can use irony, let alone sarcasm.

(Jimmy & de Oliveira Andreotti, 2021, p.127)

Part of the issue with Westernised learning is that education has become a commodity and not something that needs to be truly earned. Most learners come into the higher education space not actually wanting to give up or challenge their privileges, views or beliefs, and there is no system currently set up to hold them to account for this. Here we see a perpetuation of colonisation.

Many settlers hope to transcend colonial privilege without giving anything up. We see certain behaviours repeatedly in systems that contribute to ongoing colonisation. For example, many learners and settler staff that are new to the space claim 'ethics' (Chatterjee, 2019) as a barrier to their accountability to continuing colonisation. Being ethical leads many to claim they are against colonisation and violent systems that eradicate self-determination. These learners use words such as reconciliation, but actually do not see that by just by being in this country, they are actually complicit and therefore accountable. They use ethics and moral stances to seek innocence but also to avoid responsibility. This means learners and settler staff see themselves as sitting outside of the system, viewing themselves and their philosophical beliefs in terms of goodness, and thus non-complicit—rather than them benefiting from the status quo.

The second behaviour that is very common is that of recentring. Many settlers also gaslight Aboriginal peoples' experiences in this process by acknowledging that things were bad back in 1880, but now things are better and we should all get over it. Here we often see people struggle with the fact that they may have had a hard life / feelings / experiences, but these are actually incomparable to those of Aboriginal peoples due to white supremacy and ongoing privileges. Acknowledging this makes settlers feel uncomfortable, and it appears people will try to avoid this discomfort, so they get angry, defensive or closed off to further learning and growth (Lensmire et al., 2013).

All too often we see settlers demand simple, guaranteed answers to complex problems. This demand for certainty shows a level of arrogance and ignorance where people have often been in a position of privilege to previously have control in their lives and to know exactly what is going to happen, when, where, why and how (Jimmy & de Oliveira Andreotti, 2021). From an Indigenous perspective, not everyone should, or needs to know everything. This is inconceivable from a Western perspective. When we insist that there continues to be diversity in every culture and that issues are layered with hundreds of years of policies, programmes and harmful people, many learners and settler staff will move to 'the higher ground'. By this we mean they will often 'settlersplain' to us. They demand respect due to their qualifications, life experience, experience with Aboriginal people, marriage to Aboriginal people, children with Aboriginal people, and demand entitlements to direct and determine content, discussion and appoint themselves as an authority and therefore as having unrestricted autonomy in the space. These types of settlers often also go for the grants, the publications and the gaps in research as an 'ally', whilst basically reducing Aboriginal peoples' ability to represent, speak and voice them/ourselves.

Lastly, we have experienced the behaviour of the 'victim'. These settlers often decide and determine what is valuable and deserving of their time. They often use their student/minority/international/settler status to decide, judge and compare colonisation, and to not accept true learning and growth due to their own life experiences—whilst positioning themselves always as being hard done by, struggling or in any way and for any reason also in a minority status. They will also deal out punishments—particularly in anonymous student evaluations but also in complaints to peers and management—and they can and will seek to do harm if they feel disrespected, uncomfortable, or if in any way their authority or privilege is challenged in interactions.

Finally, we see ongoing colonisation through ignorance and lack of engagement with protocol and available information about how to engage with First Nations peoples. This is expressed within organisations where Aboriginal staff are expected to have a 'footprint' everywhere, creating an additional cultural load (Nair & Selvarj, 2021) and burden that is often not expected of non-Indigenous staff. It is effectively saying, 'you WILL represent', whilst at the same time having an expectation of how that representation will look and that Aboriginal staff will be compliant, well behaved and eternally grateful. This is unfortunately often made worse with Reconciliation Action Plans (RAPs) and strategies that are designed for tokenistic representation, with little to no comprehensive alignment or depth of learning (for example, many lack evaluation or measurement in the design). Further, the Western system requires that we are all assessment driven and maintains that we as humans will largely not do some things unless we are made to. For academics, our professional performance reviews (PPRs) are the assessment method we are held accountable to, and currently Aboriginal and Torres Strait Islander learning, accountability and responsibilities are not part of this process. So, how can we really state we are being successful?

## Creating new and sustainable systems

It is difficult to speak truth to those more powerful. This is where conflict and discomfort occur. Speaking truth to power is actually considered a non-violent political tactic (Corkindale, 2011). However, we believe it comes at much physical and emotional cost. Speaking truth to power can place one's position at risk. Those in power have many means to intimidate and, when someone publicly questions those in power, they can be labelled not a team player, or a troublemaker (Hirschmann, 1970). We ourselves have at times been labelled troublemakers when pushing back against colonisation. Therefore, most people choose the path of least resistance—to remain quiet or simply move on from an organisation ('a principled resignation'), according to Hirschmann (1970). Ultimately, our collective experiences have led us to resign from positions due to a lack of safety. However, it is the silence of management and other staff that contributes to it being difficult to recruit and retain Indigenous staff, and, until speaking truth to power becomes more common practice, recruiting and retaining Indigenous staff will remain a problem.

There is also a type of wilful blindness (Hall, 2019) (or wilful unseeing, we prefer to articulate) that occurs in institutions such as the academy (Hall, 2019). Generally speaking, 'willful blindness' is a term used to describe a situation where a person seeks to avoid legal liability for a wrongful act by intentionally keeping themselves unaware of facts that would otherwise render them implicated (Luban, 1999). Racism and violence are ignored, not labelled, and not addressed in a manner where the institution holds itself accountable. In fact, the term 'racism' is rarely articulated, as if the word is difficult to form in one's mouth.

The embodiment of IWAcT means one may become uncomfortable when speaking truth to power and addressing wilful blindness. However, we contend this discomfort is necessary fodder to address systemic violence and to decolonise and a-colonise the system. As Fanon (1961, p. 27) states, "decolonisation is always a violent phenomenon". IWAcT also requires a reorientation of language because we contend the theoretical act of decolonisation in the academy is not enough. We wish to propel social and political action, through discussion about what currently exists and what is possible. With a change in language comes a change in mindset—and, with a change inmindset, comes possibility. This is why we have chosen the language a-colonial and a-colonise. We are proposing a radical decentring of whiteness, a provocative act to push to the theoretical margins of discourse. In a way we are also calling for an urgent revival of anti-colonial thinking and practice. This is an act of resistance and reclamation, and it also offers an opportunity to design our own future.

We are appealing for an Indigenous women's approach to the reinvigoration of anti-colonial discourse, a more radical mindset and a level of fearlessness that provokes debate and encourages ground-level change within the academy and other systems. It is our hope IWAcT can—in a small way—add to the body of knowledge and nurture the creation of new frameworks, theories and knowledges that can be embedded in the academy by fostering the use of Indigenous concepts and models theoretically and in practice. The butterfly effect—a small change can result in a large difference—has occurred this way previously, in the 1970s in the case of *Roe vs Wade* (a landmark decision by the US Supreme Court that ruled that the US Constitution conferred the right for women to have an abortion)—a correlated decrease of crime was noted two decades later (Donohue & Levitt, 2001; Dubner, 2019). However, we need to note that in 2022, *Roe vs Wade* was overturned by the US Supreme Court. Current US president Joe Biden stated it was a "sad day for the court and the country" and also stated that the health and life of women in the United States would now be at risk (ABC News, 2022). It is our hope the addition of IWAcT to Indigenous Knowledges on decolonising theory will, despite recent setbacks, continue to have a butterfly effect.

This is also the beginning of exploring the possibility of how new systems—a-colonial systems—can come to life that are unique to Indigenous Knowledges. We are particularly interested in how new systems might look and function. The combined messages of all the theories that influence IWAcT, enhanced by an Indigenous women's standpoint, bring into sharp focus the necessity for new systems to grow and develop, using ancient knowledges. By taking a holistic Indigenous approach, new systems will be a-colonised from conception. We believe this is necessary for future generations. New systems are required for a more sustainable, accessible and equitable future. Although still being referred to as decolonising, cutting-edge computational technology and artificial intelligence are discussing new approaches to systems development (Birhane, 2020; Irwin & White, 2019; Mohommed, Png, & Isaac 2020). While they are discussing technological systems, we are interested in bringing an a-colonial approach into the corporeal world and applying it to the development of new systems and structures for communities.

Unfortunately, true and deep learning around Aboriginal and Torres Strait Islander peoples and issues requires great discomfort for non-Indigenous peoples, especially if they are white and settlers. This means, to really engage requires the ability to not need to be rescued from/or avoid this discomfort. Instead of wanting to feel good and comfortable, it is vital that learners try to see how they are complicit in being responsible and accountable in the continued and ongoing colonisation and systemic harm occurring constantly around us. This means being truly interested in 'in-depth' education—not just in reaffirming one's own learnings, thoughts, beliefs and views. Therefore, it means enabling, learning and enacting skills in which one can create a 'growth zone' and 'sit with' one's emotions using emotional regulation and avenues such as supervision to continue learning and remaining resilient. Some further suggestions we have include:

1. Instead of expecting to 'feel good', try un-numbing to the collective pain of historical and systemic violence that subsidises our comforts, sensitising yourself to your complicity and responsibility in relation to historical/systemic harm and the pain of the land metabolism we are part of.
2. Instead of expecting to performatively 'look good', try interrupting your socially conditioned narcissism and 'grow up': embrace the responsibility for composing your insecurities, projections, fragilities, harmful entitlements and aspirations, and desires for certainty, innocence, authority, autonomy, protagonism, praise, attention and validation.
3. Instead of expecting to 'do good', try showing up differently to the collective work, doing what is needed and what you can do, rather than what you want to do; develop stamina for the mess, the frustrations and the storms ahead.
4. Instead of expecting to 'move forward', try digging deeper and relating wider, learning to sense and stay at the edge, learning from failure and from mistakes, mapping the ditches; emphasising the integrity of the process and maintenance of ethical relationships, rather than the pace or the destination.

## Conclusion

In this chapter we have included discussion on the four theories, anti-colonial discursive framework, CART, intersectionality and complexity theory, that influence a new theory we have developed—what we call an *a-colonial* approach to systems development—the Indigenous women's' a-colonial theory (IWAcT). Our overall aim is to contribute to the emerging literature and to the Indigenous body of knowledge with the IWAcT. This theory is the beginning of a-colonial processes and draws on the above four social theories to further shape a discursive a-colonial process that privileges an Indigenous women's perspective.

We aspire to regenerative narratives and new story systems. These are the core, fundamental elements of the IWAcT, and embodying these elements is a core tenet. While we have significant and serious concerns about the current state of Western colonised systems and structures, such as the academy, in the end we remain optimistic about the future of decolonising and a-colonising processes in the academy and institutional spaces—and we are very excited about the potential for the development of new, a-colonial systems that are accessible, sustainable and equitable, and that facilitate Indigenous social mobility through professional advancement and achievement.

For this to succeed, it is our contention that we need to work collectively to abolish colonial violence in education and address healing for Aboriginal peoples. To do this, there is a requirement for settler staff and learners to 'sit with' a truth-telling process—despite the discomfort. By prioritising this learning, we can decide to do this together and own up, show up and repurpose education for the next generation—collectively. Otherwise, what is education actually for and what has the past taught us?

## Glossary of terms

**A-colonial**: spaces and systems that privilege Indigenous voices are new and not colonised, from conception.

**Accountability:** is to answer for your actions and take responsibility for your mistakes, to be responsible to another and to be able to explain what happened.

**Allies/Ally:** someone who supports disenfranchised, minority and underrepresented groups of people

**Anti-colonial discourses**: Dei and Asgharzadeh (2001) state their "aim [with the anti-colonial discursive framework] is to envision a common zone of resistance in which the oppressed and marginalized groups are enabled to form alliances in resisting various colonial tendencies" (2001, p. 297).

**Bias:** is a tendency, inclination or prejudice toward or against something or someone.

**Black Feminism:** is centred on Black women's experiences and the way colonisation has shaped them; placed in Black communities; theorises agency for Black women and promotes a humanistic visionary pragmatism.

**Blank Slate:** someone just waiting to be filled with knowledge, assuming they have none.

**Butterfly Effect:** the "phenomenon of large, disproportionate change [...] [that] illustrates that initial conditions form unique influences on a non-linear system" (Schneider & Somers, 2006, p. 354).

**Critical Anti-Racism Theory (CART)**: Dei (2013, p. 3) argues CART is a set of ideas about the "salience and centrality of race".

**Colonisation**: the invasion and attempted genocide of Great Britain over First Nations peoples of Australia and the continued systems that cause oppression, marginalisation and power imbalances.

**Complex trauma:** occurs as a result of repeated trauma experienced by a child or young person, although it can also occur as a result of experiences as an adult.

**Complexity theory:** enables understanding of complex and diverse systems that are only partially understood by traditional scientific methods (Schneider & Somers, 2006).

**Country:** For Aboriginal peoples, culture, nature and the land are all linked. Aboriginal communities have a cultural connection to the land, which is based on each community's distinct culture, traditions and lore. Each community is named a Country (e.g. Gamilaraay).

**Culture:** the arts, beliefs, customs, institutions, and other products of human work and thought considered as a unit, especially regarding a particular time or social group.

**Cultural safety:** is about creating a workplace where everyone can examine their own cultural identities and attitudes and be open-minded and flexible in their attitudes towards people from cultures other than their own.

**Decolonising:** Colonisation is more than physical. It is also cultural and psychological in determining whose knowledge is privileged. In this, colonisation not only impacts the first generation colonised but creates enduring issues. Decolonisation seeks to reverse and remedy this through direct action and through listening to the voices of First Nations people.

**Discourse:** the use of words to exchange thoughts and ideas.

**Economic inequality:** is the unequal distribution of income and opportunity between different groups in society.

**Elder:** someone who has gained recognition as a custodian of knowledge and lore, and who has community and spiritual permissions to disclose knowledge and beliefs.

**Emotional labour:** refers to how one manages or regulates one's own and others' emotional expressions in a workplace.

**Epistemic violence:** is violence exerted against or through knowledge, and is probably one of the key elements in any process of domination. It is the structural prerogative that a system of knowledge is self-perceived as more accurate and valuable over another system of knowledge, which it deems to be inferior and uncertain. Epistemic violence exists when methods are used that lead to the extermination, annulment and destruction of certain knowledge and its bearers, reaching the extreme of their irrevocable loss, known as epistemicide.

**Ethics:** are based on well-founded standards of right and wrong that prescribe what humans ought to do, usually in terms of rights, obligations, benefits to society, fairness or specific virtues.

**First Nations Peoples:** The first peoples of Australia—Aboriginal and Torres Strait Islander peoples.

**Gaslighting:** is a form of psychological abuse in which a person or group causes someone to question their own sanity, memories or perception of reality.

**Governance:** patterns and practices of rule by which Indigenous people govern themselves in formal and informal settings.

**Higher education sector:** The Australian higher education system is made up of around 170 higher education providers. These are registered by the national regulator the Tertiary Education Quality and Standards Agency (TEQSA).

**Holistic:** means to provide support that looks at the whole person, not just their mental health needs. The support should also consider their physical, emotional, social and spiritual well-being.

**Horizontal violence:** is hostile and aggressive behaviour by individual or group members towards another member or groups of members of the larger group. This has been described as intergroup conflict.

**Indigenous Knowledge Paradigms:** a culturally specific discourse based on Indigenous peoples' premises, values and world view

**Indigenous Knowledge Systems:** The complex set of spiritual values developed by Aboriginal people and that are part of the Dreamtime include self-control, self-reliance, courage, kinship and friendship, empathy, a holistic sense of oneness and interdependence, reverence for land and Country, and a responsibility for others.

**Indigenous Women's A-colonial Theory (IWAcT):** seeks to privilege Indigenous women's perspectives, creating an Indigenous women's zone, to decentre whiteness and further challenge systemic race-based violence by radically challenging colonial systems and framing a-colonial spaces.

**Indigenisation:** is a multilayered and holistic university-level and university-wide organisational change initiative (Pidgeon, 2016). It is the incorporation of Indigenous perspectives, content and knowledges within the curriculum, including pedagogy, Indigenous facilitators and a shift in values and attitude from wider personnel with overall governance.

**Indigenous Space/ Space:** the creation of shared understandings, skills and philosophies, as developed by First Nations communities and societies with a millennia of interconnectedness with Country, natural surroundings and Mother Earth.

**Intergenerational Trauma:** refers to trauma that is passed from a trauma survivor to their descendants. It can also be referred to as transgenerational or multigenerational trauma.

**Interpersonal violence:** occurs when interactions between people serve to maintain or exacerbate the unequal distribution of opportunity across ethnoracial groups (Berman & Paradies, 2010, p. 207).

**Interracial violence:** when a white person takes their misinformation and stereotypes towards another group and performs an act of harassment, exclusion, marginalisation, discrimination and hate.

**Performative:** the practice of words, posts and gestures that do more to promote an individual's own virtuous moral compass than actually help the causes that they're intending to showcase.

**Intersectionality:** is a framework that postulates multiple identities or social categories intersect at an individual (micro) level that reflect the macro-level systems which expose the privilege and oppression that occur in said systems, such as racism, ageism, sexism and ableism (Crenshaw 1995).

**Marginalised:** the act of treating a person or group as though they are insignificant by isolating and/or disempowering them.

**Pedagogy:** is the study of optimal frameworks and techniques for teaching and learning and their execution.

**Positioning:** is the social and political context that creates one's identity in terms of race, class, gender, sexuality and ability status.

**Protocol:** observing customs that demonstrate respect for cultural traditions and histories.

**Privilege:** refers to certain social advantages, benefits or degrees of prestige and respect that an individual has by virtue of belonging to certain social identity groups. Within American and other Western societies, these privileged social identities—of people who have historically occupied positions of dominance over others—include whites, males, heterosexuals, Christians and the wealthy.

**Race:** is any one of the groups that humans are often divided into based on physical traits regarded as common among people of shared ancestry; also: the fact of dividing people, or of people being divided, into such groups.

**Racism:** is the process by which systems and policies, actions and attitudes create inequitable opportunities and outcomes for people based on race. Racism is more than just prejudice in thought or action. It occurs when this prejudice—whether individual or institutional—is accompanied by the power to discriminate against, oppress or limit the rights of others.

**Race-based systemic violence:** refers to the systems in place that perpetuate racial injustice, has three primary components: 1) It's historically specific, meaning the systems maintaining racial injustice change over time (and sometimes based on location). 2) It is a distinctly structural phenomenon, meaning the practices and behaviors that perpetuate racism within a system are baked into the system itself. 3) If the system provides advantages for some, it disadvantages others.

**Reconciliation:** is about strengthening relationships between Aboriginal and Torres Strait Islander peoples and non-Indigenous peoples, for the benefit of all Australians.

**Reconciliation Action Plans (RAPs):** a tool that enables organisations to make their contribution to a reconciled Australia.

**Safe:** free from harm or hurt—so feeling safe means you do not anticipate either harm or hurt, emotionally or physically (Preisler, 2013).

**Self-determination:** an ongoing process of choice to ensure that Indigenous communities are able to meet their social, cultural and economic needs.

**Settlers:** Whether others have come here via choice or colonisation consequences, our land was never ceded, and we, as First Nations peoples, are the Sovereign peoples.

**Settler splain:** explaining something in a slightly condescending, patronising manner, while a) assuming the person you're talking to is not knowledgeable about the subject, b) likely believing you know more about it than you actually do, and c) thinking they must need to hear your wisdom.

**Stolen Generation:** Since colonisation, numerous government laws, policies and practices resulted in the forced removal of generations of Aboriginal and Torres Strait Islander children from their families and communities across Australia.

**Systemic violence:** refers to institutional practices or procedures that adversely affect groups or individuals psychologically, mentally, culturally, economically, spiritually or physically.

**Tokenistic:** the person doing tshi wants to seem like they are helping a group of people who are treated unfairly in society, but their action is not meant to make lasting changes to how those people are treated.

**Trauma:** is the emotional, psychological and physiological residue left over from heightened stress that accompanies experiences of threat, violence and life-challenging events.

**Violence:** does not just refer to physical violence but also social, emotional, psychological, economic and spiritual violence.

**Westernisation:** the adoption of the practices and culture of Western (in Australia, Euro-British) countries.

**White:** the dominant cultural space with enormous political significance, with the purpose to keep others on the margin. It refers to the privileges and power that people who appear white receive because they are not subjected to the racism faced by people of colour and Indigenous people.

**Wilful blindness**: is a legal term used to describe a situation where a person seeks to avoid legal liability for a wrongful act by intentionally keeping themselves unaware of facts that would otherwise render them implicated (Luban, 1999).

## References

ABC News. (2022, 25 June). United States Supreme Court Overturns Roe v Wade, erasing constitutional right to abortion. www.abc.net.au/news/2022-06-25/united-states-supreme-court-overturns-roe-v-wade/101183036

Alessandrini, P. (2022). FivesSuggestions for an aspiring composition teacher: Towards an inclusive compositional pedagogy. *Tempo, 76*(302), 42–51.

Balla, P. (2019). Mother tongue: She who must be obeyed loved and Aboriginal women's stories. *Metro Magazine: Media & Education Magazine*, 202, p. 74–79.

Bastos, J. L., Harnois, C. E., & Paradies, Y. C. (2018). Health care barriers, racism, and intersectionality in Australia. *Social Science & Medicine, 199*, 209–218.

Berkes, F., & Berkes, M. K. (2009). Ecological complexity, fuzzy logic, and holism in indigenous knowledge. *Futures, 41*(1), 6–12.

Berman, G., & Paradies, Y. (2010). Racism, disadvantage and multiculturalism: towards effective anti-racist praxis. *Ethnic and Racial Studies, 33*(2), 214–232.

Birhane, A. (2020). Algorithmic colonization of Africa. *SCRIPT-Ed, 17*(2), 389–409. https://doi.org/10.2966/scrip.170220.389

Bishop, A. (2020). *Becoming an ally: Breaking the cycle of oppression in people*. Fernwood.

Bodkin-Andrews, G., & Carlson, B. (2016). The legacy of racism and Indigenous Australian identity within education. *Race Ethnicity and Education, 19*, 1–24. https://doi.org/10.1080/13613324.2014.969224

Bowleg, L. (2012). The problem with the phrase women and minorities: intersectionality—an important theoretical framework for public health. *American Journal of Public Health, 102*(7), 1267–1273.

Carlson, B. (2019). Disrupting the master narrative: Indigenous people and tweeting colonial history. *Griffith Review, 64*, 224–234.

Carlson, E. (2017). Anti-colonial methodologies and practices for settler colonial studies. *Settler Colonial Studies, 7*(4), 496–517.

Chatterjee, S. (2019). Immigration, anti-racism, and Indigenous self-determination: Towards a comprehensive analysis of the contemporary settler colonial. *Social Identities, 25*(5), 644–661.

Corkindale, G. (2011, 11 February). The importance of organizational design and structure. *Harvard Business Review, 1*. https://hbr.org/2011/02/the-importance-of-organization

Crenshaw K. (1991). Mapping the margins: intersectionality, identity politics, and violence against women of color. *Stanford Law Review, 43*(6), 1241–1299.

Crenshaw K. (1992). Whose story is it anyway? Feminist and antiracist appropriations of Anita Hill. In T. Morrison (Ed.), *Raceing justice, engendering power*. Pantheon.

Crenshaw, K. (1989). Demarginalizing the intersection of race and sex: A black feminist critique of antidiscrimination doctrine, feminist theory and antiracist politics. *University of Chicago Legal Forum, 1989*(1), Article 8. https://chicagounbound.uchicago.edu/uclf/vol1989/iss1/8

Crenshaw, K. (1995). Mapping the margins. In K. Crenshaw, N. Gotanda, G. Peller, & K. Thomas (Eds.), *Critical race theory: The key writings that formed the movement* (pp. 357–383). The New Press.

Cullen, P., Mackean, T., Walker, N., Coombes, J., Bennett-Brook, K., Clapham, K., ... & Longbottom, M. (2022). Integrating trauma and violence informed care in primary health care settings for First Nations women experiencing violence: a systematic review. *Trauma, Violence, & Abuse, 23*(4), 1204–1219.

Darity, W., & Nembhard, J. G. (2000). Racial and ethnic economic inequality: The international record. *American Economic Review, 90*(2), 308–311.

Davis, K. (2020). Who owns intersectionality? Some reflections on feminist debates on how theories travel. *European Journal of Women's Studies, 27*(2), 113–127.

Dei, G. J. S. (1999). The denial of difference: Refraining anti-racist praxis. *Race Ethnicity and Education, 2*(1), 17–38.

Dei, G. J. S., & Asgharzadeh, A. (2001). The power of social theory: The anti-colonial discursive framework. *Journal of Educational Thought (JET)/Revue De La Pensée Éducative, 35*(3), 297–323.

Dei, G. J. S., & Lordan, M. (2013). Chapter eleven: Conclusion: Where does critical anti-racism theory lead us? Considering educational, policy, and community implications. *Counterpoints, 445*, 183–185.

Denzin, N. K., Lincoln, Y. S., & Smith, L. T. (Eds.). (2008). *Handbook of critical and indigenous methodologies.* SAGE.

DiAngelo, R. (2018). *White fragility: Why it's so hard for white people to talk about racism.* Beacon Press.

Donohue. J., & Levitt. S. (2001). The impact of legalized abortion on crime. *Quarterly Journal of Economics, 116*(2), 379–420, https://doi.org/10.1162/00335530151144050.

Doyle, M. W., & Stiglitz, J. E. (2014). Eliminating extreme inequality: A sustainable development goal, 2015–2030. *Ethics & International Affairs, 28*(1), 5–13.

Dubner, S. J. (2019). Abortion and crime, revisited [Ep. 384], Freakonomics. https://freakonomics.com/podcast/abortion/

Elwood, J., & de Oliveira Andreotti, V. (2021). Conspicuous consumption economies of virtue and the commodification of indigeneity. *Public, 32*(64), pp. 121–133. https://doi.org/10.1386/public_00077_1

Fanon, F. (1961/2004). *The wretched of the earth* (Richard Philcox, Trans.). Grove Press.

Fanon, F. (1963). *Sur la culture nationale.* Australian HR Institute.

Fanon, F. (1970). *Black skin, white masks.* Paladin.

Gaywsh, R., & Mordoch, E. (2018). Situating intergenerational trauma in the educational journey. *in education, 24*(2), 3–23.

Hall, C. (2019). *Social work as narrative: Storytelling and persuasion in professional texts.* Routledge.

Hand, S. (2005). *Catholic Voices in a World on Fire.* Traditional Catholic Reflections and Reports. Lulu.com.

Hankivsky, O., & Cormier, R. (2011). Intersectionality and public policy: Some lessons from existing models. *Political Research Quarterly, 64*(1), 217–229.

Hirschmann, A. O. (1970). *Exit, voice and loyalty: Responses to decline in firms, organizations, and states.* Cambridge, MA: Harvard University Press.

Howitt, R., Muller, S., & Suchet-Pearson, S. (2009). Indigenous geographies. In *International encyclopedia of human geography* (pp. 358–364). Elsevier.

Irwin. R., & White. T. (2019). Decolonising technological futures: A dialogical tryptich between Te Haumoana White, Ruth Irwin, and Tegmark's artificial intelligence. *Futures, 112.* https://doi.org/10.1016/j.futures.2019.06.003

Jimmy, E., & de Oliveira Andreotti, V. (2021). Conspicuous consumption: Economies of virtue and the commodification of Indigeneity. *Public, 32*(64), 121–133.

Kauffman, S. A. (1993). *Origins of order: Self-organization and selection in evolution.* Oxford University Press.

Kezelman, C. (2014, 12 June). *Trauma informed practice.* Mental Health Australia. https://mhaustralia.org/general/trauma-informed-practice

Kovach, M. (2015). Emerging from the margins: Indigenous methodologies. In S. Strega & L. Brown (Eds.), *Research as resistance: Revisiting critical, Indigenous, and anti-oppressive approaches* (pp. 43–64). (2nd ed.). Canadian Women's Press.

Kovach, M. (2021). *Indigenous methodologies: Characteristics, conversations, and contexts.* University of Toronto Press.

Lee, E. (2017). Performing colonisation: The manufacture of Black female bodies in tourism research. *Annals of Tourism Research, 66*, 95–104.

Lensmire, T., McManimon, S., Tierney, J. D., Lee-Nichols, M., Casey, Z., Lensmire, A., & Davis, B. (2013). McIntosh as synecdoche: How teacher education's focus on white privilege undermines antiracism. *Harvard Educational Review, 83*(3), 410–431.

Luban, D. (1999). The Warren Court and the concept of a right. *Harvard Civil Rights-Civil Liberties Law Review, 34*, 7–37.

Martin, K., & Mirraboopa, B. (2003). Ways of knowing, being and doing: A theoretical framework and methods for indigenous and indigenist re-search. *Journal of Australian Studies, 27*(76), 203–214. https://doi.org/10.1080/14443050309387838

Mattsson, T. (2014). Intersectionality as a useful tool: Anti-oppressive social work and critical reflection. *Affilia, 29*(1), 8–17.

McIntosh, P. (1988). *White privilege and male privilege: A personal account of coming to see correspondence through work in women's studies* (Working Paper 189: 1–20). Wellesley, MA: Wellesley Center for Research on Women.

McIntosh, P. (2018). White privilege and male privilege. In M. Kimmel & A. Ferber (Eds.), *Privilege* (pp. 28–40). Routledge.

McMillan, M., & Rigney, S. (2018). Race, reconciliation, and justice in Australia: From denial to acknowledgment. *Ethnic and Racial Studies, 41*(4), 759–777.

Menzel, K. (2021). *Shaken, not stirred. An Aboriginal woman's experience of the academy.* [Unpublished doctoral dissertation]. Deakin University.

Menzel, K., & Cameron, L. (2021). A meeting of freshwater and saltwater: Opening the dialogue of Aboriginal concepts of culture within an academic space. In T. McKenna & P. Onesta (Eds.), *Indigenous knowledges* (pp. 117–146). Brill.

Merton, T. (1967). *Mystic and Zen master.* Farrar, Strauss and Giroux.

Mohamed. S., Png. M., &Isaac, W. (2020). Decolonial AI: Decolonial theory as sociotechnical foresight in artificial intelligence. *Philosophy & Technology, 33*, 659–684. https://doi.org/10.1007/s13347-020-00405-8

Moodie, N., Maxwell, J., & Rudolph, S. (2019). The impact of racism on the schooling experiences of Aboriginal and Torres Strait Islander students: A systematic review. *Australian Educational Researcher, 46*, 273–295. https://doi.org/10.1007/s13384-019-00312-8

Museus, S. D., & Griffin, K. A. (2011). Mapping the margins in higher education: On the promise of intersectionality frameworks in research and discourse. *New Directions for Institutional Research, 2011*(151), 5–13.

Nair, N., & Selvaraj, P. (2021). Using a cultural and social identity lens to understand pandemic responses in the US and India. *International Journal of Cross Cultural Management, 21*(3), 545–568.

O'Sullivan, S. (2019). A lived experience of Aboriginal knowledges and perspectives: How cultural wisdom saved my life. In J. Higgs (Ed.), *Practice wisdom* (pp. 107–112). Brill.

Pickens, I. B., & Tschopp, N. (2017). *Trauma-informed classrooms.* National Council of Juvenile and Family Court Judges.

Pidgeon, M. (2016). More than a checklist: Meaningful Indigenous inclusion in higher education. *Social Inclusion, 4*(1), 77–91.

Preisler, J. (2013). Being safe vs. feeling safe. *Views of Foster Care and Adoption in North Carolina. Fostering Perspectives, 17*(2). Being Safe vs. Feeling Safe

Rigney, L. I. H. (2003). *Indigenous education, languages, and treaty: the redefinition of a new relationship with Australia.* Aboriginal Studies Press.

Schneider, M. (2002). A stakeholder model of organizational leadership. *Organization Science, 13*(2), pp. 209–220.

Schneider. M., & Somers. M. (2006). Organizations as complex adaptive systems: Implications of Complexity Theory for leadership research. *Leadership Quarterly, 17*(4), 351–365. https://doi.org/10.1016/j.leaqua.2006.04.006

Science in Australia Gender Equity (SAGE). (2015). SAGE pathway to Athena Swan. https://scienceg enderequity.org.au/sage-accreditation-and-awards/sage-pathway-to-athena-swan/

Simmons, M., & Sefa Dei, G. J. (2012). Reframing anti-colonial theory for the diasporic context. *Postcolonial Directions in Education, 1*(1), 67–99.

Smith, L. T., Tuck, E., & Yang, K. W. (Eds.). (2018). *Indigenous and decolonizing studies in education.* Routledge.

Uhl-Bien, M., Marion, R., & McKelvey, B. (2007). Complexity leadership theory: Shifting leadership from the industrial age to the knowledge era. *Leadership Quarterly, 18*(4), 298–318.

United Nations. (2007). United Nations Declaration on the Rights of Indigenous Peoples. www.un.org/development/desa/indigenouspeoples/wp-content/uploads/sites/19/2018/11/UNDRIP_E_web.pdf

Universities Australia. (2022). *Indigenous Strategy 2022–25*. Universities Australia. www.universitiesaustralia.edu.au/wp-content/uploads/2022/03/UA-Indigenous-Strategy-2022-25.pdf

Van der Kolk, B. (2022). Posttraumatic stress disorder and the nature of trauma. *Dialogues in Clinical Neuroscience, 2*(1), 7–22.

Vizenor, G. (1999). *Manifest manners: Narratives on post Indian survivance*. University of Nebraska Press.

Wintoneak, V., & Blaise, M. (2022). Voicing Derbarl Yerrigan as a feminist anti-colonial methodology. *River Research and Applications, 38*(3), 435–442.

# 8

# INDIGENOUS VOICE AS SELF-DETERMINATION

## Co-designing a shared future for all Australians

*Bronwyn Fredericks*

### Introduction

The Uluru Statement from the Heart invites the broader Australian public to "walk with us in a movement of the Australian people for a better future" (Uluru Statement from the Heart, 2021). Since its inception in 2017, the movement to enact the Statement's three guiding principles of Voice, Treaty and Truth, has gained significant momentum. Despite numerous roadblocks and the actions of those who have sought to misrepresent the reforms proposed, support amongst the wider Indigenous and non-Indigenous community continues to grow.

In this chapter, I provide an account of the progression of the Uluru Statement from the Heart (hereafter 'the Statement') by drawing on peer-reviewed literature and media gathered until the time of writing in 2022. I approach the discussion from a reflexive futurist perspective where I imagine a future in which a constitutionally enshrined First Nations Voice to Parliament has successfully been decreed by the Australian public via a referendum.

Future-proof practices that draw on networks of relationality and emphasise obligations to past, present and future generations is a defining feature of many Indigenous epistemologies (Martin and Mirraboopa, 2003). Some First Nations knowledge systems in North America, for example, apply 'seventh generation' principles in which decisions are made with consideration of the impact for seven generations into the future. Speaking on seventh-generation principles, Clarkson, Morrissette, and Regallet (1992, p. 76) argue that

> The concept of inter-generational equity, embodied in the teaching of the seventh generation, points out the necessity of ensuring the survival of future generations to a society whose heavy discounting of the future has resulted in a massive degradation of the world inherited from their parents and grandparents.

While the idea of past and present generations is commonly referenced in Acknowledgements to Country in Australia,[1] along with words that speak to 'a better future', the degree to which policy decisions truly reflect this sentiment is questionable. It is disturbing to note that many of the injustices and disparities between Indigenous and non-Indigenous peoples,

DOI: 10.4324/9781003271802-10

which existed seven generations in Australia's past (approximately during the turn of the century), remain pervasive today (Lowitja Institute, 2021). If outcomes do not change, the same injustices will extend well into the future.

I ask that you now walk with me through my words on these pages in a future that I hope will come to fruition in the coming years. As you do, contemplate whether this is a future you desire for yourself, your family, friends and communities—a future where intergenerational equity is assured and protected. Think of the world in seven generations' time, the steps needed to make it a reality, and the importance of creating constitutional reform via enshrining a First Nations Voice to Parliament. In this chapter, I have written of an imaginary future where a referendum for a Voice has been successfully voted in by the Australian public. I do so in hope of emphasising its plausibility and potential to be a life-changing event in Australia's modern history.

## What is the Uluru Statement from the Heart?

The Uluru Statement from the Heart is the culmination of 13 regional dialogues held with Indigenous communities throughout Australia from 2016 to 2017 (Davis & Williams, 2021). The dialogues were facilitated by the Referendum Council, a federally funded Indigenous-led body assigned to investigate and document Indigenous communities' views on how constitutional reform should look and the steps needed to achieve it (Davis et al., 2018a; Referendum Council, 2017). Previous discussions on constitutional reform had overlooked the voices of Indigenous communities, despite it being on the Indigenous agenda for years. According to constitutional lawyer Megan Davis, governments were in the habit of prioritising the voices of a select group of 'elites' who purported 'to speak on the mob's behalf' with no authority to do so (Davis et al., 2018b).

On 23 to 26 May, 2017, the First Nations National Constitutional Convention was held on the lands of the Anangu people in the Northern Territory to discuss the findings of the dialogues and how this should be disseminated to the public (Appleby & Davis, 2018; Larkin & Galloway, 2018). Some 250 delegates attended the convention, representing each region consulted. While the convention involved robust discussion amongst delegates, one point of consensus was that reforms must be lasting and meaningful. This sentiment was the product of decades of governmental disregard of Indigenous voices and advisory bodies (Moreton-Robinson, 2009). Indigenous peoples were adamant towards rejecting the piece-meal offering made by former governments, including having Aboriginal and Torres Strait Islander peoples symbolically recognised in the preamble of Australia's constitution without assurance of meaningful systemic change (Huggins, 2018; Morris & Pearson, 2017).

Through the dialogues, Aboriginal and Torres Strait Islander peoples were demanding greater representation in the parliamentary process and the political decisions that impact their interests and rights (Appleby & Davis, 2018; Synot, 2019). Instead of proposing a legislated body appointed by government, which would be susceptible to changing political agendas and budgets, delegates sought that a representative voice be written into Australia's constitution, guaranteeing its continuation (Martin, 2018).

On 30 June 2017, the Referendum Council's final report was delivered to the then prime minister, Malcolm Turnbull, and the leader of the opposition, Bill Shorten. The report fully endorsed the Uluru Statement from the Heart and recognised it as a reflection of the wishes of over 1,200 Indigenous delegates consulted. It took just four months for the Turnbull government to reject the statement, describing it as neither "desirable or capable of winning acceptance in a referendum" (Davis & Williams, 2021, p. 173). Turnbull believed the reforms were not 'saleable' to the public due their being too 'radical', with no realistic prospect of passing a referendum (Wahlquist, 2017). As observed by Megan Davis (2018a), Shorten's willingness to break the trend of bipartisan agreement on Indigenous affairs and commit his support to an enshrined Voice to the Parliament was promising (Davis, 2018a; Fredericks & Bradfield, 2021a). The coalition's stranglehold of government for the years that followed, however, significantly hindered progression, with the successive then prime minister Scott Morrison indicating that there would be no policy change under his government (Karp, 2018).

In the years that followed, some vocal and high-profile politicians, including the then-deputy prime minister, Barnaby Joyce, and Turnbull's successor, former prime minister Morrison, sought to derail the campaign by misrepresenting the Voice as a 'third chamber' of Parliament (Fredericks & Bradfield, 2021a; 2021b). The misrepresentations were carried on by commentators and the media (Fredericks & Bradfield 2021c; 2021d). This false characterisation, described by the now minister of Indigenous affairs, Linda Burney, as an act of 'scaremongering', suggested that the Voice to Parliament would interfere with Australia's parliamentary and legislative process (Hobbs & Jones, 2022; Karp, 2018).

The Voice to Parliament (as opposed to a voice *in* parliament and a voice to *government*) was never intended to hold parliamentary powers to legislate or veto policies (Dolar, 2019). It was always intended, and is now operating, as a non-binding advisory body through which Indigenous perspectives may be voiced and considered during discussions (Davis & Williams, 2021). This standpoint was clearly documented by the Referendum Council (2017, p. 38), which stated that the "proposed Voice would not interfere with parliamentary supremacy, it would not be justiciable, and the details of its structure and functions would be established by Parliament through legislation that could be altered by Parliament".

The Voice has offered a practical way of inserting Indigenous perspectives into parliamentary debates, encouraging politicians to confront and address Indigenous peoples' questions, concerns, opinions and suggestions before decisions are made and legislation voted on (Davis & Williams, 2021). While the 2022 election resulted in a record number of Indigenous candidates being elected across all parties—three in the house of representatives and seven in the senate (Zaunmayr, 2022)—it does need to be remembered that a politician's stance on policy is shaped and constrained by their party's political agenda and the directives of the parliamentary whip. That is, while they are Indigenous peoples, they represent their political parties, and their respective political party policy platforms, and all the constituents in their individual electorates.

Despite the increase in Indigenous people in parliament, Indigenous peoples as a distinct group have long been under-represented in the Australian political system. The First Nations Voice to Parliament offers an opportunity to integrate community representation into debates in a way that accommodates Indigenous peoples and is free from the constraints that are often attached to political parties. It inserts a uniquely 'Black' voice that honours Indigenous self-determination as enshrined in international documents such as the United Nations Declaration on the Rights of Indigenous Peoples (UN General Assembly, 2007). Roy Ah-See, one of the leaders of the Uluru Statement awareness campaign, History Is Calling, declared our collective will by stating that we "don't want a green voice, we don't want a red voice, we don't want a blue voice: we want a black voice" (Cassidy, 2022, para. 6). However, as I discuss in further detail below, this 'Black Voice' can both coexist with, and remain independent of, Western political structures.

### Can the Statement coexist with the sovereignty of the Crown?

In his call for new ways of thinking about critical Indigenous well-being, Brendan Hokowhitu (2017, p. 3) contends that "the future is merely a manifestation of how we perceive the present, or rather what we see as lacking in the present". Hokowhitu (2020; 2007) argues for a future where Indigenous sovereignty is re-centred and the superiority and dominance of Western epistemologies and frameworks, challenged. The re-centring of Indigenous sovereignty must recognise Indigenous cultures as fluid, diverse and free of romanticisation (Hokowhitu, 2017; Hollinsworth et al., 2021; Langton, 1994). Indigenous voices should not be enclosed or essentialised but provided a space that honours them and enables them to coexist—but not necessarily conform or align—with Western structures on equal terms. If the future is 'what we see as lacking in the present', what was lacking in 2017 in Australia was a constitutionally enshrined First Nations Voice that assured that Aboriginal and Torres Strait peoples were adequately represented and given the opportunity to express their sovereignty during parliamentary discussions.

The enshrinement of a First Nations Voice was a long, arduous and hard-fought campaign. It did not come easy and was met with criticism by numerous critics who sought to sidetrack its progression (Fredericks & Bradfield, 2021a; Hobbs & Williams, 2019). Prior to the 2022 federal election, the campaign was met with resistance from some Indigenous critics (Larkin & Maguire, 2020), the government and high-profile commentators who ignored the will of the Australian public who overwhelmingly expressed support for a constitutionally enshrined Voice (Hobbs & Jones, 2022). Post-election, the mood had shifted to a more optimistic outlook. However, the wording of the referendum question and the structure of the Voice mechanism posed additional challenges that needed ironing out. While public debate is valid and necessary, activists within the campaign did not want it becoming a distraction which would delay or sidetrack progression. Some individuals, such as Yiman and Bidjara scholar Marcia Langton, who was appointed co-chair of the Senior Advisory Group overseeing the Indigenous Voice Co-design Process alongside Kungarakan human rights campaigner Tom Calma, emphasised her opinion that all details of the mechanism should be finalised *before* the referendum was put to the public (Brown, 2022).

Others, including the prime minister, however, argued that a referendum was not predicated on finalising such details, but rather should affirm the public's will to establish a First Nations Voice to Parliament (Wright, 2022). The referendum is an enabling provision (Davis, 2022b); it is a first step from which the Voice can be further debated, hashed out and molded in response to how Indigenous stakeholders wish to have their views represented. The Voice is not designed to be bounded within the constitution but rather protected by it (Appleby, 2021). It should remain fluid enough to shift and adapt to the will of Indigenous peoples over time. In response to criticisms that the campaign was lacking direction, Megan Davis (2022b, para. 17) wrote:

> The idea that there is no meat on the bones of what a voice might look like is a furphy. The model of the voice has been developed since 2017 over three key processes that

have involved Indigenous-run dialogues, a parliamentary inquiry and a government-led consultation.

As the years advanced, we eventually arrived at a future where a First Nations Voice to Parliament provided a space where systemic problems could be addressed, while the diversity of communities' needs and the different approaches to addressing them could be considered. The Uluru Statement from the Heart speaks to a present where the social injustices towards Indigenous peoples continue, recognising the obligation to create a better future for forthcoming generations,

> Proportionally we are the most incarcerated people on the planet. We are not innately criminal people. Our children are alienated from their families at unprecedented rates. This cannot be because we have no love for them. And our youth languish in detention in obscene numbers. They should be our hope for the future.
>
> (The Uluru Statement, 20122, para. 6)

In seeking a constitutionally enshrined First Nations Voice to Parliament in 2017, Indigenous activists, scholars, lawyers and community members were calling to establish a space where Indigenous peoples could insert their voices and sovereign rights in a manner that "co-exists with the sovereignty of the Crown" (The Uluru Statement, 2022, para. 3). Indigenous sovereignty is described by Goenpul scholar Aileen Moreton-Robinson (2020, p. 259) as being "in and of the earth", existing beyond the Western state and systems of law. Indigenous peoples' sovereign and custodial right to land is also recognised in the Statement, which declares:

> sovereignty is a spiritual notion: the ancestral tie between the land, or 'mother nature', and the Aboriginal and Torres Strait Islander peoples who were born therefrom, remain attached thereto, and must one day return thither to be united with our ancestors.
>
> (The Uluru Statement, 2022, para. 3)

Previous political structures have long failed to recognise the link between humans and place, or what Aboriginal and Torres Strait Islander people now call Country. Political decisions are predominantly made from Western ontological standpoints that separate the so-called natural environment from human society. This fails to recognise the land as a parent to which Indigenous peoples hold responsibilities to protect and nurture (Moreton-Robinson, 2020). The Uluru Statement, however, has provided a mechanism that is beginning to balance Western-centric decision-making by ensuring representation of Country and community in dialogues. The Voice to Parliament has effectively inserted Indigenous understandings into political discussions, forcing a reorientation of how some policies are constructed and implemented. As a result, new partnerships where multiple disciplinary backgrounds intersect have emerged (Neale et al., 2014).

Without continuing and sustained pressure for lasting change, policies can quickly turn into tokenistic gestures, empty promises and acts of 'white benevolence' (Foley & McKinnon, 2008). Speaking on former prime minister Kevin Rudd's apology to the Stolen Generations in 2007, Foley and McKinnon (2008, p. 1) have observed how such acts often become "part of future white Australian mythology about how wonderfully they have always treated the Aboriginal people. It will become part of white Australia's long history of denial". Rudd's apology was his government's first act in Parliament, yet rates of child removal continued to parallel those of the Stolen Generations (Sue-Anne et al., 2021), as did incarceration rates, despite the findings of the Royal Commission into Aboriginal Deaths in Custody (Dodson, 2018; Dodson et al., 1991).

Fifteen years after Rudd's apology, the current prime minister Anthony Albanese committed to holding a referendum on a First Nations Voice to Parliament in the opening statement of his acceptance speech. While this was a momentous occasion, we have long known that political rhetoric and commitments do not always translate to meaningful action. The Voice to Parliament, which proved to have overwhelming public support during the referendum when it was finally held during Labor's first term of government, has successfully held governments to account by providing context and testimony that help prevent discourses from falling into colonial habits of denial and self-gratuity. It has provided representation on Indigenous people's own terms—expressed and articulated in a manner less likely to be manipulated by predominantly non-Indigenous governments, and political parties. McKinnon (2014, p. 376) has further argued that Indigenous texts:

> are not dependent upon our relationships with colonisation or contact with white people. Understanding the texts we produce as a part of the practice of being from a sovereign Aboriginal group, not limited by colonial concepts of time, but moving beyond those borders assists us to wrestle the Aboriginal texts from all-encompassing colonial encounters.

The Voice to Parliament that we had long waited for since the referendum was announced in 2022 provides a mechanism through which Indigenous texts are shared and inserted into national dialogues in ways where Indigenous peoples retain autonomy and sovereignty of their own representation. Referring to Aboriginal writers, but equally applicable to the community and regional representatives who form the Voice, McKinnon states, "through the stories that they tell, Aboriginal writers add the experiential and lived dimension to the government and organisational reports which statistics and figures cannot capture" (McKinnon, 2019, p. 210).

It has long been known within Indigenous health and Aboriginal Community Controlled Health Organisations that the most successful health programmes have invested in preventative and early-interventionist strategies (Gubhaju et al., 2019); have worked in an integrated manner with their partners; and have maintained self-governance (Crooks et al., 2020; Dudgeon et al., 2012). Gubhaui and colleagues (2019) have called for more longitudinal studies that examine health trajectories of Indigenous peoples over time. While the Voice to Parliament does not function as a research body, it nonetheless plays a role in documenting and reporting outcomes via parliamentary discussions and records. The Voice to Parliament has the potential to provide longitudinal evaluation of how the Government *responds* to the evidence it is provided with—resulting in greater and mutual accountability (Davis, 2022b).

In the National Empowerment Project, community members from the Toomelah community expressed the importance of having a clear vision for the future whilst healing community via addressing and moving forward from past injustices, a view that is shared among many Indigenous communities (Dudgeon et al., 2014). Community ownership, culturally and locally appropriate programmes, strengths-based approaches, flexibility, and respect for gender were all identified as contributing to Indigenous communities' healing. The need to heal is also recognised in the Uluru Statement, which declares: "Makarrata is the culmination of our agenda: the coming together after a struggle. It captures our aspirations for a fair and truthful relationship with the people of Australia and a better future for our children based on justice and self-determination" (The Uluru Statement, 2022, para. 10).

During consultations for the design of the Voice to Parliament, Indigenous peoples spoke on the importance of a community-led design which would enable communities to come together, work together and ultimately heal (Australian Government 2021, p. 41). Colonisation and racism continue to have intergenerational impacts on health, education and other outcomes. For many Aboriginal people, such as Tracey Bunda (in Manathunga et al., 2020, p. 16), truth is a collaborative exercise that demands non-Indigenous "settler invaders speak, know and embody" colonial and Indigenous truths, recognising the myths of terra nullius, the legal fiction that classified the land now known as Australia as uninhabited, and accepting the continuation of Indigenous sovereignties. Pat Dudgeon (2020, p. 103) has also noted how strengths-based apporaches help heal communities, for they build "the capacities of individual, families, and communities to survive adverse life events across generations and enable practitioners to build on existing capabilities".

## An appetite for change

Public support leading to the referendum for constitutional change was consistent and strong throughout the Uluru campaign. In 2017, 71 per cent of the public supported a referendum to constitutionally enshrine a First Nations Voice to Parliament (Centre for Governance and Public Policy, 2017), with online polling showing an overwhelming preference to formally recognise Indigenous peoples in the constitution (Referendum Council, 2017). By 2020, Reconciliation Australia's 'Reconciliation Barometer Survey' showed that 81 per cent of the public felt it important to constitutionally protect an Indigenous representative body. The Australian Constitutional Values Survey (Centre for Governance and Public Policy, 2021) also indicated that 60 per cent of respondents wanted a First Nations Voice to Parliament, with 51 per cent expressing a desire for it being constitutionally enshrined. Only 21 per cent of respondents were against this prospect (Deem et al., 2021).

In 2021, the Australian government opened public submissions as part of its co-design process, which would inform the scaffolding of a future First Nations Voice. Of the 2,554 public submissions assessed by the UNSW Indigenous Law Centre (3062 public submissions were received in total), 90 per cent supported constitutional change, with 87 per cent directly calling for constitutional enshrinement (Phelan, 2021). Submissions represented a cross-section of the Australian public with 61 per cent coming from non-Indigenous organisations and individuals (Larkin et al., 2021).

In the wake of the federal election in 2022, surveys by the Australian Broadcasting Corporation (ABC) indicated that three-quarters of Australians were in favour of constitutional change, with the majority coming from Labor (82 per cent) and Greens (92 per cent) voters, as opposed to 43 per cent amongst Liberal-National voters (Wellauer & Brennan, 2022). Whilst statistics slightly varied between polls, they consistently demonstrated that most of the Australian public would overwhelmingly support a constitutionally enshrined Voice to Parliament, should they be given the opportunity to have their say via a referendum—which history proved accurate.

In 2021, the Uluru Statement was awarded the Sydney Peace Prize for its contribution in providing a clear and measured pathway towards realising reconciliation in Australia (Dale, 2021; Fredericks, 2022a). Archie Law, chair of the Sydney Peace Foundation, said that the Statement "provides the leadership that we desperately crave to achieve respect, recognition, and reconciliation" (Sydney Peace Foundation, 2021, para. 13). Acknowledgement via awards such as these helped solidify the campaign as one that was of relevance to all Australians, Indigenous and non-Indigenous alike.

The Statement promotes peace through its emotive language that emphasizes unity and inclusivity in a manner atypical of legal documents. Anandakugan (2020, para. 6) stated that it is "regarded as a political deeply human statement seeking to secure dignity for Australia's First Nations". The Uluru Statement from the Heart is unlike any other declaration previously presented to the government. It is a concise one-page testimony that outline's Indigenous peoples' will for a better future for Aboriginal and Torres Strait Islander peoples, and for the nation. What distinguishes it from previous documents such as the Barunga Statement (1988), or the Yirrkala Bark Petition (1963) is that a conscious decision was made to gift it to the Australian people as opposed to the government (Mayor, 2020). Pat Andersen, co-chair of the Referendum Council that released the final report in 2017, stated that Indigenous peoples did not want to see the Statement 'imprisoned' behind glass walls, but rather that it should remain in community until its proposed reforms have been implemented (Zhou, 2021).

The Statement, therefore, is a living document that travelled across the country, allowing people to witness it and add their own names on subsequent documents and petitions. The Uluru Canvas (From the Heart, 2020), organized as part of the From the Heart campaign, for example, provided an opportunity for the public to put a face to their messages of support, creating far-reaching networks on social media (Fredericks & Bradfield, 2021a, 2021b, 2021c, 2021d). Whilst an enshrined Voice to Parliament has now been achieved. The importance treaty and truth-telling continues and the Uluru Statement lives on.

## An intergenerational fight for change

In April 2022, delegates from across Australia, including representation from multiple Aboriginal Lands Councils,[2] Indigenous leaders, and emerging Indigenous leaders, youths and lawyers, along with Elders, many whom also campaigned for constitutional change in 1967, met in Cairns and Yarrabah to reaffirm their support for the Uluru Statement. This was a pivotal moment in the campaign as 2023 marked the 56th anniversary of the 1967 referendum (Karp, 2022; Wellauer, 2022). With this date looming, and the nation heading towards an election where the incoming government would have significant influence on when (and if) a referendum would be called, delegates, of whom I was one, were acutely aware of the need to act *immediately*. I remember the words of Anangu man Sammy Wilson, Custodian of Mutitjulu and past chair of the Central Land Council, talking about what it meant to him, and his people, and the sense of *urgency* that was needed.

I recall listening to Elders such as Alfred Neal—a key figure in the 1967 campaign—who provoked me to think of all those who fought and campaigned for constitutional reform before me, many of whom had passed away before seeing it come to fruition (D. Butler, 2022). We found ourselves in a similar position 55 years later. I was left questioning whether figures such as Megan Davis, Pat Anderson, Noel Pearson, Eddie Synott, Dani Larkin, Sally Scales, Janine Coombs, Janine Gertz, Hannah McGlade, and many, many thousands of others, including myself, would ever see constitutional reform in our lifetimes—and if the same fight would continue in seven generations' time. We owed it to those who struggled before us (and for the future generations who would carry on their legacy) to make a substantial push for constitutional change.

It was decided that a referendum should be held on 27 May 2023, the anniversary of the 1967 referendum and six years since the gifting of the Uluru Statement from the Heart. An alternate date of 27 January 2024 (Gooley, 2022) was also decided to allow for an extended awareness campaign. We outlined this in the Yarrabah Affirmation where we stated, "Who would have thought that history and the future would coincide and give us such a day? There is great premonition in this" (Yarrabah Affirmation, 2022, para. 9).

Since the European arrival, necessity, and an obligation to fight injustice, has transferred from one generation to the next. In *Growing Up Aboriginal in Australia* (Heiss, 2018), Anita Heiss' anthology of Indigenous peoples' reflections on their Indigeneity, Ambelin Kwaymullina (cited in Heiss 2018, p. 111) reflects on her vision for Australia's future:

> I want to be old in the way my ancestors were old, those brave, wise men and women who survived the colonial cataclysm. Their lives were ones of grinding injustice and yet they never lost their sense of hope or their sense of humour. It was they who carried the future and held it safe within themselves in the face of determined efforts to destroy all of what makes Indigenous people who they are. Like them, I look forward to an Australia in which everyone can breathe. Perhaps I will never see it in my lifetime.

While we knew the struggle would continue, we retained hope that a Voice to Parliament would help Australia 'breathe', and that it was very much achievable in our lifetime. Regardless of the results of the 2022 election, we knew that pressure had to be sustained. If a Liberal and National Party Morrison-led government retained power, its trajectory towards establishing a legislated Indigenous voice to government, or the prolonged wait for a so-called consensus to be reached, had to be redirected towards the wishes of the Australian public, who overwhelmingly were demanding constitutional enshrinement.

If the Australian Labor Party a government, its leader, Anthony Albanese, had to be held to his commitment of holding a referendum in the first term of government. While we would not be dissuaded by the possible outcome of the election, we knew that we had to act immediately, and history proved us right. Only six weeks after we had met in Cairns, the Australian Labor Party won the 2022 election with Albanese indicating his support for a referendum in his opening statement, declaring,

> I begin by acknowledging the traditional owners of the land on which we meet. I pay my respects to their Elders past, present and emerging. And on behalf of the Australian Labor Party, I commit to the Uluru Statement from the heart in full.
>
> (in ABC News, 2022, para. 3)

This was a significant moment in the campaign and gave Indigenous peoples hope that the horrific gaps across numerous health, education, employment, housing, justice, and other social outcomes would finally be guided by the voices and needs of Indigenous peoples.

## The Voice as a pathway to treaty and national reform

In their submission to the Queensland Productivity Commissions' (QPC) inquiry into service delivery in remote and discrete Aboriginal and Torres Strait Islander communities (2017), the Cape York Institute (CYI) highlighted the need to develop the 'right policy framework' to reach the goal of Closing the Gap[3] across numerous outcomes for Indigenous peoples. The QPC's report, which the CYI described as "the most important policy document produced in the state of Queensland since the *Protection Act* was legislated in 1897" (CYI 2017, p. 3), provided a framework for reform at a state level. They say that the state and local governments might have been willing to support local communities to "ensure that the right structures and processes" were in place and that a coherent system of good governance, capable of enabling development and "the long-term viability of First Nations and discrete Indigenous communities" existed (CYI 2017, p. 4). As the presiding commissioner for the inquiry, I knew what the submissions all said, and what I had heard at round tables, and in meetings, and through the public forums. Community members, local governments and Indigenous organisations wanted systemic and structural change.

In addition to the QPC's report, along with Queensland's Tracks to Treaty project (Queensland Government, 2018), and the subsequent processes, other states such as South Australia were pursuing their own voice mechanism (McLoughlin & Boisvert, 2022); the Noongar in Western Australia had secured the South West Native Title Settlement, worth over 1.3 billion dollars (Piesse, 2018; South West Aboriginal Land and Sea Council, 2018); and Victoria had created a First Peoples' Assembly (Allam, 2019; First Peoples' Assembly Of Victoria, 2022) and were well on their way towards drafting a Treaty. Federal support, however, is still needed to create meaningful and lasting change at a national level. Now that a constitutionally enshrined First Nations Voice to Parliament has been established, Indigenous peoples finally have a political forum to amplify the success of state and local treaties and partnerships, opening an inclusive dialogue that will work towards the negotiation of a federal/national treaty.

A national treaty process was always envisioned as part of the reforms proposed at Uluru in 2017. In the years that preceded the enshrinement of the Voice, however, there was some debate over the sequence of Voice, Treaty, Truth, and concerns about sovereignty and a preference to push for a treaty rather than constitutional reform (Rigney, 2021). Some individuals and political parties spoke against the sequencing of the Statement (J. Butler, 2022). Some were preferencing Truth and then Treaty before Voice, while others were preferencing Treaty before Truth and Voice (Parkin, 2020). Their opposition was premised on the idea that constitutional recognition can only come *after* a process of truth-telling was engaged and a treaty reached (Le Grand, 2020).

Very careful consideration to the sequencing of Voice, Treaty and Truth, however, was given by the delegates at the First Nations National Constitutional Convention. During the regional dialogues, communities expressed their concerns at the restructuring of the Indigenous Advancement Strategy by the Nation Audit Office, which resulted in funding cuts and a convoluted application/evaluation process. The criteria according to which organisations and service providers received funding were unclear, undocumented and seemingly arbitrary to community workers and representatives. Concerns over the Native Title process (and the rift it often causes between families), as well as the need for the processes of a national treaty/treaties, were all raised as issues in need of immediate address (Davis, 2018b). A feeling of discontent was evident, with many communities feeling that tokenistic and invasive enquiries and commissions into issues such as Aboriginal deaths in custody exposed truths but rarely resulted in structural change (Dale, 2021). The need for immediate change was noticeable.

Communities expressed that a national representative Voice would allow greater Indigenous involvement and transparency of political processes, providing a line of communication where the interests of local communities could flow into national dialogues and vice versa. Constitutional lawyer and member of the Referendum Council Megan Davis (2018a, p. 40) recognised this, stating:

> One of the innovative decisions of the dialogues was that the Voice could provide a front-end political limit on the parliament's power to make laws for Indigenous peoples [...] [it] is about bringing back to the state the footprint of First Nations and imbuing the decision-making of the government and bureaucracy with the cultural authority and cultural legitimacy of the foundation of Indigenous culture, the land and its ancient polities.

Having a representative Voice as the first component of the Uluru Statement—and it being mandated by the public via a successful referendum—has provided a mechanism that now advises 'both chambers of Parliament on laws and policies' which impact Indigenous peoples. It has allowed discussions of a national treaty to be appropriately framed and designed in partnership with Indigenous peoples (Larkin & Galloway, 2021, p. 194). The Voice is now guiding the national treaty-making process and providing a platform on which First Nations people can work in partnership with parliament and negotiate equitable outcomes for the future (Larkin & Maguire, 2020). Greater participation in the political system is encouraged, providing Indigenous peoples with the institutional political power that was lacking before the referendum. With constitutional enshrinement, the Voice provides the Uluru Statement with political legitimacy and empowers Indigenous people with the political capital and tools necessary to unsettle and challenge the Australian legal system from within. Now that we have passed a referendum for a representative First Nations Voice to Parliament, our attention can be directed towards negotiating a treaty process.

## The Voice is a means, not an end

Despite the progress made since the enshrinement of the Voice, there is still much to be organised and negotiated about drafting a treaty and implementing initiatives that work towards Closing the Gap in a meaningful way. History and international examples have demonstrated that treaties are notoriously difficult to come to fruition, and when they do, they are easily broken or are limited due to statutory powers existing outside its formal instruments (Appleby & Synot, 2020; Pearson & Morris, 2017; Young & Hobbs, 2021). Davis (2022a) has also noted that not all communities are ready or equipped with the same capital to negotiate a treaty. We still have some way to go on the federal front. In 2017, the need for immediate action was recognised by the delegates at Uluru, along with the awareness that time was a luxury we simply do not have. Throughout the campaign, activists repeated the mantra 'the time for action is now!' (Fredericks, 2021, 2022b), until action was finally taken via a referendum. As declared throughout the campaign (counter to highly publicised false characterisations of how the Voice would operate), the Voice does not function as a third chamber, nor does it give the representative body veto powers. The gears of the Westminster political system continue to turn, and at times churn.

The First Nations Voice to Parliament, however, has secured Indigenous peoples a seat at the table where representatives contribute to political dialogues using our own voices that are free of political party allegiances and which are accountable to the communities they represent. The CYI (2017, p. 4) identified that the greatest and often most neglected challenge to bureaucratic reform relates to how reforms are implemented and its assurances that they are "long term [and] learns from past mistakes and successes". Enshrining the First Nations Voice within Australia's constitution has secured its longevity. Learning from past mistakes and successes, however, is an ongoing process.

Australia is still very much on the journey towards Makarrata[4] and continues to 'come together after a struggle'. For better or worse, the struggle will always be remembered. Hokowhitu (2017, p. 2) has highlighted that while Indigenous peoples do not want to recall colonial histories,

> it is similarly one we cannot suppress in relation to Indigenous wellbeing for if colonisation did anything it made Indigenous peoples unwell through the confinement of the Indigenous body, the subjugation of Indigenous political resistance, and the obliteration of Indigenous ways of knowing.

In seven generations' time, it is hoped that such subjugation and obliteration will become a distant memory rather than a transgenerational inheritance. The enshrined Voice to Parliament has proven effective in providing a line of communication that links local, regional and state agreements to federal agendas. We are beginning to see the turning of the tide where policies pertaining to Indigenous peoples are now being implemented in ways that empower Indigenous communities whilst building capacity. The Voice has been successful in holding existing parliamentary chambers and governments to account, while also providing a consultative source of information that has helped co-design effective and culturally responsible policy. Years have passed since preparations were made in 2022 for a referendum on a First Nations Voice, and over those years Indigenous peoples have successfully partnered with governments to fully realise the targets long sought in Closing the Gap (Coalition of Peaks, 2020). Life expectancy gaps between Aboriginal and Torres Strait Islander peoples, for example, have closed significantly via policies informed by Indigenous expertise in health.

There is still much work to be done to address the disadvantages that continue to plague our communities. When co-designing the Voice, we were never under the illusion that a representative body would instantly translate to social justice for Indigenous peoples. Improved outcomes remain partly dependent on non-Indigenous peoples and systems *listening* and responding to what Indigenous peoples are telling them. What we were fighting for, however, was a genuine opportunity to create lasting and meaningful change.

The Coalition of the Peaks—the peak body for Indigenous service provision, formed in July 2020—has made strides in closing disparities between Indigenous and non-Indigenous Australians by improving services, yet they initially struggled to hold the government to account. The National Agreement on Closing the Gap (Coalition of Peaks, 2020) was fast in danger of becoming yet another empty promise characterised by government 'intent' that manifested in indifference and inaction.

Now that we have a First Nations Voice to Parliament, we have been able to demand accountability by holding the government's policies, commitments and rhetoric to account. We have provided valuable input that has shaped meaningful and culturally appropriate policies that are framing prosperous Indigenous futures. Our voices have directly called out government inaction within the very systems where promises, policies and praxes are decided on. We have been able to propose community-led solutions that are continuing to create new trajectories for Indigenous peoples. While the political paradigms we work in remain centred within white ontological structures, Indigenous voices are playing a significant role in shifting the Australian polity.

Indigenous peoples have long envisioned this, as outlined in the *Wiyi Yani U Thangani (Women's Voices)* report conducted by the Australian Human Rights Commission in 2020. This report, led by Aboriginal and Torres Strait Islander Social Justice Commissioner June Oscar AO, outlines (Australian Human Rights Commission, 2020, p. 86):

> Our right to self-determination can, and must, be fulfilled within a united Australian polity. It will, however, require Australian governments to imagine a future outside of the bounds of rigid Western models: a future in which we are given room to rebuild structures that reflect who we are as distinct peoples; and a future which allows for our structures to be interwoven into the fabric of a reconciled nation.

The Uluru Statement from the Heart was always intended to be a marathon, not a sprint, and while we still have some way to go before arriving at our destination of a 'reconciled nation', the Voice to Parliament is an indication that 'base camp' is now behind us. Irene Watson (2012, p. 14) once spoke of Aboriginal peoples' burden of having to prove 'our continuing sovereignty' while the state's lawful authority went uncontested. To this we say no more. Indigenous peoples' voices to Australia's parliament—now protected by the constitution—have allowed us to assert our sovereign right to govern our lives, build policy for the benefit of all people (Indigenous and non-Indigenous alike), and challenge the very authorities that seek to impose their will on us, without us.

## Conclusion

Over the course of seven generations past, Aboriginal and Torres Strait Islander peoples have been subjugated by countless dehumanising government policies that have sought to control every aspect of Indigenous peoples' lives, denying Indigenous sovereignty and humanity. Despite this, Indigenous peoples have continuously practised their cultures on unceded lands, resisting oppressive colonial regimes by 'talkin up' (Moreton-Robinson, 2021) to the systems that seek to deny their very existence and stunt their wealth, progression and success. In this chapter, I have taken a somewhat optimistic position that imagines a future where a First Nations Voice to Parliament has already passed a referendum. This future, however, is yet to be decided.

In 2023/4, all voting Australians will have their chance to answer a question (yet to be worded) that will ask if they support a First Nations Voice to Parliament. As discussed throughout this chapter, an enshrined First Nations Voice has the potential to build the infrastructure that will help design the policies that will Close the Gap across numerous disparate outcomes, and create a more equitable future, now and in seven generations' time. If this opportunity is squandered, it is possible that the mistakes of the past will be doomed to be repeated; the current Indigenous-led successes that are already having real impact on communities will not reach their full potential; and seven future generations will inherent the same exhausting fight for basic human rights and recognition. The Uluru Statement from the Heart reads: "In 1967 we were counted, in 2017 we seek to be heard" (The Uluru Statement, para. 12), and to this I add: in 2022 we ask that you accept our invitation to walk with us in a movement of the Australian people for a better future.

## Notes

1   An Acknowledgement to Country is a verbal or written expression of respect where a person recognises the Traditional Owners and their ancestors of the location(s) on which they gather. Both Indigenous and/or non-Indigenous people from any location can perform an Acknowledgement to Country whilst a Welcome to Country can only be performed by someone who has kinship and cultural ties to that specific place.
2   Aboriginal Land Councils are bodies of elected Indigenous members who oversee land and sea management and advocacy for local Aboriginal populations at the state level of government.
3   Closing the Gap is a political agenda that seeks to address the disparities between Indigenous and non-Indigenous populations across a range of social outcomes. In 2022, this was expanded to focus on increasing Aboriginal and Torres Strait Islander participation and input in the design and delivery of policies, programmes and services.
4   *Makarrata* is a Yolngu word associated with conflict resolution and one that translates to "come together after a struggle" (Gaykamangu, 2012). The Uluru Statement calls for a 'Makarrata Commission' to supervise agreement-making and truth-telling between all levels of government and Indigenous peoples.

## References

ABC News. (2022, 22 May). Read incoming prime minister Anthony Albanese's full speech after Labor wins federal election. *ABC News.* www.abc.net.au/news/2022-05-22/anthony-albanese-acceptance-speech-full-transcript/101088736?utm_campaign=abc_news_web&utm_content=link&utm_medium=content_shared&utm_source=abc_news_web.

Allam, L. (2019, 11 April). Victoria a step closer to Indigenous treaty with creation of First Peoples' Assembly. *The Guardian.* www.theguardian.com/australia-news/2019/apr/11/victoria-a-step-clo ser-to-indigenous-treaty-with-creation-of-first-peoples-assembly.

Anandakugan, N. (2020, 6 January). The Uluru Statement from the Heart: Contextualizing a First Nations Declaration. *Harvard International Review,* https://hir.harvard.edu/the-uluru-statement-from-the-heart-contextualizing-a-first-nations-declaration/

Appleby, G. (2021. 22 January). An Indigenous 'Voice' must be enshrined in our Constitution. Here's why. *The Conversation.* https://theconversation.com/an-indigenous-voice-must-be-enshrined-in-our-constitution-heres-why-153635

Appleby, G., & Davis, M. (2018). The Uluru statement and the promises of truth. *Australian Historical Studies, 49*(4), 501–509. https://doi.org/10.1080/1031461X.2018.1523838

Appleby, G., & Synot, E. (2020). A First Nations Voice: Institutionalising political listening. *Federal Law Review, 48*(4), 529–542. https://doi.org/10.1177%2F0067205X20955068

Australian Government. (2021). *Indigenous Voice Co-design Process: Final Report to the Australian Government.* National Indigenous Australians Agency: Canberra. https://voice.niaa.gov.au/sites/default/files/2021-12/indigenous-voice-co-design-process-final-report_1.pdf

Australian Human Rights Commission. (2020). *Wiyi Yani U Thangani (Women's Voices): Securing Our Rights, Securing Our Future—Report.* https://humanrights.gov.au/sites/default/files/docum ent/publication/ahrc_wiyi_yani_u_thangani_report_2020.pdf

Brown, G. (2022, 11 July). Voice should be fuly formed before poll: Langton. *The Australian.* www.theaustralian.com.au/subscribe/news/1/?sourceCode=TAWEB_WRE170_a_GGL&dest= https%3A%2F%2Fwww.theaustralian.com.au%2Fnation%2Findigenous-voice-should-be-fully-formed-before-referendum-marcia-langton%2Fnews-story%2Fb310e07ed641cfb5b73c1d075 b824d0e&memtype=anonymous&mode=premium&v21=dynamic-high-test-score&V21spcbe haviour=append

Butler, D. (2022, 11 April). Yarrabah Affirmation calls for Voice referendum in next parliamentary term. *NITV News.* www.sbs.com.au/nitv/article/yarrabah-affirmation-calls-for-voice-referendum-in-next-parliamentary-term/xpm4ww1de

Butler, J. (2022, 14 October). Lidia Thorpe wants action on treaty and truth before campaigning for Indigenous voice. *The Guardian.* www.theguardian.com/australia-news/2022/oct/14/lidia-thorpe-wants-action-on-treaty-and-truth-before-campaigning-for-indigenous-voice

Cape York Institute (CYI). (2017). CYI submission in response to the draft report. *Queensland Productivity Commission Inquiry into Service Delivery in Queensland's remote and discrete Indigenous Communities.* Queensland Productivity Commission. www.treasury.qld.gov.au/queenslands-economy/office-of-productivity-and-red-tape-reduction/former-queensland-productivity-commission/

Cassidy, C. (2022, 9 May). Australians urged to back Indigenous voice to parliament in History is Calling campaign. *The Guardian.* www.theguardian.com/australia-news/2022/may/09/australi ans-urged-to-back-indigenous-voice-to-parliament-in-history-is-calling-campaign

Centre for Governance and Public Policy. (2017). *Australian Constitutional Values Survey 2017: Results Release 2.* https://news.griffith.edu.au/wp-content/uploads/2017/10/Griffith-Univers ity-UNSW-Australian-Constitutional-Values-Survey-Sept-2017-Results-2.pdf

Centre for Governance and Public Policy. (2021). *Australian Constitutional Values Survey 2021: Results Release 1,* Brisbane, CQ University. www.cqu.edu.au/__data/assets/pdf_file/0021/ 190092/australian-constitutional-values-survey-2021.pdf

Clarkson, L., Morrissette, V., & Régallet, G. (1992). *Our responsibility to the seventh generation: Indigenous peoples and sustainable development.* International Institute for Sustainable Development Winnipeg. www.iisd.org/publications/our-responsibility-seventh-generation

Coalition of Peaks. (2020). *New national agreement on closing the gap.* https://coalitionofpeaks.org. au/new-national-agreement-on-closing-the-gap/

Crooks, K., Casey, D., & Ward, J. S. (2020). First Nations people leading the way in COVID-19 pandemic planning, response and management. *Medical Journal of Australia, 213*(4), 151–152. https://doi.org/10.5694/mja2.50704

Dale, A. (2021). *From the heart: Enshrining constitutional recognition.* Law Society of New South Wales. https://lsj.com.au/articles/from-the-heart-enshrining-constitutional-recognition/ #:~:text=In%202017%2C%20the%20Uluru%20Statement,for%20Voice%2C%20Treaty%20 and%20Truth

Davis, M. (2018a). The long road to Uluru: Walking together—truth before justice. *Griffith Review, 60.* www.griffithreview.com/articles/long-road-uluru-walking-together-truth-before-just ice-megan-davis/

Davis, M. (2018b). Voice, treaty, truth. *The Monthly.* www.themonthly.com.au/issue/2018/july/153 0367200/megan-davis/voice-treaty-truth.

Davis, M. (2022a). Speaking up: The truth about truth-telling. *Griffith Review, 76,* 25–35.

Davis, M. (2022b). A voice of recognition. *Weekend Australian.* www.theaustralian.com.au/inquirer/ a-voice-of-recognition/news-story/c0901c504bee2a467f0fbea358c8e631

Davis, M., & Williams, G. (2021). *Everything you need to know about the Uluru Statement from the Heart.* UNSW Press/NewSouth Publishing.

Davis, M., Dixon, R., Appleby, G., & Pearson, N. (2018a). The Uluru Statement. *Bar News: The Journal of the NSW Bar Association* (Autumn 2018), 41. https://search.informit.org/doi/10.3316/ agispt.20180726000224

Davis, M., Saunders, C., Mckenna, M., Morris, S., Mayes, C., & Giannacopoulos, M. (2018b). The Uluru Statement from Heart, one year on: Can a First Nations Voice yet be heard? *ABC.* www.abc. net.au/religion/the-uluru-statement-from-heart-one-year-on-can-a-first-nations-v/10094678

Deem, J., Brown, A. J., & Bird, S. (2021, 8 April). Most Australians support First Nations Voice to parliament: survey. *The Conversation.* https://theconversation.com/most-australians-support-first-nations-voice-to-parliament-survey-157964

Dodson, P. (2018). Constitutional recognition. *International Journal of Applied Psychoanalytic Studies, 15*, 124–127. https://doi.org/10.1002/aps.1574

Dodson, P., Wootten, H., O'dea, D., Wyvill, L., & Johnston, E. (1991). *Royal Commission into Aboriginal Deaths in Custody: Final Report.* National Archives of Australia. www.naa.gov.au/explore-collection/first-australians/royal-commission-aboriginal-deaths-custody

Dolar, S. (2019). Law Council explains government's key misunderstanding of the Uluru Statement. *Australasian Lawyer.* www.thelawyermag.com/au/news/general/law-council-explains-governments-key-misunderstanding-of-the-uluru-statement/208247?m=1. 5 November

Dudgeon, P. (2020). Decolonising psychology. In B. Hokowhitu, A. Moreton-Robinson, L. Tuhiwai-Smith, C. Andersen, & S. Larkin (Eds.), *Routledge handbook of critical indigenous studies,* (pp. 100–113). Taylor & Francis Group.

Dudgeon, P., Cox, A., Walker, R., Scrine, C., Kelly, K., Blurton, D., Bolardaras, J., Bracknell, C., Brennan, T., & Butorac, A. (2014). *Voices of the People: The National Empowerment Project: National Summary Report 2014: Promoting Cultural, Social and Emotional Wellbeing to Strengthen Aboriginal and Torres Strait Islander Communities.* University of Western Australia. https://research-repository.uwa.edu.au/en/publications/voices-of-the-peoples-the-national-empowerment-project

Dudgeon, P., Cox, K., D'anna, D., Dunkley, C., Hams, K., Kelly, K., Scrine, C., & Walker, R. (2012). *Hear our voices: Community consultations for the development of an empowerment, healing and leadership program for Aboriginal people living in the Kimberley, Western Australia.* Centre for Research Excellence, Aboriginal Health & Wellbeing.

First Peoples' Assembly of Victoria. (2022). *Treaty for Victoria: First Peoples' Assembly of Victoria.* www.firstpeoplesvic.org/

Fredericks, B. (2021, 23 March). An Indigenous voice: The time for action is now! *Westender.* https://westender.com.au/an-indigenous-voice-the-time-for-action-is-now/

Fredericks, B. (2022a, 27 May). Time to wear your uluru heart on your sleeve. *Westender.* https://westender.com.au/time-to-wear-your-uluru-heart-on-your-sleeve/

Fredericks, B. (2022b). Why I still hear it on the radio and I 'still' see it on the television: Treaty and the Uluru statement from the heart. *Journal of Australian Indigenous Issues, 25*, 3–21. https://search.informit.org/doi/10.3316/informit.692861368672485

Fredericks, B., & Bradfield, A. (2021a). Co-designing change: Discussing an Indigenous voice to Parliament and constitutional reform in Australia. *M/C Journal, 24*(4). https://doi.org/10.5204/mcj.2801

Fredericks, B., & Bradfield, A. (2021b). 'More than a thought bubble…': The Uluru Statement from the Heart and an Indigenous voice to Parliament. *M/C Journal, 24*(1). https://doi.org/10.5204/mcj.2738

Fredericks, B., & Bradfield, A. (2021c). 'Seeking to be heard': The role of social and on line media in advocating the Uluru Statement from the Heart and constitutional reform in Australia. *Journal of Alternative & Community Media, 6*(1) Special Issue: Community and activist media: resistance and resurgence, 29–54. https://doi.org/10.1386/joacm_00092_1

Fredericks, B., & Bradfield, A. (2021d). Addressing the roadblocks of constitutional change through mobilising Indigenous voices online. *Journal of Global Indigeneity, 5*(2). www.journalofglobalindigeneity.com/article/29806-addressing-the-roadblocks-of-constitutional-change-through-mobilising-indigenous-voices-online

From the Heart. (2020). *The Uluru Statement—From the Heart.* https://fromtheheart.com.au/

Gaykamangu, J. G. (2012). Ngarra law: Aboriginal customary law from Arnhem Land. *Northern Territory Law Journal, 2*, 236–248.

Gooley, C. (2022, 11 April). Indigenous leaders lay out referendum dates as action urged on Voice. *Sydney Morning Herald.* www.smh.com.au/politics/federal/indigenous-leaders-lay-out-referendum-dates-as-action-urged-on-voice-20220411-p5ack3.html

Gubhaju, L., Banks, E., Ward, J., D'este, C., Ivers, R., Roseby, R., Azzopardi, P., Williamson, A., Chamberlain, C., & Liu, B. (2019). Next Generation Youth Well-being Study: Understanding the health and social well-being trajectories of Australian Aboriginal adolescents aged 10–24 years: Study protocol. *BMJ open, 9*(3). http://dx.doi.org/10.1136/bmjopen-2018-028734

Heiss, A. (2018). *Growing up aboriginal in Australia.* Black Inc.

Hobbs, H., & Jones, B. T. (2022). Egalitarian nationhoods: A political theory in defence of the voice to parliament in the Uluru Statement from the heart. *Australian Journal of Political Science, 57*(2), 1–16. https://doi.org/10.1080/10361146.2022.2028720

Hobbs, H., & Williams, G. (2019). Trust and the constitution. In M. Evans, M. Ngrattan, & B. Mccaffrie (Eds.), *From Turnbull to Morrison: Australian Commonwealth Administration 2016–2018—understanding the trust divide.* Melbourne University Publishing.

Hokowhitu, B. (2007). Voice and the postmodern condition. *Junctures: The Journal for Thematic Dialogue, 9*, 7–13.

Hokowhitu, B. (2017). Weaving past, present and future. *Journal of Indigenous Wellbeing: Te Mauri–Pimatisiwin, 2*(1), 2–3.

Hokowhitu, B. (2020). Introduction. In B. Hokowhitu, A. Moreton-Robinson, L. Tuhiwai-Smith, C. Andersen, & S. Larkin (Eds.), *Routledge handbook of critical indigenous studies*, (pp. 1–5). Taylor & Francis Group.

Hollinsworth, D., Raciti, M., & Carter, J. (2021). Indigenous students' identities in Australian higher education: Found, denied, and reinforced. *Race Ethnicity and Education, 24*(1), 112–131. https://doi.org/10.1080/13613324.2020.1753681

Huggins, J. (2018). Reflections on the reconciliation journey. *Journal of Australian Indigenous Issues, 21*, 72–77.

Karp, P. (2018, 26 September). Scott Morrison claims Indigenous voice to parliament would be a third chamber. *The Guardian.* www.theguardian.com/australia-news/2018/sep/26/scott-morrison-claims-indigenous-voice-to-parliament-would-be-a-third-chamber

Karp, P. (2022, 7 July). Labor plans to hold referendum on Indigenous voice to parliament in 2023. *The Guardian.* www.theguardian.com/australia-news/2022/jul/07/labor-plans-to-hold-referendum-on-indigenous-voice-to-parliament-in-2023

Langton, M. (1994). Aboriginal art and film: The politics of representation. *Race & class, 35*(4), 89–106. https://doi.org/10.1177%2F030639689403500410

Larkin, D., & Galloway, K. (2018). Uluru Statement from the Heart: Australian Public Law Pluralism. *Bond Law Review, 30* (2), 335. https://doi.org/10.53300/001c.6796

Larkin, D., & Galloway, K. (2021). Constitutionally entrenched Voice to Parliament: Representation and good governance. *Alternative Law Journal, 46*(3), 193–198. https://doi.org/10.1177%2F1037969X211019807.

Larkin, D., & Maguire, A. (2020, 7 July). Lidia Thorpe wants to shift course on Indigenous recognition. Here's why we must respect the Uluru Statement. *The Conversation.* https://theconversation.com/lidia-thorpe-wants-to-shift-course-on-indigenous-recognition-heres-why-we-must-respect-the-uluru-statement-141609

Larkin, D., Buxton-Namisnyk, E., & Appleby, G. (2021). What did the public say about the government's Indigenous Voice co-design process? *UNSW Sydney Newsroom.* https://newsroom.unsw.edu.au/news/business-law/what-did-public-say-about-government%E2%80%99s-indigenous-voice-co-design-process

Le Grand, C. (2020, 25 June). Without treaty, incoming senator can't feel part of 'Team Australia'. *Sydney Morning Herald.* www.smh.com.au/national/without-treaty-incoming-senator-can-t-feel-part-of-team-australia-20200625-p55649.html

Lowitja Institute. (2021). *Leadership and Legacy through Crises: Keeping Our Mob Safe.* Close the Gap Campaign Report 2021. The Close the Gap Campaign Steering Committee and Indigi Print.

Manathunga, C., Williams, P., Bunda, T., Stanton, S., Davidow, S., Gilbey, K., & Raciti, M. (2020). Decolonisation through poetry: Building First Nations' voice and promoting truth-telling. *Education as Change, 24*(1), 1–24. https://doi.org/10.25159/1947-9417/7765

Martin, K., & Mirraboopa, B. (2003). Ways of knowing, being and doing: A theoretical framework and methods for indigenous and indigenist re-search. *Journal of Australian Studies, 27*, 203–214.

Martin, W. A. (2018). Constitutional Law Dinner 2018 Address. 23 February, 2018. Parliament House, Sydney. www.supremecourt.wa.gov.au/_files/Speeches/2018/Constitutional%20Law%20Dinner%202018%20by%20Martin%20CJ%2023%20Feb%202018.pdf

Mayor, T. (2020). When the heart speaks. *Griffith Review*, 10–17. https://search.informit.org/doi/abs/10.3316/informit.655973771771383

Mckinnon, C. (2008). Duplicity and deceit: Gary Foley's take on Rudd's apology to the stolen generations. *Melbourne Historical Journal, 36*, 1–7.

Mckinnon, C. (2014). From scar trees to a 'bouquet of words': Aboriginal text is everywhere. In T. Neale, C. McKinnon, & E. Vincent (Eds.), *History, power, text* (pp. 371–383). UTS ePress. https://doi.org/10.5130/978-0-9872369-1-3.v

Mckinnon, C. (2019). The lives behind the statistics: Policing practices in Aboriginal literature. *Australian Feminist Law Journal*, 45(2), 207–223. https://doi.org/10.1080/13200968.2020.1800931.

Mcloughlin, C., & Boisvert, E. (2022, 12 June). Consultation to start on SA Indigenous Voice to Parliament ahead of 2023 launch. ABC News. www.abc.net.au/news/2022-06-13/consultation-to-start-on-sa-voice-to-parliament/101147480

Moreton-Robinson, A. (2009). Imagining the good indigenous citizen: Race war and the pathology of patriarchal white sovereignty. *Cultural Studies Review, 15*, 61–79.

Moreton-Robinson, A. (2020). Incommensurable sovereignties: Indigenous ontology matters. In B. Hokowhitu, A. Moreton-Robinson, L. Tuhiwai-Smith, C. Andersen, & S. Larkin (Eds.), *Routledge handbook of critical indigenous studies* (pp. 257–268). Taylor & Francis Group.

Moreton-Robinson, A. (2021). *Talkin'up to the white woman: Indigenous women and feminism*. University of Minnesota Press.

Morris, S., & Pearson, N. (2017). Indigenous constitutional recognition: Paths to failure and possible paths to success. *Australian Law Journal, 91*(5), 350–359.

Neale, T., Mckinnon, C., & Vincent, E. (2014). *History, power, text: cultural studies and indigenous studies*. UTS ePRESS.

Parkin, D. (2020). The Uluru statement is not Lego. The Greens can't rearrange it to suit their ideals. *Crikey*. www.crikey.com.au/2020/10/16/greens-uluru-statement-position/

Pearson, N., & Morris, S. (2017). *A rightful place: A road map to recognition*. Black Inc.

Phelan, A. (2021, 3 May). Indigenous Voice: Overwhelming support for constitutional enshrinement. *UNSW Sydney Newsroom*. https://newsroom.unsw.edu.au/news/business-law/indigenous-voice-overwhelming-support-constitutional-enshrinement

Piesse, E. (2018, 17 October). Australia's biggest native title settlement, worth $1.3b, registered three years after deal struck. ABC News. www.abc.net.au/news/2018-10-17/australia-biggest-native-title-claim-worth-$1.3b-registered/10386774

Queensland Government. (2018). *Tracks to treaty: Statement of commtment*. www.datsip.qld.gov.au/resources/datsima/programs/tracks-to-treaty/tracks-to-treaty-soc.pdf

Queensland Productivity Commission. (2017). *Service delivery in remote and discrete Aboriginal and Torres Strait Islander communities*. Queensland Productivity Commission. https://apo.org.au/sites/default/files/resource-files/2018-06/apo-nid179581_1.pdf

Referendum Council. (2017). *Final report of the Referendum Council*. Department of the Prime Minister and Cabinet (Australia). www.referendumcouncil.org.au/sites/default/files/report_attachments/Referendum_Council_Final_Report.pdf

Rigney, S. (2021). On hearing well and being well heard: Indigenous international law at the League of Nations. *TWAIL Review, 2*, 122–153. https://twailr.com/wp-content/uploads/2022/04/6.-Rigney-Indigenous-International-Law-at-the-League-of-Nations.pdf

South West Aboriginal Land and Sea Council. (2018). *About the Settlement Agreement*. South West Aboriginal Land and Sea Council. www.noongar.org.au/about-settlement-agreement

Sue-Anne, H., Burton, J., Blacklaws, G., Soltysik, A., Mastroianni, A., Young, J., Jones, M., Jayakody, N., Bhathal, A., & Krakouer, J. (2021). The Family Matters Report 2020: Measuring trends to turn the tide on the over-representation of Aboriginal and Torres Strait Islander children in out-of-home care in Australia. www.familymatters.org.au/family-matters-report-2020-reveals-aboriginal-and-torres-strait-islander-children-continue-to-be-separated-from-families-and-culture-at-an-alarming-rate/#:~:text=The%20report%20reveals%20a%20concerning,the%20age%20of%2018%20years

Sydney Peace Foundation. (2021). *2021–22 Uluru Statement from the Heart*. https://sydneypeacefoundation.org.au/peace-prize-recipients/2021-uluru-statement-from-the-heart/

Synot, E. (2019). The Universal Declaration of Human Rights at 70: Indigenous rights and the Uluru Statement from the Heart. *Australian Journal of International Affairs, 73*, 320–325. https://doi.org/10.1080/10357718.2019.1631252

Uluru Statement from the Heart. (2021). *The Statement—Uluru Statement from the Heart*. https://ulurustatement.org/the-statement

UN General Assembly. (2007). *United Nations Declaration on the Rights of Indigenous Peoples.* www.un.org/development/desa/indigenouspeoples/declaration-on-the-rights-of-indigenous-peoples.html

Wahlquist, C. (2017, 26 October). Indigenous Voice proposal 'not desirable', says Turnbull. *The Guardian.* www.theguardian.com/australia-news/2017/oct/26/indigenous-voice-proposal-not-desirable-says-turnbull

Watson, I. (2012). The future is our past: We once were sovereign and we still are. *Indigenous Law Bulletin, 8*(3), 12–15.

Wellauer, K. (2022, 11 April). Indigenous leaders say 'it's time for a referendum' on First Nations Voice to Parliament. ABC News. www.abc.net.au/news/2022-04-11/aboriginal-leaders-call-for-referendum-on-voice-to-parliament/100982290

Wellauer, K., & Brennan, B. (2022). Vote Compass data finds most Australians support Indigenous Voice to Parliament—and it has grown since the last election. ABC News. www.abc.net.au/news/2022-05-04/indigenous-voice-to-parliament-vote-compass/101031774?utm_campaign=abc_news_web&utm_content=link&utm_medium=content_shared&utm_source=abc_news_web

Wright, S. (2022, 31 July). Detail of Indigenous Voice to come after referendum: Albanese. *Sydney Morning Herald.* www.smh.com.au/politics/federal/detail-of-indigenous-voice-to-come-after-referendum-albanese-20220731-p5b5zj.html

Young, S., & Hobbs, H. (2021). Treaty-making: Critical reflections on critiques from abroad. In A. Whitaker, H. Hobbs, & L. Coombes (Eds.), *Treaty-making two hundred and fifty years later* (pp. 156–178). Federation Press. http://hdl.handle.net/10453/150149

Zaunmayr, T. (2022, 23 July). FULL LIST: Record number of Indigenous MPs voted in to serve the Australian people. *National Indigenous Times.* www.nit.com.au/full-list-record-number-of-indigenous-mps-voted-in-to-serve-the-australian-people/

Zhou, N. (2021, 26 May). Uluru Statement from the Heart awarded 2021 Sydney Peace Prize. *The Guardian.* www.theguardian.com/australia-news/2021/may/26/uluru-statement-from-the-heart-awarded-2021-sydney-peace-prize

# 9

# FUEL, FLAME AND SMOKE

## On Indigenous fantasy

*Travis De Vries*

### Introduction

I am a storyteller, artist and cultural critic. I create work of aspirational futurism that often involves violence as a mechanism to attain the aspirational political futurism. For context, I was born as a Gamilaroi person on occupied territory and I live as a Gamilaroi person on occupied territory. This is the reality of my existence.

I am not an academic. I have been described as an independent scholar. I am not an expert on economic, political or social issues. I am, however, a lived experience expert in being 'Aboriginal' and in understanding my place in relation to the state of 'australia'. I feel strongly about telling the stories that I, as an individual, believe should be told.

This is the reality of being that I bring to my fiction writing, my characters, my sense of place. All of it comes from this well.

### Fuel

It is often difficult to know what to write down from a story, particularly one that is yet to be told. How does one choose what are the important parts of a story? Of course, we should consider who the audience is. Who the reader will be. However, often the reader will come from a varied background with varied levels of contextual information and experiences that they bring that pollute their reading. No reader is a neutral party—more so when they are presented with what could be considered a work that is of a sensitive political nature. Work, for example, that presents a view with characters who ascribe to anarchist ideologies, characters who appear to be the 'heroes' central to the plot.

We should still consider the audience. However, we should not consider who the audience is; this is a variable that is ultimately outside of our control. Rather, we should speculate who we want the audience to be. Who is the ideal audience for this writing? Is it the young First Nations person with budding energy and ideas for change who could potentially emulate the characters contained wherein? Or do we write for the White gaze? Do we look to inspire within our own people, or look to change the minds of the people who currently have a hold over us?

DOI: 10.4324/9781003271802-11

The question of what to include in a story is very much centred on who the audience is. More so when we think of cultural stories and what they are used for: the passing on between generations and between groups of knowledge both public and secret. Parts of a story are kept back from certain people for a multitude of reasons. Certain younger people within the cultural group may not be judged ready for certain parts of the story at this time by the Elders of the cultural group. This is a tradition that is central to many First Nations cultural storytelling traditions (see Dillon, 2012).

What are the mechanisms within the writing that we use to withhold information within the work? There are a number of technical devices we can utilise from the Western traditions, alongside the First Nations traditions of storytelling to hide information, sometimes even in plain sight. These techniques include: red herrings, the planting of false information by characters, sleight of hand, the mishearing of conversations, and unreliable narrators. I would note that this list is not exhaustive (Laney et al., 2008). Storytelling traditions in my community often include an 'unreliable narrator' (Nünning, 2015) to hide information. At times this can also include letting the listener know that they are not ready for the information the story entails. Curiously, as most storytelling within this tradition is accompanied by associated cultural practices such as painting, song, dance or ceremony that the listener is often participating in, the omission of details within the framework of the story feels less important (Fricke, 2019). As an 'audience', you are conditioned to not be ready for certain parts of the story. For the Western audience, this omission of facts feels akin to a trick the writer is playing on them, or potentially even a lack of talent on the part of the writer (from the audience's perspective).

One of the other key devices for the withholding of information, and one that I attempt to use more and more, is 'implied action' (Duffield & Whitty, 2016). This is when a scene happens 'off camera' so the reader doesn't get to witness it from the perspective of the narrator. The audience only gets hints of what happens from the characters through their recounting of experiences or through their conversations about how they feel post-action. This device is a powerful tool if used well as it can keep tension high for the reader whilst allowing the writer to not have to spell out each and every moment of a scene. If writing from a first-person perspective, the writer can construct a sequence where, for obvious reasons, the character misses key action moments, or misses conversations or their experience of certain information, or actions are clouded by their own lack of knowledge. Using this device for storytelling has been a powerful way for me as writer of contemporary First Nations work to be able to choose what information an audience is 'allowed' to know from a cultural point of view.

Combining the concept of holding back specific cultural information with inter-community political discussions alongside impactful storytelling creates a vehicle for me as a writer and a First Nations person to explore what I view as potentially contentious ideologies that are much-needed discussion to be had within our communities. These ideologies will likely become more apparent in the reading of the short story and across more of my work. They range from social uprising of First Nations peoples, through to the use of violence and guerrilla warfare against an occupying force on stolen land, through to more micro discussions that should only be had in specific cultural communities.

In the following story I have ruminated on this practice and purposefully kept information back from the reader, information that may be pertinent to the crucible of the characters and to the story; however, arguably nothing is lost from the story and the reader can still follow the plot and enjoy the story. This is the public version of the story. There is another version that is not meant to be read by those who are not ready for it. There are titillating hints within this story of information that is yet to be known. There is the beginning of what I believe to be an important political conversation to be had. As Dillon (2012, p. 3) reminds us, "writers of Indigenous futurisms sometimes intentionally experiment with, sometimes intentionally dislodge, sometimes merely accompany, but invariably *change* the perimeters of sf [science fiction]". As such, this work fits perfectly within the speculative fiction genre of Indigenous Futurism.

It was late afternoon on the summer solstice, the longest day of the year. The cavern floor was clean and dry and smelt of sand, not the type of sand you find near water but sand that has been shaped by the slow decay of stone which has never felt sunlight upon its rough face. The cavern also smelt like wood smoke and a rich tea, a pot of which sat brewing beside a fire midway back into the cavern, the light barely noticeable from the cavern mouth.

A group of six people huddled together in the centre of the cavern, alternating between staring at the fire and at the old bent woman who sat nearby. A man came from the darkness at the rear of the cavern and with one badly scarred hand, lifted the teapot from its small iron table beside the fire. He took it to the old woman and poured her a deep cup of tea before offering it in turn to each of the other members of the group. A nod here or a guttural noise signalling a no there, he made his way around all of them slowly and with purpose before also taking a seat and looking expectantly at her.

The light of the fire flickered for just a moment and extinguished, and the cave went dark. A faint pink orange light still came in from the sunset streaming in through the mouth of the cavern nearly half a minute's walk away. The coals of the fire still glowed and spat sparks at each other. A breath of anxiousness went through the group as the man stood and gathered more sticks and logs from the cave wall and carried them in one trip to the firepit. He placed them with certainty, fed the fire and coaxed it back into flames as the darkness outside the cave became blue, then black.

'Feed it before it goes out next time, Fallon', the woman said and made a clicking noise at him with her lips.

Fallon, the man who had brewed the tea, smiled, his face lit by the now healthy fire. He signalled for one of the others to collect an armload of wood from the cave wall. 'Set it next to you and keep the fire going, or our Beloved Mother will have my head', his voice clear and dripping with honey. He was one of those men you could tell had been beautiful in his youth. The acolyte did as they were told and soon was poking the fire with one of the stouter branches.

The older woman sighed as she took a long sip of her tea and then wrapped the cup in the sleeves of her robes and folded it all in towards her stomach. She smiled and shook her head as she chuckled and her long hair spilt down around her shoulders. The light of the fire lit up her features. Her eyes were piercing and reflected the flame back at the group. She looked almost owlish perched up on her chair.

The fire also illuminated the ceilings and walls of the cavern. Sandstone, ancient and fragile. There were ochre drawings across the walls and parts of the ceilings, although they were too tall for even the tallest man to have been able to reach them. Gods, their arms outstretched or power radiating from their heads or stomachs, animals, humans, plants and landscape. A hundred, hundred stories must have been told on those walls.

The woman sat once more in mute silence for a moment. Maybe remembering, maybe lost in thought. A smile again made its way onto her face, starting at her chin and moving up into her cheeks. Shadows and light danced across the lines of her face, only for a moment and then the smile was gone, replaced with a look of hard determination.

'Shall we begin again?' Her voice was clear and was only punctuated by the crackle and hiss of the fire playing steadily once more in its place. A chorus of nods, grunts and murmurs of agreement.

'You are to listen, you are to hear, you are to remember. You will not write anything down. That is our way. We are storytellers. One day, one of you may tell this story, and it may change a little with your telling. Today you will listen and you will listen well.

'Your problem is you all want heroes. Everyone wants a story: big flashy magic, gods, forbidden love. You don't realise that what is real can be really messy. You don't always get heroes, or even if they are heroes to you now, in the moment, they didn't know what the fuck they were doing. We didn't know what the fuck we were doing.

'We didn't know what we were doing and yet we did it anyway. We made this world what it is now, and maybe this world isn't what it could be, but it's the one we have and we fought to make it this way'.

'First, we take Gamilaroi, then we can help everyone else'. Fallon's voice carried across the room and the seven seated around the table looked towards me, the eighth and newest member. The sounds of their own conversations quickly fading and forgotten, absorbed by the clear note of Fallon's that bounced tinnily around the plywood walls.

One of them, an Uncle, stood up from his chair and leaned against the table. 'No. We need to mobilise every tribe. It's all or nothing. Or we lose our allies in this'. Uncle Len was the eldest and usually any decision he made was taken on by the rest of the group and subsequently everyone in their community.

'If we take Gamilaroi, we could become a sanctuary for so many', Fallon argued with him. Not many ever did. You could tell Len was used to being the final word.

Another voice came from across the table. Aunty Sara was Uncle Len's cousin and backed him on everything. She huffed. 'Or we become a target. Mob will turn against us in droves if we stick out like tall poppies. A prize they only need to cut down for their own ascension'.

Fallon turned to stare sharply at her. Then I watched as his eyes softened. My plan was to get her and Len and everyone else at the table on my side, not get shut down before I'd even had a chance to get going. Fallon nodded towards where I was sitting.

'But if we were to unite everyone together and strike as one, there would be no stopping us. We are stronger together', I said.

Uncle Len spoke again, 'We don't even need to strike. If we are united, we will be listened to, our voices will be from the heart of all of us'.

'Or we all get wiped out together ...' The voice came from the back of the room. My voice. The shadows deep, the dust swirling in little eddies as the warm golden light from the fading sun streamed in through the window. 'Why would they decide to listen to us now? What could have possibly changed this year as opposed to the two hundred years of shit we've endured?'

'This goes against all of our cultural protocols, it goes against everything I believe in'. Sara spoke again, her head shaking and staring straight across the table and Uncle Len. They would try to stop us.

'Fuck the cultural protocols, Sara. They're just another weapon the whites have implanted to make us passive and complacent. There is no handbook for what we are about to do, there are no rules to this', Fallon said.

I echoed his voice. 'We've been planning this action for months; it's been in train for years if not decades if you'd remember my grandfather. You're getting cold feet now?'

My Grandfather had been a key member of the group. His death still stung me hard when I thought too much about it.

'It's not cold feet. I still think we should be moving but we should be doing it the right way …'

'What right way?' I cut in on Sara. These kinds of community conversations didn't always end. They never felt like there was an agreed conclusion. That's community though; it's messy. Everyone weighs in and has a say about a situation, and then people still go and do what they want to anyway. There is contempt that boils for months and even years within a community. There's also love and respect.

'With everyone, every single mob coming together with a collective voice. There's no point in just us making a move and then sticking out like a sore thumb'.

One of the others in the room spoke up from where they sat in their chair. 'When they arrived here on these shores, two hundred and fifty years ago, did we all fight together against them?'

'No, I wasn't there and you weren't either, Elaine', Sara almost spat at her. Those two had hated each other for years. At least a couple of meetings had ended with the two of them ready to fight. I knew I needed to step in or I'd lose them all.

I walked up towards the table and stood next to Uncle Len.

'No, we didn't all come together. They hit Dharug and they hit Darkinjung, then Awabakal, then us, then Wiradjuri. They took us each out one by one and we fell one by one. No one came to our aid. We called for assistance but no one came. No one understood until the white scourge fell onto them. Fuck some of those desert mob, didn't see any of them till the seventies'.

'And so shouldn't we try a different way now?' Uncle Len had turned to me. 'Shouldn't we try to keep talking, with everyone, and go together, be a part of a larger conversation?

'We are trying a different way. People have been trying all last century to bring everyone together, to create a unification, to speak to them on their terms. We need to speak to them on ours, though. We need to sit in our power, on our land'.

'You'd damn us all. If you fail, things will be worse than they ever were'. Sara's words were desperate although true. Things could be bad.

'It's better than doing nothing. I can't sit around like you lot have and wait for someone else to do something. I can't wait for someone to come and save all of us'.

I felt myself staring into the distance, replaying the conversation from the night before over and over in my head. I'd been going to the meetings for a long time, with Grandfather, with Uncle, with Dad. None had ever ended like that as far as I could remember. I needed to prove my point to them.

'Billie, you look hard right now', Fallon observed. Rosy smirked and let out a grunt and raised one eyebrow at me as she leaned out of the passenger seat window.

I was filling the car up, leaning onto the car with my hand holding the nozzle of the petrol hose. I suppose I looked good from his angle in the back of the car.

147

'What do you mean by that?' I questioned. 'I feel—'

'Nothing sexual la, just that you seem fired up, you look calm, I can feel your confidence from over here'.

'I was thinking about last night again'. I shrugged as the nozzle clicked and I tapped it twice before putting it back on the pump.

'So was I', Rosy said. Rosy had been in the room; she was the group secretary and would scribe things down. 'I stopped writing halfway through that. You were all so fired up, I wasn't sure what to write'.

'We can't wait any longer. I'm going to make a move, tonight'.

We were in the car, driving back into town after going out to the forest. Rosy, Fallon and me. Fallon was driving; it was his car. I was in the passenger seat and Rosy was slouched in the back. We'd been out at the grandmother tree, where we always went to talk about the things that were just for us.

'My dad had this theory … He'd tell me about when we'd be on long drives through country, when we'd be passing these big farm properties all owned by generations of white fellas who probably only owned them cause they'd killed mob or looked the other way while others did'.

'What was the theory, Billie'? Rosy could never let a story just happen the way a story was meant to. She always had questions, trying to keep it on a straight track.

'I'm getting there. We'd be driving past these big farms—houses were old, sheds were old, made from old trees, and the fences were wood and barbed wire. Half the time the farms weren't even growing anything anymore. The fences were all fallen down or falling down'. My voice fell into a cadence, like it always did when I'd tell, the same as my Grandfather's had. Rising and falling in volume and pitch. Letting certain words or phrases ring out. He'd never taught me how to do it. I'd just been around for so many of his stories that it had rubbed off. He could hold a whole pub in thrall with one of his stories.

'Dad would talk about how the whites gave all these places names from their homelands. All names from Britain, Scotland, France and Italy, but our country doesn't look a lick like those places. For one, the fences. Dad was always going on about the fences. In Europe and England their farm fences are all made of stone and rock. They're built to last like Stonehenge. Their fences over there are like that 'cause they're meant to be there.

'Here, though, all of the fences are made of wood and barbed wire. If they want to keep their fences, they have to replace them every twenty years or something, a couple of times a generation'.

'So, is that his theory? Fences?' Rosy rightly interrupted me again.

'Shut up, Rosy, I'm getting to it', I laughed.

'They built them like this out here because deep down somewhere, they know they're not meant to be here. Country doesn't want them here. They give our lands their own names to try to change that, try to cover over what Country is telling them, but they can't lie to themselves on a psychic level.

'On a psychic level they're not meant to be here. They weren't ever welcomed here. Their fences, their houses out here are so incredibly temporary. That was Dad's theory. I want to take it one step further though'.

'Oh yeah, what's one step further than not meant to be here?' Fallon only asked questions during stories when it was something he was interested in. He could be so reserved most of the time, though if you piqued his interest, he would be so intensely focused.

'Well, the rocks they built with down on Dharug country, they're Dharug rocks. They probably don't want them here either, and all we need to do is wake them back up and they'll do what they need to do'.

'They're just rocks, Billie, like in your head. What you going to do, speak them into turning into dust'?

'I don't know yet, alright, Rosy? I really don't know. It's still just theory at this point'.

'That's why we have this'. Fallon held up the petrol can. 'We can't rely on your fucking fence and rock theory'.

Fallon poured the petrol onto the floor of the room and then dropped the can. The noise of the can hitting the old, wet rug. The patterns of the rug showed its age and mixed with the darker colours where the petrol had flowed across it and onto the old wood floors. The smell of the petrol was overpowering and mixed with the smells of the room, the wood oil, the old rug smell. I felt my mind swim a little. The fumes made the room wave a little, like an old television just off-channel.

Rosy stood looking at a solid wooden and glass cabinet filled with different items and their labels. Among the items was an old wooden camera along with some black and white photographs of the town during a parade, a hat from a soldier named Douglas Howe who had gone to some war overseas, a wooden nula, carved with nails stuck into it, and a crystal stone with what appeared to be wax and hair on one end of it.

'Hey, come take a look at these', Rosy called to Fallon and me.

Fallon blew out the match he'd just lit, careful not to let a spark leave the tip and fall to the ground where it would certainly take up quickly. He and I walked to the cabinet and looked.

'Some of this stuff shouldn't go up with the rest of the chambers', Rosy said.

'Definitely not!' Fallon remarked. 'You want any of it?'

'I'd like the camera, actually. It's pretty cool', Rosy replied.

'You know we can't get caught with any of this stuff. If we do, we're done'. I stood looking into the cabinet intently for a moment, then I sighed.

'Go on then'. The words ran together. The soft vowel sounds bleeding into each other. 'Gorn then'.

Fallon stepped back for a moment, then kicked the front glass of the cabinet hard. The glass pushed in at the edge, splintering the wood, and then smashed with a sound that caused the three of us to wince the way only the sound of glass smashing can.

'Watch it!' I shouted.

'Taxi!' Rosy's voice rang out across the room and the three of us burst into laughter. What we were doing was ridiculous. Our tensions were high and we were nervous.

Fallon walked forward and picked up the nula. He gripped it in his right hand and held it up towards the roof. He looked like a warrior. Rosy picked up the wooden camera, curled its strap around her arm. She smiled.

'What about you, Billie?' Rosy asked. 'You taking anything from here? Then we'll light her up'.

I shook my head. 'Nah, nothing for me'.

The three of us turned back towards the petrol-soaked rug. Fallon pulled the lighter back out of his pocket. He flicked it, once, and the flame jumped to life on the wick. He made a motion to toss it onto the rug and then stopped.

'No point in losing my good lighter'. He turned back to the cabinet and grabbed one of the splinters of wood. He stood there lighting it on fire. I went over to the cabinet to look at the crystal stone. It was purple and light pink and looked like quartz. What had looked like wax before was actually resin mixed with hair and animal fur. I picked it up.

'Either of you ever seen something like this before?'

The others turned around to look as I held out the stone, about the size of my palm.

As they turned, the flame on the splinter of wood Fallon was holding, jumped off and fell onto the floor. All too suddenly we felt all of the air suck out of the room, replaced with heat as flames leaped to life from the floor in the centre of the room.

Before Fallon and Rosy could move the flames rushed at them, the petrol had run along a valley in the wooden floor towards where they had been looking at the items in the cabinet. Now the room was split almost in two by the huge circle of flame and the line of flame running across it. Fallon and Rosy were separated from me. My eyes darted around the room. I had the door on my side that we'd broken in through and a fire extinguisher was hanging beside it. Fallon and Rosy had a huge old window on their side of the room.

The air in the room was getting hotter by the second and it felt hard to breathe. Fallon moved to jump through the flame and Rosy grabbed him just as he left the ground. The force as she pulled him back forced his hand forward and the arm of his sweater caught fire.

'Idiot!' Rosy yelled at him and pushed him into the wall of the room, smothering the flame. The material had melted into his forearm and an ugly red welt was welling up through the still smoking cloth.

'We have to get Billie', he snarled at Rosy.

'She can handle herself. You however would have lit up like a candle with what you're wearing'. She gestured down at his basketball shorts. A horrified look filled Fallon's face, both the pain of the burn and the realisation that Rosy had just saved his life.

'I've got the door on my side', Billie called.

The flames of the carpet leaped higher and the line of fire reaching from the main blaze to the cabinet that Fallon had nearly tried to jump through, exploded as the cabinet took fire as well. The flames moved faster than flames should, the dry wood mixed with the fumes of the petrol amplifying the flammable properties of both.

The storage compartment underneath the cabinet lit up and all of the oxygen in the room was sucked out once again. The whole cabinet burst into huge flames.

The three of them were blown back from the force of it, and all too luckily, as the wave of heat rippled out at them.

'Fuck', Billie shouted as she pulled herself up from the floor. 'Rosy, Fallon, out of here. I'll sort myself'.

Fallen looked at Rosy, who had been blown backward into the wall with the force of the explosion. He grabbed at her as her eye tilted and she fell back.

'Billie!' Fallon screamed.

Billie stared. She could see the scene she was in, playing through her head. She could see the future of it if it went badly. She could see the newspaper article that would be written if the three of them burned in the council chambers in the fire they had started. She could see the Gamilaroi council falling apart, everything she had spoken about, everything she had dreamt, everything she could be coming to nothing.

Billie closed her eyes for a second as time seemed to stretch around her. She breathed in sharply and her eyes flew open.

'The nula', she yelled at Fallon. 'Break the window and get her out now. I'm going this way, I'll meet you at the car'.

Fallon didn't hesitate. He gripped the shaft of the generations-old weapon that he had just stolen, no not stolen: reclaimed, and he swung it at the window above him. The sound of smashing glass rang out once again, cutting over the noise of the flames as the window shattered. He smashed the broken shards of glass out from around the window frame and picked Rosy's unconscious body up, the hot, bright red of her blood dripping onto the floor from a wound on her forehead. He lifted her fairly easily; he was a large young man. And as gently as he could, he got her through the now open window and onto the garden bed outside. As he looked back, he thought he saw Billie, now sitting on the ground across the room before the fire grew in ferocity again and he had to move both himself and Rosy away from the heat.

Rosy opened her eyes and took a few moments to realise where she was: laid out on the back seat of the car. She could hear two people talking. There was a throbbing feeling, deep in her skull though, and she couldn't make out the words yet. They felt jumbled, in the wrong order or around the wrong way. A conversation that was already well into being over.

After a moment of deep concentration, she realised she was in a car. She could see specs of light thousands of years away in a sheet of blackness that was the sky through the window of the speeding car.

I sat in the passenger seat while Fallon was driving, holding the steering wheel with one hand. 'I thought I saw you, in the room still after I got out of the window?' Fallon asked curiously, glancing across at me, one eye still trained on the road.

'I was', I said. 'I was still in the room'.

'How are you alive'?

'I did it, I spoke to the stones'.

It was the last thing Rosy heard before she drifted back into the mute darkness of unconsciousness. The blood from her head wound crusted over and matted with her hair.

*'I was so worried about losing both Fallon and Rosy that night'. The old woman's voice cracked and she looked at Fallon across the fire. 'I'm so glad I didn't. He makes a great tea which, I would note, I'm still waiting on my second mug of'. She unfolded her arms from inside her robes and held the cup out.*

*Fallon rose from where he was sitting, motioning for the acolyte who had moved to get the pot of tea before him and held it up.*

*'I'll have to make some more; this has steeped too long for you, Beloved One'.*

*One of the acolytes spoke, 'You went against protocols?'*

*'Yes, of course. They are guides for how we leave with each other when everything is fine. When everything is not fine, when we are dogs that have been kicked too many times, then the protocols no longer dictate how we should be'.*

*'How do you decide what to follow and what to break?' another asked.*

*Billie breathed for a moment, a slow, drawn-out breath as though she was chewing over the answer.*

*She stood up from her seat and towered above the group. She was an incredibly tall woman. Her robes flowed and dragged on the ground as she moved over to the cave wall where a bench sat covered in items and tools.*

*She picked up a green quartz crystal, resin and hair covering one end. It sat in the palm of her hand. When she finally spoke, her voice resounded against the wall of the cave and echoed out to the fire, distorting the sound.*

'We decided to do what we had to, just as you may decide you will do what you have to'.
The aroma from the pot of tea Fallon was stirring over the fire began to drift around the room.

'Shall we continue the story then?' Billie asked the room. 'We have much more to tell and only two more days to get through this'.

## Smoke

It is often difficult to know what to write down from a story, particularly one that is yet to be told. In this piece I follow on from a previous work published as a short story in *Black Light* (2022) that follows the 'radicalisation' of the protagonist. This work explores elements of friction in intercultural relationships and the contrast of the needs of the individual in respect to the wants of those who would speak for the community. It is not a perfect representation, nor does it claim to be.

As mentioned in the pre-essay 'Fuel', I have utilised the mechanism of the unreliable narrator and I have displayed implied action to keep potential culturally sensitive material out of the reader's view. It is an 'if you know, you know'. To be completely clichéd, where there is smoke, there is fire. There is only so much we as writers can do to keep secret knowledge held back.

With the always open question: 'Who is your audience?' we come to another struggle. Do we as storytellers and writers get to choose the hands that gain access to our work?

My question culturally is: how do we choose who is allowed to tell what story and when, particularly in the light of broken cultural connections?

## References

Dillon, G. (2012). *Walking the clouds: An anthology of Indigenous science fiction.* University of Arizona Press.

Duffield, S., & Whitty, S. J. (2016). How to apply the Systemic Lessons Learned Knowledge model to wire an organisation for the capability of storytelling. *International Journal of Project Management, 34*(3), 429–443.

Fricke, S. N. (2019). Introduction: Indigenous futurisms in the hyperpresent now. *World Art, 9*(2), 107–121.

Laney, C., Kaasa, S. O., Morris, E. K., Berkowitz, S. R., Bernstein, D. M., & Loftus, E. F. (2008). The Red Herring technique: A methodological response to the problem of demand characteristics. *Psychological Research, 72*(4), 362–375.

Nünning, V. (2015). Unreliable narration and trustworthiness: Intermedial and interdisciplinary perspectives. In V. Nünning (Ed.), *Intermedial and interdisciplinary perspectives* (pp. 1–30). De Gruyter.

# 10
# THE VOICE OF COUNTRY
## Our obligation and responsibility to listen

*Noeleen Lumby*

### Introduction

Over the past five decades, there has been an increase in Indigenous language revitalisation, as Indigenous people feel safer to openly participate in cultural practices and return to our own ways of knowing, being and doing (Martin, 2003). Following on from the year of Indigenous languages, the United Nations General Assembly declared 2022 as the commencement of the decade of Indigenous languages, to draw attention to the critical status of Indigenous languages, globally, and to promote their preservation and revitalisation (United Nations, 2021). Prior to colonisation, on this continent colonially known as Australia, we had the most linguistically diverse landmass, with conservatively over 250 language groups and 800 dialects spoken (Dixon, 2002; Walsh, 1993).

Colonisation has been and continues to be a violent and oppressive system that has endorsed the demise of our languages. Our children were taken from their ancestral lands and their families, and moved to settler-controlled institutions, including Christian-managed mission schools where in many instances brutal indoctrination in the ways of 'Christianity' were daily life. Aboriginal children within this settler colonial structure were violently reprimanded for speaking their own language and this contributed to the severing of intergenerational transmission of our languages. Wurundjeri Elder Joy Wandin Murphy speaks about her grandmother's time at Coranderrk mission:

> The tribal language was not allowed to be spoken. And my Granny was one who said they would not stop them speaking language. She was a leader and herded all the women together in her house and they would sit around and talk language.
>
> (McConchie, 2003, p. 48)

As a result, many of us are now relearning our languages and, unlike our ancestors, many of us are learning our languages in settler education institutions, such as schools. Although this involves community members, who are language speakers, to teach within such a setting, this environment, is fraught with trauma for many Aboriginal peoples who have experienced the violence of the settler schooling system (Fletcher, 1989). Aboriginal scholars

DOI: 10.4324/9781003271802-12

Gawaian Bodkin-Andrews and Bronwyn Carlson argue that "it is indisputable that we have faced a long history of educational inequalities [...] that even in contemporary times we are still fighting for educational equality" (Bodkin-Andrews & Carlson 2016, p. 785).

Most Indigenous language programmes across this continent are dependent on government funding, and like most government funding for anything Indigenous, the conditions are generally short-term or one-off opportunities. The struggle, then, is how communities can continue this important work once the funding is discontinued (Mahboob et al., 2017).

This chapter investigates the way communities are working towards the revitalisation of our languages within a settler colonial regime. Firstly, I will discuss how settler colonialism has been a pivotal and an ongoing force in the linguicide of our languages. This chapter will also discuss the long and violent history Aboriginal peoples have endured within settler colonial education institutions, followed by an exploration of how communities in New South Wales navigate the complexities of settler education institutions, government policies and funding opportunities when revitalising their languages.

As James Cook sailed the *Endeavour* along the east coast of this continent, he sat on the deck feasting his eyes on our beautiful Country. In an unlawful act, he claimed everything he saw in the name of the king (Carlson & Farrelly, 2022). Later, with the arrival of settlers, the practice continued, and they renamed our homelands after themselves, wiping out tens of thousands of years of knowledge and linguistic diversity. Our languages are embedded within Country, this is our grounded normativity, this is who we are, and our languages reflect the intricate relationships we have with Country (Foster, 2020).

For example, viewing Gulaga, a spiritual and sacred place for the various clans of the south coast of New South Wales, Cook set about renaming this significant ancestor 'Mount Dromedary' as it reminded him of a camel (Foster, 2020). It is in more recent times that the correct name, Gulaga, has been reinstated. Djiringanj Yuin knowledge holder Warren Foster (2020) explains the relationship with Gulaga, whom he refers to as 'Mother Mountain' and notes many creation stories are held by Gulaga and it is a significant site for ceremony. Settler sociologist Anthony Moran argues that the process of renaming is a central act of colonialism:

> Through discrete acts of naming the white explorers mapped out a country as much in their own minds as in the charts that they drew up. This imaginative mapping and naming was a central aspect of the act of colonisation. It filled, or rather formed, the new space in which the colonisers were to live, with a combination of old and new names, most deriving from England, and many a result of the whims and accidents of experience of the explorers and surveyors who set out to 'discover' the country [...] Cancelling out the Aboriginal relationship to the land was central to the colonial project.
>
> (Moran, 2002, p. 1023)

From the first colonial impact site at Kamay, renamed in 1788 and now known as Botany Bay, the century-long drift of settler colonisation spread across this continent, working towards the destruction of Aboriginal peoples, cultures and languages. The multitude of languages across what is now known as New South Wales endured the longest impact of settler colonial destruction. Settler historian Henry Reynolds (2006) argues that colonisation was rolled out in a 'patchwork' style, resulting in some communities being immediately and devastatingly impacted while other communities were able to remain on their own

Country for more lengthy periods of time. This has resulted in some communities being able to retain some or all their languages and still have fluent speakers, while leaving other communities with only a few words and phrases (Wafer & Lissarrague, 2008). The retaining of our languages is not a result of any settler benevolence but due to the strategic efforts of Aboriginal people, who would often continue to speak their languages in private and away from the settler gaze. This was a risk, as the invading forces, the colonisers, including Christian missionaries, wanted their language, English, to be spoken. Many of our people were punished for defying this rule but continued to share their languages secretly in private spaces. This demonstrates the tenacity of our Elders to keep our languages alive, for which we are forever grateful.

The destruction of our languages is referred to by settler scholar Gerard Roche (2020) as 'linguistic colonialism', and is equally as treacherous as other forms of colonial violence. Its sole purpose was to erase Indigenous knowledges of the way we understand and speak of our relationships with each other and with Country. This practice is still evident today. Eliminating Aboriginal cultures and languages is core to the epistemic and ontological violence of settler colonialism. Settler colonial violence operates as structural violence that discursively challenges the 'authenticity' of Indigenous identities (Carlson, 2016). Prior to colonisation, there were hundreds of self-identifying Aboriginal groups across this continent. The homogenisation of us as 'the aborigines' began the colonisers' work to strip away our unique and complex identities. For centuries after the arrival of the British, settler linguists, historians and anthropologists concerned themselves with collecting our languages, among other cultural artefacts and technologies, in what Carlson describes as 'rescue' or 'salvage' work (Carlson, 2016, p. 30). The intent was to gather all that they could from a population deemed to be a 'dying race'. Our languages formed part of this rush to salvage information. They believed, the inevitable demise of Aboriginal people would also result in the demise of their oral languages and the need for the settler to record the language and assume control. This notion that our ancestors would 'naturally die out' was shared through the nineteenth and early twentieth centuries by anthropologists and other researchers who 'confidently predicted the imminent extinction of the race' (McGregor, 1993; Nakata, 2007; Carlson, 2016). This meant that settler practices and later, policies regarding our ancestors were designed without a future in mind and were to ensure we assimilated into settler culture; this included our languages (Elkin, 1963; Carlson, 2016; Walsh, 2012).

Artefacts, such as word lists and recordings, were collected for settler intrigue and curiosity given our categorisation as a 'dying race'. These artefacts have, in the present day, become useful for some communities in their language revitalisation journey (Yallop, 2012; Walsh, 2012). Revitalisation of language brings language back to Country and empowers community to reclaim cultural practices and strengthen cultural identity. There are many approaches communities take to this process including confronting, marginalising and dismantling the secondary discourse of alienation carried by the invading language (Fettes cited in Walsh, 2010, p. 307). Relearning and returning our languages to Country, in a settler colonial environment, means we must think differently about how we use our languages in today's changing world. Reimagining what this might look like will be different for each community.

Aboriginal linguist Jakelin Troy and fellow linguist Michael Walsh (2010) argue the general perception of many settlers is that languages in the southeast of the continent, including New South Wales, have been lost and presumed dead and therefore cannot be revived. This perception is flawed and over the past 20 years has been proven inaccurate. Troy and Walsh explain, "remarkable developments in a considerable variety of languages that have been described as 'extinct'" (2010, p. 176) are flourishing today. Because settlers are unaware, it does not mean language speakers do not exist. It would appear in some communities that language is still alive, being shared and spoken on Country. Our connection to culture and Country is embedded within us; our languages evolve like all languages to fit into the world we know today.

Colonisation continues to be a violent and oppressive structure that has seen the genocide of our people, the taking of our land and the attempted demise of our languages (Wolfe, 2006). Our children were taken from their ancestral lands and families and moved to Christian-managed mission schools where in many instances, brutal indoctrination in the ways of 'Christianity' were daily life. Kamilaroi scholar Bob Morgan (2019, p. 113) describes the purpose of mission schools was to enforce 'Eurocentric education' and was an "exercise in social engineering and not-so veiled form of cultural genocide". The initial impact and ongoing effects of settler colonisation interrupted the intergenerational transmission of language (Bell, 2000; Rademaker, 2019). Settler colonial policies of assimilation and the forcible removal of Aboriginal children to mission schools ensured a continuation of this break in language transmission (Haebich, 2015). Our languages were forbidden to be spoken and only the language of the coloniser was allowed to pass our lips and be heard. Our connections to Country, culture and language are further severed by the ongoing over-representation of Aboriginal children in 'Out of Home Care' that we currently witness, who have been removed from their families and into state care (Krakouer et al., 2018). This practice continues to occur at an alarming rate with the ongoing traumatic practice of child removal causing a break in cultural connection. including the ability to learn and speak their languages (Atkinson, 2002, p. 57).

Learning our languages in a settler colonial institution under these conditions and using the language of the coloniser as the dominant language of instruction does compromise the learning of language and cultural practices that being on Country can afford. Settler colonial systems are grounded in authoritarian power and hierarchy which is often in direct conflict with our ways of knowing, being and doing (Simpson, 2017). Colonisation has changed the way we use our languages and practice culture. They have in some instances taken on a different form and evolved, and these are now undertaken within a restricted context; however, we do continue to maintain these practices. Yagera and Dulingbara linguist Jeannie Bell (2000, p. 47) argues our cultural practices are a "natural and integral part of who we are" and notes: "The form and use of our languages has changed dramatically over the past 50 to 100 years [...] but the continuity of connection to country and language has remained" (2000, p. 49).

New South Wales is linguistically diverse. Precolonisation, an estimated 35 Aboriginal languages and approximately 120 dialects were spoken (Wafer & Lissarrague, 2008). Many of these languages are not regularly spoken today in what De Costa (2021, p. 357) describes as a state of sleep awaiting Aboriginal people to learn and speak to Country again. There has been over recent decades, an exciting linguistic renaissance and a determination to rebuild languages (Bell, 2000; Troy & Walsh, 2010). Bell (2000) considers the environment in which our Elders were trying to survive, and why many had little choice but to learn English and settler ways of living, and argues:

> members of our parents' generation who had left the missions in the 1940s and
> 1950s were trying hard to assimilate into this new environment, attempting to take

advantage of the limited education and job opportunities now available to them and their families. Many of them believed that traditional language and culture was a thing of the past and must be left behind.

(2000, p. 45)

While many Aboriginal communities continue to fight for the revival of their languages, they also lament the loss that has occurred and the violence our ancestors endured.

Truscott and Malcolm (2010) remind us that these assimilatory policies have been and continue to be destructive to Indigenous languages. Government policies of today are not as visibly focused on assimilation, but arguably continue to work against continuity and success of language revitalisation (Mahboob et. al., 2017). Although it appears the federal and state governments provide a large amount of funding to language revitilisation programmes, on further analysis there is a very different reality. For individual communities wanting to fund their language revitalisation programme, the process can be daunting and complicated.

For Aboriginal people, the commencement of a language revitalisation programme can be overwhelming due to the complex web of bureaucracy, community politics, relationships and contested histories that all need to be navigated. Developing a language revitalisation programme necessitates expertise in several fields that usually require cross-cultural collaboration (Bracknell, 2020). The current state of language programmes within the New South Wales school system poses many challenges. Confined by the requirements of settler governments, the programmes are rarely flexible and often do not meet the changing and frequently complex needs of the community. Often, teaching Indigenous languages is not seen as a priority and the time devoted to teaching is minimal and not integrated across all curriculum areas, or indeed a whole school approach is not implemented. Language programmes delivered in schools need a consistent and sustained approach to be successful.

The number of primary school students now engaged in language learning may look positive; however, even with a substantial increase, this number equates to just on 1.5 per cent of primary school students, Indigenous and non-Indigenous, in New South Wales public schools who are learning the language of Country (NSW Government, 2021b). In addition, of the 20 language communities involved in the school-based language revitalisation programmes, less than a quarter of the programmes have run continually during that time (NSW Government, 2021b).[1] This could be interpreted as a funding issue, with funding opportunities being competitive and, in some instances, a 'one off' opportunity. The figures for continuation of language learning in secondary school and tertiary education decline significantly (NSW Government, 2021a). This has further implications for the future of language revitalisation, as the paucity of language learners will have a compounding effect on the availability of qualified language teachers in the future (Troy & Walsh, 2010).

While De Costa (2021, p. 358) argues that educational institutions can help in revitalising sleeping languages, it is our epistemologies and methodologies that are important to the process and critical that revitalisation occur on our terms (Rhydwen, 2010). Language revitalisation programmes need to be a collaborative process, and colonial epistemologies and methodologies may hold some usefulness. Learning our languages in a settler colonial institution and using the language of the coloniser as the dominant language of instruction does compromise the learning of language and culture. Commencing the teaching of an

Aboriginal language in the school environment is complex, and communities are sceptical about teaching in a settler education system. However, they have the potential to assist us to navigate settler systems. Schools may have the physical infrastructure to provide space for language learning to occur, although many in the Indigenous community believe language and culture should be taught using our epistemologies and methodologies, on Country. It is good to remember that these institutions are on our Country.

If the government were truly committed to language revitalisation, then communities would be better resourced to undertake this work. Educational institutions can be seen as a place of change and radical possibilities "where meaningful relationships and partnerships between community, learners and teachers can promote positive outcomes" (Anyon, 2014). Support for Indigenous language revitalisation within schools, is multifaceted, and dependent on many factors including leadership changes and budget constraints. Settler anthropologist Teresa McCarty and Hopi scholar Sheila Nicholas argue, much of the funding of Indigenous language programmes is given to education institutions to administer whereby our languages and cultures are compromised (McCarty & Nicholas, 2014). With future discussions on sustainability, funding and the lack of hours allocated to learn a second language, the return of languages to Country becomes difficult. Purdie and colleagues (2008) highlighted these issues that continue to impact on communities engaging in language revitalisation programmes within schools. The criteria, terms and conditions in which a community must work within educational institutions can be seen as overly restrictive and not in line with Indigenous pedagogical approaches. If we are to strengthen our linguistic connections to Country, we need to have control over the process (McCarty & Nicholas, 2014). There are many Indigenous communities which want to continue to maintain autonomy over community language programmes. They are sceptical about their move into the education system and question the sharing of language with all students, particularly when Indigenous children may not be the priority. Firstly, while on the surface this is not necessarily an issue, many Indigenous people do not trust institutions, with good reason, and secondly, they feel this would provide more access to our languages to settler children than our own children (Purdie et al., 2008; McCarty & Nicholas, 2014).

With funding opportunities targeting schools rather than communities, the power of decision-making is given to school leadership rather than Indigenous people, language speakers and communities. This could have devastating impacts, as articulated by Hesquiaht scholar Layla Rorick (2019, p. 225), who argues that language cannot be taught without culture, stating, the "key to the resurgence of Indigenous knowledge systems, through decolonising educational approaches, is recovering and re-strengthening connections to our languages". Language planning and programming within schools must be directed by the community and incorporate local language and culture. Rorick (2019, p. 227) also notes the intersection between Indigenous language, culture of Country and spirituality for the development of educational programmes, referring to this as a "curriculum grounded in place" and that is achievable if Indigenous pedagogies are valued and embedded in learning. Communities which undertake language revitalisation programmes on the southeast of this continent, for example, have identified essential factors that are vital for the success and longevity of language programmes (Troy & Walsh, 2010). This includes Indigenous consultation and control from the initial stages and throughout the programme. Communities also have deep concerns regarding control over the revitalisation of their languages and over protecting such intellectual property (Janke, 2021). Many communities have developed policies and protocols to protect their languages. These processes are in place to inform participating settlers involved in the way the community requires their language to be taught, maintained and shared. It is expected protocols should be acknowledged and respected when education institutions engage with community in language revitalisation programmes (Janke, 2021).

Communities also have concerns about working within the formal education system to revitalise their language and may recall negative experiences, including older generations who remember children being stolen from schools or times when Aboriginal children were excluded. Even today, many Aboriginal people find schools are not always welcoming, and parents have expressed feelings of alienation and disengagement from the system, and indeed Indigenous students today continue to experience racism in schools (Bodkin-Andrews et al., 2021). While on the surface educational institutions do not necessarily pose an issue, many Indigenous people have good reason to distrust such places.

Standard Australian English is the national language used across this continent and it is the standard by which all children are assessed within the educational system. Ultimately, it is about whose language and knowledge is valued (De Costa, 2021). Aboriginal languages, Aboriginal English and Kriol are very rarely seen as valuable (Rhydwen, 2005). Settler colonial influence over Indigenous language revitalisation projects is further reinforced by government policy and funding opportunities. One of the challenges for community-led language revitalisation work is the necessity to rely on government funding opportunities. These opportunities are available through a vetting process whereby communities compete for a share in the funding allocation (Olawsky, 2020). This may mean a language programme could be funded for the first round and then miss out on the second round of funding. Torres Strait Islander scholar Sana Nakata and settler colleague Sarah Maddison argue that "For Aboriginal and Torres Strait Islander people, the experience of constant policy change has been frustrating, destabilising and disempowering, underscoring settler disregard for Indigenous sovereignty and autonomy" (2019, pp. 408–409). These policies and funding opportunities continue to perpetuate the settler colonial agenda of linguicide and are a point for Aboriginal people to protest for genuine and meaningful opportunities, and ongoing funding for language revitalisation (Roche, 2022). The notion of linguistic justice for Aboriginal peoples is vital in order for a language programme to be successful, and community control of such programmes is the most advantageous way forward.

In 2020, the New South Wales Government established the Aboriginal Languages Trust to "provide a focused, coordinated, and sustained effort" (NSW Government, 2021b) in promoting and revitalising Aboriginal languages. In the 2022/23 state budget, the New South Wales Government pledged over $138 million over the next decade for Aboriginal language programmes. This equates to just under $14 million a year for all language revitalisation programmes across this state. This may seem like a significant figure and a sustained approach to revitalising our languages; however, with over 2,200 public schools in New South Wales alone, this is a mere drop in the ocean for real engagement and sustainability of language revitalisation programmes. Without a sustained long-term strategic approach and adequate funding incorporating self-determination, many opportunities for communities to teach their languages will not be achieved. As Troy and Walsh argue (2010, p. 180), "there is a tension between accountability to various government authorities who control the purse-strings and real control by Indigenous people". The constant change in policies and related media attention to government commitment of funding for Indigenous languages are often seen as an opportunity for government to 'celebrate' their commitment to working with Indigenous people and supporting language revitalisation programme. There are certain barriers and obstacles hidden behind the rhetoric of government support. One need only look at the Closing the Gap initiative to see that government-led initiatives often fail Aboriginal peoples. Indeed, since 2020, Aboriginal languages have been included as a federal government Closing the Gap target, stating a "sustained increase in number and strength of Aboriginal and Torres Strait Islander languages being spoken by 2031". The Closing the Gap initiative over the last ten years has continued to fail to improve conditions for Indigenous people across many areas, including health, school attendance and decreased incarceration numbers. Being categorised as a 'target' within the Closing the Gap initiative may not be the best way forward for our language revitalisation programmes. It is well known that targets under Closing the Gap are rarely achieved (Driese et al., 2021).

At a federal level, the recently elected Labor government allocated a further 14 million dollars to support language learning in 60 schools across this continent. These 'one off' funds will be rolled out over a three-year period, with the first year allocated to planning and the following two years to teaching. As with most funding for language programmes, there may be little opportunity to continue the programmes without further funding after the initially funded three years, and the schools involved in the initiative may have to join the other communities that need to apply for competitive funding to support the continuation of their programmes.

Working within the constraints of the settler colonial educational system further hinders the success and sustainability of language programmes. Indeed, our language and cultures should be taught on Country by all community members who have the knowledge to share with the younger generation, with no need for an overseer.

Most, if not all language learning programmes in New South Wales are language revitalisation programmes (Walsh, 2001). As such, this usually includes community members as teachers or knowledge contributors. For example, there may be Elders and others in the community who can speak their language and can support the development of a language revitalisation programme and teach other community members. Often, learning a language also comes with a deeper understanding of Country and other cultural knowledges (Bell, 2013). Who can teach our languages is a question for individual communities to answer, and in many instances the answer is as varied as our languages themselves. One challenge that faces language revitalisation efforts is a real shortage of community members who still reside on Country and are willing and able to participate. Often ill-health and a myriad of other commitments can impact availability. Some communities have made decisions that only those with ancestral connections to the community should be given permission to teach the local language. This can pose some limitations, and especially if there is no one with the knowledge and skills, time, and commitment to undertake this work. If language is offered via the educational system, then these types of decisions may not always be made by the community themselves.

For thousands of years, there has been no need for formal training, which is now becoming increasingly required to teach in a school setting. This need for a formal qualification is another way settler colonial frameworks control the teaching and learning of our own languages (NSW Department of Education, 2021). Many school programmes are now requiring language tutors to hold a formal qualification, in their target languages regardless of whether they can speak their own language fluently. This certification is available through local TAFE[2] institutions. It is desirable for a tutor to have a minimum Certificate III level for school tutoring. This study can take time. Progression from a Certificate I through to a Certificate III can take up to 18 months to complete. Language-funding programmes have criteria, which include time constraints for the spending of funds. Unfortunately, this required certification impedes the commencement of programmes and the availability of language teachers. In some instances, community members may already have the knowledge to teach language in a school setting and are required to undertake further learning or to apply for recognition of prior learning, which can take some time to navigate. Training of community members to tutor language in schools can be seen as a step forward; however, if a community language teacher does not have a formal teaching qualification, then a qualified teacher, regardless of their expertise in language teaching, must be present in the classroom while lessons are taking place. Paying both a teacher and tutor to be in one classroom impacts on individual school budgets and influences the longevity of a language revitalisation programme and the employment of community members.

Qualified community language tutors are paid at substantially lower levels than qualified teachers. The difference in pay scale speaks volumes regarding what is considered of value in the classroom. The hourly rate has been set in many schools participating in language revitalisation classes (NSW Coalition of Aboriginal Regional Alliances, 2018). Arguably, this is a tactic to ensure that language revitalisation is difficult to achieve. As Olawasky (2020, p. 4) argues, the Australian government fails to see the "significance of Indigenous language for employment, education and social wellbeing including health". As we know, feeling connected to culture and community provides nourishment and increased well-being for Indigenous peoples. We cannot put a 'set price' on the transmission and sharing of our cultures and languages, and there is a need for proper renumeration for community language teachers.

Language programmes delivered in the educational setting require a consistent and sustained approach. This has been the case for successful second language programmes in Europe. As Samantha Disbray argues, "consistent, high-quality programmes with between two to four lessons per week over the first four years and three to five lessons in the upper primary years [are required] to develop communicative competence" (Disbray et al., 2018, p. 8). This approach also been used successfully in other countries. Unfortunately, the New South Wales Government funding for language revitalisation programme initiative falls short of this target, with an allowance for language learning with a three-hours-per-school allocation. This may seem a significant time allocation; however, it does not take into consideration schools with larger numbers of students who may require multiple community tutors to teach (NCARA, 2018).

With future discussions lacking on sustainability, funding and the necessary hours required to learn a second language, there is a real concern for the return of all our languages to Country. Purdie and colleagues (2008) highlighted these issues and their continued impact on communities engaged in language revitalisation programmes in schools. The criteria, terms and conditions in which community must work within educational institutions across this continent can be seen as overly restrictive and not in line with self-determined Indigenous pedagogical approaches (McCarty & Nicholas, 2014).

Our languages are still endangered. Communities must navigate the complexities of settler colonial policies to ensure their languages are again spoken on Country. Currently, communities must partner with government institutions, which have a variable success rate on returning language to Country. New South Wales government funding for revitalisation programmes is ephemeral and given over to education institutions to manage. Community must work within the parameters of such institutions to enable them to teach their language.

There are concerns about the longevity of language revitalisation programmes when funding ceases. Very little has been put in place to ensure continuity for future generations to learn the language of Country. Communities have worked hard to navigate this space and should be proud of the work that has been done to bring our languages back, to hear our children speak the language of their homeland. Indigenous people, however, must control the language revitalisation process; we should have autonomy over where and how our languages are taught. This can prove difficult due to the way governments write policies that result in many restrictions and challenges, as argued by Simpson: "it can appear or feel as if the state is operating differently because it is offering a slightly different process to Indigenous peoples" (2017, p. 45). We must resist the colonial imperative to govern us in all aspects of our lives including the return of language to Country. The current situation sees the government determine which of our languages are deemed relevant and important enough to be revitalised based on governmental criteria and not the value that the community sees. Many of the larger and stronger languages of New South Wales that are being funded through the New South Wales Government Education Department programmes are seeing more federal funding applications approved over smaller community language applications (Australian Government, 2022). By resisting settler colonial governance and control over our language revitalisation programmes, we begin to enrich the language and embed our ways of knowing, being and doing through our activism and efforts (Simpson, 2017).

Settler colonial policies and institutions have damaged our cultures and languages, but we must resist referring to the demise of our languages as a forlorn outcome. The settler language of 'lost', 'dead and dying' and the 'last of' are linguistically violent and produce a discourse that sees our languages and cultures firmly relegated to history and devalued in the present. Through the passion and dedication of Indigenous communities, and teachers, enormous strides are being made in bringing our language back to Country. Navigating settler colonial institutions, policy and ephemeral funding opportunities is challenging. Our languages sit in a relationship to Country, and to understand and converse with Country, we need to relearn our languages. This is our obligation and responsibility to our ancestors.

## Notes

1  This relates to data collected over the last ten years in public schools.
2  www.closingthegap.gov.au

## References

Anyon, J. (2014). *Radical possibilities: Public policy, urban education, and a new social movement*. Routledge.

Atkinson, J. (2002). *Trauma trails: Recreating songlines: The transgenerational effects of trauma in Indigenous Australians*. Spinifex Press.

Australian Government. (2022). *Department of Infrastructure, Transport, Regional Development, Communications and the Arts, Indigenous Languages and Arts Program*. www.arts.gov.au/funding-and support/indigenous-languages-and-arts-program

Australian Labor Party. (2020). Labor's Plan to Teach First Nations Languages in Schools. www.alp.org.au/policies/labors-plan-to-teach-first-nations-languages-in-schools

Bell, J. (2000). Linguistic continuity in colonised country. In J. Henderson and D. Nash (Eds.), *Language in native title* (pp. 43–52). Aboriginal Studies Press.

Bell, J. (2013). Language attitudes and language revival/survival. *Journal of Multilingualand Multicultural Development, 34*(4), 399–410. http://doi.org/10.1080/01434632.2013.794812

Bodkin-Andrews, G., & Carlson, B. (2016). The legacy of racism and Indigenous Australia identity within education. *Race Ethnicity and Education, 19*(4), 784–80. https://doi.org/12/1080/13613 324.2014.969224

Bodkin-Andrews, G., Foster, S., Bodkin, F., Foster, J., Andrews, G., Adams K., & Evans, R. (2021). Resisting the racist silence. In M. Shay & R. Oliver (Eds.), *Indigenous education in Australia: Learning and teaching for deadly futures* (pp. 21–37). Routledge.

Bracknell, C. (2020). Rebuilding as research: noongar song, language and ways of knowing. *Journal of Australian Studies, 44*(2), 210–223. http://doi/10.1080/144443058.2020.17463800

Carlson, B. (2016). *The politics of identity: Who counts as Aboriginal today?* Aboriginal Studies Press.

Carlson, B., & Farrelly, T. (2022). Monumental upheavals: Unsettled fates of the Captain Cook statue and other colonial monuments in Australia. *Thesis Eleven, 169*(1), 62–81.

Costa, P. (2021). Indigenous language revitalization: How education can help reclaim 'sleeping' languages. *Journal of Language, Identity & Education, 20*(5), 355–361. https://doi.org/10.1080/15348458.2021.1957684

Disbray, S., Barker, C., Raghunathan, A., & Baisden, F. (2018). *Global lessons: Indigenous languages and multilingualism in school programs.* First Languages Australia. www.firstlanguages.org.au/global-lessons

Dixon, RWM. (2002). *Australian languages. Their nature and development.* Cambridge University Press.

Dreise, T., Markham, F., Lovell, M., Fogarty, W., & Wighton, A. (2021). *First Nations Regional and National Representation: Aligning Local Decision Making in NSW with Closing the Gap and the proposed Indigenous Voice* Working Paper No.141/2021). Centre for Aboriginal Economic Policy Research, Australian National University. https://doi.org/10.25911/65M2-V536

Elkin, A. P. (1963). Aboriginal languages and assimilation. *Oceania, 34*(2), 147–154. www.jstor.org/stable/pdf/40329423.pdf

Fletcher, J. J. (1989). *Clean, clad and courteous: A history of Aboriginal education in New South Wales.* Southwood Press.

Foster, W., & Australian Broadcasting Commission. (2020). *Mount Gulaga the sacred Mother and Gurunggubba the greedy pelican* [Video]. YouTube. www.youtube.com/watch?v=fbd-YG5om_s

Haebich, A. (2015/2016). Neoliberalism, settler colonialism and the history of Indigenous child removal in Australia. *Australian Indigenous Law Review, 19*(1), http://jstor.org/stable/10.2307/2642330

Janke, T. (2021). *True tracks: Respecting Indigenous knowledge and culture.* University of New South Wales Press.

Krokouer, J., Wise, S., & Connolly, M. (2018). We live and breathe through culture: Conceptualising cultural connection for Indigenous Australian children in out of home-care, *Australian Social Work, 7*(3), 265–276.

Maddison, S. (2019). *The colonial fantasy: Why white Australia can't solve Black problems.* Allan & Unwin.

Mahboob, A., Jacobsen, B., Kemble, M., & Xu, Z.C. (2017). Money for language: Indigenous language funding in Australia. *Current Issues in Language Planning, 18*(4), 422–441. https://doi.org/10.1080/14664208.2017.1331497

Martin, K. (2003). Ways of knowing being and doing: A theoretical framework and methods for Indigenous and Indigenist re-search. *Journal of Australian Studies, 27*(76), 203–214.

McCarty, T., & Nicholas, S. (2014). Reclaiming Indigenous languages: A reconsideration of the roles and responsibilities of schools. *Review of Research in Education, 38*(1), 106–136.

McConchie, P. (2003). *Elders: Wisdom from Australia's Indigenous Leaders.* Cambridge University Press.

McGregor, R. (1993). The doomed race: A scientific axiom of the late nineteenth century. *Australian Journal of Politics and History, 39*(1), 14–22.

Moran, A. (2002). As Australia decolonises: Indigenizing settler nationalism and challenges of settler/Indigenous relations. *Ethnic and Racial Studies, 25*(6), pp. 1013–1042.

Morgan, B. (2019). Beyond the guest paradigm: Eurocentric education and Aboriginal peoples in NSW. In E. McKinley & L. Tuhiwai Smith (Eds.), *Handbook of Indigenous education* (pp. 111–128). Springer.

Nakata, M. (2007). *Disciplining the savages, savaging the disciplines.* Aboriginal Studies Press.

New South Wales Government Aboriginal Languages Trust. (2021). *Aboriginal Languages Trust.* www.alt.nsw.gov.au/

NSW Coalition of Aboriginal Regional Alliances (NCARA). (2018). *A Step Closer: A Report with Recommendations from NCARA to the New South Wales Government following Stage One of the OCHRE Evaluation.* www.aboriginalaffairs.nsw.gov.au/conversations.orchre/about/aboutochre/evaluation-implementation/NCARA-Report-08-18.pdf

NSW Department of Education. (2021). *Aboriginal Outcomes and Partnership Directorate. Aboriginal Language and Culture Nests Guidelines.* https://education.nsw.gov.au/content/dam/main-education/teaching-and learning/aec/media/documents/Guidelines_Aboriginal_Languages_and_Culture_Nests.PDF

NSW Government. (2021a). Data from: *Language participation for Years 7–9 by gender and school year (2012–2021) NSW Department of Education.* https://data.cese.nsw.gov.au/data/dataset/language-participation-for-years-7-9-by gender-and-school-year

NSW Government. (2021b). *Data from: Primary students in NSW government schools studying a language other than English (2012–2021).* https://data.cese.nsw.gov.au/data/dataset/primary-students-in-nsw government schools-studying-a-language-other-than-english

Olawsky, Knut. (2020, August). *Concerns over Australian Government funding for Aboriginal and Torres Strait Islander languages.* Commissioned by Mirima Dawang Woorlab-gerring Language and Cultural Centre. http://mirima.org.au/wp content/uploads/2020/08/Concerns-over-Federal-funding-for_Australian-Indigenous languages_RELEASE-1.pdf

Purdie, N., Frigo, T., Oxolins, C.,Noblett, G., Thieberger, N., & Sharp, J. (2008). Indigenous languages programs in Australian schools: A way forward. Australian Council for Education Research, Australia. https://research.acer.edu.au/cgi/viewcontent.cgi?article=1017&context=indigenous_education

Rademaker, L. (2019). *The great Australian silencing: The elimination of Aboriginal languages and the legacy of colonisation.* ABC Religion & Ethics. www.abc.net.au/religion/the-elimination-of-aboriginal -languages-and the-legacy-of-colon/10731474

Reynolds, H. (2006). *The other side of the frontier: Aboriginal resistance to the European invasion of Australia.* University of New South Wales Press.

Rhydwen, M. (2005). Kriol: The creation of a written language and a tool of colonisation. In M. Walsh & C. Yallop (Eds.), *Language and culture in Aboriginal Australia* (pp. 155–168). Aboriginal Studies Press.

Rhydwen, M. (2010). Strategies for doing the possible: Supporting school Aboriginal language programs in NSW. In J. Hobson, K. Lowe, S. Poetsch, & M. Walsh (Eds.), *Reawakening languages; Theory and practice in the revitalisation of Australia's Indigenous languages* (pp. 253–262). Sydney University Press.

Roche, G. (2020). Abandoning endangered languages: Ethical loneliness, language oppression and social justice. *American Anthropologist, 122*(1), 64–169.

Roche, G. (2022). Linguistic human rights in Tibet: Advocacy and denial. In T. Skutnabb Kangas & R. Phillipson (Eds.), *Handbook of linguistic human rights.* Wiley & Blackwell.

Rorick, c. L. (2019). waɬyaʕasukʔi naatnaniqsakqin: At the home of our Ancestors: Ancestral continuity in Indigenous land-based language immersion. In L. T. Smith, E. Tuck, & K. W. Yang (Eds.), *Indigenous decolonising studies in education: Mapping the long view* (pp. 224–251). Routledge.

Simpson, L. B. (2017). *As we have always done: Indigenous freedom through radical resistance.* University of Minnesota Press.

Troy, J., & Walsh, M. (2010). A linguistic renaissance in the southeast of Australia. In G. Senft (Ed.), *Endangered Austronesian and Australian languages: Essays on language documentation, archiving, and revitalisation* (pp. 175–182). Australian National University. Pacific Linguistics.

Truscott, A., & Malcolm, I. (2010). Closing the policy-practice gap: Making Indigenous language policy more than empty rhetoric. In J. Hobson, K. Lowe, S. Poetsch, & M. Walsh (Eds.), *Reawakening languages: Theory and practice in the revitalisation of Australia's Indigenous languages* (pp. 6–21). Sydney University Press.

United Nations. Department of Economic and Social Affairs. International Decade of Indigenous Languages 2022–2032. www.un.org/development/desa/indigenouspeoples/indigenous-langua ges.html

Wafer, J. W., & Lissarrague, A. (2008). *A handbook of Aboriginal languages of New South Wales and the Australian Capital Territory*. Muurrbay Aboriginal Language and Culture Cooperative.

Walsh, M. (1993). Languages and their status in Aboriginal Australia. In M. Walsh & C. Yallop (Eds.), *Language and culture in Aboriginal Australia* (pp. 1–14). Aboriginal Studies Press.

Walsh, M. (2001). A case of language revitalisation in 'settled' Australia. *Current Issues in Language Planning, 2*(2–3), 251–258. https://doi.org/10.1080/14664200108668027

Walsh, M. (2010). Why language revitalisation sometimes works. In J. Hobson, K. Lowe, S. Poetsch, & M. Walsh (Eds.), *Re-awakening languages: Theory and practice in the revitalisation of Australia's Indigenous languages* (pp. 22–36). Sydney University Press.

Walsh, M. (2012). Languages and their status in Aboriginal Australia. In M. Walsh & C. Yallop (Eds.), *Language and culture in Aboriginal Australia* (pp. 1–12). Aboriginal Studies Press.

Wolfe, P. (2006). Settler colonialism and the elimination of the native. *Journal of Genocide Research, 8*(4), 387–409. https://doi.org/10.1080/14623520601056240

Yallop, C. (2012). The structure of Australian Aboriginal languages. In M. Walsh & Yallop (Eds.), *Language and culture in Aboriginal Australia* (pp. 15–32). Aboriginal Studies Press,.

# 11
# INDIGENOUS FUTURES FOR THE SUBJECT OF ENGLISH

## A profile of practice

*Tamika Worrell*

### Introduction

White people are too often the only authorities of Aboriginal lives and histories. So powerful is the dominant colonial storying of Aboriginal peoples that the possibility of Aboriginal people having their own stories—and moreover, stories that are imbued with theoretical positions—is rendered impossible, flung to a margin to be out of sight and out of the colonisers' minds or, when heard, disavowed. Aboriginal people are not all assimilated and have not all forgotten.

*(Phillips & Bunda, 2018, p. 52)*

Aboriginal and Torres Strait Islander perspectives, histories and cultures form an integral component of learning for all students in all subject areas. The freedom that teachers of the subject English have, for resource and text selection, including the versatility and availability of texts, offers a unique opportunity to embed these perspectives. As texts form the basis for teaching a variety of skills and outcomes in English, this subject area provides opportunities for teachers to select texts which offer a range of Aboriginal and Torres Strait Islander standpoints. As Phillips, Mclean Davies, & Truman (2022, p. 171) identify, "As a curriculum area, English has been foundational to empire, invasion, and colonisation of Indigenous peoples the world over". This is further illuminated by the nature in which English has been utilised as a tool of the settler colonialism system (Wolfe, 2006). English, and language broadly, is utilised to both maintain the colonial powers, as well as the colonial norms that accompany these (Hogarth, 2019a). Hogarth (2019a, pp. 4–5) posits an important question; "Why is Standard Australian English the only means of communication advocated in Schools?" This highlights the precarious existence within which the subject of English operates.

In order to explore Indigenous futures within the subject of English, I am presenting one Profile of Practice, Yannha,[1] from my doctoral research which explores the question "How do NSW English teachers represent Aboriginal and Torres Strait Islander perspectives in Stages 4 and 5 (Years 7–10) through their text choices and pedagogical approaches to these texts?" My doctoral research builds on the pilot project (Worrell, 2019), which identified

DOI: 10.4324/9781003271802-13

there is a need to investigate the role of Indigenous knowledges representation. That is, what knowledge should be taught in the subject English in the classroom; how it should be taught and for what purpose in order to represent Indigenous perspectives. The findings of the pilot identified that whilst text selection is a deeply personal practice, it is heavily informed by school contexts including school ethos, financial supports and the learner profile of the students. It also identified that non-Indigenous teachers have a fear of both 'doing the wrong thing' and acting tokenistically (Worrell, 2019).

This Profile is a result of entering a relationality with the participant through a yarning methodology. For Indigenous peoples, yarning is an important practice which transcends Western frameworks of conversing; whilst it is about speaking, it is also about listening (Bessarab & Ng'andu, 2010; Shay & Wickes, 2017). In addition, the yarning approach extends beyond the conversations with participants as it was embedded throughout the research process. I sat with knowledges, I listened to Country, I listened to old people and knowledge holders. I connected and yarned with my Indigenous Higher Degree Research (HDR) community, and I learnt and was inspired by their profiles and practices. I sat with the data, I yarned with the data, and I yarned about the data. The strength of yarning as a methodology is the flexibility it offers to adapt to the needs of Aboriginal research as well as enable the past, present, and future to be considered (Dean, 2010). It also builds a relational accountability of research to participants, and the research (Fredericks et al., 2011; Bessarab & Ng'andu, 2010; Dean, 2010). This chapter, and the research that has been carried out here, has been written on Dharug Ngurra (in the Dharug language, this refers to Country). As a *yinnar* (woman in Gamilaraay language) from Gamilaroi/Kamilaroi/ Gomeroi Country, I acknowledge Dharug Ngurra as the Country which has raised me and grown me since birth, and the Dharug knowledge holders who carry the knowledges of this land since time immemorial.

## Curricula and policy contexts

National policy and curricula contexts have cemented the importance of Aboriginal and Torres Strait Islander perspectives as an integral part of education agendas (Education Council, 2019; MCEETYA, 2008; ACARA, 2022b) . Subject English, and the inclusion of Aboriginal and Torres Strait Islander perspectives is situated amongst a suite of state-based and national policies, guidelines, and declarations. Teachers nationally are tasked with navigating a wide range of shifting and competing priorities and mandates in their profession. This is true for English teachers, who must navigate a range of contextual pressures and demands to meet a range of professional regulations (O'Sullivan, 2020). To situate future aspirations within this area, we must first look at the layered and complex spaces which drive these curricula.

## United Nations Declaration on the Rights of Indigenous Peoples

To start at the international layer, the United Nations Declaration on the Rights of Indigenous Peoples (UNDRIP) is a key consideration. It recognises, welcomes, affirms, and considers a range of declarations relating to Indigenous peoples globally (UN General Assembly, 2007). Australia, a settler colonial nation, voted against the adoption of the UNDRIP, as one of four countries out of 158 (Davis, 2007). This was endorsed by Australia in 2009, positioning it as an "aspirational document" (Dorfmann, 2015). Prior to its acceptance in 2009, Davis wrote in 2008 of the strength the declaration offers Australia as a moral and educative tool for Indigenous peoples and the wider community. When considering the position of the present research study, this international document sets a benchmark of rights as they relate to Indigenous peoples globally. Further to this, Article 14 of the UNDRIP pertains directly to education, and our rights, as Indigenous peoples, to establish and control "educational systems and institutions providing education in their own languages, in a manner appropriate to their cultural methods of teaching and learning" (UN General Assembly, 2007, p. 5). Article 14 extends beyond this, announcing our rights to access "all levels of education without discrimination" and the right for states to take "Indigenous individuals, [...] to have access, when possible, to an education in their own culture and provided in their own language" (UN General Assembly, 2007, pp. 5–6). These three points from Article 14 outline crucial considerations when it comes to education and Indigenous peoples. Article 14 covers the role of language, cultural methods, and our communities and the importance of control. We see here the second point focuses on access to all levels of education without discrimination. The third point puts the onus on states to collaborate with Indigenous peoples to take effective measures that will result in education for us in our own cultures and languages. This global declaration offers a key exemplar of the international discourses taking place in relation to Indigenous communities. UNDRIP offers a position on what the standard practice *should be*, whether or not this takes place in practice. It situates Indigenous peoples as part of a global community of Indigenous knowledge holders.

## Australian Curriculum

The Australian Curriculum, Assessment and Reporting Authority (ACARA) is responsible for four key areas relating to "National Curriculum, National Collaboration and Leadership, National Assessment and National Data and reporting" (ACARA, 2022a). Whilst these four key areas are equally important, it is crucial to consider the positioning of the national curriculum and how it relates to Aboriginal and Torres Strait Islander peoples broadly, as well as specifically through consideration of subject English. A significant part of the Australian curriculum is the three cross-curriculum priorities (CCP) relating to core learning areas which must be included across all subject areas. These three CCPs are: Aboriginal and Torres Strait Islander Histories and Cultures; Asia and Australian's Engagement with Asia; and Sustainability (ACARA, 2022b). Of importance for the current study is the Aboriginal and Torres Strait Islander Histories and Cultures CCP. ACARA (2022b) has two distinct needs which they aim to address through this CCP. The two needs are:

1. provides Aboriginal and Torres Strait Islander students with the ability to see themselves, their identities and cultures reflected in the curriculum;
2. allows all students to engage in reconciliation, respect, and recognition of the world's oldest continuous living cultures.

(ACARA, 2022b)

These two national priorities are cemented through the inclusion of the Aboriginal and Torres Strait Islander Histories and Cultures CCP in all subject areas through the Australian curriculum. Whilst it is up to each state to interpret the National Curriculum, this is an important prioritisation that cements the implementation of Indigenous historical and cultural standpoints through all areas of teaching and learning.

## Alice Springs Mparntwe Declaration

The Alice Springs (Mparntwe) Education Declaration (Mparntwe Declaration) is a national declaration that has built upon the goals established in the Melbourne Declaration on Educational Goals for Young Australians, which was integral in driving the inclusion of the CCPs (Education Council, 2019; MCEETYA, 2008). The Mparntwe Declaration reaffirms the importance of the Aboriginal and Torres Strait Islander CCP in the Australian curriculum, and the vision for its impacts (Education Council, 2019). It states:

> This cross-curriculum priority provides Aboriginal and Torres Strait Islander students with the ability to see themselves, their identities and cultures reflected in the curriculum and allows all students to engage in reconciliation, respect and recognition of the world's oldest continuous living cultures.
>
> (Education Council, 2019, p. 15)

The Declaration reaffirms the goals and importance of the Aboriginal and Torres Strait Islander CCP and reiterates the duality of its role and impact in the classroom and beyond. Firstly, we see that Aboriginal and Torres Strait Islander students should see themselves in the curriculum and classroom. Secondly, we see that all students, including non-Indigenous students, should be able to engage in reconciliation, respect, and recognition as an effect of the CCP.

## New South Wales Education Standards Authority

As we continue to narrow down the scope and situate this study, it is important to look at the NSW context and the national considerations that inform the state drivers. The New South Wales Education Standards Authority (NESA) is an independent authority which reports to an independent board, as well as the minister for education and early childhood learning (NESA, 2012). In its current iteration, the English K–10 syllabus presents the standards of what knowledges students should hold, and the skills of what things they should be able to do from Kindergarten to Year 10 (NESA, 2012). The syllabus attributes its overarching views to the Melbourne Declaration as it reiterates the two goals of this document (MCEETYA,2008). In enacting the CCPs of the Australian curriculum, the English K–10 syllabus utilises learning across the curriculum icons to map this through the document (NESA, 2012). Indigenous perspectives are embedded in the syllabus rationale, which states that students should "engage with the literature and literary heritage of Aboriginal and Torres Strait Islander peoples" (NESA, 2012, p. 10). It is further reiterated in the stages of learning, which require students to study "a widely defined Australian literature, including texts that give insight into Aboriginal experiences in Australia" (NESA, 2012, p. 22).

As is the role of the state-based syllabus authorities, NESA includes the rationale for the CCP in its syllabus documents. It also encourages teachers to "involve local Aboriginal communities and/or appropriate knowledge holders in determining suitable resources, or to use Aboriginal or Torres Strait Islander authored or endorsed publications"; and "read the Principles and Protocols relating to teaching and learning about Aboriginal and Torres

Strait Islander histories and cultures and the involvement of local Aboriginal communities" (NESA, 2019, p. 25). This addition to the NSW English K–10 syllabus combats the problematised language of the English syllabus requiring students to experience "texts that give insights into Aboriginal experiences in Australia" (NESA, 2012, p. 22). However, because the addition does not connecting directly to the syllabus, the problem is not resolved. Whilst the syllabus is a document to be enacted, it should model and mandate best practice. This addition also moves to include Torres Strait Islander peoples; however, in the last sentence it only mentions Aboriginal peoples like the wider syllabus document.

These contexts are layered and serve to narrow down the wider picture that informs the teaching of subject English in NSW Schools. The syllabus documents and policy drivers are operationalised and enacted in different ways, and through inquiry into teacher's practice, we can see how they exist and function on the local school level.

## Profiles of Practice

Whilst the methodology adopted here draws on a case study approach (Stake, 2005; 2006; Yin, 2018), the language used to refer to these is purposefully represented as Profiles of Practice. Profiles of Practice are more reflective of the lives of people behind the 'cases'. These Profiles of Practice are teacher profiles that identify the teacher's practice, as well as the context in which it exists. It also reflects the purpose for the case study approach, to allow practising teachers, and pre-service teachers and their educators, to engage with these profiles. These profiles will be written with the consistent thought in mind of the end user, other English teachers, community members, and initial teacher education educators. I first drew on the term 'Profiles of Practice' in Worrell (2022) as a publication output of the pilot of this study, which has been transformed into a driving component of my doctoral methodology. I am defining Profiles of Practice as distinct and unique singular stories of an educator's practice that transcend beyond the static and often dehumanised nature of a case study.

## Yarning with Yannha

Yannha is an Aboriginal English and HSIE teacher and is in the 21–30 years of age range. She has two to five years of experience working at one Government School in the New England, New South Wales region as a classroom teacher. Yannha's interest in participating in this project stems from all the research that is conducted, which does not necessarily involve teachers. Yannha states, "If teachers aren't actually participating in the research, then it can't go anywhere or be accurate, I guess. And this is a topic that I'm pretty passionate about". This enthusiasm was affirming for me as a young researcher engaging in this space.

Yannha's school is located in Western NSW, in a regional location, and she works at a Secondary Government 7–12 school (ACARA, 2021). At the time of the interviews, Yannha's school had a 35 per cent Indigenous student enrolment, of a wider population of the full-time equivalent enrolment of 683 students. In addition, 5 per cent of students have a language background other than English (ACARA, 2021). ACARA (2021) categorises this school as being located in an inner regional location. The school has an Index of Community Socio-Educational Advantage (ICSEA) score of 867 and is in the fifth percentile.

I met with Yannha on two sequential Mondays at 4 p.m. via Zoom for our conversations. On our first meeting, Yannha was in the second week of virtual learning after a snap regional lockdown, which had been extended beyond our second meeting. These stay-at-home conditions prompted conversations around the inequity of at-home learning, and sympathy for students without stable internet or technology at home, and how that has impacted virtual learning planning. As I was yarning with an Aboriginal participant, I started off with the protocol of acknowledging Country, and shared my own positioning as an Aboriginal person culturally and geographically. This was reciprocated by Yannha. We bonded over shared experiences as Aboriginal women, and as teachers passionate about English and our young people. I felt an immense weight to impress Yannha, as my project is for the benefit of Aboriginal students in the classroom. I also positioned Yannha as sister, or Baawaa in Gamilaraay language, and did so when acknowledging Country.

I shared with Yannha where the passion for this project has come from. Immediately it was clear to me that this resonated with Yannha:

> I did definitely notice, when I was a student, a lot of the Aboriginal perspectives that I was seeing weren't really from Aboriginal people, and we didn't get a whole lot of information on Aboriginal perspectives. So, then going in as a teacher, I've been really conscious of bringing that in, and I've just noticed how aware I am when texts that we have to choose from aren't actually by Aboriginal people.

This cemented a shared understanding and viewpoint.

One of the early questions in our first conversation revolves around capturing both the professional identity, and the reasoning behind pursuing an English teaching career. Yannha attributes becoming an English teacher to her love of language, including Aboriginal language [language name withheld], which she is currently learning as well as introducing and teaching at school. Regarding language, Yannha stated:

> I think language is powerful, and I think that we need to be teaching more of our kids about understanding the power of language, and the power that texts and different things can have in communicating. And I guess teaching them to analyse the world around them, not just take things at face value.

I queried Yannha on who she was referring to when saying 'our' kids: Aboriginal students, or all the students at the school. Whilst in this context, she was referring to all students, she went on to say she works closely with Indigenous students. I had asked Yannha, "So, when you say you work with Mob kids, is that a formal part of your role? Is it just as an Aboriginal teacher, you just fall into it?" Yannha responded, "I think I've fallen into it more than anything. I took on junior AECG" (AECG is the Aboriginal Education Consultative Group). She added that with her language learning that was taking place, she was asked to be involved in more things. This led us to discuss the additional labour placed on Indigenous teachers in schools, and the tendency due to passion for our communities, to pick up additional roles and wear additional hats. I asked Yannha if her workload included these additional roles, to which she responded, "No. It's just extra stuff, but if it's going to help our community and help bring language into kids' lives and into the school, then it's worth it, I guess".

In my own personal reflections, I wondered if aspects of this related to the "cultural taxation" experienced by Aboriginal teachers in school settings. Padilla (1994, p. 26) coined the important term "cultural taxation", describing it as a type of taxation "which assumes that we are best suited for specific tasks because of our race/ethnicity or our presumed knowledge of cultural differences. This taxation takes many forms, with some being easier to identify than others". Hogarth (2019b, p. 49) contextualises this in the context of being an Aboriginal teacher in a school, noting "The embodied Aboriginal is indeed the very aspect that makes us attractive to institutions and yet, hidden responsibilities and roles within our job descriptions are further burdens we are expected to accept; to meet the expectations of the employer". Yannha highlights the cultural load she has inherited as an Aboriginal teacher, and the lack of value attributed to this by her employers, evidenced in a lack of work loading for the additional cultural load.

We then moved to discussing the best parts about being an English teacher. Yannha talked about the moments, whilst not always often, when students see the value that English can have on their lives. In addition, she also shared this:

> I think bringing in different kinds of texts into my students' lives and when they really respond to a text. So, for example, my year sevens, we're doing a unit at the moment that's specifically on Australia's first peoples, and texts of Aboriginal perspectives and that demonstrate aspects of Aboriginal culture. We were looking at the song by Archie Roach, Native Born, and my year sevens were loving it. We had so many good conversations and they were really getting into the song, which was awesome.

This vignette showcases the way in which powerful learning experiences aid English teachers' professional practice and motivation.

As texts, and text selection play a central role in this study, I asked Yannha to walk me through her step-by-step approach to selecting a text. Yannha begins with unit outlines, created by her head teacher. These unit outlines then inform the types of texts needed. Yannha gave an example of this: "So, if it's a unit that's focused on visual things, then I'm looking for picture books or a graphic novel or websites". From establishing the text type, Yannha then decides what she wants the students to be focused on, such as representation, or a core theme from the unit outlines such as an "Our Stories of Asia" unit. Lastly, ensuring that the text selection suits the class and students. Yannha notes that this process usually results in a wide range of texts that then needs to be narrowed down. This narrowing down is done by considering what has been done already, and seeking something different, or getting a new perspective, or selecting something that allows students to build on skills they have begun developing.

I then shifted to focusing on text selection to represent Aboriginal and Torres Strait Islander perspectives in the classroom by asking Yannha if the process changes for this content. Yannha noted that there will be a point where she consciously decides that she wants a text by an Aboriginal author, or a text that has Aboriginal and Torres Strait Islander people in it. Yannha offered other ideas about what this looks like in practice:

> When I was doing our unit for year seven at the start of the year, it's heroes, and I decided for myself it was a really important thing that the students in my class saw an Aboriginal hero. And so, our main text was, which I'd chosen because it works really well with students, was a film on a New Zealander and a sports person. I was like, all right. If I can find an Aboriginal sports person that we're going to look at

first, and then I went and looked for different people and found Adam Goodes and Cathy Freeman and looked at them obviously. And so, we looked at articles to do with those guys as heroes.

This example of practice offers a strong example of the practice of embedding an Aboriginal perspective. Beyond that, it also intrinsically speaks back to deficit discourses by representing Aboriginal and Torres Strait Islander peoples as heroes, when there can typically be a tendency to focus on us as victims. Yannha noted regarding the unit: "I can't do this without having an Aboriginal and Torres Strait Islander hero in here".

I asked Yannha if she thought this is something that non-Indigenous colleagues would consider. Yannha noted that she didn't think so and commented on her experiences from sharing this in a professional learning group:

> I brought this up as something I wanted to improve on and talk about Aboriginal perspectives, and the texts that we have because I was a little annoyed that our book room has lots of Aboriginal centred texts, and are not actually by Aboriginal authors.

This importantly illustrates how the conversation organically transitioned into discussions of Aboriginal authorship, and the prevalence of non-Indigenous authored texts which centralise Aboriginal themes, peoples and histories. Yannha expanded on this, sharing that when she explored the texts in the book room, "when I did some research on the authors, I only found two or three maybe, that were actually by Aboriginal authors, to which I was like, 'Can we change that?'". She responded that this prompted the head teacher to realise they needed to consider their practice.

I was able to yarn to Yannha about the complexities and considerations around the role of Aboriginal authors to tell Aboriginal stories. I noted to her that it felt strange asking her this, as mob; however, I was able to treat it as a stepping stone in our conversation. I knew Yannha's perspective would be significant for other educators to read, whilst also being a timely reminder that not all Indigenous peoples share the same points of view. Yannha responded to this passionately:

> Definitely. I mean, obviously it's not the only thing that we can and will and should tell, but it's really important that we do express those aspects of our identity, considering how significant our culture is to us. But also, in terms of connecting with others all around, and showing those around us that it is a beautiful thing and something that we should be proud of, and helping, like we talked about last time, young people seeing representations of themselves and how important that is as well.

This conversational extract offers us an important consideration: whilst our voices should be the ones telling our stories, we can and should tell stories across genres. Drawing on Yannha's response, I followed this up with a question about practice. I asked her, "if you were including a text that wasn't written by an Aboriginal person but was centralised, let's say, around Aboriginal themes and characters and stories, what kind of approach would you have to a text such as that one?" Once again, Yannha gifted me with a wonderful example of her own practice:

Well, I do include texts like that when I look at Aboriginal texts. I do make sure students know that it's not written by an Aboriginal author, and I do it, more often than not, in conjunction with texts that are written by Aboriginal authors. And I like to do that in a way of looking at authority and the differences in authority over texts, and then talking about what sort of aspects we're seeing, like the differences between how the ideas are presented, as well. And I find that leads to a conversation about the genuine ideas that are presented within the text, and how we see the difference between, say, Archie Roach's *Native Born*, and *Fat and Juicy Place*. There's some things that those sort of texts can't really portray, represent.

This is an important consideration that Yannha employs in practice, illustrating the role that non-Indigenous authored texts can play in the classroom. She touches on the powerful theme of authority, and the subsequent conversations this inspires with her students. She went on to continue this thought:

Or using things like symbols and whatnot that are part of visual representation, and that line in the syllabus that talks about using cliches and stereotypes and symbols and whatnot, and I'm like that's not something we should be doing in this unit. And it's just … I think there's a lot of lack of understanding about how we can incorporate Aboriginal perspectives in a respectful manner and still meet parts of the syllabus we need to.

Regarding this, I commented to Yannha that it sounds like she's fighting a battle on her own, and that there is tension in her English faculty because of this. To this, Yannha linked back to our first conversation, commenting that she has a young colleague she collaborates with often, who is on the same page as Yannha. She went on to say, "But my other colleagues don't necessarily understand, or they do but they do to an extent, and so there is very much a lack of, I guess, being on the same page about all of this and stuff". This challenge, particularly as an early career teacher and an Aboriginal teacher, illustrated a layer suite of challenges that Yannha faces. This led us to yarning about professional development as well as cultural safety.

Yannha was openly vulnerable and humble in our conversations, noting that she does not bring Aboriginal perspectives "brilliantly and flawlessly" into the English classroom. I feel this humility is incredibly powerful; as Aboriginal teachers, we are often positioned as experts, and whilst we are closer to experts than our non-Indigenous counterparts, we too are learning and developing professionally. Yannha identified that professional development that assisted with blending the syllabus and culture to "help empower me to lead" would be beneficial. This type of professional development that Yannha calls for is clearly layered. She wants something that will refine her skills as well as build in the leadership and confidence to lead in this area. This aligns closely with Yannha's commentary around her faculty, describing going up against teachers who have very well-established careers of 20 or 30 years. She comments that her age as well as her inexperience in comparison can make it difficult to step up into the space and state, "Well, I don't agree with this", or "Maybe we shouldn't be doing it that way, maybe we need to do this instead". A layer of complexity exists here, as we are taught to respect our Elders; however, in the Western school system, we can often be at odds with the knowledges senior staff are presenting.

Aside from the collegial challenges Yannha touched on, there are also a range of professional challenges that exist and are well documented within the teaching profession. I asked Yannha if she reads for leisure, to which she said, "No, not anymore". When she reads, she reads on the basis of determining suitability for the classroom. She is conscious that long novels will disengage her students. She went on to tell me about the directive in the faculty to draw on what's available in the book room, sharing that she has wasted time reading some of the texts available in the book room: "I don't have time to sit there and read it for … to only decide that I don't want to use it". I could sense the frustration as she shared with me, and I got the sense this was a repeated disappointment she experienced. She shared an example of this:

> And recently I read *Samurai Kids*, thinking, "Oh, this'll be great for my unit on stories of Asia", and then, as I was getting through it, I was like, "This guy was not actually Japanese himself, was he?" It's just so obvious. There's so many better things that I could use.

Yannha is clearly aware and attuned to the importance of authority in texts, and prioritising the voices of those with lived experience. Yannha further touched on the time-poor nature of the profession and the decisions this creates. Part of her last remarks in our last conversation: "I don't like judging a book by its cover, but sometimes I feel that I just make those snap decisions. I'll have a look at the cover, look at the size, and be like, 'Yeah' or, 'No'" illustrate the reality of the English profession, particularly for Yannha, who is balancing a level of cultural taxation, as well as the standard role of being a subject English teacher.

Towards the end of our second conversation, we tackled professional development, discussing how Yannha stays up to date with both English curriculum and contemporary Indigenous affairs.

> Well, I'm on social media a fair bit in terms of my teaching things. I really only look at stuff on Facebook and Instagram now, in terms of teaching. And then I follow quite a few organisations or people in general on various social medias, which then allows me to see new things that come up, and then I can go and take that and investigate a little bit further myself. And especially when it comes up on teaching platforms, like the ETA Facebook page, for example, so I use that as a starter

Yannha reiterates the role that social media plays in both professional and cultural aspects. Social and digital media has been transformative for Indigenous peoples and the ways we connect at all levels: local, national, and global (Carlson & Dreher, 2018; Carlson & Frazer, 2020). Teachers are now better situated with access to Indigenous digital and social media to stay informed on Indigenous affairs as well as teaching ideas, resources, and texts. For Yannha, she identifies two platforms for her social media use relating to her teaching practice.

Yannha was generous in her sharing, and it was important to reciprocate her generosity. Due to the considerable time prediction of the interview being one to two hours total across two interviews per participant, it was important to reciprocate my appreciation with a gift for the participants' time. The gifts that are selected as incentives are the 2020 publications *Fire Front: First Nations Poetry and Power Today*, edited by Gomeroi scholar

Alison Whittaker, and *Who Am I? The Diary of Mary Talence*, by Wiradjuri author Anita Heiss. The reciprocity related to these gifts offers value for the participant's time, as well as being a potential resource with which to engage. It aligns with the premise of this project valuing Indigenous authorship. The incentive was identified in the participant information and consent forms to contribute to the transparency and ethics of the process.

## Conclusion

Yannha's Profile of Practice offers us a glimmer of hope for the future of Indigenous perspectives in subject English. There is a need to prioritise the teaching of Indigenous-authored texts in the subject of English in the classroom, and through the example of Yannha, we know there are Indigenous teachers doing the groundwork. Subject English is informed by a range of contextual and curricula contexts; however, there is often a disconnect between how these are enacted. It is necessary to provide support to Indigenous teachers to pay them and value the cultural loads they are carrying within school systems (Padilla, 1994; Hogarth, 2019). There is room to further consider what professional development is vital to aid in teachers' critical reflection in order to do this well. In imagining Indigenous futures for education, we can look to Indigenous education sovereignty as envisioned by Gamilaroi scholar Michelle Bishop (2021, p. 421): "education that is grounded in Indigenous axiologies, ontologies, epistemologies and methodologies, for the benefit of all students". Whilst this study still fits within the realm of critiquing and changing the current Western system to include our perspectives, histories, and cultures, Bishop (2021) highlights the Indigenous futures we can aspire to. Through engaging with practicing Indigenous peoples who are English teachers, we can identify different ways of good practice in this area.

Ultimately here, I aim to illuminate an Indigenous education future where Aboriginal and Torres Strait Islander voices are the default choice for teachers when selecting a text as a way to include Aboriginal and Torres Strait Islander peoples. To return to the opening of this chapter, Phillips and Bunda (2018) say that settlers should no longer be the gatekeepers or spokespeople for our peoples. Our voices must be prioritised for all students to engage with in the English classroom. Yannha highlights the prevalence of non-Indigenous authored texts in the book room that are drawn upon. As Langton (1993) identifies, it is not reasonable to demand a sort of censorship where Indigenous peoples control all of our representation. What Langton (1993) does suggest is that we should discover the possible points of control and produce our own self-representations. For English teachers, we should be encouraging a critical reflection of the power of choice in the classroom. Teachers must be conscious of the voices they silence when selecting texts that all students will be engaging with, when it comes to Aboriginal and Torres Strait Islander histories, cultures, and understandings.

## Note

1 Pseudonym selected by the participant to protect anonymity and school site in line with State Education Research Application Process (SERAP) clearance.

# References

Australian Curriculum, Assessment and Reporting Authority. (2021). School Site [Deidentified for anonymity] My School Website. (Address withheld).

Australian Curriculum, Assessment and Reporting Authority. (2022a). *The Australian Curriculum Version 9.0*. ACARA. https://v9.australiancurriculum.edu.au/

Australian Curriculum, Assessment and Reporting Authority. (2022b). *Understand This Cross-Curriculum Priority. Aboriginal and Torres Strait Islander Histories and Cultures*. ACARA. https://v9.australiancurriculum.edu.au/teacher-resources/understand-this-cross-curriculum-prior ity/aboriginal-and-torres-strait-islander-histories-and-cultures

Bessarab, D., & Ng'andu, B. (2010). Yarning about yarning as a legitimate method in Indigenous research. *International Journal of Critical Indigenous Studies, 3*(1), 37–50. https://doi.org/ 10.5204/ijcis.v3i1.57

Bishop, M. (2021). A rationale for the urgency of Indigenous education sovereignty: enough's enough. *Australian Educational Researcher, 48*(3), 419–432. https://doi.org/10.1007/s13384-020-00404-w

Carlson, B., & Dreher, T. (2018). Introduction: Indigenous innovation in social media. *Media International Australia Incorporating Culture & Policy, 169*(1), 16–20. https://doi.org/10.1177/ 1329878X18803798

Carlson, B., & Frazer, R. (2020). 'They got filters': Indigenous social media, the settler gaze, and a politics of hope. *Social Media + Society*. https://doi.org/10.1177/2056305120925261

Davis, M. (2007). The United Nations Declaration on the Rights of Indigenous Peoples. *Indigenous Law Bulletin, 6*(30), 6–8. https://doi.org/10.3316/agispt.20080171

Davis, M. (2008). Indigenous struggles in standard-setting: The United Nations Declaration on the Rights of Indigenous Peoples. *Melbourne Journal of International Law, 9*(2), 439–471. https://doi. org/10.3316/agis_archive.20090400

Dean, C. (2010). A yarning place in narrative histories. *History of Education Review, 39*(2), 6–13. https://doi.org/10.1108/08198691201000005

Dorfmann, J. (2015). Undermining paternalism: UNDRIP and Aboriginal rights in Australia. *Harvard International Review, 37*(1), 13–14.

Education Council. (2019). *Alice Springs (Mparntwe) Education Declaration*. Education Council. www.educationcouncil.edu.au/site/DefaultSite/filesystem/documents/Reports%20and%20publi cations/Publications/Alice%20Springs%20Declaration/Alice%20Springs%20(Mparntwe)%20Ed ucation%20Declaration%20(accessible).pdf

Fredericks, B., Adams, K., Finlay, S., Fletcher, G., Andy, S., Briggs, L., & Hall, R. (2011). Engaging the practice of Indigenous yarning in action research. *ALAR Action Learning and Action Research Journal, 17*(2), 12–24. https://doi.org/10.3316/informit.463112109856313

Hogarth, M. (2019a). Y is standard oostralin English da onlii meens of kommunikashun: Kountaring White man privileg in da kurrikulum. *English in Australia, 54*(1), 5–11. https://doi.org/10.3316/ aeipt.224527

Hogarth, M. (2019b). Racism, cultural taxation and the role of an Indigenous teacher in rural schools. *Australian and International Journal of Rural Education, 29*(1), 45–56. https://doi.org/10.3316/ aeipt.222825

Langton, M. (1993). *'Well, I heard it on the radio and I saw it on the television …': An essay for the Australian Film Commission on the politics and aesthetics of filmmaking by and about Aboriginal people and things*. Australian Film Commission.

Ministerial Council on Education Employment Training and Youth Affairs (MCEETYA). (2008). *Melbourne Declaration of Education Goals for Young Australians*. www.curriculum.edu.au/verve/ _resources/National_Declaration_on_the_Educational_Goals_for_Young_Australians.pdf

New South Wales Education Standards Authority. (2012). *English K-10 Syllabus*. Updated 2019. Education Standards. https://educationstandards.nsw.edu.au/wps/portal/nesa/k-10/learning-areas/ english-year-10/english-k-10

New South Wales Education Standards Authority. (2019). *English K-10 Syllabus. Updated 2019*. Education Standards. https://educationstandards.nsw.edu.au/wps/portal/nesa/k-10/learning-areas/ english-year-10/english-k-10

O'Sullivan, K-A. (2020). Personal and professional identities: Exploring the relationship between NSW secondary English teachers' beliefs and values about literature and its role in their classrooms. *English in Australia, 55*(1), 44–55.

Padilla, A. M. (1994). Ethnic minority scholars, research, and mentoring: Current and future issues. *Educational Researcher, 23*(4), 24–27. https://doi.org/10.2307/1176259

Phillips, L., & Bunda, T. (2018). *Research through, with and as storying.* Routledge. https://doi.org/10.4324/9781315109190

Phillips, S., McLean Davies, L., & Truman, S. E. (2022). Power of country: Indigenous relationality and reading Indigenous climate fiction in Australia. *Curriculum Inquiry, 52*(2), 171–186. https://doi.org/10.1080/03626784.2022.2041978

Shay, M., & Wickes, J. (2017). Aboriginal identity in education settings: Privileging our stories as a way of deconstructing the past and re-imagining the future. *Australian Educational Researcher, 44*(1), 107–122. https://doi.org/10.1007/s13384-017-0232-0

Stake, R. E. (2005). Qualitative case studies. In N. K. Denzin & Y. S. Lincoln (Eds.), *The SAGE handbook of qualitative research* (pp. 443–466). SAGE.

Stake, R. E. (2006). *Multiple case study analysis.* Guilford Press.

UN General Assembly. (2007). United Nations Declaration on the Rights of Indigenous Peoples: Resolution / adopted by the General Assembly, 2 October 2007, A/RES/61/295. www.refworld.org/docid/471355a82.html

Wolfe, P. (2006). Settler colonialism and the elimination of the native. *Journal of Genocide Research, 8*(4), 387–409. https://doi.org/10.1080/14623520601056240

Worrell, T (2019). *Text choice: Teaching Aboriginal and Torres Strait Islander perspectives in English.* [Unpublished master's thesis]. Macquarie University.

Worrell, T. (2022). Profiles of practice: Influences when selecting texts to include Aboriginal and Torres Strait Islander perspectives in English. *English in Australia, 57*(1), 5–15. www.aate.org.au/documents/item/2691

Yin, R. K. (2018). *Case study research and applications: design and methods* (6th ed.). SAGE.

# PART II

# Intimacies

This theme explores the complexity of Australian Indigenous life and identity, and uses this to understand possibilities for Australian Indigenous futures, including:

- Who and what is 'Indigenous' in Australia and how this might change in the future
- Relations of care, reciprocity, obligation and responsibility
- Australian Indigenous queer identities and cultures

DOI: 10.4324/9781003271802-14

# 12

# UNSETTLING THE SETTLER STATE AND BEING ON THE FRONT LINE OF INDIGENOUS RESISTANCE

*Lynda-June Coe*

## Preface

Since the arrival of the First Fleet onto Gadigal Country on 26 January 1788, Indigenous people have defended our homelands. From open warfare on the frontier plains to petitions and strike action, Indigenous resistance has evolved not only from a fundamental need to survive but to also seek a future where we thrive. 'Australia Day' is held on 26 January as a national day of celebration. It is a day to reflect on settler sovereignty, history, identity and what it means to be 'Australian'. For Indigenous peoples, however, the day is a reminder of dispossession, genocide and racial exclusion. These are two very distinct and opposing positions.

## Introduction

Yiradhu marang yuwin ngadhi Lynda-June Coe. Bala-dhu dyiramal Wiradjuri yinaa galari giyalang.

Hello, my name is Lynda-June Coe. I am a proud Wiradjuri woman of Galari (Lachlan River). My home and community are beautifully located along a hilltop overlooking our ancestral place, our river, Galari-bila. Galari-bila (renamed by colonisers as the Lachlan River) is one of four major river systems on Wiradjuri Lands. We are river people, freshwater people, and our connections with Country have lasted since time immemorial, since the first sunrise and sunset.

I am a student of the Aboriginal Sovereignty Movement.[1] My Elders and teachers were pioneers of the Aboriginal Land Rights Movement[2] and are founding members of the Aboriginal Tent Embassy.[3] The student–teacher relationship branches from a vast family tree deeply embodied in Wiradjuri ways of knowing, being and doing. The majority of my Elders/teachers have now passed on to the place of murriyang, our sky camp, and I honour their investment and legacy by giving voice and prominence to their knowledge and values throughout this chapter. In my culture, the web of knowledge does not belong to anyone or to a singular authority, which is customary to Western paradigms, but belongs to the collective, the nation and the community, and more importantly, to the Ancestors of yesterday and tomorrow. I am but one tiny, miniscule strand in this 80,000-year-old web determined to uphold and regenerate its connectivity to the next. As a Wiradjuri Koori,[4] that is my obligation, purpose and intention across all facets of life.

Wiradjuri people have been at the vanguard of efforts to have Indigenous rights to life, liberty and property officially recognised across this continent now known as Australia. We were there at the Day of Mourning and Protest in 1938 (Maynard, 2007), at the Tent Embassy in 1972 (Foley, 2011), and at the High Court in 1979 (Falk & Martin, 2007). We worked on the first publication calling for a Treaty (Maddison, 2009), on the New South Wales Land Rights Act (McDonald & Marcus, 2004), and were at the High Court again in 1993 (Falk & Martin, 2007). And yet, in the settler colonial nation of Australia, Wiradjuri people, as a people, do not exist. We have no legal status or recognition of our sovereignty. Our efforts to build up a significant economic and political presence through the 1980s with the Wiradjuri Regional Aboriginal Land Council were smashed with the stroke of a government pen as it amended the Aboriginal Land Rights Act of 1983 (McDonald & Marcus, 2004). Today, Wiradjuri mob, including myself, are engaged in front-line activism continuing the fight that our Ancestors started.

My extended family were there at the 1938 Day of Mourning and Protest, and it is here that my focus begins. This chapter explores the social and political impacts of Indigenous-led protest on January 26, which is colonially referred to as 'Australia Day', but is known to Indigenous people as 'Invasion Day' and/or 'Survival Day'. From 1788, Indigenous people have registered their objection to the coming of the British and their insistence on staying. The arrival in 1788 is referred to as an invasion by many Indigenous people as it constitutes uninvited actions that led to the dispossession of our homelands and to the deaths of many of our people. January 26 is a day of Indigenous–settler conflict and contention, with the dominant discourse of white possession exclusively silencing Indigenous people through a historical process of invisibility. This chapter amplifies Wiradjuri voices and their contributions to the struggle of Indigenous movement-building since the 1938 Day of Mourning of Protest to the present. I acknowledge the struggle and resistance began long before this date. As a Wiradjuri warrior engaged in the resistance, this chapter includes my own voice as an agitator and organiser against settler domination.

## Being on the frontlines

I am a representative and member of the organisation 'Fighting in Solidarity Towards Treaties' (FISTT). FISTT is an Indigenous-led people's movement aimed at liberating Indigenous peoples through social and political campaigns, protest and disruption (see Gregoire, 2018). FISTT is a next-generation collective of warriors raising public awareness, leading and co-organising events such as protests focused on Black Lives Matter, Aboriginal Deaths in Custody, Aboriginal child removals and Invasion Day (see Ollivain, 2021). We are a Warrane-based (Sydney) group, and like the Warriors of Aboriginal Resistance (WAR) (see DeWitt, 2015) of Meanjin (Brisbane) and Naarm (Melbourne), we continue to unsettle the settler state through the amplification of Indigenous voices and the presence of refusal, activating 'the streets' and building awareness through social media platforms. Principled on our unceded sovereignty and right to self-determination, we are the frontline of Indigenous resistance.

Following in the footsteps of my Ancestors, I am drawn to the frontlines in an effort to challenge settler violence in all its forms and to assert my birthright as a Wiradjuri warrior fighting to make the world a better and safer place for our people, communities and Ancestors to come. I am compelled to take to the streets to voice my disgust at the way settlers use their institutions of power, such as the media, to rain their hatred and violence upon us. In one example of many, in 2018, the morning Channel 7 television show *Sunrise* ran a segment with a panel of all white settlers: journalist and television presenter Sam Armytage, commentator Prue MacSween and radio host Ben Davis. In this segment the panel suggested that a second Stolen Generation is needed to 'help' Aboriginal children because, according to their opinion, we are incapable of looking after our own children (Carmody, 2018). Aboriginal children are removed from their families at staggering rates. MacSween stated, "just like the first Stolen Generation where a lot of kids were taken for their wellbeing, we need to do it again" (cited in Carmody, 2018, para. 6). Armytage also made comments about Aboriginal parents which were proven to be untrue—blatant lies (Richards, 2020). Channel 7 was forced to apologise. Like all settler apologies, this one was performative. By 'performative', I am suggesting that it is about the person apologising receiving the credit for the act as opposed to anything changing for those who are wronged (see Fredericks, Carlson, & Bargallie, 2020). The pre-recorded statement aired at 6:47 a.m. on a Monday morning, suggesting the network was keen to ensure as little viewership of the apology as possible (Carmody, 2018).

In 2020, we were again compelled to take our protest to the streets even in the midst of the Covid-19 pandemic. The killing of George Floyd by the police in the United States added fuel to the fire of the everyday pain felt by Indigenous people here, especially due to the seemingly endless and unaddressed Aboriginal deaths in custody (Carlson, 2021). Thousands of us, accompanied by many non-Indigenous supporters, took to the streets to demonstrate our frustration and rage against the racism, discrimination and violence we endure (Coe, 2020). And as we protested, there were still more deaths in custody (Allam et al., 2020; Carlson, 2021). As I have previously written (2020, para. 6): "The settler state must confess ownership of its historical wrongdoings and abuse of power. Like any violent perpetrator if it is to recover and transform from a place of denialism, they must take ownership".

Like many political movements, our call to the streets is fuelled by injustice. As Castel (2015) argues:

> The usual horses of humanity's apocalypse ride together under a variety of their hideous shapes: economic exploitation, hopeless poverty, unfair inequality, undemocratic polity, repressive states, unjust judiciary, racism, xenophobia, cultural negation, censorship, police brutality, warmongering, religious fanaticism (often against others' religious beliefs), carelessness towards the blue planet (our only home, disregard of personal liberty, violation of privacy, gerontocracy, bigotry, sexism homophobia and other atrocities in the long gallery of portraits of the monsters we are.
>
> (2015, p.12)

Nearly all of the above list is a daily reality for Aboriginal and Torres Strait Islander peoples. The fact of the matter is, settler-Australia has a track record of killing Indigenous people, and this continues today (McQuire, 2022; Watego, 2021). As I have previously argued, from an Indigenous perspective, we have lived an undeclared colonial war since 1770 when the continent was proclaimed the possession of Britain, under the lie of terra nullius, which in turn refused the existence of our sovereignty (Coe, 2020). The denial of our rightful sovereignty manifests in the denial of our right to exist. This formed the fundamental relationship that our people have had with the colonial state since then. It has also seen our mobilisation as political subjects. Every year on January 26, we take to the streets to remind settlers that their celebration of the nation is a celebration that is built on a hope that we would not be here.

In this chapter I include the story of two significant protests launched by Indigenous people to counteract the commemoration of 'Australia Day'. I discuss the 1938 Day of Mourning and Protest, and the 1972 Aboriginal Tent Embassy as both transformative 'ground zero' sites of Indigenous sovereignty and front-line resistance. I also include the contributions of my own people—the Wiradjuri. As an Indigenous protest organiser of today's generation, it is imperative we understand the historical lessons learnt by our Ancestors, Elders and Grandparents in order to map, navigate and strategise pathways that ultimately work towards our disentanglement from the colonial regime. My focus on Wiradjuri peoples is not to show any disrespect for any other Indigenous people involved. This is to highlight the way in which Wiradjuri have demonstrated their involvement in fighting against colonialism and demanding our sovereignty since 1788.

## Indigenous resistance

> The Aboriginal community has a strong history of resistance: from the early days of the colony with leaders like Pemulwuy and Yagan, to the Coranderrk petitions, the Australian Aboriginal Progressive Association's defiance of the NSW Aborigines Protection Board, to the day of mourning protests in 1938, the Pilbara strike and the Wave Hill walk off, to the Aboriginal Tent Embassy and the anti-Bicentennial march in 1988. There is a rich history of marching in the streets, protesting through boycott and keeping a visible, challenging and confrontational presence.
>
> (Behrendt, 2015, p. 2)

The "challenging and confrontational presence" Eualeyai Kamillaroi scholar Larissa Behrendt (2015, p. 2) refers to in the above quote is the grassroots mobilisation and activism Indigenous people across this continent have deployed against racial violence and colonial oppression since the eighteenth century. From wooden spears and nullas-nullas (wooden clubs) on the open frontier plains to petitions and protest, our people have resisted the white conquering of our cultural identities and rights to land (Foley, 2015). Through 200 years of concerted effort and various waves of resurgent activity, Indigenous people have sustained our presence through a defiant struggle of refusal, based on the central argument to all debates surrounding Indigenous people: our unceded sovereignty (Foley, 2015; Gilbert, 1973). Indigenous resistance can be described as "all of the ways Black people combat the physical and emotional wages of the system of White Supremacy" (Rankin & Solomon, 2019, p. 6).

In defending our homelands against settler invasion, the narrative of our Ancestor warriors who kept the settlers from expanding inland as quickly as they had intended to as well as our continuing survival against the onslaught of colonial terrorism, is a point of pride for our people (Gilbert, 1993; Goodall, 1996). The frontline on this continent commenced with Bidgigal warriors such as Pemulwuy on Dharug Ngurra ('Country') as colonists expanded west from Gadigal Country.[5] Pemulwuy led an armed rebellion and resistance against Governor Arthur Phillip and it was through the spearing of his game-keeper, John McEntire, who was reported to have shot and killed Aboriginal people during his hunting expeditions, that Governor Phillip set the precedent for what was to amount to a nationwide assault on Aboriginal people (Dutto, 2019; Willmot, 1987; Woodroffe, 1993). Phillip, in retribution ordered six Aboriginal people be killed and two captured to be publicly execution (Turbet, 2011, p. 55). Pemulwuy was later killed, his head decapitated and sent to Joseph Banks in London (Woodroffe, 1993, p. 27).

Two hundred years since Pemulwuy was killed and his head shipped off to England, being Aboriginal or Torres Strait Islander in Australia can lead to negative experiences early in life that can have a serious impact, and even result in death (Carlson, 2021; McQuire, 2022; Watego, 2021). From our infancy to adolescence, structural racism and violence force us to walk a fine line in our interactions with whiteness and coloniality, where hopefully our good manners will be enough to save us from being criminalised and institutionalised (see Rigney, 2020; Watego, 2021). For example, in my experiences within the school system, I was sometimes a confident and academically driven student, whereas my sister was an artist and expressed herself in different ways, as is the case for many Indigenous children. Our different experiences with settler teachers and institutions would set the trajectory of being capable or incapable of navigating the Western world as an adult. My sister experienced racism from her settler teachers, as did I, but she was singled out, disliked and made an example of because she was non-compliant with the norms of the institution and refused to blindly obey. Like many Indigenous children, she had questions when things made no sense to her—she could not just accept our position as dictated by the various lessons about what it means to be 'Australian'. I was tolerated to an extent based on my capacity to produce the work that was required to meet the settler standards of the educational system. Western education was an unsafe space for my sister's learning needs, and due to her failure to comply with the framework of assimilation which is embedded in Australia's education system, she was eventually expelled. Like many, her experiences left her feeling disillusioned and resulted in her being unable to fulfil her educational aspirations (Bodkin-Andrews & Carlson, 2016).

To be an Aboriginal and Torres Strait Islander person and to freely live as such continues to be a struggle. We continue to deal with hostile settler attitudes and structures which have denied our existence based on the violent dispossession of a continent—violence that we have never willingly surrendered to. Our resistance is a story of a will to win and to survive (see Miller, 1985) as we deploy every means necessary to ensure our ways of being continue to exist for the younger and next generations to follow. Since the 1920s, Indigenous peoples have been largely internationally influenced by Indigenous and Black activism of other settler societies, such as across Turtle Island (United States and Canada) and Aotearoa (New Zealand), to raise our presence politically and give voice to Indigenous rights amongst the dominant culture who have come to stay in our ancestral homelands.

## Day of Mourning

This was the big fight, not with your fists but with your brains.
(Pearl Gibbs cited in Goodall, 1996, p. 230)

The 1938 'Day of Mourning' was the starting point of the Aboriginal political movement in Australia, and a prominent Wiradjuri presence was front and centre with the Ingram family, who belong to the same clan group as my own, and Erambie 32 Acres mob (relatives). Within the first century after invasion, coloniality, race and power had produced a white-centred nation which experimented with the concept of racial exclusion as policy (Curthoy, 2003). The colonial states and territories became a federation in 1901 and at the same time legislated the White Australia Policy, encouraging white British people to migrate to the continent (Schech & Haggis, 2004). Indigenous people had already been relegated to the margins of settler society, and our exclusion became formally legislated under the Aborigines Protection Board 1909 (Carlson, 2016, pp. 22–26). It is these unbearable and unjust conditions that saw the rise of agitation, leading to organised political action.

The modern Indigenous political movement in Australia was launched in an era of complete government regulation and control. My old people were confined to Aboriginal missions and reserves and lived under a regime of assimilation, segregation and exclusion. In the 1920s, Indigenous political campaigning was growing. In 1924, prominent Indigenous activists such as Fred Maynard, William Cooper, Bill Ferguson and Pearl Gibbs laid the foundations for Indigenous political activism by establishing the first Indigenous-led and organised group in the country, known as the Australian Aboriginal Progressive Association (AAPA). The AAPA demanded self-determination, land rights and civil rights as well as Aboriginal control of Aboriginal affairs and the end to the practice of removing Aboriginal children from their families. This was a strong assertion of Indigenous sovereignty and a distinct political identity not yet seen by settlers (Foley, 2011; Maynard, 2007; Perheentupa, 2020). Inspired by the activism in the United States particularly (see Maynard, 2007), the AAPA began holding rallies and protests in the streets. They also used other methods such as writing letters and petitions.

Strongly influenced by the African American struggle and voices like Marcus Garvey, Aboriginal people in New South Wales began to organise themselves in the first deployment of modern Aboriginal political activism (Maynard, 2013). Wiradjuri people were instrumental throughout this period and the quest for equal rights and self-determination was originated. One person in particular, William 'Bill' Ferguson, who was born in Darlington Point in 1882, would become a pioneer within the movement alongside Fred Maynard, Jack Patten, William Cooper and Margaret Tucker. Ferguson launched the Aboriginal Progressive Association (APA) in June 1937 in Dubbo, Wiradjuri Country, in response to the growing discriminatory race powers Aboriginal people were being subjected to under the Aborigines Protection Act (1909) (AIATSIS, 2021; Maynard, 2013; Briscoe, 2013).

By the 1930s, three prominent Indigenous political organisations had been established: the Australian Aborigines League, founded by William Cooper, Doug Nichols, Bill and Eric Onus in Naarm (Foley, 2007); the Aboriginal Progressive Association, under the leadership of Bill Ferguson and Pearl Gibbs in western New South Wales; and the coastal AAPA, which was by then driven by Jack Patten (Goodall, 1996, p. 230). All three organisations shared fundamental aspirations for Indigenous rights that were underpinned by sovereignty and self-determination (Foley, 2007; Goodall, 1996).

On 26 January 1938, the APA instigated the Day of Mourning in Sydney to coincide with Australia's sesquicentenary and 150th anniversary of European settlement. Thomas (1988, p. 77) suggests that "anniversaries of this kind appear to reveal much about the societies they celebrate: sometimes they provide possibilities for oppositional representations of history; invariably they speak the high rhetoric of imagined histories and ever more glorious futures". Settlers engaged in a spectacle of celebrations that included a re-enactment of the landing of the First Fleet and a parade. Local Aboriginal people, however, were not interested in celebrating their dispossession and refused to participate. To provide an imagined 'reality' of the day, the organisers brought 26 Aboriginal people from Aboriginal reserves in Menindee and Brewarrina (western NSW), who were tasked with waiting on the shores for the arrival of the British. The cohort were chosen due to their particular 'traditional appearance' to appease the racial stereotyping of a traditional aesthetic (Goodall, 1996). After the short re-enactment, the next event entailed the 'Australia's March to Nationhood', which consisted of a parade of 120 floats through the streets of Sydney (Thomas, 1988, p. 79). The celebrations were heavily condemned by Indigenous activists involved in the Aborigines Progressive Association (Goodall, 1996); they were considered a total disregard of Indigenous suffering and oppression and recognised as a deliberate design to celebrate white superiority and white possession (Maynard, 2007).

Two weeks prior to 26 January1938, Jack Pattern and William Ferguson released a statement, titled 'Aborigines claim citizenship rights!' which stated:

> The 26th of January 1938, is not a day of rejoicing for Australia's Aborigines; it is a day of mourning. This festival of 150 years' so called "progress" in Australia commemorates also 150 years of misery and degradation imposed upon the original native inhabitants by the white invaders of this country. We, representing the Aborigines, now ask you, the reader of this appeal, to pause in the midst of your sesqui-centenary rejoicing and ask yourself honestly whether your "conscious" is clear in regard to the treatment of the Australian blacks by the Australian whites during the period of 150 years' history which you celebrate?
>
> (Aborigines Progressive Association, Patten & Ferguson, 1928, para. 1)

The APA advertised a conference to be held at the same time as the parade, called the Day of Mourning and Protest, which was attended by at least 100 Aboriginal people. The thinking at the time by members of the APA was a complete defiance of the status quo in an era where Aboriginal dissonance and disruption was relatively unheard of given the powers of the state, which had consumed the livelihood of Aboriginal people and communities. As Gary Foley (2007, p. 122) mentions: "By opposing the 150th Anniversary celebrations, Cooper, Nicholls, Patten and others were asserting that ultimately it was Aboriginal land, and they were implicitly and explicitly challenging the legitimacy of the imposed sovereignty of Australia".

While the Day of Mourning and Protest called for equality and citizenship, the contemporary movement encompasses more nuanced demands such as land rights, climate justice, police violence, deaths in custody, child removals, closure of Aboriginal communities and an end to all forms of discrimination and violence (Behrendt, 2003; Birch, 2018; Carlson, 2021). Most importantly, the contemporary movement asserts sovereignty instead of requesting citizenship, and continues to disrupt the lie of terra nullius and the myth of peaceful settlement. Indigenous people across the continent continue to hold space for our

Ancestors and future Ancestors, challenging the nation state with their humanity, pride and dreams of a just future.

With the various stages of colonisation which have occurred over two centuries, Indigenous society and lifeways suffered significantly and, in some parts people, languages and cultures neared extinction, but to the dismay of the colonial regime, we have survived and continue to reverse the residue of our suffering set by the foundations of our leaders of the 1920s and 1930s. The protests we see today on 'Invasion Day' were born out of this era against the same system of white supremacy that connects Indigenous people in struggle. As Rankin and Solomon (2019, p. 6) write:

> the "system of White Supremacy" defines the realities of Black people and is not merely a belief that being White is better but is a political, cultural, and economic system premised on the subjugation of people who are not white. This system of subjugation manifests in multiple ways and is enforced, policed and reinforced again with varied degrees of "physical violence, mental abuse and robbery".

In the context of Australia, the system of white supremacy and coloniality has been fundamentally built into every corridor of power.

## Aboriginal Tent Embassy

The 1960s in Australia saw a significant rise in Indigenous political activism and protest challenging settler occupation and its institutions (Foley, 2007). Inspiration was further encouraged by adopting language and approaches from the plight of other Indigenous people and Black people around the globe, and particularly the United States, for example, the American civil rights movement (Dierenfield, 2013); the American Indian movement (Whittstock & Salinas, 2015), and the Black Power movement (Maynard, 2007; Slate, 2012).

The international Black struggle, particularly, represented and called for civil and equal rights in political, economic and social rights. The Indigenous articulation of this was based on uprising and protest of their exclusion, denial of culture and rights to land. As Gilbert (1993, p. 2) explains: "Our people have endured historical land theft, attempted genocide, oppression, denial of human rights, actual and de facto slavery, ridicule, denigration, inequality and paternalism".

Indigenous blockades to the system of white supremacy, which has contained our displacement and entanglement within the Western-colonial paradigm, continues to be fought against by people using both creativity and agency to challenge the status quo. Indigenous-led campaigns such as the 1965 Freedom Ride in New South Wales (see Libesman, 2019) and the Gurindji walk-off at Wave Hill in Northern Territory (see Duncan, 2017), along with the promise for social change of the 1967 Referendum (see Goodall, 1996), political consciousness and the actions which occurred throughout this period, impacted and defined the agenda of Indigenous land rights and self-determination like no other time before. By the 1970s, the Black Power movement had been established in Redfern (Foley, 1991). Known as the Black Caucus, this group was made up of young Indigenous activists at the time including Lyn and Peter Thompson, Billie Craigie, Gary Williams, Gary Foley, Tony Coorey and my dad's older siblings Uncle Paul and Aunty Isabell Coe (Foley, 2014). According to Foley (2014, p. 26):

These young activists by now had accumulated a significant degree of knowledge and experience in a range of areas, including political agitation and organisation, establishing major community self-help programmes, creating a sophisticated public relations network that clearly was able to out-manoeuvre and outwit the highly paid public servants presenting government perspective [...] thus the young Black Power activists seized control of the initiative and political agenda.

On the night of 25 January 1972, four Aboriginal activists in Redfern, Tony Coorey, Billy Craigie, Bertie Williams and Michael Anderson, travelled to Ngunnawal Country (where Canberra is located) to protest against the then-prime minister William McMahon's Australia Day statement (see Carlson, 2022). McMahon, in his address, stated that there would be no Aboriginal land rights and instead introduced 50-year general purpose land leases in the Northern Territory to favour mining companies. Nabalco mine in the Gove, which the Yirrkala people has been opposing, was given approval, citing that it was in "the national interest" (Robinson, 2013a, p. 4).

The following day, the nation woke up to the news that the four Aboriginal activists were sitting on the lawns of Parliament House underneath a beach umbrella holding a placard reading 'Aboriginal Embassy' (Foley, 2013; 2011). The first statement to the media by the Aboriginal Embassy representatives was delivered by Michael Anderson (cited in Robinson, 2013b, p. 5), who stated: "As soon as they start tearing up Arnhem Land we're going to start tearing up bits of Australia [...] the land was taken from us by force [...] we shouldn't have to lease it [...] our spiritual beliefs are connected with the land".

In the following days, members of the Black Caucus arrived as well as supporters from all over the continent. By July, the camp had gathered and harnessed such public attention that the Federal Opposition Leader, Gough Whitlam, met with the activists to discuss their terms (Newfong, 2014). As described by renowned Indigenous journalist and member of the Aboriginal Embassy John Newfong (2014), the Embassy had compiled a five-point plan for land rights which contained the following demands:

1. Control of the Northern Territory as a State within the Commonwealth of Australia; the parliament in the NT to be predominantly Aboriginal with title and mining rights to all land within the Territory.
2. Legal Title and mining rights to all other presently existing reserve settlements throughout Australia.
3. The preservation of all sacred sites throughout Australia.
4. Legal title and mining rights to areas in and around all Australian capital cities.
5. Compensation monies for lands not returnable to make the form of a down payment of six billion dollars and an annual percentage of gross national income (p. 139).

Arguably, the Aboriginal Tent Embassy was established to protest the very meaning and representation of 'Australia Day' and settler legitimacy. The Aboriginal Tent Embassy has become, according to Behrendt (2015, p. xxiv), "an iconic act of resistance and of sovereignty".

On 26 January 2012, the 40th Anniversary of the Tent Embassy was organised to coordinate a national day of protest and a conference on Ngunnawal Country. I had a small part to play in assisting with the organisation of this event and it was my introduction and involvement of frontline movement-making. My older cousin, Nioka Coe, the daughter of

Uncle Billy Craigie and Aunty Isabell Coe, was instrumental in ensuring the embassy site was prepared for a large encampment and a three-day conference with workshops to discuss the future direction of the movement. I was visiting Canberra in late 2011 and staying with Nioka for a short period when one afternoon, we went for a walk to the house of a Gomaroi sister who had been playing her part in sorting the concert and music for the day. We walked into her home as she was preparing music and a PowerPoint for a media announcement. I lent my voice as narrator for the advertisement of the 40th anniversary and, little did I know and understand at the time, that little *Call Out* clip was sent to every Black media and radio station across the continent. My voice had been streamed far and wide to encourage mob to mobilise for a day of action in our fight for sovereignty. I was happy to have contributed in some small part.

Following the events of 26 January 2012, one of the major outcomes of the conference was the establishment of Tent Embassies across the continent to assert sovereignty and demands for self-determination and the return of land. According to the First Nations Sovereign Union (2021), Aboriginal embassies were set up in Brisbane and Woomera (QLD); Cowra-Wiradjuri, Moree, and Kuradji (NSW); Portland, VIC; Port Augusta, SA; and Swan Valley, Noongar and Walmadan (WA). My father and I organised the Cowra-Wiradjuri embassy, along with guidance from my Aunty Isabell.

## Always was always will be

Over the past decade, Indigenous peoples have continued to converge in organised spaces. Younger groups have taken up the frontline through a resurgence of Indigenous resistance. One such group is the Warriors of the Aboriginal Resistance (WAR). Co-founder Meriki Onus (cited in DeWitt, 2015, para. 4) affirms:

> It's no accident. We are Warriors of Aboriginal Resistance. Without resistance the white man succeeds in taking our land and country so our purpose is not to attack but defend and protect. We want to revive the warrior spirit in our people by facilitating a culture of resistance.

In 2020, I was invited by the Metropolitan Local Aboriginal Land Council to give a Keynote Speech at the Day of Mourning and Protest site—Australia Hall, Elizabeth Street, Sydney. To stand in the hall, 82 years from the original Day of Mourning and Protest in 1938, was an incredible honour—one that I will cherish for my lifetime as I research, write and draw strength from the pioneers of the Aboriginal movement. I am reminded of the responsibilities and cultural obligations to uphold my values and beliefs in every space and opportunity that is placed in front of me. Being Wiradjuri demands this.

In closing, I finish with the words of my dear dad, Les Coe, who passed away in April 2019. Dad spent the last ten years of his life organising and speaking at the Tent Embassy and travelling around the country with his sisters Aunty Isabell and Aunty Jenny, with deep conviction and belief in what the embassy represents for our people and our survival. We co-authored this statement one afternoon up home in Cowra after much deliberation on the meaning of 'Aboriginal Sovereignty'. I have kept and treasured this statement. Together, we wrote:

Aboriginal Sovereignty Never Ceded [...] what does it mean?

It means Aboriginal people of Australia have not ever willingly or freely acknowledged or given the right for a foreign power to occupy our country and impose its laws and political systems on a free willed and peaceful people.

It means that Aboriginal people have not freely or willingly given up the right to self-determination or self-rule.

It means that Aboriginal people have not given up the right to own our lands, waters and natural resources.

It means that Aboriginal people have not given up the right to live and exist as free people in our own country.

It means that Aboriginal people be afforded a basic human right of speaking and teaching our own languages.

It means that Aboriginal people have not freely or willingly given up the right to practice our own religion.

It means that Aboriginal people have not given up the right to practice our own culture.

It means that Aboriginal people may one day be free from this constant and relentless fixation Australian politicians have in wanting to steal our children.

It means that Aboriginal people have not been free and willing participants in Australian political systems and their uniquely Australian idiosyncratic forms of Aboriginal engineering.

It means that Aboriginal people have not given up the right to support and sustain our way of life as a free and independent people.

It means that Aboriginal people are not free and willing participants in the occupation of our country by a ruthless and merciless foreign power.

Aboriginal Sovereignty raises a legal and political discourse that I will talk about next time.

Both the Day of Mourning and Protest, and the Aboriginal Tent Embassy represent significant actions which laid the foundation for contesting the legitimacy of settler sovereignty, for calls for treaty and for a redress package to compensate for dispossession and the denial of our humanity and uniqueness as a nation of Indigenous nations.

Early in 2022, I attended the 50th anniversary of the Aboriginal Tent Embassy and reflected on the previous ten years with pride, passion and love for my people, my family, those who are no longer with us and to the future of Indigenous people across this continent (Carlson & Coe, 2022a; 2022b). I am drawn to the words of Behrendt (2015, p. xxiv), who highlights the transformative and revolutionary impact of the Tent Embassy, and this includes the efforts of our people from the 1920s and 1930s who laid the way for the Tent Embassy and the contemporary political movement:

Today, the Tent Embassy stands as a transformative, revolutionary moment in Australian political history and a profound moment in worldwide anticolonial protest. It is timely that this important moment is reflected upon, critiqued, but most importantly of all, celebrated.

(Behrendt, 2015, p. xxiv)

My chapter set out to highlight the efforts of Wiradjuri warriors who have endlessly stood strong against the colonisers who have waged a war on Aboriginal people for over 200 years. My mob were there at the 1938 Day of Mourning and Protest and stood their ground at the Aboriginal Tent Embassy. As an agitator and organiser, I continue the work of my Ancestors and maintain the rage and keep the resistance movement going as we fight for our freedom and sovereignty.

## Notes

1 The Aboriginal Sovereignty Movement is an Indigenous-led grassroots political movement of the twenty-first century which was organised and mobilised from the Aboriginal Tent Embassy 40th anniversary gathering in 2012.
2 The Aboriginal-led Land Rights Movement was founded in the 1920s and 1930s, and called for land rights and Aboriginal control over Aboriginal affairs (Libesman, 2019; Maynard, 2007).
3 The Aboriginal Tent Embassy was established by Aboriginal people involved in the Black Power Movement known as the 'Black Caucus', in Redfern on 26 January 1972 on the lawns of the Old Parliament House as a result of Prime Minister McMahon's announcement and opposition to land rights in the Northern Territory.
4 The term 'Koori' specifically refers to Indigenous people originating from southeast Australia. The Wiradjuri people refer to themselves and each other as Wiradjuri Koories (Coe, 2020; Lambert-Pennington, 2012).
5 See 'The Australian Wars', a 2022 three-part series focused on "the bloody battles fought on Australian soil", directed by Rachel Perkins, www.sbs.com.au/ondemand/tv-series/the-australian-wars.

## References

Aborigines Progressive Association, Patten, J. T., & Ferguson, W. (1938). *Aborigines claim citizen rights! A statement of the case for the Aborigines Progressive Association.* http://nla.gov.au/nla.obj-241787110

Allam, L., Wahlquist, C., & Evershed, E. (2020, 6 June). Aboriginal deaths in custody: 434 have died since 1991, new data shows. *The Guardian.* www.theguardian.com/australia-news/2020/jun/06/aboriginal-deaths-in-custody-434-have-died-since-1991-new-data-shows

Behrendt, L. (2003). *Achieving social justice: Indigenous rights and Australia's ruture.* The Federation Press.

Behrendt, L. (2015, 9 June). Who's afraid of the Indigenous middle class? *The Guardian Australia.* www.gooriweb.org/news/2000s/2015/guardian9jun2015.pdf

Birch, A. (2018). 'On what terms can we speak?' Refusal, resurgence and climate justice. *Coolabah* (24&25), 2–16. https://doi.org/10.1344/co201824&252-16

Bodkin-Andrews, G., & Carlson, B. (2016). The legacy of racism and Indigenous Australian identity within education. *Race Ethnicity and Education, 19*(4), 784–807.

Briscoe, G. (2014). The origins of Aboriginal political consciousness and the Aboriginal Embassy, 1907–1972. In Gary Foley, Andrew Schaap, & Edwina Howell (Eds.), *The Aboriginal Tent Embassy: Sovereignty, black power, land rights and the state* (pp. 74–85). Routledge.

Carlson, B. (2016). *The politics of identity: Who counts as Aboriginal today?* Aboriginal Studies Press.

Carlson, B. (2021). Data silence in the settler archive: Indigenous femicide, deathscapes and social media. In S. Perera & Joseph Pugliese (Eds.), *Mapping deathscapes: Digital geographies of racial and border violence* (pp. 84–105). Routledge.

Carlson, B. (2022, 30 September). Made in 1972, the documentary Ningla-A' Na is a powerful look at the establishment of the Aboriginal Tent Embassy. *The Conversation.* https://theconversation.com/made-in-1972-the-documentary-ningla-ana-is-a-powerful-look-at-establishment-of-the-aboriginal-tent-embassy-191499

Carlson, B., & Coe, L. J. (2022a, 12 January). A short history of the Aboriginal Tent Embassy: An indelible reminder of unceded sovereignty. *The Conversation*. https://theconversation.com/a-short-history-of-the-aboriginal-tent-embassy-an-indelible-reminder-of-unceded-sovereignty-174693

Carlson, B., & Coe, L. J. (2022b, 31 March). The Aboriginal Tent Embassy at 50: a history of an ongoing protest for Indigenous sovereignty in Australia podcast. *The Conversation*. https://theconversation.com/the-aboriginal-tent-embassy-at-50-the-history-of-an-ongoing-protest-for-indigenous-sovereignty-in-australia-podcast-180216

Carmody, B. (2018, 13 March). 'So many mistruths': Sunrise cops heat over Aboriginal adoption segment. *Sydney Morning Herald*. www.smh.com.au/entertainment/tv-and-radio/so-many-mistruths-sunrise-cops-heat-over-aboriginal-adoption-segment-20180313-p4z46h.html

Castells, M. (2015). *Networks of outrage and hope: Social movements in the Internet age*. John Wiley & Sons.

Coe, L. J. (2020). Black liberation—it's time to be on the right side of history. *IndigenousX*. https://indigenousx.com.au/black-liberation-its-time-to-be-on-the-right-side-of-history/

Curthoys, A. (2003). Liberalism and exclusionism: A prehistory of the white Australia policy. In L. Jayauriya, D. Walker, & J. Gothard (Eds.), *Legacies of White Australia: Race, culture and nation* (pp. 8–32). University of Western Australia Press.

DeWitt, C. (2015, 27 January). We interviewed Australia's Warriors of Aboriginal Resistance. *Vice*. www.vice.com/en/article/7b7n3q/interview-with-the-warriors-of-aboriginal-resistance

Dierenfield, B. J. (2013). *The civil rights movement* (Rev. ed.). Routledge.

Duncan, A. (2017, 11 May). Andrew Bolt insists Indigenous Australians weren't here first. *Pedestrian*. www.pedestrian.tv/entertainment/andrew-bolt-insists-indigenous-australians-werent-here-first/

Dutto, M., 2019. *Legacies of Indigenous resistance: Pemulwuy, Jandamarra and Yagan in Australian Indigenous film, theatre and literature*. Peter Lang.

Falk, P., & Martin, G. (2007). Misconstruing Indigenous sovereignty: Maintaining the fabric of Australian law. In A. Moreton-Robinson (Ed.), *Sovereign subjects. Indigenous sovereignty matters* (pp. 33–46). Allen and Unwin.

Foley, G. (1991). Redfern Aboriginal medical service: 20 years on. *Aboriginal and Islander Health Worker Journal*, 15(4), 4–8.

Foley, G. (2007). The Australian Labor Party and the Native Title Act. In A. Moreton-Robinson (Ed.). *Sovereign subjects: Indigenous sovereignty matters* (pp. 118–139). Allen & Unwin.

Foley, G. (2011). Black power, land rights and academic history. *Griffith Law Review*, 20(3), 608–618.

Foley, G. (2013). A reflection on the first thirty days of the Embassy. In G, Foley, A. Schaap, & E. Howell (Eds.), *The Aboriginal Tent Embassy: Sovereignty, black power, land rights and the state* (pp. 22–41). Routledge.

Foley, G. (2014). ASIO and the Aboriginal Rights Movement 1951–1972. In M. Burgmann (Ed.). *Dirty secrets: Our ASIO files*, Newsouth Publishing.

Foley, G. (2015). Timeline of significant moments in the Indigenous struggle in South East Australia. *The Koori History Website*.

Fredericks, B., Carlson, B., & Bargallie, D. (2020). 'Nothing about us without us': performative allyship and telling silences. *Croakey Health Media*. www.croakey.org/nothing-about-us-without-us-performative-allyship-and-telling-silences/

Gilbert, K. (1973). *Because a white man'll never do it*. Harper Collins.

Gilbert, K. (1993). *Aboriginal sovereignty. Justice, the law and land*. Burrambinga Books

Goodall, H. (1996). *Invasion to embassy: Land in Aboriginal politics in New South Wales, 1770–1972*. Allen & Unwin.

Gregoire, P. (2018). Time for a treaty: An interview with FISTT's Lynda-June Coe. *Sydney Criminal Lawyers*. www.sydneycriminallawyers.com.au/blog/time-for-a-treaty-an-interview-with-fistts-lynda-june-coe/

Lambert-Pennington, K. (2012). "Real Blackfellas": Constructions and meanings of urban Indigenous identity. *Transforming Anthropology*, 20(2), 131–145.

Libesman, T. (2019). Dispossession and colonisation. In L. Behrendt, C. Cunneen, T. Libesman and N. Watson (Eds.), *Aboriginal and Torres Strait Islander legal relations* (pp .3–18). Oxford University Press.

Macdonald, G., & Marcus, J. (2004). *Two steps forward, three steps back: A Wiradjuri land rights journey: Letters to the Wiradjuri Regional Aboriginal Land Council on its 20th anniversary, 1983–2003*. LhR Press.

Maynard, J. (2007). *Fight for liberty and freedom: The origins of Australian Aboriginal activism*. Aboriginal Studies Press.

Maynard, J. (2013). Tracking back: Parallels between the 1920s Aboriginal political movements and the 1972 Tent Embassy. In G. Foley, A. Schaap, & E. Howell (Eds.), *The Aboriginal Tent Embassy: Sovereignty, black power, land rights and the state* (pp. 84–97). Routledge.

McQuire, A. (2022). The act of disappearing. *Meanjin*. https://meanjin.com.au/essays/the-act-of-disappearing/?fbclid=IwAR0k1Q5NWRRZCzopjrNSFj4Xg0CB31NCZxs6xObSqb_BqI71BZ3o8nrC5Co

Miller, J. (1985). *Koori, a will to win: The heroic resistance, survival & triumph of black Australia*. Angus & Robertson.

Newfong, J. (2014). Camping indefinitely at the Embassy (February–June 1972). In G. Foley, A. Schaap, & E. Howell (Eds.), *The Aboriginal Tent Embassy: Sovereignty, black power, land rights and the state* (pp. 139–143). Routledge.

Ollivain, C. (2021, 5 June). First Nations group boycotts SBS and NITV over Palestine coverage: Members of FISTT have previously participated in the news outlets' reporting of the Black Lives Matter movement. *Honi Soit*. http://honisoit.com/2021/06/first-nations-group-boycotts-sbs-and-nitv-over-palestine-coverage/

Perheentupa, J. (2020). *Redfern: Aboriginal Activism in the 1970s*. Aboriginal Studies Press.

Rankin, K., & Solomon, A. (2019). *How we fight white supremacy: A field guide to black resistance*. Bold Type Books.

Richards, J. (2020, 11 June). 'Sunrise' is being sued for that segment where they called for another Stolen Generation. *Junkee*. https://junkee.com/sunrise-sued-stolen-generation-segment/257279

Rigney, L. (2020). *Socially just education*. Lecture for the Australian Association of Research Education (AARE) seminar [Video]. YouTube. https://youtu.be/0Hk_axTFAvQ

Robinson, S. (2013a). Regulating the race: Aboriginal children in private European homes in colonial Australia. *Journal of Australian Studies*, 37(3), 302–315.

Robinson, S. (2013b). The Aboriginal embassy: An account of the protests of 1972. In G. Foley, A. Schaap, & E. Howell (Eds.), *The Aboriginal Tent Embassy: Sovereignty, black power, land rights and the state* (pp. 35–53). Routledge.

Schech, S., & Haggis, J. (2004). Terrains of migrancy and whiteness: how British migrants locate themselves in Australia.. In A. Moreton-Robinson (Ed.), *Whitening race: Essays in social and cultural criticism* (pp. 176–191). Aboriginal Studies Press.

Slate, N. (Ed.). (2012). *Black Power beyond borders: The global dimensions of the Black Power movement*. Springer.

Thomas, J. (1988). 1938: Past and present in an elaborate anniversary. *Australian Historical Studies*, 23(91), 77–89.

Thomas, S. (2014 16 June). Voices from the past: Aboriginal protests remembered. *Sydney Morning Herald*. www.smh.com.au/entertainment/art-and-design/voices-from-the-past-aboriginal-protests-remembered-20140616-zs8um.html

Turbet, P. (2011). *The first frontier*. Rosenberg.

Watego, C. (2021). *Another day in the colony*. University of Queensland Press.

Willmot, E. (1987). *Pemulwuy: The rainbow warrior*. Matilda Media.

Wittstock, L. W., & Salinas, E. J. (2015). A brief history of the American Indian Movement. AIM History. University of Arizona. www.u.arizona.edu/~salvador/Spring/Spring%20Documents/Civil%20Rights/A%20Brief%20Histry%20of%20AIM.pdf

Woodroffe, R. D. (1993). Pemulwuy. *Ngoonjook* (9), 23–31.

# 13

# VISUAL LIBERATIONS AND EMBODIMENTS OF ANCESTRAL MEMORY

## Exploring the relational engagements of Indigenous queer artists

*Dylan Barnes*

### Terminology

In this chapter the terms 'Aboriginal' and 'Indigenous' are used interchangeably, but their meanings are contextually defined. The term 'Aboriginal' refers to the first peoples of the (so-called) Australian continent and encompasses all Aboriginal language groups and their respective communities. The term 'Indigenous' is used to represent First Nations peoples on a global scale and within this chapter includes both Aboriginal, Torres Strait Islander, and other global Indigenous communities. 'Aboriginal' is usually accompanied with the term 'Torres Strait Islander' because of the Torres Strait's geographical and sociocultural proximity to Australia and Australian discourse. I have, however, included 'Torres Strait Islander' under 'Indigenous' as this chapter specifically discusses Aboriginal peoples, cultures, and intricacies. When discussing cultural meanings, languages, or practices that are specific to a certain language group or locality, I have used the name of the language group where relevant.

'LGBTQIA+' is an umbrella term that represents identities which exist outside of heteronormative sexual and gender identities. The term 'queer' as a collective identifier also represents the multitude of identities that exist outside of heteronormative sexual and gender binaries and is perceived by some as a more inclusive—and less restrictive—term to the identities within the LGBTQIA+ acronym. Although both 'LGBTQIA+' and 'queer' are often used interchangeably, this chapter uses the term 'Indigenous queer' peoples to refer to communities within so-called Australia who identify as both Indigenous and 'queer' (or under the umbrella term LGBTQIA+). It is important to note that both 'queer' and 'LGBTQIA+' are colonial terms that are rooted in European institutions of heteropatriarchy and Indigenous erasure (Monaghan, 2015, p. 201). These terms do not capture the complexity of Indigenous queerness that exists outside of these colonial binaries.

DOI: 10.4324/9781003271802-16

## Introduction

Indigenous queer peoples experience unique challenges within settler society due to their intersecting racial, sexuality, and gender identities (Carlson et al., 2022). One of these challenges is the isolation of Indigenous queer peoples from both LGBTQIA+ and Indigenous communities as a result of settler heteropatriarchy, which places many Indigenous queer peoples in a position of cultural disconnection and longing for community (Farrell, 2021). For many Indigenous queer peoples, art is an essential practice that reconnects us with our communities, ancestors, Country, and our own identities. As Indigenous queer peoples, our methods of communicating our ancestral stories are deeply interwoven into how we relate to each other and Country. All aspects of our lives are defined and embodied through our relationships to each other, Country, and to our ancestors—to which we are able to restore these relationships through the cultural knowledges that are communicated within our art. This chapter explores the ways in which Indigenous queer artists embody the cultural memories of our ancestors through artistic and relational explorations of identity, Country, community, and liberation.

In this chapter, I first define the concept of 'relationality' and how this term is foundational to, and embodied within, Aboriginal ontologies, epistemologies, and axiologies (Martin & Mirraboopa, 2003, pp. 209–211). I then analyse the physical, emotional, and cultural symbolism of various artworks by me and other queer Indigenous artists and explore how we communicate our relational connections to Country, ancestors, and each other through creative mediums. This analysis aims to increase understanding of the artistic manifestations of relationality of Indigenous queer artists and exemplify how relationality is central to how Indigenous queer peoples identify, coexist, and thrive. These findings highlight alternative ways to understand and practise relationality through the works of Indigenous queer artists and provide insight into how different Indigenous artistic styles and symbols are reflective of relational practices.

## Positionality

I am a Wiradjuri person from the Riley and Ferguson mobs in Dubbo, central New South Wales, and have cultural connections to the Darkinjung peoples of the Central Coast of New South Wales and the Ngardi peoples of East Arnhem Land. I was born on Darkinjung Country where I spent my childhood until I moved onto Dharug Country (broader area now referred to as Sydney) to study Indigenous Studies at Macquarie University. I openly identify and live as an Indigenous queer, non-binary artist and scholar with interests in Indigenous Queer Studies, relationality, and art.

As an Aboriginal artist, I have over four years of practical experience selling my own art, but I have been immersed in Aboriginal—specifically Wiradjuri and Ngardi—artistic techniques and knowledges from a young age. Although I was raised off-Country and quite isolated from my community and extended family around New South Wales, I had several opportunities to connect with my cousins during our family visits that happened once every one to five years. Three of my cousins in particular, Uncle Michael (Gararroongoo) (Mick) Huddleston (a Ngardi man from the Roper River region of East Arnhem Land), Aunty Karen (Mungarrja) Lee (a Wiradjuri woman from the Western Sydney area in eastern NSW), and Aunty Linda (Nungjingi) Huddleston (a Wiradjuri and Ngardi woman from Katoomba) were instrumental in my development as an artist. All three of my cousins possess over

20 years of experience as Aboriginal artists alongside their lifelong connections with their communities and ancestral knowledges. The knowledges and techniques my cousins have taught me throughout my life, such as Wiradjuri and Ngardi artistic symbols, dot-work and Raark (cross-hatching) painting techniques, and Dreaming stories play a significant role in my artistic expressions and navigation of my cultural identity and connections.

My knowledge of the interweavings of art and Indigenous queer communities and relationalities is directly informed by my lived experiences as an Indigenous queer person and artist. The intersections of my queerness, Indigeneity, and geographical separation from community and Country have brought about complex challenges in my journey to reconnect with my culture and be part of community. My existence on the outskirts of heteronormative Indigenous communities and non-Indigenous LGBTQIA+ communities has directly informed my artistic works, through which my art has become an expressive tool of reconnection to my ancestors, communities, and to Country. While I stress that my positionality does not place me as an authority on what constitutes Indigenous queer art, identity, or experience, it does provide me with a relevant understanding and mutuality of the artistic, symbolic, and thematic explorations of Indigenous queer artists in relation to their identities, experiences, and cultural navigations, making me an appropriate participant within this discourse.

## Relationality

The concept of relationality recognises that all aspects of humanity, land, space, spirit, and the subconscious are interconnected and possess a reciprocal relationship with one another (Moreton-Robinson, 2016, p. 71). Indigenous peoples possess a connection to Country that is physical, emotional, spiritual, and ancestral, to which all aspects of this interwovenness are fluid and living (LaPensée, 2017, p. 193). In this sense, reciprocity exists in the mutual exchange of knowledges, resources, and respect between humans, Country, non-human presences such as animals and plant life, and more-than-human presences such as ancestral spirits, time, and space (Kwaymullina & Kwaymullina, 2010, p. 201). Relationality acts as the foundation to all Indigenous epistemologies and ontologies (Watson, 1997, p. 39). It forms the foundations of our cultural histories and social relations, which are all interwoven. These foundations emerged from the metaphysical concept known as 'the Dreaming'. The Dreaming (explained in further detail in the following section) is a complex philosophical term that Aboriginal peoples use to describe the multiplicity, non-linearity, and interconnection of everything, everywhere, and everywhen (Kwaymullina & Kwaymullina, 2014, p. 35). Our identities, stories, communities, journeys, and understandings are directly informed by the Dreaming. Forming relationships with the physical, metaphysical, and spiritual world around us is how we communicate and embody the Dreaming. Relationality helps us acknowledge who we are and who we claim to be, how we interact with each other and other-than-humans, and how we as physical and spiritual beings are interconnected with Country (Moreton-Robinson, 2016, p. 71).

As Aboriginal people, we exist relationally (Tynan, 2021). We exist in relation to each other, to Country, our ancestors, time, space, and to our pasts, presents, and futures. When we are 'in relation' to the world around us, we connect to, live through, and embody the past, present, and future of everything around us through Country (Rey, 2019, p. 310). Our kinship systems transcend colonial definitions of family and community—that are inherently human-centric and heteropatriarchal (O'Sullivan, 2021a). Our ways of knowing, experiencing, and connecting with everyone and everything around us are tied to Country. Indigenous conceptions of kin and community include animals, plants, sacred sites, spirits, and other more-than-human beings—all which we consider our kin to some degree of connection (Kwaymullina & Kwaymullina, 2014, p. 37).

We define and identify ourselves through our relationships. We introduce and speak of ourselves in relation to who/what/when we are connected to. To identify and situate ourselves within the world, we introduce ourselves through who we are connected to; where we were born' what land we are connected to; where our parents, grandparents, and further ancestors were born; who our communities are; who our non-human relatives are; and who our closest kin are (Watson, 2015, p. 69). Defining ourselves through who/what/when we are related and connected to is part of the greater nexus of Aboriginal epistemologies, ontologies, and axiologies. Who we are in relation to Country is directly linked to who we are in relation to other humans, animals, spirit, time, space, and our ancestors. Our relationships and kinship systems go beyond the practical definition; they are the foundations of our knowledge, communities, and law/lore (Dudgeon & Bray, 2019, p. 3). We learn about ourselves, Country, and all of its human, non-human, and more-than-human presences through our relationships.

Relational philosophy is integral to Indigenous storying. Our stories are passed down to us by our kin and ancestors to teach us our place and purpose within the physical and metaphysical world. Storying teaches us how to engage and care for ourselves, each other, Country, our ancestors, and the non-human and more-than-human beings we exist alongside (Sium & Ritskes, 2013, pp. 3–4). Oral storytelling is the relational engagement of observing, listening, connecting, belonging, and caring that transcends the expectation of 'knowledge transfer' (Rey, 2019, pp. 113–114). Storytelling is a holistic methodology that gives meaning and place to the individual and their community, while situating themselves within the relational space of Country and its presences (Rey, 2019, p. 114). Through storytelling, we communicate knowledge that has been taught to us by our ancestors, who learned from their ancestors, who ultimately learned these knowledges through their experiences and engagements with Country and the Dreaming. Everything we are taught comes from what our ancestors knew, experienced, and embodied. Our connections to the Dreaming and our ancestors' knowledges come from storytelling and engagements with Country that act as the medium through which we learn, play, connect, thrive, and heal. We are taught these knowledges through oral, visual, and sensory mediums that can only be taught by our own communities and through our complex and relational engagements with Country.

### Understanding 'the Dreaming'

I refer to 'the Dreaming' frequently throughout this chapter. The concept of 'the Dreaming'—and the lived embodiment that we as Aboriginal peoples are familiar with—is one of extreme complexity, nuance, and cultural significance. 'Dreaming' is an English translation (Stanner, 1979, p. 23) of a complex concept that insufficiently describes the epistemological and ontological 'web' of relations that exist beyond time and space (Rey, 2019, pp. 49–50). Each Aboriginal language group around so-called Australia possesses a unique definition or conception of 'the Dreaming' that cannot be directly translated into English or other Aboriginal languages (Kwaymullina & Kwaymullina, 2014, p. 35). For example, the Yolŋu people of North East Arnhem Land in the Northern Territory use the term 'wetj' to describe the relational ontology that underpins the ways that Yolŋu people live, act, engage, feel, and thrive (Bawaka Country et al., 2013, pp. 186–187). Both 'wetj' and 'the Dreaming' are terms that seek to conceptualise the timeless web of relationships that Aboriginal peoples— or specific language groups and communities—possess with everything, everywhere, and everywhen. The relationships that we share with non-humans and more-than-humans are created, informed, and passed down by our ancestors' histories and knowledges through the Dreaming.

Our understandings of and connections to each other, the world, and beyond-the-world are deeply rooted within the Dreaming, which is communicated through methods such as oral storytelling, performance, art, traditions, and interactions with Country, non-humans, and more-than-humans. Dreaming stories have been passed down and shared with us by our ancestors and kin since creation. These stories teach us about our physical and spiritual connections, creation stories, relationalities, and interactions with human, non-human, and more-than-human presences that are held within the timeless web of the Dreaming. Our Dreaming stories are ancient geographical relationships that connect us to the everywhen (Saunders, 2022). As Aboriginal peoples, we maintain the eternal web of the Dreaming through embodied memories (Rey, 2019, p. 48). Through our stories, artworks, performances, and traditions, we are maintaining our ancestral knowledges and identities by sharing our knowledges with each other and other presences. Larrakia Elder and scholar Bilawara Lee (2013, p. 12) describes our relational embodiments as a 'seed' that is infused into the earth, similar to how a flower leaves behind another seed to continue its life and spirit. We keep our ancestral memories alive through song, dance, ceremony, and art which are all interwoven with/into Country, the non-human and more-than-human, and the cosmos (Rey, 2019, p. 48).

The processes of tending to and embodying our ancestral memories are actions of healing for ourselves, our communities, our ancestors, and the non-human and more-than-human beings we are intertwined with (Allen, 1999; Di Giminiani, 2016). Embodying ancestral memory through song, art, tradition, and relating are ways that we are able to heal intergenerational traumas brought upon us by colonial occupation and violence (Rey, 2019, p. 59). When we practise ancestral memory, we are performing and expressing knowledge to our communities and our youth that has been passed down to us by our ancestors. Our art is an embodiment of Dreaming knowledges that locate our identity, cultural connections, community, experiences, and our historical context (Taçon, 2019, p. 10).

## Art as identity, knowledge, and connection

The art we produce is imbued with historic cosmology, spirituality, law/lore, and relational connections which are expressed using both traditional and contemporary symbolism that possesses significant cultural meaning (Somerville, 2014, p. 406). These symbolic meanings are sometimes deeply contextual to specific language groups and their complex histories and relationalities, but some symbols are recognised and used by many language groups, such as the sitting person or campfire symbols. The use of symbols aims to tell stories of our histories, the geography of the land, and our connections to other beings, human, non-human, and more-than-human. Our art is a visual and symbolic acknowledgement of Aboriginal peoples' physical, emotional, spiritual, and cultural connection to the land, ancestral spirits, and all non-human and more-than-human presences around us (Kleinert & Neale, 2000, p. 241). Aboriginal art forms before and during colonial occupation commonly centred around depictions of our creators' spirits, totemic animals, and layouts of the land through mediums such as rock art, wood engravings, and sand drawings (Kleinert & Neale, 2000, p. 241).

Aboriginal rock art is a key example of ancestral memory that we are able to access through our engagements with Country. Rock art can take various forms such as stone engravings, paintings, drawings, and sculptures, which are found in almost every area of the continent and vary depending on the language group and locality (Taçon, 2019, p. 5). Our rock art is sacred as they are direct creations and embodied memories of our ancestors' knowledges that were formed thousands of years ago. In some language groups, some rock art bodies were created by spiritual beings during creation, or 'the Dreaming', which further solidifies their importance to Aboriginal knowledges and relations (Taçon, 2019, p. 7). Both the physical presence of rock art and its location are important and sacred to their respective communities. The depicted artwork and its placement on Country tell us stories of how our ancestors lived and protected each other and Country, the formation of the land, the historical events of their time, and the sacred law/lore that they learned and passed down to us. Rock art and the site of its creation is a direct connection to our ancestors, traditions, spirits, and the Dreaming (Taçon, 2019, p. 13).

When we are present with the artistic creations of our communities and ancestors—whether they are rock paintings, carvings, land formations, or traditions—we are sitting with, embodying, and remembering the memories that have allowed us to live and thrive to this day, as if they were being spoken to us (Taçon, 2019, p. 13). We are able to perform and express these teachings through art, song, dance, and performance using our knowledge of traditional practice and contemporary methods such as digital art, film, performance art, mixed media art, and many other forms of expression and creation. With a multitude of methods to communicate, express, and embody the memories of our ancestors and connect with our communities, many Indigenous queer artists today are utilising these artistic forms to convey the complexities, dichotomies, and lived experiences of Indigenous queer survivorship within the settler state.

## Artistic expression as relational engagement

For many Aboriginal peoples who are artists today, particularly those whose Aboriginality intersects with other marginalised identities, a resounding theme within our creative expressions is resistance and survival. As marginalised peoples within the settler colony, we are both physically and spiritually subject to debate, policy, violence, exclusion, and critique from the settler majority. We are targets for violent legislation that impacts us on economic, community, bodily, and political levels. Our cultural, gendered and non-gendered, sexual, and political identities are critiqued, demeaned, and isolated by settler hegemonies that seek to erase Indigeneity from the landscape (Whittaker, 2015, p. 226). Many of us are subject to the intersectional abuses of racism, sexism, queerphobia, transphobia, ableism, and classism from settlers and, as a result of the forced internalisation of settler institutions, even from our own communities (Carlson & Day, 2021, pp. 187–188). It is for this reason that Indigenous queer art as we see it today—and a multitude of art produced by Aboriginal peoples in the past few decades, which goes beyond the scope of this chapter—is rooted in themes of survival, resistance, and community. Indigenous queer bodies on a physical, metaphysical, spiritual, and political level are actively resisting the violent confines of settler colonialism. Through their expression of deep love, connection, and community, they reject colonial categorisations of queerness that are rooted in heteropatriarchy (Day, 2020, 2021). Indigenous queer existence challenges the settler colonial regime by finding ways to live, thrive, and relate with ourselves, our communities, and our ancestors within a system that prioritises our erasure (Monaghan, 2015, p. 198). Indigenous queer peoples are utilising creative mediums to express alternative futurisms that centre Indigenous communities, knowledges, and relational ontologies which prioritise Indigenous liberation.

The term 'Indigenous Futurisms', coined by Grace Dillon (2016), is a useful concept that contextualises the cultural, historical, and relational foundations of Aboriginal art and its importance within Aboriginal ontologies, resistance, and liberation. As a creative movement, Indigenous Futurisms represents a conceptual and realistic reimagining of the world through the lenses of Indigenous resurgence and decentring of colonial systems. Dillon (2016, p. 2) argues that "Indigenous Futurisms are not the product of a victimized people's wishful amelioration of their past, but instead a continuation of a spiritual and cultural path that remains unbroken by genocide and war". The creative expressions of Indigenous queer people commonly explore themes of cultural and community reconnection, self-love, and ancestral storying, which is encapsulated within Indigenous resistance and survival within the colony (Farrell, 2021). The themes and realities of Indigenous survival and liberation are central to the exploration of Indigenous Futurisms, which is exemplified further when Indigeneity intersects with other marginalised identities—in this case, Indigenous queer identities. The concept of survivance is a core component within 'Indigenous Queer Futurisms' as it asserts an Indigenous queer presence and establishes that Indigenous queer peoples can imagine and experience identities, senses of place, and relational connections that transcend colonial binaries (Farrell, 2021, p. 2). Indigenous queer identities and expressions are rooted in relational ontologies that are interwoven with our experiences of colonialism, resistance, legacies, and connections to Country and community (Farrell, 2020)—through which our creative expressions exist in direct relation to our lived experiences, ancestral knowledges, connections to Country, and our imagined futures.

The remainder of this chapter presents an analysis of the artworks of three Indigenous queer artists—Wiradjuri and Ngiyampaa artist Charlotte Allingham (known commonly by their Instagram username '@coffinbirth'); Yuwi, Torres Strait and South Sea Islander artist Dylan Mooney (known by their Instagram username '@dylanmooney__'); and myself (known by '@dylan.barnes.art')—with a focus on how their art visually explores and navigates themes of Indigenous queer resistance, community, and futurism, and how these themes are interwoven with relational ontologies.

### Charlotte Allingham

Much of Allingham's work possesses a common theme of resistance through community solidarity, connections to Country, and pride in identity. The work I will discuss[1] depicts two feminine presenting Indigenous people, one who is standing upright and adorned with a crown of native flowers, and another who is lying down holding a wooden spear. Within this piece, Allingham asserts the importance of Indigenous matriarchy and resistance by amplifying the power that matriarchs possess within our communities. Indigenous women have been pivotal in maintaining our relational engagements with Country and our communities. To us, land is the giver of life, and women are the custodians (Wilson & Laing, 2018, p. 135). Indigenous women, femmes, and life-givers are both our creators and carers. They carry our stories and knowledges, maintain our kinship structures, care for our communities and for Country, and fight for our right to exist in the past, present, and future (Oscar, 2018). In Allingham's work there is an intentional depiction of the Indigenous feminine body in front of the sun, adorned with native leaves and flowers, depicted with the ability to control and create leaves from her fingertips. All of these elements convey a story of Country, one that amplifies Country as a life-giver and our creators as protectors and the life forces of Country.

Dreaming knowledges of many different language groups, particularly Yolŋu stories, state that the Sun—or Sun-person—lights a small fire every morning and carries it across the skies from east to west, until she reaches the western horizon and puts out her torch (Norris & Hamacher, 2011, p. 100). The Sun as a physical and spiritual presence is a provider of warmth, daylight, and life force. The Sun protects us and guides us into the new day. It is a keeper and producer of ancestral knowledge that helps us navigate the memories of our ancestors. As a life-giving presence within many Aboriginal Dreaming knowledges, the Sun represents a caregiver and a creator of life force—mirroring the roles and depictions of Indigenous women, femmes, and birth-givers within our communities. The connections we have with the Sun are interwoven with our relationships with fire—which are depicted in the eyes of each woman in the artwork. Our ancestors would use fire to cultivate and distribute plant life, trap animals for hunting, and for ceremonial, war, and cleansing purposes using smoke (Pascoe & Gammage, 2021, pp. 56–57). With a large portion of this continent's plant life requiring fire in order to regenerate and germinate (p. 57), fire plays a vital role in the protection of Country and the living memories and knowledges of our ancestors.

Allingham's use of fire in this artwork represents both an ongoing relationality between Aboriginal peoples and Country, and a theme of resistance where fire denotes destruction—specifically destruction of colonial institutions. We see fire as a motif that conveys grief and pain through events such as bushfires and housefires, but also as a motif of protest, violence, and resistance against the colony. The theme of resistance is further conveyed through the wooden spear in the sitting figure's hand. The spear represents a relationality between humans, Country, and ancestors—where the human crafts the spear with wood that was sourced from Country, using the knowledge that was passed down from our ancestors to guide our construction of the spear, and following sacred law that tells us what and when to hunt specific animals using the spear. The spear-holding person wears a white T-shirt displaying the text "NEVER UNDERESTIMATE OUR FIRE IN OUR BONES: WALKING TOWARDS THE SUN". This statement expresses a deep resistance towards colonial institutions on a communal, bodily, and relational level. The use of 'our' signifies a fire that is felt within the bodies of Indigenous peoples—a fire of resistance and anger towards the colony, and a fire of healing, regeneration, and cleansing that our communities and ancestors have utilised since creation. The statement on the sitting person's T-shirt acts as a visual culmination of resistance and relationality where the motifs of the spear, fire, creation and care, and native flora reflect an ongoing connection to Country and ancestral knowledges.

In another artwork,[2] Allingham explores a similar theme of resistance through visual elements of queer identity, love, and fantasy. This artwork depicts two naked Indigenous people sharing a kiss in a loving embrace, with their groin areas covered by native flora. Both people possess long, elf-like ears, and the rightmost person has fairy wings protruding from their back and two scars on their chest under each nipple. The use of native flora to obstruct each person's genitalia explores a similar theme of relational connections with

Country, similar to the depictions in the first artwork discussed. Allingham utilises the obscuring placement of the native flora as a means of portraying sexually and gender-diverse characters to her audience that cannot be 'assigned' to a certain sexual or gendered category. This idea is furthered by the two scars on the rightmost person's chest that are indicative of a person who has undergone a bilateral mastectomy (colloquially known as 'top surgery') (Cheung et al. 2019, p. 130). 'Top surgery' is performed predominantly on trans and gender-diverse individuals who were assigned female at birth to remove breast tissue—which usually results in scarring on the individual's chest, similar to the rightmost person depicted in this artwork. The representation of trans identity through these top surgery scars communicates a notion of futurism that not only recognises the existence and experiences of trans, gender-diverse, and queer Indigenous peoples, but visually portrays the imaginings and realities of Indigenous queer love.

Allingham's depiction of Indigenous queer love explores both a lived reality of many Indigenous LGBTQI+ peoples, and a realm of fantasy and futurism that exists as an idealistic reimagining of the world we live in. The use of fairy wings and elf-like ears is reminiscent of fantasy-like imagery in fiction that is associated with fairies, magic, living nature, and storytelling. The popular concept of fairies is personified by a delicate whimsy that is accompanied by magic, spirits, and connections to nature—through which this artwork captures this natural whimsy through the inclusion of native flora and pastel colours and tones. The fusion of fantasy motifs, Country, and Indigenous queerness reflects a form of Indigenous queer futurism that locates our experiences, relational connections to Country and community, and understandings of our identities within a fantastical world that gives primacy to our liberation and relationalities. Allingham's depictions in both artworks tell stories of ongoing relationalities where community connection and protection of Country are the foundations of our humanity—through which Indigenous matriarchy and Indigenous queer love are acts of resistance and liberation.

## Dylan Mooney

Much of Mooney's work explores the beauty and disruptive nature of Indigenous queer bodies and radical queer love by interweaving themes of resistance, relationality, and identity. As Indigenous queer peoples, we understand and love ourselves in relation with our communities, ancestors, and human and more-than-human presences around us (Day, 2020, p. 371). When we can exist openly as Indigenous queer peoples within our communities, we are able to access our communities' knowledges, navigate our identities and culture, continue our connections with family and Country, and open ourselves to love from our families, communities, Country, and other Indigenous queer people. Mooney's artwork[3] visually explores the interweavings of Country and Indigenous queer love through elements of native flora and fauna and Indigenous queer futurism. This artwork depicts two Indigenous, masculine-presenting people who are lovingly staring into each other's eyes, with the text "AND THEN LIFE WAS BEAUTIFUL" above the couple's heads. Each person possesses coloured hair with small wisps protruding from them—mimicking the native grevillea flower and that has been utilised by our ancestors for its sweet nectar since creation. Mooney's use of the grevillea as hair explores a relational engagement between Country and the Indigenous queer body. The idea that the grevillea is naturally 'growing' out of each person's scalp conveys the notion that Country—and its non-human and more-than-human presences within it—exist physically and relationally within our bodies. Country and the knowledges of our ancestors and communities run deeply within our bodies, through our blood, through our thoughts, and through our engagements. This idea is further supported by the native leaves protruding from the leftmost person's shirt, and the grevilleas that are placed around the edges of the artwork. The grevilleas that surround the couple communicate their place on Country, through which the love and connection they share as Indigenous queer people exists in relation to Country and its presences.

The relationship and connection between the couple in the artwork is subtly supported by the imagery of the rainbow lorikeet on the rightmost person's shoulder and head. Within the context of this work, the lorikeet symbolises both a relational presence that is interwoven with Country, and also a subtle visualisation of the rainbow colour scheme motif that is associated with the LGBTQIA+ pride flag. The rainbow lorikeets that lie in the rightmost person's hair tell us a story of the lorikeet's diet, which mainly consists of pollen and nectar from flora such as the grevillea and banksias. The relationship between the lorikeet and the Indigenous queer body is one that is ever-present and ongoing. Our relational engagements with Country still thrive even under the violent institutions of colonialism that attempt to isolate us from our communities. We still persist and resist. Even within marginalised bodies, we are still creating and maintaining communities, continuing our relationship with Country and its presences, and finding new ways to love and protect each other. This notion of Indigenous queer resistance through love and community culminates in the statement "AND THEN LIFE WAS BEAUTIFUL". This statement conveys a tone of contentment and hope that is achieved only through Indigenous queer love and relationality. Mooney conveys that the couple's love and connection between themselves, their communities, and Country, is one that is obtainable and timeless—even within the confines of colonialism. This artwork is a visual and thematic exploration of Indigenous queer futurism that is communicated through love, community, and Country. Under the colonial regime, our bodies, identities, and relationalities will always be in constant threat of violence and erasure (Monaghan, 2015, p. 198), but we continue to resist these threats and exist authentically with ourselves and our communities.

Mooney further explores the interconnectedness between Indigenous queerness and Country within another artwork.[4] The visual depiction of native flora between the two masculine-presenting Indigenous people communicates a relationality where Country exists physically and spiritually within the Indigenous body. This motif is further conveyed through the smoke that wafts between each person and into the star-laden sky at the top of the artwork. The smoke and embers convey a similar story to the fire motif within Allingham's work discussed above. Both works utilise the visual elements of fire to communicate themes of resistance and regeneration; however, Mooney's work emphasises the restorative and healing properties of fire and smoke. As a relational practice and more-than-human presence, fire—when used to burn eucalyptus leaves—creates a cleansing smoke that heals our bodies and spirit, harbours connections within our communities, and demonstrates care towards Country and its presences (Rey, 2019, pp. 318–319). The smoke in Mooney's artwork follows an intentional path that weaves between the two bodies before wafting into the skies—which symbolises a regenerative connection between the Indigenous queer body and the ancestors that watch over us in the skies. The cleansing smoke within this artwork represents the healing of our relationalities with our communities, ancestors, Country, and our own bodies, which is the foundation to our liberation. Those of us whose bodies were—and still are—victims of violence, dispossession, and isolation as a result of the colonial project are able to heal those wounds with the cleansing smoke. Being able to reconnect with our communities that we were once isolated from because of our marginalised identities, is a form of resistance that gives primacy to restoring our relationalities and community structures.

Within the artwork, Mooney shares an ongoing story of resistance and community love that is deeply interwoven within our ancestors' memories and knowledges. The mutual respect, protection, and care for our communities and Country is the foundation for all Indigenous ways of being, doing, and knowing (Rey, 2019, p. 320). Our ancestors have kept this foundation alive since our creation, and although the colonial project has attempted to destroy our relational engagements and knowledges, we are carrying on these relationalities by understanding and sharing our ancestral stories, healing our communities, and resisting the colonial institutions that seek to erase us. As Indigenous queer people, our work towards Indigenous liberation is an ongoing, relational engagement that weaves our complex identities, cultural knowledges, and mutual care for our communities. Our work, whether it be within academia, the arts, or other areas of society, carries on the memories of our ancestors through our relational engagements. When our work prioritises community care and liberation, knowledge sharing, and protection of Country, we are maintaining the seed of ancestral knowledge that requires our relational engagements to grow and thrive (Lee, 2013, p. 12). Indigenous queer art plays a significant role in nourishing the seeds of ancestral knowledge as these visual relationalities and stories are gateways for both the (re) integration of Indigenous queer peoples within their communities, and the revitalisation of our community and kinship structures.

I turn now to my own art.

## Dylan Barnes

The artwork entitled *United Souls* (see Figure 13.1) is an original painting of mine that encapsulates the themes of community revitalisation, ancestral storying, and Indigenous queer resistance within its symbolism. This artwork draws inspiration from my own experiences as a non-binary, trans, Aboriginal person—specifically my experiences of cultural and community isolation on the basis of my queerness, transness, and geographical separation from my community and family. There are two recurring, culturally significant symbols within this work, which are the 'U' shape and the dot symbols, both of which are artistic symbols that are used in my family, and in Wiradjuri and Ngardi Country generally. According to my Uncle Mick (Gararroongoo) and Aunty Linda (Nungjingi), the 'U' symbol represents a sitting person, with its artistic origins dating back to the time of our creation. The symbolism of the 'dot' represents either an individual person, a piece of knowledge, or an ancestral memory, depending on the artist's language group, cultural context, and meaning of the artwork. The 'U' and dot symbols are utilised together to convey a large community of people who are connected through their experiences, identities, and connections to others.

Both the people ('U' symbols) and knowledges and memories (dots) in the work are scattered into five lined sections—two light blue lines at the top and bottom, two light pink lines towards the centre, and one white line in the centre. The blue, pink, and white colour scheme emulates the colour order of the transgender pride flag designed by Monica Helms in 1999, where the three colours represent masculine, feminine, and intersex or gender non-conforming identities respectively (International Transgender Historical Society, n.d.). The interweaving of cultural symbolism with the trans flag conveys a visual relationality

*Figure 13.1* 'Ngumbadalngilanha Dhulubang-galang' (United Souls).

Source: Artwork depicting several 'U'-shaped symbols in a similar layout to the transgender pride flag. Painted in Sydney in 2021. Own work.

that acknowledges and explores Indigenous queer experiences and identities. The visual and cultural exploration of Indigenous transness is a form of resistance that asserts both the survivance of Indigenous queer peoples and identities, and also the collective power to define and locate ourselves as a unified collective of Indigenous queer peoples (Finley, 2011, p. 37).

The central themes of Indigenous queerness and community building within the work reinforce a greater, ongoing story of resistance and futurism that is rooted in Indigenous liberation. As Indigenous queer peoples have been isolated from both heteronormative Indigenous communities and non-Indigenous LGBTQIA+ communities because of colonially entrenched heteropatriarchy, queerphobia, and homonormativity (Whittaker, 2015, p. 226), the formation of Indigenous queer communities has become an action of safety, solidarity, hope, and cultural reconnection for many Indigenous queer people. The overarching story in *United Souls* encapsulates the opportunities of hope and safety that Indigenous queer peoples can achieve when we can finally feel connected with a community. When we possess a true sense of community with other Indigenous queer peoples, we can exist and thrive alongside each other and navigate our personal and cultural identities and relationalities without fear of violence or isolation.

As a queer Indigenous person in their early 20s, I have spent the greater portion of my life yearning for community. My childhood and young adulthood were plagued with the possibility that I could never experience closeness or solidarity with anyone *like* me. However, my situation now is far different from how it was growing up. After moving to Sydney in 2019, I have been able to meet and connect with many other Indigenous queer peoples who I feel genuine solidarity with (Keovorabouth, 2022). I have the privilege of working alongside other Indigenous queer scholars who are making significant contributions within the Indigenous Queer Studies field (Day, 2020; Farrell, 2021; O'Sullivan, 2021b; Sullivan, 2018). My situation now is only possible because of the work and grassroots activism of Indigenous and Indigenous queer community members, activists, and scholars that have paved the way for Indigenous queer liberation. My artwork is a love letter to the trans and queer Indigenous peoples—both past and current—who are actively resisting colonial institutions and creating spaces for Indigenous queer peoples to live authentically and relationally. This artwork expresses an ongoing story that weaves my experiences as a queer Indigenous person, the knowledges I have learned from my ancestors and family, and the relationalities between myself, Country, and the communities that I am connected to.

## Conclusion

The examples explored within this chapter illustrate the ways in which Indigenous queer artists embody the knowledges and memories of our ancestors through our art and relational symbolism. Indigenous queer resistance, especially through our art, represents a relational storying of community healing and Indigenous liberation that continues the memories of our ancestors which are defined as reciprocity and care for Country and all of its presences. Indigenous queer art challenges colonial limitations of what it means to be 'Indigenous' and 'queer' by exploring the relationalities of Indigenous queer bodies, identities, and communities. With the emergence of Indigenous Queer Studies within the academic discourse, the prioritisation of Indigenous queer perspectives, experiences, and relationalities is pivotal to the growth of this field. Indigenous queer artistic expressions possess a multitude of complex stories and knowledges that are interwoven with our ancestors and close communities. The further exploration of Indigenous queer art from a wider variety of artists from different localities will prove beneficial for ongoing discussions of relationality and Indigenous queer liberation.

## Notes

1 See www.instagram.com/p/CN6QC4pMatZ/?igshid=YmMyMTA2M2Y%3D
2 See www.instagram.com/p/CZqglouDX4D/?igshid=YmMyMTA2M2Y%3D
3 See www.instagram.com/p/CJhqy4TAG95/?igshid=YmMyMTA2M2Y%3D
4 See www.instagram.com/p/CevOHOVPpaa/?igshid=YmMyMTA2M2Y%3D

## References

Allen, C. (1999). Blood (and) memory. *American Literature, 71*(1), 93–116.
Allingham, C. [@coffinbirth]. (2021, 21 April). I am so honoured to be able to donate this work for the @dhadjowa_foundation art action for their fundraising event, along side other [Photograph]. Instagram. www.instagram.com/p/CN6QC4pMatZ/?igshid=YmMyMTA2M2Y=
Allingham, C. [@coffinbirth]. (2022, 7 February). that's the look, that's the look, the look of looovve. the look of love ♥ [Photograph]. Instagram. www.instagram.com/p/CZqglouDX4D/?igshid=YmMyMTA2M2Y=
Carlson, B., & Day, M. (2021). Love, hate and sovereign bodies: The exigencies of aboriginal online dating. In A. Powell, A. Flynn, & L. Sugiura (Eds.), *The Palgrave handbook of gendered violence and technology* (pp. 181–201). Palgrave Macmillan.
Carlson, B., Kennedy, T., & Farrell, A. (2022). Indigenous gender intersubjectivities: political bodies. In M. Walter, T. Kukutai, A. Gonzales, & R. Henry (Eds.), *The Oxford handbook of Indigenous sociology* (pp. 1–30). Oxford University Press.

Cheung, A., Wynne, K., Erasmus, J., Murray, S., & Zajac, J. (2019). Position statement on the hormonal management of adult transgender and gender diverse individuals. *Medical Journal Of Australia, 211*(3), 127–133. https://doi.org/10.5694/mja2.50259

Country, B., Suchet-Pearson, S., Wright, S., Lloyd, K., & Burarrwanga, L. (2013). Caring as Country: Towards an ontology of co-becoming in natural resource management. *Asia Pacific Viewpoint, 54*(2), 185–197. https://doi.org/10.1111/apv.12018

Day, M. (2020). Indigenist Origins: Institutionalizing Indigenous Queer and Trans Studies in Australia. *TSQ: Transgender Studies Quarterly, 7*(3), 367–373. https://doi.org/10.1215/23289252-8553006

Day, M. (2021). Remembering Lugones: The critical potential of heterosexualism for studies of so-called Australia. *Genealogy, 5*(3), 71.

Di Giminiani, P. (2016). Being from the land: Memory, self and the power of place in indigenous Southern Chile. *Ethnos, 81*(5), 888–912.

Dillon, G. (2016). Introduction: Indigenous Futurisms, Bimaashi Biidaas Mose, Flying and Walking towards You. *Extrapolation, 57*(1–2), 1–6. https://doi.org/10.3828/extr.2016.2

Dudgeon, P., & Bray, A. (2019). Indigenous relationality: Women, kinship and the law. *Genealogy, 3*(23). https://doi.org/10.3390/genealogy3020023

Farrell, A. (2020, 13 June). Queer and Aboriginal in a regional setting: Identity and place. *Archer.* http://archermagazine.com.au/2020/06/queer-and-aboriginal-identity-and-place

Farrell, A. (2021). Feeling seen: Aboriginal and Torres Strait Islander LGBTIQ+ peoples, (in)visibility, and social-media assemblages. *Genealogy, 5*(57). https://doi.org/10.3390/genealogy5020057

Finley, C. (2011). Decolonizing the queer native body (and recovering the native bull-dyke): Bringing 'sexy back' and out of Native Studies' closet. In Q. Driskill, C. Finley, B. Gilley, & S. Morgensen (Eds.), *Queer Indigenous Studies: Critical interventions in theory, politics, and literature* (pp. 31–42). University of Arizona Press.

International Transgender Historical Society. (n.d.). History of the pride flag. http://transgendersociety.yolasite.com/tg-pride-flag-history-timeline.php. Archived at https://web.archive.org/web/20210308005146/http://transgendersociety.yolasite.com/tg-pride-flag-history-timeline.php

Keovorabouth, S. T. (2022). The queer urban Indigenous city: Understanding the impacts of the settler-colonial state on urban Indigenous and two-spirit identity. *Journal of Global Indigeneity, 6*(1), 36062.

Kleinert, S., & Neale, M. (2000). *The Oxford companion to Aboriginal art and culture* (pp. 40–244). Oxford University Press.

Kwaymullina, A., & Kwaymullina, B. (2010). Learning to read the signs: Law in an indigenous reality. *Journal of Australian Studies, 34*(2), 195–208.

Kwaymullina, B., & Kwaymullina, A. (2014). Indigenous holistic logic: Aspects, consequences and applications. *Journal of Australian Indigenous Issues, 17*(2), 34–42.

LaPensée, E. (2017). Relationality in Indigenous food and medicine games. *Resilience: A Journal of the Environmental Humanities, 4*(2–3), 191–200. https://doi.org/10.5250/resilience.4.2-3.0191

Lee, B. (2013). *Healing from the Dilly Bag.* Xlibris.

Martin, K., & Mirraboopa, B. (2003). Ways of knowing, being and doing: A theoretical framework and methods for indigenous and indigenist re-search. *Journal of Australian Studies, 27*(76), 203–214.

Monaghan, O. (2015). Dual imperatives: Decolonising the queer and queering the decolonial. In D. Hodge (Ed.), *Colouring the rainbow: Blak queer and trans perspectives* (pp. 195–207). Wakefield Press.

Mooney, D. [@dylanmooney__]. (2021, 2 January). 2nd work for UniSA/Museum of Discovery ❤ 🐊 [Photograph]. Instagram. www.instagram.com/p/CJhqy4TAG95/?igshid=YmMyMTA2M2Y=

Mooney, D. [@dylanmooney__]. (2022, June 13). Been a while since I've done a drawing 🐊 [Photograph]. Instagram. www.instagram.com/p/CevOHOVPpaa/?igshid=YmMyMTA2M2Y=

Moreton-Robinson, A. (2016). Relationality: A key presupposition of an Indigenous social research paradigm. In C. Andersen & J. O'Brien (Eds.), *Sources and methods in Indigenous Studies* (7th ed., pp. 69–77). Routledge.

Norris, R., & Hamacher, D. (2011). Astronomical symbolism in Australian Aboriginal rock art. *Rock Art Research, 28*(1), 99–106.

O'Sullivan, S. (2021a). The colonial project of gender (and everything else). *Genealogy, 5*(3), 67.

O'Sullivan, S. (2021b). Saving lives: Mapping the power of LGBTIQ+ First Nations creative artists. *Social Inclusion, 9*(2), 61–64. https://doi.org/10.17645/si.v9i2.4347

Oscar, J. (2018). *'BECAUSE OF HER, WE CAN' National Aboriginal and Torres Strait Islander Women's Conference* [Speech transcript]. Host site. https://humanrights.gov.au/about/news/speec hes/because-her-we-can-national-aboriginal-and-torres-strait-islander-womens (Thursday, 12 July 2018)

Pascoe, B., & Gammage, B. (2021). *Country: Future fire, future farming*. Thames & Hudson Australia.

Rey, J. (2019). *Country tracking voices: Dharug women's perspectives on presences, places and practices* [Unpublished doctoral dissertation]. Macquarie University.

Saunders, M. (2022). Everywhen: Against 'the power of now'. *Griffith REVIEW* (76), 115–125. https://search.informit.org/doi/10.3316/informit.468911687120179

Sium, A., & Ritskes, E. (2013). Speaking truth to power: Indigenous storytelling as an act of living resistance. *Decolonization: Indigeneity, Education & Society, 2*(1).

Somerville, M. (2014). Developing relational understandings of water through collaboration with indigenous knowledges. *Wiley Interdisciplinary Reviews, 1*(4), 401–411. https://doi.org/10.1002/wat2.1030

Stanner, W. E. H. (1979). *White man got no dreaming: Essays 1938–1973*. Australian National University Press.

Sullivan, C. (2018). Majesty in the city: Experiences of an Aboriginal transgender sex worker in Sydney, Australia. *Gender, Place & Culture, 25*(12), 1681–1702. https://doi.org/10.1080/09663 69x.2018.1553853

Taçon, P. (2019). Connecting to the ancestors: Why rock is important for Indigenous Australians and their well-being. *Rock Art Research, 36*(1), 5–14.

Tynan, L. (2021). What is relationality? Indigenous knowledges, practices and responsibilities with kin. *cultural geographies, 28*(4), 597–610.

Watson, I. (1997). Indigenous peoples' law-ways: Survival against the colonial state. *Australian Feminist Law Journal, 8*(1), 39–58.

Watson, I. (2015). *Aboriginal peoples, colonialism and international law*. Routledge.

Whittaker, A. (2015). The border made of mirrors: Indigenous queerness, deep colonisation and (de) fining Indigenousness in settler law. In D. Hodge (Ed.), *Colouring the rainbow: Blak queer and trans perspectives* (pp. 223–237). Wakefield Press.

Wilson, A., & Laing, M. (2018). Queering indigenous education. In L. T. Smith, E. Tuck, & K. W. Yang (Eds.), *Indigenous and decolonizing studies in education* (pp. 131–145). Routledge.

# 14

# UTOPIANISM, ECO-CRITICISM AND COLONIAL FANTASY

## Germaine Greer's *White Beech* as a case study in settler futurity

*Arlie Alizzi*

### Introduction

This chapter is an attack on the Western utopian format from a critical Indigenous Futurist perspective. In it, I briefly trace the history of utopianism as both a genre and a practice before reflecting on Germaine Greer's 2013 memoir, *White Beech: The Rainforest Years*, as a key text for examination. I reflect on this book, which is situated on Yugambeh land, to argue that the critical habits of utopianism as both a genre and a practice are embedded in settler colonial land relations of property and possession. This possessive logic, to refer to the work of Goenpul scholar Aileen Moreton-Robinson (Moreton-Robinson, 2015), includes practices of utopianism which claim to be critical, leftist, and in Greer's case, eco-critical and feminist.

The basis of utopianism is tied to the consumption of Indigenous lands and to the appropriation of cultural and intellectual property as what Fredric Jameson (2005) calls the 'raw materials' for utopian envisioning. Greer's book applies this template with a particularly gendered lens as she fancifully speculates on Indigenous-gendered life and the sovereignty of Aboriginal people of the Gold Coast Hinterland region. This raises some unexpected connections to Greer's own personal tanglings with transgender people, and I will seek to draw this out in conversation with her land appropriation and earlier intellectual attempts to identify with a politically abstracted version of Aboriginality. While Greer's memoir has been celebrated by eco-feminists, it has also been pointed out that the work performs an insensitive white feminist cultural reading of the place it addresses, though as Lara Stevens has written, "As yet, no Indigenous Australians have published written responses to *White Beech*" (Stevens, 2018b, pp. 1–2). It is my hope that this critique will be useful for coming into an understanding of the workings of utopianism in Yugambeh Country, and I write with the intent to advocate for a rethinking of the norms of engagement with Yugambeh Country as a settler-utopian experiment in the 'good life'.

DOI: 10.4324/9781003271802-17

## On utopianism

There never was and there never will be a paradise—neither an Indigenous one, a religious or moral one, a worker's, futuristic, technological or even a physical one. This is important to understand, because the hierarchical structure of many societies gives the impression that one is always on the way to some destination, to a better position, life or world. Although this is an illusion, Western people were (and still are) habituated to the notion of 'travelling', metaphorically, toward some great unknown where they hope that what might be waiting for them is, if not Heaven, then maybe, Happiness, Love, Security, a Theory Explaining Everything.

(Graham, 2008)

Utopianism has been a key conversant (or an antagonist) for me in thinking about Indigenous Futurism. Futurism, and its companion practice of utopianism, are both modalities of activist practice, critical thinking, politics, and literature with many applications for scholars and creatives. However, I draw a distinction between Indigenous Futurism and utopianism and science fictions, despite all of these forms of writing sharing the common practice of using time and place as a 'formal strategy' (Scott, 2016) to imagine politicised visions of future worlds.

I see Indigenous Futurism as an activist practice which extends both into text and beyond it into ordinary life. My understanding of Indigenous Futurism in Australia is defined by three key aspects. Firstly, Indigenous Futurism imagines an Indigenous politics in the future. By politics, I mean that Indigenous peoples in the future are collectively organised and involved in imaginative and active forms of governance and communal action. Although some Indigenous Futurist texts represent a dim future in which structural racism and other forms of colonial violence have intensified, they also represent Indigenous peoples engaged in adaptable collective governance and resistance strategies. Dharug writer Mykaela Saunders has contributed that a key defining feature of Indigenous Futurism is that it must imagine Indigenous people in the Future, and I extend on her analysis to recognise the distinctly political elements of the texts I look at here (phone conversation with author, 23 March 2020). Secondly, Indigenous Futurism uses the future to subvert and defamiliarise colonial time. It employs time to call colonial understandings of reality into question and assert Indigenous perspectives on time. Finally, Indigenous Futurism allows for the complexity and agency of women, queers, children, and the non-human world. These often-silenced narrative perspectives are made central to Indigenous Futurist texts and other creative works.

As Kombumerri philosopher Mary Graham (2008) points out, the sensibilities and assumptions of utopianism are rooted in a Western desire for escapism; to travel to another place, and to draw from Moreton-Robinson (2015), to possess it according to the logics of whiteness and property. As I will explore, this takes place both in textual imaginings and in the material practices of land appropriation, ownership, and colonial migration, invasion, and nation-building; these are interdependent practices. Indigenous Futurism distinctively and consciously operates to imagine Indigenous presence and politics in the future while also presenting an active critique of white utopianism and science fiction in its creative output. Additionally, the recent creative outputs of Indigenous Futurists make a concerted effort to emplace Indigenous women and non-binary people in their representations of the future, paying attention to the particularities of their sovereign belonging alongside a serious consideration of non- or more-than-human entities.

Utopianism as a practice and genre has an extractive and ambivalent relationship with Indigenous peoples. It has drawn heavily from the corpus of European knowledge produced about Indigenous cultures and owes much to what Gamilaraay scholar Jared Field has called settler 'trafficking' (Field, 2020) in Indigenous knowledges, stories, and cultural property. Utopian writing and associated practices of utopian social organising rely on dispossession and colonial encounter to produce their stories and to self-actualise. As a genre, it has also declared itself in some ways to belong exclusively to an elite Western philosophical tradition of imagining a good life. In literary theory, the Utopian genre's 'origin story' is commonly located in Europe, most often beginning with Thomas More's 1516 text *Utopia*. *Utopia* established a literary 'tradition' rooted in settler colonist explorations which drew on colonial travel writing and diarising, and other forms of circulation of information from the early settler/invaders back to Europe, to narrate a journey by boat to an alternative society.

The utopian narrative structure provides an image of a faraway country which is organised differently to the home country that the narrator eventually returns to; the 'journey' for European writers creating a vehicle for imagining possibilities for new means to arrange society and power structures (Vieira, 2013, pp. 4–5). Sociologist Krishan Kumar names More as the father of the genre, which by his definition, produces an idea of the "good society" (Kumar, 2003, p. 68). The belief in ideals of the good society or 'good life' remains one of the important threads across textual and academic work on the topic, but again, its relationship to Indigeneity is complex.

Portuguese utopian studies scholar Fatima Vieira writes about the origins of utopian texts in the early colonial era, as travel writing cultivated a relationship between Europe and its 'others', bringing about speculation on new ways of organising society and framing new explorations of possibility and futurity:

> More wrote his Utopia inspired by the letters in which Amerigo Vespucci, Christopher Columbus and Angelo Poliziano described the discovery of new worlds and new peoples; geographical expansion inevitably implied the discovery of the Other. And More used the emerging awareness of otherness to legitimize the invention of other spaces, with other people and different forms of organization.
>
> (Vieira, 2013, p. 4)

Vieira and others (Claeys, 2010a, 2010b; Kumar, 2003) also attempt to situate Utopia within global political histories and European ideas of "social betterment", human aspiration, and social and political critique (Vieira, 2013, p. 22). At the same time as they align utopian writing with positive philosophical projects which respond to social crises, scholars in the field acknowledge its role in informing colonial ideologies which "not only reinforced the superiority of the 'Old World' but justified and naturalized the extensive appropriation and colonization of the 'New World'—as we have seen in Thomas More" (Pohl, 2010, p. 59). More's Utopia, emerging from the diaries of colonists as they moved around the Americas, is seen as the origin point for a proliferation of textual types and futurist practices, and the interrelationship between visions of the 'good life' in utopian thinking and colonisation have persisted well beyond the origins of the genre in More's text.

Utopias and dystopias are also described by theorists like Claeys and Jameson (2005) as responses to political, social, and cultural crises or problems, mobilising an imagination of the future to attempt to "intervene on the present" (Tuck & Gaztambide-Fernández, 2013, p. 80). However, the idea of the critical or leftist utopia has not escaped this problematic relationship. Marxist scholar Fredric Jameson argues that utopian visions of the future can reveal the limits of the imagination of the author, as they are shaped by the author's own understanding of their social reality. He notes as an example that while early utopias tended to eliminate property or money from their vision, in more modern utopias, money remains a persistent feature. In modern utopias, it is "an absence which [...] become[s] unthinkable when the use of money is generalized to all sections of the "modern" economies" (Jameson, 2005, p. 17). As Jameson writes, "our imaginations are hostages to our own mode of production", and thus utopias have the "negative purpose of making us more aware of our mental and ideological imprisonment" (Jameson, 2005, p. xiii). Similarly, in reference to science fiction and utopianism, he writes that since the end of the Cold War, "it is easier to imagine the end of the world than the end of capitalism" (Jameson, 2005, p. 199). In futurist movements in twenty-first-century Australia, while the end of capitalism or even the end of so-called anthropocentrism might be imaginable to white people, the end of colonialism remains unimaginable.

Jameson also describes the interest of utopian writers in Indigenous cultures during early colonial times as one of its foundational aspects. *Utopia* offers a template example in which Jameson identifies a literary fascination with Indigenous societies that arose during the period of exploration and colonisation of the Americas. In More, he notes an "identification with the Inca empire, whose 'communistic' social system has not ceased to fascinate the West" (2005, p. 24). Utopia, he then explains, is a bricolage of material from the past and present to form an idealised other world. During the exploration of the so-called 'New World', Indigenous societies became one of the 'raw materials' of these utopian texts. Christopher Kendrick explains:

> What are the ultimate elements of Utopian society? It represents an imaginary combination of modes of production, including major aspects of at least four distinct modes. First, its economic arrangements are partly modelled upon those of tribal communism [...] The encounter with tribal communism in the New World doubtless provoked Utopian communism, yet More's island—mirror for England that it is—hardly takes the print of New World tribalism in any sort of serious way [...] Yet, utopian communism can hardly be accounted for as a modernized version of the tribal system, it must also be drawn from the representation of 'accomplished' communism.
>
> (Kendrick, 1985 cited in Jameson 2005, pp. 27–28)

The Marxist definition of 'primitive communism' or 'tribal communism' is at play in a surprisingly explicit way here in relation to utopianism, and Karl Marx, for his part, conceptualised Indigenous societies in this way in his description of the main forms of precapitalist modes of production. The 'bricolage' of this conception along with the writer's own political inclinations forms the practice of utopia.

The observation that utopian writers use Indigenous cultures as a material for their future-building and political visioning indicates a representational relationship evident in the body of science fiction more generally. European writers employ Indigenous social structures in their writing in a way that shows a Western form of longing for an out-side; a romantic, often anti-capitalist sensibility which sees Indigenous cultures as holding solutions to the ills of modern society. The consequent use of Indigenous societies as aesthetic and intellectual 'raw material' for a bricolated representation of a yet-to-be-realised communistic future happens concurrently alongside the exploration and exploit-ation of Aboriginal lands. It also entails the conceptualisation of Indigenous societies as static, not fully realised, and unable to modernise, only to be consumed and merged with the political will of the utopian author. Jameson's analysis presents the utopian writer as having a "workshop like the inventor's, a garage space in which all kinds of machinery can be tinkered with and rebuilt" (Jameson, 2005, p. 14), while Indigenous society becomes a "representational code" among many others, all of which are tools in the inventor's toolbox (Jameson, 2005, p. 25).

By positioning Indigenous peoples in this way, Jameson implies a lack of coordinated, conscious, or intentional political organising on the part of Indigenous peoples. Utopianism requires the use of Indigenous people by Western thinkers, but through "the constant effort of a process that seeks to combine them" and to unify them into a "whole political program" (Jameson, 2005, p. 25). This involves identifying their "still existing social spaces" which are "barely surviving from the past" as deficient, lacking in political will and complexity (Jameson, 2005, p. 25). Indigenous societies then can only be part of the utopian canon to the extent that they may form the passive raw materials of it. In the case of More's *Utopia*, this meant creating a synthesis of "Greece, the medieval, the Incas, Protestantism" as four elements of the new, perfect, society, from which "new ideological values might be incarnated" (Jameson, 2005, p. 24).

Reviewing the body of work on utopian theory, I argue for a definition of utopianism as a process of mobilising Aboriginal lands and peoples in service of a settler political identity. Utopia involves two interdependent processes: the occupation and invasion of Indigenous lands, and the extraction of Indigenous knowledges and cultures as the "raw materials" of utopian visions (Jameson, 2005 p. xiii). This is reflective of an overall relationship between Indigenous peoples and Western theory which is, as Bundjalung poet Evelyn Araluen writes, "structurally and conceptually embedded in the intellectual products of nineteenth-century imperialism, such as notions of civilization and the Other, reflecting geographic and economic forces of appropriation, expropriation, and incorp-oration" (Araluen, 2019, p. 482).

Araluen's critique of literary theory for how it has failed to respond to, or to even approach, the lived experience of Aboriginal people, urges new ways of theorising uto-pianism which account for the lived effects of its processes.

Debate continues on the distinctions between utopia as a genre of writing and utopia as a practice of imagining of 'real' political worlds and possibilities. Kumar's definitions of utopia and anti-utopia, for example, emphasise the fictive rather than the 'real' or the aspirational political utopias, and insist on distinctions between the two. Utopia and anti-utopia, two interdependent genres, he argues, need "the literary imagination to proclaim [their] message" (Kumar, 2003, p. 71). Texts, then, can appear as 'blueprints' for action, and utopian actions are associated with literary movements. Utopian theorist Lyman Tower Sargent's work on utopianism makes even bolder claims about the deep connections between text and practice, acknowledging the utopian desires inherent to settler colonial processes in Australia and Aotearoa, New Zealand. In his work on the utopianism of national identity, he has identified utopian wilfulness in the construction of nations as well as smaller-scale utopian endeavours like intentional communities. Intentional communities or communes, he explains:

> were once called by many other things, including utopian communities, utopian experiments, and practical utopias [...] an intentional community is a group of five or more adults and their children, if any, who come from more than one nuclear family and who have chosen to live together to enhance their shared values or for some other mutually agreed upon purpose.
>
> (Sargent, 2010b, p. 7)

Looking at the settler colonial context, Sargent has noted that utopia is now used "as a label for many types of social and political activity intended to bring about a better society", claiming that "all utopian practice is about the actual rather than the fictional transformation of the everyday" (Sargent, 2010b, p. 6). Settler colonial nation-building is a utopian practice, and for Sargent, countries like New Zealand and Australia are considered intentional communities for this reason. While religious desires and political desires often provide the incitement for settler colonial migration, the desire for an improved life, "a full stomach, decent shelter [...] and a better future for themselves and their family" are also utopian visions which motivate and sustain colonisation and land occupation (Sargent, 2010a, p. 200). Sargent's work singles out Australia in this respect as a strong example of the utopian impulse bound up with colonisation:

> The most significant aspect of Australian utopianism has been in practical attempts to put utopia in place. While historically the number of Australian intentional communities was not great, from the 1970s on Australia has produced more such communities per capita than any country other than Israel.
>
> (Sargent, 2010a, p. 209)

The history of intentional communities in the country must be seen as utopianism at work; what Sargent calls putting "Utopia in place" (2010a, p. 209), and the act of the occupation of land itself is inherently tied to utopian impulses in Sargent's reading. For Sargent, utopianism situates settler possession of and presence on Aboriginal land itself as an act of hopeful imagining in search of the good life. On the sensibilities of utopian literature, he observes that the most significant works of utopian literature reflect the logics of colonial activities on the ground; "More's Utopians simply did not consider the inhabitants of the area to be colonised to be important, and this attitude is frequently repeated in utopian literature set in colonies" (Sargent, 2010a, p. 202).

Unangax̂ scholar Eve Tuck and Rubén Gaztambide-Fernández offer a definition of settler futurity which is relevant here, which they name as the "permanent virtuality" of the "settler on stolen land" (2013, p. 80). They argue, following Patrick Wolfe (2006), that settler coloniality is constituted by futurity in its logic of elimination and replacement which requires the "continued and complete eradication of the original inhabitants of contested land" and the incorporation of Indigenous peoples with a view to further emplacing settlers (Tuck & Gaztimbide-Fernández 2013, p. 80).

I want to pause here to attempt to situate Yugambeh Country in its own right before attempting to conceptualise it within its relationship to the Western utopian impulse as expressed in Greer's memoir. Yugambeh people and Yugambeh Country were compellingly put into writing in an Aboriginal academic voice in the 1990s by the late Ysola Best. Speaking back to colonial ethnographies and histories, Best put on the record that Yugambeh people existed and have their own genealogies, relations to land and people, economic systems, spiritual beliefs, and distinct language, and she set a research agenda for a project of undoing colonial narratives of Southeast Queensland. She noted that there is a need for continued in-depth writing on the subjects of contact and conflict in south-east Queensland;

> I have attempted to briefly assess some early historical records to determine, from an Aboriginal perspective, how Yugambeh people adapted to a changing environment and survived through an uneasy co-existence with newcomers to their land. I will conclude by questioning what benefit Yugambeh people gained by assisting the newcomers who moved into their country illegally, usurping the right of Yugambeh people to access their economic resource—the land. Indeed, had those many early European arrivals to southeast Queensland respected appropriately those Aboriginal individuals and communities who assisted their progress and aided their survival, the 'contact history' would have been easier to interpret.
>
> (Best, 1994, p. 88)

Best asserts in her work a distinct Yugambeh ontology, and also notes my own ancestor Jenny Graham's influence in the region in the twentieth century, alongside other Yugambeh ancestors such as Bilin Bilin, in advocating for and ensuring the survival of Aboriginal people in south-east Queensland since colonisation. In her critical history work on contact history, Best engages with settler accounts to argue that previous writing on contact and conflict in pastoral and frontier history in the south-east was Eurocentric, lacking proper understanding and consideration of Aboriginal peoples' genealogies, linguistics, and belief systems.

Best contributes to the historical record at the time that the Yugambeh language is part of a dialect chain which encompasses family groups from the Logan, Albert, Pimpama, Coomera, and Nerang Rivers, "including all the adjacent streams and creeks" (Best, 1994, p. 87). Contemporary Yugambeh people have diverse ways of identifying and describing themselves, but generally, family groups are known as the Kombumerri, Wangerriburra, Migunburri, Munanjali, Gugugun, Birrinburra, Bolongin, and Minjinbul. We have family and linguistic connections all the way down to the Tweed River and into Bundjalung country, across the New South Wales border, until you reach to the country of the Gumbaynggir to the south, whose language is distinct from the Bundjalung/Yugambeh dialect chain. Most importantly, Best made the particular point of arguing that Aboriginal people in the Yugambeh nation were in possession of their own distinct economic systems, contesting the popular perspective on frontier conflict history that Yugambeh and settler conflict occurred due to Yugambeh people's desire to control and share in the economic overabundance of the settler society. She argues instead that conflict arose not from jealousy or a failure to adapt, but from the Yugambeh demand to protect what they already had: water, land, and people. Dr Mary Graham further argued the following on the resistance of the contemporary Yugambeh community:

> Aboriginal people have a kinship system which extends into land; this system was and still is organised into clans [...] it does not matter how western and urbanised Aboriginal people have become, this kinship system never changes. (It has been

damaged by, for example, cultural genocide/Stolen Children/westernisation etc, but has not been altered substantially).

(Graham, 2008, p. 2)

Both Best and Graham have set out to contest persistent notions within the settler academy that Yugambeh people's language and culture have been eradicated, arguing instead that Aboriginal communities, sensibilities, and kinship systems in the region are continuing, and becoming stronger over time.

The point made by Best on the economic component of Yugambeh belonging on the Gold Coast and surrounds feels ever more salient when examining how Country is engaged with today. Yugambeh Country has many lives, and it lives those lives primarily alongside the settler utopian dream of retirement. The Gold Coast and its surrounding areas, as the state of Queensland understands it, is a consumer product for property developers, investors, tourists, and retirees. Non-Aboriginal residents and visitors to the Gold Coast tend to belong to two categories: those in pursuit of a fun holiday or those in pursuit of a happy retirement. Life—either the life which takes place during the holidays, the fretful periods between work, or the life that is possible after retirement, which a productive worker is promised to enjoy after a certain age—is bought, sold, and possessed. The retirement and the holiday are therefore two forms of what I think of as utopian settler engagements with Yugambeh country. Another is the tree-change, which is an escapist engagement with land as property that was explored in Goorie writer Melissa Lucashenko's *Mullumbimby*, which presented a complex and layered Indigenous conversation with the ideal of the 'good life' in Western literary culture. Tree-changers and sea-changers are more permanent escapists from the productive life of city cultures who are hoping to get back to a simpler life in communion with nature. Yet another kind of utopia found there in the area which Yugambeh Country encompasses, mainly in the hinterlands, are alternative communities, a form of utopian settler colonial possession with land which, as Sargent has noted, is invested with a particular kind of political zeal that represents a radical impulse but remains continuous with the projects of settler nation-building, settler futurity, and colonial possession.

## Germaine Greer

I mean the thing that makes us Australian I reckon is Aboriginality. You look at our kids running round. All they own is a surfboard and a beaten up wagon and loincloth. Aboriginality will take over eventually.

(Schofield, 2000)

Germaine Greer is a well-known white Australian public intellectual who has lived, worked, and studied in both Europe and Australia for the length of her long academic career. In recent years, Greer has been the subject of an episode of 'deplatforming', a forced withdrawal from several significant public speaking engagements at universities and writers' events for making derogatory and inflammatory comments about trans women. The views she expressed publicly about trans women during the period between 2015 and 2018 seemed particularly focused on asserting a definition of womanhood as a political category of experience tied to the body, which she argued trans women had no access to, especially when a full medical transition either does not occur or occurs later in life (see Nagouse & Edwards, 2018; Wahlquist, 2016). Performative public rejections of Germaine by several writers' festivals and universities in the late 2010s happened alongside a conversant and short-lived public *platforming* of Greer in mainstream media and feminist circles, due to her willingness to express her views about trans people publicly and the responsive generation of outrage by media outlets. Further heroising her, the University of Melbourne, her alma mater and the place where I earned my PhD in Indigenous Futurism, purchased and acquired Greer's archive for the collection of the University library in 2017 as I was busy compiling research on utopianism as a genre.

Across the last ten years, the University of Melbourne came under fire both internally and from the outside for playing host to a number of transphobic professors and lesser academic characters, and was the site of multiple public forums on trans people's identities, bodies, and civic and human rights and belonging (Johnson et al., 2019). Between 2019 and 2021, there was a concentration of emotive and intense episodes of debate regarding university policy around free speech and its relationship to matters of transgender rights and recognition on campus. One such public event involved groups of protesters and counterprotesters circling campus for hours, and the words 'trannies OUT!' being graffitied on a window in the Old Arts building (Carey, 2021). The university's own policy positions on LGBT staff and students have also shifted internally as increasing numbers of people internally are identifying as openly gender diverse. On the level of workplace relations (as well as discourse as expressed by institutional machinery and policy, student life, and subject curriculum), recognition of transgender and non-binary subjectivity through the rights of either workers or consumers/customers of the university is being highlighted and reconfigured.[1]

I couldn't—and still can't—look away from Greer's bizarre television appearances from this time. I have been fascinated by any and all scandals involving anti-trans feminist ideologues since my own encounters with the teaching materials of former professor Sheila Jeffreys at the university. I was focused on how much the increasing cultural and political demand to recognise the complexity and legitimacy of transness deeply bothers Greer. Greer's intellectual identity has been outwardly fugitive and tied to being countercultural, and who, as Lara Stevens noted in her review of *White Beech*, has never "identified easily with her sisters", maintaining an "openly hostile and antagonist attitude" towards many other feminist critics (Stevens, 2018a, p. 117). During some recorded interviews from this time period, she appears flustered and enraged, fervently discussing madness, cancel culture, identity politics, undescended testicles, Caitlyn Jenner, steroids, aging, sagging breasts, and castration.

Prior to the episode of 'deplatforming', Greer had been advocating for the value of transcending the limits of white Australian identity and becoming Aboriginal. Her argument that "Aboriginality would take over eventually", from an interview with Nell Schofield in the year 2000, commenting on the heated debates about the potential for a national apology to Aboriginal people under the rule of the then prime minister John Howard (1996–2007) gestured towards a strange future vision which I found hard to picture. She argued in the same interview for a literal form of becoming Aboriginal which would transcend racial categories and embrace cultural adoption as good for the nation: "all Australians could be Aborigines. The Aborigines are not racist, the Aborigines would be very prepared to incorporate white people in an Aboriginal system, but we have to be very much more daring than we are" (Greer, 2003, p.2). Her 2003 essay *Whitefella Jump Up: The Shortest Way to Nationhood* proselytised more formally on the potential benefits of reckoning with Aboriginality as a necessary component of positive white political identity in settler

Australia. 'Jump up' she translates in the subtitle as "from Kriol, of cattle, to leap up to a higher level; hence, of people, to be resurrected or reborn" (Greer, 2003, p. 10). She names the state of being colonial "the white man's burden", and she argues that while Aboriginal misery is a common spectacle in the mainstream media, "whitefella spiritual desolation is seldom admitted, let alone discussed" (Greer, 2003, p.10). The possibility of healing and transformation for her is in reckoning first with dispossession, and next with becoming Aboriginal: "The second step in the journey is a second statement to the self in the mirror: 'I was born in an Aboriginal country, therefore I must be considered Aboriginal' [...] soul-searching about Australian identity has gone on for years without even the glimpse of a resolution" (Greer, 2003, pp. 19–21).

Her commitment to this as the resolution to both a collective misery and a crisis of self, as well as to a host of ecological, social, and political issues by extension, plays out in multiple personal–political public actions. She makes it plain that seeking cultural adoption and education is a part of this, and encourages white society to become more like an approximation of what Aboriginality looks like to her through seeking out Aboriginal people as instructors in law, kinship relations, and proper behaviour. She periodically refused to return to Australia until a treaty was reached between white people and Aboriginal people, and on some occasions, asked to be met at customs only by Aboriginal people as an attempt at lawful engagement only with "Black Australia" rather than white Australia. Flippant but persistent references to trans life emerge at different points in her speech on this transition into an Aboriginal state of being:

> I don't think I can move in; I mean I don't want to be like those transsexuals who have their operation on Monday and start talking for women on Tuesday. I don't know what it is to be an Aborigine, and I would never ever, ever, speak as an Aborigine. I may decide though, I mean when it comes to decisions time, I may decide that that's what I should do.
>
> (Greer, 2004)

It is Greer's fixation with the construction of a positive identity for herself as a white settler-occupier that brings her to her ecological legacy project near Cave Creek in the Numinbah Valley, on Yugambeh Country.

## White Beech: The Rainforest Years

I have discussed already how utopian forms of thinking and writing are political and critical ways of engaging with the future which emerge in response to perceived problems or crises in the contemporary society. They often come from anti-capitalist and eco-critical frameworks. For Greer, a central crisis is white identity, and her proposed solution is to look at how Aboriginality can be reinterpreted as a pathway to construct a healthier white nation and address a guilt-afflicted and miserable settler psyche.

*White Beech* (2015) narrates the story of Greer's return to Australia from the United Kingdom after her resolution to leave white Australia. When she returns, it is with the intent to establish an ecological conservation land care project as a means of repairing or redeeming her own participation in invasion and dispossession and the resultant destruction of ecosystems. The work has been heroised by eco-critical theorists and public intellectuals as a work that cements her as an eco-critical activist and a participant in the cutting edge of

eco-feminist and new materialist critique (see Stevens, 2018a). Greer's search for and purchase of the land she intended to rehabilitate and rewild began in 2001, one year following
her 'tearful' declaration that she would never return to 'white Australia', and her comments
to Nell Schofield that she did not want to be 'like those transsexuals who have their operation on Monday and start talking for women on Tuesday', and that she would always ask
to be welcomed at customs by Aboriginal people. *White Beech* begins with Greer recounting
her search for an appropriate tract of land to make into a rehabilitation and rewilding
scheme. She notes that she initially has particularly romantic visions of living in the desert:

> What I really wanted was desert. For twenty years I had been roving back and forth
> over central Australia, hunting for my own patch of ground [...] one of my fantasies
> has always been to lie in my own bed and watch the desert landscape slowly turn
> violet while fat yellow stars pop out in the inky sky and owlet-nightjars shake the
> still-warm sand.
>
> (Greer, 2015, p. 55)

These desert notions evaporate as it becomes clear that a suitable plot of land must be one
which both fulfils her fantasies of remote wildness and closeness to the earth, while not
interrupting her idea of herself as a proponent of Aboriginal sovereignty. Central Australia
is too close to the politics of dispossession and native title, and too tied in with visible
Aboriginal presence from her perspective. She notes with some complaint the psychological
complexities of dealing with land which is open to potential native title claims. Her sister
questions her:

> Jane said,
> 'You wouldn't contest the validity of any Aboriginal land claim, would you?'
> 'No'.
> 'Never? No matter what?'
> 'Never. no matter what'.
> 'So that's that?' 'That's that'.
> And that was that.
>
> (Greer, 2015, p. 77)

Instead, Greer and her sister Jane go coastal, seeking out plots of land in Eden and Bega
before eventually acquiring freehold land in the Numinbah Valley. Exploring the possibility
of acquiring freehold land in Eden further south on the NSW coast (which she derisively
calls a 'backwater' (2015, p. 51), Greer explains that she feels she can't quite connect with
the available land there due to the crowding in of waves of new development, industry, and
persistent environmental damage and pollution:

> If I had bought [this] parcel of forest, I'd have had a munitions wharf and storage
> depot, a chip mill working twenty-four hours every day, and 163 timber lorries a day,
> and fifty hectares of mussel farm to look at and listen to, as well as several battles
> to fight [...] I wondered whether it might not be my destiny to be caught up in the
> struggle to preserve the forests of the south east.
>
> (Greer, 2015, pp. 53–52)

The search is then on for a piece of land she can both save, but which is not too far gone to save. For her, the plot of Yugambeh Country in the forest hinterland serves multiple purposes. It represents damaged goods, but it is not 'unsaveable', and is suitably undisturbed by active industry (although the presence of tourists disturbs her peace occasionally). The question of Aboriginal land claims in the area is also, in her mind, settled enough. She sets out trying to discover the Aboriginal lineage of the plot of land she's acquired, seeking knowledge of the place and whether it has any significance to local Aboriginal people. She also discusses her fantasy for a 'welcome ceremony' and a traditional name to decorate her project:

> The first thing I did, once the documents were signed and the transfer completed, before I had spent a single night [...] was to go in search of the traditional owners. At the Minjungbal Aboriginal Cultural Centre at Tweed Heads I thought I would find somebody who could tell me the property's true name, and whom I should approach for permission to camp there. I even dared to hope I could find someone to perform a welcome ceremony for me. I in turn would have been more than happy to let Indigenous people use the land as they wished.
>
> (Greer, 2015, p. 114)

Greer's wording recalls the work of Aileen Moreton-Robinson. In *Talkin' Up to the White Woman* (2002), Moreton-Robinson discusses her positioning to white feminism in relation to a few experiences from her academic practice, one in particular which involves a similar request for a welcoming:

> Being asked by a university (with one day's notice) to be part of a welcoming committee to meet a white feminist professor at the international airport at 5.30am. The professor had been invited to receive an honorary doctorate from the university, but she threatened not to come to Australia unless she was met and welcomed by Indigenous women. This seemingly noble but colonial gesture by the professor was soon eroded by her questioning us on what we were going to do at the Sydney Olympics about the denial of Indigenous rights in this country. She offered her unsolicited advice about what we should do and wanted us to advise her about what we might want her to do. Finally I responded by asking her to tell us what the limits were to what she would do. She did not answer my question—instead she changed the subject.
>
> (Moreton-Robinson, 2002, p. xvii)

The 'welcome to Country' by Aboriginal women is here positioned as a performance of both the anti-colonial and the feminist values of the unnamed white professor. The incident forms part of Moreton-Robinson's relations with white feminism as one of extractiveness, of demanding entitlement, and of engagement with Aboriginal women as a utility to perform a white woman's politics of virtue. The charge of welcoming the white woman to Country, when not properly performed, spurs her into a wholesale rejection of Aboriginal sovereignty in the area. Moreton-Robinson's extensive work on virtuosity and the possessive logics of whiteness provide important tools for understanding Greer's work as a public intellectual and her actions in occupying the Numinbah Valley.

The story of *White Beech* is consistent with the utopian relationship of extraction of Aboriginal world views, representations, and cultural and intellectual property along with land as a 'raw material' which can be used to interpellate the radicalism and criticism of the utopian author. Greer's descriptions of Yugambeh Country reflect the same problems identified in Ysola Best's (1994) critique of Eurocentric histories of Yugambeh Country and culture. In Greer's mind, the country she's occupying has no valid Aboriginal land claim on it, or if it does, she is willing to negate it. Greer's book targets my own bloodline, the Graham family, by name, among 12 other families, in arguing against the sovereignty of Aboriginal people to the area she has purchased. Assessing for herself the validity of Aboriginal rights to the forest, she comments that "descendants of a single small kin group can hardly lay claim to such a huge swathe of territory. it doesn't add up" (2015, p. 117). Whether or not Aboriginal people in the area, Yugambeh or otherwise, have a connection to the place, Greer's work recalls Tuck's definition of a settler futurity which is ensured "through an understanding of Native-European relations as a thing of the past, and the inclusion of Native history as a past upon which a white future is ensured" (Greer, 2015, p. 77). It is clear that in order to legitimise her project to 'save' the forest, Greer needs to erase the being and integrity of any Indigenous peoples who might have connection to it. Greer's white eco-feminist standpoint is also reflected in her conceptualisation of one site in the area, the Natural Bridge, that she surmises to be a place of 'sacred women's business'. Arguing that it appears as "an image of titanic intercourse" (Greer, 2015, p. 127), she guesses that "the cave was a place of serious women's business, even of pilgrimage in time of special need. Infertility. Unwanted pregnancy. Maybe even infanticide" (Greer, 2015 p. 128). Meditating on this, Greer and her sister contemplate the Natural Bridge and recite Coleridge to it. Responding to this act of uninformed "conjecture", Stevens criticises this act as a detraction to the overall radicalism of the text;

> Though Greer has attempted to reconcile with her privileged relation to Australian sovereignty through writings such as *Whitefella Jump Up* (2003) and her claim in *White Beech* that she does not own Cave Creek: "[i]t would never have occurred to me that my whitefella freehold title endowed me with proprietorial rights" (*White Beech* 114), in her interpretation of Natural Bridge, she does not seem to recognise the dangers of her uninformed cultural reading as a white subject and privileged public voice.
>
> (Stevens, 2018b, p. 168)

Greer's writing reflects that she is hoping to actualise both her anti-colonial and eco-feminist political identities through her possession of Aboriginal land. As she erects fences around the freehold land she's purchased, marking it with signs declaring she will prosecute any trespassers or people who take anything from the land without permission, she confides in the reader that she believes the restoration project is "in no-man's land", remarking:

> Whenever I look at the forest, and the creek, and the animals and the birds who live here, it seems utterly barmy that anyone could imagine that she owned all this [...] according to Australian law I don't own any mineral wealth that lies under the soil, but apparently I can lay claim to the rare creatures that live above it. I can certainly prosecute anyone removing materials animal or vegetable from the property without

my permission. The only way I can make sense of my anomalous situation is to tell myself that I don't own the forest, the forest owns me.

(Greer, 2015, p. 141)

It is important that Greer's writing of the land, not just her occupation of it and her practice of supposed care, becomes part of this performance of radical identity. This is especially highlighted in her fantasising about the Natural Bridge formation near Cave Creek as a "sacred women's site" or, at another moment, a "place of demons" (Greer, 2015, p. 141). Her purchase of the land is articulated as a process of becoming responsible, of situating herself in a relation of care with land through a rewilding process, but it appears more clearly to be a practice of possession and political self-construction which aims to soothe the troubled identity she articulated in *Whitefella Jump Up* (2003). She describes having "little plastic signs made, screw[ing] them onto star pickets and ha[ving] them put up all along the unfenced boundary" (2015, p. 104), while attempting to evade the colonial politics of dispossession by avoiding buying land with any legally viable Aboriginal claim of native title. That the plot of forest is bought through freehold title is assumed to absolve her of responsibility to the sovereignty for the surrounding Aboriginal nations. By doing this, she perpetuates at once the utopian impulse of an occupation of and writing of the story of land in a way that is invested with a radical political will and a logic of settler possession. Blocks of land in the hinterlands of Byron Bay and the Gold Coast are frequently advertised using the same language deployed by Greer of sacred femininity, solitude, privacy, paradise, even describing individual properties as an 'Eden' where one can retreat. While she expresses disdain and disapproval for the ways in which colonial dispossession has affected the area, her own language perpetuates the same utopian mindset—that the rainforest is an Eden-like country desired for possession.

## Conclusion

*White Beech* reveals how utopian thought is invariably built using Indigenous societies as inspiration, as "raw materials" from which the European imagination generates its own politics. Utopia is an act of imagining which imagines settler futurity on stolen land. While it generates a political critique of aspects of the dominant settler colonial society, even critiquing colonialism, it consumes Indigenous societies as the raw materials for the envisioning of its political and social desires. Utopianism is the consumption of Aboriginal lands and societies in service of Western political and personal aspirations for various forms of 'good living'. *White Beech* reveals the limits of utopian radicalism in how it perpetuates settler colonial possessive logics which require the disappearance of Aboriginal people. It is also valuable for how it can bring about a conversation about the entanglement between colonialism and transphobia. Fees received for the Greer archive purchased by the university during a time of heightened transphobic discourse, in which both Greer and the University were participants, went towards Greer's charity project for Cave Creek Rehabilitation Project, The Friends of Gondwana Forest. As a transgender Yugambeh critic, I hope this piece can contribute towards a critical rethinking of Yugambeh Country by white intellectuals which encourages a rigorous turn away from its conceptualisation as a utopian place, free for physical occupation and epistemological possession by eco-critical colonists.

## Note

1 The consultation period for the university's newly written Gender Affirmation Policy became a key site for this intellectual battle. It can be read in full here: https://policy.unimelb.edu.au/MPF1364

## References

Araluen, E. (2019). The limits of literary theory and the possibilities of storywork for Aboriginal literature in Australia. In J. Archibald Q'um Q'um Xiiem, J. De Santolo, & J. Lee-Morgan (Eds.), *Decolonizing research: Indigenous storywork as methodology* (pp. 382–414). ZED Books.

Best, Y. (1994). An uneasy coexistence: An Aboriginal perspective of 'contact history' in Southeast Queensland. *Aboriginal History Journal, 18*(2), 87–94. https://doi.org/10.22459/AH.18.2011.08

Carey, A. (2021, 18 June). Transgender debate a free speech stress test for Melbourne University. *The Age*. www.theage.com.au/national/victoria/transgender-debate-a-free-speech-stress-test-for-melbourne-university-20210617-p581r8.html

Claeys, G. (2010b). The origins of dystopia: Wells, Huxley and Orwell. In G. Claeys (Ed.), *The Cambridge companion to utopian literature* (pp. 107–132). Cambridge University Press. http://universitypublishingonline.org/ref/id/companions/CBO9780511781582A009

Claeys, G. (Ed.). (2010a). *The Cambridge companion to utopian literature*. Cambridge University Press.

Field, J. (2020, 7 September). *Gamilaraay kinship dynamics* [Lecture; Video]. YouTube. www.youtube.com/watch?v=i0GNEd6VhGc&list=WL&index=79&t=993s

Graham, M. (2008). Some thoughts about the philosophical underpinnings of Aboriginal worldviews. *Australian Humanities Review, 45*. http://australianhumanitiesreview.org/2008/11/01/some-thoughts-about-the-philosophical-underpinnings-of-aboriginal-worldviews/

Greer, G. (2003). Whitefella jump up: The shortest way to nationhood. *Quarterly Essay* (11), 1–78.

Greer, G. (2004, 19 June). We can dream too. *The Guardian*. www.theguardian.com/world/2004/jun/19/australia.bookextracts

Greer, G. (2015). *White Beech: The rainforest years*. Bloomsbury.

Jameson, F. (2005). *Archaeologies of the future: The desire called utopia and other science fictions*. Verso.

Johnson, E., Zhang, S., & Zhang, S. (2019). *Petitions, protests and sex based events*. Farrago. https://umsu.unimelb.edu.au/news/article/7797/2019-09-24-petitions-protests-and-sex-based-events/

Kendrick, C. (1985). More's Utopia and uneven development. *Boundary 2, 13*(2/3), 233–245.

Kumar, K. (2003). Aspects of the Western utopian tradition. *History of the Human Sciences, 16*(1), 63–77.

Moreton-Robinson, A. (2002). *Talkin' up to the white woman: Indigenous women and feminism*. University of Queensland Press.

Moreton-Robinson, A. (2015). Introduction. In *The white possessive: Property, power and indigenous sovereignty* (pp. xi–xxiv). University of Minnesota Press.

Nagouse, E., & Edwards, K. (2018, 6 June). Germaine Greer: From feminist firebrand to professional troll. *The Conversation*. http://theconversation.com/germaine-greer-from-feminist-firebrand-to-professional-troll-97645

Pohl, N. (2010). Utopianism after More: The Renaissance and Enlightenment. In G. Claeys (Ed.), *The Cambridge companion to utopian literature* (Vol. 1, pp. 51–78). Cambridge University Press.. https://doi.org/10.1017/CCOL9780521886659.003

Sargent, L. T. (2010a). Colonial and postcolonial utopias. In G. Claeys (Ed.), *The Cambridge companion to utopian literature* (pp. 200–222). Cambridge University Press.

Sargent, L. T. (2010b). *Utopianism: A very short introduction* (UniM INTERNET resource). Oxford University Press.

Schofield, N. (Director). (2000). Germaine Greer 25th July 2000. In *Arts Today*. ABC Radio National. www.abc.net.au/rn/legacy/programs/atoday/stories/s155190.htm

Scott, C. (2016). (Indigenous) place and time as formal strategy: Healing immanent crisis in the dystopias of Eden Robinson and Richard Van Camp. *Extrapolation, 57*(1–2), 73–93. https://doi.org/10.3828/extr.2016.6

Stevens, L. (2018a). From the Female Eunuch to White Beech: Germaine Greer's ecological feminism. In L. Stevens, P. Tait, & D. Varney (Eds.), *Feminist ecologies* (pp. 117–133). Palgrave Macmillan.

Stevens, L. (2018b). Mother? Nature?: Germaine Greer, contemporary feminisms and new materialisms. *Hecate, 44*(1–2), 156–171.

Tuck, E., & Gaztambide-Fernández, R. A. (2013). Curriculum, replacement, and settler futurity. *Journal of Curriculum Theorizing, 29*(1), 18.

Vieira, F. (2013). The concept of utopia. In G. Claeys (Ed.), *The Cambridge companion to utopian literature* (pp. 3–28). Cambridge University Press.

Wahlquist, C. (2016, 12 April). Germaine Greer tells Q&A her trans views were wrong, but then restates them. *The Guardian Australia.* www.theguardian.com/books/2016/apr/12/germaine-greer-tells-qa-her-trans-views-were-wrong-but-then-restates-them

Wolfe, P. (2006). Settler colonialism and the elimination of the Native. *Journal of Genocide Research, 8*(4), 387–409.

# 15

# YARNING WITH THE ARCHIVES

*Jacinta Walsh and Lynette Russell*

## Introduction

An archive is a knowledge stored. It is an accumulation of records or materials in any form. Indigenous peoples' archival sources have been stored and curated for millennia through transgenerational memory, spiritually centred cultural practices, daily rituals, kinship networks, art, dance, song lines, and storytelling.[1] These archives hold memories and are expressions of 'Country'[2] (Supernant, Baxter, Lyons, & Atalay, 2020). Mother Earth[3] herself is an invaluable life-creating and supporting entity that holds her own infinite physical and physiological non-human records and memory. In this Country we now call Australia, in addition to the archives created and stored by Indigenous peoples and Mother Earth, we now have the records created by those who have travelled from other places to settle. Non-Indigenous settlers to Australia have left behind an extensive web of archival material and stories intrinsically linked to Indigenous peoples' lives, to Land, Water, and Sky, and to all living things. Overwhelmingly, these records tell stories of Indigenous and non-Indigenous human encounters, and imperialistic attempts to conquer and control Indigenous peoples, and Land, Water, and Sky (McKemmish et al., 2011; McKemmish, Faulkhead, & Russell, 2011; Nakata & Langton, 2005; Russell, 2006; Russell, 2018). All the archives available to us, in all their forms, are the layers of recorded activity and memory that are human and non-human, and provide a treasure trove of infinite information.

Aboriginal and Torres Strait Islander individuals, families, and communities can draw immense strength, resilience, and empowerment from reconnecting with the ancestral stories that live within family memory, cultural artefacts, and Country (Harkin, 2014 & 2019; Justice, 2018; McKemmish et al., 2011; McKemmish, Faulkhead, & Russell, 2011; Nakata & Langton, 2005; Russell, 2018; Russell, 2006; Travis & Haskins, 2020; Wickes, 2008; Wright, 2018). Connections with Country, Culture, and Kinship relationships are integral to many Indigenous people's identity formation. Understanding these relationships can be akin to knowing one's first point of orientation, one's true self, at the very core, as a cultural and spiritual being (Atkinson, 2002; Gumillya Baker & Rosas Blanch, 20 July 2022; Harkin, 2014, 2019). The colonisation of Australia has had a devastating and lasting influence on the ability of Indigenous families and communities to remain connected

DOI: 10.4324/9781003271802-18

to their spiritual selves. The archives created by the colonisers were primarily designed as instruments of oppressive regimes, often targeting the very sanctuary that is an Indigenous family (Haebich, 2000; McKemmish et al., 2011). These records document Eurocentrically informed technologies, a powerful and violent discourse that has told and continues to tell First Nations families and communities not to love themselves or their Cultural heritage. Ironically, for families who have experienced significant separation from each other, from their cultural connections, the archives created by the colonisers, have become critical sources, providing families with opportunities to locate the very moments in time they were disconnected from each other and from Culture, Country, and Spirit, the moments in time they were told not to love themselves. The documents created by the colonisers have become an invaluable source for understanding the colonisers' behaviours, motivations, and aspirations. When an Indigenous family has access to all this knowledge, they can repatriate their position of knowing, of power. Most importantly, Indigenous family reconnections with new and old archives enable them the opportunity to remember (not find for the first time), but 'remember' their embodied memory of Spirit, Culture, and Love that has and will always run through their veins. Always was, Always will be. A connection with any archive relating to a family's ancestral lineage directly supports their ability to search for, locate, and remember their ancestral, cultural, and spiritual identity and their rights to and relationships with Country (Commonwealth of Australia, 1997, pp. 281–309; Harkin, 2019; Russell, 2008). With access to these records, a family can peel back the layers of their transgenerational story and rediscover themselves, their culture, identity, and sense of ancestral power, place, and belonging (Healing Foundation, May 2021, pp. 49–50). The deep wounds created through colonisation can be healed and they can repatriate, giving agency and voice to the love they have always held for themselves.

This chapter is a conversation, a yarn, that will echo the voices of many others who have engaged with archives to remember and share the glory of their ancestral lineage. Indigenous writers, musicians, artists, and those inside and outside the academy have for millennia engaged with archives in all forms to celebrate and share cultural knowledge and, more recently, challenge settler-colonial policies and practices. These stories remind us of our cultural connections, and the emotional relationships we have with each other, and often utilise the power of story to effect personal and social change (Brewster & Berg, 2000; Harkin, 2014; Huggins, 1998; Justice, 2018; Russell, 2020b; Travis & Haskins, 2021; Wickes, 2008; Wright, 2018). Inspired by this ancient and dynamic practice of storytelling, Lynette and I write this chapter intending to provide our reflections on the journey, the vortex that is ancestry life story research and writing. I will lead this discussion and pose three questions for Lynette to consider. Together, we hope our reflections and personal insights into our journeys to remember ourselves are valuable to this ongoing and vital conversation.

## Let's yarn

My name is Jacinta Walsh. I am a Jaru / Jawuru woman and a PhD candidate in the Monash Indigenous Studies Centre at Monash University. My thesis will document 60 years of the life lived by my biological Great Grandmother Mabel Ita Eatts (née Frederick), a Jaru woman, a Stolen Generations survivor, who was born on Country, in Ceremony, in about 1907 in an Aboriginal Women's birthing place at Lugangarna (Palm Springs), near Halls Creek in the East Kimberley Region of Western Australia. Through an analysis of over 100 archival documents, and with my Great Uncle and Birth Father's living memory, our family is remembering and sharing our story. I have asked my PhD primary supervisor and mentor, Professor Lynette Russell AM, a Wotjobaluk woman and acclaimed historian, to join me in a yarn to reflect on how important the written and oral archives are to us, to our story-telling, our healing, our identity formation and reformation, and to knowledge creation more broadly. Lynette has written extensively on the importance of the archives to families, and the 'affect' and the risks for the families as they process what is found (Mckemmish et al., 2011; Mckemmish, Faulkhead, & Russell, 2011; Russell, 2018; Russell, 2006; Russell, 2005; Russell, et. al., 2008). Lynette is supporting me on my research journey, has helped many families through the process of ancestry research, and has authored her memoir, *A Little Bird Told Me: Family Secrets, Necessary Lies* (Russell, 2002; Russell, 2020a). We will share our experiences of Indigenous family-derived research methodologies that embrace heartfelt epistemological approaches. We aim to demonstrate to the reader what it feels like to explore the archives and unravel Indigenous family life stories that bring to light newly remembered realisations of self. As many have before, we will affirm that narratives derived by Indigenous families through their access to archives are essential to tell and hear.

### Yarning with the archives and access: Jacinta's story

One encounter with an archive that relates directly to us can alter our view of the world in an instant. It can be enlightening and devastating all at once. I know this to be true. My first known encounter with an archive changed the course of my life forever. I am an adoptee. I was born in Melbourne in September 1973. I was placed in foster care initially and then adopted in May of 1974. Growing up in a non-Indigenous, multicultural Catholic family with three other adopted siblings, I had a happy and loving childhood. While I knew I was of Aboriginal heritage, growing up in a non-Indigenous family and community, I could not understand what being an Aboriginal person 'was supposed to feel like'. In 1997, at the age of 24 years, I decided to contact Link Up, an agency that supports the reunification of First Nations families. On 14 January 1998, I received a letter informing me of my appointment with the Catholic Family Welfare Bureau, adoption services in Melbourne. The appointment was set for 11 a.m., on 2 February 1998. This was the day I was to receive my personal adoption file.

On Monday, 2 February 1998, I arrived at the adoption services and pregnancy counselling office in East Melbourne. Within moments of arriving, I was sitting in a consult room and in conversation with a counsellor. She was holding my adoption file in her hand, which was resting on her lap. We chatted for a little while, and then she handed me my file. I received a manila folder containing photocopies of the legal and administrative documents regarding my adoption and the paperwork created in 1973 by the St Joseph Babies Home in Broadmeadows at the time of my birth. This meeting quickly escalated into a series of unexpected, highly charged, and deeply emotional moments. I was not an academic researcher then. In fact, I had no idea what an archive was. I certainly had no idea that documents held and stored by government and non-government agencies could have such an immeasurable effect on me. It was the moment my reconnection with my birth family and my ancestral lineage became stronger, became possible. The counsellor respectfully left the room to allow me to meet my biological family, on paper, for the first time. I felt overwhelmed and terrified, but in a good way, struck by the intuitive realisation that I was about to know more of my true self.

The documents themselves were difficult to read, not physically but emotionally. The terminology used in the 1970s to describe my Birth Parents, Adoptee Parents, and me, was steeped in Westernised hierarchies of race and morality. "Apart from skin tone. S.W. did not feel at this stage that the baby has pronounced aboriginal features. Regardless, couple seem extremely happy and have accepted their little girl" (St Joseph Babies Home, Broadmeadows Admission form, 11 September,1973).

I was recorded as an "illegitimate" child with Aboriginal ancestry born to a nameless "¼ caste aborigine". I was overcome with shock at how my family and I, and our circumstances were categorised and described. I had never seen anything like this before.

If that were not enough, inside my file was a letter from my Birth Mother, written in 1991. She had posted this letter to the agency, hoping that one day I would contact the agency and receive it. This document sat in the archives of the Catholic Family Welfare Bureau for seven years. Thankfully, it found its way to me. This letter was a pure expression of love, written by a mother who had spent over 20 years not knowing if her daughter was safe and loved. I knew in this moment that my life, and hers, would never feel the same again.

Through this encounter with an archive, at the age of 24, I remembered that I had a Birth Mother who loved me. I remembered that I was born in Melbourne but was from Western Australia. I remembered that my Birth Father was an Aboriginal man, and my Birth Mother was of Irish heritage. I had my Birth parents' contact details available to me. Receiving these documents from the adoption services in Melbourne began what has now become over 20 years of reconnection with my birth family in Western Australia, a reconnection that has bought me a sense of peace and a place and belonging.

In 1997, serendipitously, a biological cousin on my Birth Father's side, whom I did not know, applied to the State Records Office of Western Australia to locate the historical government records related to his Great Grandmother. In 1998, the same year I contacted the family, a file of copied historical records was sent to us all. In this file were microfilm copies of Mabel Ita Frederick's 'personal file', created in 1929 by A. O. Neville, the chief protector of Aborigines in Western Australia. There were over 34 letters, telegrams, and certificates dated between 1929 and 1939, authored by Mabel Ita Frederick; the man she married, Jack Albert Eatts; various police officers from Derby and Broome; and the chief and deputy chief protectors from the Aborigines Department in Perth. When I received these documents, I had no idea of the context in which they were created, nor their purpose or significance. I was also unsure who Mabel Ita Frederick or Jack Albert Eatts were, or how their lives were part of mine.

### Listening to our Elders: oral (living) history

After receiving Mabel's files and having numerous conversations with my Birth Father and family, I learned that Mabel Ita Eatts (née Frederick) was my Great Grandmother and that she had six children. Her first Daughter was Roseleen (Rose) May, my Grandmother and my Birth Father's mother. In 1999, I met my Great Uncle Walter (Waldo) Eatts, Mabel's fifth Son. I never met Mabel or Rose. All of Mabel's children, except for my Great Uncle Walter, had passed away before I contacted my birth family in 1998. Meeting my Great Uncle Walter Eatts was then and continues to be profoundly important to me.

In 1998, Uncle was writing his memoir and had already written many poems about his life (Eatts, 2014; Poetry published in Eatts, 2014). My Uncle's memoir, *Somewhere*

*Between, Not White, Not Black, Not Wanted* (2014), has since become a pivotal source for my PhD. He wrote about his mother's life as a Stolen Generations survivor (Commonwealth of Australia, 1997) and his life as a young child, teenager, and adult. He described what he knows from his living memory, archival evidence, and his own original research. Meeting my Great Uncle, reading his life story, and then rereading the archival material in Mabel's file, my own story began to reveal itself in ways I had never imagined possible. I could see and feel my life was embedded within a thread of intergenerational lived experience.

My Great Uncle's recollections and willingness to share them are pivotal to our family's understanding of Mabel's life and our own. Our family knows how lucky we are. So many First Nations Elders have lived experiences they cannot share; they do not want to remember. Like all our family's Elders, Uncle Wally is a living archive, an invaluable repository of memory. He wants our family story to be remembered. Having read Uncle Wally's books and poetry and having spent the last 20 years exploring further the archival documents in Mabel's personal files, our family now recognises Mabel's life as having incredible influence over all of ours. We have identified an intergenerational trajectory of events that help explain how our family has come to be in the present. We are also reading our family's documents against the grain and listening to our Uncle Wally as he and we identify our ancestral links to Land, Water, and Sky. Not only are we reconnecting with each other, but we are also remembering our place, ourselves, and our position as ancestral beings. This is where access to the archives has power for Indigenous families.

Shawn Stanley Wilson, a Cree scholar, in his PhD dissertation titled *Research as Ceremony: Articulating an Indigenous Research Paradigm* (2004), describes how the act of research can be, itself, an act of ceremony. Sharing our story as a family around the dinner table, listening to each other with compassion and love, these are the moments our family finds our point of orientation. In these moments, we reconnect with each other as Kin and often imagine that our ancestors are with us. They are moments we identify with and that express our Aboriginality and assert our family's self-determination. These are the moments that optimise Wilsons's articulation that research really is, for our family, an act of ceremony.

### Searching for our stories: knowledge repatriation

Lynette, in October 2020 you gave a lecture titled 'Memories and Narratives, an Ongoing Reflection' (Russell, 23 October 2020), and you were talking about the writing of your memoir, *A Little Bird Told Me: Family Secrets, Necessary Lies* (2002). You said that initially, you were writing about your journey to discover the life stories of your Grandmother Nanna, and your Great Grandmother Emily, for your father. You suggested that he was your initial motivation but that you later realised the story was important to your Sons. In your memoir, however, you say: "I, too, felt that unless I knew my Grandmother and her secrets, I could not know myself" (Russell, 2002, p. 18). You are a university professor, who knows well the academy's historical bias against life history writing as an academic genre. And yet, one of your earliest publications was your memoir. In it, you wrote:

> This is a story of identity, memory, remembering and madness—all inextricably linked together. Emily, Nanna and Jack's life stories cannot be completely reclaimed but at least I can revisit them. Importantly, Emily's story can be heard and hopefully her pain can be understood. I want her suffering not to be in vain. this book is my

attempt to understand Nanna, to appreciate her for all her strengths and weaknesses, and to recognise that hers was a life lived the only way she knew how.

(Russell, 2002, p. 28)

Could you tell me a little about your Nanna and your Great Grandmother Emily, and why you thought it was important that you shared their stories, despite being aware of any institutional bias against the academic merits of this genre?

### *Lynette*

Many of my earliest memories involve my Grandmother Gladys. On weekends my father would take me to my grandparents' home, where he and my grandfather would work on cars in the garage. Sometimes they would go rabbit hunting (with ferrets), leaving me to spend the whole day with my Nanna. Even though my grandparents lived in Melbourne's suburbs, they were very nearly self-sufficient. We would spend hours tending the vegetable plot, making jams with the fruit from their fruit trees, all the while Nanna would sing to me and tell me stories. As I got older, I came to understand that for all that closeness, she was holding back secrets, things she thought too shameful to speak out loud. After I finished high school and chose to study archaeology and history at university, I saw in her a distress that I was getting too close to her truth. As an adult, I would call her every Sunday, and we would talk for over an hour. The usual topics were my children, their antics, and what they'd been up to. When I spoke about my studies, she'd often become silent.

On one occasion, I was writing an essay on kinship for my anthropology class, and our lecturer suggested we each create a family tree and explore our various heritages. When I questioned my Nanna about her family, I was rebuked. "The past can still hurt" was the refrain she said over and over. I increasingly realised that she had Aboriginal heritage and a lifetime of being told to hide it. The past had led to her fearing being exposed. This seemed incredibly sad to me, and I felt compelled to further my research, but I also knew I needed to do so in a sensitive and ethical way. I recall speaking to my PhD supervisor, saying I wanted to make this study part of my doctoral studies, and he made an astute assessment. He implied that I should follow up the family research alongside my academic work and pursue it more fully after finishing my dissertation. There was such hostility to autoethnography and family history within the academy then. He was concerned that I would not be taken seriously as a scholar. He was right. The academy was not ready then to validate First Nations family life writing. After completing the thesis and the subsequent book, I then pursued in earnest the writing of "A Little Bird Told Me". That decision was over 30 years ago, literally half my lifetime.

One of the joys over the past three decades is to see that the academy has shifted, and a project such as yours, Jacinta, is not merely possible but supported, even celebrated. I hope I have played a role in that process.

Lynette, you have.

Three years into my PhD candidature, having gained an awareness of the importance, purpose and nature of archival research, I planned my family's first visit to the State Records

Office of Western Australia (SROWA) to view original historical documents relating to our story. On Tuesday, 26 April 2022, I walked into the State Records Office, located on level three of the State Library in the city of Perth, with my Birth Father, my Half-Sister, her 14-year-old Daughter, and my three Sons, aged 14, 15, and 16 years old. This visit was a long and much-anticipated event, three years in the making. I had arranged with a senior archivist for our family to see records in their original form created in 1911 by Father Thomas Bachmair from the Beagle Bay Mission (Colonial Secretary's Department, Aborigines and Fisheries. Subject: Beagle Bay Mission. Return of Natives at Mission dated July 1911, SROWA). Knowing the magnitude of this moment, our family gathered together outside of the reading room to reflect on what we were about to view. Together we reflected on the significance of this moment: this was the day three generations were about to view documents still in existence in their original form, from the Beagle Bay Mission, from the year Mabel was institutionalised there.

Three generations entered the reading room, were handed the file by a librarian, and within moments were viewing Beagle Bay Mission documents created in 1911. We were looking at a ledger condition report with columns recording and reporting to the "Department of Aborigines and Fisheries" the number, name, sex, age and condition of the Aboriginal people living at the Beagle Bay Mission. The file cover page reads: 'Subject: Beagle Bay Mission. Return of Natives at Mission dated July 1911'. This file contains pages and pages of names of children as young as five years old and other Aboriginal people of varying ages who lived on-site at the Mission. There were 126 names recorded as having arrived and been detained or as living on-site between February and July 1911.

At this moment, we believed we had found Mabel's name on the typed ledger report. We believed that Mabel was recorded as 'Ida', 'No. 107', 'Sex ... F', 'Age... 5', and 'Condition ... H.C. Girl'. Under the category of 'Condition', the description of each person in this report, their whole being was reduced to only one or two words, or worse, one or two letters. To see it now is shocking, despairing.

'H.C.' (Half Caste),
'Fl. Bl.' (Full Blood),
'Idiot' (person with learning or developmental disorder),
'Old' (person Fifty years or older),
'No man' (unmarried woman),
'Infirm' (physically weak),
'No man with child' or 'with little child' (unmarried woman with a young child),
'Cripple' (physically disabled)
'H. Blind' and 'Blind'. (Visually impaired)

To be categorised in this way, to be reduced to a number, a letter, what must that have felt like? In that moment, I had a flashback to my own birth and adoption records. Alarmingly, I could see, in the early 1970s, that my Birth Father and I had been described with a similar crude and demeaning simplicity (St Joseph Babies Home, Broadmeadows Admission form, 11 September 1973).

Our family has had access to digital and paper microfilm copies of Mabel's files for over 20 years. While the content of the files was confronting, there was something very different about seeing these documents in their original form. The 100-year-old beige-coloured, coffee- and ink-stained, almost see-through thin paper somehow transported us back to the very moment this report was created. Seeing the handwritten and typed descriptions of the children was unnerving. My Birth Father felt as though he was there in that moment, at the Mission, a five-year-old child admitted into an institution. He knew what that was like.

Our whole family was fully engaged. I have never seen my Sons and Niece so entangled in our family story. My Niece was captivated and curious about every detail. My youngest Son was leaning into the documents and smelling them. "They smell like old men", he said. "They are recorded like cattle; it was as though 'who' they were didn't matter, only 'what' they were", my Half-Sister said. We could feel the tone of accomplishment in the author's records, each name listed as an achievement. My three Sons and my Niece were pointing to words and asking questions. "What is this word?" "What does this mean?" "Why did they write that?" "Can you read that name?" "Are these names real, or were they made up?" These were important questions, and the young people were engaged wholeheartedly with what was in front of them. My three Sons and my Niece could see and feel the power of words as a mechanism of control, oppression, and violence. My Birth Father was deeply affected by the file cover page. It read: ABORIGINES & FISHERIES. Several times he said: "We were classed as animals". Discussing with my Birth Father, my Half-Sister, and our children how these terms were used over 100 years ago to describe Aboriginal people was heartbreaking. They could see and feel the pain these words were causing their Pop, my Birth Father. We discussed early twentieth-century Eurocentrically informed scientific beliefs and Evangelistic movements to 'save First Nations peoples from themselves' (Choo, 2001). Understanding the context of Mabel's childhood through these documents allowed our family to imagine Mabel's lived experience, feel her pain and be proud of her resilience and strength, both then and later in her life. We wanted to hug Mabel and say to her, "we were not with you then, but we are here with you now".

We know through our family's living memory that Mabel lived her life resenting her treatment as a child. She carried the pain of her removal from her mother and her institutionalisation to her grave. On Tuesday, 26 April 2022, in the reading room of the State Records Office of Western Australia, an intergenerational, emotional, and transformative conversation was taking place. Three generations, representing a family that has experienced significant intergenerational disconnection and relocation, were together in conversation with Mabel. We were overcome by deep sorrow; however, healing was taking place. We were remembering our transgenerational story, locating the deep wounds our family has carried, and reconnecting with our story of love, resilience, and strength (Atkinson, 2002; Mehl-Madrona, 2010). Through this experience emerged a grounding sense of peace.

### Finding our place: affect

Lynette, you have written about the significance of viewing archival materials in their original form. You have said: "Archives can be tactile, visceral, aural and olfactory, something that is certainly reduced when the physical becomes digital" (Russell, 2018, p. 205). You have written extensively about the experience of 'affect' in the archives (Russell, 2018). I am particularly intrigued by an archive's powerful ability to transport us to 'place'. In the lecture you gave in October 2020, you were reflecting on the time you were writing *A Little Bird Told Me* (2002); you talked about viewing Emily's mental asylum records in the basement of the actual building she was kept in. In your memoir, you described walking through the building that was once the Sunbury asylum, looking for the room in which you believed Emily was imprisoned (Russell, 2002, p. 100). Can you describe why those moments, being in the actual place where Emily was detained, were so impactful for you? How important is 'place' in our family life stories?

## Lynette

The great historian Greg Dening wrote of the doing of history; the experiential engagement historians have with their subject matter (Dening, 1996). With that in mind, I sought out all the places my Great Grandmother had been held. These were the asylums she was imprisoned in and the various institutions that held her. Touching history in that way gave me a connection to Emily that felt tangible. I was able to share her pain and anxiety despite being separated from it by more than over half a century. This was the relationship with her I wished I could have had in life, but through the act of doing and performing history, I was able to create an attachment both to her and to her place(s).

I also spent lots of time on her Country. I walked it, drove it, breathed it, and allowed the presence of the Land to wash over me. To hear the birds sing and the trees rustle as they would have when she lived there. The town she was born in is called Lillimur, which means "black wattle" in the Weragia language. On my desk, I have a small stone I found on my walk over Country, and I touch it every day to remind me of being grounded. I also had a name plaque made for our house. It is called "Lillimur", and every day, I can recall where she came from and, by extension where I come from too.

I think for most Aboriginal people, place is incredibly important. It may not be Country per se, as so many people have been physically removed from the traditional Lands and through no fault of their own. There are many ways for us, as Aboriginal people, to re-connect with our Country. For me personally, I connect with Country through the simple pleasure of time spent in my suburban backyard tending to my vegetable garden.

### Our futures: transgenerational storytelling

Lynette, I also enjoyed how you were able to read Emily's asylum documents against the grain, and notice her connections to her ancestry and Country, notice her power. From a loving family standpoint, you have talked about how through story, you were able to give voice to her experiences and give agency to her journey (Russell, 2005, p. 164). You have written about the necessity for you to reinterpret the mental asylum records, try to read them from Emily's perspective. You have said: "[she] is now reconfigured as an Aboriginal woman who talked to her spirits and her Wotjabaluk ancestors, who had practiced, and now through archival research, had passed on (some) of her Indigenous cultural knowledge" (Russell, 2005, p. 164).

To say that you were able to reimagine Emily as an Aboriginal woman is powerful. To reset and reidentify her as she was born to be. A Wotjabaluk woman who talked and sang with her ancestors. Her story, documented by the staff of the asylum institutions, could not or would not recognise her as an ancestral being. For me, this exemplifies the importance of life writing from Indigenous family standpoints. We can peel back the layers of archival records created by historical colonial agents, see through the cloud that is imperialism, and reconnect with our Indigenous selves, our ancestral archival knowledge in all its forms and in all its wonder. Lynette, how else could you describe the value of First Nations Family life writing?

## Lynette

Indigenous family narratives derived from written, oral, and all other archives that relate to them provide unique and essential contributions to our understandings of the past and present. These narratives showcase, at a micro level, the complexities in the relationships that have and continue to exist with and between First and Second Nations peoples. They are commonly written through an intergenerational lens, through epistemological and ontological beliefs that time is synchronous. The past lives in the present and in the future, always and at once. They often display methodologies of relational accountability (Wilson, 2004, p. 7). An Indigenous family writing their story is accountable to their community, to their ancestors, and to future generations. Their writing requires mutual respect, reciprocity, empathy, and compassion. Rigorous research can encompass all these things. Indigenous family life narratives are a repatriation of Indigenous knowledge in all its forms and are expressions of transgenerational and dynamic cultures. They bring a family's cultural knowledge back into focus and, in doing so, become vehicles for sharing critical Australian historical viewpoints, contemporary cultural understandings, and spiritually informed perspectives. They are an assertion of agency to the family that writes them, to their culture, their community, to other Indigenous communities, to their ancestors, and to future generations. Importantly, an Indigenous family's life story will humanise, decolonise, and disrupt 'whitestream' Australian narratives that have and continue to misrepresent, or excluded their point of view and their historical and ongoing connections to Country and Spirit.

A family's ability to remember, know, and share their truth is intrinsically linked to their access to all archives that relate to them. Issues of access, then, are imperative. Asserting our right to access any archive that relates to us can require bravery, patience, determination, and persistence and can often result in grave disappointment. While the right to have ceremonial objects and human remains repatriated is recognised in the UN Assembly, Declaration of Human Rights (61/295. Fforde, McKeown, & Keeler, 2020; McKemmish et al., 2011; United Nations Declaration on the Rights of Indigenous Peoples, 2007, Article 12.2, p.12), the repatriation of archival documents that relate to Indigenous families and communities is not. Many records created by the colonisers have been destroyed, lost, or have been made unavailable (Commonwealth of Australia, 1997, p. 282; Marsh & Kinnane, 2003). In 1991, the Royal Commission into Aboriginal Deaths in Custody asserted First Nations families' moral right to access their archival material (Commonwealth of Australia, 1991, Recommendation 53). In 1996, the Bringing Them Home National Inquiry into the Separation of Aboriginal and Torres Strait Islander Children from their families received testimonials from many Indigenous families and archivists nationwide, highlighting significant barriers for Indigenous families to access their historical records. Recommendations 21 to 30B of the Bringing Them Home Royal Commission Inquiry Report aimed to address these issues (Commonwealth of Australia, 1997, pp. 281–309). Most of these recommendations are yet to be implemented. In 2007, Lynette Russell and a team of researchers undertook an extensive study titled *Koorie Archiving: Trust and Technology* (2008). Under the heading 'Strategies for Law Reform', this report suggested Australia create a new law, an 'Indigenous Knowledge Act', which directly and comprehensively gives Aboriginal and Torres Strait Islander people rights over their knowledge in all its forms. The report suggested this Act could bring together many strands of law reform to address issues of access and preservation of 'Indigenous knowledge' held in archival collections (Russell et al., 2008, p. 28). This idea has not been implemented. In 2021, the Healing Foundation published a report titled *Make Healing Happen: It's Time to Act*. Again, this report called for greater access for First Nations families to all archival material held about them, and culture- and trauma-informed support for them to process what is found (The Healing Foundation, May 2021, pp. 49–50). These recommendations have yet to be supported by the Commonwealth and implemented. Traditional ancestral land rights are caught up within the Commonwealth's ownership and legal control over Country. The Australian Commonwealth 'Archives Act 1983' (Commonwealth of Australia, 1983) protects the interests of the legal governing State and does not mention or acknowledge First Nation people's rights to material about them or relating to them.

So, we are not done yet. This conversation is ongoing; in fact, it will never end. Lynette and I, and many others, will continue to imagine a future that enables the rights of First Nations families to reconnect with the stories that reside in the archives through community-based, culture- and trauma-informed repatriation programmes nationwide. We will continue to envision the makings of a task force of Indigenous peoples supporting Indigenous families to remember, celebrate, and share their ancestral stories. That's a future to look forward to.

## Conclusion

Both Lynette and I have spent years searching, reflecting, and touching the past. I began my life journey far away from my point of orientation. In my early adult years, I first encountered archival material that enabled a lifelong journey of reconnection with my bloodline. Meeting and knowing my birth family is central to me remembering who I am and where I come from. I have found my point of orientation. The written archives have made this possible. Knowing my Great Uncle Walter Eatts, my guiding Elder, our family's knowledge holder, we are blessed. I have been inspired by his determination to share our family story and to give voice to his life and the life of his mother, Mabel Ita Eatts. Inspired by his storytelling, my PhD project was born. With the support and guidance of my mentor, Professor Lynette Russell, a knowledge holder of First Nations history, archival research, and an expert in storytelling from inside the academy, I became a professional early career history researcher at the age of 46. I will continue my Great Uncle's legacy and share our family story. I am proud of my research relationships with my three Sons, my Niece, my Half-Sister, my Birth Father, and my Great Uncle Walter Eatts. I hope our story echoes the voices of many other First Nations families who are looking deeply into living family memory, Country, and to the archives created by the colonisers, to remember their ancestral lineage, reconnect with their Spirit, and remember their love for themselves.

For Lynette, the role of archives in telling the story of Australia's chequered history has been a lifelong commitment. She has pushed back on the academy's bias against First Nations' family life writing. As an emerging scholar, almost a lifetime ago, she says, she shared her own story with the academy, and, thank goodness, she did. It is upon the shoulders of such scholars as Lynette Russell, Natalie Harkin, Jackie Higgins, Judi Wickes, Ali Baker, Faye Blanch, and many others that emerging Indigenous scholars can now do the same. Students now seek Lynette out, to support them in their voyage into community, into the past, and into the territory of archival research. It is the source of her greatest pride to know she has helped others on their journey.

Together we have experienced the importance of archives, their accessibility, and the need for cultural safety. Our access to the written and oral archives is at the very centre of this transformative journey. With these resources, we are creating new narratives; we are writing for our futures. Our storytelling is itself a living oral archive that will exist for generations to come. For ourselves, our families now, and for future generations to come, we are remembering ourselves and 'Finding our Place'.

## Notes

1 All references to cultural understandings represent the authors' own world views and are based on their own understandings of First Nations people's connections with Country, Kin, and Spirit.
2 Australia's Aboriginal and Torres Strait Islander communities are recognised as the oldest cultures in the world, having existed for over 60,000 years. There are over 500 different Aboriginal clan groups on this continent we now call Australia, each with distinctive cultures, laws, beliefs, and languages. Aboriginal culture has a profound spiritual connection to Land, Water, and Sky. Each clan group is connected to specific regions, and these regions are referred to as 'Country'. Country is sacred. It represents family, culture, and identity. Aboriginal law and extensive and complex kinship (family) networks are deeply linked to relationships with one's Country. Knowing one's family kinship networks is central to identity formation and one's sense of belonging to Country.
3 Jacinta Walsh has intentionally capitalised all references to her Birth Father, Birth Mother, Half-Sister, Sons, her Great Uncle, Country, and Mother Earth herself, to honour and highlight her relational accountability to them. Uncle Walter Eatts is affectionately also known and referred to by family as Uncle Wally, Uncle, Pop, and Pop Wally.

## References

Atkinson, J. (2002). *Trauma trails, recreating song lines: The transgenerational effects of trauma in Indigenous Australia*. Spinifex Press.

Australian Government. *Archives Act 1983*. www.legislation.gov.au/Details/C2016C00772

Brewster, A., & Berg, R. V. den. (2000). *Those who remain will always remember: An anthology of Aboriginal writing*. Fremantle Arts Centre Press.

*Chief Secretary's Department, Aborigines, Subject: Half-Caste—Mrs Mabel Ita Eatts of Derby, Personal file*, 1935, SROWA. The specific location of family archival documents is not being disclosed out of respect for our family's personal and cultural connections to the material.

Choo, C. (2001). *Mission girls: Aboriginal women on Catholic missions in the Kimberley, Western Australia, 1900–1950*. University of Western Australia Press.

*Colonial Secretary's Department, Aborigines and Fisheries. Subject: Beagle Bay Mission. Return of Natives at Mission dated July 1911*, SROWA, Item 1911/1439 (Beagle Bay).

Commonwealth of Australia. (1991). *Royal Commission into Aboriginal Deaths in Custody National Report*. Vol. 5: "Aboriginal society today", Recommendation 53. www.austlii.edu.au/au/other/IndigLRes/rciadic/national/vol5/

Commonwealth of Australia. (1997). *Bringing Them Home; Report of the National Inquiry into the Separation of Aboriginal and Torres Strait Islander Children from Their Families*. https://humanrights.gov.au/our-work/bringing-them-home-report-1997

Commonwealth of Australia. (1997). *Report Recommendations, Bringing Them Home; Report of the National Inquiry into the Separation of Aboriginal and Torres Strait Islander Children from Their*

*Families. Recommendations Related to Indigenous Family Archival Access*: Recommendations 21 to 30B. https://bth.humanrights.gov.au/the-report/report-recommendations

Dening, G. (1996). *Performances*. Melbourne University Press.

Eatts, W. (2014). *Somewhere between not white not black not wanted*. Twelfth Planet Press

Fforde, C., McKeown, C. T., & Keeler, H. (2020). *The Routledge Companion to Indigenous Repatriation: Return*, Reconcile, Renew. Routledge.

Haebich, A. (2000). *Broken circles: Fragmenting Indigenous families, 1800–2000*. Fremantle Press.

Harkin, N. (2014). The poetics of (re)mapping archives: Memory in the blood. *Journal of the Association for the Study of Australian Literature: JASAL*, 14(3), 1–14. https://openjournals.libr ary.sydney.edu.au/index.php/JASAL/article/view/9909

Harkin, N. (2019). *Archival-poetics*. Vagabond Press.

Healing Foundation. (2021, May). *Make Healing Happen: It's Time to Act*, pp. 49–50. https://healin gfoundation.org.au/make-healing-happen/

Huggins, J. (1998). *Sister girl: The writings of Aboriginal activist and historian Jackie Huggins*. University of Queensland Press.

Justice, D. H. (2018). *Why Indigenous literatures matter*. Wilfrid Laurier University Press.

Marsh, L., & Kinnane, S. (2003). Ghost files: The missing files of the Department of Indigenous Affairs Archives. [Paper in: History and Native Title, Choo, Christine and Hollbach, Shawn (eds.).]. *Studies in Western Australian History*, 23, 111–127. https://search.informit.org/doi/abs/ 10.3316/ielapa.200307138

McKemmish, S., Faulkhead, S., & Russell, L. (2011). Distrust in the archive: Reconciling records. *Archival Science*, 11. https://doi.org/10.1007/s10502-011-9153-2

McKemmish, S., Iacovino, L., Ketelaar, E., Castan, M., & Russell, L. (2011). Resetting relationships: Archives and Indigenous human rights in Australia. *Archives & Manuscripts*, 107– 144. https://publications.archivists.org.au/index.php/asa/article/view/10125

Mehl-Madrona, L. (2010). *Healing the mind through the power of story: The promise of narrative psychiatry*. Bear & Co.

Nakata, M. N., & Langton, M. (2005). *Australian indigenous knowledge and libraries*. Australian Academic & Research Libraries.

Poems authored by Walter Eatts, published in Eatts, W. (2014). *Somewhere between not white not black not wanted*. All in One Book Design: "Somewhere Between", p. 4; "Camooweal", p. 43; "Stockman and his Dreams", p. 4; "A Drover's Dream", p. 52; "Min-Min Lights", p. 54; "My Brother, the Bushland, his Home", pp. 67–69; "1905 Act", p. 92; "Lost Tears", p. 97; "Life's Corridors", p. 99; "Mother's Land", p. 101; "What is Love", p. 109; "I Had a Good Time", p. 111

Russell, L. (2002). *A little bird told me: Family secrets, necessary lies*. Allen & Unwin. https://ebook central.proquest.com/lib/monash/reader.action?docID=128241

Russell, L. (2005). Indigenous knowledge and archives: Accessing hidden history and understandings. *Australian Academic & Research Libraries: Australian Indigenous Knowledge and Libraries*, 36(2), 161–171. https://doi.org/10.1080/00048623.2005.10721256

Russell, L. (2006). Indigenous records and archives: Mutual obligations and building trust. *Archives and Manuscripts*, 34(1), 32–43. https://search.informit.org/doi/abs/10.3316/apaft.05528089 5547821

Russell, L. (2018). Affect in the archive: Trauma, grief, delight and texts. Some personal reflections. *Archives and Manuscripts*, 46(2), 200–207. https://doi.org/10.1080/01576895.2018.1458324

Russell, L. (2020a). What the Little Bird Didn't Tell Me. *Victorian Historical Journal*, 91(1). https:// search.informit.org/doi/abs/10.3316/informit.273178010242922

Russell, L. (2020b, 23 October) *Memories and narratives, an ongoing reflection*. University of Queensland. https://hass.uq.edu.au/event/7941/memories-and-narratives-ongoing-reflection

Russell, L., McKemmish, S., Schauder, D., Williamson, K., Johanson, G., & Heazlewood, J. (2008). *Koorie Archiving: Trust and Technology. Final Report*. ARC Linkage project, Monash University. www.monash.edu/__data/assets/pdf_file/0008/2373848/Koorie-Archiving-Trust-and-Technology-Final-report.pdf

*St Joseph Babies Home, Broadmeadows Admission form*, September 11, 1973, original document held by Catholic Family Welfare Bureau (CFWB).

Supernant, K., Baxter, J. E., Lyons, N., & Atalay, S. (Eds.). (2020). *Archaeologies of the heart*. Springer Nature.

*The Commonwealth of Australia Act 1983.*

Travis, K. A. P., & Haskins, V. (2021). Feminist research ethics and First Nations women's life narratives: A conversation. *Australian Feminist Studies, 36*(108), 126–141. https://doi.org/10.1080/08164649.2021.2004537

United Nations, 61/295. *United Nations Declaration on the Rights of Indigenous Peoples.* Resolution adopted by the General Assembly on 13 September 2007, Article 12.2, p.12. www.un.org/development/desa/indigenouspeoples/declaration-on-the-rights-of-indigenous-peoples.html

United Nations. (2007). *United Nations Declaration on the Rights of Indigenous Peoples*, Resolution adopted by the General Assembly on September 13 2007, Article 12.2, p.12. www.un.org/development/desa/indigenouspeoples/declaration-on-the-rights-of-indigenous-peoples.html

Wickes, J. (2008). 'Never really heard of it': The certificate of exemption and lost identity. In P. Read, F. Peter-Little, & A. Haebich (Eds.), *Indigenous Biography and Autobiography* (pp. 73–92).

Wilson, S. (2004). *Research as ceremony: Articulating an indigenous research paradigm* [Unpublished doctoral dissertation]. Monash University. https://trove.nla.gov.au/version/15943257

Wright, A. (2018). What happens when you tell somebody else's story? *International Journal of Applied Psychoanalytic Studies, 15*(2), 136–139. https://doi.org/10.1002/aps.1576

www6.austlii.edu.au/cgi-bin/viewdb/au/legis/cth/consol_act/aa198398/

# 16

# DIGITAL INDIGIQUEERS

## Locating queer mob in the literature

*Andrew Farrell*

### Introduction

Research which centres Indigenous LGBTIQ+ (lesbian, gay, bisexual, transgender, intersex and queer) peoples requires situated and intersecting textual analysis beginning with LGBTIQ+ Indigenous authors, subjects, theories and critique. In this chapter, I explore a range of texts that inform my ongoing research on Aboriginal and Torres Strait Islander LGBTIQ+ peoples and social media. This work is undertaken with an investment in the territorialising and the self-determination of academic research that produces knowledge about Aboriginal and Torres Strait Islander LGBTIQ+ peoples. Across the continent colonially known as Australia, academic institutions are built on unceded lands where Aboriginal and Torres Strait Islander peoples retain their position as sovereign subjects (Moreton-Robinson, 2020). The knowledges produced across the settler-colonial landscape have largely prescribed an understanding of Aboriginal and Torres Strait Islander peoples through the lens of settler, cis-gendered and heterosexual people. I prescribe to queer knowledges and critique which point to prevailing discourses on settler-colonial cis-heteropatriarchy as hierarchies which dominate settler-colonial society and render Indigenous peoples into categories of heteronormative, cis-gendered, binary gendered and patriarchal systems and norms. These containers and hierarchies are challenged by texts that assert "Indigenous Sovereign Erotics" (Driskill, 2004), which will be explored in the context of Aboriginal and Torres Strait Islander LGBTIQ+ use of social media and the internet.

Please note, throughout this chapter I use terms such as 'queer mob' interchangeably with 'Aboriginal and Torres Strait Islander LGBTIQ+ community'. This is done with respect to our endless diversities.

### Indigiqueer resistance

Anti-colonial Indigiqueer (Whitehead, 2017) resistance includes the evaluation and criticism of sources that position settlers as knowers and Indigenous peoples as subjects. Settler academic work has had a substantial role in the colonisation of Indigenous society, leading to Indigenous peoples being generally regarded as the most researched group in

DOI: 10.4324/9781003271802-19

the world (Fredericks, 2007; Tuhiwai-Smith, 1999). Settler knowledge production since 1770 has mistranslated and homogenised hundreds of unique societies as heterosexual and cis-gendered (Konishi, 2012; Nakata, 2007). Where observed to be deviant, settlers took action to eliminate Indigenous sovereignty through gendered and sexual violence by enforcing settler ideas about gender and sexuality through mechanisms such as state institutions (Carlson et al., 2021). In recent times, Indigenous queer scholars globally across settler-colonial contexts, have and continue to intervene in research about Indigenous people and provide a critical queer voice (Driskill, 2010; Farrell, 2021a, b; Justice, 2010; Laing, 2021; Monaghan, 2015; O'Sullivan, 2021; Sullivan, 2020; Wilson, 2015).

My research on Indigenous LGBTIQ+ peoples and social media continues the trajectory of Indigenous research towards the embedding of complexities around Indigeneity, gender, sex and sexuality which is negotiated both on and offline. Situating Indigenous LGBTIQ+ peoples both on and offline emphasises Indigenous LGBTIQ+ agency in the present day and into the future through how we engage with current and ever-changing technologies (Carlson & Berglund, 2021). My research is situated in sites of recognition and truth-telling which prioritises previously excluded and erased LGBTIQ+ voices. Indigenous queer research is highly transformative and often challenging to perceptions about Aboriginal and Torres Strait Islander peoples. It challenges the centralising notion that Aboriginal and Torres Strait Islander societies were heterosexual, cisgendered and gender binary. It goes beyond these categorisations to say that all Aboriginal and Torres Strait Islander peoples exist beyond the scope of Western epistemologies and ontologies through the notion of what Gender Studies scholar Qwo-Li Driskill (2004, p. 51) calls 'sovereign erotics' as an erotic "healing from the historical trauma that First Nations people continue to survive". This chapter continues the contemporary traditions of queer Indigenous interventions by challenging the stigma of multiple minority research as being 'too hard' and challenging. Situated in Indigenous Queer Studies and the emergence of the field across this continent, this work is multidisciplinary, highly creative and experimental. I have found that I have had to develop unique approaches to engage with the literature which is inspired by Indigenous LGBTIQ+ scholars and activists nationally and globally—for example, Turtle Island (North America), the Pacific Islands, and across this continent known as Australia. I have also considered non-queer and settler texts to facilitate conversations that seek to recognise Indigenous LGBTIQ+ peoples in the context of this continent.

### Context: settler-colonialism, cis-heteropatriarchy, identity and authenticity

Aboriginal and Torres Strait Islander peoples form vastly diverse communities, across hundreds of nations, whose histories are over 65,000 years old and are the world's oldest living cultures. Since the illegal claiming of terra nullius by British explorer James Cook and subsequent settlement in 1788, Aboriginal and Torres Strait Islander peoples have endured waves of settler-colonial violence which strive to eliminate Aboriginal peoples through what Wolfe terms the settler-colonial "logic of elimination" (Wolfe, 2006, p. 387). This erasure includes the widely recognised forms of targeted violence through policies emergent in settler colonies which, for decades, segregated, institutionalised and attempted to assimilate Aboriginal and Torres Strait Islander peoples into a white Australia (Moreton-Robinson, 2015). Genocidal aims embedded across racially and culturally targeted policies attempted to dissolve Indigenous cultures through intervening in Indigenous ontologies and epistemologies and the relationalities which structure

241

Aboriginal and Torres Strait Islander peoples' lives (Tuck & Yang, 2012; Wolfe, 2006). Mississauga Nishnaabeg scholar Leanne Betasamosake Simpson (2017, p. 93) argues that settler-colonialism "work[s] to destroy the fabric of Indigenous nationhoods by attempting to destroy our relationality by making it difficult to form sustainable, strong relationships with each other". Colonisers targeted our genders and sexualities as a part of a greater settler-colonial project of genocide (Morgensen, 2012; Picq, 2019). Enduring settlement, Aboriginal and Torres Strait Islander peoples have been subjected to academic research which has played a central role in the surveillance and control of Indigenous peoples. Gendered and sexual violence, particularly against Indigenous LGBTIQ+ peoples, is still endemic in contemporary academic works which reproduce settler-colonial frameworks of gender and sexuality and erase queer peoples (Carlson et al., 2021; O'Sullivan, 2021). Indigenous Queer Studies has developed across this continent to explore the ways that Indigenous peoples have been subject to settler-colonial epistemologies and ontologies of gender, sex and sexuality (Day, 2020). Indigenous Queer Studies decentres settler-colonialism by challenging normative settler-colonial ontologies and epistemologies which prioritise and enforce patriarchal, cisgendered and heterosexual society, as well as identify settler-colonialism through emergent frameworks of sexuality that continue to prioritise settler-colonialism such as homonormativity and homonationalism. (Picq, 2019; Puar, 2017) These frameworks occupy and define Indigenous ways of being and doing gender, sex and sexuality.

Settler-colonial heteropatriarchy across this continent is situated within the broader scope of Western European imperialism and settler-colonialism, and settler-colonialism remains the overarching power system in place that still tethers 'Australia' to the British empire. The extension of social and cultural norms generated from imperial rule continues to have a great impact in the lives of Indigenous people in all contexts of settler-colonialism. Nations such as Australia, the United States and Canada have not only physically occupied Indigenous lands but have cast settler-colonial imaginaries that have occupied the social and cultural mores of Indigenous society through the violent assertion of settler identity (Whittaker, 2016). As argued by Morgensen (2011, p. 10), Indigenous elimination "proceeds through settler regulation of sexual relations, gender identity, marriage, reproduction, and genealogy, and all similar means for restricting resistant indigenous national difference". Morgensen (2015) puts forward a theory of 'settler sexuality' which describes the use of Western sexuality as an oppressive force. Settler sexuality is described as a "white national heteronormativity [and increasingly homonormativity] that regulates Indigenous sexuality by supplanting them with the sexual modernity of settler subjects" (Morgensen, 2011, p. 106) and as "the heteropatriarchal and sexual modernity exemplary of white settler civilisation" (in Tallbear, 2018, para. 9). This is reiterated in the work of scholars such as Jonathan Katz (2007, p. 143), who argues that "Without realizing it, usually, we are all deeply embedded in a living, institutionalized [and colonized] heterosexual/homosexual distinction". Heterosexuality prevails as do the support mechanisms of patriarchy, gender power systems, race and racism which uphold Western settler-colonial cis-heteropatriarchy.

In the late Victorian era, the term 'heterosexuality' evolved to diagnose sexual pathology and then become descriptive of 'normal' sexuality in Europe and settler-colonial societies (Katz, 2007). This has evolved from Western notions of gender and sexuality which centre nglicized ideas of reproduction and purity to prescribe Cartesian binary systems in a post-Enlightenment Europe (Norman et al., 2019). From the beginning of normative sexual formations and the beginning of sexual identity, the West has continued to dominate discourses of gender, sex and sexuality. Beyond being cognisant of these developments, Indigenous people continue to resist as they have always done (Simpson, 2017).

Indigenous people have been subject to the full extent of settler-colonial cis-heteropatriarchy. Outright acts of gendered violence are described through Maureen S. Heibert's concept of gendercide, and expanded by Deborah A. Miranda (2010), a Chumash person from the Ohlone-Costanoan Esselen Nation, as inclusive of genders outside of the settler-colonial gaze. Heibert (cited in Miranda, 2010, p. 258) argues:

> Gendercide [is] an attack on a group of victims based on the victims' gender/sex. Such an attack would only really occur if men or women are victimized because of their primary identity as men or women. Moreover, it must be the perpetrators themselves, not outside observers making ex-poste analyses, who identify a specific gender/sex as a threat and therefore a target for extermination.

Miranda (2010) responds by proposing the addition of a third gender. This expansion of the definition centres Indigenous ontologies through the recognition of more than two genders. From that position we can read history though Indigenous queer critique, which reaches further outside of the Western paradigm to assert Indigenous ontologies. Indigenous queer critiques of historical events, such as Miranda's analysis of the extermination of the 'joyas', the Spanish name for third-gender people, describe entrenched European notions of gender and sexuality in which Indigenous people were killed in barbaric and inhumane ways such as throwing them "to the [Mastiff] dogs" for their perceived gender transgressions (Miranda, 2010, p. 257). Anishinaabe activist, economist and author Winona LaDuke (1995, para. 10) argues:

> we are often in the role of the prey to a predator society, whether for sexual discrimination, exploitation, sterilization, absence of control over our bodies, or being the subjects of repressive laws and legislation in which we have no voice. This occurs on an individual level, but equally, and more significantly on a societal level.

LaDuke also points to the ways that Indigenous ontologies are erased or rendered dormant as settler societies reproduce settler patriarchies in "that [Native] matrilineal societies, societies in which governance and decision making are largely controlled by women, have been obliterated from the face of the earth by colonialism" (in O'Dea Schenken, 1999, p. 774; see also Keovorabouth, 2021). With a range of Native queer critiques established across Turtle Island, Indigenous gender, sex and sexual heterogeneity is rendered visible. As argued by Picq (2019, p. 170), "Indigenous sexualities are as diverse as the peoples who prace them, ranging from non-monogamous relations and crossdressing to homo-affective families. Sexual diversity has historically been the norm, not the exception". Picq (2020) points to the precondition that Indigenous societies largely exist outside of colonial translation and understanding. These arguments have implications for understanding Indigenous approaches to digital sites.

The installing of settler-colonial heteropatriarchy can also be explained by social fractures that occurred through colonial violence. Across this continent, efforts were made to assimilate Aboriginal and Torres Strait Islander peoples and civilise us into Western modernity, beginning with children's institutes such as the Parramatta Native Institute[1] and subsequent children's homes which segregated and indoctrinated Indigenous children according to Western gender norms (Cruickshank & Grimshaw, 2019). From the perspective of Indigenous LGBTIQ+ peoples, it will always be a sensitive topic to approach where we, through difference, highlight the problematic, toxic and violent relationships that mirror settler-colonial heteropatriarchy and, to an extent, accept the roles and power associated with settler-colonial logics of sex and gender. While difficult to negotiate, conversations around gender, sex and sexuality are necessary, critical and life-saving, yet are silenced through violence, shame and stigma, which feed into the aims of settler-colonialism: elimination (Wolfe, 2006).

Current and recent discourses of Aboriginal identity have been shaped by Indigenous LGBTIQ+ scholars who speak to settler-colonial cis-heteropatriarchy and the prevalence of fundamentalist thinking which produce anti-queer racist sentiment and violence (Alizzi, 2014). As argued by Nyungar scholar Braden Hill (2014, pp. 10–11), Indigenous activism in settler-colonial Australia has been underscored through sites of difference having "the potential to, and in some instances do, invoke the notion of culture and identity as an oppressive site of authority in a way that is, in practice, fundamentalist" and how "notions of culture, tradition and authenticity to construct a site of authority in a way that is absolute and oppressive". Hill's argument is generative of discourses around authenticity which can apply, for example, to Alizzi's (2015b) argument which centres queerness and the politics of recognising gender and sexual diversity against authoritative heteropatriarchal definitions of Aboriginal identity. Aboriginal scholar Bronwyn Carlson (2016, p. 119) contends that there are many sites of identity conflicts in which:

> the diverse and complex expressions of Aboriginal identity that have been produced through varied colonial experiences raise questions and demands to extend the collective right to self-determination to individuals demanding to have their experiences recognised and authenticated as evidence of the "Aboriginal" experience.

This argument is expansive of the definition of Aboriginality to recognise the multiplicity of experiences that Aboriginal and Torres Strait Islander peoples endure under colonial occupation—such as the 'Aboriginal' experience Carlson refers to. My position is that gender and sexual diversity are traits of humanity and that Indigenous LGBTIQ+ peoples join their broader Indigenous communities in the project of recognising our collective humanity as we heal relational structures (Graham, 2014). A proponent of fundamentalist and conservative sentiment is the conceptualisation of purity which inhabit definitions of Indigeneity. The private and intimate lives of Aboriginal and Torres Strait Islander peoples are broadly documented in the period of occupation and heterosexualisation. However, conversations about purity often address racial dimensions of purity rather than gendered, sexed or sexual sovereignty, as demonstrated by religious indoctrination of Aboriginal and Torres Strait Islander peoples in mission and reserve life. (Cruickshank & Grimshaw, 2019).

Indigenous LGBTIQ+ politics of inclusion and exclusion are situated between queer and Indigenous distinctions yet have needs separate from both. Themes of belonging are woven out of a range of autobiographic and biographical works (see Hodge, 2015). Belonging is often associated with visions of a queer Indigenous past. As global conversations address Indigenous gender and sexual diversity, Australia has formed its own specificities around discourses of gender, sex and sexually diverse histories that attempt to revive our queer roots. Jawoyn artist and scholar Troy-Anthony Baylis takes a revisionist historical approach in reading Aboriginal history. Referencing the Mimi spirits, which are part of his cultural legacy, Baylis recasts them through a queer Indigenous lens. As genderless spirits, Baylis (2014, para. 20) argues that "Mimi spirits are transformative figures that have a gift with language, including visual language. They luxuriate in the chaos of [embodied] ambiguity and can be used to manipulate meaning" in terms of their genderless and sexually analogous qualities. The argument that Indigenous history requires a critical queer reading is reflected in Oscar Monaghan's (2015, p. 509) work, which argues that:

> the queering we do is not undertaken with a view to arriving at some idealised Indigenous authenticity; rather, it is as much about naming the settler state as heteropatriarchal and White as it is about recovering subordinated histories and recognising that the sexual and gendered formations found in those histories was neither heteronormative nor queer.

These perspectives intervene in Indigenous Studies and expand it simultaneously. Discourses of identity and authenticity are commonplace in digital settings. Indigenous life writing as well as critical scholarship make these tensions accessible through granting context, history and a written legacy. Aboriginal and LGBTIQ+-identified scholars such as Gomeroi scholar and poet Alison Whittaker (2016) and Yugambeh scholar Arlie Alizzi (2014) speak to the mythologising of queerness in precolonial times. Whittaker (2016, para. 14) argues that Aboriginal people "are cast off as being incapable of queerness and trans-ness, and of loving queer and trans Aboriginal people", embedded in the notion that queerness is incompatible with Indigeneity. Recalling the ways that Aboriginal and Torres Strait Islander cultures became 'straight' through processes of colonisation, Whittaker (2016) points to the ways that Indigenous people are always already savage, a paradox in which Indigenous queerness is produced through deficit discourses and, in contemporary times, are recast as regressive through stereotypes that claim that Indigenous culture and society does not accept LGBTIQ+ identities.

Homophobia and transphobia are viewed as a product of colonisation and colonial thinking which becomes a normative perception in Indigenous society. Alizzi (2014) argues that current knowledge around Indigenous intimate and family life does not reflect the lived complexities of Aboriginal and Torres Strait Islander LGBTIQ+ peoples, that there is acceptance, love and care which reflects the continuity of traditional modes of relationality. Many activists and scholars across Aboriginal and Torres Strait Islander LGBTIQ+ sites have criticised the narrowing of Indigenous peoples into a cis-heterosexual binary, and are broadly opposed to attempts to represent Aboriginal and Torres Strait Islander cultures as a monolith (Gorrie, 2019; Monaghan, 2015; O'Sullivan, 2021; Whittaker, 2016). Not only do these scholars innovate discussions of anti-colonialism, but they also intervene in the coloniality of queer and identity discourses, which for many years have been rendered marginalised, silent and oversaturated by the critical mass of heteronormative society both Indigenous and non-Indigenous. Alizzi (2015, p. 592) makes an important intervention that accounts for Indigenous queer well-being, stating "we don't need to be able to construct ourselves in written historical accounts in order to consider ourselves real and whole". We do not need to justify ourselves to a wide audience to validate and value our lives.

## Digital life

An important site for the recognition of Indigenous LGBTIQ+ peoples are social media platforms. Access to Indigenous queer thinkers and knowledge is a powerful tool against the shame and stigma that has gone unchallenged. The ability to speak to power has been inhibited by the significant barriers that these communities have faced offline. As well, social media sites have been used to silence, discriminate against and exclude queer mob (Carlson & Frazer, 2021; Donnelly, 2016; Farrell, 2021b; Lim et al., 2020). Conflict which targeted queer mob included online debates on marriage equality (O'Sullivan, 2021). I am tentative about using the term 'lateral violence' to describe instances of intracommunity conflict as there are glaring inequalities within the community between those with cis-heterosexual and patriarchal privilege and those without. Queer Wiradjuri scholar Corrinne Sullivan (2020, p. 348) articulates the complex dynamic of belonging for people "whose lives and experiences may be considered wrong, deviant, or incongruent with the organisation/community" through the example of Indigenous sex workers, both queer and non-queer. Community sites are constructed through centralising ontologies (O'Sullivan, 2015) and generative cultural norms around gender, sex and sexuality which result in further policing of our identities. Such complexities can also be understood by considering the intersubjectivities of power and oppression in Indigenous communities, in which "each of us lives within a system that vests us with varying levels of power and privilege" determined under the conditions of settler-colonialism (Hill Collins, 1993, p. 78). Such complexities determine our power and powerlessness in all digital social and cultural sites and, increasingly, these complexities are performed online. Carlson identifies that both online and offline activity has implications for each context. (Carlson, 2013; 2016; 2020)

Settler research examining digital technologies fits into two broader categories of 'non-Indigenous' and either (1) White or (2) People of Colour (POC) research. It is viewed as such under the distinction that to be a settler, one doesn't always fit into categories of whiteness. The distinction also carries with it the interruption of the binary between Indigenous and non-Indigenous by recognising non-Indigenous peoples' intersubjectivities of race, ethnicity, nationality, gender, sex and sexuality online (Noble, 2018). Non-Indigenous research does not often include the specificities of Indigenous peoples online, and especially Indigenous LGBTIQ+ peoples. I have approached these texts with a queer Indigenous lens which enables careful correlation and criticism. Queer social media research across this continent, for example, provides us with minority discourses of social media use and experience specific to oppressed groups such as the LGBTIQ+ community (Burnwell, 2010; Hanckel et al., 2019). At the same time, these texts often fall short of Indigenous inclusion through minimal representation and sometimes reflect non-white LGBTIQ+ peoples, as demonstrated by an article titled 'Grindr Is Deleting Its 'Ethnicity Filter'. But racism is still rife in online dating published in *The Conversation* (Lim et al., 2020). Such collaborative work puts inclusion into action through co-authorship (Lim et al., 2020). This is also informed by the chapter 'Peopling the Empty Mirror: The Prospects for Lesbian and Gay Aboriginal History' (in the edited collection *Gay Perspectives II: More Essays in Australian Gay Culture*), which was conceived by a group of Indigenous and non-Indigenous LGBTIQ+ peoples who formed the Gays and Lesbians Aboriginal Alliance (1993). This text reflects the complexities, differences and commonalities shaped by race, culture, gender, sex and sexual discourses in Australia during the 1980s and 1090s. While these can be seen as unrelated texts, it is through the Indigenous queer lens that intersections of power, privilege and oppression can be extracted and understood.

The literature on LGBTIQ+ Aboriginal and Torres Strait Islander identities, particularly autobiographical formats, paints a picture of queer Indigenous life under settler-colonialism in this settler colony referred to as Australia. Carlson and Berglund (2021) demonstrate that globally, Indigenous people are utilising digital technologies to assert our perspectives, experience, truth-telling and recognition of Indigenous peoples (see also Duarte, 2017; O'Carroll, 2013). The settler-colony known as Australia is thoroughly condemned for its historical and current treatment of Indigenous peoples through social media activism. Of those who experience more than one form of oppression and disadvantage, Aboriginal and Torres Strait islander LGBTIQ+ written and spoken testimonies demonstrate the severe, violent and life-threatening oppression and disadvantages faced by queer mob, often implicating our own peoples in instances of violence against us as well as the broader non-Indigenous society (Farrell, 2021a; Kerry, 2014). Compounding these issues are the structural responses which continue to ignore calls for greater attention to Indigenous LGBTIQ+ health and well-being that are accessible in online articles (Bonson, 2016). Complex interventions into the health and well-being of Indigenous LGBTIQ+ peoples are emphasised in recent research where the framing of these interventions is directed towards societal and structural failings regarding queer Indigenous peoples and communities (ATSISPEP, 2016; Day et al., 2022; Hill et al., 2022. Indigenous LGBTIQ+ writings point at structural, societal and intimate relationships as a call to attention and action. Testimonies of violent and horrifying themes present across the literary niche of Indigenous queer writing are a call to action and empathy, and compel important autonomous, local, critical and justice-based research which must be led and informed by queer mob to ensure that we are safe to scrutinise and 'speak up' (Moreton Robinson, 2002).

Homophobic and transphobic violence is a harrowing standard in life writings of queer mob. Investigating anti-LGBTIQ+ sentiments is integral on the path to justice (Gays and Lesbians Aboriginal Alliance, 1993; Hill et al., 2022; Petray & Collin, 2017; Wilson, 2015). Homophobia and transphobia online are complex in terms of how they are cast and layered onto community, for example, where racism, homophobia and sexual violence are singularly leveraged against mob online (Farrell, 2022a). There is also the susceptibility of the broader non-LGBTIQ+ identifying community to being targeted by gender, sex and sexual discrimination regardless of how they identify, showing that this is an issue that should be of concern to all. (Carlson, 2020)

Digital technology has been used by queer mob to challenge multiple forms of oppression since its early stages. On the margins, allied activism can be seen online as grassroots efforts against queerphobias with groups such as Queers for Reconciliation (n.d., n.p.), who, in the 1990s, formed a "commitment to initiating positive change in the relationships between Indigenous and non-Indigenous communities" through approaches against homophobia online. The landscape of activism has changed dramatically for queer mob, shifting from strains of reconciliation and into equity and justice and a push towards recognising that queerphobia cannot be understood without the broader context of settler-colonialism which has imported sexual and gendered violence as an act of imperialism (Whittaker, 2016). Digital studies that centre Aboriginal and Torres Strait Islander peoples can address these acts of violence and oppression, as shown in the work of Carlson (2020). Inclusive research is developing to address multiple marginalised groups, including queer mob, to highlight the complexities of violence against Aboriginal and Torres Strait Islander peoples as not only racialised, but as experiencing violence which is also gendered, sexual, sexed and tied closely to settler-colonialism (Carlson, 2020). Recent research cites an alarming data set which shows that an overwhelming majority of Aboriginal and Torres Strait Islander people experience negativity online, including 78 per cent of respondents witnessing hate speech weekly (Carlson & Frazer, 2021; Kennedy, 2021a; Kennedy, 2021b). Noble (2018, p. 180) argues:

> [African American] identities are often a commodity, exploited as titillating fodder in a network that traffics in racism, sexism, and homophobia for profit [...] [and] the onus for change is placed on the backs of Black people, and Black women in the United States in particular, to play a more meaningful role in the production of new images and ideas about Black people.

Similarly, as settler-colonialism persists on- and offline, Aboriginal and Torres Strait Islander peoples undertake the work to reclaim and reterritorialise social media images of ourselves (Carlson & Berglund, 2021; Duarte, 2017). Online studies also extends to identifying key trends in the literature which limit the scope of Indigenous queer critique, such as the limitations produced by a focus on justice in primarily health and well-being settings offline (ATSISPEP, 2016; Donelly, 2016; Dudgeon, 2015; Hill et al., 2022; Lezard et al., 2020).

Indigenous digital studies across this continent advances the important work of global Indigenous scholarship. Based on a tradition of critical Indigenous scholarship, Indigenous digital technologies studies canvases all critical themes such as race/racism, culture, identity, sovereignty and settler-colonialism. Beyond that, Indigenous digital technology studies is highly innovative, along with the embedding of diverse identities including Indigenous LGBTIQ+ genders and sexualities. Indigenous academics working in the field are few but impactful. Carlson's contribution has formed a significant basis from which future scholarship is possible. Since her Stanner Award-winning *The Politics of Identity: Who Counts as Aboriginal Today?* (2016), Carlson has explored digital technologies, social media, memes, dating applications and help-seeking online (Carlson, 2013, 2020; Carlson & Berglund, 2021; Carlson & Day, 2022; Carlson & Frazer, 2021). As a contributor to the field, my own work has been provoked by the critical dearth of literature on queer mob across Indigenous Studies broadly. Through digital technology studies, I have contributed to the growing literature on the topic and have published on social media platforms, drag, digital archiving, Indigenous queer visibility online, and queer Indigenous activism (Farrell, 2016; 2017; 2021b; 2022). As an Indigenous queer-identified person, my research, teaching, activism and responsibilities prioritise Indigenous queer people beginning with queer mob across this continent and then expanding to our global relatives. This includes a growing network of queer Indigenous scholars and Indigenous and non-Indigenous allies. As my work feeds into academic discourses online, I too am enabled by community online. Queer mob are often overlooked and unseen in the digital landscape, and I wanted to participate in the historicising of their importance to our communities through research recognising queer mob. Aboriginal business entrepreneur Leesa Watego (2015, n.p.) argues that Aboriginal and Torres Strait Islander peoples' use of digital sites demonstrates our unsurprising "ability to adapt to new ways and new technologies, and the importance and necessity of challenging colonisation". The assertion of our existence online reminds settler-colonisers that we are present and thriving. Cutting through the racist tropes and deficit discourses associated with Indigenous peoples and technology, Carlson (2013) highlights that Aboriginal and Torres Strait Islander peoples use social media at a higher rate than their non-Indigenous counterparts. As demonstrated by current literatures, through self-determined data and research practices, we can take ownership of constructive and critical community-informed scholarship which collectively transforms our future (Walter, 2021).

## Conclusion

I am of the belief that digital technologies have underpinned transformative justice, making progress increasingly viable. I also acknowledge the limitations and prospects of research on its trajectory. Being online, as well as community and institutional responses to us, raises endlessly interesting provocations about Indigenous life as the harbinger of innovative, autonomous research. What the current literature tells us is that beyond the clear interventions into settler-colonialism, there are those who are invested in research outside the typical scope of Indigenous Studies and who are pushing the limitations of it with mindfulness and care towards our diversities and difference. To achieve the position of knowing more about queer mob, a challenge to settler-colonial norms and violence relating to gender, sex and sexual norms must exist across all sites of human connection. The scholarship that we produce has implications tied into the ongoing humanisation and restoration of the sovereignty and dignity of Indigenous peoples. Texts which inform this work include those that capture broad themes of Indigeneity, gender, sex, sexuality and digital sites such as social media. A dearth of academic writings on Indigenous communities have historically failed to capture and include the experiences of Indigenous LGBTIQ+ peoples; however, this has not stifled its emergence. Across this continent there is a move in research towards more inclusive futures for Aboriginal and Torres Strait Islander LGBTIQ+ peoples. Meanwhile, we must also recognise the many queer mob who constitute digital sites through fiction and non-fiction literatures, visual art, poetry, theatre, television and beyond, which you can find on virtually any platform.

## Note

1  For more information, see https://dictionaryofsydney.org/entry/parramatta_and_black_town_nati ve_institutions

## References

Aboriginal and Torres Strait Islander Suicide Prevention Evaluation Project (ATSISPEP). (2016). *Inaugural National Aboriginal and Torres Strait Islander Suicide Prevention Conference Report.* www.atsispep.sis.uwa.edu.au

Alizzi, A. (2014). Against authenticity. *Overland.* https://overland.org.au/previous-issues/issue-215/feature-maddee-clark/

Alizzi, A. (2015a). Indigenous subjectivity in Australia: Are we queer? *Journal of Global Indigeneity,* *1*(1). http://ro.uow.edu.au/jgi/vol1/iss1/7

Alizzi, A. (2015b). Are we queer? Reflections on 'Peopling the Empty Mirror' twenty years on. In D. Hodge (Ed.). *Colouring the rainbow: Blak queer and trans perspectives* (pp. 583–616). Wakefield Press.

Baylis, T. (2014, 15 April) The art of seeing Aboriginal Australia's queer potential. *The Conversation.* http://theconversation.com/the-art-of-seeing-aboriginal-australiasqueer- potential-25588

Bonson, D. (2016, 5 May). No data exists on suicide among gay and trans Indigenous Australians. *The Guardian.* www.theguardian.com/australia-news/2016/may/05/no-data-exists-on-suicide-among-gay-and-trans-indigenous-australians

Burnwell, C. (2010) Rewriting the script: Toward a politics of young people's digital media participation. *Review of Education, Pedagogy, and Cultural Studies, 32*(4–5), 382–402.

Carlson, B. (2013). The 'new frontier': Emergent Indigenous identities and social media. In M. Harris, M. Nakata, & B. Carlson (Eds.), *The politics of identity: Emerging indigeneity* (pp. 147–168). University of Technology Sydney E-Press.

Carlson, B. (2016). *The politics of identity: Who counts as Aboriginal today?* Aboriginal Studies Press.

Carlson, B. (2020). Indigenous killjoys: Negotiating the labyrinth of dis/mis trust. In T. Moeke-Pickering, A. Pegoraro, & S. Cote-Meek (Eds.), *Critical reflections and politics on advancing women in the academy* (pp. 105–123). IGI Global.

Carlson, B., & Berglund, J. (Eds.). (2021). *Indigenous peoples rise up: The global ascendency of social media activism.* Rutgers University Press.

Carlson, B., & Day, M. (2022). Love, hate and sovereign bodies: The exigencies of Aboriginal online dating. In A. Powell, A. Flynn, & L. Sugiura (Eds.). *The Palgrave handbook of gendered violence and technology* (pp. 181–202). Springer.

Carlson, B., & Frazer, R. (2021). *Indigenous digital life: The practice and politics of being indigenous on social media.* Palgrave Macmillan.

Carlson, B., Kennedy, T., & Farrell, A. (2021). Indigenous gender intersubjectivities: Political bodies. In M. Walter, T. Kukutai, A. A. Gonzales, & R. Henry (|Eds.). *The Oxford handbook of Indigenous sociology* (pp. 1–21). Oxford University Press.

Collins, P. H. (1993). Toward a new vision: Race, class, and gender as categories of analysis and connection. *Race, Sex & Class, 1*(1), 25–45.

Cruickshank, J., & Grimshaw, P. (2019). *White women, Aboriginal missions and Australian settler governments: Maternal contradictions.* Brill.

Day, M. (2020). Indigenist origins: Institutionalizing Indigenous Queer and Trans Studies in Australia. *Transgender Studies Quarterly, 7*(3), 367–373.

Day, M., Bonson, D., Farrell, A., & Bakic, T. (2022). *Aboriginal & Torres Strait Islander LGBTQISB+ people and the COVID-19 pandemic: A survey of impacts experienced as at mid-2021.* Black Rainbow.

Donnelly, B. (2016, 18 April). Gay minorities speak out against racist slurs on Grindr. *Sydney Morning Herald.* www.smh.com.au/national/gay-aboriginal-man-publishes-racist-slurs-on-dating-app-20160418-go8zov.html

Driskill, Q. (2004). Stolen from our bodies: First Nations two-spirits/queers and the journey to a sovereign erotic. *Studies in American Indian Literatures, 16*(2), 50–64.

Driskill, Q. (2010). Doubleweaving two-spirit critiques: Building alliances between Native and Queer Studies. *GLQ: A Journal of Lesbian and Gay Studies, 1*(69), 69–92.

Duarte, M. E. (2017). Connected activism: Indigenous uses of social media for shaping political change. *Australasian Journal of Information Systems, 21*, 1–12.

Dudgeon, P., Bonson, D., Cox, A., Georgatos, G., & Rouhani, L. (2015). *Sexuality & Gender Diverse Populations Roundtable Report.* The Healing Foundation. Canberra.

Farrell, A. (2016). Lipstick clapsticks: A yarn and a Kiki with an Aboriginal drag queen. *AlterNative: An International Journal of Indigenous Peoples, 12*(5), 574–585.

Farrell, A. (2017). Archiving the aboriginal rainbow: Building an aboriginal LGBTIQ portal. *Australasian Journal of Information Systems, 21*.

Farrell, A. (2021b). The rise of Black Rainbow: Queering and Indigenizing digital media strategies, resistance, and change. In B. Carlson & J. Berglund (Eds.), *Indigenous peoples rise up: The global ascendency of social media activism* (pp. 140–156). Rutgers University Press.

Farrell, A. (2022). *Indigenous LGBTIQ+ community online.* [Unpublished doctoral dissertation]. Macquarie University.

Farrell. A. (2021a). Feeling seen: Aboriginal and Torres Strait Islander LGBTIQ+ peoples, (in)visibility, and social-media assemblages. *Genealogy, 5*(2), 57–68.

Fredericks, B. (2007). *The changing nature of Aboriginal and Torres Strait Islander health research.* Guest Public Lecture Series, Oodgeroo Unit, Queensland University of Technology, Kelvin Grove, 26 October.

Gays and Lesbians Aboriginal Alliance. (1993). Peopling the empty mirror: The prospects for lesbian and gay Aboriginal history. In R. Aldrich (Ed.), *Gay perspectives II: More essays in Australian gay culture* (pp. 1–62). Department of Economic History, University of Sydney.

Gorrie, N. (2019). Rob, and queer family. In B. Law (Ed.), *Growing up queer in Australia* (pp. 16–21). Black.

Graham, M. (2014). Aboriginal notions of relationality and positionalism: A reply to Weber. *Global Discourse, 4,* 17–22.

Hanckel, B., Vivienne, S., Byron, P., Robards, B., & Churchill, B. (2019). 'That's not necessarily for them': LGBTIQ+ young people, social media platform affordances and identity curation. *Media, Culture & Society, 41*(8), 1261–1278.

Hill, B. (2014). Searching for certainty in purity: Indigenous fundamentalism. *Nationalism and Ethnic Politics, 20*(1), 10–25.

Hill, B., Dodd, J., Uink, B., Bonson, D., Bennett, S., & Eades, A. M. (2022). Aboriginal and Queer identity/ies in Western Australia: When there is a need to know in therapeutic settings. *Qualitative Health Research, 32*(5), 755–770.

Hodge, D. (2015). *Colouring the rainbow: Blak queer and trans perspectives.* Wakefield Press.

Justice. D. H. (2010). Notes towards a theory of anomaly. *GLQ: A Journal of Lesbian and Gay Studies, 16*(1–2), 207–242.

Katz, J. (2007). *The invention of heterosexuality.* University of Chicago Press.

Kennedy, T. (2021a, 11 June). 97% of Indigenous people report seeing negative social media content weekly. Here's how platforms can help. *The Conversation.* https://theconversation.com/97-of-indigenous-people-report-seeing-negative-social-media-content-weekly-heres-how-platforms-can-help-162353

Kennedy, T. (2021b, 3 June). Indigenous peoples' experiences of social media: The good and the bad. *Facebook Australia Blog.* https://australia.fb.com/post/indigenouspeoples-experiences-of-social-media-thegood-and-the-bad/

Keovorabouth, S. T. (2021). Reaching back to traditional teachings: Diné knowledge and gender politics. *Genealogy, 5*(95), 1–9.

Kerry, S. (2014). Sistergirls/brotherboys: The status of indigenous transgender Australians. *International Journal of Transgenderism, 15*(3–4), 173–186.

Konishi, S. (2012). *The Aboriginal male in the Enlightenment world.* Pickering & Chatto.

LaDuke, W. (1995). *The Indigenous Women's Network: Our Future, Our Responsibility Statement of Winona LaDuke.* United Nations Fourth World Conference on Women, Beijing, China, 31 August 1995. https://ratical.org/co globalize/WinonaLaDuke/Beijing95.html

Laing, M. (2021). *Urban Indigenous youth reframing two-spirit.* Routledge.

Lezard, P., Prefontaine, Z., Cederwall, D.M., Sparrow, C., Maracle, S., Beck, A., & McLeod, A. (2020). *MMIWG2SLGBTQQIA+ National Action Plan Final Report.* https://mmiwg2splus-nationalactionplan.ca/wpcontent/uploads/2021/06/2SLGBTQQIA-Report-Final.pdf

Lim, G., Robards, B., & Carlson, B. (2020, 7 June), Grindr is deleting its 'ethnicity filter'. But racism is still rife in online dating. *The Conversation.* https://theconversation.com/grindr-is-deleting-its-ethnicity-filter-but-racism-is-stillrife-in-online-dating-140077

Miranda, D. A. (2010). Extermination of the joyas: Gendercide in Spanish California. *GLQ: A Journal of Lesbian and Gay Studies, 16*(1), 253–284.

Monaghan, O. (2015). Dual imperatives: Decolonising the queer and queering the decolonial. in D. Hodge (Ed.). *Colouring the rainbow: Blak queer and trans perspectives: Life stories and essays by First Nations people of Australia* (pp. 195–207). Wakefield Press.

Moreton-Robinson, A. (2002). *Talkin' up to the white woman: Indigenous women and feminism.* University of Minnesota Press.

Moreton-Robinson, A. (2015). *The white possessive: Property, power, and Indigenous sovereignty.* University of Minnesota Press.

Moreton-Robinson, A. (Ed.). (2020). *Sovereign subjects: Indigenous sovereignty matters.* Routledge.

Morgensen, S. L. (2011). *Spaces between us: Queer settler colonialism and indigenous decolonization.* University of Minnesota Press.

Morgensen, S. L. (2012). Theorising gender, sexuality and settler colonialism: An introduction. *Settler Colonial Studies, 2*(2), 2–22.

Morgensen, S. L. (2015). Cutting to the roots of colonial masculinity. In R. A. Innes & K. Anderson (Eds.), *Indigenous men and masculinities: Legacies, identities, regeneration* (pp. 38–61). University of Manitoba Press.

Nakata, M. (2007). *Disciplining the savages, savaging the discipline*. Aboriginal Studies Press.

Noble, S. U. (2018). *Algorithms of oppression: How search engines reinforce racism*. New York University Press.

Norman, M. E., Hart, M., & Petherick, L. (2019). Indigenous gender reformations: Physical culture, settler colonialism and the politics of containment. *Sociology of Sport Journal, 36*(2), 113–123.

O'Carroll, A. D. (2013). Virtual whanaungatanga: Māori utilizing social networking sites to attain and maintain relationships. *AlterNative: an International Journal of Indigenous Peoples, 9*(3), 230–245.

O'Dea Schenken, S. (1999). *From suffrage to the Senate: An encyclopedia of American women in politics* (Vol. 1). A-M, ABC-CLIO.

O'Sullivan, S. (2015). Queering ideas of Indigeneity: Response in repose: Challenging, engaging and ignoring centralising ontologies, responsibilities, deflections and erasures. *Journal of Global Indigeneity, 1*(1), 1–6. http://ro.uow.edu.au/jgi/vol1/iss1/5

O'Sullivan, S. (2021). The colonial project of gender (and everything else). *Genealogy, 5*(3), 67–76.

Petray, T. L., & Collin, R. (2017). Your privilege is trending: Confronting whiteness on social media. *Social Media + Society, 3*(2), 1–10.

Picq, M. (2019). Decolonizing Indigenous sexualities: Between erasure and resurgence. In M. Rahman, S. M. McEvoy, & M. J. Bosia (Eds.), *The Oxford handbook of global LGBT and sexual diversity politics* (pp. 169–184). Oxford University Press.

Puar. (2017). *Terrorist assemblages: Homonationalism in queer times*. Duke University Press.

Queers for Reconciliation. (n.d.). https://reconciliation.tripod.com/

Simpson, L. B. (2017). *As we have always done: Indigenous freedom through radical resistance*. University of Minnesota Press.

Sullivan, C. (2020). Who holds the key? Negotiating gatekeepers, community politics, and the 'right' to research in Indigenous spaces. *Geographical Research, 58*(4), 344.

TallBear, K. (2018). Yes, your pleasure! Yes, self-love! And don't forget, settler sex is a structure. The Critical Polyamorist. www.criticalpolyamorist.com/homeblog/archives/04-2018

Tuck, E., & Yang, K. W. (2012). Decolonization is not a metaphor. *Decolonization: Indigeneity, Education & Society, 1*(1), 1–40. www.latrobe.edu.au/staff-profiles/data/docs/fjcollins.pdf

Tuhiwai-Smith, L. (1999). *Decolonizing methodologies: Research and Indigenous peoples*. Zed Books.

Walter, M. (Ed.) (2021). *Indigenous data sovereignty and policy*. Routledge.

Watego, L. (2015, November). Reterritorialising social media. NotQuiteCooked.com. https://ratical.org/co-globalize/WinonaLaDuke/Beijing95.pdf

Whitehead, J. (2017). *Full-metal Indigiqueer*. Talonbooks.

Whittaker, A. (2016, August). Queerness and Indigenous cultures: One world, many lives. *Archer Magazine*. https://archermagazine.com.au/2016/08/queernessindigenous-cultures/

Wilson, A. (2015). Our coming in stories: Cree identity, body sovereignty and gender self-determination. *Journal of Global Indigeneity, 1*(1). https://ro.uow.edu.au/jgi/vol1/iss1/4/?fbclid=IwAR2eEHiCYobNXK7cgRY8ShkPja9V9Mr1SBeHgyp99iFSmJHqOxq-XWvJao

Wolfe, P. (2006). Settler colonialism and the elimination of the native. *Journal of Genocide Research, 8*(4), 387–409.

# 17

# THE EDGE OF THE TIDE

Exploring the complexities and futures of
Aboriginality from the critical perspectives of
Indigenous researchers

*Stephanie Gilbert, Tracey Bunda, Bronwyn Fredericks
and r e a (Regina Saunders)*

## Introduction

This chapter provides reflections of our experiences as Aboriginal academics and researchers within the complexities of who and what it is to be 'Aboriginal' in Australia, how change has occurred across our lifetimes, and how changes might be shaped in the future. The context of the future is absent of a definitive lineal time location but rather is offered as a space where we will predominantly not be present.

We commenced writing this work together, retreating to the relative quietness and slowness of Minjerribah/Stradbroke Island in Quandamooka Country in the second year of the Covid-19 pandemic. Together the four of us explored—driving, talking, walking, photographing and capturing visual and soundscapes. We experienced the space as newcomers through to those of us who had been visitors over many decades to those with familial and country connections to place. We filled ourselves with the sacred physicality of Country to focus our thinking for writing and on a challenge set by Stephanie, who asked us to think deeply into our own axiological positionings as Aboriginal academics and researchers to contemplate Lethabo King's (2019, p. 3) concept of the "shoal" as an offshore geological formation that is neither land nor sea—as metaphor, mode of critique and methodology.

Using this concept has been helpful to lean into with its resultant images of shifting land and changing tidelines. Within our own contexts we consider the shoal as the "edge" (Lethabo King, 2019, p. 3), the place which washes over the presence of our time and from which future possibilities are held for and within Aboriginal identities in a differing ecotone of the future. The authors' voices are separate and yet connected through their embodiment of space and the time spent together on Minjerribah/Stradbroke Island.

DOI: 10.4324/9781003271802-20

## Stephanie: the shoal ecotone and constructing my introduction

The transition zone at the edge of the sea is such a foreign and familiar place for me. Born in western New South Wales to people of western New South Wales, I know its smell. I love its plains and the sky so huge above, that tell so many stories in one minute and a whole new set a minute later. I love its riverbeds and, as in Lethabo King's words, I am reminded that the blood of my people flows through the river systems to meet the sea (2019), that all the chemicals, beings, knowledges and experiences since forever and on into the future meet in the land, rivers, and finally, the seas. This also reminds me of the wind. Perhaps it is the unsettled feelings of the strange and unknown that come with the wind, and the wind that is unique in smell to the sea. Water presents itself in all of the spaces I discuss here. Even in its absence it is a presence. Recollet (2019, p. v) speaks of water, including the movement and migration of water, of "the radical reorientational capacities of water [...] Water is that which moves between the maps fluidly, forcefully, and fiercely". Recollet (2019, p. v) calls this a kinstillatory connection for the displaced like me, the "water's migratory relationality—akin with the Milky Way—illuminates spatial freedoms in ways that produce 'home' as ephemeral yet also quite rooted". We are both grounded and celestially connected. Waters act to imprint upon us in the ways Lethabo King describes.

The sea is so often accompanied by the wind and helps this seashore transition zone blending the land and sea. Unusually for a body so constructed by the western inland plains, I have lived near the sea for much of my life. I do not love the sea, but I do love the shoreline itself. In it I feel my smallness, the wild unknown, and recognise the inland and sea coming together as in the shoal. Lethabo King uses the concept of ecotones to describe spaces such as these. She says, "ecotones are spaces of transition between distinct ecological, social and ontological systems" (2019, p. 113). So how to consider this shoreline, the water and my transitional space and placement within it? I utilise Burgess (2013, p. 13) to speak to my transition zone: my identity in three ways. She says:

1. Tell the story of your names: all of your names;
2. Tell the story of your community, however each [...] defines 'community';
3. Tell the story of your gifts.

### *My names?*

"When you tell the story of your names you tell the story of your people, your family, and what you feel about your names" (Burgess, 2013, p. 13). I am Stephanie, disappeared, adopted, fostered, incarcerated in legislation and by my name. I have multiple middle and surnames because of these very same processes. Each name has a story. I am named for my mother and grandmother. I was renamed in my removal. I have populated my name, leaving behind the bits that I don't want (including people) and being conscious about those parts I do. I do not feel able to go back to my birth name nor totally remove that name I now live in.

My first and middle names speak of my grandmother, who left my mother at the mission with the family when my grandmother went to get work on stations. To her death, my grandmother would speak of not knowing my mother, me and others in our family even though we had relationships with her that spanned many, many years. Her connection to us had been broken in a deeply distressing lifelong way and in a way, like my own broken storyline. Yet I am named for her.

My first name is the name given to me at birth; however, when you are adopted, your family name changes to the parents' name you gain. For me, I am an English Gilbert. My adoptive parents were immigrants from England themselves. Being named Gilbert in Australia is a colonising indicator of two groups of Aboriginal people, in New South Wales and far North Queensland whom I am not related to at all. Introducing myself has often required correcting this misnaming. Linking to family networks and geographical place is core to establishing a relationship to other Aboriginal people in Australia; hence, it is difficult when your name doesn't match who you are and where you're from and you don't have that information to give anyway. For many years, I could not answer who my biological family was and where they came from. I regularly introduced myself as Stolen Generations. Although this has been my experience and was less common when I was young, I now see many Aboriginal people who do not know their history and their name. I know how difficult this makes negotiating Indigenous spaces and recognise many new ways that have developed in this absence of information. These include claiming a broader tribal grouping rather than family name alone.

Burgess (2013) asks, who is my community? I have recently felt like my community is both empty and full. Moving back to my adolescent home city has felt like a new place and meant restarting, re-meeting places and people so that my local community has felt quite empty. My family communities are made up of blood family and other family. It has included biological, adoptive, fostered and families of choice. It is made up of those who support me, but as I am learning new ways of being, my community is shifting.

My community identity plays in multiple communities and is ever shifting and complex. I have been a part of many family-based communities. My first memories are of being a Gilbert. In my adulthood, I have come to describe this experience as being like a cult member, and being a member certainly damaged me. Leaving the cult has also had so many implications, not least of which was watching my siblings self-destruct. To this day it is a story of attachment and lack of attachment. Both parents damaged the children in many ways, and I was again removed permanently into care. I learnt that family meant nothing and that relationships will always end, and yet the family that self-destructed changed its narrative again when my brother, who had been missing to us for 30 odd years, suddenly reappeared. This created much confusion and turmoil.

Another of my communities is made up of those whom I spent time with as a family member in a foster family in my teenage years. That family continues to include me in their family. This is a privilege and a grounding I find hard to describe. They are not Aboriginal people, but I did much of my investigation of my Aboriginality in their family and in the years since I became an adult.

I also have a community made up of my biological family. In my early twenties, I reconnected with them. At this point of reintroduction, I had a very beginning understanding of the Stolen Generations (not called that at that point in time). I went home to meet people who lived an Aboriginality I was not familiar with. I had grown up away from Aboriginal people and then everyone I met in my biological family was Aboriginal. I can't remember much of that time, but I know I was a stranger, and they were strangers to me. I however looked and sounded like them. I just lived in silence. How do you speak in this emptiness, this lack of knowledge and the lack of commonality? To this day, the literature on Stolen Generations struggles to do this and struggled with those who came home with such different values and experiences.

## *Gifts*

Burgess challenges us to "wonder what their family, organization, or community would be like if it were gift-based and not just skill-based" (2013, p. 13). These words challenge us to think about what we bring to any gathering. If you do not identify what paid work you do in your introduction into a space, what would you speak about? As I believe one of my gifts is being open to telling my truth, doing this creates an opportunity to create a space for caring, to share how I think things through and seek to understand how others with whom I share the space also see. My challenge to learning this gift is to listen better, and some days I am very challenged to listen more effectively.

I am taken by the idea, as I sit here in Booloor-chambinn Enoggera Brisbane (State Library Queensland, 2022), that the space or zone we know as the shoreline may have existed anywhere like three kilometres into the sea from where it is now. That means that it lay far beyond what we now consider land or the shoreline. I am again reminded by the idea that all of the chemicals which have created us, remain in our world. People lived on what is now the sea. We are land and we are water. I am the blood spilled on my mother's land. Why am I taken by this this idea of relatedness to all things, including what has come before and what is to come? What I know, though, is that as reinforced by the shoal and the shoreline change is guaranteed. That change will include the understanding of Aboriginal people like me who have not grown up in Aboriginal families and spaces and that whose only experience was from adolescence onwards. That being said, it is also true that the experience of Aboriginal people in Australia led to the creation of my life experience and continues to impact our communities and indeed my own family. We are the change, but we are the change in all of the spaces, including the shore, shoal, the sea and the land as well.

## Tracey

Lethabo King's work (2019) reminds me of the fascination-come-challenge I hold in needing to explain the depth of the seemingly every-day-ness of our lives inherent within our identities. In exploring the complexities and futures of Aboriginality, there is a politically treacherous territory to enter into. The known, unknown, knowing and unknowing are everywhere.

We write on my mother's Country. We make ourselves known to Country and Ancestors who will see us as visitors. We are within their scope. We visit the beach closest to our accommodation. There is something about a winter beach. Stephanie and I take a large piece of log as our seat and watch r e a at work. They are a study in technicality, capturing sounds and images with their iPhone.

We move from the beach to another, more sheltered, with a small grove of paperbark. It is here I peel back the layers of paperbark, exposing the design left behind by the small creatures who make this their home, their nursery. Perhaps these creatures, these relations, are still there but are invisible. In the design, in the seemingly endless meandering behaviour of the lines etched into the firmer bark of the tree, I feel compelled to theorise these shapes. I look to Gilles Deleuze and Félix Guttari's *A Thousand Plateaus* (1987) and consider the value of the rhizome as a useful theoretical link to explain the photographic image below. There is something of the rhizome in the patterning, and in the patterning, there is definitely something of the ancestral to Ngugi (my mob), curatorial connections to kin, kin in all its

Ancestral lineage, the multiple branches signifying family, all remaining connected. This is an Ancestral lineage who would have known my mother and would have seen her forcibly removed from her Island home with her family. In this Country the ecotone—ecological in Country—harsh in its historicity of raced policy, came to adversely impact upon my mother's life, enacting an abrasion to the ways of knowing her Ngugi world of that time. A violent wrenching across the shoals and into the open seas. The effects of this family history linger as I stand on my mother's Country and wonder as to what is being enunciated here in reference to my own claims of identity.

In what ways are there familiarities, lived relationalities when one is born from Ancestors of this Country but never having had the privilege of living on Country? Is there an essence of who I am to be found in this Country, or perhaps the better question is, does this country know me? Do the Ancestors see a commonality in me connecting me back to my mother, and other kin, connecting me to those family branches? Perhaps there is a trace, lying small, hidden/preserved in the etchings of lines in the paperbark—an ecotone of Country—a trace of the sense of myself linking me to my Ancestors (See Figure 17.1).

We walk the second beach, which is hardly occupied. Closer to Mooloomba than Pulan Pulan, r e a has moved beyond us to record it all with their trusty iPhone. Stephanie and

*Figure 17.1*   Peeling back the paperbark.

Source: Photograph by Tracey Bunda, 2020.

*Figure 17.2*   Curridgee circa 1927 (Aunty) Eva Livinge [back row left], Mrs McConnell [back row right], Nellie Dalton [front row left], (Aunty) Lottie Levinge, daughter of (Aunty) Eva Levinge [front row right].

Source: Michael Aird Collection sourced from Aunty Lottie Levinge.

I move together; sometimes we are our single selves, other times we come back together. We watch r e a be methodical. Their recordings now will shape artistry later. Maybe. A winter beach. It captivates. The constancy of its rhythmic charms. Tall and skinny paperbarks crush onto nature's borderline where sand and vegetation gammon sit neatly out of each other's way. One is really trying to be the boss of the other. Pools of water nestle against the high rise of sand. The wind ripples the surface.

There is only one photograph (See Figure 17.2) I have in my collection of my mother as a young girl. It was given to me by another colleague. She would have been four years old. There is her familiar round face and some of her hair has escaped from underneath her hat. She is sort of smiling for the camera. Her friend, the aunt of the colleague who has given me the photograph, sits beside her and her expression is more surprise, caught in the moment by the camera. The two are sitting, playing with the sand, and together they foreground the photograph. In the background sit two Aunties, legs outstretched. I imagine a lazy day at the beach, children playing, Aunties talking.

Not long after this photograph was taken, my mother's family was expelled from Minjerribah, and not long after that, at the age of six my mother was taken from her family and incarcerated at the Purga Aboriginal Mission in Ipswich. If in the ecotone there is held transition, then in the transition again and again and again, being forced across socially abrasive spaces, there is fragility, vulnerability, a denial to the ecotones of pleasure. As I represent my mother's future, have I, in the generational transitioning, been able to hold on to an ontological sameness in identity? Perhaps. Perhaps not. Perhaps not all of the sameness. The tides that transitioned my time marked difference—culturally, historically, socially—and as my daughter signifies my future, her identity is also marked in difference from my own and her grandparents' and her other Ancestors' times.

What is the tenor of the ecotone of the future? What Aboriginal essences will be found in the structural castings? Shall there be an all-encompassing digital ecotone—one in which the body itself has transitioned to the cyborgian—machine and human inextricably linked in the same body? How might the component parts that constitute the Aboriginal identity be recognisable? Or shall we find an environmental ecotone where an identity of humanness has been laid to waste as much as our Country too has had its identity threatened? In this situation, will Aboriginal identities be maintained ontologically without a land to stand upon?

Or shall that which is Aboriginal and ontological be maintained, uplifting the next generations through stories (Phillips and Bunda, 2018), a passing on of what it means to be Aboriginal in and for the world? That zone of transition, at the edge, where the shallows step into the depth of an unknown future, an unknowing in some respects of what will be. It is in this space that we simultaneously brace/embrace ourselves for change—a preparedness either way that draws from traditions and practices that have positionality and relationally in our connections to people, to Country (Bunda, 2013). This is the foundation of our knowledge systems. It is a rhythm that cascades across time, into itself, and it is in this rhythm that we, as Aboriginal peoples, will continue to be. What then is the shape of a future Aboriginal identity?

We shall watch the tides move across deep water to the shallows of the shoals and wait and see.

## Bronwyn

As I arrive within Quandamooka Country, I find myself surrounded by stunning Country filled with animals, plants and knowledges that fully sustained Aboriginal people for hundreds of generations before Europeans arrived. I look forward to fresh seafood, some walks and maybe an open fire in the evenings. Country provides all the nutrition and sustenance we need, for both body and spirit, and I feel this as soon as I step off the ferry (See Figure 17.3).

Although today we eat a catered meal, the importance of sharing food and yarns continues This is something we have always done and will continue to do (See Figure 17.4). As we enjoy our food, however, my privileged position is not lost on me. Many Indigenous peoples live with food insecurity, daily, struggling to access and afford the very basics (Fredericks & Bradfield, 2021a). The pandemic exacerbated this, particularly for some community members.

As I look over the vast bodies of water within Quandamooka Country—in the sea, lakes, rivers and creeks—I feel the eternal presence of Country. I smell and taste the salt in the air as the wind blows from the ocean. As it does, it kisses my cheeks and unfolds

*Figure 17.3* Quandamooka Coast (light).
Source: Photograph by r e a (2020).

memories: some good, some sad, some of times gone by in my lifetime and those of others before me. It's a place I have been many times. I have spent time here as a teenager, as an adult and now as an older woman. The ancestors, the trees, the animals all have a sense of me, and I have a sense of them. Within the knowing there is also an acceptance.

Even when I am active and busy, I feel a sense of peace and stillness. A calmness comes over my mind, and within my body and spirit. My mind no longer jumps back and forth, trying to manage multiple demands and every chaos and crisis that arises. I think of life, and of people, relationships, place, Country. I am reminded in a good way of where we have been, who I am as an Aboriginal woman from south-east Queensland, and how I know myself and my responsibilities. My thoughts wander and linger on some of my relationships, past thoughts and spoken words, actions and writings, which is why I draw on them here. I also think about what is still to be done.

*Figure 17.4*    Quandamooka Coast (shellfish).

Source: Photograph by r e a (2020).

Throughout my life I have had support from my family, friends, community and mentors, each of whom has encouraged me to pursue further education as a means to make meaningful change. Their love and support remain with me, and like the coastal winds of Quandamooka, they whisper reminders of my responsibilities to continue to fight social injustice and create a better future for forthcoming generations. We are all gathered for this writer's retreat with a shared commitment to advance our knowledge and skills so that our scholarship can help create a better future.

The wind here stirs me at times. The same winds that carry the waves that crash along the coastline, remind me of the water's capacity to both destroy and renew. I walk and observe the waves, hills and cliffs, and the way the waves pound them, one after the after, sometimes in a gentle melodic rhythm and sometimes as if almost lashing the coastline as a form of punishment for unknown wrongdoing. And yet, while the rocks might suffer some damage, they are sculptured, and transformed into the most beautiful, wondrous shapes (See Figure 17.5). They replicate the essence of our own sculpting, our becoming. Almost like the wonder of our own existence as we move through time, space, place and Country, and as our edges become sharper, rougher, prickly, or weathered, rounded and smooth. Country reminds me that it is a life force and has its own agency. It creates and co-creates with humans. It's not passive but has an active presence in our lives, and in the changes within our lives.

It's through weathering the changes that I seek to develop and learn. Sometimes my confidence grows a little, too, and I imagine I'm like the dolphins just off the headland who learn to ride waves in the sunshine. I know, too, as they do, not to be too confident and that sometimes we might need to relearn, to go to greater depths, and to find greater learning along with goodness and compassion, even for myself when I have done wrong. When I am still and truly within the presence of Country, I know that layers are revealed of it, and myself. The more receptive I become, the more layers I find and the more I see the profound and the implications for wisdom. Country speaks. Country transmits. Country teaches. And Country remembers. It is a hidden inexhaustible source of truth, and is not linear in time.

*Figure 17.5*  Quandamooka Coast (rock formation).
Source: Photograph by r e a (2020).

Sometimes my greatest learning has come at times like this, and from understanding the good I have worked towards, and the wrong I have done or caused. The learnings enable me to make sense of it all, and to work with Country to be better, learn, affirm and not cause harm again (Gilbert, 2019a, 2019b). I know that this is the only way I can become more open, more compassionate and more focused on who I am becoming. In this, I know that while we might think the rocks, hills and blowholes have been here for thousands of years, and thus are the same, they aren't. They've also changed and are still changing. They are still becoming, as I am. These are the chains of delusion, or the thoughts we use to fool ourselves about the world in which we all live.

I reflect on how people tell themselves certain stories, and how Country has stories about them which are embedded within their very being. These are reflected in stories of past summers here, fish eaten, campsites made, the people encountered. This is in the same way that Phillips and Bunda (2018) refer to stories of one's lives and the stories of Country. There are also stories of plants, animals, objects and peoples embedded within Country on the island, and within Quandamooka Country (Moreton-Robinson, 2000). Country lives within us, and we are reminded of this through our daily interactions or via the works of scholars, innovators and artists such as r e a Saunders (2022), whose work draws inspiration from Country as a means to "examine the bonds between our bodies, our politics, our memories, our place and our futures" (p. 1).

Sometimes the waters of storms and the Brisbane Basin wash down and across the bay, causing the freshwater and saltwater to converge, along with the flora, fauna and objects of Country swept up and along. They exist in relationship to each other and are part of ongoing renewal. Shoals often occur in brackish waters where salt and freshwater meet, creating a swirling and bubbling effect. As we wrote in the introduction, scholars such as Lethabo King have used shoals as metaphors for transitional zones in which worlds collide. The pushing and receding of the waves along the coastline, and the bubbling foam it creates, direct my thoughts to the transitional potential of the Uluru Statement from the Heart (Fredericks & Bradfield, 2021b, 2021c; Uluru Statement, 2017).

Like the waters that surround me, the future lives in the past and present, flowing through time. At the same time, I hear and feel the growing unrest and frustration in young Indigenous people who are unhappy with the same old status quo, and slow steps forward, and steps backwards too. They seek real and substantive change as many of my contemporaries do, and those people before us did. This desire, and demand for change has been there for decades, and is gaining momentum like a fountain bubbling, increasing in intensity over time.

For now, I/we continue to survive, fight and work towards improving outcomes for our continued survivance so that we will thrive today and well into the future. This compulsion and sense of responsibility to drive better outcomes flows through my blood and is embedded in my bones. Like the rocks on Quandamooka, however, I weather, I change, I grow, I decay—I am a product of Country. I am inspired by the knowledge I have been gifted during the retreat, gifted from the brilliant minds of those I have collaborated with and the lifeforce and omnipresence of Quandamooka Country.

## rea

I am from the central west area of New South Wales; my Country sits on the border between two nations (the Warrumbungles) Wailwan Country (paternal), and the (Pilliga Scrub) on the northern side, Gamilaraay Country (maternal). I was raised on the banks of the Castlereagh River, a once lush waterway, which provided our food and drinking water, where we bathed and learnt to swim in this mighty river like most mob. When I first arrived at the ocean edge in Eora Country (Sydney) in 1968, my first sighting of this vast unknown ocean was more than I could imagine—was it even safe? Over the years, my fear has reduced somewhat as I continue to be drawn to the ocean's edge. I love feeling salt water on my skin, it's very cleansing and it re-energises my mind and body. I have learnt to respect the vast seas that surround the land masses of the world.

My first visit to Quandamooka Country was in the late 1990s. During a long weekend, my partner and the company (previously known as Rock'n'roll Circus) were working on a new circus-based performance—*The Dark*—which was about to go on tour. On arrival on the island, I immediately felt concerned about how far I would have to swim to make it back to the mainland (See Figure 17.6). I sometimes experience anxiety around water, and it doesn't matter what kind of water it is—pool, river or ocean. My fear comes from what adults see as a fun thing to do, which is to throw children into water with the assumption that this will somehow teach them how to swim! Eventually I learnt to swim on my own terms, but my fear of water has remained. But now that I am older, I have a better

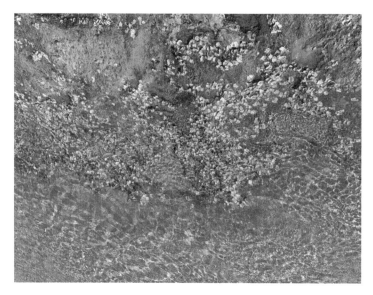

*Figure 17.6* Quandamooka (edge of the water).
Source: Photograph by r e a (2020).

understanding culturally about my relationship to water. It is about feelings of calm and peace–a spirituality.

Water is a metaphor for many things.

> I can't help wondering how many ways water shapes the body,
> how the body shapes desire, how desire moves water, how water
> stirs color, how thought rises from land, how wind polishes
> thought, how spirit shapes matter, how a stream that carves
> through rock is shaped by rock.
> (Ehrlich, 1991, p. 81)

In 2020, I made my second trip to Quandamooka Country with my work colleagues from the University of Queensland for a research retreat. This time I was introduced to this Country through Professor Tracey Bunda, who has cultural connections to North Stradbroke Island. So, the inspiration to write about our experiences came from numerous conversations that we had, which explored the ideas that ultimately inform our multifaceted approaches to research, as Indigenous academics. We should also never underestimate the importance of conversations, which undoubtedly take place over food, and the value of walking repetitively on Country, essential to our collective sharing and reflective processes. Creativity and thinking are constantly mapped by my sensorial experiences of Country. Everything I do is informed by how my senses are activated—when I am walking on the beach, I feel my face being brushed by the ocean breeze and my nose reacts to ubiquitous smells of the ocean. As a creative person, my senses are ultra-important, as they influence how I navigate the world.

My eyes are the primary collectors of my experiences; these visual links then locate themselves somewhere in my body as personal memories. I have learnt to trust my senses, as they are a direct connection to my personal, 'cultural' archive that is contained within my body. Every day that we visited the beach during our research retreat, flashes of spirit-cleansing occurred. We all felt a strong sense of regeneration which then opened us up, collectively, to new ideas and which ultimately inspired this chapter. Personally, I was moved by the ever-changing land–seascape and the boundless energy that I felt on this beguiling Country. When you are on Country, home is intuitively experienced. It is emotionally important to feel how our own Country is embodied in us.

As Indigenous people, location means a number of important things to us. It is not simply a geographical place or the location from which we come, but rather it locates you and your family within the broader Aboriginal framework of identity, culture, knowledge, authority and responsibility. Locating oneself on Country is how Indigenous people identify with each other; it is how we introduce ourselves in order to know how to relate to others. As Sinclair (2003, p. 122) reminds us, location is interconnected: revealing our identity to others, who we are, where we come from, our experiences that have shaped those things, and our intentions for the work we plan to do. Hence, 'location' in Indigenous research, as in life, is a critical starting point. Location for my family is embodied in who we are; it is literally about *locating* our cultural language in an Indigenous (Aboriginal) knowledge system that has been passed down by our Elders. The passing down of knowledge connects us not only to our Country, but also to a long history of storytelling, language, song, dance and other cultural forms that are embedded in Country. As Langton (1993, p. 71) notes, the importance of understanding location is crucially part of an Aboriginal research methodology and cultural protocol. This point is echoed by Absolon and Willett (2005, p. 97) as well as by Langton (1993, p. 67), who argues that the concept of location goes beyond Country; it is inclusive of cultural kinship and spiritual and community traditions and practices that may appear to have been lost or destroyed by invasion and colonisation.

In developing Aboriginal methodologies of storytelling, I am informed by the embodiment of sensorial experiences that come essentially from a stillness—by taking the time that is needed to observe, listen, smell, taste and feel the energy around me, I am able to observe my senses, my responses. By taking photographs when I visit other Indigenous people's Country, I consciously create a visual catalogue, a series of 'seen' reflections of my in-the-moment experiences. Photographs are vitally important for our people. Sometimes, our private family photographic collections contain photographs sourced from public museums, galleries, libraries or other colonial collections, recontextualised and repurposed for the telling of our histories and stories. Sometimes these images inspire me to consider new ways of seeing and thinking, but as time shifts my experiences, my embodiment of the original experience is often prompted by a set of completely new feelings. We all have sensorial experiences that provoke and stimulate our memories and often stay within us for a long, long time, and there is no doubt that they make a significant contribution to shaping who we are and inform how we interpret the world.

I am frequently moved by the subtle nuances of how all the elements of Country (in this case, Quandamooka Country) connect the past, the present and give me a fleeting sense of the future. In her call for Indigenous working methodologies to be taken up within academic and cultural institutions, Indigenous Cree and Métis academic Emma LaRocque (1996, p. 13) argues: "Native scholars and writers are demonstrating that 'voice' can be, must be, used within academic studies not only as an expression of cultural integrity but also as an attempt to begin to balance the legacy of dehumanization and bias entrenched

*Figure 17.7*   Quandamooka Coast (water, sky).

Source: Photograph by r e a (2020).

in [...] studies about Native peoples". For many Indigenous people, photographs, films and video have become tools for generating historic links to their Indigenous heritage; often these mediums can activate formal processes towards reclaiming heritage and sovereignty (See Figure 17.7). Through such acts of reclamation, it becomes possible to reinscribe Indigeneity and decolonise dominant representations.

We as Indigenous peoples want to tell our own stories, write our own versions, in our own ways, for our own purposes. It is not simply about giving an oral account or a genealogical naming of the land and the events which rage over it, but a very powerful need to give testimony to and restore a spirit, to bring back into existence a world fragmented and dying. The sense of history conveyed by these approaches is not the same thing as the discipline of history, and so our accounts collide, crash into each other (Tuhiwai Smith, 1999, p. 28). Drawing on Country to tell stories and to decolonise history is a vital aspect of all practice-led Aboriginal research. Indigenous research methodologies are slowly beginning to be recognised within the academy, through theoretical and critical frameworks which have been developed by key Indigenous researchers such as Absolon and Willett, Langton, Nakata, Tuhiwai Smith and Rigney (in Foley, 2003, p. 45) elaborate on the importance of Country to Aboriginal research. Indigenous peoples in Australia and the Pacific must look to new anti-colonial epistemologies and methodologies to construct, rediscover and reaffirm their knowledge and cultures. By identifying the importance of site-responsive and site-located cultural responses, I give value to my personal presence, as subject, artist and researcher, and I am always mindful of the *we-identity* that operates for us as Indigenous (Aboriginal) artists and researchers (Seran, 2015, p. 662). As an artist and producer of ideas, research and writing, I make my work on colonised lands that have never been ceded. Therefore, I am both the researcher and the researched; this is an ambiguous and uncomfortable space that I constantly reflect on within my work. I exist in the liminal space of the shifting sands and changing tides. As Indigenous researchers, we all work from our own narratives and we position ourselves at the outset of our work because the only thing that we can draw on with authority is ourselves (Absolon & Willett, 2005, p. 97). The conceptualisation of *embodiment* as a performative act of walking, belonging and being on Country locates the work that we do as Indigenous people, as one that is "rooted in a deep sense of kinship responsibility, a responsibility that relays a culture, an identity, and a sense of belonging" (Wilson, 1998, p. 27).

## Conclusion

In this writing by four strong Aboriginal researchers, we have entered an exploration of our interaction and embodiment of heritage, our sense of being and our engagement with Country and 'shoal'. The chapter sees themes emerge in each section of self-reflection of the shoal metaphor, asserting our sense of being in place on Minjerribah/Stradbroke Island and that experience becoming a site of struggle, discomfort, growth and comfort. Each author articulates other relationships to the shoreline, to the essential nature and function of the shoreline, and to how we see that embodied in our own lives. Each section is deeply nuanced by the author to carry out our metaphor of the shoal and sets a challenge for the course of our individual lives into the future, including how we might model this for our communities and younger generations. Each author has utilised words or concepts to set a course through their past, their consciousness of present and setting a course for the future. We hope that in presenting these interactions with the metaphor of the shoal, we illuminate how we navigate our, sometimes rocky, shores and paths through our lives. We acknowledge a future we will not be a part of, but hope for a continuance of our knowledge that the space and place we are in, the smell, the water and our knowledge of our Elders, Ancestors and young community members will affirm a sure footing for the future.

## References

Absolon, K., & Willett, C. (2005). Putting ourselves forward: Location in Aboriginal research. In L. Brown & S. Strega (Eds.), *Research as resistance: Critical, Indigenous, and Anti-Oppressive approaches* (pp. 97–126). Canadian Scholars Press.

Bunda, T. (2013). *The relationship between Indigenous peoples and the university: Solid or what!* [Unpublished doctoral thesis]. University of South Australia.

Burgess, P. (2013). Building the beloved Community: A life practice. *Hūlili: Multidisciplinary Research on Hawaiian Well-Being, 9*, 11–34.

Deleuze., G., & Guttari, F. (1987). *A thousand plateaus*. University of Minnesota Press.

Ehrlich, G. (1991). *Islands, the universe, home*. Viking.

Foley, D. (2003). Indigenous epistemology and Indigenous standpoint theory. *Social Alternatives, 22*(1), 44–52.

Fredericks, B., & Bradfield, A. (2021a). Indigenous Australians and COVID-19: Highlighting ongoing food security issues. *International Journal of Home Economics, 14*(1), 53–65. www.google.com/url?sa=t&rct=j&q=&esrc=s&source=web&cd=&ved=2ahUKEwjGt4G9wrP4AhWjg2MGHdnjAkgQFnoECAMQAQ&url=https%3A%2F%2Fwww.ifhe.org%2Ffileadmin%2Fuser_upload%2Fe_Journal%2Fvol_14_1%2FP4_Fredericks-Bradfield.pdf&usg=AOvVaw3FE6wEipvoCdHDftQta9nE

Fredericks, B., & Bradfield, A. (2021b). 'More than a thought bubble…': The Uluru Statement from the Heart and Indigenous Voice to Parliament. *M/C Journal, 24*(1). https://journal.media-culture.org.au/index.php/mcjournal/article/view/2738

Fredericks, B., & Bradfield, A. (2021c). Co-designing change: Discussing an Indigenous Voice to Parliament and constitutional reform in Australia. *M/C Journal 24*(4). https://journal.media-culture.org.au/index.php/mcjournal/article/view/2801

Gilbert, S. (2019a). The treadmill of identity: Treading water, paddling like a duck but still in the same pond. *Australian Feminist Law Journal, 45*(2), 249–26.

Gilbert, S. (2019b). Living with the past: The creation of the stolen generation positionality. *AlterNative: An International Journal of Indigenous Peoples, 15*(3), 226–233.

King, T. L. (2019). *The black shoals.* Duke University Press.

Langton, M. (1993). *'Well, I heard it on the radio and I saw it on the television…': An essay for the Australian Film Commission on the politics and aesthetics of film making by and about Indigenous people and things.* Film Commission.

LaRocque, E. (1996). The colonization of a Native woman scholar. In P. M. Chuchryk & C. Miller (Eds.), *Women of the First Nations: Power, wisdom, and strength* (pp. 11–18). University of Manitoba Press.

Lethabo-King, T. (2019). *The black shoals: Offshore formations of Black and Native Studies.* Duke University Press.

Moreton-Robinson, A. (2000). *Talkin' up to the white woman: Indigenous women and feminism.* University of Queensland Press.

Phillips, L. G., and Bunda, T. (2018). *Research through, with and as storying.* Routledge Focus.

Recollet, K. (2019). Relational constellation. In G. Henry Jr & E. LaPensée (Eds.), *Sovereign traces* (Vol. 2, pp. v–vi). Michigan State University Press.

Saunders, R. (2022). *r e a—artist | curator | activist | academic | cultural educator.* [Online]. https://rea-noir.com/

Seran, J. (2015). Australian Aboriginal memoir and memory: A Stolen Generations trauma narrative. *Humanities, 4*(4), 661–675.

Sinclair, R. P. (2003). Indigenous research in social work: The challenge of operationalizing worldview. *Native Social Work Journal, 5*, 117–139.

State Library of Queensland. (2022). *Aboriginal Place Names.* www.brisbanehistory.com/aboriginal_place_names.html

Tuhiwai Smith, L. (1999). *Decolonizing methodologies: Research and Indigenous peoples.* Zed Books.

Uluru Statement from the Heart. (2017). *The Statement—Uluru Statement from the Heart.* https://ulurustatement.org/the-statement

Wilson, A. C. (1998). Grandmother to granddaughter: Generations of oral history in a Dakota family. In D. A. Mihesuah (Ed.), *Natives and academics: Researching and writing about American Indians* (pp. 27–36). University of Nebraska Press.

# 18

# OUR YOUNG PEOPLE ARE OUR FUTURE

## Cultural Continuity and the Illawarra Flame Trees

*Jodi Edwards*

### Introduction: Kiama

The three principles of learning are watching, listening, and seeing. If we don't follow these principles then we don't learn anything.

(Harrison, 2009, p. 59)

In 2021, I completed my PhD. I was definitely one of those people who never dreamed I was capable of completing such an undertaking. But I did. I didn't do it alone—like most Indigenous peoples, rather, it was a collective effort and shared journey of learning and teaching with other Indigenous peoples. My PhD is focused on cultural continuity and, particularly, for Dharawal and Yuin cultures given our close proximity to 'ground zero' where the first colony was established. One of the most joyous parts of my PhD journey was supporting young people in the Illawarra to know more about their histories, cultures and cultural practices. A significant part of this was the formation of the Illawarra Flame Trees—an Indigenous youth performing arts group. Watching young Indigenous people bursting with pride as they learned and showcased their cultural knowledge, and seeing their Elders, parents and other community members experience such joy in bearing witness to this gave me much hope for the future. Our young people are our future and it is our job to nurture that and ensure they know they are exactly who their ancestors would want them to be.

I begin this chapter with the story of Kiama (pronounced Kia-ma) and her sistas (the term more commonly used by many Aboriginal peoples for 'sisters'), which was told to me by Aunty Julie Freeman. While the story has a somewhat tragic ending, it is ostensibly about sisterhood and the connection between the girls in the story. The narrative provides a basis for the young women and girls who came together in 2013 to establish the Illawarra's first Aboriginal girls performing dance troupe, the Illawarra Flame Trees (IFT). The IFT had the aim of learning language, songs and dance that belong to Dharawal Country. The group's intention was to inspire new forms of cultural practices

DOI: 10.4324/9781003271802-21

where young future ancestors could imagine a time centred on their Aboriginal cultural heritage and their Aboriginal identities. I told this story of Kiama and her sisters to the group at Shellharbour Aboriginal Community Youth Association (SACYA) hall. The purpose for sharing the story was twofold: first, to help the young women understand the strength of connection between sistas and, secondly, to share the story through dance to the broader community.

I retell this story here as it was told to me by local Elder Aunty Julie Freeman. I tell it as best as I remember it, as is our practice of storytelling:

Kiama lived a long time ago in this place near Bombo with her two older sistas. There were three sistas and Kiama was the baby. Their Mother used to tell the two older sistas not to go out into the far wild seas in their canoes, but they always did. They were always told to take Kiama with them, and they must stay in the safe part of the harbour in the safe part of the sea.

They used to always put Kiama on the headland at Bombo when they went out into the wild sea fishing and tell her not to tell their mother they went into the rough sea in the deep. They would say, 'stay don't move till we come back to pick you up'. One day the mother said make sure you don't go into the deep-water because there is a big storm. The sistas disobeyed their mother and they went out leaving Kiama on the headland and said, 'don't you leave until we come back, cause if Mum finds out we have taken you and gone out into the deep water we will get in big trouble'. The two sistas went way out into the deep and then the storm blew in. It blew their canoe far away. Kiama waited and waited long into the dark for her two sistas to come back, but they didn't, and sadly, they were drowned on that day.

The girls stated that they felt a strong connection with the story. They listened intently and their body language spoke of their acknowledgement of the lessons being told. One of the parents in attendance, who I later interviewed as part of my doctoral research, said, "my daughter understood the story well and what it meant to have loyalty to your siblings" (6F). Even those in the group who did not have siblings felt the story spoke to their connection with each other as members of the IFT. Parents were impressed that their children were being taught culture and lore through a local Dreaming story. One parent stated that they had seen how the storms roll in very quickly at Bombo, near Kiama, and how it whips up the sea. Parents also expressed how much more connected they felt to their Country by hearing the Aboriginal story of the place.

While many Dreaming stories are often allegorical in nature and focus on teaching cultural Law, they also act in many ways to instil cultural pride. This story is central to the region which I am ancestrally connected to, and to the sensibilities of many Aboriginal coastal dwellers. For the girls' dancing troupe, it provides a basis for understanding the importance of taking responsibility for each other and teaches respect for rules set in place by Elders, who deserve respect for their wisdom. The rules are also to ensure safety and survival. Collective responsibility is vital to the girls' success as dancers; they learn to 'see' what each other are doing, and to 'look out' for one another as members of a collective whose performance depends on mutual recognition and respect. I have no doubt that this and other stories told to the dancers impacted positively on their understanding of culture and their desire to be part of its continuity.

## Establishing the Illawarra Flame Trees

Initially, the IFT dance troupe was born from the Tullimbah Youth Leadership Program in 2013 and 2014. In the first few weeks, funding was successfully applied for through the Higher Education Participation and Partnership Program (HEPP) through the University of Wollongong. The initial funding was to support public speakers and the filming of the 12 young members. Once funding was available, the new focus was to embed into the programme a range of cultural knowledge that would incorporate cultural practices. The purpose of this was to re-enculturate the dancers so that their art would become a reflection of parts of local culture that had been lost or laid dormant because of the violence of colonisation. This was to be an intense learning process. In addition, the dancers would work with an Aboriginal choreographer, Sharni Potts. The members of the group and Sharni worked well together to produce several contemporary dances, many of which were connected to local Dharawal Dreaming stories. Some dances incorporated ochre, and the young dancers designed and wore specific outfits for dances made either by themselves or a professional dressmaker. An example of the outfits and dance combinations was the Ochre Dance. This dance emulated the use of ochre in body art, or 'painting up' to dance. The skirt for this was a light brown shade with dark brown and white, contrasting colours of the earth, and the white ochre often utilised by women dancers. There is also a dance about the Five Islands, an island group off the coast in the Illawarra. This dance was adorned by a light blue dress representing the ocean. The dancers also had a black and bright red costume that represented the IFT. The IFT name was agreed on by the young women. The tree itself is well known in the Illawarra area—it is sturdy and native to the region and is a beautiful sight when in bloom. It is a deciduous tree with magnificent scarlet blooms that occur in late spring. In precolonial times, the seeds were toasted and eaten, so the tree has significance for its provision of food as well as its beauty. It was agreed that the tree represented a perfect metaphor for the dance troupe, who could aspire to the tree's beauty, vigour and longevity, and its strong connection to Country.

Local community grants assisted the IFT to pay a choreographer to help create contemporary cultural dances. This was a creative process that involved the girls and, in addition to invoking precolonial cultural ways of dance, also introduced contemporary dance and movement forms. Culture is a living breathing gift to us from our ancestors, and everyday Aboriginal people create new and interesting cultural artefacts (Burgess, 2019). A music teacher was employed to provide singing tuition and to introduce the dancers to the rudiments of timing and vocal techniques. In addition, funds were useful for the purchase of material for performance outfits. The funding was therefore a crucial aspect of the inception of the troupe as it allowed for creative thinking about the possibilities for its overall professional development.

The establishment of the IFT was about ensuring that cultural practices were both revived and reinstated into a local knowledge system that would ensure their continuity as daily ritual. Membership was open to young women based on their connection to the Illawarra through Wodi Wodi or Dharawal heritage, or for those who were now residing in the Illawarra and in the process of establishing Aboriginal cultural bonds with the region. Parents were invited to be part of the group by taking up membership on an advisory committee. Connecting with Elders has been an important part of the design of the IFT.

Elders have generously shared stories of their lives and the Dreaming as these have been told to them by their parents and Elders. The young women were encouraged to practice deep listening known as the cultural practice of 'dadirri' (Ungunerr, 2017). According to Ngan'gityemerri educator Miriam-Rose Ungunmerr (2017), dadirri is 'inner, deep listening and quiet, still awareness' (p. 14). Ungunmerr explains:

> Through the years, we have listened to our stories. They are told and sung, over and over, as the seasons go by. Today we still gather around the campfires and together we hear the sacred stories. As we grow older, we ourselves become the storytellers. We pass on to the young ones all they must know. The stories and songs sink quietly into our minds and we hold them deep inside.
>
> (Ungunmerr, 2017, p. 14)

Listening in this way required some practice; the young people, and indeed their parents, were not accustomed to stopping and being quiet and simply being still. The act of listening intently required patience and an ability to suspend one's own impulse to interrupt, to ask questions and be part of the story. This is a cultural skill our people have clearly mastered as evidenced by the longevity of many of our stories and their circulation throughout various Countries. When everyone stopped and listened, they understood that there was much to learn from the Elders. Listening provided an opportunity to hear stories passed down by parents and grandparents about this place and people's connection to it. As Ungunmerr (2017) explains, the stories penetrate quietly as they are repeated. The dancers knew they were privileged to receive the wisdom of the Elders, and they knew it would impact positively on their performance because the stories reinforced for each dancer her sense of who she is and where she comes from.

## Cultural education

As the IFT grew in popularity and were called on to perform at many events, their parents were keen to ensure that the young women remained grounded and remembered why they came together in the first place. The importance of listening to the Elders was paramount to their cultural education. In 2014, the IFT participated in a workshop with members of the Bangarra[1] Dance Theatre called 'Rekindled'[2] that was held at Killalea Reserve at Shellharbour. Regardless of their fame and achievements, Bangarra has always provided community workshops that teach young Indigenous people about dance and storytelling. A local Elder who was present spoke to the IFT. I also interviewed this person for my doctoral research. They stated:

> When I was young, we had to go working, not learning the old ways of work. We had to go picking, you know, like peas. We travelled up and down the coast picking. We pick for hours and days on end. We weren't even allowed in the picture show until it started and then we had to be out before it ended. You're lucky you get to learn all our old ways, that's what we all fought for.
>
> (1E)

The IFT had numerous opportunities to listen to Elders' stories. A Dharawal person spoke about growing up when segregation was normalised and when Aboriginal people were considered less than human. They told the young women, "Blacks were not permitted to drink from the same taps as the whites" (1E). The young women were not aware this type of racial segregation had existed here on this continent and were shocked, believing this type of violence was more common in the United States or South Africa. In addition to Dreaming stories, therefore, the dancers were learning their history and the histories that impacted their ancestors as part of the colonial project. As so much local history has been hidden, erased and in some instances, lost, those aspects of colonial history are an important reminder to the dancers of the impact of their dance as an acknowledgement of the endurability of colonial history in contemporary times—of the continuity of culture that is evident despite attempts to eradicate Aboriginal people.

In 2015, the young women performed at a variety of events, including many opening events for the University of Wollongong and various performances for local and state government Reconciliation events. The troupe also went to local schools and performed during NAIDOC[3] week. One of the events was held specifically for the young women with internationally renowned choreographer Jo Clancy. This event took place at Hill 60, a local Aboriginal heritage site at Port Kembla in the Illawarra and a site of significant historical and cultural significance for Aboriginal people. During this event, the IFT had the opportunity to listen to the stories of local Elders. I also interviewed this person as part of my PhD research. They are a Yuin person and they explained to the IFT:

> See here, this is all known as Hill 60. Our people we used to fish from up the top here spotting the fish and waving to the others down there on MM beach. Our mob used to live over there in the back of the sandhills in sugar bag huts, that's before we got them houses now at Coomaditchie. Now we can see Grandmother mountain there, Geera and if we look this way, we can see her five naughty sistas. That's the story of Oola Boola Woo. If we look just a little bit over there, we can see Grandfather mountain. His job is to watch over us make sure we all safe.
>
> (16E)

Learning the significance and connection of the landscape reinforced in the young women a sense of place and connection to Country. The knowledge imparted at some of these events was crucial in the development of dance and the choreographic work designed to tell stories. The IFT and their parents loved these opportunities and felt there was a real sense of connection to each other and to Country. The importance and usefulness of narratives, storytelling and yarning are gaining momentum as recognised research methods in the academy (Geia et al., 2013, p. 13). However, Indigenous people have always recognised the power of storytelling. First Nations educators Melanie Maclean and Linda Wason-Ellam (2014, p. 9) articulate the importance of storytelling as a vehicle for survival and the laws of communal relationships in Indigenous cultures:

> Stories hold the key to the traditions, the rituals, and the social ways of Indigenous passed on messages about loyalty, respect, responsibility, honesty, trust and sharing all those qualities that helped them within the relationships in their daily lives. Storytelling was much more than a pastime. Storytelling was a social institution, an "oral university" that taught people young and old about being "human"—that is, how to function in the community.

One of the more significant camps the IFT attended was held in the Royal National Park, located between the Illawarra and Sutherland Shire on Dharawal Country. The event began with a Welcome to Country to situate us and provide us with the knowledge we needed to ensure appropriate behaviour and adherence to local protocols while on Country. A smoking ceremony was performed next and we were dusted with gum leaves to ensure safe passage as we travelled on this Country. This event included the making of a bark nuwi (canoe). Elders and significant knowledge holders were invited to share what they had learned about making nuwi and to lead the building of the nuwi.

## The nuwi (bark canoe)

A camp of Dharawal and Yuin Elders and significant community members was held with the IFT and their families for the purpose of sharing the tradition of making a bark nuwi. The IFT were taught about the varying roles community members play in its construction. For example, a respected Dharawal man, and another of my PhD participants, explained:

> Men would have responsibility of removing the bark from the tree. Women used bark canoes to fish from and collect duck eggs. Men used to fish and took them out whaling, this weekend you will all be a part of a cultural immersion experience.
>
> (1M)

After a cultural welcoming and smoking ceremony, which included a formalised ritual of requesting permission from the tree for its transformation into a nuwi, members of the group worked together to strip a sheet of bark from a tree located in the Royal National Park. The process of removing the bark from the tree was then followed by placing it in the river, where it would lay soaking and softening overnight. The purpose for this was two-fold: the soaking of the bark allowed for the swelling or expansion of the wood, thus aiding in the tightening and strengthening of the individual fibres to assist in shaping and the buoyancy. Secondly, soaking the bark also allowed for the individual fibre strands to be stripped easily as they became softer. The next morning, a group of people retrieved the bark and began the process of stripping it, strand by strand. This was a long process that was instrumental in breaking down barriers between young and old and enriching relationships of mutual trust through working together and storytelling. Conversations were exchanged around aspects of cultural life prior to colonisation. Discussion took place about the value of working alongside one another and how young people swapped tools with old people to allow both parties to have a break to rest or eat. The young people would learn that nuwis were used to fish the estuaries and that in Lake Illawarra, some nuwis would have square backs so those fishing could easily drop the nets. The older participants taught the young the art of turning the individual strands into string and rope to help bind the nuwi. The young women learned how sustainable our ancestors were and how adept they were at conserving resources so there was no excess or waste; all parts of the tree had a purpose. Parents talked to their children about collecting strands and bark pieces to help with starting a fire, while others also showed the young people how fires could be lit with wet bark or wood. The Dharawal man mentioned above went on to explain:

> Many people think when it's raining you cannot go camping; however, our ancestors knew how to start a fire and keep it going; otherwise, they would be cold and hungry

during that wet season. Our old people were scientists, they knew many things about the bush.

(1M)

The bark was then soaked with water and heated over a fire to assist in the shaping process of the canoe and binding it into its final form. The nuwi then needed to be left to dry out so it could harden. As it dried, it shrunk, sealing all the fibres together. Where small holes may exist, the resin from the xanthorrhoea tree (commonly known as the grass tree) was heated and smeared to further act as a sealant to ensure the nuwi was watertight. The lessons learned by the making of nuwis, like many cultural activities practices by Aboriginal people, are metaphorical in nature. Each part of the process speaks to patience, the art of listening, of understanding responsibility to the landscape, respecting Elders knowledge and ensuring survival. The finished nuwi becomes a mascot of pride, a material cultural emblem of survival whereby a multitude of lessons are passed on. Like the nuwi, these teachings 'travel' through the Country to carry the culture as a physical, living breathing entity that has not, and will not die.

During the camp, the IFT and their parents would also learn how to make 'Johnny cakes'. Johnny cakes are flattened dough cakes made from flour, water and salt. They are cooked on an open fire and are something of a staple for many Aboriginal people as they provide a delicious hearty meal in the absence of other food sources. Many of the young people were unfamiliar with what a Johnny cake was, and this amused their parents, who often ate Johnny cakes regularly growing up. Johnny cakes are made with the seeds from the lomandra bush. Most of the adult participants enjoyed the hands-on aspect of working with their children and making and eating the Johnny Cakes, which we served with tea. Parents commented in their responses to the survey that the event promoted family and community and they were pleased with being involved.

While working and sharing food, the young women heard stories of loss, hardship and of being abused and violated by non-Aboriginal people and governments. They learned new knowledge about Country and of the terrain and the life and rocks and surrounding landscape. The act of working and eating together allowed for vast knowledge to be passed on. This way of experiential learning covered topics such as history, maths, science and geography, but all learning took place outside in the open as a community. These were not the teachings regulated by classroom settings but the informal, deep learning that comes from collective action with the goal of producing and reproducing cultural knowledge.

## The business of performance

The initial community grant funding received by the troupe was a short-term solution to its maintenance and professional development. The group had to decide on a way forward where they could be self-funded. It was determined that one way to approach this was to charge a fee for performances. The group had been in constant demand for event openings and to perform at NAIDOC and Sorry Day[4] and other cultural events. This strategising was important for the young women so they could determine their future and work out ways in which the continuation of the IFT could be financially viable. Many of the Elders and other community members offered their time for no charge; however, the group decided they would pay for services wherever possible. The Elders were clear that their participation on most occasions was part of their cultural responsibility to pass on their knowledge and to participate in the efforts of local youth to engage with the importance of cultural continuity. Their generosity was appreciated, and their mentorship and teaching have proved enormously beneficial for the young women in instilling an appreciation of the connection between Elders and younger people in the community.

Four of the young women aged 13 and 14 took on a leadership role. They established the business framework of the Illawarra Flame Trees. They asked the parents to register the troupe as a business and to set up a bank account. Because the young women were underage, the parents took responsibility for initiating a finance committee to act on behalf of and guide the young women. The young women worked together to set up a website and Facebook page.[5] They set up individual profiles on the web page and established a fee structure. One of the younger dancers initiated a meeting with the Freemasons of Kiama to request funding. I was also involved in seeking sponsorships and obtaining partnerships with local businesses and organisations. From these initiatives, some funding flowed and the IFT were able to expand their creative aspirations and purchase more costumes and maintain tuition for their development. The IFT continued to perform on a regular basis at various local functions where partners showed support for the troupe by purchasing various items for them and by promoting them through their own organisational networks.

The young women would meet before rehearsals with the parent advisory group and consult with them about various ideas regarding how the funding might be spent, for example, the purchase of material or some publicity for the troupe through local media coverage, or someone to assist with public speaking and the protocols of event organising. There were make-up requirements and, at times, transport costs, food costs and so on. There were always expenses and new ideas coming forth that required money to expedite. With the help of the parents committee, the IFT became quite savvy regarding finances. Some of the activities the young women were keen to engage in were costly. Buying costumes, ochre, paying for dance and singing lessons, and being able to provide transport and shared meals were all incurred expenses. The IFT learned not to be entirely dependent on external funding but rather, to stand proud and be self-funded through various fundraising initiatives that enabled them to pay for choreographers, artistic directors, singing teachers, and costumes. It was important for their longevity to develop practices of mutual obligation in the community, to help others where possible while ensuring their own employment remained viable. The troupe made a decision to seek payment from those who had the means to pay, but also, to continue to support community-led events without payment.

In addition to developing prowess regarding organisation and finance, the troupe needed to consider a succession plan that would ensure continuity into the future. The older group members decided that a partnership for each older dancer with a younger member would initiate a built-in mentorship whereby learning about various aspects of the management protocol would be passed on. This model was set in place and continues to be a workable solution to ensuring the continuity of the troupe.

### The Illawarra Flame Trees: the young matriarchs

As a cultural custodian, it is of great importance to me that the young women both know and understand the nature of matriarchal society. This factor is particularly significant in the postcolonial domain of the very tightly structured, patriarchal, broader society in which they live and learn. The group were taught about what had been written about us as Aboriginal women by the colonisers, and also what had been left out of historical recordings, such as the crucial roles women played in the sharing and preservation of culture (Balla, 2017). The dancers were taught how anthropology, for example, was often undertaken by men and how, in academic circles particularly, it is their notes and publications that people often draw on to determine the cultural life of Aboriginal people pre-invasion. Our lives were understood through the cultural lens of the colonisers and the way in which their society was formed. This meant that most anthropologists were men and they sought to record the activities of Aboriginal men as assumed leaders in our society and too often ignored the lives and roles of Aboriginal women, as noted by Brock (2020, p. 33): "it is for this reason that reports by male anthropologists of the non-existence of women's secret ceremonies in an area are not always to be trusted".

Dharawal and Yuin people have a long-held tradition of strong and competent women whose knowledge and spiritual dedication have built strong communities for tens of thousands of years. We know of this through various passed-on stories, and through the position that Aboriginal women have continued to maintain since colonisation. The colonial separation of gender roles and responsibilities clearly inflected the ways in which Aboriginal people saw themselves post-invasion (see Carlson et al., 2022; O'Sullivan, 2021). It seemed important to me that the young women know and understand that the ways of their ancestors did not correspond with the gendered rules about labour that were transported here. It was important for the young women to recognise that gender roles were important and that some practices were shared with all people, and others were only for specific people based on their gender. For example, there are dances that are only performed by women and others only performed by men. These dances may represent different roles and responsibilities. There are also dances where everybody participates, for example, our Mara Mara, or fishing dance. The men teach the boys the appropriate men's way to dance the Mara Mara dance, which includes simulating the practice of hunting techniques with a spear. The women teach the girls the same dance, deploying the movements associated more specifically with women's fishing techniques. Women fished with fishing lines, not spears, so the fishing dance for women teaches the technique of how to throw the fishing line and how to reel it back in. In this way, the women's and men's fishing dance is represented by different movements that relate to the differing gendered roles of our society. These are not perceived or judged in accordance with introduced perceptions of gendered hierarchy or notions of patriarchal dominance. Rather, they reflect different but equally important roles in the preservation and survival of our people. Women's participation in social and cultural life was often reduced by anthropologists to being less important than that of men and in many cases has been completely ignored (Brock, 2020).

It is important for the young women to see older women dancers from the Yuin and Dharawal nations and to understand the gender differences in relation to Aboriginal cultural mores rather than Western dictates of gender. This opportunity was provided by the Djajawaan Dancers. The Djajawaan Dancers are a women's dance group based in Narooma on the far south coast and comprise both Dharawal and Yuin women. The IFT were able to witness the dancers participate in ceremony just for women, with no men present. In 2017, the Djajawaan Dancers invited the IFT to dance with them at a significant women's event in Sydney in honour of Barangaroo. Barangaroo was an Aboriginal woman of the Cammeraygal clan of the Dharug nation in Sydney's coastal region. She was fierce and is remembered as a strong woman who did not take lightly to the arrival of the British and refused to engage in their ways of life, including wearing their clothes.[6] It is vital for our young women to hear the stories of our women ancestors and their role in defending our Country and culture. These are details typically left out of colonial accounts of communication.

It is the case that British, and European more generally, notions of gender relations were transported to all places that were colonised (Lugones, 2007). These values were based on economic precepts that assured male dominance in all things pertaining to wealth, property ownership and the running of all business outside of the home (Lugones, 2007). This neat hierarchical division brought with it a division of labour that deemed men's work more important, more lucrative and more worthy of status (Mies, 2014). This was not the case for many Aboriginal cultures where a form of matriarchal pride ensured that women and children were protected by women's labour; the gathering of food, for example, was often paramount to survival, where hunting was not productive, or easily accessed (Gale, 1990). Many women's dances speak to the roles women played—as is the case for men's dances. However, these dances are not viewed as different in terms of a hierarchical structure where one is deemed better than the other because of the messages conveyed. This lesson was difficult for many IFT dancers who had grown up and partially absorbed the gender relations intrinsic to all aspects of Western education, to all societal institutions and indeed, to many Aboriginal people (Nichol, 2011). Learning that dances conveyed an equivalence of importance in roles and responsibilities was an important aspect of cultural training.

## Performing pride

Ceremonial performances are salient to cultural life; music, song, ceremony, performance and dance were and are still very important elements of Aboriginal life and culture. There are songs for every occasion, some of which are expressed in special ceremonies, a practice that the IFT are continuing. In late 2013, the young women performed for the very first time in Wollongong at the signing of the Regional Partnership Agreement between the Department of Aboriginal Affairs and members of the Illawarra community. This was a significant event, one in which the Illawarra community wanted to showcase cultural connection with dance and stories and the youth. The New South Wales minister for Aboriginal Affairs was at the event and commented, "what we're seeing with these young women are leaders of the future. Performing arts has become a mechanism where people are seeing and talking about sharing Aboriginal Culture".[7]

The IFT performances became well known and they soon had bookings to perform at a range of events, including community cultural events, government and various education venues and some high-profile sporting events, in addition to Reconciliation and NAIDOC events. The popularity of the troupe became widespread and they were in demand as representatives of local Aboriginal culture, which was now being widely showcased throughout the region. In 2014, the curator of the Australian Museum in Sydney extended an invitation for the IFT to perform at the opening night of the *Garrigarang: Sea Country*[8] exhibition held at the Australian Museum. This invitation was to perform a dance to a song in language which was written and sung by one of the members of IFT and was a part of the exhibition. The young women and their families were invited as they had participated in the making of a bark canoe on Country which featured in the exhibition. They had also been instrumental in weaving a fish net from bark; this was also included in the exhibition. The IFT gave a spectacular performance on this occasion that was commented on by many of the spectators.

The IFT have been booked every year at multiple NAIDOC events, Reconciliation events, 'Australia Day' events, and school performances, including Southern Stars. Their fame has become widely known and appreciated by the local Aboriginal community, and significantly, by the broader community in the region. At all times, it has been evident that the younger women form bonds and take more responsibility as the older dancers approach adulthood and spend more time pursuing study or career options. Leadership roles and qualities are passed on and demonstrated through the carrying out of responsibilities for one another and the collective. This was demonstrated during the 2018 NAIDOC event at Macquarie University where I was completing my PhD at the time. The event was held in Sydney at the Macquarie University city campus. The NAIDOC event was significant to the dancers for many reasons, not least of which was the range of prominent Indigenous people in attendance. Local lands council people attended in addition to a broad section of Indigenous academics and other professionals. This was to be an event where the dancers would be viewed by Aboriginal adults who would be assessing their ability to act as cultural performers and carriers of knowledge. The dancers knew of the significance of this event and that the spotlight would be on their performance; they were aware that this performance must be flawless. They prepared assiduously. Prior to the day, it became known that some of the community Elders could not attend or provide transport to the event. Other arrangements were speedily made and the young dancers arrived and prepared for the event. There was a significant amount of feedback from those in attendance, all of which was positive and a testament to the troupe's dedication and preparedness.

## Dance rites and songlines

On average, the IFT were booked at least 24 times a year at paid events. It was due to this commitment and dedication by the young women that they were noticed and invited by organisers to perform at a national event. In 2018, the IFT participated in the national Aboriginal and Torres Strait Islander dance event Dance Rites.[9] Over 300 dancers and singers competed in this national event. There was a $20,000 prize at stake for the dancers deemed to be the best over the two-day event. Dancers were required to perform three dances: a welcome dance, a farewell dance and a 'wildcard' dance. The young women performed the dance Kia'ma. To accompany the dance, one of the members also sang the story. This performance ignited both the Aboriginal and non-Aboriginal audience, who whistled, clapped and cheered for the young women as they left the stage. One of the performers at the event, after watching the IFT performance of Kia'ma, commented that "classics are the pinnacle of all societies and cultures, and these are our classics—our songlines are the archiving and mapping of this country".[10] As a cultural performance troupe, it was important for the young dancers to understand that their performances were being linked to songlines and their significance in the Dharawal and Yuin nations. Songlines are tracks or lines of travel that designate routes and their astronomical and geographical features connecting people to place and culture. This information assisted the young women to form their identity and sense of belonging to the Illawarra and to their own Elders. In Dreaming stories, songlines are the markings of communication that helped shape the landscape and define Country. They are the stories that tell of the landscape and its people from creation to the present. As a contemporary dance troupe, it was important for the IFT to understand that singing and dancing in language had cultural significance in that it formed part of the basis for spiritual belief. Songlines are therefore the tracks of cultural narratives that speak to us and teach us about ancestors and their spirits. Songlines in our communities provide guidance, and IFT came to understand the contribution songlines made to establishing and maintaining language groups. The young women and their families would learn that songlines were more than just walking tracks to follow from one area to another. Songlines, as the dancers would learn in contemporary times, would ignite energy—a form of spiritual strength that prepared Aboriginal people and the young women mentally for performance and life. Uncle Max Harrison (2009, p. 33) describes the impact of songlines as

> such an important part of our mental and spiritual structure. They are lines of energy that run between places, animals, and people. We know at times where the songlines are and we like to follow them for the energy, not only because we can send a message to other neighbouring tribes but so we can keep in touch with animal and bird life. We follow the songlines of the animals to know where they are and to see if they have moved on. If they have moved on, then we can start a burn off to create more life without hurting the animals.

The power of understanding the energy of songlines helps to understand the sacredness and connection from one spiritual site to the next. For instance, the connection between Geera, grandmother mountain (Mt Keira), and the Five Islands, her sisters, is an example of an established songline. When someone interferes with the structure of a songline, they disturb the energy of that track. This was explained to the IFT in terms of cutting down the trees to make way for mountain bike tracks, or tourist zip lines, or other features desired and authorised by non-Aboriginal people. This activity breaks the energy between the people and Country and thereby disturbs the narrative that belongs to that area. While explaining this to the IFTs so they could create a dance, I used the example Uncle Max Harrison (2009, p. 37) refers to about the cutting down of the trees at the base of Gulaga mountain (Mt Dromedary),

> People don't understand about the sacredness and those songlines, those Dreaming lines. They say cutting trees down at the base of the mountain is not touching the sacred sites up top, but they don't understand about the short circuiting of the spiritual connectedness from one place to the other.
>
> (Harrison, 2009, p. 37)

Learning about the significance of songlines is vital for our young people to understand the connection our old people have, and that they have inherited, to the land and sea. This cultural connection allows our people to connect with marine life and with the water itself: sea Country. This connection was mentioned when our old people called in the winds to help the fish. Michael Organ (1990) also noted the existence of recordings of Aboriginal people singing dolphins, who were believed to be the spirits of their Fathers, to help with fishing, driving the fish towards the shore (Field, cited in Organ, 1990, p. 334).

In one of the last recorded ceremonies held in the Illawarra in 1939–1940, Aboriginal people from Kiama, Wollongong, Liverpool, Brisbane Water and Newcastle were observed singing about the coming of the settlers. Anglican pastor W. B. Clarke (cited in Organ, 1990, p. 52) observed the proceedings, and comments on the topic being sung;

the white man came to Sydney in ships and landed the horses in the saltwater. It is of such ridiculous subjects that the Blacks of New Holland make their songs–and any trifling event is celebrated by a song.

Like many colonisers, the pastor did not understand the importance of singing our histories. The songs tell future generations about the event and about its impact. These songs about the arrival of the British and subsequent colonisation tell us important things about the event. Far from being 'ridiculous' or 'trifling', such songs tell our people of the beginning of attempts to eradicate us, and of our ability to memorialise such events in song for future generations.

The reinvigoration of cultural pride is central to all aspects of cultural continuity, but is particularly notable with the IFT. This is due to the visual aspect of their performances, which are steeped in a wide variety of body movements, languages and facial expressions that convey enjoyment and the desire to dance well and bring their cultural knowledge to the spectators, many of whom taught this knowledge to them. In this way, the cultural pride expressed in the dances becomes a gesture of reciprocity—a kind of gifting back to the community and the Elders and an acknowledgement of learning. Dancing thus becomes a pedagogical experience that involves both teachers and learners.

As a parent, I often had the benefit of hearing the conversations between the young people and between the other parents. I was happy to hear they were inspired by the focus of the group on sharing cultural practices, and to see our culture living and being enjoyed by young people and that parents were engaged equally as learners as well as educators. Participants 4F and 5M were two such parents who acknowledged that they learned many traditional practices that had not been passed down and now they could share them with their children, and one day their grandchildren:

> We have been so fortunate to learn many practices through the Illawarra Flame Tree experience, some of which I have not seen before. I would never have known how to make a canoe or traditional weave [and] now I know both. I can share them with the younger kids.
>
> (4F)

> Wow, my son feels like a part of the community and we have friends we now call family. What I have learned I can share with the kids and the grandkids that's down to the Illawarra Flame Tree programme.
>
> (5M)

Along with the sense of community and the continuity of knowledge and cultural practices being shared, there have been a range of other positive outcomes. The young women stated that they felt strong in their culture and as a result felt they could achieve whatever goals they set for themselves. Three of the young women who joined the IFT when they were only 13 years old, have now enrolled in university degrees. One young woman is now in a trainee manager position. Another who started when she was 11 years old has just been accepted to do a double degree at university. The young women have developed a strong repertoire of cultural capital that anchors them. The younger members are still in school and still dancing and participating in cultural activities. They remain high profile, and in

2019 were asked to open for the international singer from United States, Charley Pride, one of the biggest-selling country music artists who is well loved by Aboriginal people. Charley Pride, sadly, passed away in December 2020.

## Contemporary historical pathways

The IFT demonstrate the need for more localised youth groups that focus on cultural continuity. The sadness expressed by some of our Elders and parents at not having these opportunities and having to live under oppressive government policies is partially offset by their joy at seeing the gratitude of young people who now have these opportunities. The eagerness of young men to join the group indicates that young people are very keen to learn more about our culture and languages.

The IFT created a pathway or contemporary songline for young people to understand the past via physical and spiritual encounters with Aboriginal cultural stories, language and cultural landscapes. Their performances developed a framework that allows young women and young men to learn and express local culture through a performing arts platform which has encouraged other young people to want to pursue similar activities through performance. The troupe continue to flourish like the bright red leaves that adorn the native tree. It is uplifting to have witnessed the transformation of these young people into such culturally informed and confident individuals. The most rewarding part has been to see the engagement from Elders and the broader community. I was humbled by the responses from parents and community members who were grateful for my involvement and inspired by the young people's enthusiasm. I am reminded of my non-Aboriginal parents, who made sure I always had a connection to my culture and who supported me in my efforts to locate my birth parents and connect with my Aboriginal family and Country. It is through their diligence that I understood who I was. This knowledge has enabled me in turn to provide support for these young people. Parents noted the way in which the young people engaged with learning and the potential for these practices to be continued:

> Your role here is to guide a generation of young people to understand the strength of our culture. Lead them to the knowledge and they will scoop it up like a fisherman in the middle of a mullet haul. They will hear, see and sing our songlines and create the new ones.
>
> (3E)

> Culture runs through our veins like the rivers run through our country, that's the song you must learn them young ones. Once they can see and hear the connection is continuous, they will embrace it well into their future. Then you will see and hear their strength. Always teach them respect, responsibility, resilience, reciprocity, and reconciliation.
>
> (27E)

## Where are The Illawarra Flame Trees?

In 2019, many of the senior young women began to forge new career pathways, handing over the responsibility of the IFT performances to the next generation of young people. At a Destination New South Wales event held at Killalea State Park, IFT performed for the last time in its current format. On that night, they performed before the Ngargins, a cultural dance troupe of young people based in the Illawarra. The Ngargins also had Yuin and Dharawal kinship connections. After the performance, the IFT and Ngargin performers talked over tea about sharing, learning and performing together as one family. The IFT and Ngargins decided to unite and became the Gumaraa Dancers. This partnership allowed more young men to be a part of the group while allowing the inclusion of more senior women. Gumaraa Dancers would explore historical cultural dance styles performed in the Dharawal and Yuin nations. This partnership allowed for the inclusion of didgeridoo players, clap sticks, and for local song man and dance teacher Richard Campbell to assist the group in learning historical cultural dances. This ensured the Gumaraa Dancers continued to be taught a range of perspectives when dancing. Of the original Illawarra Flame Trees, the youngest member has just completed their higher school certificate. Of the older members, two have successfully completed an undergraduate university degree and two others are working towards completion of their undergraduate degrees. Three others are fully employed in careers of their choice that focus on Aboriginal cultures. I completed my doctorate, the first in my family to do so. I am now continuing my work as a Vice Chancellor's post doctorate research fellow. I continue, however, to focus on cultural continuity and on working for my community.

## Conclusion

The Illawarra Flame Trees hold a very specific place in local culture and provide a significant demonstration of Aboriginal cultural survival in the locale. The young people who continue to perform are living emblems of the vitality of our rituals, practices and belief systems. They are testament to the life and vigour of Aboriginal cultural life passed down and now manifest in the popular art of contemporary performance. The continuing forms expressed through dance and movement, and their 'flow-on' effect through inspiration to other younger members of communities, are testament to endurance, and to the power of kinship and the potential for strong relations between Elders and young people. The dancers are living, corporeal symbols of resistance to colonial rule in their determination to pursue, create, illustrate and preserve Aboriginal culture and to overlay the devastation of colonialism with cultural pride.

## Notes

1 Bangarra is an Aboriginal and Torres Strait Islander organisation and one of Australia's leading performing arts companies.
2 Bangarra's Rekindling project is based on working with young people and Elders to share Aboriginal knowledges and express these in a community performance. Bangarra's choreographer, Frances Rings, has been an advocate for the project since its inception, speaking to Illawarra Performing Arts Centre and for local school programmes.
3 NAIDOC is a national week of celebrating Aboriginal and Torres Strait Islander cultures. See www.naidoc.org.au
4 A national day to remember the children who were forcibly removed from their families, now referred to as The Stolen Generations. See www.reconciliation.org.au/national-sorry-day-2020/
5 See www.facebook.com/theillawarraflametrees/
6 For more information about Barangaroo, see: www.barangaroo.com/see-and-do/the-stories/barangaroo-the-woman/
7 Victor Dominello was Minister for Aboriginal Affairs during this time and his focus was on culture and youth—he announced he was there to announce the 'Illawarra Regional Partnership Agreement', *Community Based Working Group*, 12 November 2013.

8 For more information about Garrigarang: Sea Country exhibition, see: https://australian.mus
  eum/exhibition/garrigarrang-sea-country/
9 For more information about Dance Rites 2018, see: www.abc.net.au/news/2018-12-15/sydney-
  opera-house-dance-rites-2018-indigenous-dance-competition/10567690?nw=0
10 See: www.abc.net.au/news/2018-12-15/sydney-opera-house-dance-rites-2018-indigenous-dance-
  competition/10567690?nw=0

## References

Balla, P. (2017). Writing Blak to the future: Situating the ways Aboriginal matriarchs protect and resist with art and story. *Writing+ Concepts 2017*, 150–156.

Brock, P. (Ed.). (2020). *Women, rites and sites: Aboriginal women's cultural knowledge*. Routledge.

Burgess, C. (2019). Beyond cultural competence: Transforming teacher professional learning through Aboriginal community-controlled cultural immersion. *Critical Studies in Education*, 60(4), 477–495.

Carlson, B., Kennedy, K., & Farrell, A. (2022). 'Indigenous gender intersubjectivities: Political bodies'. In M. Walter, T., Kukutai, A. Gonzales, & R. Henry (Eds.), *The Oxford handbook of Indigenous sociology* (pp. 1–30). Oxford University Press.

Gale, F. (1990). The participation of Australian Aboriginal women in a changing political environment. *Political Geography Quarterly*, 9(4), 381–395.

Geia, L. K., Hayes, B., & Usher, K. (2013). Yarning/Aboriginal storytelling: Towards an understanding of an Indigenous perspective and its implications for research practice. *Contemporary Nurse*, 46(1), 13–17.

Harrison, M. (2009). *My People's Dreaming: An Aboriginal Elder speaks on life, land, spirit, and forgiveness*. Finch Publishing.

Lugones, M. (2007). Heterosexualism and the colonial/modern gender system. *Hypatia*, 22(1), 186–219.

Mies, M. (2014). *Patriarchy and accumulation on a world scale: Women in the international division of labour*. Bloomsbury.

Nichol, R. (2011). Traditional socialisation and education in Australia. In R. Nichol (Ed.), *Growing up Indigenous* (pp. 49–57). Sense Publishers. https://doi.org/10.1007/978-94-6091-373-0_3

O'Sullivan, S. (2021). The colonial project of gender (and everything else). *Genealogy*, 5(3), 67.

Organ, M. K. (1990). *Illawarra and South Coast Aborigines 1770–1850*. Aboriginal Education Unit in Wollongong University.

Ungunmerr, M. R. (2017). To be listened to in her teaching: Dadirri: Inner deep listening and quiet still awareness. *EarthSong Journal: Perspectives in Ecology, Spirituality and Education*, 3(4), 14–15.

# 19

# BE(COM)ING IN THE CITY

## Indigenous queer relationalities and community building

*Corrinne T. Sullivan*

### A note to the reader...

I am the community, well, not entirely of course, but I am a part of it. I am a queer/lesbian Wiradjuri ciswoman, though I have lived and been nourished by Dharug Country for most of my life. I am also a board member of BlaQ Aboriginal Corporation, which I will mention throughout this chapter. BlaQ Aboriginal Corporation is a community-based organisation located on Gadigal Country (otherwise known as Sydney, Australia) that serves and supports the Aboriginal and Torres Strait Islander LGBTIQ+ community. Therefore, I write this chapter as a community member and as a board member, though I readily acknowledge that I cannot, and do not want to, know or share all things. So, whilst I can attest to what I feel, experience and what I have observed, as well as to that which has been written by others, I do not claim this chapter to be reflective of everyone's experience/s—this is not, nor should it ever be read as a grand master narrative. However, it is important to recognise that there are shared experiences and understandings among Indigenous queer mob, and even if what is reflected upon in this chapter is not demonstrative of all individual experiences, I will be so bold to say that even if this is not your experience, you know of others who do share these experiences.

I use the terms 'Indigenous', 'queer' and 'mob' in this chapter. I use the term 'mob' to refer to Aboriginal and Torres Strait Islander peoples. I do so to arouse a sense of who we are 'in common' and who see that commonality as influential for their sense of culture and identity, as well as my own. The term 'Indigenous' is used to denote First Nations/ Aboriginal and/or Torres Strait Islander peoples of so-called Australia; however, I recognise that all these terms are problematic. I use the term 'queer' to refer potentially to anyone who sees themselves under the common umbrella label of LGBTIQ+ (Lesbian, Gay, Bisexual, Trans*, Intersex, Queer, and those that see themselves as being sexuality and/ or gender diverse but may not fit neatly or entirely into any of those terms/labels). I also invoke the term 'queer' as a political statement to advocate against the narrow definitions of the label/s LGBTIQ+ that can hold sexuality and/or gender static, rather than fluid and complex.

DOI: 10.4324/9781003271802-22

## *Reflection*

I begin this chapter sitting at my computer at my desk. Growing up, if I was to write anything, it would be by pen and paper. If I was to research any topic, I would walk to the local library and consult the *Encyclopedia Britannica*. If we had the money and the phone was connected, I would call my grandmother—she was the smartest and most thoughtful person I knew. My Aunties and Elders in my communities were the font of cultural Knowledge and information, but some topics are just off limits. Neither my Grandma, Aunties, Elders nor the library could help with my topic at hand. You see, I am of an age, as I am sure you have figured out, that did not grow up with the internet, and there was nowhere else to turn.

The complicated twists of my life, of my story, are mine, but are also shared. Here is why. I am a queer Wiradjuri woman. Growing up to be able to understand what that meant would be framed by listening to the ways in which my 'parents', kin and communities talked about gay people. Hearing words like 'fag' and 'dyke', and 'fuckin' queers' was very, very, normal. Even my beloved Grandma would always refer to my older cousin who is lesbian as 'Sandra, you know, the lesbian'—Sandra remains on the margins of our family and kin. There were other gay family and community members, and they were always discussed in hushed tones that inferred that something was wrong with them.

Being different in my family and community was something I did not want to be. I wanted to be loved, included, not gossiped about. I wanted my Grandma to be proud of me. I did not want to be lesbian, queer, a dyke. I never did go to the library to look up anything 'gay' or 'queer'—too shame for that. Could you imagine if anyone saw? What if I got caught? What would people think? I would be admonished for being queer, for being a dirty deviant. I can recall the deep-seated shame of masturbating and fantasising about women. I do not know what I thought would be more shameful, being caught masturbating or people knowing what I was getting off to.

I knew I had 'dirty thoughts' growing up; however, I never linked them with my being gay. No, these were just my (hidden) dirty sex thoughts—not my sexuality. I laugh now, how naive, how ridiculous that I could not link, could not imagine, admit, that my fantasies should be, could be, were, my (hidden) reality. My lived 'reality' led me to living a lie for a really long time, until I could no longer. I had all these questions, but nowhere to go for answers. As I grew older and my world/s widened, the false veils of my 'reality' began to slip—and then they crashed.

Some questions I had needed to ask remained tightly held, vaulted away until they exploded. And then I started to ask all the questions and slowly made revelations about myself. I was terrified of who I might lose. Most of all I was scared that I would lose my family and communities, that I would be rejected by my Elders. I could no longer hold myself in, knowing that if I continued to live a 'reality' that did not match my soul, then I would die. With the recognition that I was already dead, I then thought I might as well let myself come to life and give my 'reality' the death it needed so that I could live, to be, to know, to do. And then I came to life.

## Introduction

I live on land that is not my own, far from the lands of my many ancestors; this land continues to care for and nurture me. The Gadigal People of the Eora nation, like so many other First Nations peoples, continue to survive and resist the ongoing settlement of their land in a myriad of ways. It is here that I do gender and sex and love in a way that the settler deems perverse, and it is here that the settler state mars me out for death as both Indigenous and Queer. It is here, also, that I have come to find my liberation to be inextricably bound up at the intersection of Queer and Indigenous.

(Monoghan, 2015 p. 206)

As Indigenous people, we are our relationships with other people. This is how we do culture, our way of being, knowing and doing (Martin & Mirraboopa, 2003). Alfred and Corntassel (2005) suggest that relationships "are the spiritual and cultural foundations of Indigenous peoples" (p. 605). How Indigenous people relate to each other is a central aspect of how we connect and belong to our Country, communities, each other, and to ourselves. Belonging and connection is a social, cultural and political experience that is relational, intimate, embodied and affective (Sullivan, 2022). A sense of belonging and connection is assembled at a young age, stemming from our ontological relationships with Country and kin (Moreton-Robinson, 2003; Tynan, 2021), and our ongoing recognition and acceptance as a collective member of our community/ies (Carlson, 2016). The way in which we operationalise socially, culturally and politically is often formed within our respective community/ies; however, the very concept of what or who is the community remains a vexed and thorny issue (Sullivan, 2020b). Currently, concepts of Indigenous 'community' remain fixated on what could be understood as Western ontological assumptions about our very own existence that have undercut our abilities to reap the benefits of other, more robust relational ways of being (Carlson, 2016; Tynan, 2021).

However, what happens when those relationships, belonging and connectedness are tested? For Indigenous queer mob, our birthrights to have relationships with Country and kin can be disrupted due to our 'deviant' sexualities and/or gender diversities. The advent of the invasion and ongoing colonisation of so-called Australia has resulted in an endurance of the colonial project of gender enforced on Indigenous communities (O'Sullivan, 2021). The overtures of Westernisation and Christianisation have led us all to the precipice of heterosexuality in this country now known as Australia (Day, 2021). Colonio-centric views are dominated by the fixation of heteropatriarchy and governed by the authority of the White, heterosexual male. This fixation manifests itself in dictating (hetero)sexual conformity, gender expression and role compliance (O'Sullivan, 2021). These views have infiltrated Indigenous communities and become infused by virtue of the colonial project to become cultural dogma (Sullivan, 2020b). The conflation of heterosexuality, Westernisation and Christianity has emerged as something which some Indigenous people and communities struggle to become disentangled from. The entanglement of heterosexuality, Westernisation and Christianity within Indigenous communities produces a variety of contradictory social and cultural expectations of what or who counts as 'Indigenous' (Sullivan, 2020a). Heterosexuality is seen as the 'norm' by some Indigenous people and their community/ies due to the reinforcement of colonial ideologies and the interruption of their own deep knowledges and histories (O'Sullivan, 2021). Therefore, colonial and cultural constructions are a process to be understood, but should not been seen as constitutive of the way in which Indigenous sexualities, gender diversities and identities are, or should/could be, recognised and represented (Sullivan, 2020a).

Indigenous peoples whose sexualities and genders may be categorised as 'diverse', or queer, forge possibilities for belonging and connection through purposeful destabilisations of heteropatriarchal 'Indigenous communities' whilst simultaneously reinforcing the very concept of community—insofar as bringing together Indigenous peoples who are queer to build new communities is a radical and fundamentally sovereign way to undermine the colonial project (O'Sullivan, 2021). This chapter will draw to attention the way in which Indigenous queer mob make space and create communities in the city, together with discussion of the conditions in which Indigenous queer mob feel in place/out of place in the city. The city, therefore, is chosen as a site of exploration due to the decades-long tradition of queer people (Gorman-Murray, 2004), including Indigenous queer mob, mobilising (Sullivan et al., 2022), migrating and placemaking in the city (Sullivan, 2022). The manner in which Indigenous queer mob community build and 'space/place make' goes beyond the borders of the city; they are also emerging across digital online spaces (Farrell, 2021a, 2021b), including online dating apps (Carlson, 2020). Indigenous queer mob community building (re)shifts dominant social and cultural special orders to (re)define and effect the myriad ways in which Indigenous queer mob do, know and be culture, gender and sexuality, as intimated by Valentine, who states that once "identities are 'done' differently in particular temporal moments they rub up against, and so expose [...] dominant spatial borderings that define who is in place/out of place, who belongs and who does not" (Valentine, 2007, p. 19).

## A kind of Indigenous community building

To appreciate the ways in which Indigenous queer mob build community, it is important to first understand how Indigenous mob broadly build community. Aboriginal and Torres Strait Islander peoples have always built communities, or what would be more aptly labelled kinship systems, being a manifestation of our belonging and connections to each other, our relationality. Indigenous relationality has a central tenet that 'all things exist in relatedness' and has 'sets of conditions, processes and practices' that remain in alignment as kin (Martin, 2008, p. 69). As all things exist in relatedness, it is "inconceivable that an entity, idea or person could exist outside" of this kinship system (Tynan, 2021, p. 601).

This relationality of kinship is culturally specific and is built on complex knowledge systems of who and how we relate to each other and Country (Dudgeon & Bray, 2019; Tynan, 2021). However, kinship and relationality both with land and each other have been, in some ways, disordered and disrupted by the continuing avalanche of colonisation. The invasion and ongoing colonisation of the country now known as Australia include the dispossession of land from Aboriginal and Torres Strait Islander peoples. This dispossession of land has resulted in the dispersing of people through forced removals (Dudgeon & Bray, 2019), child removal (Menzies, 2019), and involuntary movement in order to find food/shelter/work (Goodall, 1996). It is important to note that Indigenous peoples have always employed voluntary movements to places/spaces external to what were smaller geographically contained kinship communities, mobilising to trade, to visit kin beyond localised borders, and to participate in cultural ceremony, for example (Standfield, 2018). Subsequently, the dispossession and dislocation of Indigenous peoples from their lands and family/kinship systems shifted, in some ways, the conditions in which Indigenous communities organise.

The contemporary shifting and (re)making of Indigenous communities was established, in part, via the colonial project. The expression of 'Indigenous community' in popular and cultural discourse emerged in the 1970s as a way in which government-controlled funding could be syphoned to Indigenous peoples through the institution of Indigenous organisations. This resulted in Indigenous organisations curating the expression 'Indigenous community' to secure authority within communities in order to continue to secure this funding (Peters-Little, 2000). How and to whom the resources were disseminated formed part of that authorisation, constituting a significant and ambiguous source of power (Hunt & Smith, 2018). These organisations are then positioned, or position themselves as 'the community', a co-becoming with its membership that acts as a commanding force which has considerable and oft times indisputable control of all matters related to the community, including the people, in which the organisation serves (or is supposed to) (Carlson, 2016; Peters-Little, 2000).

Predominantly, it is the Indigenous community organisations that determine who is part of the community. This is somewhat shaped by government policies, in particular the three-part definition of Aboriginality developed by the Department of Aboriginal Affairs in the 1980s. The definition states:

> An Aboriginal or Torres Strait Islander is a person of Aboriginal or Torres Strait Islander descent, who identifies as an Aboriginal or Torres Strait Islander and is accepted as such by the community in which they live.
>
> (Gardiner-Garden, 2003, p. 4)

Indigenous communities/organisations are principally constructed from the conceptions of Indigenous identity and the expression of that identity. In each organisation, the diversity of that identity is assiduously measured and controlled (Carlson, 2016; Peters-Little, 2000; Sullivan, 2020), leaving limited room for fluidity in identities, resulting in a singular and homogenised Indigenous identity (Carlson, 2016). Who and therefore which identities are considered part of the Indigenous community is complicated and can be manipulated by those within these organisations. Individuals who do not participate, or are not allowed to participate, in these organisations are often viewed as outside the community. If an organisation, ergo 'the community', determines who belongs and who does not, it is also choosing who is represented and how that representation occurs. Such decision-making has a broad impact on not only who belongs and is connected to the community but also on how that belonging and connection are felt and sensed, or not. For Indigenous queer mob, this decision-making may mean that they are not considered or accepted, and are often invisible or silenced, and are at significant risk of rejection by the community/organisation (Spurway et al., 2020; Sullivan, 2021).

## Indigenous queer mob and 'community'

Some Indigenous queer mob do not feel that they are allowed, able or willing to participate in Indigenous communities/organisations. Such feelings can lead to a sense of isolation, rejection, lack of belonging and connection, and can have considerable and damaging effect on cultural identity and sense of self. Developing and maintaining a strong sense of cultural identity is challenged when you are not accepted by your community, whether that be your family, wider kinship networks or the broader Indigenous community/ies.

This can create 'self-doubt, identity confusion and anguish' (Fredericks, 2004, p. 31) for Indigenous queer mob. The colonisation of so-called Australia is underpinned by the values and beliefs of Western Eurocentric regimes that are deeply embedded with the doctrines of Christianity (O'Sullivan, 2019, 2021). These doctrines established ideologies of homophobia and transphobia that have permeated many Indigenous communities, and thus the colonial project is working as it is supposed to writ large (O'Sullivan, 2021). For many Indigenous queer mob, our sexualities, genders and our bodies have been colonised by these ideals. The sexual and gender diversities of Indigenous peoples remain mostly absent from popular, academic and community discourses (Day, forthcoming); rather, our identities and bodies are pigeonholed and bounded by the hard edges of heterosexuality (Clark, 2017; Day, forthcoming). The limitations of these Westernised discourses tend to render Indigenous queer mob as oppressed and subordinated by heteropatriarchal structures and performances (Clark, 2017; Day, 2021, forthcoming).

Heteropatriarchal structures comprise a heterosexist "ideological system that denies, denigrates, and stigmatizes any non-heterosexual form of behaviour, identity, relationship or community" (Herek, 1990, p. 316). This heterosexism enforces and normalises negative attitudes and behaviours towards those who disrupt Western conventions of sexuality and gender. Where heterosexism exists in Indigenous communities, so too do homophobia and transphobia. For Indigenous queer mob, such environments can be severely detrimental to health and well-being (Bonson, 2017; Dudgeon et al., 2015; Soldatic et al., 2021), as well as their sense of self (Sullivan, 2021). Some Indigenous queer mob find their kinship and/ or localised communities are welcoming and safe places for queer mob to be themselves (Baylis, 2015; Clark, 2014), others not so much (Farrell, 2021a). For the latter, managing and negotiating their queer identity within their kinship or community may result in either choosing or being forced to move away; some make their way to the city.

Cities and urban spaces are often sought as a place/space in which to understand, reconcile, explore and transform (Gorman-Murray, 2004). This is particularly true of cities, which are synonymous with being 'gay neighbourhoods' or for 'gay tourism' (Gorman-Murray & Nash, 2014). Sydney, Australia, is an example of an urban city that is known for its gay scene and as a site of gay tourism, specifically Sydney's 'gaybourhood' that has Oxford Street at its heart and that unfurls across inner west suburbs such as Darlinghurst, Newtown, Surry Hills, Enmore, Paddington and Erskinville (Gorman-Murray & Nash, 2014). Sydney has become a destination for many queer people, most certainly due to its array of gay and queer-friendly bars and clubs, creative and art spaces, and annual Mardi Gras parade (Gorman-Murray & Nash, 2014). It is a place which queer people visit, or move to, that can offer opportunities for belonging and connection, a journeying that has been referred to as "queer quests for identity" (Knopp, 2004 p.122).

## Sydney: the playground of dreams

my monthly train hops to Sydney, sometimes alone and sometimes I brought along mates. This was all quite innocent but we had some fun. Sydney was the playground of dreams [...]

Sydney in the late seventies was still forming its own gay liberation movement. Together with four mates, we would frequently drive to Sydney for the weekend, going to Oxford Street venues such as the Tropicana and Flo's Palace.

(O'Donnell, 2015, pp. 53–58)

The creation of Sydney as a gay community or gaybourhood can be traced to the gay and lesbian liberation movement of the 1970s and 1980s; however, the area first saw gay commercial and residential venues in the post–World War Two era (Gorman-Murray, 2004). The gay and lesbian liberation movement was primarily generated internationally by the Stonewall riots in the USA in 1969, a protest that saw thousands take to the streets in response to a police raid of a gay bar (Stein, 2019). Stonewall is a key moment in LGBTIQ+ history that ignited activism globally. In Australia, there was increasing activism of the liberation movement, a significant moment marker being the Sydney Gay and Lesbian Mardi Gras in 1978. The 1978 Mardi Gras was a protest march against the social oppression that the queer community in Sydney were facing—in New South Wales homosexuality remained a criminal offence until 1984—and the annual Mardi Gras march has since developed into a celebration, or parade, of pride (Gorman-Murray, 2004). Indigenous queer mob have been part of the Sydney LGBTIQ+ movement since its beginnings (Russell, 2017), with issues pertaining to Indigenous queer mob gaining recognition through Indigenous and allied queer political community activism (Farrell, 2021b).

Indigenous queer mob have been known to be part of the Sydney queer community for decades (Farrell, 2021b). Our leadership and participation in the queer community and through various activist channels is highly visible at the Sydney Mardi Gras parades. The first known Indigenous group to march did so in 1980, with the first Indigenous float, the infamous 'Captain Cook', appearing in 1988 (Farrell, 2021b). Over the ensuing decades, Aboriginal and Torres Strait Islander peoples and floats have been a regular presence at Mardi Gras. Since the early 2000s, the first float of every parade has been an Indigenous float employed to lead the parade as a customary 'Welcome to Country' (Farrell, 2021b). Since around 2013, the AIDS Council of New South Wales (ACON's) Aboriginal Project has facilitated the inclusion of the Indigenous float (Grose, 2012). Leading the parade in 2021, the Indigenous float, or First Nations float, was a community-led, co-presented entry by ACON's Aboriginal Project and BlaQ Aboriginal Corporation, showcasing the Indigenous LGBTIQ+, or Indigenous queer mob, community (Sydney Gay and Lesbian Mardi Gras, 2021).

The BlaQ Aboriginal Corporation emerged in 2019 as a community-led response to increase and strengthen the visibility of Indigenous queer mob and build a safe and inclusive space of belonging and connection (BlaQ, 2019). Although Indigenous queer mob have been part of broad queer communities for several decades, many have felt that they were not always welcomed or that these spaces were inclusive. Racism and discrimination is rampant in queer communities (Kerry, 2014; Tran et al., 2022); consequently, many Indigenous queer mob do not feel that they are safe, or that they can (or want to) belong to and connect in those communities (Kerry, 2014; Sullivan, 2018). Similarly, Indigenous queer mob are subject to discrimination in their own kinship and/or local communities due to homophobia and transphobia. Therefore, the need to build and create our own spaces has become vital.

Feeling like you belong and connect is fundamental to health and well-being, and to one's sense of self. Spaces that can provide this sense of belonging and connection can then be crucial. Given that not all Indigenous queer mob are the same— we have different Countries, histories, experiences and geographies—wide and varied responses are required. Over the years, Indigenous queer mob have worked to build our own sense of community/ies, led by individuals and collectives to provide spaces for our mob to feel that they have somewhere to go, digitally and physically (for further details, see Farrell, 2021b).

These communities have been built in pockets across the nation. Some are incorporated organisations and others are less formally developed. Digital spaces, particularly on social media sites such as Facebook, have been markedly popular over the last decade (Carlson, 2013, 2020; Carlson & Kennedy, 2021; Coe, 2022). There are many active Indigenous queer spaces online, and those groups attract hundreds of members across the country (Farrell, 2021a). Digital spaces have provided Indigenous queer mob with an important platform in which to share information, to find like-minded people, and to create a sense of belonging and community that is fused with our shared social, cultural and political ways of being, knowing and doing (Carlson, 2021).

Whilst digital and social media spaces have become decidedly important, they have not reduced the significant need for physical spaces. As previously stated, many queer and Indigenous queer mob make their way to cities and urban environments to placemake, to visit and to find or explore their sexual and gender identities, and Sydney is one of these important places. Sydney can be seen as an urban playground, a 'playground of dreams', as poignantly described by Indigenous man O'Donnell (nom de plume) at the beginning of this section. However, it can also be non-inclusive. Like many queer gaybourhoods, it is unashamedly racist and discriminatory against Indigenous peoples, as well as other minorities (Ruez, 2016). For this reason, the emergence of physical spaces that cater for Indigenous queer mob are essential. Recently, there have been known Sydney clubs and bars that are ensuring that they display visible clues of inclusivity such as Aboriginal flags, stickers or acknowledgements of Country. Further, in recognition of the need for an Indigenous queer mob space due to the mobilisation of Indigenous queer mob to Sydney, the BlaQ Aboriginal Corporation has sought to provide a physical community hub for its members and allies in addition to their online presence. Although hampered by Covid-19, BlaQ has secured space to build this hub for Indigenous queer mob to come and go, and to feel safe and valued. It is a first stop, but not the last, for Indigenous queer mob to be(come), do and know in the city. William Trewlynn, former chief executive officer of the BlaQ Aboriginal Corporation, says:

> it's such a new environment for people to engage in and it's something that is going to require a cultural shift within not just government but within community as well. Because it hasn't been there before. We're fighting for not just authority but equity. In that, it causes a tension because we have a lot of growth to do as a community to understand the complexities of what it means to be Blak and queer—and Blak queer in regional/remote to Blak/queer in metro.
>
> (Veness, 2021 para. 6)

The creation of space, physical and/or digital, for Indigenous queer mob is important, and it is needed. However, it is not achieved easily and it is not without tension. Mindfulness to the notion of freedom to be who we are as Indigenous queer mob and to express that rests on forms of social and cultural belonging and connection that are not fully accounted for by some Indigenous communities and individuals, or by the State. As such, Indigenous queer mob struggles for recognition, respect and space are a challenge that is heightened when our own kin/families (and the State) invoke Indigenous cultures to exclude and discriminate against queer mob. By creating and taking up space, and building new communities, Indigenous queer mob are leading a challenge to fight back against the ways in which our bodies and identities have been strangled with heterosexism and the heteropatriarchy.

It is our sovereign right to have this presence, to have this future, so that our identities and bodies are seen for our Indigeneity and our queerness.

## Conclusion

This chapter explores the complex and resourceful way in which Indigenous queer people have carved out their own urban spaces. It delineates the ways in which Indigenous queer leadership in community building has contributed substantively to the development of these spaces. Indigenous queer community building is relationally configured and performed, possessing an embodied dynamism that serves to protect, support and promote our collective futures. Our collective and individual needs to belong and connect are how we relate to one another, how we build space and community, and how we form new kin and family. Indigenous queer leaders and activists have long organised in the city. Indigenous queer mob belonging and connection rely on a relationality that extends within, between and beyond our Indigeneity and our queerness. The ways in which we have built new communities over the decades for ourselves are done with social and cultural understandings; the creation of covert and overt digital and physical spaces; and for some, the co-production of be(com)ing in urban spaces. Taken together, these approaches help index unique social and cultural belonging and connection, as well as a broader sense of what is, or could be, Indigenous community.

I have drawn on the histories of how some Indigenous communities and organisations have formed to critique our lived present, and I do so to imagine future potentialities. Given the ubiquity of some Indigenous communities/organisations/individuals, it can be hard to forge forward. As an Indigenous queer person, I have been both loved and accepted. I have also felt the painful sting of rejection under the guise of 'culture'. I am angry and I wish to rage against colonisation and the beliefs and values that come with it which have tried to dismember our Indigenous queer realities. Ultimately, it is our collective and individual responses as Indigenous peoples to rise and resist colonialism—and we must.

## References

Alfred, T., & Corntassel, J. (2005). Politics of Identity–IX: Being Indigenous: Resurgences against contemporary colonialism. *Government and Opposition*, 40(4), 597–614. https://doi.org/doi:10.1111/j.1477-7053.2005.00166.x

Baylis, T.-A. (2015). Introduction: Looking in to the mirror. In D. Hodge (Ed.), *Colouring the rainbow: Blak queer and trans perspectives: Life stories and essays by First Nations people of Australia* (pp. 1–18). Wakefield Press.

BlaQ. (2019). *BlaQ Aboriginal Corporation*. Retrieved 10/11/2021 from https://blaq.org.au

Bonson, D. (2017). *Voices from the Black Rainbow: The inclusion of the Aboriginal and Torres Strait Islander LGBQTI people including, Sistergirls and Brotherboys in health, wellbeing and suicide prevention strategies*. Black Rainbow.

Carlson, B. (2013). The 'new frontier': Emergent Indigenous identities and social media. In M. Harris, M. Nakata, & B. Carlson (Eds.), *The politics of identity: Emerging Indigeneity* (pp. 147–168). University of Technology Sydney e-Press.

Carlson, B. (2016). *The politics of identity: Who counts as Aboriginal today?* Aboriginal Studies Press.

Carlson, B. (2020). Love and hate at the cultural interface: Indigenous Australians and dating apps. *Journal of Sociology*, 56(2), 133–150.

Carlson, B. (2021). Indigenous internet users: Learning to trust ourselves. *Australian Feminist Studies*, 36(107), 9–25.

Carlson, B., & Kennedy, T. (2021). Us mob online: The perils of identifying as indigenous on social media. *Genealogy, 5*(2), 52.

Clark, M. (2014). Against authenticity CAL-Connections: Queer Indigenous identities. *Overland, 215*, 30–36.

Clark, M. (2017). Becoming—with and together: Indigenous transgender and transcultural practices. *Artlink, 37*(2), 76–81.

Coe, G. (2022). Writing themselves in: Indigenous gender and sexuality diverse Australians online. *Media International Australia*, https://doi.org/10.3390/genealogy5030071

Day, M. (2021). Remembering Lugones: The critical potential of heterosexualism for studies of so-called Australia. *Genealogy, 5*(3), 71. www.mdpi.com/2313-5778/5/3/71

Day, M. (forthcoming). Sociology, coloniality and heterosexuality. *Journal of Global Indigeneity.*

Dudgeon, P., & Bray, A. (2019). Indigenous relationality: Women, kinship and the law. *Genealogy, 3*(2), 23.

Dudgeon, P., Bonson, D., Cox, A., Georgatos, G., & Rouhani, L. (2015). *The Aboriginal and Torres Strait Islander suicide prevention evaluation project (ATSISPEP): Sexuality and gender diverse populations (lesbian, gay, bisexual, transsexual, queer and intersex—LGBTQI): Roundtable report.* Healing Foundation.

Farrell, A. (2021a). Feeling seen: Aboriginal and Torres Strait Islander LGBTIQ+ peoples, (in)visibility, and social-media assemblages. *Genealogy, 5*(2), 57. www.mdpi.com/2313-5778/5/2/57

Farrell, A. (2021b). The rise of Black Rainbow. In B. Carlson & J. Berglund (Eds.), *Indigenous peoples rise up: The global ascendency of social media activism* (pp. 140–156). Rutgers University Press.

Fredericks, B. (2004). Urban identity. *Eureka Street, 14*(10), 30–31.

Gardiner-Garden, J. (2003). *Defining Aboriginality in Australia* (Current Issues Brief No. 10 2002–03, Issue).

Goodall, H. (1996). *From invasion to embassy: Land in Aboriginal politics in New South Wales, 1770–1972.* Allen & Unwin.

Gorman-Murray, A. (2004). Gay and lesbian public history in Australia. *Public History Review, 11*(8–38).

Gorman-Murray, A., & Nash, C. J. (2014). Mobile places, relational spaces: Conceptualizing change in Sydney's LGBTQ neighborhoods. *Environment and Planning D: Society and Space, 32*(4), 622–641.

Grose, M. (2012). *Mardi Gras Parade 2012 First Australians Float True Love … Tru!* https://issuu.com/aconhealth/docs/aboriginal_project_mardi_gras_2012_report_-_web

Herek, G. M. (1990). The context of anti-gay violence: Notes on cultural and psychological heterosexism. *Journal of Interpersonal Violence, 5*(3), 316–333.

Hunt, J., & Smith, D. E. (2018). *Building Indigenous community governance in Australia: Preliminary research findings.* Centre for Aboriginal Economic Policy Research, Research School of Social Sciences, College of Arts & Social Sciences, Australian National University.

Kerry, S. (2014). Sistergirls/Brotherboys: The status of Indigenous transgender Australians. *International Journal of Transgenderism, 15*(3–4), 173–186. https://doi.org/10.1080/15532739.2014.995262

Knopp, L. (2004). Ontologies of place, placelessness, and movement: Queer quests for identity and their impacts on contemporary geographic thought. *Gender, Place & Culture, 11*(1), 121–134.

Martin, K. (2008). *Please knock before you enter: Aboriginal regulation of outsiders and the implications for researchers.* Post Pressed.

Martin, K., & Mirraboopa, B. (2003). Ways of knowing, being and doing: A theoretical framework and methods for indigenous and indigenist re-search. *Journal of Australian Studies, 27*(76), 203–214. www.informaworld.com/10.1080/14443050309387838

Menzies, K. (2019). Understanding the Australian Aboriginal experience of collective, historical and intergenerational trauma. *International Social Work, 62*(6), 1522–1534.

Monoghan, O. (2015). Dual imperatives: Decolonising the queer and queering the decolonial. In D. Hodge (Ed.), *Colouring the rainbow: Blak Queer and trans perspectives: Life stories and essays by First Nations people of Australia*, (pp. 195–208). Wakefield Press.

Moreton-Robinson, A. (2003). Researching whiteness: Some reflections from an Indigenous woman's standpoint. *Hecate, 29*(2), 72–85.

O'Donnell, S. (2015). Black, gay in a wonderland of boogie. In D. Hodge (Ed.), *Colouring the rainbow: Blak queer and trans perspectives: Life stories and essays by First Nations people of Australia* (pp. 48–60). Wakefield Press.

O'Sullivan, S. (2019). A lived experience of Aboriginal knowledges and perspectives: How cultural wisdom saved my life. In J. Higgs (Ed.), *Practice wisdom:* (pp. 107–112). Brill Sense.

O'Sullivan, S. (2021). The colonial project of gender (and everything else). *Genealogy, 5*(3), 67.

Peters-Little, F. (2000). The community game: Aboriginal self-definition at the local level [Discussion paper, No. 10]. AIATSIS. https://aiatsis.gov.au/publication/35754

Ruez, D. (2016). Working to appear: The plural and uneven geographies of race, sexuality, and the local state in Sydney, Australia. *Environment and Planning D: Society and Space, 34*(2), 282–300.

Russell, S. A. (2017, 18 February). Step by step, the First Nations lead the way at Mardi Gras. SBS. www.sbs.com.au/topics/pride/mardigras/article/2017/02/17/step-step-first-nations-lead-way-mardi-gras

Soldatic, K., Briskman, L., Trewlynn, W., Leha, J., & Spurway, K. (2021). Social exclusion/inclusion and Australian First Nations LGBTIQ+ young people's wellbeing. *Social Inclusion, 9*(2), 42–51. https://doi.org/https://doi.org/10.17645/si.v9i2.3603

Spurway, K., Soldatic, K., Briskman, L., Uink, B., Liddelow-Hunt, S., Hill, B., & Lin, A. (2020). The social and emotional wellbeing of Indigenous LGBTQA+ young people: a global perspective. *Irish Journal of Psychological Medicine,* 1–10. https://doi.org/10.1017/ipm.2020.83

Standfield, R. (2018). Moving across, looking beyond. In R. Standfield (Ed.), *Indigenous mobilities: Across and beyond the antipodes* (pp. 1–34). ANU Press.

Stein, M. (2019). *The Stonewall riots: A documentary history.* NYU Press.

Sullivan, C. (2021). 'Hot, young, buff': An Indigenous Australian gay male view of sex work. *Social Inclusion, 9*(2), 9. https://doi.org/10.17645/si.v9i2.3459

Sullivan, C. T. (2018). Majesty in the city: experiences of an Aboriginal transgender sex worker in Sydney, Australia. *Gender, Place & Culture, 25*(12), 1681–1702.

Sullivan, C. T. (2020a). Indigenous Australian sexualities explored through the lens of sex work. In L. Johnston, E. Olson, P. Hopkins, A. Datta, & J. Maria Silva (Eds.), *Routledge international handbook of gender and feminist geographies* (pp. 17–26). Routledge.

Sullivan, C. T. (2020b). Who holds the key? Negotiating gatekeepers, community politics, and the 'right' to research in Indigenous spaces. *Geographical Research, 58*(4), 344–354.

Sullivan, C. T. (2022). When the city calls: Mapping Indigenous Australian queer placemaking in Sydney. In M. Blidon & S. D. Brunn (Eds.), *Mapping LGBTQ spaces and places: A changing world* (pp. 293–303). Springer International. https://doi.org/10.1007/978-3-031-03792-4_18

Sullivan, C., Coe, G., Spurway, K., Briskman, L., Trewlynn, W., Leha, J., & Soldatic, K. (2022). Mobility tactics: Young LGBTIQ+ Indigenous Australians' belonging and connectedness. *Journal of Global Indigeneity, 6*(1), 1–15.

Sydney Gay and Lesbian Mardi Gras. (2021). LGBTQI+ communities will RISE at 2021 Mardi Gras Parade. www.mardigras.org.au/news/lgbtqi-communities-will-rise-at-2021-mardi-gras-parade

Tran, D., Sullivan, C. T., & Nicholas, L. (2022). Lateral violence and microaggressions in the LGBTQ+ community: A scoping review. *Journal of Homosexuality, 70*(7),1–15. https://doi.org/10.1080/00918369.2021.2020543

Tynan, L. (2021). What is relationality? Indigenous knowledges, practices and responsibilities with kin. *cultural geographies, 28*(4), 597–610.

Valentine, G. (2007). Theorizing and researching intersectionality: A challenge for feminist geography. *The Professional Geographer, 59*(1), 10–21.

Veness, A. (2021, 28 October). Ten Meets William Trewlynn. *10 Magazine Australia.* www.10magazine.com.au/articles/ten-meets-william-trewlynn?fbclid=IwAR2Igm20U4COUKYnC3REGPBgRNV05-s6UEtQCKULe2lZn0JwLFN0YyS9ZsU

# 20

# INDIGENOUS FUTURES AND DEEP TIME CONNECTIONS TO PLACE

*Lou Netana-Glover*

### Introduction

A life lived lawfully patterns human behaviour into the laws of a fully sentient nature […] The 'disconnect' between people and place is a sign of lawlessness that is having significant and detrimental impacts on the web of relationships between humans and the environment.

(C.F. Black (Bundjalung) 2016, p. 165)

When considering Indigenous futures, it is common for Indigenous people to look to the past, the deep past, even the prehuman past for wisdom from our Ancestral law—laws of place that have kept our worlds in balance and generated life before settler colonial inundation started interloping in our natural relationships (Watson, 1997, 2000; Simpson, 2017; Jones, 2019). Aboriginal peoples across so-called Australia have previously lived through climate change eras, sea-level inundation, and are currently living through settler-colonial inundation. The major difference between these two types of inundation is the settler-human disregard for the law of the land. The importation of foreign 'laws' and mentalities that settler colonial inundation has brought with it, has inverted lawful authority on place. Those with the least knowledge of how, and moral sense of responsibility, to maintain Country wield the most power. This inversion began when Lieutenant James Cook first patterned lawlessness onto place. The normalisation of settler lawlessness parading as law is further sustained by the colonial state apparatus' (mainstream media) negative representations of proper law holders, that continue to shape mentalities of the majority of the settler population (Moreton-Robinson, 2009).

This chapter applies and expands Fernand Braudel's historiographical lens of *la longue durée* to convey Indigenous deep time connections to place, and bridge cultural gaps of understanding between Indigenous and Western knowledges. Viewing the interface of the Aboriginal *longue durée* and the colonial *longue durée* through the lenses of time, law and lawlessness conveys the wisdom of Indigenous knowledge systems and why Indigenous peoples persist in creating futures built from ancestral wisdom and law. Indigenous scholars

DOI: 10.4324/9781003271802-23

from so-called Australia, Aotearoa (so-called New Zealand), and Turtle Island (colonially known as the Americas) are called upon together to acknowledge our solidarity in Indigenous values and convey an essence of global Indigeneity (Carlson et al., 2023).

I write from the lands of the Yuin people on the south-eastern coast of so-called Australia. I am of Ngāti Whātua, Ngāpuhi and Tainui descent and I belong to Yuin mob[1] by adoption and marriage. Dharug, Dunghutti, Dharawal and Yuin Country raised me. I was unaware that I am Māori for most of my life. I have previously written my story— a complex story of relations between Country, Tūpuna (Ancestors), Wairua (spirit), and people connected by Te Moana-nui-a-Kiwa (the Pacific Ocean) (see Netana-Glover, 2021; 2023), where I describe what it was like to find my whānau (family) at 50 years old. Before then, I understood myself to be Aboriginal (Netana-Glover, 2021). This is relevant because as an Indigenous academic, relationality is an inherent part of methodology. Placing ourselves in relation to our research is an extension of greeting protocols that happen on place itself. It could seem odd that a Māori wahine (woman) is writing about Aboriginal deep time and places, even though white scholars do it all of the time on these lands. I am still culturally Aboriginal, and family history indicates that I may have an Aboriginal bloodline, an avenue I have not had time to investigate as I have been immersed in meeting my whānau, Te Ao Māori (the Māori world), and processing the whole experience of learning of the five-decade long deception around my genetic identity. Identity is a complex system of belonging and relationships that surpasses any colonial ideas of who counts as being Indigenous based on blood quantum or any other colonial categorisations.

Even though it is likely the cause of this deception was a young woman covering her infidelity in a monogamous marriage, the insistence of my mother to identify me as a (white) Australian resonates with colonial *longue durée* logic of elimination patterning, where those who were not eliminated by frontier killings and massacres, were eventually subject to indoctrination and other psychological conditioning strategies of colonisation (Carlson, 2016; Netana-Glover, 2021; Wolfe, 2006). Despite a personal paradigm and identity expansion of epic proportions, my inner drive for knowledge production is still invested in championing truth-telling about the genius of Aboriginal culture and law. We are still resisting the globalisation process that started in the 1700s in the Southern hemisphere.

## Lawless foundations

In 1770, in a bay on Gweagal Country of Dharawal people north of what is now commonly known as the south coast of New South Wales, Lieutenant James Cook alighted his ship. According to Cook's ship's log, after ignoring the shooing-away communications of the local Aboriginal people, Cook threw some beads and nails in their direction.[2] Assuming his trinkets had been accepted, Cook headed towards the people, who then expressed their wishes for Cook to leave Country via 'dart' throwing and verbal commands. Cook then shot his musket at them. Some of his shot connected with one of the local men. The men chose to retreat. Cook responded by trespassing deeper into Aboriginal Country and insisted on trading unwanted trinkets by leaving them in a hut and taking in 'return' weapons that had previously been placed outside. The local people refused Cook's offer. They had retreated into the bush, hiding from the threat of further musket fire (Cook & Wharton, 1893; Mumbler, 1979). Cook's actions created the blueprint for duress, at fear of violence, which would continue to pattern across Aboriginal Country as the terms of engagement forced by settler-colonial society. These terms stand to this day.

Cook had not finished trespassing. He further helped himself to the estate. After fishing the waters without permission, stealing fresh water and wood, and burying one of his dead crewmen at a watering hole, Cook eventually made contact with another non-human being of Country. He mutilated a tree by carving his arrival date and ship's name into it (Cook & Wharton, 1893; Kwaymullina & Kwaymullina 2010, p. 196). This act sent a message that it was not just people under threat, but their non-human kin were in danger. His act of mutilation itself was a transgression of ancient law of place. Cook's lawlessness and disrespect for life was to ripple out. Almost every realm of Indigenous life would soon be inundated by capitalist-settler-colonialism. The violent nature of Cook's first actions on Country was the harbinger of the physical and spiritual violence that colonial inundation brought. Cook inaugurated a patterned settler presence into place as a paradigm of law-lessness, duress and disrespect. His actions were the genesis of the structural foundation of the colonial *longue durée*. Duress is now codified in legal statute through various forms of legislation that centralises power with interloping authorities.

Duress is a nullifying factor in Western contract law and is generally applied between individual parties who can seek remedy by a court (Beatson, 1974). The notion of *mass* duress is that which "imperial formations produce as ongoing, persistent features of their [capitalist-colonial] ontologies" (Stoler, 2008, p. 192). Mass duress draws attention to an unequal social contract with the state that Indigenes, and to a lesser extent settlers, are born into. Settler anthropologist David Graeber referred to the bureaucracies in place in our capitalist paradigm as structures of violence.

> All of these [bureaucracies] are institutions involved in the allocation of resources within a system of property rights regulated and guaranteed by governments in a system that ultimately rests on the threat of force. Force, in turn, is just a euphemistic way to refer to violence.
>
> (Graeber, 2012, p. 112)

In other words, the modus operandi of colonising forces all over the world has included the creation of (violent) state structures that enable capitalist domination (Harvey, 2010).

Disregarding original lawful authority means disregarding tens of thousands of years of empirical knowledge building; hence, knowledge itself is inverted in a settler colonial paradigm. The knowledges that can reverse the damage done by the settler colonial inundation have been positioned at the bottom of the social and political hierarchy of the settler state in the colonial *longue durée*. This positioning is essential to keep Aboriginal lands as a possession controlled by successive governments for global corporate capitalist interests (Moreton-Robinson, 2015).

## La longue durée

In the early twentieth century, French Annales historians expanded the role of the historian by adopting an interdisciplinary approach to history and multi-temporal approaches to historical time scales. Fernand Braudel created an historiographical tool to consider fuller, richer historical perspectives known as *la longue durée*: a three-tiered model of temporal distinctions that is geographically based and considers socio-economics and *mentalities* of overlapping time spans (Curthoys & Docker, 2015; Burke, 1990; Tosh, 2015). Put simply,

Braudel's model proposed short-, medium- and long-term ways of historical thinking that crosses disciplinary boundaries.

In Braudel's model, trends from the long term (geographical time) affect both the medium and the short term, and these terms interrelate on each other. For Braudel and the school that coalesced around his work, the long time span—*la longue durée*—considers centuries. The *longue durée* concept became the functional and structural base to the model, "from which permanent values can be detected' along with the 'slow unfolding of structural realities"' (Braudel, 1972, pp. 20–23). Long-term patterns span decades and give rise to the second tier of social time, consisting of approximately 10, 20 or 50 years. Therefore, patterns of continuity and change detected in long and mid scales give rise to the short term—*l'histoire evenementielle*—the history of events (MacGrath, 2015; Braudel, 1980, p. 28). Braudel called this short time span individual time, "proportionate to individuals, to daily life, to our illusions, to our hasty awareness"—above all, the time of the chronicle and the journalist (Braudel, 1980, p. 28).

Of course, since Braudel's era, representation and media proliferation have accumulated more reach and exacerbated the power of such surface disturbances to affect the short and medium terms. In the colonial *longue durée* of so-called Australia, dehumanising representations of Aboriginal people have swelled historically to inform the reporting of events about Aboriginal people and culture, having the effect of silencing the multi-millennial, empirical wisdom traditions and sustainable management practices that Aboriginal law has to offer humanity (Birch, 2016).

If Braudel saw the history of events as "a surface disturbance, the waves stirred up by the powerful movement of tides" (Griffiths, 2000, p. 1), then the most telling events of colonial long-term lawlessness that occurred in recent times were the Australian bushfires of 2019 and 2020. Yuin law man and song man Warren Foster refers to those fires as "the worst bushfires in our history. It's never gone up like this. Our people never knew fires like this" (cited in Reynolds, 2020, para. 20). When Foster said "never", he meant for the Aboriginal *longue durée*. As a senior knowledge holder, Foster would know if fires of this size had occurred in the deep past.

When viewed through the colonial *longue durée*, the inverted paradigm we live in is again made obvious. The long-term, structural patterns of inverted authority devaluing Aboriginal voices and the lawless exploitative relationship to Country and its people led to the biggest fires in living, and passed down, memory (Rowley et al., 2020; Williamson et al., 2020). Yuin Senior law woman Aunty Vivian Mason says, "Aboriginal people knew these fires were coming a long time ago [...] People choose not to listen. There were plenty of signs given to us and we knew that something was going to happen" (cited in Reynolds, 2020, para. 4). No matter what the immediate cause of the fires, they are a result of the removal of the competent and lawful manager/carers of Country from their homelands, and the ignoring of their law. The colonial *longue durée* has consisted of approximately 240 years of mismanagement by inverted and immoral authority structures that dictate from imposed and imagined state jurisdictions that have proven themselves unmanageable in size.

Yet the tides of the Aboriginal *longue durée* had already stirred up numerous Aboriginal people ready to respond after these events with cultural burning knowledge. Groups like the Firesticks Alliance had been meeting for over a decade to build and pass on cultural fire knowledge and seek funding to continue to care for Country through cultural burning. It is a tragic irony that it took catastrophic fires to attract the awareness of cultural burning in the settler-public realm, albeit scant coverage (Williamson et al., 2020). In New South Wales, a Cultural Fire Management Unit has been established by the government (Williamson, 2021) to "support Aboriginal community aspirations to connect to and care for Country through cultural fire management on [National] parks"; and more recently, an "Aboriginal led" working group to "develop an Aboriginal cultural fire management strategy" has been established (New South Wales Government, Department of Planning and Environment, 2021, para.1 & 2022, para. 1). Time will tell if these initiatives will empower Aboriginal people and allow them to properly manage this aspect of caring for Country without government and settler interference.

When viewed through the Aboriginal *longue durée*, Aboriginal fire practitioners and those who lobbied for the initiatives named above are simply original people of place doing what comes naturally and lawfully— nurturing life by caring for Country. Dharawal Elder Frances Bodkin shares that there is a time cycle referred to as the Mudong Cycle of approximately 11 or 12 years in which the majority of fire behaviour was tracked and management practices occurred around the observations made of the behaviour of elements of Country (Bodkin, 2007, p. 25). Bundjalung and Wonnarua scholar Vanessa Cavanagh and Firesticks Alliance ally Peta-Marie Standley's description of cultural burning relates the deep interconnections of people and law in managing Country:

> Cultural burning is inherently connected to identity. It is about knowing your Country, knowing what is in it, how it functions, and knowing how to apply fire in response to the cultural landscape and cues held within Country. There are different levels of knowledge holding and practice of cultural fire, and this knowledge is inter-generational.
>
> (Cavanagh & Standley, 2020, p. 14)

Aboriginal people with access to their homelands have been conducting their own cultural burns. If they do not have (interloper government) title to these homelands, they risk "hefty fines or imprisonment for practicing culture, caring for the land through fire, managing indigenous counties in accordance with specialist ecological knowledge and rights and responsibilities handed down for over 2,000 generations" (Reynolds, 2020, para. 13). I have relations on Yuin Country who watched the fire go around their property. The family had been practicing cultural burning in the years leading up to the 2019 mega fires. To their north, Yuin Elder Noel Webster led 40 people conducting a cultural burn on the property of Gavin Brook and his (Aboriginal) family in June 2019. The famous Currowan Fire burned "360 degrees around [their] home", yet their "brick bungalow, grassy yard and thriving garden look like a green oasis amongst a brown and burnt landscape" (Higgins, 2020, para. 7–8). Uncle Noel describes cultural burning as "more than just about reducing fuel load [...] it's a reset for the whole landscape [...] It makes sick country healthy again" (cited in Higgins, 2020, para. 37 and 34).

*La longue durée* is a useful tool to apply to the Australian settler-colonial context because Australian history is only around two and a half centuries old. Its focus on the observation of patterns is compatible with Indigenous ways of knowing. However, to attempt to tell any part of the history of the cultural and material changes that occurred as a result of sea-level inundation approximately 6,000 or 7,000 years ago, Braudel's model needs considerable expansion. Attempts at such expansion were proposed in the Integrated History and Future of People on Earth project. The project publication (2007), *Sustainability or Collapse: An Integrated History and Future of People on Earth*, is structured in three parts: 'The Millennial Timescale: Up to 10,000 Years Ago'; 'The Centennial Timescale: Up to 1000 Years Ago'; and 'The Decadal Timescale: Up to 100 Years Ago' (Bashford, 2013, p. 342). This is an expansion on Western world history scales of centuries. Apart from occasional dalliances in millennial scales, it cannot, however, account for the deep time history of the original people of so-called Australia—Aboriginal history.

It is widely acknowledged amongst the broader settler-colonial population that the Aboriginal *longue durée* was approximately 60,000 years (National Museum Australia, 2022). A prior Western academic history that in the 1960s had placed Aboriginal occupation at 13,000 years and expanded to 65,000 years in 2017 informs this (T. Griffiths, 2000i; B. Griffiths, 2018, National Museum Australia, 2022). This period may further increase over time, the more that Western scientific research methods develop and are applied to Aboriginal Country. Regardless of science not being at a point to determine a definitive time frame, it is unlikely that the Aboriginal *longue durée* can be quantified with linear time-scale methods for axiological reasons.

## Indigenous time

Linear time is not an organising principle in an Indigenous world view, yet it can be used as a measuring tool. Various Indigenous and settler scholars have attempted to commit to paper explanations of 'time' in Indigenous realities. Palyku scholars Ambelin and Blaze Kwaymullina give a succinct explanation of 'time' that resonates with most Indigenous understandings of temporality as explained to me through my own Aboriginal law teachers and in scholarship:

> In an Aboriginal worldview, time—to the extent that it exists at all—is neither linear nor absolute. There are patterns and systems of energy that create and transform, from the ageing process of the human body to the growth and decay of the broader universe. But these processes are not 'measured' or even framed in a strictly temporal sense, and certainly not in a linear sense.
>
> (Kwaymullina & Kwaymullina, 2010, p. 199)

To speak of Indigenous 'time' is to speak of systems of energy, patterns, relationships and law. In an Indigenous world view, the universe is a sentient "pattern comprised of other patterns". All life exists in relationship to everything else. Everything is alive and knowledge exists in relationships. The Western division of disciplines is tantamount to ridiculous because to exist in isolation is impossible: "intellectual, emotional, physical and spiritual understandings of the world cannot be divorced from one another" (Kwaymullina & Kwaymullina, 2010). Law and 'time' are linked through relationality and responsibility. In an Indigenous world view, relationships are not limited to human-to-human interaction. Unlike Western discourse, humanity is not the centre or pinnacle of the world order. Humans are another important cherished component of life that has roles and responsibilities in the continual creation and renewal of life, just as animals, plants, waterways, wind, sky, sun, moon and ocean do (Black, 2016; Kwaymullina & Kwaymullina, 2010; Simpson, 2017; Jones, 2019).

Hence expanding the *longue durée* model is not just a linear timeline expansion but a multidimensional awareness informed by a relationally aware past and present, where "life lived lawfully patterns human behaviour into the laws of a fully sentient nature" (Black, 2016). Thinking in terms of law, boundaries of Country form the original 'jurisdictions'. Boundaries both connect and make distinctions between. They are geographical and/or lingual. The Aboriginal *longue durée* is an unknowable history as a whole due to there being multiple perspectives of multiple geographies with unique beings of place. This is true of the colonial *longue durée* as well, but the construction and promotion of national narratives give the settler public the illusion of a shared history.

Yuin people of the south coast of so-called New South Wales are Sea Country people and have adeptly lived through and created knowledge from sea-level inundation. Scientific studies tell us that the most recent sea-level inundation steadied around 7,000 years ago. This climate change event of the Aboriginal *longue durée* created histories, technologies and teaching stories (Nunn & Reid, 2016). The changes to south coast Country shaped the cultural fishing practices that continue to this day (Tran et al., 2016, pp. 182–185; Cruse et al., 2014, pp. 7–10). This knowledge is held in Yuin communities and has been shared on the public record as the interest for deep time history has grown. From any account of Aboriginal history, two things are certain: Aboriginal law does not change, and life thrived on precolonial Aboriginal Country (Pascoe, 2014; Marshall, 2017, pp. 21–22). The law, together with the beliefs and values inherent in it, feature in Aboriginal world views to this day. These principles do not change (Watson, 1997, p. 40). They function to strengthen resilience and survival through inundation, and to create Indigenous futures by caring for people and place.

The permanent values of the Aboriginal *longue durée* that are common to all Aboriginal peoples are that "ecologies of mutual benefit promote synergistic entanglements across species and country such that life is enhanced through beneficial connectivities" (Bird Rose, 2005, p. 300). As explained by Kwaymullina and Kwaymullina (2010, p. 203), "[T]he fundamental role of the law is to sustain, maintain and renew the network of connections between all life". The abundant health of Country at the time of British invasion is also evidenced by the pens of early Western 'explorers'. Early invader accounts give detailed testament to the health of the land—land that had been managed by Aboriginal people for tens of thousands of years (Gammage, 2012; Pascoe, 2014). Settler mentalities forged in the colonial *longue durée* project their own separation of people and place onto Aboriginal lands and people which "continues to strip away non-European notions of reciprocity between humans and the world around us" (Fletcher et al., 2021). This history gave rise to the wilderness myth—the idea that Country has maintained itself without humans caring for it (Fletcher et al., 2021). In 2014, then-Australian prime minister Tony Abbott contributed to actively maintain this myth in the public psyche by saying Sydney was "nothing but bush" before the arrival of the first fleet, and "the convicts and the sailors [...] must have thought they had come almost to the moon" (cited in Henderson, 2014, para. 4).

It has been proven that Indigenous peoples have been actively creating, managing and maintaining most of the Earth's landscapes for thousands of years (Fletcher et al., 2021; Ellis et al., 2021). Dharawal peoples have knowledges grouped into seasons whose time periods range from annual, to 12,000- to 20,000-year cycles. They have law that informs human action pertaining to each cycle, usually signified by the actions of other beings of Country such as flowering plants, or animal behaviour (Bodkin, 2008).

## South coast sea country

We call the humpback whale Jaandah. Whales have their own songline that went inland to the mountain. There was a flood and people used Gulaga to rest. You should never turn your back on Gadu, the sea, he is the provider. We must show respect, and then we can get a feed. In the old days they used to sing to calm the ocean down, it kept him happy.

(Warren Foster south coast original owner, Batemans Marine Park consultations, 2015, cited in Donaldson and Feary, 2016, p. 43)

The long connections to Country that constitute the Aboriginal *longue durée* make it hard to discern whether the flood Foster is referring to above is from the last sea-level rise or one before that. This difficulty comes to mind because Guluga (colonial name, Mount Dromedary) is inland from the ocean at its current level.[3] If the people rested on Guluga at the time of a great flood, we can deduce that the last sea-level rise either involved a period of flooding before stabilising to where it is now (and has been for approximately 7,000 years), or Foster is talking about a previous sea-level rise. The latter is the most feasible, based on archaeological records of the gradual progression of the most recent sea-level rise. Dharawal people, Yuin's northern neighbours, account for sea-level rises in Garuwanga—the Dreaming Cycle, a cycle of time consisting of 12,000 to 20,000 years. In the Darimi Ganbi (time of fire) period of that cycle "the sea levels rise, peaking with the most violent of storms" (Bodkin, 2008, p. 28).

Ecological humanities scholars have drawn on the physical sciences to assert that "oceans rising and falling, separating and connecting great areas of land [...] has long formed part of the account of an Australian human and natural past" (Bashford, 2013, p. 344). Determining which sea-level inundation Foster is talking about, however, becomes irrelevant when applying the evidence to a key concern of this chapter, lawful futures. The fact that Bodkin's and Foster's Ancestors have lived through tens of thousands of years, as recorded in contemporary histories, morally and lawfully provides a prima facie case for the assertion of sovereignty. 'He who is earlier in time is stronger in law' (Duhaime, 1998; Fellmeth & Horwitz, 2021) is a maxim at law of the interlopers themselves. The history that resides in the deep time rhythms of a rising and receding ocean attests to the intricate links of south coast Aboriginal people to Sea Country. It positions Yuin as the lawful authority and knowledge holders of Yuin Country. Indigenous territories provide the original 'jurisdictions' of place and have been proven as manageable by the precolonial histories of every colonised Indigenous peoples on the planet.

Given that sea-level rise was approximately 7,000 years ago, many south coast sites of significance are underwater now. The ocean floor has songlines that were walked, sites where ceremonies were performed, and artefacts that reflect how Yuin people lived their daily lives in periods of deep time. Relationships with the ancestors under Sea Country are significant and active today and will be into the future. Although they are buried underneath the water of sea-level inundation, they are still a loved and cared about part of community. They created the Indigenous futures that followed them. Adherence to lawful culture led their people to safety in Foster's example above.

Whereas sea-level inundation was of a known relation (Gadu, the sea), settler colonial inundation has brought a deluge of foreign interlopers. Settler colonial money and law systems use the language of water—currency, banks, (cash) flow and fluidity—but money and the legal codes of foreigners that govern its use is a violent proxy for the provisioning Gadu and his freshwater relations have always provided.[4] Similarly, linear time has proven a vicious replacement for life-affirming relational obligations as an organising principle.

## Weaponised time

Within Braudel's social time (medium length) of the Australian colonial *longue durée*, the ramifications of this disjuncture in Western and Indigenous perceptions of time have affected every aspect of Indigenous 'Australian' lives. Kwaymullina and Kwaymullina (2010) note that linear time enables representations of Aboriginal people as 'backward' with 'no future'; land is 'discovered'; law and culture 'begin[s]' with the British. Yet Native Title claimants across so-called Australia must prove their continuing connection to Country through linear time despite being subject to massacres, forced removals, assimilation and protectionist policies that included the stealing of children by the state (Kwaymullina & Kwaymullina, 2010; Strelein, 2009, 2014). Indeed "where written evidence exists that may demonstrate some sort of interruption, proof of continuity in the face of interruption is expected" (Strelein, 2014, p. 7).

It is beyond the scope of this chapter to investigate the level of purposefulness of this use of linear time by the British Admiralty and their imperial masters; however, it is interesting to consider the words of Arthur Phillip, commander of the First Fleet, as they arrived on Dharawal and Dharug Country, "that the country will hereafter prove a most valuable acquisition to Great Britain (and) time will remove all difficulties" (Mackaness, 1937, p. 165). The interloping judicial system demonstrated how the colonial inundation of linear time could serve Phillip's vision when, in 1998, Justice Olney claimed that the 'tide of history' had 'washed away' any 'real' Yorta Yorta Native Title claim to land (Genovese, 2003).

While the invasion and colonisation of the whole continent is one massive appropriation, the amelioration of responsibility brought with linear time and the national narrative that "we are all Australians", distances general public awareness from the continual acts of appropriation (theft) that have to continue to keep Australia as a settler-colonial possession (Moreton-Robinson, 2015, p. xiii). Sovereignty, law and the multiple millennia of evolving cultural knowledges are for the most part dismissed by invader governments and populations, while the colonial-capitalist-industrialised lifestyle of the nation almost destroys ecosystems in its wake.

Despite the grimness of the events of the colonial *longue durée*, the Aboriginal *longue durée* provides a foundation of hope and strategy for Indigenous futures. The hope lies in the historical resilience and the cultural foundations of lawful values that have not changed since the beginning of life and have survived the colonial *longue durée*.

Aboriginal culture is thriving across the continent and on Yuin Country, as evidenced by the availability of multiple cultural tours and workshops and the existence of multiple dance groups. Language revitalisation has brought about the Djinama Yilaga Choir who sing in the Dhurga language of Yuin people and tour beyond Yuin Country. Private, familial and community continuations of culture are the backbone all of these public events. Ancestors and descendants have not stopped creating futures by practising their ancestral culture and holding and practising their law. They are imagining and creating strong Indigenous futures.

Colonial *longue durée* patterns of control are observable and hence offer warnings. Doublespeak is normalised in an inverted paradigm. The Aborigines Protection Board (APB) was formed by the NSW government in 1883. Its name reflects the inversion of law that had been patterned into place by the lawlessness of Cook. Instead of protecting Aboriginal people, the APB 'systematically destroyed' the high degree of agency that south coast people had retained throughout the initial years of settler-colonial inundation (Rose, 1990, p. 42). The APB was replaced by the Aborigines Welfare Board in 1940 and continued to carry out racist policies to control and oppress Aboriginal people. The government habit of naming a statutory body the opposite of its actual teleological function is, I emphasise, a further expression of the lawlessness of the colonial *longue durée*. The names 'Aborigines Protection Board' and 'Aborigines Welfare Board' likely appealed to a settler sense of righteousness and work to allay guilt for usurping Aboriginal lands, keeping the illusion of lawfulness alive.

An authentically lawful paradigm would involve restoring the proper hierarchy of the lawful original jurisdictions, First Nations sovereignty. This would offer all life across so-called Australia some much-needed nourishment. It would not exclude the settler population but offer a sustainable law to live under. Restoring lawful sovereignty is seemingly unlikely in our current paradigm but still a worthy goal. The colonial *longue durée* has shown us that nation state-size jurisdictions governed by interloping governments have proven themselves destructive to life. Yet governments have been steadily expanding top-down jurisdictions run by foreign interests by further by signing 'their' nations on to United Nations initiatives such as Agenda 2030 and foreign unelected corporate 'world' bodies such as the World Health Organisation; or by increasing the influence of unelected corporate bodies such as the World Economic Forum (WEF) by putting forward political candidates who are WEF members, thereby giving uber-foreign interlopers overt *and* covert power in areas of governance concerned with health, economics and environment. Meanwhile, the so-called Australian government has never formally adopted the United Nations Declaration on Rights of Indigenous People (Law Council of Australia, 2022). These conditions are government colonial *longue durée* patterns of control in the name of protection, empowering inverted authority foreign to Country and performing the doublespeak of morality whilst acting immoral.

In a structural violence paradigm, agents of this patterning acting on the ground do not need to be mentally or politically on board with or aware of the colonisation process to enact the violence of colonial patterning on place, as the following example demonstrates. In 2015, so-called Australia signed on to the United Nations 2030 Agenda for Sustainable Development (Australian Government Department of Climate Change, Energy, the Environment and Water, 2022). Goal 14.5 of Agenda 2030 aimed to "[b]y 2020, conserve at least 10 per cent of coastal and marine areas, consistent with national and international law and based on the best available scientific information" (United Nations General Assembly, 2015, p. 24). This goal *sounds* noble. Around the same time, Yuin people were consulted by the New South Wales state government about the creation of a marine park on their Country:

> I had a meeting with them when the marine park first started coming in here. They said to me, "If you don't mark down on the map all these important places where you do your cultural fishing you will lose it and you got no argument against it". I said to them that we had done meetings with fisheries before and whatever we told them

what we wanted, those were the first things to be forgotten. So I marked it down on the map anyway and we still lost important beaches. (Participant 27, pers. comm., Schnierer & Egan, 2012, p. 94)

When the bloke [from government] that come down [...] I was reluctant to show him anything, tell him anything, because you're always a little responsible where you're talking. I said, well what do you want to know for? He said, they're the ones we want to protect for youse; these are things they told us. Paradise, Glasshouse, Punkala, so I told them all the places and that's all the places they put in there as sanctuary, we can't go. (R Mason 2015, pers. comm., 25 August).

(Donaldson & Feary, 2016, p. 94)

Due to the clash of values between Aboriginal and Western cultures as expressed through the inversion of law, acts of goodwill or good faith work against Aboriginal people in the long and medium terms of the colonial *longue durée*. This has been evidenced on the south coast "several times" when the colony was saved from starvation or drowning during the early days of the colonising project in the nineteenth century (Cameron in Donaldson & Feary, 2016, p. 10). In the example above, Mason and the other 'informant' gave information to the government believing that it was in the interest of protecting their cultural fishing grounds that their families have been managing for thousands of years. They were tricked. Participant 27 was threatened with explicit language of duress and Mason was given a false promise.

Blocking access to sites that these families belong to and whose relationships with these places have managed Country sustainably for tens of thousands of years is typical of short-, medium- and long-term colonial *longue durée* destruction patterning inherent in the continual attempt to eliminate the relationships between original people of place and their Country. It also reveals how an inverted law paradigm transposes knowledge. By 'managing' Country from imported mindsets and in unnatural, ever-growing jurisdictions, top-down messaging can assert untruths as truths and ignorance as wisdom. The *marketed* logic of marine parks or national parks rests on the wilderness myth that has driven 'conservation' efforts throughout the twentieth century to the present day (Laming et al., 2022), at great cost to our non-human kin. So-called Australia "hosts the most national parks of any country on Earth [which are] largely removed of human influence and are regarded as important sanctuaries for biodiversity on a continent that is experiencing the second-fastest rate of biodiversity loss on Earth" (Laming et al., 2022). It is no wonder that to most Aboriginal people, wilderness is known as "sick country: land that has been degraded through a lack of care through use" (Fletcher et al., 2021 p. 4).

The wilderness myth has been used to effect logic of elimination patterning globally. The UN's Harmony with Nature statement declares that since 2009, the goal of the General Assembly of the UN has been looking to create a new world with a new relationship between humankind and the Earth, and "has been to define this newly found relationship based on a non-anthropocentric relationship with Nature" (United Nations, 2022, para. 4). Indigenous cultures already have a non-anthropocentric relationship with nature that does not entail the removal of humans from Country but the opposite, as Uncle Noel Webster articulates: "when we have disconnection and remove people from the landscape, we begin to see imbalance" (cited in Reynolds, 2020, para. 22). In 2022, Wiradjuri scholar Michael-Shawn Fletcher and team found that "areas mapped as wilderness across tropical biomes have been profoundly shaped by humans in deep time, and continue to be occupied and used by diverse Indigenous and local populations today" (Fletcher et al., 2021 p. 2). The

Harmony with Nature statement chronology of events on the website makes one mention of Indigenous people, in the 2014 determined goal to "promote harmony with the Earth, *as found in indigenous cultures*, to support efforts being made from the national down to the local community level to reflect the protection of nature" (United Nations, 2015, para. 47, my emphasis). This statement typifies top-down structural authority and sets up settler governance bodies to appropriate aspects of Indigenous culture in the name of protection, excluding meaningful engagement with or stewardship by Indigenous peoples. Worse, it ignores the fact that "nearly all tropical landscapes being home to Indigenous and local peoples who have actively created and managed them for millennia" (Fletcher et al., 2021, p. 2).

Colonial *longue durée* events and patterning strongly suggest we are on a trajectory to increased global governance. This is another large step in the opposite direction of successful land and life management. Worse, it risks expanding the settler colonial nation-state modus operandi into a global protection racket. Observation of the micro and macro patterns of removal and control in the name of protection of the colonial *longue durée*, and speaking the lawlessness of settler-colonial national and state formations can serve our futures in our readiness to pre-empt and respond to oncoming aggressions veiled as protection. However, our strengths are much deeper than what can ever be articulated in the academy, or even on the public record. Indigenous futures have strong foundations from our ancestral *longue durée* values, law and cultures.

The settler *mentalité* of prescribing Indigenous people as separate from Country, relationships and other people, is the psychological ground zero that has paved the path of destruction which is currently being lamented worldwide through climate change concerns. It is a *mentalitie* that allows for the politics of identity to overshadow lived ways of being and hence exclude the experts on climate change (Indigenous peoples) from the conversation. It creates the grounds for lawless existences to cause cruel destruction. The twists and turns of my identity journey have afforded me experiences and knowledges that have brought unique relational responsibilities. I am obligated to share truths from the perspectives my journey has privileged me with. I choose to view the timing of my identity journey as Country stirring up more bonds of connection across Te Moana-nui-a-Kiwa, as we co-create our Indigenous futures for us and/as Country from the wisdom of our Ancestors.

## Notes

1   Local vernacular for members of an Aboriginal community
2   Gweagal accounts assert that Cook fired shots at this stage of the exchange (Daley, 2016), which is congruent with settler-colonial patterns of violence against original peoples of place.
3   Guluga was colonially named as Mount Dromedary by James Cook, and is the mother mountain southern Yuin people, the place of origin, a teaching site.
4   Foster is a Yuin lawman who has gendered Gadu as male. I use 'his' to honour my learnt understandings of relating to the ocean entity from Yuin Country.

## References

Australian Government. Department of Climate Change, Energy, the Environment and Water. (2022, November). 2030 Agenda for sustainable development and the sustainable development goals. www.dcceew.gov.au/environment/international/2030-agenda

Bashford, A. (2013). The Anthropocene is modern history: Reflections on climate and Australian deep time. *Australian Historical Studies, 44*(3), 341–349.

Beatson, J. (1974). Duress as a mitigating factor in contract law. *Cambridge Law Journal, 33,* 97–101.

Birch, T. (2016). Climate change, mining and Indigenous traditional knowledge in Australia. *Social Inclusion, 4*(1), 92–101.

Bird Rose, D. (2005). An Indigenous philosophical ecology: Situating the human'. *Australian Journal of Anthropology, 16*(3), 294–305.

Black, C. F. (2016). On lives lived with law: Land as healer. *Law Text Culture, 20,* 165–188.

Bodkin, F. (2008) *D'harawal natural resource management practices.* National Heritage Trust and NSW Department of Education.

Braudel, F. (1972) *The Mediterranean and the Mediterranean world in the age of Philip II,* vol. 1. William Collins and Sons.

Braudel, F. (1980). History and the social sciences. In *On History* (S. Matthews, Trans.) (pp. 26–30). Weidenfield and Nicholson.

Burke, P. (1990). *The French historical revolution: The Annales School 1929–1989.* Polity Press.

Carlson, B. (2016). *The politics of identity: Who counts as Aboriginal today?* Aboriginal Studies Press.

Carlson, B., Kennedy, T., & Day, M. (Eds.). (2023). *Global networks of indigeneity: peoples, sovereignty and futures,* Manchester University Press.

Cavanagh, V., & Standley, P. (2020). Walking in the landscapes of our ancestors—indigenous perspectives critical in the teaching of geography. *Interaction, 48*(1), 14–16. https://search-informit-org.simsrad.net.ocs.mq.edu.au/doi/10.3316/ielapa.039036093412381

Cook, J., & Wharton, W. J. L. (1893). *Captain Cook's journal during his first voyage round the world made in HM Bark 'Endeavour', 1768–71. A literal transcription of the original mss.: with notes and introduction.* (W. J. L. Wharton, Ed.). Elliot Stock

Cruse, B., Stewart, L., & Norman, S. (2014). *Mutton Fish: The surviving culture of Aboriginal people and abalone on the south coast of New South Wales.* Aboriginal Studies Press.

Curthoys, A., & Docker, J. (2015). *Is history fiction?* UNSW Press.

Daley, P. (2016, 25 September). The Gweagal shield and the fight to change the British Museum's attitude to seized artefacts. *The Guardian.* www.theguardian.com/australia-news/2016/sep/25/the-gweagal-shield-and-the-fight-to-change-the-british-museums-attitude-to-seized-artefacts

Donaldson, S., & Feary, S. (2016). *Managing the Aboriginal Cultural Values of Batemans Marine Park.* NSW Department of Primary Industries–Fisheries.

Duhaime, L. (1998). Qui prior est tempore potoir est jure. *Legal dictionary.* https://bnblegal.com/qui-prior-est-tempore-potior-est-jure/

Ellis, E. C., Gauthier, N., Klein Goldewijk, K., Bliege Bird, R., Boivin, N., Díaz, S., … & Watson, J. E. (2021). People have shaped most of terrestrial nature for at least 12,000 years. *Proceedings of the National Academy of Sciences, 118*(17), e2023483118.

Fellmeth, A. X., & Horwitz, M. (2021). *Guide to Latin in international law* (2nd ed.). Oxford University Press. www.oxfordreference.com/view/10.1093/acref/9780197583104.001.0001/acref-9780197583104-e-1795?rskey=t0eyYN&result=1807.

Fletcher, M. S., Hamilton, R., Dressler, W., & Palmer, L. (2021). Indigenous knowledge and the shackles of wilderness. *Proceedings of the National Academy of Sciences, 118*(40), e2022218118.

Gammage, B. (2012). *The biggest estate on Earth: How Aborigines made Australia.* Allen & Unwin.

Genovese, A. (2003). Turning the tide of history. *Griffith Review, 2,* 209–216. www.griffithreview.com/articles/turning-the-tide-of-history/

Graeber, D. (2012). Dead zones of the imagination: On violence, bureaucracy, and interpretive labor. The 2006 Malinowski Memorial Lecture. *HAU: Journal of Ethnographic Theory, 2*(2), 105–128.

Griffiths, B. (2018). *Deep time dreaming: Uncovering ancient Australia.* Black.

Griffiths, T. (2000). Social history and deep time, *Tasmanian Historical Studies, 7*(1), 21–38.

Griffiths, T. (2000, 1 June). Travelling in deep time: la longue durée in Australian history. *Australian Humanities Review, 18.* http://australianhumanitiesreview.org/2000/06/01/travelling-in-deep-time-la-longue-dureein-australian-history/

Harvey, D. (2010). *The enigma of capital and the crises of capitalism.* Oxford University Press.

Henderson, A. (2014, 14 November). Prime Minister Tony Abbott describes Sydney as 'nothing but bush' before First Fleet arrived in 1788. ABC. www.abc.net.au/news/2014-11-14/abbot-describes-1778-australia-as-nothing-but-bush/5892608

Higgins, I (2020, 18 January). Indigenous cultural burn a factor in helping save home from bushfire, as fire experts call for more investment. ABC. www.abc.net.au/news/2020-01-18/cultural-indigen ous-burn-saves-home-in-bushfire-threat-area/11876972

Jones, C. (2019). Indigenous law/stories: An approach to working with Māori law. In J.-A. Archibald et al. (Eds.), *Decolonizing research: Indigenous storywork as methodology* (pp. 120–136). ZED Books.

Kwaymullina, A., & Kwaymullina, B. (2010). Learning to read the signs: Law in an Indigenous reality. *Journal of Australian Studies, 34*(2), 193–199.

Laming, A., Fletcher, M. S., Romano, A., Mullett, R., Connor, S., Mariani, M., ... & Gadd, P. S. (2022). The curse of conservation: empirical evidence demonstrating that changes in land-use legislation drove catastrophic bushfires in southeast Australia. *Fire, 5*(6), 175. https://doi.org/10.3390/fire5060175

Law Council of Australia (2022). Australia must formally adopt the UN Declaration on Rights of Indigenous People. www.lawcouncil.asn.au/media/media-releases/australia-must-formally-adopt-un-declaration-on-rights-of-indigenous-people

Mackaness, G. (1937). *Admiral Arthur Phillip*. Angus and Robertson.

Marshall, V. (2017). *Overturning aqua nullius: Securing Aboriginal water rights*. Aboriginal Studies Press.

McGrath, A. (2015). Deep histories in time, or crossing the great divide. In A. McGrath & M. A. Jacob (Eds.), *Long history, deep time: Deepening histories of place* (pp. 1–31). ANU Press.

Moreton-Robinson, A. (2009). Whiteness, epistemology and Indigenous representation. In A. Moreton-Robinson (Ed.), *Whitening race: Essays in social and cultural criticism* (pp. 61–79). Aboriginal Studies Press.

Moreton-Robinson, A. (2015). *The white possessive*. University of Minnesota Press.

Mumbler, P. (1979). *Asian Bureau Australia newsletter*. South Coast Voices Collection, AIATSIS.

National Museum Australia. (2022). *Evidence of First peoples*. www.nma.gov.au/defining-moments/resources/evidence-of-first-peoples

Netana-Glover, L. (2021). Complexities of displaced Indigenous identities: A fifty year journey home, to two homes. *Genealogy, 5*(3), 62.

Netana-Glover, L. (2023). Oceanic intimacies: Country, tūpuna and wairua relationality. In B. Carlson, T. Kennedy, & M. Day (Eds.), *Global networks of Indigeneity: peoples, sovereignty and futures* (pp. 1–20). Manchester University Press.

New South Wales Department of Planning and Environment. (2021, May). *Cultural Fire Management Policy*. New South Wales Government. www.environment.nsw.gov.au/topics/parks-reserves-and-protected-areas/park-policies/cultural-fire-management

New South Wales Department of Planning and Environment. (2022, November). *Aboriginal working group for cultural fire management*. New South Wales Government. www.nsw.gov.au/media-relea ses/aboriginal-working-group-for-cultural-fire-management

Nunn, P., & Reid, N. (2016). Aboriginal memories of inundation of the Australian coast dating from more than 7000 years ago. *Australian Geographer, 47*(1), 11–47.

Pascoe, B. (2014). *Dark emu: Black seeds: Agriculture or accident?* Magabala Books.

Reynolds, A. (2020, 27 May). After the fire: A journey through Yuin Country. *Atmos magazine*. https://atmos.earth/australia-wildfire-indigenous-fire-practices-history/

Rose, D. (1990). *Gulaga. A report on the cultural significance of Mt Dromedary to Aboriginal people*. Forestry Commission of NSW; NPWS 1990.

Rowley, J. J., Callaghan, C. T., & Cornwell, W. K. (2020). Widespread short-term persistence of frog species after the 2019–2020 bushfires in eastern Australia revealed by citizen science. *Conservation Science and Practice, 2*(11), e287.

Schnierer, S. B., & Egan, H. (2012). *Impact of management changes on the viability of indigenous commercial fishers and the flow on effects to their communities: Case study in New South Wales*. Fisheries Research Development Corporation.

Simpson, L. B. (2017). *As we have always done: Indigenous freedom through radical resistance*. University of Minnesota Press.

Stoler, A. L. (2008). Imperial debris: Reflections on ruins and ruination. *Cultural Anthropology*, *23*(2), 191–219.

Strelein, L. (2009). *Compromised Jurisprudence: Native Title Cases since Mabo*. Aboriginal Studies Press.

Strelein, L. (2014). Reforming the requirements of proof: The Australian Law Reform Commission's Native Title Inquiry. *Indigenous Law Bulletin, 8*(10). www8.austlii.edu.au/cgi-bin/viewdoc/au/journals/ILB/2014/2.html

Tosh, J. (2015). *The pursuit of history*. Routledge.

Tran, T., et al. (2016). What's the catch? Aboriginal cultural fishing on the NSW South Coast. *Australian Environment Review, 31*(5), 182–185.

United Nations General Assembly. (2015). *Transforming our world: The 2030 agenda for sustainable development*. https://documents-dds-ny.un.org/doc/UNDOC/GEN/N15/291/89/PDF/N1529189.pdf?OpenElement

United Nations. (2022). *Harmony with nature*. www.harmonywithnatureun.org/

Watson, I. (1997). Indigenous peoples' law-ways: Survival against the colonial state. *Australian Feminist Law Journal, 8*, 39–58.

Watson, I. (2000). Kaldowinyeri Munaintya in the beginning. *Flinders Journal of Law Reform, 4*, 3.

Williamson, B. (2021). Cultural burning in NSW: Challenges and opportunities for policy makers and aboriginal peoples. Working Paper No.139/2021. Centre for Aboriginal Economic Policy Research, Australian National University. https://doi.org/10.25911/Q1PY-8E04

Williamson, B., Markham, F., & Weir, J. K. (2020). *Aboriginal peoples and the response to the 2019–2020 bushfires*. Working Paper No. 134/2020. Centre for Aboriginal Economic Policy Research, Australian National University. https://doi.org/10.25911/5e7882623186c

Wolfe, P. (2006). Settler colonialism and the elimination of the native, Journal of Genocide Research, *8*(4), 387–409. https://doi.org/10.1080/14623520601056240

# 21

# THE QUESTION, OR WHO ASKS FOR EVIDENCE OF QUEERNESS IN ABORIGINAL CULTURE?

*Madi Day*

*Aboriginal and Torres Strait Islander readers are advised that this chapter contains the names of people who are now deceased*

A version of this chapter was originally delivered as a keynote at the Digital Intimacies conference at Macquarie University in December 2022. The theme was Relational Futures. I wrote the keynote in a hotel room on Wallumattagal Country (North Sydney). I was in between housing while I was trying to recover from a recent death in my community as well as a harmful intimate relationship. This was my first ever keynote. While I was truly honoured by the opportunity, I couldn't bring myself to deliver a conventional research presentation. Throughout 2022, while I was researching and writing on suicide and gendered violence, as well as white settler violence on the internet, I was also surviving the impact of suicide and such violence in my own life. When I took to the podium, I could barely hold back tears, but when I looked up, I saw the faces of Indigenous[1] friends and colleagues who had held me throughout the year. In the crowd, I saw the faces of people who had brought me flowers and books, who made me cups of tea and who baked my birthday cake. I was reminded of how Blak[2] women taught me to become a hero in my own life, instead of a victim. I remembered that my work is a love letter to Aboriginal and Torres Strait Islander[3] LGBTQ+[4] people. And so, I started the yarn.

When it comes to Indigenous Studies on this continent, settler researchers are quick to overlook the significance of pop culture. I could give you hundreds of examples of this, but instead, I'd challenge you to find any work by settler researchers about Indigenous people that compares in complexity, multiplicity and future-thinking to works by Aboriginal and Torres Strait Islander people. This is in no small part due to settler resistance to understanding Aboriginal and Torres Strait Islander people as embedded in the present and future, rather than solely custodians of a precolonial past. Aboriginal and Torres Strait Islander researchers, on the other hand, dedicate significant time and effort to

DOI: 10.4324/9781003271802-24

understanding Aboriginal and Torres Islander people and cultures as living, adaptive and inventive. Here I am thinking of some key works like Marcia Langton's work on media, art and representation (1994, 2008) and Bronwyn Carlson's work on social media and country music (2016a, 2016b, 2017), but also others which I discuss below. I'm also thinking about Sandy O'Sullivan's more recent work (2021b) which explores how we as Indigenous LGBTQ+ people may see or imagine ourselves into different forms of pop culture even when we are not directly represented.

I love pop culture, especially movies. When I was 16, I had a girlfriend who worked at VideoEzy, a video rental store, here on Wallumattagal Country. After 5 p.m., I used to show up there, kick off my shoes, and eat Pizza Hut and marathon movies on a small television with a video player in the attic of the store. Sometimes I miss having a finite selection of movies and shows to browse with my fingers on a shelf. There weren't many queer or transgender stories in movies available at that time though, and even f ewerwith Blak narratives. Fifteen years and inestimable variations of screen and video technology later, there are still very few popular enough to be shown at the cinemas or to have made the shelf at VideoEzy. I still look for myself in pop culture, and I still settle for either queer, or transgender, or Blak representation—never all three and, God forbid, never a Blak non-binary dyke raised in the 1990s.

I recently went to a cinema on Gadigal Country (Glebe, Sydney) with my best friend. We've both had a difficult year and sometimes, when things are hard it helps to hold someone's hand and watch a romcom. We went to see *Bros* (2022), a romantic comedy about a neurotic white gay cisgender man who feels obscure in a broader white gay community where machoism and stoicism seem highly valued. *Bros* has been lauded as one of the first large-scale queer Hollywood romances, with a budget of 22 million dollars (Sims, 2022). The main character, Bobby, played by Billy Eisner, who also co-wrote the movie, hosts a queer history and politics podcast called *The Eleventh Brick at Stonewall*, a joke about the ancillary nature of white gay men in contemporary LGBTQ+ activism. Bobby is also working to open an LGBTQ+ history museum in New York City when he meets a 'hot but boring' man called Aaron, played by Luke McFarlene. A cat-and-mouse romance ensues, and the movie explores the complexities of love and masculinity in an age of dating apps, queer politics, poppers and group sex.

There were a lot of things I liked about this movie as a queer person. I liked the snappy relay of pop culture references, the bop-heavy soundtrack and the pokes at heterosexuality. I also enjoyed the museum as a site of contention between different perspectives in the LGBTQ+ community. There were a couple of supporting characters who were Black and trans, and some other minor characters who were white and bisexual or lesbian. Most of their lines are during arguments with Bobby on the museum committee. Acknowledging that as questionable representation, watching queers argue about marriage or whether they will hang a giant Jodie Foster poster in the centre of the museum, makes for some of the better scenes. Eventually, Bobby's frustration with his relationship with Aaron culminates in an epic tantrum aimed at other members of the museum committee. Bobby tears apart an exhibit before the museum opens because the other committee members refuse to accept that Abraham Lincoln was gay.

This scene stood out to me for two reasons. Firstly, it tickled me watching a room of different LGBTQ+ people bicker about politics and history because, honestly, I could relate. As both a researcher and a community member, I have been in many meetings where competing views and needs for LGBTQ+ people who otherwise have little in common, result in heated arguments and epic tantrums like Bobby's. Like many Indigenous, queer and transgender people, I have also joined committees ready to contribute ideas and knowledge, only to watch (usually, but not always white) gay men tank entire projects rather than incorporate other marginalised perspectives. However, secondly, and more importantly, I was fascinated to see an LGBTQ+ museum committee contemplate whether they could represent a prominent historical figure as gay.

Bobby argues that there is evidence, including letters, that imply that Abraham Lincoln had an intimate relationship with a man whom he sometimes slept with in the same bed. A white bisexual member of the committee points out that Abraham Lincoln had a wife and children, so that would mean he was in fact bisexual, not gay. The other committee members are not convinced there is enough evidence for this claim and are concerned about backlash against the museum. To this Bobby says that history needs to be represented through a queer lens and that they cannot let the 'heterosexual terrorists' win. He goes on to say that, of course, it is difficult to know that a person is queer in retrospect when all aspects of society at the time were committed to their erasure.

The assertion that due to the epistemological violence of heteronormativity, it is difficult to document queer people retrospectively may not seem that radical, especially not in a movie that features anal and group sex. Indeed, this is a complication for queer historians in the real world. However, I was struck by the self-awareness exhibited by Bobby in this moment, or at least awareness of his own cultural and social setting. I was surprised to see this in a Hollywood movie. I was surprised because at every presentation, in every classroom, in every reviewer comment returned to me, and in almost every conversation I have had with a white settler about my work, I have received variations of the same question, 'Is there evidence of queerness and transness in Aboriginal culture prior to colonisation?'

My immediate response to Bobby's claim that we can only apply queerness as a lens from our own time and place was: 'They know'. White settlers know that violent systemic suppression of queer people drives us into hiding and systematically erases our existence. Or they know that for themselves.

I should mention that I'm not a historian, or at least, I never set out to be. My love of movies turned into a media degree, and my love of writing and thinking by mob turned into a career in Indigenous Studies. Indigenous Studies is unique in its capacity to centre outwards from a decidedly anti-colonial standpoint. It is an intricate, community-connected, transdisciplinary field concerned with the nature of knowledge and a politicised intellectual legacy. There is no Indigenous Studies on this continent without the Big Playas—Professor Martin Nakata and Professor Aileen Moreton-Robinson, among others. There are two connected contributions from Nakata and Moreton-Robinson that steer Indigenous Studies now. The first is tension and affiliation with feminist and post-structuralist works that help articulate the culturally embedded and embodied nature of power and knowledge— particularly Donna Haraway (1988) and Michel Foucault (1990, 2004). Related to this is the second, a generative space where Western and Indigenous knowledges both clash and/ or mix. Nakata calls this the Cultural Interface—sites of discourse where Western and Indigenous politics, history, economics, technologies and social practices interact which are always shaped and bounded by power relations (2007, p. 9). Like Nakata, Moreton-Robinson (2015) sees tension between Indigenous and Western ways of knowing not simply as incommensurable cultural differences but rather as opportunities for exogenous examination and critique of the Western world. In this sense, conflict and contestation between Western institutions and Indigenous knowledge systems are in fact generative of new Indigenous knowledges.

This is important to Indigenous queer knowledges, because as Nakata points out, continued practices that sustain knowledges "renew its meanings in the here and now" (2007, p. 9). The propensity to cleave apart Indigenous knowledges and realities from the time and societies in which we are embedded, is a project of reductive differentiation. It is to say that we are legitimate insofar as we are culturally distinct from the modern world. Nyungar scholar, and gay man Braden Hill (2014) calls this the quest for certainty in purity, a kind of Indigenous fundamentalism. Hill likens these demands for uninterrupted, traditionalist productions of Indigeneity in favour of cultural distinction to the demands placed on Aboriginal and Torres Strait Islander people for Native Title and Land Rights:

> Claimants must be able to prove their identity and, thus, a maintained connection to an ancestral past. Furthermore, in doing so, the [Land Rights] Act necessarily elicits, from claimants, the performance of a narrow, essentialist form of Aboriginality in order to satisfy the requirements of the legislation. The native title process is similarly burdened with such difficulties.
>
> (Hill, 2014, p. 15)

The demands placed on Aboriginal and Torres Strait Islander people to perform and articulate traditional, precolonial versions of us are both endless and impossible. Necessarily, Indigenous scholarship continues to offer interventions to the contrary, particularly in the feminist and queer space.

Bronwyn Carlson's book *The Politics of Identity: Who Counts as Aboriginal Today?* (2016a) outlines the material impact of colonial policy, laws and legislation, and administrative regulation of Aboriginality. She demonstrates how primary sources of historical evidence of who Indigenous people are, and are not have been produced primarily by white bureaucrats and anthropologists. Moreton-Robinson has shown how such anthropological accounts are used in Native Title and Land Rights claims where being recognised as a "Traditional Owner" (i.e. legal access to homelands) relies on patrilineage or for women, the race of a male partner (Moreton-Robinson, 1998, 2000, 2015). In *Talking Up to the White Woman* (2000), Moreton-Robinson shows how white women anthropologists produce knowledge about Indigenous women representing a traditional versus contemporary binary:

> If she exists, she does only what anthropology decides for her, and she has completely escaped colonisation. Her lack of subjectivity means she is an object, whom anthropologists have constructed in their imagination and on paper. The traditional woman is the woman against whom all Indigenous women are measured, yet in her pristine state she does not exist.
>
> (2000, p. 88)

The quest for pure and pristine Indigeneity is troubled time and again by Indigenous scholars building on Carlson, Nakata and Moreton-Robinson's intellectual legacies.

Given that white researchers and bureaucrats have been committed to narrow productions of Indigeneity, how then would they account for complexity around gender and sexual agency? Corrinne Sullivan (2018) has shown how the moral landscape in the early colonial era resulted in primary texts like First Fleet officer accounts devoid of Indigenous women's agency. In these texts, she writes, "Indigenous women are framed in terms of sexual (use) fulness rather than possessing sexuality, and as victimised by Indigenous men who are represented as violent, barbaric, and predatory" (2018, p. 402). Sullivan is part of a cohort of queer Aboriginal scholars who research colonial impositions on Aboriginal and Torres Strait Islander gender and sexuality, and the realities and complexities of Aboriginal and Torres Strait Islander LGBTQ+ lives. As Sullivan has shown, this includes using sex work and sex for favours as a means for navigating both historical and contemporary conditions. Sullivan notes that, although we have no evidence of sex work among Indigenous communities prior to colonisation, we certainly have evidence since (2018, p. 403), and even then, there are any number of social, political and bureaucratic strategies, including university and industry ethics committees that prevent and inhibit research in this space. (See Sullivan (2020), *Who Holds the Key? Negotiating Gatekeepers, Community Politics and the 'Right' to research in Indigenous Spaces* for more on this.)

As Andrew Farrell (2022) points out, the question of cultural authenticity has been raised and addressed by queer and trans Aboriginal scholars including Arlie Alizzi and Alison Whittaker. Alizzi addressed authenticity in *Overland* (2014) in response to Anthony Mundine's backlash against a queer couple on *Redfern Now*. Alizzi argued that the Australian media went into a frenzy when Mundine said that homosexuality was not part of Aboriginal culture on social media because there is nothing non-Indigenous people love more than "watching Indigenous people fight each other publicly, especially if the topic is culture" (2014, p. 31). Whittaker (2016) has also highlighted that non-Indigenous people have a fascination with both precolonial gender and sexuality in Aboriginal and Torres Strait Islander cultures, as well as homophobia and transphobia in our communities. She argues that this is a reproduction of the myth of social regression in Aboriginal and Torres Strait Islander communities not dissimilar to the representations of Indigenous men and women in early colonial texts that Sullivan (2018) critiques.

More recently, Sandy O'Sullivan has offered a critical intervention of the colonial project of gender—a clear articulation of gender as a European colonial imposition on Aboriginal and Torres Strait Islander lives and relations. O'Sullivan is currently writing a book on the systematic symbolic annihilation of queer and transgender Indigenous people, and how Indigenous artists have challenged and do challenge this. The late David Hardy, Sandy's brother, brought our attention to the continuity of Indigenous queer resistance in the last hundred years with *Bold: Stories from Older Lesbian, Gay, Bisexual, Transgender and Intersex People* (2015), which features several stories from older Aboriginal people including Aunty Dawn Daylight and Aunty Fay June Ball. O'Sullivan's and Hardy's works speak to an international consensus between Indigenous scholars in Anglo settler colonial nations that emphasises the significance of creative practice to speak back to the erasure of queer and trans Indigenous peoples in colonial records. Farrell has written about drag (2016) and social media (2022), and Alizzi on trans video works (2017) to this end too.

Aboriginal and Torres Strait Islander queer bodies of knowledge insist that "we always will be"—they are future oriented. They are practices that produce and sustain knowledge inseparable from embedded and embodied Indigenous peoples that renew meaning as it lives, as Nakata puts it. This is different to North American literary approaches in the vein of Driskill et al. (2011) and Tatonetti (2014) which place emphasis on evidence that queerness predates coloniality. As I have discussed in *Trans Studies Quarterly* (see Day,

2020), settler queer and transgender scholars take more quickly to the latter approach because it enables them to recognise themselves in precolonial identities. Focusing on precolonial identities allows settlers to bypass the production of their own identities in the context of coloniality—the very fabric of the culture and societies in which they occur. It makes room for them to consume Indigenous cultures on the grounds of celebrating queerness and transness, without adequately addressing violence and harm, resulting in the necessity for these terms. Aboriginal and Torres Strait Islander approaches, on the other hand, leave no room for consideration of gender and sexuality without integrated anti-colonial analysis. They entail a practice of deconstructing and denaturalising settler genders and sexualities as relevant despite culture, time and place. They are cognisant that there is no queerness or transness without colonialism because these are terms that describe digression from a rigid system of categorising norms.

Coming back to how I'm not a historian, usually when I am asked for evidence of queer and transgender people prior to colonisation, I am writing or speaking about heterosexuality and the colonial/modern gender system. The discursive and institutional formation of European gender, sex and sexuality, alongside colonial projects of expansion in the nineteenth century is well documented by white historians (See Laquer, 1990; Caine & Sluga, 2000; Katz, 2007). The modern European propensity to name, claim and contain the natural world enabled white 'men of science' like Lieutenant James Cook and Joseph Banks to travel to the Pacific on voyages funded by the Crown and Royal Societies. Patricia Fara (2004) has shown that sex was always a driving force of exploration for scientists like Banks, who even imbued systems of naming plants with sexualised and gendered terms. Alongside this, European theories of evolution from Charles Darwin's *On the Origin of Species* (originally published 1859[2004]) provided scientific foundations for categorising and hierarchising race. Much of early natural history and biological science was the business of wealthy elites fascinated with the natural world. Unfortunately, with colonial expansion, they were empowered to name, claim and contain Indigenous people, too, which is why Royal Societies and natural history museums in Australia still hold so many ancestral remains and items to this day.

Early sciences of sexuality were primarily concerned with degeneracy and the regression of social and national values. The regulation of gender and sexuality in Europe postmodernity, and later settler colonial societies, has been to maintain social order and nationhood (Caine & Sluga, 2000, p. 89). As anti-colonial scholar Maria Lugones (2007) has shown, gender and heterosexuality were introduced to Indigenous societies as a civilising force—to reorder Indigenous peoples in European systems of power instead of according to their own social and cultural values. The colonial project of gender, as O'Sullivan contends (2021a), is only necessary precisely because Indigenous kinship and governance systems are incompatible with formations of colonial power like the patriarchal nuclear family. Aboriginal and Torres Strait Islander queer and transgender people do not need evidence that heterosexualism was introduced to our people and communities because we are embedded in living systems of knowledge and relations that affirm our existence (Day, 2021). Read that again. Relationality and kinship are living systems part of everyday Aboriginal and Torres Strait Islander realities that are incompatible with colonial hierarchies and power (Graham, 2014; Kwaymullina & Kwaymullina, 2010). They are not evidence of a precolonial queer and/or transgender past.

To put this another way, you do not have to remove people from their communities and put them in sites of incarceration like Blacktown and Parramatta Native Institute and re-educate them in concepts like gendered labour and dress if these behaviours are in fact universal. You do not need to introduce patterns of violence and dysfunction to berate and beat desire and affinities from generations of people if heterosexuality and unequal, binary gender relations occur naturally. So, when people ask if there is evidence of queer and trans people prior to colonisation, I say, no, there's not, but there is substantial evidence that Europeans developed heterosexuality and gendered violence. Aboriginal and Torres Strait Islander researchers have done and are doing significant work to articulate the violence of colonial gender. It is well established European settlers introduced cultures of gendered abuse and harm to Aboriginal and Torres Strait Islander people (Atkinson, 1990; Atkinson, 2000). Given that relationships are the foundation of our societies and systems of governance, gendered violence and heterosexualism are highly effective tools of settler colonialism. Introducing dysfunction to Aboriginal and Torres Strait Islander communities through policy, violence, incarceration and coercion ultimately damages our connections to each other, which are also our connections to culture and place. Settlers use this tactic in Anglo settler colonial nations worldwide—one need only look to the comparative prevalence of gendered violence against Indigenous women and LGBTQ+ people, and emerging rates of Missing and Murdered Indigenous People in continental North America and Aotearoa for evidence of that.

I'm not a historian because heterosexualism works just as well to eliminate queer and transgender Indigenous peoples now. In the last year alone, I have worked on research findings that indicate Aboriginal and Torres Strait Islander LGBTQ+ people are likely to be one of, if not the most at-risk group in Australia for both gendered violence and suicide. There is likely an interplay between these two things (Dudgeon et al., 2015). In an online survey I worked on with Black Rainbow (Day et al., 2022) documenting Aboriginal and Torres Strait Islander LGBTQ+ people's experiences of responses to the Covid-19 pandemic, almost half of 112 participants said they had suicidal thoughts during lockdown. Fifty-one per cent said they felt unsafe where they lived because they were LGBTQ+. This same survey was run online for a few days by an overwhelm of bad faith responses from people who self-identified as white and heterosexual. This was no surprise to me after working on research finding that white settlers violently target Aboriginal and Torres Strait Islander women and LGBTQ+ people on dating apps and online (Carlson & Day, 2021. All existing research into Aboriginal and Torres Strait Islander LGBTQ+ people's social and emotional well-being stresses the detrimental impact of discrimination and the importance of community support to counter it, including the *Breaking the Silence* report from Hill et al. (2021) and the *Dalarinji* report from Sullivan et al. (2021). Research by and for Aboriginal and Torres Strait Islander LGBTQ+ people in this space is invaluable because the forthcoming national Aboriginal and Torres Strait Islander Action Plan to End Violence against Women and Children (Department of Social Services, 2023) and emerging national responses to Missing and Murdered First Nations Women and Children (Parliament of Australia, 2022) are yet to incorporate the stories and urgent needs of Aboriginal and Torres Strait Islander LGBTQ+ people. Even in national responses to gendered violence in Aboriginal and Torres Strait Islander communities, we are left behind.

In the Black Rainbow survey (Day et al., 2022), a quarter of Aboriginal and Torres Strait Islander LGBTQ+ respondents said they did not feel there was any service that could adequately support them. Similarly, on another national project funded by Australia's National Research Organisation for Women's Safety Limited (ANROWS) (Carlson et al., 2021), we found that there are currently no funded organisations, services or even roles that cater to Aboriginal and Torres Strait Islander LGBTQ+ people experiencing gendered and family violence, but that Aboriginal and Torres Strait Islander LGBTQ+ people are presenting to Aboriginal and Torres Strait Islander specific and community-run services all the time which do not feel adequately resourced to support them. On the ground, community members and community-run programmes take care of mob with little if any government investment. A great example of this is Darwin Indigenous Men's Service which offers a weekly barbecue and check-ins for local queer and trans mob, and the Tiwi Island Sistergirls who fund local services through community-run events like bingo. Community enterprises founded and run by and for Aboriginal and Torres Strait Islander LGBTQ+ people like Black Rainbow[5] and BlaQ Aboriginal Corporation[6] also do essential work caring for their communities but cannot be expected to cater to their every need. Even where violence and discrimination aren't overt from settlers and their governments, there is oversight and neglect. We fend for ourselves.

Returning to the film *Bros*, if I imagine myself into that room with Bobby and the other museum committee members, into that argument about which LGBTQ+ heroes deserve to be commemorated, I'd have no precolonial contributions. Given the violent and avid way that settlers erase Indigenous people, and target Indigenous queer and trans people specifically, I may not be able to tell you of anyone from as far back as Abraham Lincoln. I couldn't offer you a picture of someone like We'wha—a Zuni hero who is also briefly depicted in *Bros* (2022). I could, however, give you countless names of Aboriginal and Torres Strait Islander LGBTQ+ heroes who have resisted colonial violence for the last 100 years. I could tell you of fallen heroes like Uncle Jack Charles, who was a survivor of the Stolen Generations that went on to be a beloved Elder and highly decorated actor (Butler, 2022), or Aunty Vanessa Smith, who was a relentless activist for the rights of transgender and HIV positive mob (Hill, 2020). I could tell you of the 78ers like Aunty Chris Burke, who walked in the first Gay and Lesbian Mardi Gras protesting police brutality against LGBTQ+ and Aboriginal and Torres Strait Islander people (Ross, 2022). I could tell you of Veronica Baxter, who police arrested after Mardi Gras in 2009 and placed in a men's prison, which killed her. Her family and her story continue to demand carceral justice for transgender Aboriginal women (Gregoire, 2020). I could tell you of living legends like Aunty Dawn Daylight, who was also stolen from her family and forced into domestic slavery at a private Catholic institution, and who is a highly respected activist, truth-teller and musician (Murray, 2019), or of Uncle Noel Tovey, who survived arrest and prison time for buggery and who is a world-renowned dancer and choreographer (Tovey, 2011). I could go on.

Systemic and epistemological violence erases Aboriginal and Torres Strait Islander LGBTQ+ people, then demands that we provide evidence of our histories to authenticate our existence. To whom? Settlers. Aboriginal and Torres Strait Islander LGBTQ+ people know we exist, and we have established roles in our respective knowledge systems and broader communities. Those of us who are still seeking that knowledge can begin our journeys with the myriad artistic and intellectual works by Aboriginal and Torres Strait Islander people which are not even close to being covered here. In the face of settler violence, Aboriginal and Torres Strait Islander LGBTQ+ people contribute to vibrant cultures of thought, care and resistance, and political legacies that are living and thus ever evolving. Instead of looking into a precolonial imaginary for evidence of Aboriginal and Torres Strait Islander LGBTQ+ people, look around you. We're busy with the mess you brought to us.

## Notes

1  I'm using 'Indigenous' here to include the First People of this continent and others. Throughout, I use 'Indigenous' when speaking about First Peoples globally
2  I use 'Blak' here in the way Erub/Mer (Torres Strait) and K'ua K'ua (Cape York) artist Destiny Deacon introduced it—encompassing the complex way Aboriginal and Torres Strait Islander people understand themselves as politically Blak while resisting racial discrimination and colonial categorisation. I specify Blak when I talk about myself and people close to me because that's the term I'd use colloquially. For more on this, see: www.sbs.com.au/nitv/article/why-blak-not-black-artist-destiny-deacon-and-the-origins-of-this-word/7gv3mykzv
3  I use 'Aboriginal and Torres Strait Islander' throughout to refer to the First People of the continent known in the colonial context in Australia and some of the surrounding islands.
4  LGBTQ+—Lesbian, Gay, Bisexual, Transgender, Queer and the plus speaks to the limitation of the acronym in representing a whole diverse community of people that live outside and beyond heteropatriarchal ciscentric genders and sexualities.
5  See https://blackrainbow.org.au
6  See https://blaq.org.au

## References

Alizzi, A. (2014). Against authenticity CAL-connections: Queer Indigenous identities. *Overland*, 215, 30–36.

Alizzi, A. (2017). Becoming-with and together: Indigenous transgender and transcultural practices. *Artlink*, 37(2), 76–81.

Atkinson, J. (1990). Violence in Aboriginal Australia: Colonisation and gender. *Aboriginal and Islander Health Worker*, 14(2), 5–21. https://search.informit.com.au/documentSummary;dn=291270013921347;res=IELAPA

Atkinson, J. (2000). *Trauma trails, recreating song lines: The transgenerational effects of trauma in Indigenous Australia*. Spinifex Press.

Butler, D. (2022). Beloved Indigenous Elder Uncle Jack Charles passes away. NITV. www.sbs.com.au/nitv/article/beloved-elder-uncle-jack-charles-passes-away/i8ir2x3zg

Cain, B., & Sluga, G. (2000). *Gendering European history 1780–1920*. Leicester University Press.

Carlson, B. (2016a). *The politics of identity: Who counts as Aboriginal today?* Aboriginal Studies Press.

Carlson, B. (2016b). Striking the right chord: Indigenous people and the love of country. *AlterNative: An International Journal of Indigenous Peoples*, 12(5), 498–512.

Carlson, B. (2017, 27 April). Why are Indigenous people such avid users of social media? *The Guardian*. www.theguardian.com/commentisfree/2017/apr/27/why-are-indigenous-people-such-avid-users-of-social-media

Carlson, B., & Day, M. (2021). Love, hate and sovereign bodies: The exigencies of Aboriginal online dating. In A. Powell, A. Flynn, & L. Sugiura (Eds.), *The Palgrave handbook of gendered violence and technology* (pp.181–201). Palgrave Macmillan.

Carlson, B., Day, D., & Farrelly, T. (2021). What works? Exploring the literature on Aboriginal and Torres Strait Islander healing programs that respond to family violence. ANROWS. www.anrows.org.au/publication/what-works-exploring-the-literature-on-aboriginal-and-torres-strait-islander-healing-programs-that-respond-to-family-violence/

Darwin, C. (1859[2004]). *On the origin of species*. Routledge.

Day, M. (2020). Indigenist origins: Institutionalizing Indigenous queer and trans studies in Australia. *Transgender Studies Quarterly*, 7(3), 367–373.

Day, M. (2021). Remembering Lugones: The critical potential of heterosexualism for studies of so-called Australia. *Genealogy*, 5(3), 71.

Day, M., Bonson, D., Farrell, A., & Bakic, T. (2022). Aboriginal & Torres Strait Islander LGBTQISB+ people and the COVID-19 pandemic: A survey of impacts experienced as at mid-2021. Macquarie University. https://researchers.mq.edu.au/en/publications/aboriginal-amp-torres-strait-islander-lgbtqisb-people-and-the-cov

Department of Social Services. (2023, 13 January). Help inform Australia's first Aboriginal and Torres Strait Islander Action Plan to End Violence against Women and Children. www.dss.gov.au/about-the-department/news/65771

Driskill, Q. L., Justice, D. H., Miranda, D., & Tatonetti, L. (Eds.). (2011). *Sovereign erotics: A collection of two-spirit literature*. University of Arizona Press.

Dudgeon, P., Bonson, D., Cox, A., Georgatos, G., & Rouhani, L. (2015). *Sexuality & gender diverse populations roundtable report (Lesbian, gay, bisexual, transsexual, queer & intersex–LGBTQI)*. Aboriginal and Torres Strait Islander Suicide Prevention Evaluation Project. Healing Foundation.

Fara, P. (2004). *Sex, botany and empire: The story of Carl Linnaeus and Joseph Banks*. Icon Books.

Farrell, A. (2016). Lipstick clapsticks: A yarn and a Kiki with an Aboriginal drag queen. *AlterNative: An international journal of indigenous peoples, 12*(5), 574–585.

Farrell, A. (2022). *Indigenous LGBTIQ+ community online* [Unpublished doctoral dissertation]. Macquarie University.

Foucault, M. (1990). *The history of sexuality: An introduction* (vol. 1). (Trans. Robert Hurley, Trans.). Vintage.

Foucault, M. (2004). '*Society must be defended': Lectures at the Collège de France, 1975–1976*. Penguin.

Graham, M. (2014). Aboriginal notions of relationality ansd positionalism: A reply to Weber. *Global Discourse, 4*(1), 17–22.

Gregoire, P. (2020, 10 June). Veronica Baxter's death in custody: A trans woman neglected in a male prison. Sydney Criminal Lawyers. www.sydneycriminallawyers.com.au/blog/veronica-baxters-death-in-custody-a-trans-woman-neglected-in-a-male-prison/

Haraway, D. (1988). Situated knowledges: The science question in feminism and the privilege of partial perspective. *Feminist Studies, 14*(3), 575–599.

Hardy, D. (2015). *Bold: Stories from older lesbian, gay, bisexual, transgender and intersex people*. The Rag & Bone Man Press.

Hill, B. (2014). Searching for certainty in purity: Indigenous fundamentalism. *Nationalism and Ethnic Politics, 20*(1), 10–25.

Hill, B., Uink, B., Dodd, J., Bonson, D., Eades, A. M., & Bennett, S. (2021). *Breaking the Silence: Insights into the Lived Experiences of WA Aboriginal/LGBTIQ+ People: Community Summary Report 2021*. Kurongkurl Katitjin, Edith Cowan University.

Hill, L. A. (2020). The Proud Awards 2020: Aunty Vanessa Smith joins the Hall of Fame. Out in Perth. www.outinperth.com/the-proud-awards-2020-aunty-vanessa-honoured-in-hall-of-fame/

Katz, J. (2007). *The invention of heterosexuality*. University of Chicago Press.

Kwaymullina, A., & Kwaymullina, B. (2010). Learning to read the signs: Law in an indigenous reality. *Journal of Australian Studies, 34*(2), 195–208.

Lacquer, T. (1990). *Making sex*. Harvard University Press.

Langton, M. (1994). Aboriginal art and film: The politics of representation. *Race & class, 35*(4), 89–106.

Langton, M. (2008). Trapped in the Aboriginal reality show. *Griffith Review, 19*, 143–159.

Lugones, M. (2007). Heterosexualism and the colonial/modern gender system. *Hypatia, 22*(1), 186–219.

Moreton-Robinson, A. (1998). Witnessing whiteness in the wake of Wik. *Social Alternatives, 17*(2), 11–14.

Moreton-Robinson, A. (2000). *Talkin' up to the white woman: Indigenous women and feminism*. University of Queensland Press.

Moreton-Robinson, A. (2015). *The white possessive: Property, power, and indigenous sovereignty*. University of Minnesota Press.

Murray, C. 2019. *Lost daylight* [film]. Brisbane Indigenous Media Association.

Nakata, M. (2007). The cultural interface. *Australian Journal of Indigenous education, 36*(S1), 7–14.

O'Sullivan, S. (2021a). The colonial project of gender (and everything else). *Genealogy, 5*(3), 67–76.

O'Sullivan, S. (2021b). Saving lives: Mapping the power of LGBTIQ+ First Nations creative artists. *Social Inclusion, 9*(2), 61–64.

Parliament of Australia. (2022, 4 August). *Missing and Murdered First Nations Women and Children*. www.aph.gov.au/Parliamentary_Business/Committees/Senate/Legal_and_Constitutional_Affairs/FirstNationswomenchildren

Ross, S. (Curator) (2022). *Deadly|Solid|Staunch: A celebration of our First Nations LGBTQIA+ community*. Exhibition. Boomalli Aboriginal Artists Co-operative. 24 February 2022 to 9 April 2022.

Sims, D. (2022, September). *Bros* is a rom-com as entertaining as it is therapeutic. *The Atlantic*. www.theatlantic.com/culture/archive/2022/09/bros-romantic-comedy-billy-eichner-review/671602/

Stoler, N. (Director) (2022). *Bros* [film]. Apatow Productions.

Sullivan, C. (2020). Who holds the key? Negotiating gatekeepers, community politics, and the "right" to research in Indigenous spaces. *Geographical Research, 58*(4), 344–354.

Sullivan, C. T. (2018). Indigenous Australian women's colonial sexual intimacies: Positioning indigenous women's agency. *Culture, Health & Sexuality, 20*(4), 397–410.

Sullivan, C., Spurway, K., Briskman, L., Leha, J., Trewlynn, W., & Soldatic, K. (2021). *Dalarinji: 'Your story'—roadmap & report to community*. Western Sydney University.

Tatonetti, L. (2014). *The queerness of Native American literature*. University of Minnesota Press.

Tovey, N. (2011). *Little black bastard: A story of survival*. Hachette UK

Whittaker, A. (2016, August). Queerness and Indigenous cultures: One world, many lives. *Archer Magazine*. https://archermagazine.com.au/2016/08/queernessindigenous-cultures/

# 22

# FUTURE TWEED

## Envisioning the possibilities of Bundjalung Country, community and culture through speculative fiction

*Mykaela Saunders*

### Introduction to Goori[1] Futurism

From 2017 to 2021, I undertook a Doctor of Arts in creative writing at the University of Sydney. My thesis was titled *Goori Futurism: Envisioning the Sovereignty of Country, Community and Culture in the Tweed*. This thesis has two components: the creative component is a short story collection called ALWAYS WILL BE: Stories of Goori Sovereignty, from the Future(s) of the Tweed and the critical component is an exegesis in three parts. The overarching question that the whole thesis asks is: what might our Country, community and culture look like in a Future Tweed, given the reassertion of Goori sovereignty? ALWAYS WILL BE offers17 different answers to this question, and the exegesis considers the research and writing that led to the answers. The project initiates the Goori Futurism as a new genre of speculative fiction that envisions Goori sovereignty in various futures in the Tweed (Minjungbal-Nganduwal land, Bundjalung Country/far northern New South Wales), using Blackfella Futurism[2] themes and tropes. The project also articulates a philosophy and aesthetics of the genre and delineates its boundaries while resisting prescriptive genre protocols.

The stories in the collection ALWAYS WILL BE are tied together by politics, setting and genre: each of the stories in this collection explores different expressions of Goori Sovereignty; all of the stories are set in the Tweed, in different versions of the Future, with various climate scenarios, population dynamics and political structures; and each story responds to the prevailing themes and tropes within the Blackfella Futurism genre. ALWAYS WILL BE is a forward-thinking collection that refuses cynicism or despair, and instead offers original, entertaining stories that imagine more liberating paradigms, and that celebrate Goori ways of being, knowing and doing—and becoming.[3]

To imagine the variety of ways that Gooris might live after reasserting sovereignty, the short story collection is epic in scope and features a diverse cast of Goori characters, and explores their complex relationships inside and across Country, community and culture. Many of these worlds are *truly* postcolonial, and the local Goori community has reasserted sovereignty in different ways in each story—sometimes reclaiming Country, or exerting

DOI: 10.4324/9781003271802-25

full self-determination over our affairs, or by incorporating non-Indigenous people into our social networks—all while practising creative, sustainable and ancestrally approved ways of living with climate change. Some of the stories envision the lifeways of thriving, autonomous characters who embody sovereignty as a utopian ideal. Some stories also comment on community politics, such as lateral violence, belonging and exclusion, and notions of authenticity tied into relational politics, by exploring these present tensions in the future tense.

To create these stories, I devised The Goori Futurism Research Framework (see Figure 22.1), which is made up of three interdependent reading and writing frames: Politics: Goori Sovereignty, Setting: Future Tweed, and Genre: Blackfella Futurism. These frames are examples of both research-led practice and practice-led research. The research within these frames informs ALWAYS WILL BE, and the writing situates the stories in their worlds of politics, local knowledge production and spec fic respectively. This chapter will discuss the second frame, Future Tweed, in depth.

Before we go any further, it is important to locate myself so that you know where I belong, and to whom, so that we can move through this chapter relationally. I am a descendent of Dharug, Lebanese and Irish people, and I belong to the Tweed Goori community, which is Minjungbal/Nganduwal land and part of the broader Bundjalung nation, located on the colonial border of New South Wales and Queensland, on the eastern seaboard of the Australian continent.

Though I am not a Bundjalung descendant, I am Goori by acculturation. I grew up in the Tweed and I belong to the Goori community through my Bundjalung and South Sea Islander family and other relationships, having been involved in my community since I was young through learning and teaching, sports, disability support, research and community arts. Tweed Gooris are the people I belong to and the people who claim me. In this project I never claim to write or speak as a traditional Bundjalung owner, but as a lifelong and active part of my community, and my writing of place and people is based in my own lived experiences, from which my imaginings grow. All of my academic and creative work to date has been rooted in my community, which is where I come from and where I'll always return. My work will always be firmly situated in this grassroots community context, never

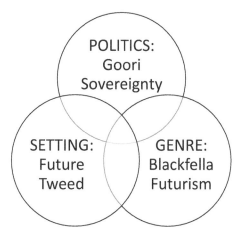

*Figure 22.1*  The Goori Futurism Research Framework.

in a generalised pan-Indigenous setting. My cultural responsibilities inform my ethical imperative to write Goori Futurism—to give hope to our jahjums (young children).

## The Goori Futurism Research Framework

The Goori Futurism Research Framework is a threefold methodological approach to creating this new genre of spec fic (speculative fiction). This research methodology is comprised of three separate but interrelated reading and writing frames. To guide my creative practice and research into creating Goori Futurism, and to feel out the parameters of the research frames, I devised three lines of questioning to pursue, each corresponding to one of the frames. For the Politics frame: Goori Sovereignty, I ask, given the reassertion of sovereignty, what might our countries, communities and cultures look like? For the Setting frame: Future Tweed, I ask, what could this look like for Goori people in Bundjalung Country, in the future, given different climate and population concerns? For the Genre frame: Blackfella Futurism, I ask, how might the Blackfella Futurism canon inform these situations?

Future Tweed will later be unpacked in-depth, but I'll briefly introduce each frame here together and in terms of their relationships to each other, to illustrate the overarching approach I've used for this project:

- The Politics frame: Goori Sovereignty uses the structure of a Goori world view to focus the needs of a sovereign Country, community and culture, and draws on sovereignty-focused literature to theorise these needs. The reading and writing in the Goori Sovereignty frame informs the philosophy and ethics of the stories, which situates them as grassroots politics.
- The Setting frame: Future Tweed draws on local Goori histories and lifeways, as well as projections for life on our planet, to imagine the localised future of Tweed's Country, community and culture. The reading and writing in the Future Tweed frame informs the climate considerations and social dynamics of the stories, which situates them as local knowledge production.
- The Genre frame: Blackfella Futurism studies the ways that our sovereign-minded texts write the future of Country, community and culture to extrapolate the genre conventions of the canon. The reading and writing in the Blackfella Futurism frame informs the conventions, themes and tropes of the stories, which situates them as spec fic.

The reading and writing in all three frames were examined through the lenses of Country, community and culture.[4] In this way, the three frames can stack on top of each other; for example, questions that arose for Country in one frame could be addressed by the other frames too. Conversely, if we focused first through Country, community and culture, the three research frames could stack on top of each other too (see Figure 22.2 and Figure 22.3).

This project has been both a research-led practice as well as practice-led research. My prior knowledge, or lack thereof, in each of the frames guided the reading and writing journey in different ways. Out of the three frames, I knew most about Goori Sovereignty, having grown up thinking and talking about it, and having taught and learnt about it over the last two decades. This frame was more practice-led than the others; I wrote my ideas out first, and afterwards I would read (or reread, more often than not) key texts to bolster

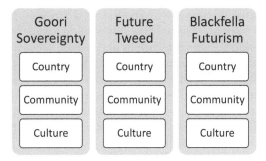

*Figure 22.2*   Goori Sovereignty, Future Tweed, Blackfella Futurism.

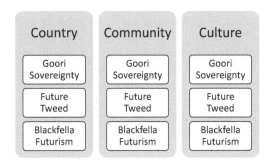

*Figure 22.3*   Country, Community, Culture.

and add nuance to what I'd written. Next, the Future Tweed frame was a mishmash of knowns and unknowns. I did know a lot about the Tweed, but I only knew something of its possible futures. I began with what I did know to pinpoint what I didn't know. In these two frames, my prior knowledge, borne from experience, fed the writing more than anything, which then determined the direction of the reading. The Blackfella Futurism frame was very different. It was the most research-led by far, as I had never written spec fic before, nor had I read most of the canon either, and so I read widely before attempting any writing. My reading informed the genre conventions, themes and tropes for my own writing.

Regardless of my prior knowledge or ignorance of each frame, the reading within each often inspired exploratory, generative writing, and vice versa. This was mostly a scaffolded and cyclical process, with my writing exposing gaps in what I needed to read, and then the reading generating ideas that turned into writing, and so on. There were not really any clear or linear ways through this process. It was a messy, sometimes frustrating but ultimately very rewarding exercise. I came to know Goori Futurism holistically by reading and writing about ideas in tandem rather than by treating reading and writing as separate activities, so I am not going to parse them out to discuss them that way.

With much of what I read and wrote I asked myself the following questions, and I used the answers as creative writing prompts: What does this idea say about Goori Sovereignty? What would this look like in my community, in a Future Tweed? What conventions from Blackfella Futurism could speak to this idea?

These were not isolated questions with individuated answers. For example, in identifying a type of Goori sovereignty, I asked how this would look in Tweed, in the future, and then I'd ask which Blackfella Futurism themes and tropes could best embody this sovereignty. In identifying Future Tweed scenarios, I asked: What are the opportunities for sovereignty in this future? What are the challenges? And then, what types of Blackfella Futurism has already engaged with these ideas—and how might I subvert or extend these ideas in a Tweed Bundjalung context? Finally, in identifying Blackfella Futurism themes and tropes, I asked: What kinds of sovereignty can I explore through this genre? And, how might these themes and tropes operate in a Bundjalung future?

When I had satisfying answers to these questions, to turn them into creative writing prompts, I'd then ask, what kinds of characters could embody or conflict with these storylines? These clusters of questions yielded many interesting lines of inquiry to pursue through world-building, which then allowed me to think about what kinds of characters might live in these worlds, and what storylines might emerge in their relationships with Country, community and culture.

In this way I generated ideas for stories from the reading, and I generated leads for reading from the stories. It would have been impossible to read everything in every field I studied, so I employed 'affective hermeneutics' as a guide—something I learned from Allanah Hunt (2019), Barkindji writer and scholar, and my co-panellist at the Science Fiction Research Association (SFRA) conference in Honolulu, in her paper from the conference. Anna Wilson (2016, para. 1.3) defines affective hermeneutics as "a set of ways of gaining knowledge through feeling". I've interpreted this as a hedonistic methodology that encourages the researcher to pursue leads based on what makes them feel good, or what excites them most.

The following section is not intended to be an exhaustive review of all the literature I read for the setting frame; rather, this section presents the literature that helped theorise the frame. In reading within the frame, and wherever possible, I always privileged the work of Aboriginal writers as good decolonial praxis. Where I've used non-Aboriginal works, I've selected them for the way that theory or argument gels well with Aboriginal world views and ways of knowing.

The following section maps my reading and writing within the frame Future Tweed. For this section, I will outline what I read and discovered in reading, and the writing that came from this, to theorise and think through the problems and opportunities in and of Country, community and culture in each frame.

## Setting frame: Future Tweed

Goori Futurism is specific in people, place and temporality. Goori Futurism stories can be set on any of the lands and communities that Gooris are from, in any version of the future that centres these peoples. In this case, my version is set in the Tweed.[5]

The Tweed, shortened from the Tweed Valley, is the north-eastern-most part of Bundjalung Country, named for the area of the language spoken by many smaller clan groups. Bundjalung Country mostly encompasses the northern rivers area of northern New South Wales, and extends over the state border into Queensland too—though it's important to remember that tribal borders were not hard lines that were policed or drawn on maps; rather, they consist of landmarks like hills, mountains and rivers that were mutually cared for by neighbouring nations. Neighbouring (and overlapping) language groups of

Bundjalung Country are: Yugembeh, which is the northern Bundjalung nation, covering the Kombumerri people's Gold Coast area; Yuggera, even further north on Meanjin/Brisbane; Ngarabal to the west, encompassing the Tenterfield area; and Gumbaynggirr to the south, from Yamba to Nambucca Heads, covering the Coffs Coast and inland. The Pacific Ocean borders Bundjalung Country to the east.

Goori Futurism is location specific, centring Goori peoples on Bundjalung Country. While a pan-Indigeneity may be politically useful for grassroots politics to connect across the continent and show solidarity under the 'one mob' banner, a pan-Indigenous story-telling erases local histories of struggle and triumph, which then flattens any uniqueness in present or future identities.[6]

As a setting that connects to future Goori places, and features future Goori peoples, it then follows that future Goori cultures must feature in any stories. Future Goori cultural themes would include the saltwater oceans, the freshwater rivers and the in-between estuaries, and feature activities such as fishing and swimming. A Future Tweed would also be concerned with current day over-development and gentrification, as well as complex issues of belonging and identity. This setting frame is built from research and knowledge about my community's past and present situations. I read and wrote into the same three main spheres as the other frames: Country, community and culture, though in the future. This helped generate ideas about what possible worlds could unfold.

To write about a place in the future, you need to know it in the now, but to know it now, you y need to understand its history. For this I largely drew on my lived experience of growing up in the Tweed, and my cultural knowledge, learnt from my family and other community people, especially Elders. I bolstered this prior knowledge by reading local literature to contextualise the now. I sought out stories that were rooted in Bundjalung Country, that could not have been set anywhere else because the place is not just setting but a character and consciousness too.

I had planned to use some of these local stories as frameworks or templates for plot points set in the future, but this didn't eventuate because I found that the futures I imagined yielded their own plots and problems. Despite these stories not contributing much to my own stories, it was still important to read other peoples' stories, especially the stories of traditional owners and people who have much longer ties to the community than myself. Reading a multi-gendered, multi-generational community of voices gave me a multi-perspectival view of the Tweed. This helped affirm what I already knew to be important for my characters by way of talking, relating, loving and fighting, and their ways of sorting things out. It also kept me grounded in my community's world view and cultural values.

There isn't too much Aboriginal fiction set in the Tweed in any time. *The Kadaitcha Sung*, by Sam Watson (1990), is set in multiple places and multiple realties, and one of these is present-day Fingal or Booningbah where the protagonist Tommy Gubba goes to stay (pp. 254–301). In his book chapter "Tales of Mystery and Imagination from the Tweed River: Shaping Historical-Consciousness", Philip Morrissey (2014) tells old stories he learnt from growing up along the Tweed River, some of which I already knew but some which I didn't. Looking further afield to other areas of Bundjalung nation uncovers some, such as Bundjalung Goorie author Melissa Lucashenko's *Mullumbimby* (2013) and *Too Much Lip* (2018), but they weren't very useful for this frame. Instead I drew on local Tweed history and memoir. The following literature supplemented my prior knowledge of community history and stories.

*Minjungbal: The Aborigines and Islanders of the Tweed Valley*, by Gail Finlay and Jolanda Nayutah (1988), is a text I have been reading since my high school Aboriginal Studies days. This slim but rich book offers research-based accounts of lives of Blackfellas of the Tweed Valley, which includes precolonial lifestyles, food, movement patterns, languages and activities (pp. 1–51). The book then discusses the ways that the community has adapted its lifeways through successive waves of colonisation and industry (pp. 52–75).

Another lovely book I consulted for inspiration, when thinking about the Tweed changing through time, is *An Aboriginal Elder Remembers 80 years*, by Tweed Goori Elder Aunty Kathleen Lena (2012). This is a retrospective of Aunty Kath's life, starting when she was born in 1928. Aunty Kath has lived through so many social changes, and she writes about her experiences of family, work, culture, education and the Tweed community at large. In *Wajehla Dubay—Women Speaking: Aboriginal Women's Essays, Stories and Poems*, eight local Goori women offer prose and poetry to paint a multi-perspective picture of Tweed in the 1990s, with some reminiscing on BC (Before Cook) times, and many old stories complement my knowledge of the Tweed from before I was born (Appo et al., 1997). Many of these stories feature water, which is a source of food, medicine, sport, leisure and pleasure, as well as language and art, and of course of spirituality and stories.

I also revisited my 2014 master's thesis, titled "Yarning with Minjungbal Women", which is a collaborative story-sharing project, authored by me but with significant input from five Goori women from the Tweed Minjungbal-Nganduwul community, who contributed anonymously for privacy reasons. Our combined meta-narrative explores transgenerational trauma as the result of past government policies, and the ways we spread strength and healing.[7] The thesis shares many past and recent stories of the Tweed, as well as anecdotes of community cohesion and conflict (Saunders, 2014, pp. 27–45). The stories these women shared with me—and not just for my thesis but through a lifetime of stories unconnected to my research—have always grounded my knowledge of how to be a good, community-minded person, which is a running theme in many of my stories.

When I switched from reading about the known to thinking about the unknown, I used the Tweed's old stories as a launching pad. I swung from the past into the future as if I were on a rope swing. As I swung from the past and passed over the present, the rope split off into multiple strands, each with a version of myself holding onto it. Each of these versions of myself jumped off her separate strands of rope and landed with a splash in a different version of the future—but all in the Tweed, in Bundjalung Country, though each future and each version of the Tweed were very different. Each version of myself walked around these new worlds, seeing and hearing and smelling and touching each iteration of what Bundjalung Country could become, give or take a few things. I learnt about each world's climate, population, the people, the politics and the stories that emerged from each world. From the comfort of the present, I tapped into each version of me in each version of the future, and from these exciting new future worlds I tapped back into me here and now, and communicated back to myself the stories that I learnt.[8] In this way my imagination, informed by reality, became a portal through which ideas from Country and community were able to emerge.

This might sound quite arcane but it is really very unexceptional. All my life, including recently, I've been part of community gatherings—festivals, celebrations, funerals, camps, cultural tours, education, surf meets, sports carnivals and meetings—and so I was able to observe my community interacting in real time, or else to mine my memories of these experiences, to imagine them in their sovereignty, in various futures, in various ways. I know the now of Tweed through living on Country and in community, through studying local histories and engaging with culture as much as a non-Bundjalung person has been able to. I used my knowledge of the now as a launching pad to project into the future. I mostly used my imagination to envision the unknowns of this frame, which has been hugely informed by my lifelong lived experiences, and from absorbing the news and ambient global anxieties about climate change. I used predictions for various climate and social scenarios and mapped them onto the Tweed, and I also drew parallels with other fictional worlds that dealt with similar scenarios, which I will discuss in the following sections, and, combined with generalised global predictions for future climates and populations, I was able to imagine many different futures for the Tweed while ensuring that the stories were anchored in the place and people, and that our unique local history, world views and lifestyles were embedded in the stories (IPCC, 2021).

I mostly engaged in more esoteric, experiential research to write within this frame. Whether I was physically there or far from home, I wrote by connecting with the Tweed, by asking Country and community about their futures. This involved walking and swimming in Bundjalung Country—either physically or imaginatively—and asking the place what it might be or may become, give or take a few things, and deep listening and feeling out the answers. This technique of deep listening to Country was taught to me by community people.[9] I would then write notes about whatever came to me.

## Future Country and climates of Tweed

In envisioning the future of Bundjalung Country, my mind first went to overdevelopment and gentrification, and how this impacts low-income Gooris not just in terms of land ownership and land rights but also rental increases. This included dreaming up ways to resist dispossession, and ways to return home even when it's hard to. With an ever-expanding Coolangatta city business district and new high-rises shooting up every year, the Tweed could soon look like Surfers Paradise, or Honolulu or Kuta, in no time.[10] This will cause significant problems for locals as the council approves more and more development but does not invest in the infrastructure to support a rapidly growing population, nor protect our plant and animal life, including in the waters. Humans are animals, too, and we need space and silence and the freedom to move. Unchecked development and expansion, and ecocide resulting from intensive industry would produce land, sea and sky pollution. With this taken to its logical conclusion, the Tweed could some day end up as a cyberpunk dystopia like Los Angeles in the *Blade Runner* films (Scott, 1982; Villeneuve, 2017), and in the book *Snow Crash* (Stephenson, 1993); the city is a crucible of disease and hotbed of crime in both worlds.

Various dystopian climate futures are possible—worlds of global warming, fires and floods, rising oceans, dizzying weather—but there are also creative opportunities within each of these climate change scenarios. Bushfires will become a more urgent issue with rising global temperatures, which, along with deforestation, dries the land, reducing rainfall and creating drought. A thinning ozone means extreme radiation, heatwaves and skin cancers. Traditional cultural burning practices may help mitigate some of the disastrous effects of bushfires, by managing fuel loads and the rates of consumption, and creating areas where bushfires won't be able to tear through and destroy (see Harney, (2014); "Chapter 5: Fire" (Pascoe, 2014), pp. 161–176; Steffenson (2020)). This won't have an effect of global temperatures but will instead be a local solution to the issue.

As a place of many waters, the Tweed is often flooded and affected by annual torrential rain, huge swell from cyclones off the coast, tidal surges and king tides. What is now seasonal rain could become unpredictable and more constant, like in Steven Amsterdam's (2009) story 'Dry Land' where the protagonist moves through a ceaselessly raining landscape. Cyclone season hits the coast annually, often around March, causing huge swell and pumping waves. This is the perennial delight of surfers. Waves are always packed with locals and tourists anyway, but more so in these times of pumping surf. Increased force and frequency of cyclones, and the heavy beating of the wind on the land could see a quickened depletion of topsoil and salination of the soil, which would mean failing crops in a place renowned for rich red soils and fertile farmland.

As Earth's ice caps melt, releasing more water into the ocean, the already rising seas are predicted to rise further. The cemetery at Fingal is already vulnerable to wild weather and is at risk of going underwater (Browning, 2017). Using Google maps, I drew what the Tweed might look like given the ocean rises one, two, three, four and five metres. At an at extreme sea-level rise, the islands off the Tweed coast would disappear and other places will become islands, or peninsulas. With riverbanks eroded, the Tweed River might start to chop and change direction like a mad cut snake. Creeks and streams might possibly become rivers, and rivers might become great lakes.

Other scenarios could arise that aren't necessarily linked to our current, realistic trajectory of global warming. For example, during the Covid-19 pandemic from 2020 to 2021, the Queensland-New South Wales state border, which was never a physical boundary, became a hard border, patrolled by cops checking the documents of people trying to cross. This border softened and hardened on and off over the next few years, depending on each state's restrictions. This got me thinking about a version of Tweed that is walled off by a permanent hard border. How would the Tweed culture grow and change inside a siloed-off town? Unlikely, though never impossible, I imagined what would happen if Wollumbin awakened. The sacred mountain is the caldera of an ancient volcano; the entire Tweed Valley is its crater. Wollumbin is a rainmaker and creator of Tweed's spectacular storms. Water mining, the act of siphoning the mountain for bottled water, could disturb the sleeping giant (Tweed Water Alliance Inc.) Also, fracking for gas is known to cause earthquakes, which could mean trouble in the cauldron of the Tweed Valley.[11]

Even less likely, but fun to think about, was a frozen Tweed. After reading Ursula K Le Guin's sci fi novel *Left Hand of Darkness* (1969), and watching Bong Joon-ho's sci fi film *Snowpiercer* (2013), I wondered what the Tweed might look like under snow, perhaps as a result of interference from geoengineering. With the Tweed's hills and mountains covered in snow, it could become a snowboarder's paradise. I imagined the Tweed's surfing culture translating into a snowboarding one, and seasonal beach tourism booms transferring over to snow seasons.

Despite the mostly grim prospects and predictions for climate, I also forced myself to imagine positive climate futures and utopian worlds of sustainability, afforded by the rest and regeneration of seasonal lifeways. In *Minjungbal*, Gail Finlay and Jolandah Nayutah provide visual and written accounts of what an undeveloped Tweed might look like (1988, pp. 2–51). I loved looking at these and other old photos of past Bundjalung Country. Could the Tweed ever be that green again? Even later photos of the Tweed were helpful aids, all the way from the beginning of farming, clearing and deforestation, and then the rapid twentieth-century development of the area through real estate grabs (Nayutah & Finlay,

1988, p. 53). Bill Gammage's *Biggest Estate on Earth* (2011) also helped me imagine what a big 'Tweed estate' could look like, rewilded.

I was a little inspired by the ethos of the solarpunk and hopepunk genres, which grew out of the previously mentioned cyberpunk; the former two use clean energy and human ingenuity to dream up more utopian cities than the latter. I was also encouraged by the real-world mass climate mobilisations of recent years. Protests and direct action may yet bring the world back from the brink of disaster. Millions of trees could be planted; we could mandate a tree-to-human ratio, ensuring that most of these are native species, to encourage the return of totemic wildlife. There could be a halt on overdevelopment, a limit on high-rises and sprawl, and the Tweed could be powered with solar and wind. Sugarcane fields and Western-style farms could be commandeered to grow native foods and attract native animals. Many clever examples of agriculture and aquaculture inspired my world-building and writing in this frame (see Diamond, 2005)and Pascoe, 2014).

### Future community and demographics of Tweed

Writing about a future Goori community meant thinking about the demographics of the wider society, too, and the social structures that exist today, and how these might change. At the 2016 census, Aboriginal and Torres Strait Islander people made up 4 per cent of the Tweed's population (Australian Bureau of Statistics, 2016). This is a slightly higher number than the national average of 2.8, and reflects the reality that in a regional area like Tweed with its population of 91,371, we all live pretty well side by side (Australian Bureau of Statistics, 2016). Lots of Gooris have white family and vice versa. Sam Watson must have seen this, too; in *The Kadaitcha Sung*, there are white hippies who live in good spirits with the Blackfellas at Fingal, unlike the social dynamics in the dystopian Meanjin/Brisbane (Watson, 1990).

There are countless ways that current population dynamics could transform in the future. One possibility is that the Goori population could shrink while the other expands, rendering us a minority on par with the national ratio or worse. As more and more people are moving to the Tweed each year, this pushes property prices up and pushes poorer people out, so this isn't so far-fetched. If non-Indigenous society goes on like this, we'd have to keep up by having more kids or adopting more people into our families; otherwise, the Tweed could turn into a white supremacist dog-eat-dog dystopian climate future like in the *Mad Max* franchise (Miller, 2015), where our extinction goes hand in hand with eco-cide.[12] Knowing my people, though, we'd never roll over and give up, or die out, though we'd likely become more invisible to white society, and have to fight harder for our rights. Sovereignty would then be conditional, as we'd probably exist in small pockets in parts of the Tweed.

Ecofascist thought holds that a good plague will solve the anthropocentric environmental crises, perhaps not knowing that we've already survived one.[13] In 1789, a smallpox pandemic broke out in Dharug Country, in Sydney, one year after the First Fleet arrived. The disease spread faster than the colonists did, owing to the interconnectivity of communities across the continent. It is estimated that in some communities, up to 90 per cent of our people died from smallpox and other diseases (Warren, 2014).

At the beginning of Australia's Covid-19 pandemic in March 2020, although the Tweed was barely affected by the virus itself, it got me thinking about how a disease might run through our town. Would our people be decimated? Historically, we've been laid low by disease. Nayutah and Finlay say that "before 1890, smallpox, dysentery, diarrhoea, venereal diseases, measles, and the common cold killed more Aborigines than white man's guns did" (1988, p. 52). However, thanks to our strong community-controlled health organisations Bugulwena, Krurungal and Kalwun, programmes and vaccination awareness would keep our community healthy and safer than the rest of the population, many of whom are anti-vaxxers (Lovejoy, 2021). This could allow a smaller population to start afresh, similar to the 'cosy catastrophe' of Stephen King's (1991) sci fi fantasy novel *The Stand*.

Another scenario is that our population could increase so much that the Tweed could be solely or mostly Blackfellas, either through our higher fertility or a mass exodus of non-Indigenous people. To my mind, the most likely way this could happen is that, through cross-cultural relationships and deepening community connections, the distinctions between Blackfella and whitefella would become so blurred as to become useless—or, put another way, whitefellas eventually become absorbed into our families and our ways. With the Tweed as majority Blackfellas, sovereignty could ideally be full and immediate for place and for people, dismantling white supremacy and whiteness in positions of power.

As mentioned earlier, the Tweed is not very culturally diverse, and the overculture is dominantly white Australian (Australian Bureau of Statistics, 2016). Whether Gooris and non-Gooris segregate from each other, by force or by choice, or whether we all remain integrated, we could all open up to welcome other cultural groups and become more multi-cultural. Whatever the population ratios and demographics, I suspect, if neoliberal late capital doesn't die, rich people will form gated communities in all the best real estate, the hills and headlands near the beaches. This often happens in dystopian fiction such as *Snow Crash* (Stephenson, 1993).

## Future culture and lifestyles of Tweed

For future lifestyles, I wrote about how different scenarios of people and place might combine in various way to create new situations that stay true to local lifeways. The Tweed always was and always will be, a water place, no matter the kinds of futures that come about, and surfing, paddleboarding, kayaking, fishing, swimming and not-yet-invented sports will be just as important as they are now. A new local annual gathering is the Jurakai Surf Culture Festival, along with the Mullet Festival, which has ancient roots; both festivals celebrate surfing and fishing respectively in a cultural way. Along with these and other newer festivals like the previously mentioned Kinship Festival that grew out of Kids Caring for Country, Tweed Goori mob have always participated in various communal celebrations, in myriad incarnations. A Bunya Festival, for example, was traditionally held every three or so years whenever there was a bumper crop of the fatty, protein-rich football-sized bunya tree nuts in what is known as the Bunya Mountains in Queensland's South Burnett region. Wakka Wakka and Kabi Kabi peoples invited all other related groups who shared the Bunya songline—the northern Gureng Gureng, the southern Yuggera and Bundjalung, the western Barranggam—as well as many other guests from further afield, to partake in the bunya nut bounty, and to share technology and information, to settle grievances, plan ahead and marry up, as well as dance, teach culture, gossip and see family.[14] This ancient festival has seen a revival in recent years thanks to Kabi Kabi Elder Aunty Beverly Hand, who was inspired by the spirit of the ancient festival in initiating the inaugural Bunya Dreaming Festival on the Sunshine Coast in 2007, which has continued up until

2019, before Covid-19 restrictions paused the gathering from 2020 (Kinninment, 2019). It's exciting to think how far into the future this, and newer festivals, could continue.

Various political paradigms are possible in the future—dependent on the ways Country and community change, and how they interact with each other. Many kinds of catastrophes are possible—plagues, fires, floods, colonisation—and the societies that emerge would depend on the scale of catastrophe, how many people are left and who they are, and what skills they have. Society could be a mix of both, or somewhere in between utopia and dystopia if wealth were not evenly distributed, just like now. A Goori utopia would see Goori control of affairs, and this could read as a dystopia for people who live in ways that are incompatible to ours. Conversely, a Goori dystopia would see us without much control over our destiny; this was certainly true in the past and it is still true for many aspects of life now. For example, overdevelopment, the destruction of sacred sites and welfare's interference in families could be considered dystopian storylines in fiction, but many Gooris are living through these circumstances in the here and now.

## Conclusion

We've now considered what different Future Tweeds could look like in terms of climate, demographics and lifestyles. We've looked at the texts I used to theorise the Future Tweed frame, and the ways the readings helped me understand the spheres of Country, community and culture. We've also looked at some of the ideas that came from the readings that sparked exploratory writing. Here at the end of this chapter, the time and place where the separated strands of rope come back together, I'll conclude with some thoughts about the significance of Goori Futurism and a reflection on this chapter.

The stories in ALWAYS WILL BE are so far the only local stories that explore our futures, and the project as a whole is the first of its kind that centres my community in the Tweed. The research I conducted is an addition to the field of research about Bundjalung Country, community and culture, especially in the future, and it adds to local knowledge produced by Goori academics. I intend to further develop Goori Futurism in ongoing creative and critical work, and it's my hope that it continues to expand through the contributions of other Gooris.

The project is a substantial contribution to both Indigenous spec fic and to its scholarship. The Goori Futurism Research Framework is the first to articulate a holistic reading and writing methodology in this way, and the thesis maps out the process of transfiguring academic research into creative practice and has produced an original short story collection, one of a small number of Aboriginal-written spec fic works that imagines our sovereignty in the future. This expands the fields of Blackfella Futurism and, by extension, Indigenous Futurism, while at the same time as carving out a brand-new niche of Goori Futurism.

## Notes

1 Goori is the demonym used by the Bundjalung and Gumbaynggirr peoples (northern New South Wales) and the Yugembeh, Kombumberri and Quandamooka peoples (South East Queensland).
2 I have theorised Blackfella futurism as a genre of a sovereign-minded speculative fiction. In addition to being authored by an Aboriginal and/or Torres Strait Islander writer and set in the future, Blackfella futurism stories must feature at least one identifiably Aboriginal and/or Torres Strait Islander protagonist who is not the last of their race.

3  This framework adapted from the work of Veronica Arbon (2008)
4  The structure of 'Country, community and culture' is informed by my lived experience of Goori lifeways. It is a framework I first used in my 2012–2014 master's research thesis *Yarning with Minjungbal Women*. In this thesis I explored transgenerational trauma through relationships with Country and culture, community, and family (2014, pp. v–vi). I class community as the human relational sphere; all other non-human relationships come under Country.
5  Some prefer the spelling 'Goorie'.
6  'One Mob' is a grassroots slogan that embraces all 500 plus Aboriginal and Torres Strait Islander peoples together as one, expresses solidarity with each other, and acknowledges a common experience under colonisation.
7  A foundation text for my research was Yiman and Bundjalung scholar Judy Atkinson's ground-breaking book *Trauma trails: Recreating songlines: The transgenerational effects of trauma in Indigenous Australia* (2002).
8  This metaphor comes from an artist talk I gave in November 2020, 'Piss and Vinegar, an Autotheory'.
9  Miriam-Rose Ungunmerr (1988) famously articulated this practice as *dadirri*.
10  Coolangatta is just over the state border, so it's in Queensland, but it always was and always will be Bundjalung Country, and so it's also part of the Tweed. I visited Honolulu, Hawaii, and Kuta, Indonesia, during my degree, and both places influenced the stories.
11  This seems unlikely as the Tweed Shire Council voted to be Coal Seam Gas Free in 2014.
12  I think about this world as neoliberalism's logical conclusion.
13  Ecofascism typically looks to totalitarian government to solve environmental issues. One contemporary ecofascist rallying point that reflects the movement's origins in German Nazi fascism (which was also preoccupied with eugenics), is the myth that overpopulation is the cause of the environmental crisis. However, this is often a Malthusian excuse to vilify nations of the global south and the working poor of wealthier nations, as research shows that the top 5 per cent of wealth is responsible for around 80 per cent of global warming and pollution. For a thorough explanation of this and other ecofascist talking points and their refutations, see (Thomas & Gosink, 2021) For a history of eco-fascism in Australia, see (Fleming, 2021).
14  Songlines are tracks that have specific songs attached to them. These are both sung and walked on the land, and are also mapped onto the sky. Songlines criss-crossed this entire continent and many were shared by different language groups. In this way they are the oldest continuing transnational literatures. For more on how songlines function mnemonically, see 'Chapter 3: Memory spaces in a modern world' (Kelly, 2016, pp. 64–79).

# References

Amsterdam, S. (2009). *Things we didn't see coming*. Sleepers Publishing.

Appo, J., Bekue, S., Brown, M., Chisholm, M., Currie, D., Harris, J.,... & Summers, J. (1997). *Wajehla Dubay–women speaking: Aboriginal women's essays, stories and poems*. Keeaira Press.

Arbon, V. (2008). *Arlathirnda Ngurkarnda Ityirnda: Being-Knowing-Doing: De-Colonising Indigenous tertiary education*. Post Pressed.

Atkinson, J. (2002). *Trauma trails, recreating song lines*. Spinifex Press.

Australian Bureau of Statistics. (2016). *Australia | New South Wales | Local Government Areas: Tweed (A)*. quickstats.censusdata.abs.gov.au/census_services/getproduct/census/2016/quickstat/LGA17550

Browning, D. (2017, 27 June). Erosion from tides and human intervention threaten historic beach cemetery at Fingal Head. *ABC News*. www.abc.net.au/news/2017-06-27/abc-rn-daniel-browning-takes-the-road-back-home-to-fingal/8364704

Diamond, J. (2005). *Collapse: How societies choose to fail or survive*. Penguin.

Fleming, A. (2021, Jun e). The meanings of eco-fascism. *Overland Literary Journal*. overland.org.au/2021/06/the-meanings-of-eco-fascism

Gammage, B. (2011). *The biggest estate on earth: How Aborigines made Australia*. Allen & Unwin.

Harney, B. (2014). Burning off: Fire law. *Yubulyawan Dreaming Project: Preserving Australian cultural heritage*. Yubulyawan Dreaming Project.

Hunt, A. (2019, 21 June). *We write down made-up stories to tell the truths we wish we could say out loud: Utilising popular culture in Aboriginal literature.* Paper presented at the Facing the Future, Facing the Past: Colonialism, Indigeneity, and SF, Chaminade University, Honolulu, Hawaii.

Intergovernmental Panel on Climate Change (IPCC). (2021). *Summary for Policymakers, Contribution of Working Group I to the Sixth Assessment Report of the Intergovernmental Panel on Climate Change.* www.ipcc.ch/report/ar6/wg1/downloads/report/IPCC_AR6_WGI_Full_Report_smaller.pdf

Joon-ho, B., dir. (2013). *Snowpiercer.* Moho Film.

Kelly, L. (2016). *The Memory Code: The traditional Aboriginal memory technique that unlocks the secrets of Stonehenge, Easter Island and monuments the world over.* Allen & Unwin.

King, S. (1991). *The stand.* Hodder and Stoughton.

Kinninment, M. (2019, 25 February). Ancient Aboriginal tradition celebrating football-sized bunya gets revival in Queensland. ABC News. www.abc.net.au/news/2019-02-25/aboriginal-bunya-dreaming-festival-revived-in-queensland/10806994

Le Guin, U. K. (1969). *The left hand of darkness.* Ace Books.

Lena, K. (2012). *My life: An Aboriginal elder remembers 80 years.* Keeaira Press.

Lovejoy, H. (2021, 1 October). Tweed Heads freedom protest draws big crowd. *The Echo.* www.echo.net.au/2021/10/tweed-heads-freedom-protest-draws-big-crowd/

Lucashenko, M. (2013). *Mullumbimby.* University of Queensland Press.

Lucashenko, M. (2018). *Too much lip.* University of Queensland Press.

Miller, G., dir. (2015). *Mad Max: Fury road.* Village Roadshow Pictures (Australia), Warner Bros. Pictures (International).

Morrissey, P. (2014). Tales of mystery and imagination from the Tweed River: Shaping historical-consciousness. In V. Castejon, A. Cole, O. Haag, & K. Hughes (Eds.), *In turn in turn: Ego-histoire, Europe and Indigenous Australia* (pp. 271–280). ANU Press.

Nayutah, J., & Finlay, G. (1988). *Minjungbal: The Aborigines and islanders of the Tweed Valley.* North Coast Institute for Aboriginal Community Education.

Pascoe, B. (2014). *Dark Emu: Black seeds: Agriculture or accident?* Magabala Books.

Saunders, M. (2014). *Yarning with Minjungbal Women: Testimonial narratives of transgenerational trauma and healing explored through relationships with country and culture, community and family.* [Unpublished master's thesis]. University of Sydney. https://ses.library.usyd.edu.au/handle/2123/13059

Scott, R., dir. (1982). *Blade runner.* Warner Bros.

Steffensen, V. (2020). *Fire country: How Indigenous fire management could help save Australia.* Hardie Grant.

Stephenson, N. (1993). *Snow crash.* Penguin.

Thomas, C., & Gosink, E. (2021). At the intersection of eco-crises, eco-anxiety, and political turbulence: A primer on twenty-first century ecofascism. *Perspectives on Global Development and Technology, 20*(1–2), 30–54.

Tweed Water Alliance Inc. Stop Water Mining. https://tweedwateralliance.org

Ungunmerr, M.-R. (1988). Dadirri—inner deep listening and quiet still awareness: A reflection by Miriam-Rose Ungunmerr. *Miriam Rose Foundation.* www.miriamrosefoundation.org.au/dadirri/

Villeneuve, D., dir. (2017). *Blade Runner 2049.* Warner Bros. Pictures (North America) and Sony Pictures Releasing (International).

Warren, C. (2014, 16 April). Was Sydney's smallpox outbreak of 1789 an act of biological warfare against Aboriginal tribes? ABC Radio National. www.abc.net.au/radionational/programs/ockhamsrazor/was-sydneys-smallpox-outbreak-an-act-of-biological-warfare/5395050

Watson, S. (1990). *The Kadaitcha sung.* Penguin.

Wilson, A. (2016). The role of affect in fan fiction. In I. Willis (Ed.), *The classical canon and/as transformative work* (Vol. 21). Transformative Works and Cultures.

# 23

# THE MUSEUM OF THE IMAGINATION

## Curating against the colonial insistence on diminishing Indigeneity

*Sandy O'Sullivan*

### Changing museums

Museums are dangerous places for Indigenous people. To understand why museums or other places that display the cultures of others within the container of colonialism are even relevant to a discussion on agency and our futures, we must understand the work that Indigenous peoples have done to challenge colonialism through the lens of the museum collection. For centuries, colonial collecting spaces have kept, studied and displayed the stolen bodies of our ancestors (Fforde et al., 2022; Ormand-Parker et al., 2020; O'Sullivan, 2016). Many museums have insisted on ownership of the bodies brought into their collections, as central to science and inquiry (Aranui, 2020). They have frequently required lengthy negotiations to effect repatriation or the return of ancestral remains, an extraordinary requirement for stolen bodies (Aranui, 2020; Clegg & David, 2020; Janke, 2019; O'Sullivan, 2016, 2021; Turnbull, 2020). In recent decades, the work of Indigenous practitioners challenging these 'rights', in some cases through the public shaming of museums, has resulted in the return of too few of our ancestors (Tapsell, 2020). Though frequently the return of ancestral bodies is framed as a 'gift', the tide of change has been wrought by Indigenous people naming these barbaric practices and asserting our own complex beliefs and ideas around the treatment of our ancestors (Knapman & Fforde, 2020; O'Sullivan, 2016). At the centre of these negotiations is agency and an insistent voice from Indigenous actors who have insisted on our rights, as well as on the responsibilities of the colonial museum. Across this chapter it will be argued that the literal voice of Indigenous people has worked to mitigate a diminishing view of the past by holding firm complex ideas of who we are. Insisting on the complexity of why our different communities resist being held in museum collections seems rudimentary, but insisting on a negotiation of our place—if any—in the violence of a museum requires more than a negotiation across the bad faith acts of the past. It requires understanding why we continue to allow a presence in the contemporary museum space at all.

DOI: 10.4324/9781003271802-26

## Our voices

From 2010 to 2017, I was funded by the Australian Research Council to examine the representation and engagement of First Nations' peoples in nationally significant museum spaces. With the underpinning knowledge that the bodies and objects belonging to Indigenous people had not only been held in many of these collections without permission, but also that meaningful interpretation was often outside of the scope of the museum, the project sought to examine ways that greater agency had been adopted by asking a single question of that complex negotiation: what works? (O'Sullivan, 2016).

When I began this research to explore the capacity of national museum spaces to interpret and represent First Nations peoples and communities, several key findings quickly emerged. The research focused on three countries: the United States of America, Australia and the United Kingdom, all with vastly different systems and approaches to museum management, display and engagement. Each colonial nation had an identifiable formal or informal system endorsed, to some extent, by each government. These networks and spaces, along with museums and 'keeping places' fill the gaps in these networks, and all contributed to this study that in the end included 470 museums and sites of exhibition. The starting point was a single question: 'what works' in their representation and engagement of First Nations' peoples? If the expectations at the beginning of the study were that there would be an administrative focus on income and visitor numbers, or even on reported satisfaction from Indigenous communities, a decade and 470 museums into the study, a more complex set of characteristics formed the measurement of 'what worked'. Even so, a single measure was frequently reported as a solution to this complex problem of how to see the museum as a site of worthy of engagement by Indigenous peoples and communities. That measure was, unsurprisingly, our participation at all levels, not just in consultation but in design. Indigenous museum directors, curators, education leaders and interpreters, all engaged in community consultation, would result in better outcomes while ensuring a level of accountability missing from museums of the past. This message was consistent.

The general approach in the study was a combination of heuristic analysis of the space, through exhibition, and the history of the institution and the landscape in which it operates provided the comparative backdrop to each of the museums reviewed. The second stage of the process focused on discussions with representatives of these museums, to ask the central question of what works and what is effective in the representation of communities they engage with. The obvious museum spaces in each country included, for example, the two museums of the National Museum of the American Indian (NMAI) located in Washington, DC, and New York as well as significant Tribal museums; the National Museum of Australia (NMA) and state museums throughout Australia; and in the United Kingdom the museums of the National Museum Wales, National Museums Scotland, and significant museums in England, where no formal single system exists. At this stage, any reader would be pondering why the United Kingdom is included in a study on First Nations' peoples that focuses on own-community representation. Later in the chapter this is explored, with some findings that speak to agency and a revelation around 'voice'.

Conversations with staff at the NMAI were an important starting point for collections that span Turtle Island, a landmass that has been claimed colonially as 'North America'. Both the Washington, DC, and New York sites of the NMAI museum sit within the US government-funded Smithsonian Institute. It is important to identify that the NMAI buildings and initial operations were co-funded by several Tribal governments, designed and managed by Indigenous peoples, and that because of these arrangements, the NMAI has a role both within the colonial government and a responsibility to those who have entrusted it with their cultural and actual investments (Cobb, 2005). This relationship continues to provide both a link and a set of accountabilities between these museums, government institutions, Tribal museums, and other Nations throughout the Americas and the Pacific, framed by the NMAI as the 'Western Hemisphere' (Atalay, 2006). The differences between these national spaces that saw themselves as overarching, and Tribal museums that held a more complex and direct accountability, were also a part of the landscape of study (O'Sullivan, 2016). As this research focused on the location of an Indigenous voice in the space, the NMAI provided a model for the literal location of a voice, with the presence of Indigenous cultural interpreters who continue to provide a personal and institutional perspective on the galleries and building of the NMAI. Similarly, the media teams at the NMAI, often including people from the area being represented, have managed to incorporate stories and ideas through video, audio and interactive processes that support material culture displays, that attempt to focus the museums of the NMAI on community-told story, with museum objects incorporated to assist a first-person cultural story being told (Smith, 2020). Overwhelmingly, the ways in which Indigenous curators have been central to exhibition development was pointed to as a substantial act of accountability, but also a site of literal contestation as the voice was relocated into this space. Both Indigenous cultural interpreters at the NMAI and Indigenous curators have moved beyond the frequently distanced representation of non-Indigenous people describing the 'othered' Indigene, by being both present and by articulating their relationship to the community represented (Smith, 2020).

In Australia, the Gallery of First Australians in the National Museum of Australia, and particular exemplars of representation in state museums such as Bunjilaka—not only a museum space but also an Aboriginal Cultural Centre, located within Melbourne Museum—have been developed over the last decade by moving from curatorial and management control of settler curators, to local Indigenous engagement and curatorship (Witcomb, 2014). Without this engagement, the possibility of the literal voice becomes distanced. Throughout the project, museum professionals, both Indigenous and settler, insisted that it was only through the lens of Indigenous oversight that changes could occur in the museum space. One of the strengths of the incorporation of the literal voice has been the capacity for new media forms to be used to reassert our rights in these literal spaces of our ancestors. At Bunjilaka, we see the story of Bunjil, the great creator, as a local and engaged story that is endorsed by not only Community but also the substantial Elders group that manages Bunjilaka.

National and state-based museums matter in this landscape because as colonised people, these sites of management have often not only held substantial Indigenous collections, but have also provided a settler-nation state voice to how the broader community understands Indigenous people. The complexity of this voice has often been lost, but when our literal voices are present in the space, this complexity is—as Paul Chaat Smith—frames it, undeniable (Smith, 2020).

There were many other museums that added to the research project. Museums with significant collections such as the Eiteljorg Museum of American Indians and Western Art and Chicago's Field Museum were included, with a note that many of these museums have extensive relationships with the NMAI and Tribal museums, hosting their touring exhibitions as a measure to share both cost and purpose. For this reason, changes to one of these sites can

338

create opportunity for change across the nation. This research focused on two projects that acted to provide a complex voice while also creating opportunities for extension to how others might view the worlds of Indigenous peoples: *IndiVisible: African-Native American Lives in the Americas* (NMAI, 2010), which also prompted a response from the Eiteljorg Museum with *Red/Black: Related through History* (Eiteljorg, 2010) and exhibitions that focus on the multiethnic Native communities of the US of people who share both an African American and a Native American history, and *Native Words/Native Warriors*, a project on Navajo code talkers of World War II (NMAI, 2009). In addition to the role that this touring strategy contributes to challenging tropes of identity and participation, it is also significant that these exhibitions expand their scope of display. It was not only Indigenous but also Black/African American museums that were on the touring schedule for *IndiVisible: Native Words/Native Warriors*, on Indigenous languages that operated as codification within the military in World War II, which also saw display at military museums. Where Native communities are often cast in opposition—even if sympathetically—they instead become a part of the dominant story with a further reminder about the great number of Native Americans who have served in the US military. This complexity interrogates the ways in which Indigenous people have been traditionally framed, by following individual and specific stories of people and their families. In doing so, it challenges pan-Indigenising tropes and ideas and creates strategies for First Nations people to tell the stories that matter to them (O'Sullivan, 2021; Carlson, 2016; Carlson, 2013, Kovach et al., 2013).

## The United Kingdom and the problem of 'voice'

In understanding why the literal voice does so much heavy lifting in representing who we are in the museum space, we must consider the way in which that voice has always been present in museums. Bennett (1995, p.19) contends that the European museum was never framed outside of culture, but instead began to provide a testing ground for the development of a bourgeoisie, to provide both a voice and a space of inquiry. The museum visitor's voice was present and required. Rather than engaging in an excluding European middle class engaged in a curiosity that contained the colonial world, could it now be shaped by the demands of an increasingly diverse audience? How could the museum follow and adapt to an audience, working against the construct of an institution that simply reproduces its own historical ideals of 'othered' representation? The willingness and capacity to assess that engagement, is at the core of requesting participating museums to identify their own perceptions of success in their representation of, and engagement with, First Nations peoples. It requires them to face their own journeys of representation and determine what success means for their institution, and why it matters. If Bennet is correct, and audience always dictates demands, who is the audience that demands Indigenous complexity, and how can they be heard?

In the context of colonial incursion and retrieval of our literal bodies and the objects of culture that frame our past, there has been a consistent message that the colonial museum needs to make reparation. But how—and why—do we continue to engage in these spaces? By considering Vizenor's (1999) theory of Indigenous survivance, where all understandings of our past are intangibly connected to our present and irrevocably to our future, we know that it is not only through return and repatriation, important as this project is, but it is also through our insistence that if our story is told, we are the ones to tell it. Pan-Indigenising who we are as peoples, has been a mechanism of colonialism that has allowed us to be categorised and reduced by others. To insist on our complexities is central to understanding that we are not only defined by our relationship to these colonial structures, but that the colonial is not all that matters in that landscape. It also suggests a far more overarching concern: for any group to do work that diminishes or reduces who any group are as a people, they very likely did not begin with a distanced colonial project. This theory was then played out across this project as I interrogated the ways in which the United Kingdom had understood its own people, an undertaking that began with a request from an Indigenous Elder.

In the early stages of the project, it was clear I would need to spend time examining museums in Australia and the United States of America, two sites with hundreds of First Nations' communities that shared at least some facets of colonisation and colonial control (O'Sullivan, 2016). In order to ensure community involvement and, hopefully, endorsement back in so-called Australia, I had a number of focus groups that included Indigenous Elders, to set scope and ask for suggestions. At one such event, an Elder contacted me after the event and asked if I was looking at the UK, because "you can tell a lot about how they represent us, by how they tell their own story" (O'Sullivan, 2021). I have written extensively about this inclusion and the resistance from multiple museums, including the concern from British museum professionals that this would engage a racist idea of 'Indigenous Britain' and an overarching concern that Indigeneity was not something discussed seriously in the UK. Importantly, the two findings this delivered validated the Elder's inquiry and framed a better understanding of the way that voice has not only been used consistently across the European museum since the 1700s, but also the ways in which that voice has shaped their attitude to colonisation.

When I began my research in the UK, I started with the National Museums Scotland, specifically with the Scotland Galleries of the National Museum of Scotland (NMoS) in Edinburgh. A site that uses chronology to tell the story of Scotland, the Galleries, at their base, use the term 'we' to describe their ancestors, and in more contemporary galleries, for example, Modern Scotland, they discuss identity, resistance and Scottishness. The Galleries are also an inclusive space, incorporating the diaspora that has called Scotland home in the last few hundred years, at the same time as talking about a more ancient people. It seemed very like the experience of visiting the Mashantucket Pequot Museum in Connecticut, one of the largest Indigenous museums in the world, and one that, through a combination of social history and natural history approaches, tells the story of the land, the story of the Tribe, and the story of their place in the world (Kasper & Handsman, 2015). In this way, the Scotland Galleries seemed to use some of the markers of an Indigenous gallery.

Although this question of 'First Peoples' was more difficult for English museums, when I used examples from Scotland, Wales and Northern Ireland, many of the museum professionals across English museums recognised that this was not as difficult for them to understand. It perhaps raises an important question, even with the successful inclusion of Wales and Scotland, of how the United Kingdom can possibly be included in this study. Does it show representation? Yes, but for the United States and Australia, while contested within the space of identity and Indigenous nation formation and rights, they are recognised internationally as having an Indigenous peoples that continue to be present and sovereign to this day. Their recognition exists under the United Nations Permanent Forum on Indigenous Issues (UNPFII), and it is perhaps this particular means of identifying Indigenous communities that holds dominant nations from understanding their own

Indigenous identity as something definable. The markers of Indigeneity that the UNPFII uses set one of the markers as "Form(ing) non-dominant groups of society" (UNPFII, 2007, p. 7). Can a dominant group, then, claim Indigeneity? Can Wales, Scotland and Northern Ireland be included simply because they do not dominate?

## If you call it something else, is it *actually* something else?

For this reason, the term 'Indigeneity' was abandoned for the purposes of this study during 2011 on a return trip to the UK. It also became important to explain to British participants why they were being included. It was also important to answer the question of why the UK was included, and to do this, a different—more explicitly defined—process was deployed. Instead of using the term 'Indigenous', the term 'First Peoples' was used. If the notion of a single progenitor group is challenged, and rightly so, this new definition allowed for the exploration of the representation of multiple peoples over a broader range of time. For this reason, regardless of the difficulty that it posed, it was important to consider this zone of representation. It could be argued, and this study does argue, that England has a right to ethnic representation of all its peoples whether they are from a range of cultures that have found a home in England in the last few hundred years, or from the descendants of its First Peoples. At a personal level, and invoking a reversal of the gaze, I find it enormously sad that these English institutions find it so difficult to accommodate a discussion of English ethnic and cultural space within their museums, or explore their collections more fully, to work through this. Their voice, after all, is present. They are not absent from the long—centuries-long—discussion and formation of this identity. That any zone of representation may exclude others who live within the space of Britain and England is clearly the fear of this inclusion, but the method of representation apparent in the Scotland Galleries that includes a multicultural Scotland as well as a historic ethnic treatment of its people, may prove a useful tool to frame an inclusive approach.

These complex, but also relatively clearly delineated exhibitions and zones of representation in the US and Australia were forming a pattern of representation, and ideas around success through widening audiences and relationships were being represented. In the United Kingdom, this research process became rather unstuck. For this research, however, some of these difficulties in the UK have served to provide a key to understanding what representation and cultural belonging mean in the context of displays of 'First Peoples'. The three systems of the UK that were examined for the purposes of this study included the formal systems of the National Museum Wales, the National Museums Scotland and the unsystematised range of National museums in England, interchangeably framed as Britain.

The 'unsticking' that occurred, was around the notion and relevance of a discussion of First Peoples. Initial contact with museums in the UK was in 2010 during an extended visit to that country. By this time the museums of the NMAI, several other national and tribal museums in the US, and several of the major museums in Australia had participated in the study. The Scotland Galleries seemed, as a part of the National Museum and the National Museum system, to understand the role of representation required, and they also understood the scope of the research provided in the original PDF. Their Senior Curator of Social History and Diaspora, David Forsyth, immediately understood and was able to provide significant interpretation of nation identities and First Peoples issues within the space, at the same time as discussing both a multicultural Scotland and the diaspora of Scottish peoples around the world. When asked about successful zones of engagement, it became clear that contemporary voices being incorporated into the Modern Scotland gallery were successful in that they drew from the local audiences, spoke to ideas of Scottish identity, both ancient and contemporary, and had resonances for their local audiences, exploring issues of resistance, identity and location.

## Whose voice?

Without suggesting that the approach was exactly the same, the National Museum Wales certainly demonstrates a sense of nation identity in its system and explores this notion through spaces such as St Fagans National Museum of History, an outdoor/indoor museum that operates as a national space to celebrate Welsh culture, language and life. In contrast, and not only because there is no tidily formal system, England became a kind of polite battleground of resistance in the context of this research. I approached all of the major museums in England, and in particular those that held national collections. Most of the museums wanted to discuss their work; however, many found it enormously difficult to comprehend that they could have First Peoples that they might need or want to represent— in spite of extensive collections from the past and present—and it was difficult to move the conversation beyond this point.

Many of the museum representatives vehemently challenged the notion of First Peoples ever having existed in Britain, or of them having a place in modern-day Britain. The background to this is, of course, a valid concern that the term 'Indigenous' has been hijacked by various right-wing groups to invoke an exclusive space of ownership; however, I clarified that this would be articulated in any discussion. It does, however, seem unlikely that for a country that invokes the importance of history as a valued cultural marker (Harvey, 2016), that their own social history in relation to First Peoples should not be represented (White et al., 2019). Spaces like the Museum of London understand and promote their history, both through their contemporary multicultural communities and their relationship to their past communities. But in examining the Museum of London, a space that explores place and a story of the city and the land, a greater level of complexity emerged when, as sometimes occurs with a comparative study, I mapped a transposition of the representation of Romans in the Museum of London, with the role of colonisers in Indigenous-focused museums. If we had a national Indigenous museum, would we frame our development as a people on the success and value of being colonised in the way that edification from the Roman incursion is framed in the Museum of London? From this supposition, a bigger issue emerged. If we promoted so wholeheartedly that colonisation made our world *better*, as one could argue the Museum of London has done, would we then see colonisation as edifying? Is that how British people see colonisation? Or, is this how museums have told the story of a connected colonial past?

Chantal Knowles, a then-curator at the NMoS, described her experience of working with representatives of the Canadian nation of the Tlicho, with whom the NMoS has both a significant collection, and in 2008 mounting an exhibition that focused not only on this collection, but also revised and new materials from the Tlicho. Importantly, the exhibition included the stories of both the Tlicho nation and of the relationship between Scottish people in the Tlicho lands, and how that manifested in stories, objects and the collection within the NMoS, and finally in the development of this exhibition. Knowles discusses the contentious term 'nation' in the context of a shared difficult naming for both Tlicho and

Scotland, as both inhabiting internationally unrecognised nationhood (2011, p. 242). Her discussion of this shared history goes some way towards explaining the less problematic engagement with this project than it found with English museums.

It also led to the consideration of time factors in the way that First Peoples could be understood. If the Scotland Galleries at the NMoS are able to discuss resistance, it could be as recently as the formation of the Scottish Parliament in the twentieth century. If Wales can talk about language revitalisation and the role of the media, the discussion is within the last hundred years. But for the Museum of London, a space that contributes enormously to the life of the city, and that does not shy away from genuine representation of pre-Roman First Peoples, it remains a very difficult space to explore. Do time and distance make Indigenous people, Indigenous? If so, where does Vizenor's (1999) Indigenous survivance land, we exist because we have always existed, but we are not remnants of the past. Our voices and our sites of resistance continue.

## Our voices and our choice to engage—museums or elsewhere?

So, we must ask how, in delivering a future where Indigenous peoples determine and shape our own paths, what practical work can we do to resist and challenge the colonial trappings that insist on narrow representations and a restricted recall of the past? In spaces like museums, how can we tell our stories yet make them expansive? What are the alternative public-facing strategies to break free of a focus on narrowed understandings of who we are as a people? Much of my work over the last decade has focused on the way that gender and sexuality and every other Indigenous complexity is either left out, erased or minimised within museum spaces (MacDonald, 2022; O'Sullivan, 2021), but this is changing because so many more of our people are insisting on our complexities (Day, 2020; McGeough, 2022) and refusing to engage in ideas of a reductive Indigene.

The solution to this representation may not always be in the literal museum, but in the museum of the imagination. It may be in the way that we gather and share and tell the world about who we are, who we have always been, and who we may be in the future. We do this through direct telling, and through indirect inclusion, incorporation in popular culture forms. Over the time that greater agency and work by Indigenous curators and community-engaged approaches have occurred in museum spaces, there have been similar hard-won sites of representation and engagement across other creative fields where our stories are told. In writing, film and television, across music and in the broad visual arts, we have seen greater and more complex representation insisted on by our own peoples and communities (Hendry, 2022; Knopf, 2008).

These inclusions are in the museum of the imagination, rather than in the literal museum. In the space in which we create ways of knowing and being and tell our own stories, we are often writing complexities that some may comprehend and others may not yet. The right to know, the idea that it is for all audiences, or the notion that representation must define rather than describe, is a part of the dismantling of stereotypes of who we are as Indigenous people.

The actor Olivia Lucas, who describes herself as Afro-Indigenous/Cree Metis/Nova Scotian Black, and who was cast as Thelma Bearkiller on mainstream television show *Motherland: Fort Salem*, describes two aspects of both her casting and how she approached the role. Both choices speak to the ways in which not only Indigenous people can challenge tropes of identity, but who has agency to make that happen. To have her otherwise

Indigenous character be also framed as an Afro-Indigenous character, she identifies, was a choice in the writer's room made by a writer who had children who were Afro-Indigenous (BGE & Lucas, 2022). It affirms that vested understanding will often deliver complexity. In the same way as an Indigenous curator will know the value of including complex stories that reflect the lived experiences of who we are, this casting delivered a more complex rendering of a character. Lucas also offers in the same interview that she saw her character as queer. This was not information otherwise available, but her claims were that queerness was not an issue across her community, so it seemed an obvious choice in showing Indigenous complexity (BGE & Lucas, 2022).

Again, what if the museum of the imagination were not a literal museum but all of the cultural production of our own making? What if the character that Lucas portrays and the story that an Indigenous curator tells, both in their complexity and availability to a broader audience, gave our communities a more complex rendering of who we are and who we may be? What if that rendering included popular culture iterations and understandings of what it is to be Indigenous? Our art, the characters we write, tell the stories of who we are and that complexity can be of our own making, expansive and futures-driven. Museums are a colonial problem for us as Indigenous peoples to solve, but we will not solve it by containing it within the walls of the museum. Do we wish to remain tethered to literal categorisations, creating fewer and fewer opportunities for expansive understandings of who we are? Or do we wish to take on the archive and insist on expanding it to include all the creative and cultural measures of our Indigenous survivance?

# References

Aranui, A. K. (2020). Restitution or a loss to science? Understanding the importance of Māori ancestral remains. *Museum and Society, 18*(1), 19–29.

Atalay, S. (2006). No sense of the struggle: Creating a context for survivance at the NMAI. *American Indian Quarterly, 30*(3–4), 597–618.

Bennett, Tony. (1995). *The birth of the new museum.* Routledge.

Big Gay Energy (BGE), & Lucas, O. (2022). Olivia Lucas (Thelma Bearkiller) Interview Motherland: Fort Salem. [Video]. YouTube. https://youtu.be/pNx7G3DTlkI.

Carlson, B. (2013). The 'new frontier': Emergent Indigenous identities and social media. In M. Harris, M. Nakata & B. Carlson (Eds.), The politics of identity: Emerging Indigeneity (pp. 147–168). University of Technology Sydney E-Press.

Carlson, B. (2016). Striking the right chord: Indigenous people and the love of country. *AlterNative: An International Journal of Indigenous Peoples, 12*(5), 498–512.

Clegg, M., & David, N. (2020). The return of Ancestral Remains from the natural history Museum, London, to Torres strait Islander traditional owners: Repatriation practice at the museum and community level. In C. Fforde, C. T. McKeown, & H. Keeler (Eds.), *The Routledge companion to Indigenous repatriation* (pp. 696–708). Routledge.

Cobb, A. J. (2005). The National Museum of the American Indian as cultural sovereignty. *American Quarterly, 57*( 2), 485–506.

Day, M. (2020) Indigenist origins: Institutionalizing Indigenous Queer and Trans Studies in Australia. *Trans Studies Quarterly, 7*(3), 367–373.

Eiteljorg Museum of American Indians and Western Art. (2010). *Red/Black: Related Through History.* Indianapolis.

Fforde, C., Andrews, J., Ayau, E. H., Smith, L., & Turnbull, P. (2022). Emotion and the return of ancestors. In A. Stevenson (Ed.), *The Oxford handbook of museum archaeology,* 65–84. Oxford University Press.

Harvey, D. C. (2016). The history of heritage. In P. Howard & B. Graham (Eds.), *The Routledge research companion to heritage and identity* (pp. 19–36). Routledge.

Hendry, J. (2022). *Representations of Native Americans in contemporary media: Dances with Wolves, Diane Sawyer, and Reservation Dogs* [Unpublished doctoral dissertation]. University of South Dakota.

Janke, T. (2019). *True tracks: Indigenous cultural and intellectual property principles for putting self-determination into practice.* [Unpublished doctoral dissertation]. Australian National University.

Kasper, K., & Handsman, R. G. (2015). Survivance stories, co-creation, and a participatory model at the Mashantucket Pequot Museum and Research Center. *Advances in Archaeological Practice, 3*(3), 198–207.

Knapman, G., & Fforde, C. (2020). Profit and loss: Scientific networks and the commodification of Indigenous ancestral remains. In C. Fforde, C. T. McKeown, & H. Keeler (Eds.), *The Routledge companion to Indigenous repatriation* (pp. 361–380). Routledge.

Knopf, K. (2008). *Decolonizing the lens of power: Indigenous films in North America.* Brill.

Knowles, C. (2011). 'Objects as ambassadors': Representing nation through museum exhibitions. In S. Byrne, A. Clark, R. Harrison, & R. Torrence (Eds.), *Unpacking the collection: Networks of material and social agency in the museum* (pp. 231–247). Springer.

Kovach, M., Carriere, J., Barrett, M. J., Montgomery, H., & Gillies, C. (2013). Stories of diverse identity locations in Indigenous research. *International Review of Qualitative Research, 6*(4), 487–509.

MacDonald, L. (2022). Balancing curatorial Indigenous and queer belonging: In conversation with artist and curator Adrian Stimson (Blackfoot Siksika Nation). In H. Igloliorte & C. Taunton (Eds.), *The Routledge companion to Indigenous art histories in the United States and Canada* (pp. 103–114). Routledge.

McGeough, M. (2022). Beyond queer survivance. In H. Igloliorte & C. Taunton (Eds.), *The Routledge companion to Indigenous art histories in the United States and Canada* (pp. 362–370). Routledge.

National Museum of the American Indian. (2009). *Native Words/Native Warriors.*

National Museum of the American Indian. (2010). *IndiVisible: African-Native American Lives in the Americas.*

O'Sullivan, S. (2016). Recasting identities: Intercultural understandings of First Peoples in the national museum space. In P. Burnard, E. Mcackinlay, & K. A. Powell (Eds.), *The Routledge international handbook of intercultural arts research* (pp. 35–45). Routledge.

O'Sullivan, S. (2021). The colonial project of gender (and everything else). *Genealogy, 5*(3), 67.

Ormond-Parker, L., Carter, N., Fforde, C., Knapman, G., & Morris, W. (2020). Repatriation in the Kimberley: Practice, approach, and contextual history. In C. Fforde, C. T. McKeown, & H. Keeler (Eds.), *The Routledge companion to Indigenous repatriation* (pp. 165–187). Routledge.

Smith, P. C. (2020). The terrible nearness of distant places: making history at the National Museum of the American Indian. In M. de la Cadena & O. Starn (Eds.), *Indigenous experience today* (pp. 379–396). Routledge.

Tapsell, P. (2020). The cross-cultural complexity of implementing the return of museum-held ancestral remains. In C. Fforde, C. T. McKeown, & H. Keeler (Eds.), *The Routledge companion to Indigenous repatriation: Return, reconcile, renew* (pp. 259–276). Routledge.

Turnbull, P. (2020). International repatriations of Indigenous human remains and its complexities: the Australian experience. *Museum & Society, 18*(1), 6–18. https://openresearch-repository.anu.edu.au/bitstream/1885/270143/1/International%20Repatriations%20of%20Indigenous%20Human%20Remains.pdf

United Nations Permanent Forum on Indigenous Issues. (2007). Indigenous peoples, Indigenous voices. [brochure]. www.un.org/esa/socdev/unpfii/

Vizenor, Gerald Robert. (1999). *Manifest manners: Narratives on postindian survivance.* University of Nebraska Press.

White, M., Ashton, N., & Bridgland, D. (2019, December). Twisted handaxes in Middle Pleistocene Britain and their implications for regional-scale cultural variation and the deep history of Acheulean hominin groups. In M. White, n. Ashton, & D. Bridgland (Eds.), *Proceedings of the Prehistoric Society* (Vol. 85, pp. 61–81). Cambridge University Press.

Witcomb, A. (2014). 'Look, Listen and Feel': The First Peoples exhibition at the Bunjilaka Gallery, Melbourne Museum. *Thema La revue des Musées de la civilistion, 1,* 49–62.

# 24

# LESSONS ON DECOLONIALITY FROM BLAK AND BLACK SAHULIAN ECOLOGIES AND THE ABORIGINAL PHILOSOPHY OF EVERYWHEN

*Kaiya Aboagye and L. Wilo Muwadda*

### Please note

The Indigenous Knowledges of law and lore within this chapter are spoken at the level of uninitiated children with common knowledge on the boundaries of sacred ways of being, doing and knowing the common 'lore of reciprocity'. This chapter is speaking on Blak Indigenous peoples of the Global South's sacred way of being without crossing into sacred knowledges held in strict law achieved by initiated women, men and senior custodians of religious Indigenous knowledges.

Blak, Bla(c)k and Blak Indigenous: An acknowledgement of the intentional spelling of the word 'Blak', and the removal of the 'c' to be inclusive of Aboriginal, Torres Strait, Papuan, West Papuan and South Sea Islander people, as well as all other melanated embodied Indigenous kin and (Ailan) relations. Together they constitute the Blak demography of the Sahulian-centred ontological world view of the southern hemisphere.

### Introduction

This chapter considers ideas of transformative and decolonial Indigenous futurities through the openings and liminal spaces of relational encounters between Black and Indigenous peoples in the Global South–Sahul. It negates the violence of colonialism that has separated Black and Indigenous people's lifeways by offering a praxis of constellational and reciprocal reading. It weaves and brings together knowledge entanglements between the lineages of Black radical thought traditions, Blak Indigenous philosophies, and ancestral knowledge systems of the Southern hemisphere. It reimagines the terms of our relations as they are contoured by the porosity of an ever-shifting terrain, as we (Black and Indigenous people) continue to find the language, register and forms that allow us to, as brontë velez and Tiffany Lethabo King articulate in their podcast, *The Black Shoals*, "continue to walk each other home" (Velez & King, 2022, part one/315).

DOI: 10.4324/9781003271802-27

In this chapter, we offer a cluster of thoughts in development and observations of existing ecological patterns and embodied Blak Indigenous knowledge's praxis. We use these entanglements as a way to examine questions pertaining to Blak Indigenous liberatory futures as they are increasingly situated within the crises of our time. This study employs a critical Fanonion interpretive frame (Nwankwo, 2010; Potter & Phillips, 2006; Rycenga, 2007) to speak toward decolonial Indigenous futures, a future that is marked by an age whereby we humans are entering the new geological era of the Anthropocene epoch.

To examine this, we look to the connective threads between Blak and Black relational ontologies, as a vessel both moving forward and stretching backwards to reach into Indigenous temporalities of deep time and space. In the Aboriginal ontology of the Dreaming, this is the philosophy of Everywhen (Saunders, 2022) accessed through Dadirri that calls the body back to land (Ungunmerr-Baumann, 2002). Within the African lineage, we are called to pour libation in the spirit of Sankofa, which makes past, present and future intertwine, calling spirit into flesh—a kind of weaving when read in relation to one another makes visible and reveals thematic, conceptual tools of liberation. The organising metaphors used in this reading, serve as alternative openings and intimate sites for reimagining; they offer sanctuary for the types of abolitionist politics that brings about non-colonial imagination and transformation that Blacks and Indigenous peoples have shared for centuries (King, 2019).

This chapter is a provocation of thoughts, philosophical deliberations and a series of questions. In turning our attention to the types of things we need *to think with*, in order to engage the scale and depth of black relational ontologies here. Across the Southern continental plate, we can return to that which has continued to sustain Black life and Indigenous kin on this continent—our relations. That is our relations to one another, our relations to earth, air, breath, root, soil, seas, sands, suns and other shoals, all of which offer formations and openings to Blak relational encounter. The framework used to weave together the concepts contained within this chapter is a contemplation of Blak and Indigenous liberation struggles as informed by the ecological intelligence of our non-human kin, the sentience of Country and Black Indigenous cartographies. It seeks to build ways that allow Blak-kin to meet and encounter each other as siblings and restore Blak relational ways of being to reimagine futures together outside of the gaze and violence of colonialism.

## How to read this chapter

This work subscribes to the Collabray: methodological experiment for reading with reciprocity (Liboiron, 2020). This is a project that asks us to change the way we engage academic texts, to reflexively interrogate "reading relations that tend to be extractive, rather than something more reciprocal, humble, generous and accountable" (Liboiron, 2020, p. x). This method of reading calls for us to pull away from, to push back against, the academic impulse to "mine text for what we want, what we need, and then leaving the rest […] skimming only for the answer or citation that might fit what [we] need" (Liboiron, 2020, p. x). Reciprocal reading practices dismember privileged settler epistemologies, which, as described by Eve Tuck on Twitter (9 October 2017):

> sift through our work as they ask, 'isn't there more for me here? Isn't there more for me to get out of this? Or isn't there something less theoretical […] something more practical, less radical, more possible […] can't you make something that imagines it

clearly enough for me to see it? For me to just plunk it into my own imagination [...] can't you do more work for me?

A more expansive, reciprocal reading and engagement of this work asks for deep attention to inner listening—Dadirri. This deep listening enables a praxis of form, in which to begin constellational reading (described later). It is also the method employed to write. What is required includes reading with the senses, and rereading, reading across, and listening deeply with the body and the land, listening between the cracks and bringing together many points of connection with deeper understanding. It is a call to, what King in conversation with velez suggests is to "create different kinds of attention[s] that we have within our bodies (conscious, unconsciously and energetically), where we have to listen, when we have to stop, pause and where we have to feel" (velez & King, 2019, Part One/315). Also, it is to know when to release or surrender in what we cannot or are not yet ready to receive.

The Cartesian impulse to deconstruct, and separate, is often reflected in extractive academic reading practices, which relates to the dispossessing practices of the colonial era's enlightenment project, a colonial logic that sought to dismember and separate the mind, body (land) and spirit. Alexander (2005, p. 281) articulates

> since colonization has produced fragmentation and dismemberment at both the material and psychic levels, the work of decolonization has to make room for the deep yearnings for wholeness [...] to belong to that which is both material and existential, both psychic and physical.

The Indigenous praxis of constellational writing and reading allows for a way of reading that mirrors Indigenous ways of reading Country and ecology, a register that is capacious enough to encapsulate the complexity of Black Indigenous relational ontologies, conjuring connectivity that sparks re-(re)membering between the memory of ecology, land, body, mind, and spirit.

What is also breathed into being through this framework is that which is informed through embodied Blak kustom, ritualistic ways of Blak being (which we discuss and describe later as the etymology of Smolpla tok (small talk) and Bigpla tok (big talk). This relational Blak praxis takes form and shapeshifts through Blak embodied knowledge traditions, alive within the body. These living forms of cultural work are in evolving reverence to our benevolent ancestors whom we love, and honour and are in mutual reciprocal relation with when this work takes place in real life, within community amongst one another and within the words and pages of this book theoretically. This cyclical, circular organisation of thinking and writing offers a reciprocal way of reading that mirrors the complex geological grammar of the land that moves through us. We offer this form as a portal to, "reimagined Black and Indigenous epistemologies, ontologies and historiographies that can re-write us and allow us to become otherwise" (velez & King, 2022, Part One/315).

### Preparing for Dadirri + constellational reading

We share this with you, dear reader, to briefly position ourselves within the research as well as to set out some preliminary considerations when reading and engaging with the Indigenous metre, register and the Indigenous methodologies used throughout the cultivation of this work. How the method of writing the chapter is set up and designed is described by using an analogy of mapping constellational star systems—a system mirrored in the fishing practices of Oceanic knowledge systems across the ailans (islands) of the Pacific and elsewhere.

In engaging with this work, we ask that you think of the constellations in the sky and the ways in which ancient peoples have read the stars astrologically. Matao Indigenous Knowledges practitioner and multidisciplinary artist Dakota Camacho described it as "drawing one point in the sky and then you draw another point at the sky and draw another point in the sky" (cited in Aboagye, 2022, p. 10). Then in the reading of those spaces, it is what's between those points that make up that which is critically important. It is this dimension that is porous and allows for the shape of interpretation, analysis and meaning to emerge. What is present in the spaces of absence, is as vital as the space we are presently concerned with analysing. Similarly, we cannot see that deep reef when we go fishing. Nevertheless, we know where it is by lining up landmark points on surrounding islands, a coconut tree, a peninsula point, and importantly a crossing reference point—the jetty on that island, for example. It is mapping and tracking by lining up key points.

Transferred to academia, it is a process of mapping literature by tracking methods within concepts and constructs to build context for key focus points of discussion, arguments and counterarguments. The emergent ontologies and epistemologies include cultural values and shape future protocols and procedures. These types of knowledge entanglements inform the critical practice of decolonial Indigenist methodologies. The incorporation of our ways of being and working is mirrored in our ways of writing. This way of mapping and tracking is also how findings that lead to more questions emerge within this chapter's critical engagements. This Indigenous way of being spills into our way of reading and writing. Through forms that are cyclical and constellational, ebbing, and flowing. It is this movement that is reflected back in the tone and register of the chapter's structure.

## The ritual positioning

In the spirit of Black relationality and its protocols for relating, we must outline our subject positioning. In the spirit of Black relationality and its protocols for relating, we must outline our subject positioning, our relationship to one another, the sacred knowledges referred to in this work and the communities to which these knowledges belong. The kinship ties between myself (Kaiya) and L. Wilo Muwadda link us to the ancestral homelands of the Manbarra people of Palm Island.

The Manbarra gave the new Palm Island population of Aboriginal, Torres Strait and South Sea Islander people from various nations of Queensland the name Bwgcolman, meaning 'Many Tribes, One Mob'. This honourable name now identifies people removed from their homelands to Palm Island and Fantome Island under the Aboriginal Protection Act. Government legislation forced many tribes to be removed from their traditional homelands and sent there. Together we are extended kin, historically bound by Manbarra Country, community and family ties. This connection has remained a source of nourishment. Moreover, it has opened spaces for deeper praxis, dialogue and the intellectual theorisation of Black relationalities, as well as the intricate intersections of the vast, rich and complex Black-lived realities. It offers us something for the here and now of Everywhen. It leads us towards practices and cultivations in the ways of becoming response-able, as we move through the iterations of colonial psychosis as articulated in the Fanonion schema (Barrientos, 2021).

When I (Kaiya Aboagye) asked Elder L. Wilo Muwadda to co-author this chapter, I did so with the intention of sitting alongside and at the knees of those who have come before me. It is part of L. Wilo Muwadda's lore for knowledge sharing between Elders and younger generations learnt from his Eastern Arrernte (Alyawarr) Elders. Nicholas Peterson identifies this continuum of practice within the traditional Puntipi people of the Western Desert in Australia:

> The senior generation holds the religious law and derives its authority from having undergone the process of transmission of the law from the generations senior to it. Collectively and individually, members of the senior generation are obliged to look after and nurture the succeeding generation, preparing them for holding the law. Hierarchy and authority thus come to be presented in the guise of concern and nurturing, and in consequence, generosity becomes the complement of authority.
>
> (Peterson, 1993, pp. 869–870)

In this chapter's co-authoring situation, the sharing with a cultural responsibility and obligation for the pastoral care of information is *not* the sharing or revealing of sacred religious knowledge belonging to one particular clan or Indigenous group. Sharing stories and ways is common knowledge of the kinship lore of sharing, caring, of responsibilities and obligations particular to Indigenous people worldwide. Within this chapter, the sacredness of being Indigenous is the foundation of Indigenous peoples' role as caretakers for Earth Mother, which has a lore of sharing, caring, of obligations and responsibilities.

The co-generation of this conceptual work is a deliberate act of Blak Indigenous knowledge (IK) reclamation that is in resonance with our traditional ways of sharing with care. Blak IK reclamation is a process articulated by Tynan (2020, p. 164), who reminds us to "remember that knowledge is not new, it comes from place, country and ancestors". What has emerged is a homage to the continued mission for Black intergenerational knowledge transfer and the imperative for Blak ancestral memory work that guides in all we do, as Indigenous academics working with sacred knowledges within colonial systems of academia. We, the authors, agreed that, in our convergence, we would write this to honour intersectional Black + Blak knowledge traditions. These traditions link us culturally and place our feet firmly within the rich soils and vast oceans that frame the Blak Sahulian ontological paradigm. So, it is this we would like to share in our thinking around Black and Indigenous futurities within this place.

### Critical questions and thought provocations

So now that you have prepared for Dadirri (the process for deep listening) and undergone a cultural process of Smolpla tok (which sets you up to be a good listener and tests your humility to becoming story ready), let us bring you to that bigpla tok (deeper/ bordering sacred philosophical knowledges) we want to share ethically and responsibly. These processes, structures or rituals for engagement let us return our thinking back to the original research question that asks: what do we need *to think with* in order to meet a Black/ Indigenous future and what is it that this Sahulian framework for Black and Indigenous futures might do? Working the rituals and cultural kustom practices of Blak epistemologies helped us think about the sorts of questions we might ask and consider within this framing of the future. In doing so, we frame the following as key guiding, overarching questions:

(1) Where are the intimate conduits for Blak spiritual activity that offer a vehicle to transmute truth into power and provide restorative practices for Black meaning-making in a colonial anthropogenic world?
(2) What does a Black Sahulian amelioration concept offer toward this pursuit?

These are questions that can:

• Reorient emergent strategy and assist to build mutual aid processes for the continued building of Black and Blak trans-Indigenous frames and political imperatives.
• Help us to be in and move towards greater rightful relations, as a people connected in kin and custodial obligation across the cosmos, earth and all her elements, interrogating the terms of these relations and building emergent practice and discourse towards this end.
• Restore Indigenous obligations to uphold ancestral sibling relationships in our global pursuit of liberation, freedom and collective planetary health, as this provides a pathway of healing for our ancestors too.
• Reconfigure and centralise the conditions and state of Bla(c)kness as a constant lens for global humanity—as it is upon the backs of Blak and Indigenous peoples that it has been built. For, when we Blak and Indigenous are free, everyone becomes free from extractive colonial systems intent on destroying us and the earth.

These macro-level questions are interpretive frames that further reinforce the interconnectivity of Blak relationalities as they are operationalised within the Global South—or the continental framework we use and call Sahul. This interconnectivity has and continues to provide a source of sustenance and survival. Indigenous peoples have survived the genocidal project of imperial settler colonialism. We understand what it means to encounter the Anthropocene (an end-of-the-world paradigm). We are well placed in offering something in the way of continuing our humanity to transform collective climate and planetary health as we now move through anthropogenic times.

## On Blak + Black interior intimacies of the future

This chapter began as an attempt to answer a scholarly question posed by Yoruba scholar and public intellectual Báyò Akómoláfé (2022b), who asks, "what do we need *to think with* in order to meet an Indigenous decolonial future?" And so, it began as an effort to understand: What is the nature of this future? And how might this apply to Black and Indigenous people?

The nature of our future is marked by the current humanitarian crises of our time, the future as the Anthropocene. Our contemporary human epoch is characterised by significant environmental and cultural shifts and radical advancements in technology. As the consciousness of our technology expands, so do the parameters, borders and shapes of our human inquiry, stretching into planetary realms and in more-than-human ways (Mbembe,

2017). This confluence of forms is seeding the emergence of new assemblages of knowledge that are pressing upon us to rethink everything! (Mbembe, 2017). So, in sitting with the vast movements of this question, we moved closer to another question that asks, *As we move through the Anthropocene, what are the intimate ways decolonisation in the Global South, Oceania and the African diaspora return to Indigenous forms of relationality?* Or it is otherwise framed as, *How have Black and Indigenous people continued to find openings that bring us closer to ecological and decolonial liberation?*

These types of questions are firmly placed within a broader field of enquiry found in Black and Indigenous studies in the Northern hemisphere. There is a growing scholarly field (see Quashie, 2021; Swan, 2022) doing the work to help "close the distance between the language of Indigenous sovereignty and Black freedom" (velez & King, 2022, Part One/315). These scholars and many others are thinking about the sorts of ways to inform, secure and transform Black and Indigenous people's freedoms and futures as they have continued to be marked by the encroachment of an ongoing genocidal settler colonial project and evolving catalyst of the Anthropocene epoch. This work of Blak and Black relationalities is less visible within academic spaces of the Global South; however, this is not to say that Black and Indigenous relationalities do not take shape or form here.

As we move through the Anthropocene, what are the intimate ways decolonisation in the Global South, Oceania and the African diaspora return to Indigenous forms of relationality in the meeting of our ecological liberation struggles? In asking this question, we want to make clear that we are not mounting an argument on the Anthropocene, but instead we are asking questions about what undercuts or lies beneath the surface of all this.

By grounding our analysis in the Black Sahulian ecological landscape and Aboriginal philosophical lessons provided in the teachings and tenants of Dadirri, we mount a position that centres the importance of conceptual offerings that teach us intimate ways to be in the future right here, right now—in the everywhen (Gilchrist, 2020). What is offered are our reflections, on the sorts of things we need to gather, cultivate and sit with, in the arrival of our futures. We offer a series of questions that help us think about what a Blak Sahulian amelioration concept might offer. To accomplish this effort, the chapter embeds Indigenous Knowledges from an alliance between Black Indigenous people from countries of Africa, Sahul and Melanesia—the sharing of Indigenous Knowledge systems that link all Black Indigenous people of the Global South.

The chapter embodies Blackness in the Global South across the Black Pacific, extending to include Pasifika relations, who are also our kin from neighbouring islands such as Vanuatu, the Solomon Islands, Fiji, Papua and West Papua, to name a few (Aboagye, 2018). Each of their experiences of Blackness "have shared spheres of influence, and often a historical connection to the African diaspora and Aboriginal Australia" (Aboagye, 2018, p. 72). Then often contained within these parameters, are other ways, cultural moments of trans-Indigenous encounters or Black-on-Blak relational intimacies—a confluence of sorts that opens space for vast interiorities that help us reimagine complex Black and Indigenous living and aliveness within a genocidal colonial project. This is not an uncritical essentialising or simplistic exercise in comparison between Black + Blak paradigms. It is, instead, ancestral assemblages of trans-Indigenous exchange that see, acknowledge and are grounded in ongoing differences. Moving in concentric spirals that are both di-unital and syncopated rhythms offers openings for the co-generation of Blak Sahulian /Indigenous entanglements.

## A Blak Sahulian amelioration concept

Historically and contemporaneously, our movements continue to march to the same cries of protest, seeking towards the mobilisation of Black freedom and sovereign Indigenous futures.

However, there are no longer questions about whether it is productive or not to detail the terms of our alliance and joint political mobilisation. Rather, what we are now considering pertains to how we are moving (mobilising, organising, strategising) to form deeper questions about the Blak mind, the flesh and the spirit, all conduits for our internalised conditions in the experiencing of our blackness marked by colonialism. These sites of Blak ontology transmute and free us from the colonial conditioning that stirs in us a deep transgression, and brings ancestral flesh and memory into conversation with ecology.

A Blak Sahulian concept built upon this premise helps us attend to deeper questions about the trajectories and forms of future justice and helps us critically assess where we have arrived in the here and now. This allows us to attend to questions like, "what happens when forward movement no longer leads us to interesting places?" And/or, "what do we do when justice obstructs transformation and victory keeps us tethered in carceral dynamics of state politics?" (Akómoláfé, 2022a). These provocations are critical questions for thinking about the future and building a language that provides ways to be in and ways to think with, for Blak liberatory praxis, a praxis within the context of this new geological recasting and technological reconfiguring that is producing an almost entirely new concept of human, humanness and the human condition. Chadwick Allen's (2012) notion of trans-Indigeneity offers Black and Indigenous people a way to move beyond the politics of the nation state, colonial borders or cartographies of transnationalism, transcending us to ancient cosmological realms where the intimate ecological spheres of Black/Indigenous relationalities are linked and central. Returning mirrors of land and seascapes reflect the nexus between Indigenous Africa, Sahul and Melanesia.

The retheorisation of Blak +Black relational ontologies builds a decolonial praxis of place, space and time. It is what Akómoláfé (2022b) calls "Becoming-black [...] it is not taking on black skin; it is the often pre-intentional/local flow of processes that enlists bodies of all kinds into the undoing of hegemonic stability". In a politics of refusal, Blackness seeks to incite ruptures, an upheaval of colonial consciousness and its bio-political programming. In its working, it disrupts the interiority of our own internalised colonial conditioning, as it takes on new adaptations, shapes and forms within the age of the Anthropocene. Many Black scholars are doing this work in their retheorisations of ontological Blackness (Dei, 2017; Mbembe, 2006; Moten et al., 2016; Quashie, 2021). As they work through the thread of expansiveness in the 'Blackness' of our humanity, which offers something to others in the vastness of what it means to be human. It is to this end Bla(c)k aliveness is not about skin; rather, it is an ontological disposition that intrinsically binds all of humanity together in the cyclical interconnectivity of time, land and space (the past, present and future—Sankofa). Significantly, the relational forms of inter-Indigenous kinship are those which bind Black Indigenous people in a sibling relationship. This shared, relational kinship is ontologically bound and manifest in culturally rooted epistemic obligations and responsibilities linked to ancestral lands of the respective country.

## Blak Indigenous cartography as trans-Indigenous practice

Engaging Indigenous concepts of lands and cartography opens a way for closer trans-Indigenous exchange between Africa, Sahul and Melanesia. Centring the supremacy of expansive geographical and ecological systems beneath us and across the ocean plates enables Black and Indigenous peoples to divorce themselves and racialised identities from settler notions of the nation state and multi-nationalist discourse. The Blak Sahulian paradigm is a vast discursive, geographical land space under the sociocultural custodianship of Papuan, Aboriginal and Torres Strait Islander peoples prior to the last ice age (Redd & Stoneking, 1999; Webb & Rindos, 1997). It is a cosmo-verse anchored in precolonial cartographies of space and time, linking the past, present and future. This is a cosmological order whereby ancestral, spiritual and cultural conceptions trace the ecologies of the land and sea, entering the temporalities of the spirit realm where ancestors and ecology memory reside. These knowledges are contained in the dreaming stories of the land that link vast terrains and peoples and bind them together, which in turn become rooted in and inform the ontological experiences of Sahulian Blakness and its subsequent cultural praxis.

These stories of the landscape are the connective threads that translate into Blak relational codes of ethics which determine individual social actions, obligations and responsibilities towards one another. It also forms the logic for social organisation, behaviour and relationships, and can animate the interiority of Blak Indigenous sociocultural lifeworlds. For example, the custodial values of humility in our gratitude to be custodians of the earth (whom we understand we are intrinsically a part of) cross into all our ways of doing and being. Sahul is also important as it is the historical site for organised Blak + Black political mobilisation in the Global South. Blak and Indigenous liberation struggles have existed at the nexus of decolonial, political and liberation theology.

Swan (2022) established that Melanesians have long used Black religious spaces as a means to politically organise efforts and movements against colonialism. Swan's work maps and traces Black and Blak radical traditions that have taken place since the 1970s, where Bla(c)k Melanesians embraced the political currents of a broader Black internationalism at the intersection of Black liberation theology. The amalgam of the decolonial and the spiritual lineage within the Blak Oceanic continues to be an important site of Indigenous power. This conduit reinforces the need for a continued and sustained focus on Blak Indigenous Oceanic scholarship that re-engages the political, cultural and spiritual spheres. The evidence for this is in the ancestral realms of anti-coloniality—a type of decoloniality that is harnessed and rooted in the earth and the power of African and Indigenous spiritual practices, in the same ways that Haitian revolutionaries and Maroonage communities understood the need to take freedom by any means necessary and demand sovereignty across the lineages to come.

This form of trans-Indigenous resistance is described by Shilliam (2015, p. 13) as a "decolonial science of deep relations":

> which seeks to repair colonial wounds, binding back together peoples, lands, ancestors and spirits. Its greatest challenge is to bind back together the manifest and spiritual domains. For in the latter domain there exist hinterlands that were never colonized

by Cook and Columbus, and therein lie the supports of global infrastructure for anti-colonial connectivity.

### A Fanonian Anthropocene: a new frontier for Blak liberation wars

The psychological violence of colonialism has produced a world that is increasingly debilitated by addiction, mental unwellness, the violence and brutality of the nation state, terrorism at the hands of extractive industries, exploitation and capitalist consumerism. All of these symptomatic conditions that manifest themselves out of the disease of psycho-logical colonialism as told in the prophecies of Frantz Fanon's *Wretched of the Earth* (1961) and *Black Skins White Masks* (2008), both canonical doctrines on decoloniality and Black + Blak liberation. It is now in this human age that the offerings of ancient wisdom and ori-ginal earth-based religions feel pertinent and critically important in the pervasiveness of the existential crisis of the omnipresent violence of the West Fanon predicted.

Decolonial theorists such as Achille Mbembe (2017) explain how the rejection of the Cartesian dichotomies between subject/object, society/nature, human and non-human have given rise to the intensification of the critique of Western knowledge and its systems, forms and institutions of knowledge production, presenting the need for new questions that help us make sense of our lives in new and vastly changing worlds. The emergence of crit-ical Indigenous knowledges collapses and reconstitutes the knowledge landscape into what Mbembe would call "a new ontological turn" (Mbembe, 2017).

Fanon's classical text, *Concerning Violence* (1961, p. 61), forewarned that "colonialism is not a thinking machine, nor a body endowed with reasoning faculties. It is violence in its natural state. And it will only yield when confronted with greater violence". Is the eco-logical violence of the Anthropocene the post-Fanonion moment that foretells the end of the world as we know it? Does the rising ecological agency of Earth Mother bring a new frontier for revolutionary violence, to usher in decolonial emancipation and liberation? Can the intellectual work of Black and Indigenous theorists, or the ontological turns found in our scholarship be "the votive oil that marks the end of the 'world', [seeking] out cracks in the vast terrain of the Human (the Anthropos) […] to invite decolonial practices of fugitivity" (Akómoláfé, 2022b).

In this ontological turn, the Anthropocene must be as understood as being entangled within the blood of the Black and Indigenous bodies. Akómoláfé (2022a) speaks about this notion as the 'Afrocene', and to be with this concept is to notice that

> Black bodies, over time, have suffered the weight of creating the space for the human projects to thrive, the Anthropos […] it didn't just sprout […] out of nothingness […] it was framed on death […] denial and exclusion, as it is today, our notions of justice, [are] framed upon bones, upon bones and death and grief and tears and dying.

This calls us back to the fundamental Fanonion philosophy, that is, "the colonized man finds his freedom in and through violence" (Fanon, 1961, p. 86). This means, to truly decol-onise, that is, if humanity is to ever be free of the psychotic violence of colonialism, it must be violently destroyed. In this sense, the Anthropocene as prophecy is the violent fall of colonialism. In the application of a Blak Indigenous Sahulian response, the Anthropocene and its lamenting ecological destruction, we offer some thoughts on development as an emergent strategy that might undercut a Blak Indigenous anthropogenic logic for the future.

## Blak time as a trans-Indigenous project: Sankofa and Everywhen

A porous site for Black ontological convergence (which is almost always found) is in the intimate ways Blak and Indigenous folks (globally) know and think about our relationship to time and being on time! This is about a dissident refusal that rejects colonial notions of time and urgency. The archetypal trope of Black and Indigenous folk always being late is another crack in the opening to the ways in which we can understand and theorise other intimate sites of Blak relational ontologies. This is grounded in and related back to ancestral concepts of time that push back against colonialism.

Sankofric philosophy and Akan temporality can be cross-read with contemporary Aboriginal understandings of the Dreamtime or Dreaming cosmological systems. The Dreaming is a way of being that comes from the lore of reciprocity and lives in the Dreaming of the 'Everywhen' (Joy, 2020). Jones (2003, p. 52) explains that Everywhen of the Dreaming's elusive approaches to time evades total capture, whereby, to exist in the Blak Indigenous reality of past, present and future as 'Everywhen', means a postcolonial future is already realised in the Blak Indigenous reality. This liberatory tool is the gift that is offered from Blak Sahulian cosmological realms and ecologies, the return to the infinite space of liminality found in Black + Blak time-space continua.

Sankofric dreaming is the sustenance that pulls us into deeper alignment with planetary pulls, and it is here we end where we started in the beginning. Like the constellational tides of the ocean, lulling us back and forth with movements of cyclicality, this reciprocal way of being with the past, present and future, "teaches us to pray again, to meditate, to sit with the land, to commune with each other and our lived spaces" (Archibald, 2019, p. 12). The planet moving towards a vast re-interrogation of what it means to be human in a planet that is forcing, rapid, evolving, and reorients our questions and positionings about the future. Sankofric forms of mediation and praxis of Dadirri have offered a sound vehicle and starship that help us find constellational and planetary ways back home—a place where both structural and interior strategies collide and reshape form for the here and now. It does not offer a one-size-fits-all form or even an endpoint. What it does, rather, is moves us to lifeworlds of the future that are here with us now, Tto move at a pace and place with such depth in finding our ways back into the earth. It shows us how to be in deeper resonance with the interior worlds of our being-ness and speaks life force into new/old ways of being in and with the future right here, right now—in the Everywhen.

## Dadirri as trans-Indigenous practice

The spiritual gift of Dadirri as described by Ngangikurungkurr Elder and artist Miriam Rose Ungunmerr-Baumann (2002) offers another trans-Indigenous site of Blak Indigenous temporality, an intimate internalised practice that closes the distance between humans and nature. Dadirri includes the properties of stillness, waiting and deep intuitive listening. Miriam Rose explains:

> In our Aboriginal way, we learnt to listen from our earliest days. We could not live good and useful lives unless we listened [...] Our Aboriginal culture has taught us to be still and to wait. We do not try to hurry things up. We let them follow their natural course—like the seasons. We watch the moon in each of its phases. We wait for the

rain to fill our rivers and water the thirsty earth [...] When twilight comes, we prepare for the night. At dawn we rise with the sun.

(Ungunmerr-Baumann, 2002, pp. 1–2)

To demonstrate the philosophical application of Dadirri praxis within community kustom, and embodied Blak forms of being, we discuss the notion of how to be in rightful relation with one another through the etymology of Smolpla tok and Bikpla tok. This is discussed as an iteration of this slowing-down process and preparing for deep listening as a philosophy applied within communities and implemented in Blak cultural practice.

## The etymology of Smolpla tok

The slow and steady formalities of knowledge transfer for Blak Indigenous Sahulian people have been this way for thousands of years. In preparing for slow learning, we go through a ritual of Smolpla tok (small talk), humour, banter and cups of tea before we get into the Bikpla tok (serious talk). Sometimes this takes place over days or months. Part of it is getting to know each other, a ritual in preparation before getting ready to be in alignment to connect more profoundly. All of this brings us into a process of settling down, to prepare to be in a state of Dadirri so we are listening deeply and are deemed story worthy.

Within Indigenous epistemological traditions globally, there is a critical nexus between integrity, becoming story ready, and stories carrying responsibilities. Vanessa Andreotti (2022) explains that to receive a story with integrity is to carry the responsibility that comes with receiving it. She states,

some Indigenous stories, take seven days to be told with integrity [...] [but today] we don't even have the attention span anymore to stay quiet [...] to actually listen, and [...] to listen with the number of layers that are required for you to listen to a story like that.

(cited in Akómoláfé, 2022c)

This process of Smolpla tok exemplifies this important cultural work format that sits an under the surface, quietly working away. Indigenous knowing finds wisdom in this way of being. It is a process for slowing down and preparing to listen deeply in a reciprocal, multidimensional way. It comprehends an Indigenous metre between the storyteller and the story listener that is reciprocal and relational. For example, the nature of talking changes, because what people say and share must be spoken back with skill and precision. The process of talking changes, and one must learn to read the protocols and nuances of speech, inflection and pauses in the flow of energy.

This awareness is about Blak conventions of respect and to be mindful not to incite shame through an unequal asymmetrical dynamic of colonial power relations. The tone of the conversation has been mirrored in the format and structure of this work. We must bring these often muted, or invisible aspects of Indigenous ways of being, into your conscious awareness as the reader. Stopping and starting when required to disrupt and decolonise assumptions typical to Western knowledges, and for other modes of neocolonialism and Western practices that seek to pursue things, scientifically know things, rationalise, deconstruct, be the knower and objectively quantify. For Linda Smith (2012, p. 39), decolonisation of knowledge and research does not mean and has not meant the total rejection of all theory, research or western knowledge. Rather it's about centering our concerns and worldviews and then coming to know and understand theory and research from our own perspectives and for our own purposes.

(2012, p. 39)

This Indigenist way of knowing compels us to speak back to the colonial preoccupation with finding stability, safety and security in the realm of the objective, fixed, compartmentalised and logical. Indigenous epistemologies agitate at the very seams of colonialism's uneasiness of knowing about not knowing.

## Moving closer to bikpla tok

Indigenous knowledges and custodial or sacred knowledges are things that are earnt or owned and are governed through strict processes of holistic ritual, ceremonial rites, traditional training, mentoring and higher-order learning. It cannot be freely accessed, given or bought in the same ways that Western knowledge acquisition is purchased and consumed at the individualist level. Often knowledge chooses its owner or is inherited, outside of and beyond the agency of the individual. It is earned through relationality, kinship, connection, or relationships to and with the knowledge holder or knowledges itself.

In opening a dialogue about decolonial futures within Blak Sahulian Indigenous knowledges systems, you, dear reader, have inherited a responsibility. The method we use to read and move through the metre of this work makes visible the reciprocal obligations between reader and writer. There are responsibilities that arrive with this work and sit alongside it, as a form of praxis and the deep listening required to receive this story with integrity.

In *Decolonising Research*, Jo-Ann Archibald describes the processes of Indigenous story work and the journey to 'being story-ready', explaining how "paying attention to the important cultural work" was vital in learning how "to make herself culturally worthy, to work with precious stories" (cited in Ashworth, 2021, p. 3). At this juncture, "the story listener is implicitly invited to work with the story and begin making meaning from and with the story" (Ashworth, 2021, p. 3). As described in the book: "It is here that the synergetic energies of textual encounter harmonize storyteller, story and audience. Poetic textual encounters are sensory and emotional–they reach across generations and dimensions" (Ashworth, 2021, p. 12).

These Indigenous ways of knowing to transcend the objective to resolve things, complicate and move us beyond the concept of mere justice. Smolpla tok and Bigpla tok offer a generous form of Indigenous technology for the future. It is a sustainable way of being in a world that ever is accelerating. It is a way of being with deep listening that can respond to the predicaments of our future, a future in this current political moment, which has left us with inadequate structures, policies and ideologies of justice and liberation that "no longer lead to interesting places" (Akómoláfé, 2022a). The slow ancestral forms of deep listening allow for closer introspection, a way of hyper-self-reflexivity. They reveal to us the ways in which our movements of solidarity, need for belonging and demands justice and freedom have begun to take on "the same shapes and forms as the very institutions of power we are seeking to transgress" (Akómoláfé, 2022b). This way of being unsettles the unconscious psychic terrain of our own racialised interiority. Instead, it instigates deeper questions about the ways in which we ourselves are "embroiled in energetic currents of complicity with the matters we are most vehemently opposed to" (Akómoláfé, 2022b, p. x). As Akómoláfé (2022b) describes, we have "organized so deeply, that in our attempts to organise emancipatory projects and decolonial movements with the promise of liberation and freedom, we've taken on the shapes of that which we're supposed to resist". Akómoláfé calls us to rethink our own complicity/dependence and entanglement with ideologies of justice. Calling it "the injustice of justice", it is a position that asks, "Is justice enough? What if injustice in order to be itself requires justice to function well?" (Akómoláfé, 2022b).

## Sankofa philosophy and the spiral of Indigenous temporalities

Smolpla tok and Bigpla tok reveal some of what is required of us here. The need to reorient our frames completely, to re-imagine strategies about what it means to know (unconsciously, embodied through memories of flesh, ancestrally, energetically): How do we come to know and to what ends? It is here in the multidimensional realm of the mystical that Indigenous ancestral ways become generous, porous and abundant in strategy.

The Akan, Sankofric call to 'go back and retrieve it' transports us to other times and interdimensional places that our old people once travelled long ago (Aboagye, 2022). The Indigenous West African proverb 'Sankofa' asks us to stretch our gaze behind to look back into our ancient ancestral past, not merely as a means to an end but as something more than that. It suggests to time-travel through the Indigenous multiverse where past, present and future are one in the same place and lead us to places we cannot always comprehend. And it requires us to land in the incomprehensibility of such a place, with the servitude and humility to understand the greater force that is at work.

This space makes room for the integration of the Indigenous ontological and metaphysical realms—a world view whereby to know, or the nature of knowing and knowledge can be both logical and illogical, irrational, immaterial, cosmic and non-human. Like Dadirri, it moves at a certain pace and tone that may take some time to land and arrive into conscious awareness. Moving our thinking about decoloniality and Indigenous futures into this space produces different types of outcomes. It comprehends diffractive ways of being, where justice isn't fixed to solution-oriented goals. Importantly, it poses critical provocations that force us to consider: What are the reciprocal or custodial obligations? And, what is imparted to us once the receiving or the gifting of knowledge has been attained?

The goal here isn't to revert to colonial notions of urgency to 'fix it' and find urgent solutions to colonial problems, but is something much deeper than that. The pedagogical goals that emerge from this praxis are located in the Aboriginal philosophy of Everywhen and are rooted in the sacred realms of Dadirri. Akómoláfé (2022a) eloquently articulates that: "De coloniality and fugitively call for something more than justice because justice is not enough, […] our bones cry out for resurrection, not retribution, not restitution, not a museum, she calls out for a different kind of activity altogether".

It is to know how to *be with* the disease of colonialism as described by Fanon (Ahluwalia, 2003; Kebede, 2001; Ndayisenga, 2022), and be in service to deeper ways of becoming 'response-able', as described by Akómoláfé (2020a). Being 'response-able' is to be seated in service humbly, in ways that might lead us to find alternate forms and sites of Indigenous power where ecological agency gives us humans expression and form that exist outside of our human-centric interiorities. Moreover, it generates space for emergent knowledges, which creates an emergent strategy in this urgent time of deepening anthropogenic shifts.

It forces us to relinquish power and divest it elsewhere, into entities outside of ourselves and in ways or forms that we may never fully comprehend. It also means that equally may never be fully accepted within the Western academic space as a site where knowledge lives, is verified, is produced and quantified as either authoritative or not.

What is pertinent in this process of allowing questions to emerge with their own agency, their own oracle, is the very nature of questioning and knowledge in and of itself. Questions are a form of knowledge production, and knowledge forms a part of a broader ecosystem of Blak relational kinship. Questions lead us to more questions—they shapeshift and take other forms and spaces in their meeting. Questions, therefore, become a part of the cultivation process, the sowing, the tilling, the gathering up of ideas, thoughts and concepts. It is in this generative spirit of finding Indigenous interpretive lenses through which to frame questions that the pedagogical arch of this research finds its key contention. Simply asking the question may offer an oracle that is more generative, and or a deeper constellational movement, than in the solutions that they are supposed to find and seek out. Akómoláfé calls this "post-activism, an aesthetic of listening, gathering, dying, smelling, praying, splicing and doing myriad things with cracks" (Akómoláfé, 2022a).

## Conclusion

In closing, the frameworks, concepts and ideas discussed and utilised here, we have sought to offer a series of invocation, evocations so we may come to know love and care for one another with deeper rigour and ecological intimacy. We offer these thoughts and conceptualisations as a practice towards restoring and healing the separation of Black and Indigenous relations—what Tiffany Lethabo-King calls "the critical suture of our survival that requires the Earth's health" (velez & King, 2022, part one/315). It is critical that we understand in our pursuit for decolonisation, we cannot address imperative issues of Black and Indigenous futurity in anthropogenic times divorced from the lands' refusal to be separated from the flesh, relations to one another and the vast spiritual domains in which they reside.

To close, we offer a summary, answering our original research question. What are the sorts of things we need *to think with*, to meet a decolonial Indigenous future? We summarise our closing the form of a list that offers percolations of a Blak Sahulian emergent strategy. Emergence is a concept developed by Adrienne Mare Brown. She describes Emergence as "the way complex systems and patterns arise out of a multiplicity of relatively simple interactions" (Brown, 2017, p. 3). An Emergent Strategy emphasises

> critical connections over critical mass, building authentic relationships, listening with all the senses of the body and the mind [...] to turn our human legacy towards harmony [...] and intentionally change in the ways that grow our capacity to embody the just and liberated worlds we long for.
>
> (Brown, 2017, p. 3)

### Emergent strategy 1: theories of Blackness, a constant lens for humanity

Engaging in the ontological turns rooted in the advancement of a Blak Sahulian amelioration concept demonstrates an emergent strategy for Blak and Indigenous futurity here. It offers us both the theoretical and the philosophical basis for an architecture towards the realisation of a decolonial future. In developing this work, the types of emergent strategy we foresee evolve from the cluster of ideas and philosophical entanglements explored. They have sustained centuries-long relations between Black and Indigenous people. Moreover, they speak to a continued need for theorising and sustained engagement with Black Indigenous relationalities, as well as the continued growth of critical scholarship in the Global South, in which to build a language to discuss radical decolonial futures, that are in conversation with the North.

There is a need to build the types of emergent strategies that can help us interrogate, slow down, unlearn, oscillate, push, pull and learn to be with the depths of our questions about future. We need to move in and out of realms of newly emerging ideas and ever-increasing knowledge entanglements. The retheorisation of discursive, metaphysical Black Indigenous spaces within the Oceanic context of the Global South speaks to the continued traditions of Black + Blak survival and the evolution of Indigenous technology that reorients our being and constitution within the evolving dynamics of settler-colonial society. It flows in conversation with several critical provocations that concern our sense of time, space and black ontological realities.

## Emergent strategy 2: the advancement of a Black Sahulian paradigm as belonging

Despite the changing formations of our lands and seas in the times of the Anthropocene Espoch, Sahul will remain a significant ancestral, ontological realm for Blak Indigenous Oceanic People Global South. Sahul is the ecological life force through which we can access Blak Indigenous philosophies temporalities such as the Dreaming of Everywhen. A metaphysical Indigenous concept of time and space based on the continuum of past, present and future, where time is not compartmentalised but is conseptualised as one time together (Gilchrist, 2020). Where ancestors speak through us and generations to come, speak to us through the process of Dadirri, this helps us build and sustain critical connections between spirit, ecology and flesh. This approach intentionally rejects the Cartesian model for thinking and dismantles the Western canon's process of knowledge construction, linear rationalities and objective logic. In this rejection, we return to the rightful restoration of ancient Indigenous songlines of knowledge, restoring also ancient Indigenous conceptual sites of place and boundaries. These sites are unbounded by humans; they hold their own agency, impress upon us and compel us to be in a relationship with them, rather than to human-centric subjugation.

This chapter has been a call and response—between the intersectional, interconnected cultural realities shared by Blak +Black Indigenous Oceanic populations of the Global South and the Global North. It responds in answer to Akómoláfé's macroscopic probings by offering back another question. What does the Black Sahulian ecological landscape provide in terms of philosophical lessons and Aboriginal teachings grounded in the tenants of Dadirri?

## Emergent strategy 3: Sankofric temporalities and Dreaming Everywhen

Last, this chapter's purpose has sought to provide a theoretical and philosophical base from which to define, expand and discuss the liminal space of Blak Sahul as an emergent strategy for decoloniality in the Global South. In doing so, we return to historically

Bla(c)k trans-Indigenous forms of place-making and meaning-making praxis as the core contentions. Part of this requires the return to precolonial temporalities and notions of time and space. We examine the importance and enduring significance of Aboriginal dreaming philosophies such as the Everywhen. And we put them in conversation with those similarly found in Indigenous African philosophical systems, such as the Indigenous Akan people's Adinkra system that employs the concept of Sankofa (loosely translated as looking back to go forward in the present). This forms a significant Blak trans-Indigenous project exploring Bla(c)kness.

Indigenous Oceanic time-space continua and Blak Sankofric traditions produce ontological realities of time and space that completely obliterate Western linearity and its conventions of temporality. It is the occupation and firm rooting within a space that stretches, reaches back and calls us into an ancient awareness of our old people's deeper, metaphysical, ancestral ways of being. There is an incoherent knowing that forces us to reshape the forms and parameters, that transmutes the lines and interiority of our questioning. Shifting the depth of our practice of questioning is to consider that even in the very act of our asking, there is something of significance, something that just our questions alone can do, and offer up something about the very nature of our own interrogations of the so-called future. As Akómoláfé (2022c) has expressed it, "the question in its asking is just as powerful". Not to find some end point, but that there is generosity and abundance and depth that might be the ground force swell for the types of future politics we would like to see happen one day.

# References

Aboagye, K. (2018). Australian Blackness, the African diaspora and Afro/Indigenous connections in the global south. *Transition, 126*, 72–85.

Aboagye, K. (2022). Restoring Black/Indigenous relations in Australia: An Indigenist sociological theory for Bla(c)k Indigeneity in the global south. *Journal of Global Indigeneity, 6*(1), 36058.

Ahluwalia, P. (2003). Fanon's nausea: The hegemony of the white nation. *Social Identities, 9*(3), 341–356.

Akómoláfé, B. (2020a). For the Wild podcast. In *Slowing down in urgent times*.

Akómoláfé, B. (2020b). We will dance with mountains: Into the cracks: What will we explore. https://course.bayoakomolafe.net/

Akómoláfé, B. (2022a). Slow study: We will dance with mountains: Into the cracks! with Báyò Akómoláfé (No. 20/11/2022). In *Episode 3: Failure*. https://course.bayoakomolafe.net/

Akómoláfé, B. (2022b). Slow study: We will dance with mountains: Into the cracks! with Báyò Akómoláfé. In *Episode 4: Descent*. https://course.bayoakomolafe.net/

Akómoláfé, B. (2022c). Slow study: We will dance with mountains: Into the cracks! with Báyò Akómoláfé. In *Episode 6: Sacred*. https://course.bayoakomolafe.net/

Alexander, Jacqui (2005). *Pedagogies of crossing: meditations on feminism, sexual politics, memory, and the sacred*. Duke University Press.

Allen, C. (2012). *Trans-Indigenous methodologies for global native literary studies*. University of Minnesota Press.

Andreotti, V. (2022). 10 Weaving threads that gesture. In W. Zhao, T. S. Popkewitz, & T. Autio. (Eds.), *Epistemic colonialism and the transfer of curriculum knowledge across borders: Applying a historical lens to contest unilateral logics*, (pp. 108–152). Routledge.

Ashworth, S. (2021). *Decolonizing research: Indigenous storywork as methodology*. Zed Books, 2019, Taylor & Francis.

Barrientos, K. C. (2021). Turn white or disappear: Psychological colonialism as structural violence in the work of Johan Galtung and Franz Fanon. *Academia Letters* https://doi.org/https://doi.org/10.20935/AL3859

Brown, A. M. (2017). *Emergent strategy*. AK Press.

Dei, G. J. S. (2017). [Re] framing blackness and black solidarities through anti-colonial and decolonial prisms: An introduction. In *Reframing blackness and black solidarities through anti-colonial and decolonial prisms* (pp. 1–30). Springer.

Fanon, F. (2008). *Black skin, white masks*. Grove.

Gilchrist, S. (2020). *Belonging and unbelonging: Indigenous forms of curation as expressions of sovereignty* [Unpublished doctoral dissertation]. University of Sydney.

Jones, J. (2003). Oodgeroo and her editor: The production of stradbroke dreamtime. *Journal of Australian Studies, 27*(76), 45–56. https://doi.org/10.1080/14443050309387823

Joy, R. (2020). Response to 'Danse Macabre: Temporalities of Law in the Visual Arts' by Desmond Manderson. *Etica & Politica/Ethics & Politics*. www.youtube.com/watch?v=Qa5NUW7aQAI

Kebede, M. (2001). The rehabilitation of violence and the violence of rehabilitation: Fanon and colonialism. *Journal of Black Studies, 31*(5), 539–562.

King, T. L. (2019). *The Black shoals: Offshore formations of Black and Native studies*. Duke University Press

Liboiron, M. (2020). 'Exchanging'. In K. Jungnickel (Ed.), *Transmissions: Critical tactics for making and communicating research* (pp. 89–108). MIT Press.

Mbembe, A. (2006). Nécropolitique. *Raisons politiques*, 1, 29–60.

Mbembe, A. (2017). Future Knowledges and the dilemmas of decolonization. Lecture, 20 September. Duke Franklin Humanities Institute.

Moten, F., Hartman, S., Carter, J., & Cervenak, S. J. (2016). The Black outdoors: Humanities futures after property and possession. *John Hope Franklin Humanities Institute, Duke University, 2*(4), 2.

Ndayisenga, Z. (2022). Fanon on the arbitrariness of using violence: An inevitable for both colonialism and decolonization. *Journal of Black Studies, 53*(5), 464–484.

Nwankwo, P. O. (2010). *Criminal justice in the pre-colonial, colonial and post-colonial eras: An application of the colonial model to changes in the severity of punishment in Nigerian law*. University Press of America.

Peterson, N. (1993). Demand sharing: reciprocity and the pressure for generosity among foragers. *American Anthropologist, 95*(4), 860–874.

Potter, R. B., & Phillips, J. (2006). Both black and symbolically white: The 'Bajan-Brit'return migrant as post-colonial hybrid. *Ethnic and Racial Studies, 29*(5), 901–927.

Quashie, K. (2021). *Black aliveness, or a poetics of being*. Duke University Press.

Redd, A. J., & Stoneking, M. (1999). Peopling of Sahul: mtDNA variation in aboriginal Australian and Papua New Guinean populations. *American Journal of Human Genetics, 65*(3), 808–828.

Rycenga, J. (2007). Book review: Nigel Gibson (2003) Fanon: The Postcolonial Imagination. Cambridge: Polity. *Journal of Asian and African Studies, 42*(3–4), 360–363.

Saunders, M. (2022). Everywhen: Against 'the power of now'. *Griffith REVIEW*, 76, 115–125.

Shilliam, R. (2015). *The black Pacific: Anti-colonial struggles and oceanic connections*. Bloomsbury Academic.

Smith, L. T. (2012). *Decolonizing methodologies: Research and indigenous peoples* (2nd ed.). Zed Books.

Swan, Q. (2022). *Pasifika black: Oceania, anti-colonialism, and the African world*. NYU Press.

Tynan, L. (2020). Thesis as kin: Living relationality with research. *AlterNative: An International Journal of Indigenous Peoples, 16*(3), 163–170. https://doi.org/10.1177/1177180120948270

Ungunmerr-Baumann, M. R. (2002). Dadirri: Inner deep listening and quiet still awareness. www.dadirri.org.au/wp-content/uploads/2015/03/Dadirri-Inner-Deep-Listening-M-R-Ungunmerr-Bauman-Refl1.pdf

velez, B., & King, T. (2022, 7 December). (Host) Tiffany Lethabo King on The Black Shoals Part Two (with Bronte Velez) (No. 315) [Audio podcast episode]. In *For the wild*. https://forthewild.world/listen/tiffany-lethabo-king-on-the-black-shoals-315

Webb, R. E., & Rindos, D. J. (1997). The mode and tempo of the initial human colonisation of empty landmasses: Sahul and the Americas compared. *Archeological Papers of the American Anthropological Association, 7*(1), 233–250.

# PART III

# Digital futures

This theme explores the many and varied ways in which Australian Indigenous peoples use technology and how it is entangled in their lives, including:

- How technology can bring about Australian Indigenous futures
- The opportunities in digital life, including for global community, connections, redistribution of power, and so on.
- The challenges of digital life, including surveillance, hate speech, violence, and so on.

DOI: 10.4324/9781003271802-28

# 25

# THE FUTURE OF AUSTRALIAN INDIGENOUS RECORDS AND ARCHIVES IS SOCIAL

*Rose Barrowcliffe*

## Introduction

Archives exist between two paradigms, one derived from their colonial past, which relies on text-based documents and continual custody of records in the hands of 'trusted' institutions, and another based on postmodern thought, which accepts that records exist in many forms and are created and controlled by a multitude of influences. Caught between these two paradigms is Indigenous peoples' right to self-determination, and to know about, control and manage records about us. Aboriginal and Torres Strait Islander people have long experienced frustration at not being able to find, access and control their records that are held in institutional archives. While the world changes around them, institutional archives are slowly developing ways of supporting Indigenous rights and at the same time, adapting to the rapidly evolving digital nature of record-keeping. This chapter discusses how Aboriginal people Islanders are finding their own ways to create, store and provide access to records through the use of social media. Social media sites of record-keeping act as both a complement to, and in some cases a substitution for, institutional archives. In this chapter, I suggest that by using social media to create, store, manage, provide access and pluralise records, Aboriginal people have developed a form of record-keeping that embodies self-determination. But does that mean that institutional archives will become irrelevant to Indigenous communities' record-keeping in the future?

## Recognising Indigenous rights in archives

Increased recognition of Indigenous rights over the past 30 or so years has also permeated into archival practice. The use of colonial record-keeping to control Indigenous peoples' lives means that accessing and using those same records to take back control is an act of decolonisation (O'Neal, 2015). Rights assertions, or 'warrants' (McKemmish et al., 2019, p. 286), have led to significantly improved recognition of Aboriginal and Torres Strait Islander rights in archives. Many Aboriginal and Torres Strait Islanders have been shocked and angered to find the extent of records kept about us and our ancestors. That we haven't been informed about these records that are held in state and national collecting institutions

DOI: 10.4324/9781003271802-29

engenders outrage amongst Indigenous people (Fourmile, 1989). Understanding our histories, and knowing how we connect to our community is an important part of Aboriginal identity, so much so that the Royal Commission into Aboriginal Deaths in Custody (RCIADIC) report's recommendation 53 stated that access to records was key to developing the identity and self-esteem of Aboriginal detainees (Commonwealth of Australia, 1991).

The articulation of Indigenous rights in record-keeping has evolved to go beyond record access. The *Bringing Them Home* report dedicated a full chapter (chapter 16) to explaining the importance of archives and records to Aboriginal and Torres Strait Islander people. Many of the recommendations support enacting recommendation 53 of the RCIADIC. In 2007, the United Nations released the Declaration of the Right of Indigenous Peoples (UNDRIP) which speaks about Indigenous rights to "self-determination" (Article 3); "the right to practice and revitalize [our] cultural traditions and customs" (Article 11.1); "the right to revitalize, use, develop and transmit to future generations [our] histories, languages, oral traditions, philosophies [...] and retain [our] own names for communities, places and persons" (Article 13.1); "the right to the dignity and diversity of [our] cultures, traditions, histories and aspirations which shall be appropriately reflected in education and public information" (Article 15.1); "the right to maintain, control, protect and develop [our] cultural heritage, traditional knowledge and traditional cultural expressions, as well as the manifestations of [our] sciences, technologies and cultures [...] [We] also have the right to maintain, control, protect and develop [our] intellectual property over such cultural heritage, traditional knowledge, and traditional cultural expressions" (Article 31); and "the right to determine [our] own identity or membership in accordance with [our] customs and traditions" (Article 33).

Also key to Indigenous rights in archives is Indigenous data sovereignty (IDS). IDS is supported through UNDRIP, but stands alone as an independent articulation of Indigenous rights in record-keeping. IDS is defined as: "the right of Indigenous peoples to determine the means of collection, access, analysis, interpretation, management, dissemination and reuse of data pertaining to the Indigenous peoples from whom it has been derived, or to whom it relates" (Maiam nayri Wingara & Australian Indigenous Governance Institute, 2018a, p. 1).

In the context of IDS, the Maiam nayri Wingara collective identifies data as "information or knowledge, in any format or medium, which is about and may affect Indigenous peoples both collectively and individually" (Maiam nayri Wingara & Australian Indigenous Governance Institute, 2018b, p.1). This definition of 'data' can also be considered to apply to a record. These rights are further supported in archives with the Adelaide-Tandanya Declaration (herein referred to as the Tandanya Declaration), a warrant specific to archives. The Tandanya Declaration is based on the UNDRIP and applies data sovereignty and self-determination rights specifically within an archival framework. These warrants assert Aboriginal and Torres Strait Islander rights at every stage of the record's life.

The recognition of Indigenous rights has improved dramatically in the past decades, but thus far, these assertions of rights have not led to a marked improvement in Aboriginal and Torres Strait Islander peoples' ability to access, own or control our records. The very nature of archives as keeping places for legacy narratives and legacy forms of records has meant that archives struggle to deliver on rights aspirations. While archives have signed up to a variety of warrants to support Indigenous rights in records, they are still tied to legislation and practices that make it hard to fulfil those rights.

## Daunting places with hellishly complex systems

Despite theoretical support of Indigenous rights in archives, archival institutions have struggled to embed Indigenous rights in their practice. Many of the reasons for this were laid out in the *Bringing Them Home* report released in 2006. Linda Briskman described records access as "hellishly complex" (Commonwealth of Australia, 1997, evidence 134, n.p.). Even experienced archivists like Kathy Frankland, head of Queensland's Community and Personal Histories team, recognise that archives are "daunting places" with each "us[ing] different systems" (Commonwealth of Australia, 1997, evidence n.p.). Part of the challenge is that visitors to the archive cannot browse the repository shelves themselves and therefore are completely reliant on finding aids (Commonwealth of Australia, 1997, Australian Archives submission 602, n.p.). The finding aids themselves are vague and only offer a basic insight from a non-Indigenous world view about what is in the collections.

In addition to the difficulty of navigating the systems, users face process barriers, such as privacy laws, freedom of information (FOI) processes, limitations to legislative scope and expensive fees for digitisation. Records with personal information can only be accessed by the person who is named in the record. If other people are named in the record, then their names may be redacted or withheld. This makes it difficult for archive users who are trying to find information about someone else, such as a family member. There is no legal right to access third-party files (such as a family member). There are FOI processes that, if granted, can force access to otherwise restricted records, but to use the FOI process, the exact file ID is required, and giving a subject is not sufficient. These processes and laws, while flawed, are helpful to an extent, but that extent only applies to government archives. There is no legislation guaranteeing right of access to non-government records, such as those held by religious organisations, and no laws that compel those organisations to keep their records. Archive users may negotiate all of these issues, only to find that access can be cost prohibitive. Hefty fees to obtain digital copies of records can be a barrier to those who do not have the financial means to pay for digitisation and cannot travel to the archive themselves (Commonwealth of Australia, 1997). Despite the *Bringing Them Home* report being nearly 20 years old many of these issues still exist today.

The complexity of record ownership adds another layer of frustration for Indigenous people. Government archives hold records that have been created by government agencies. State libraries are statutory bodies that acquire their collections is a variety of ways, with the majority of their acquisitions coming from donations and purchases from non-Indigenous collectors (Barrowcliffe, 2022). In both cases, the ownership of the record is derived from the person/s or agency that transfers the collection to the archive. According to the legislation that governs them, state archives become the guardian of the records in their care, but the owner is always the parent agency. State libraries often become the owner of the record at the time of acquisition (Barrowcliffe, 2022). Ownership is perceived differently by Aboriginal and/or Torres Strait Islander people, who see the records as belonging to them (Commonwealth of Australia, 1997; Russell et al., 2008). This difference in understanding of ownership is yet to be resolved within archival practice. All of these issues combine to make access to archival records prohibitive to most Aboriginal and Torres Strait Islander people, and archives remain places that contain records that are *about* us, but not *by* or *for* us.

## The narrative gap

Government archives hold large volumes of records that symbolically annihilate Aboriginal and Torres Strait Islander peoples and support deficit narratives. Symbolic annihilation is not simply whether Indigenous peoples are present or absent in the records. It is also about identifying the quality of representation. An identity-based community can be present in records, but be under-represented, maligned or trivialised in the way they are represented in those records (Caswell, 2014; Caswell et al., 2017). The term 'symbolic annihilation' also applies when intersectional identities are not represented in a community's narratives (O'Sullivan, 2021). The records are building blocks of narratives. If the records are deficient of the complexity and diversity that is in the community, then the resulting narratives will be deficit narratives.

As Indigenous peoples, we are caught in a 'data paradox' which has yielded many deficit narratives and a lack of narratives that adequately represent the aspirations, complexities and diversity of First Nations communities. The Maiam nayri Wingara Indigenous Data Sovereignty Collective argues that Indigenous people are over-represented in BADDR data. BADDR data implies blame by contrasting Indigenous people to 'normal' non-Indigenous people; aggregates Indigenous people into a homogeneous group; decontextualises data from its sociocultural context; supports deficit narratives, often linked to government reporting priorities; and all too often has restricted access (Maiam nayri Wingara & Australian Indigenous Governance Institute, 2018a). BADDR records do not reflect the diverse identities, communities, world views and aspirations of Aboriginal and Torres Strait Islander peoples.

Overcoming these deficit narratives requires gathering data, or records, that accurately represent the diverse knowledges and ways of being of Indigenous communities. Research in other identity-based communities has demonstrated that communities who feel that they are being symbolically annihilated in mainstream narratives will find ways to generate, control and share their own narratives (Caswell, 2014; Caswell et al., 2016, 2017, 2018; Zavala et al., 2017). This can often be in the form of community archives. These community archives build counternarratives which can either contradict or enrich the mainstream narrative (Dunbar, 2006). In Australia, where Indigenous community archives are relatively rare, Indigenous people are creating, storing and providing access to records through social media in ways that contradict and enrich mainstream narratives and archival practice.

## Indigenous social media use

Aboriginal and/or Torres Strait Islander people have a disproportionately high adoption rate of social media (Carlson & Frazer, 2018). Bronwyn Carlson and Ryan Fraser found that Aboriginal and/or Torres Strait Islander people use social media in ways that reaffirm their Indigenous identity, either through connecting with family and community or through sharing and seeking out Indigenous content. They also use social media in cultural ways that reflect traditional practices such as sorry business, community connection and activism (Carlson & Frazer, 2018). It makes sense, then, that Aboriginal and Torres Strait Islander people also use social media for identity-affirming record creation, storage, management and access. For tens of thousands of years, Aboriginal and Torres Strait Islander people have used non-literate methods of record-keeping. These methods include song, dance, painting, oral storytelling and marks in plants and landscapes. Aboriginal and Torres Strait

Islanders' use of social media has adapted these traditional practices into the contemporary, digital space of social media.

Three key platforms for Aboriginal and Torres Strait Islander record-keeping are TikTok, Twitter and Facebook. Each platform is used in unique ways that marries modern audiences with traditional record-keeping. While Aboriginal and/or Torres Strait Islander users reflect the dynamics of the platform (i.e. TikTok is more popular with younger record creators; Twitter is popular with academics, journalists, political commentators; Facebook is used for connecting communities and sharing photos), Aboriginal and Torres Strait Islander record creators are finding new ways to record and share cultural and historical information that relates to themselves or their mobs.[1] The various formats lend themselves to different forms of record creation and record sharing. The commonalities between these platforms is that they are being used by Aboriginal and Torres Strait Islander users and creators for identity building, providing record access and counternarratives.

Understanding whether Aboriginal and Torres Strait Islanders perceive their use of social media as a conscientious effort to create records would require further investigation. Duranti (1994) explains that from the early days of archival theory, the records that are considered trustworthy are those that are created, used and chosen for reuse in the course of everyday life. By this definition, the posts created by Aboriginal and Torres Strait Islander social media users is considered a record whether or not the post creator considers it to be so. The records continuum model, the theoretical framework that Australian archivists work within, separates the capture of information from the record creation (McKemmish et al., 2010; Upward, 2000). According to the records continuum model, to be a record there must have been a deliberate decision to retain the captured information, and this conscious choice is what differentiates a trace, information created in the course of a transaction, from a record. When considering Aboriginal and Torres Strait Islander social media use through a records continuum model lens, the process of sharing archival records on social media can also be seen as an act of pluralisation, which is part of the cycle of record creation.

It is clear that by posting archival records to social media, Aboriginal and Torres Strait Islander users intend to share those records, but how far and wide the record is pluralised on social media is mostly out of the poster's control. The person who creates the post can delete the post, but the post can be saved via screenshot and pluralised beyond the original poster's control. Even on the original post, the number of likes, shares and comments is decided by other users. As discussed later in this chapter, this can mean that social media can both support Indigenous data sovereignty and put it at risk. The examples in the next section highlight positive examples of Aboriginal and Torres Strait Islander people and communities exercising their data sovereignty through social media.

### Indigenous social media records filling the archival gaps

While institutions try to adapt to the evolving rights-based, digital environment, Aboriginal and/or Torres Strait Islander people have been adapting their record-keeping in ways that suit their needs and rights by using social media. Rather than waiting for archives to provide access to archival records, communities have found their own way to provide access through social media. Indigenous people and communities are using social media in three distinct ways that assert their self-determination and rights through records access and counternarratives.

Indigenous communities are circumventing access conditions of institutional archives by providing access to archival records via Facebook groups. These groups are based around real communities, with many members living in the community or identifying as diaspora from that community. One example of this is the Cherbourg community Facebook group. Like other Facebook groups, members regularly share photos to the group. Unlike other Facebook groups, many of the photos shared to the Cherbourg community Facebook group are archival photos that have been obtained from institutional archives. The original record remains in the archive and may still have restricted access, but digital copies are freely shared through the group. Not only does this provide access to the photos for people who are unable or unwilling to navigate archival systems, but it also means that other community members can access the record without the costs involved in digitisation of the original record. Most of the time, these posts are stored in the group feed indefinitely, but occasionally the record is only shared for a set amount of time. The original poster mentions the time frame when they post, giving other group members enough time to save the records before the post is removed. The benefits of sharing records in community Facebook groups also include the information that community members add to the record by commenting on the Facebook post. Group members comment with names of people in photos, and details of the event that the record was created at. This enrichment is invaluable to understanding the record, but also supports complex and diverse narratives about the community.

Enriching narratives with Indigenous knowledge and world views is becoming more prevalent across all social media channels. Wiradjuri astrophysicist Kirsten Banks (@AstroKirsten) uses her TikTok platform to share scientific information embedded with traditional knowledge. Banks' short videos create a record of Western and Aboriginal and Torres Strait Islander scientific knowledge of weather patterns, astronomy and appropriate terminology. Banks' TikTok account has over 350,000 followers, and some of her videos have been watched over 600,000 times, indicating that the impact of these records on narratives of Aboriginal scientific knowledge far exceeds that of mainstream archival records. A large following is not always necessary to enrich narratives, and that enrichment can flow both into and from Indigenous communities. In the early days of the Covid-19 pandemic, Dallas Mugarra and Jerry Bitting created @CaptainSanitizer on TikTok to share information about the coronavirus (Zwarta, 2021). They produced video records in a mix of English and the Murrinh-Patha language for the Wadeye community, which has a population of just over 2,200 people (Australian Bureau of Statistics, 2021). These video records complemented the existing Covie-19 messaging that was in the English language by conveying it in the Murrinh-Patha language. Furthermore, the @CaptainSanitizer videos are a record of Covid-19 responses by Aboriginal communities, helping to add a new perspective to the narrative about the pandemic. @AstroKirsten and @CaptainSanitizer create records to educate by enriching existing, non-Indigenous knowledge with Indigenous knowledges. In doing so, they create a counternarrative that complements existing narratives.

Counternarratives are used to contradict, or to speak back to existing narratives that underrepresent, malign or trivialise Aboriginal and/or Torres Strait Islander communities. One of the most prominent platforms for this is Twitter. Examples abound of Aboriginal and/or Torres Strait Islander users who create records to speak back to mainstream narratives on issues such as gender and intersectionality (@SandyOSullivan), Indigenous incarceration and police violence (@disposablehuman), the legal system (@TeelaReid), and so much more. Indigenous social media users do not just create records relating to their specialisation, but also respond to mainstream narratives to correct misinformation that relates to Aboriginal and/or Torres Strait Islanders.

Aboriginal and Torres Strait Islander social media records fill a narrative gap where archival records could and should be. In 2020, fierce debate broke out in Australia about whether the #Blacklivesmatter movement has any relevance here. The debate hinged on two key issues: whether slavery existed in Australia, and whether we have the same experience of systemic police violence. In mainstream media, the then prime minister downplayed the role of slavery in Australia's history (Australia, 2020a, 2020b), and an Australian journalist stated that Australians didn't 'understand' systemic racism and police violence (Liddle, 2020). Indigenous people took to social media, particularly Twitter, to decry this trivialisation of the very real history of slavery and police and carceral violence against Aboriginal and/or Torres Strait Islander people (Barrowcliffe, 2021). At the time, state and national archives, the very institutions that hold records on these matters, remained silent on the topic, leaving Aboriginal and Torres Strait Islander social media records to be the key counternarrative to misinformed mainstream narratives.

The importance of archives is not just that their records can and should inform narratives, but also that collecting decisions send a message about which events are important to societal memory and which are not. The #Blacklivesmatter uprising coincided with National Reconciliation Week (26 May to 3 June), and Covid-19 pandemic restrictions. The #Blacklivesmatter protests took place across Australia on 5 and 6 June, but the protests were being widely discussed across media and social media during National Reconciliation Week in the lead-up to the protests. During this time, state and national collecting institutions had ongoing collecting calls for Covid-19 ephemera and were 'celebrating' National Reconciliation Week on their social media channels but remained silent on #Blacklivesmatter (Barrowcliffe, 2021). This despite the #Blacklivesmatter protests being some of the largest protests that Australia has seen. Aboriginal and/or Torres Strait Islander social media users, on the other hand, were using their social media accounts to coordinate protest activity and record their preparations for the protests. This demonstrates a gap in collecting priorities between Aboriginal and Torres Strait Islander people and collecting institutions. Social media has been used to fill narrative gaps or provide counternarratives where institutional archives have feared to tread.

## Are institutional archives a part of Indigenous futures?

What the examples from the previous section prove is that Aboriginal and Torres Strait Islander people will find ways to create, store and share records that accurately, appropriately and respectfully represent us, with or without institutional archives. Aboriginal and Torres Strait Islander people have turned to social media platforms to fill narrative gaps left by institutional archives. So the question is: Is there a role for institutional archives in Indigenous futures?

There are many ways that collaborations between Aboriginal and Torres Strait Islander communities and institutional archives can be mutually beneficial. National and state archives still hold vast numbers of records yet to be understood from an Indigenous standpoint. As an example, Queensland State Archives alone holds over 3.5 million records, only 6.7 per cent of which have ever been accessed (Louise Howard, pers comm. 2022). There are still many opportunities to discover long forgotten records that can help inform narratives. Better yet, by centring Indigenous communities in decision-making about records, Indigenous communities have the opportunity to enrich their own community's narratives. Broader society also stands to benefit, with a better understanding our shared post-invasion history. Increasingly, it is expected that Aboriginal and Torres Strait Islander people be considered co-creators of records that relate to them (McKemmish et al., 2011), and that Aboriginal and Torres Strait Islander communities participate in archival processes as partners with equal authority as the institution. This means that understanding records in institutional archives can and should incorporate Indigenous world views.

The records created and shared on Indigenous social media accounts can facilitate more engagement than archival records in archives. Aboriginal and Torres Strait Islanders enhance archival records via social media when community members comment on the record with details about the people, place or event in the record. The comments on community Facebook pages are full of information that can help enrich the metadata of the original record that remains in the collecting institution. Connecting the enriched record back to the institution sometimes happens informally. Queensland State Archives staff occasionally provide archival records to the Cherbourg community Facebook group admin to share to the group (David Paterson, pers. comm., 2022). This enables the archive staff to understand the content of their records better, and in some cases, enrich the metadata of the original record. It is this sort of collaboration that could benefit archives and Indigenous communities by enriching record metadata and thereby making the original record more discoverable and accessible.

While large collecting institutions may not ever be as agile as social media accounts, they can learn from and work with Aboriginal and Torres Strait Islander social media users to make mainstream archival records more relevant and accessible to Aboriginal and Torres Strait Islander people. The records that social media users are creating are contemporary records of significance. They are already imbibed with Aboriginal and/or Torres Strait Islander world views and reflect issues of importance to Aboriginal and Torres Strait Islander communities at this time. The information that these records contain is exactly the sort of data that the Maiam nayri Wingara Indigenous Data Sovereignty Collective argues should be prioritised (Maiam nayri Wingara & Australian Indigenous Governance Institute, 2018a). The records they create are an assertion of rights, an exercise in self-determination and a celebration of identity. They are records that postmodern institutional archives should aspire to collect.

In recognising the advantages that social media can bring to Indigenous record-keeping, it is important also to be mindful of the dangers of rushing headlong into open access on social media platforms. Issues that are already present with open access archival records are exacerbated through social media. In the *Bringing Them Home* report, Elders expressed concerns about others accessing records that contain personal information about their lives (Commonwealth of Australia, 1997). Both in archival records and through social media, Indigenous people are faced with racism and derogatory language (Carlson & Frazer, 2018; Commonwealth of Australia, 1997). Records can contain information that can cause distress and breech cultural protocols. This can be exacerbated when the records are shared out of context. These concerns need to be weighed up when using social media to store and share records. Varying risk mitigation strategies are available on these platforms, including turning off or deleting comments, having a group moderator, or taking down records if the negative impact of sharing the record outweighs the benefits. Not surprisingly, the successful social media communities are often the ones that are supported by their own real-life communities. In the case of community Facebook groups, there is a large degree of peer review and responsiveness to community feedback that makes these social media spaces more agile in responding to the risks of open access to records. Risk mitigation responsibilities also rest with collecting institutions. Archival institutions should not be harvesting Aboriginal and Torres Strait Islander people's social media feeds without their knowledge and consent, lest they stray into the realm of surveillance. Like most techno-logical tools, social media is powerful if used with careful considerations.

What remains to be seen is whether Indigenous record creators and institutional archives can bridge the divide between informal social media record-keeping practice and institu-tional archival practice. Indigenous people have long practiced record-keeping in forms that are not recognised by mainstream archival practice. The use of social media for record-keeping is a modern iteration of that tradition. Archival institutions have broadened the definition of a record beyond text-based documents but still rarely look at social media as an important form of Indigenous record-keeping.

## Conclusion

Indigenous rights and digital technology have progressed markedly in the past 30 years, and this has affected the ways and means of record-keeping. Archives have been working to adapt to this new archival paradigm but struggle to meet the rights expectations of Aboriginal and Torres Strait Islander people, including the right to self-determination, and the right to know about, own and control records about us. Institutional archives are governed by legislation that determines what they collect and how they make it available. Archives use complex systems and rules for managing archival records, and this makes accessing archival records impractical for many Indigenous people. In addition to issues of access, institutional archives hold vast numbers of records that ignore the complexity and diversity between and within Aboriginal and Torres Strait Islander communities. These records support deficit narratives rather than supporting the aspirations and uniqueness of Aboriginal and Torres Strait Islander communities.

Aboriginal and Torres Strait Islanders have adopted social media to create their own records as well as share institutional archival records that relate to them. Through the use of social media, Aboriginal and Torres Strait Islanders are speaking back to, and enriching, narratives that symbolically annihilate them. Indigenous people are both creating new records and providing access to existing archival records through social media platforms. These records document the issues that are current and important to Aboriginal and Torres Strait Islander people. The interaction with these records is equally important. Social media audiences who engage with these records often add context to them and enrich the record with detailed information about the record content. The bridge between institutional arch-ival practice and modern Indigenous record-keeping through social media is a space of opportunity. Archives can use these social media channels as a litmus test for understanding issues important to Aboriginal and Torres Strait Islander peoples. The Indigenous know-ledge shared through social media platforms can assist in making archival records more discoverable and accessible for all users and can enrich future narratives about Aboriginal and Torres Strait Islander peoples to include our full and diverse selves.

## Note

1 'Mob' has been adapted in modern Aboriginal and Torres Strait Islander culture to mean 'community' or 'family'.

## References

Australian Bureau of Statistics. (2021). *2016 Wadeye, Census All Persons QuickStats*. www.abs.gov.au/census/find-census-data/quickstats/2016/SSC70275

Barrowcliffe, R. (2021). Closing the narrative gap: Social media as a tool to reconcile institutional archival narratives with Indigenous counter-narratives. *Archives and Manuscripts*, 49(3), 151–166. https://doi.org/10.1080/01576895.2021.1883074

Barrowcliffe, R. (2022). *NSLA Contemporary Collections audit*. www.nsla.org.au/resources/indigenous-collections-audit/

Carlson, B., & Frazer, R. (2018). *Social media mob: Being Indigenous online*. Macquarie University. https://researchmanagement.mq.edu.au/ws/portalfiles/portal/85013179/MQU_SocialMediaMob_report_Carlson_Frazer.pdf

Caswell, M. (2014). Report from the field: Seeing yourself in history: Community archives and the fight against symbolic annihilation. *Public Historian*, 36(4), 26–37. https://doi.org/10.1525/tph.2014.36.4.26

Caswell, M., Cifor, M., & Ramirez, M. H. (2016). 'To suddenly discover yourself existing': Uncovering the impact of community archives. *American Archivist*, 79(1), 56–81. https://doi.org/10.17723/0360-9081.79.1.56

Caswell, M., Gabiola, J., Zavala, J., Brilmyer, G., & Cifor, M. (2018). Imagining transformative spaces: the personal–political sites of community archives. *Archival Science*, 18(1), 73–93. https://doi.org/10.1007/s10502-018-9286-7

Caswell, M., Migoni, A. A., Geraci, N., & Cifor, M. (2017). 'To be able to imagine otherwise': Community archives and the importance of representation. *Archives and Records*, 38(1), 5–26. https://doi.org/10.1080/23257962.2016.1260445

Commonwealth of Australia. (1991). *Royal Commission into Aboriginal Deaths in Custody*. Australasian Legal Information Institute. www.austlii.edu.au/au/other/IndigLRes/rciadic/national/vol5/5.html#Heading9

Commonwealth of Australia. (1997). *Bringing Them Home Report*. https://humanrights.gov.au/sites/default/files/content/pdf/social_justice/bringing_them_home_report.pdf

Dunbar, A. W. (2006). Introducing critical race theory to archival discourse: Getting the conversation started. *Archival Science*, 6(1), 109–129. https://doi.org/10.1007/s10502-006-9022-6

Duranti, L. (1994). The concept of appraisal and archival theory. *American Archivist*, 57(2), 328–344. https://doi.org/10.17723/aarc.57.2.pu548273j5j1p816

Fourmile, H. (1989). Who owns the past? Aborigines as captives of the archives. *Aboriginal History*, 13(1), 1–8.

Liddle, C. (2020). Nine reporters called out for 'ignorance ' on Australian black history. SBS. www.sbs.com.au/nitv/article/2020/06/01/nine-reporter-called-out-ignorance-australian-black-history

Maiam nayri Wingara, & Australian Indigenous Governance Institute. (2018a). *Indigenous Data Sovereignty Briefing Paper*. www.bcfndgi.com/

Maiam nayri Wingara, & Australian Indigenous Governance Institute. (2018b). *Indigenous Data Sovereignty Communique*. www.aigi.com.au/wp-content/uploads/2019/10/Communique-Indigenous-Data-Sovereignty-Summit-1.pdf

McKemmish, S., Chandler, T., & Faulkhead, S. (2019). Imagine: A living archive of people and place 'somewhere beyond custody'. *Archival Science*, 19(3), 281–301. https://doi.org/10.1007/S10502-019-09320-0

McKemmish, S., Faulkhead, S., & Russell, L. (2011). Distrust in the archive: Reconciling records. *Archival Science*, 11(3–4), 211–239. https://doi.org/10.1007/s10502-011-9153-2

McKemmish, S., Upward, F. H., & Reed, B. (2010). Records continuum model. In M. J. Bates & M. N. Maack (Eds.), *Encyclopedia of library and information sciences* (Vol. 3, pp. 4447–4459). CRC Press. https://doi.org/10.1081/E-ELIS3-120043719

O'Neal, J. R. (2015). 'The right to know': Decolonizing Native American archives. *The Right to Know, 6*(1), 19. https://doaj.org/article/3ff7a56279ac429eaf9c8af034b05705

O'Sullivan, S. (2021). Saving lives: Mapping the power of LGBTIQ+ First Nations creative artists. *Journal of Social Inclusion, 9*(2), 61–64. https://doi.org/10.17645/si.v9i2.4347

Prime Minister of Australia. (2020a, 11 June). Interview with Ben Fordham, 2GB. [Transcript]. www.pm.gov.au/media/radio-interview-2gb-ben-fordham-live

Prime Minister of Australia. (2020b, 4 June). Interview with Ray Hadley, 2GB. [Transcript]. Media Office. https://pmtranscripts.pmc.gov.au/release/transcript-42963

Russell, L., McKemmish, S., Schauder, D., Williamson, K., Johanson, G., & Heazlewood, J. (2008). *Koorie Archiving: Trust and Technology Final Report.* Monash University. www.monash.edu/__data/assets/pdf_file/0008/2373848/Koorie-Archiving-Trust-and-Technology-Final-report.pdf

Upward, F. (2000). Modelling the continuum as paradigm shift in recordkeeping and archiving processes, and beyond—a personal reflection. *Records Management Journal, 10*(3), 115–139. www.aslib.com

Zavala, J., Migoni, A. A., Caswell, M., Geraci, N., & Cifor, M. (2017). 'A process where we're all at the table': Community archives challenging dominant modes of archival practice. *Archives and Manuscripts, 45*(3), 202–215. https://doi.org/10.1080/01576895.2017.1377088

Zwarta, H. (2021, 6 February). In the NT community of Wadeye, a new superhero joins the fight against coronavirus. ABC News. www.abc.net.au/news/2021-02-06/nt-captain-sanitiser-coronavirus-message-wadeye-tik-tok/13106068

# 26

# BEYOND ZEROS AND ONES

## Walking the daisy talk with D'harawal Elders to understand their (dis)connection with internet services

*Ros Sawtell and Gawaian Bodkin-Andrews*

### Introduction

While there is an abundance of research across developed countries reporting on older non-Indigenous people's perceptions of barriers to using information and communication technologies [ICTs], there is little research seeking to understand the perceptions of Aboriginal Elders. With greater roll-outs of online services (Australian Communications Media Authority, 2021; Digital Transformation Agency, 2018), especially for the often compulsory government services (including My Aged Care, Medicare, and the Australian Tax Office), one must be concerned that Aboriginal Elders are at risk of being further marginalised if they remain disconnected to internet services. As a result of this concern, this chapter will centre the voices of D'harawal Elders living on Country (extending from saltwater to freshwater Country in what is now known as South-West Sydney), who have shared their lived experiences regarding the complications, tensions, and traumas of engaging with ICTs and using, at times, compulsory online services.

### Positioning myself

Emanating from my, the principal author Ros Sawtell's, personal experiences, when assisting as a facilitator at my local Elders group between 2014 and 2017, I witnessed first-hand the distress caused to the attending Aboriginal and Torres Strait Islander older community members when the Australian government 'rolled out' their expanded My Aged Care programme in 2015. These older community members, who often struggled with ICTs, found that accessing information about proposed changes to services available was difficult to achieve, with 30–90 minutes wait times before even speaking to a staff member on the telephone or, alternatively, having to engage with the government's online website, which left many of these older community members even further confused and anxious. Repeated discussions at community meetings highlighted fears revolving around Elders' inability to connect with advice and also showed the importance of allowing a community's

DOI: 10.4324/9781003271802-30

concerns to be heard. From this tumultuous foundation, I found myself motivated to ensure these Elders' voices were heard.

## Background

While many reports are broadening the definition and number of digital divides, the Australian government steadfastly holds to 'cost, access, and skills' as the main reasons many citizens are not engaging with digital services (Australian Human Rights Commission [AHRC], 2018; Borg & Smith, 2018). Homogenising, limiting, and viewing issues through a prism, of simple zeros and ones, governments and businesses also continue to spruik that benefits to one's well-being will be automatic simply by engaging with online services (AHRC, 2018; United Nations, 2020). Unfortunately, this does not take into account the importance of 'choice' in human behaviour and the systemic forces that may directly influence these choices (Laumer et al., 2016; Rogers, 2003), systemic forces that for Aboriginal and Torres Strait Islander peoples, and especially Elders, can be seen as overwhelmingly negative (e.g. racism, genocide, assimilation, and Eurocentrism) (Tuck & McKenzie, 2015; Wright & Kickett-Tucker, 2017). Only acknowledging simplistic and individualistic beliefs as the basis for adoption/rejection, often faulting specific populations, especially Aboriginal peoples for non-adoption, perpetuates the dominant Western narrative of deficit.

Such Western individualistic and deficit orientations do not acknowledge how present choices for Aboriginal Elders can be influenced by the complexity of their lived experiences. The government's automatic assumption of fault does not take into account how Elders have lived and how cross-generational experiences have been systematically impacted by the deficit discourses and dehumanising negative policies targeting them since colonisation (Behrendt, 2001; Bond & Singh, 2020; Fforde et al., 2013; Moreton-Robinson, 2015; Pascoe, 2018). For Elders, contemporary individualistic and Eurocentric discourses and social pressures may directly impact their 'abilities' and 'desires' to learn, compounded by the systemic effects of historical trauma, including impacts from forced isolation, poverty, racism, and reliving past negative policies and practices (Atkinson, 2002; Wright & Kickett-Tucker, 2017). With this in mind, it is paramount that the Australian government become aware of the responsibility and stewardship it holds with regards to Elders and their lives.

This dearth of understanding on the part of the Australian government, and arguably in research itself (as there is a clear absence of research on Aboriginal and Torres Strait Islander Elder engagement with ICTs), sadly enables policy and technology training developers to continue to ignore the voices of Elders in meeting their ICT and online service needs. Rigney (2017) argues the importance of safe places where Elders voices can be acknowledged and valued. This research offered space where a small group of Elders were able to share their diverse views to barriers accessing ICTs and why they choose to have little to no engagement with online services.

## Aboriginal yarning

This chapter will report on a subset of a larger data set that utilised Aboriginal yarning (Bessarab & Ng'andu, 2010). More specifically, this chapter will engage with the voices of two female and three male Elders from the D'harawal Traditional Descendants and Knowledge Holders Circle (ages from just over 60 to 90 years). The Circle is a collection of D'harawal storytellers from the south-west Sydney area whose bloodlines and clan connections are connected to some of the major river systems within the broader Sydney basin (e.g. Georges, Nattai, and Cataract Rivers), and linked by a shared storyline. Due to a combination of pressures from Covid-19, and Indigenous protocols and ethics, the yarning sessions were varied and diverse. Social yarning was committed to through preliminary consultations within larger Circle meetings to ensure that the research was valued and governed by the Circle themselves. Social yarning (sharing of, gifting, having tea and coffee) was also conducted within the following individual yarns to further establish comfort trust and cultural comfort. The research yarning also took place within these individual yarns, where the lead researcher 'stepped back', listened deeply, and allowed the Elders to guide the yarn in the directions that suited their lived experiences most. Finally, follow-up collaborative yarning took place by providing individual transcripts and derived themes to each individual Elder, and then with a larger Circle yarn where thematic patterns were discussed and approved by the Circle members.

## Elders' voices

One key aspect of yarning with these Elders was that on the surface their narratives may appear messy and at times unrelated to the topic at hand, yet from these 'divergences' very important themes related to the topic later emerged. Any interruptions would have seen the deeper wisdom of the Elders become disrupted, and most likely trust, lost. This lesson was reinforced by Lollipop, who stated, "Mum used to say that Aboriginal people talked the daisy-talk". For this Elder, daisy-talk is a visual representation of the research topic, where discussion begins at the centre of the daisy, then meanders away around the petals, and the stories generally return to topic of their own accord.

It is from this epistemic and ontological foundation that the themes emerging from the voices, and wisdom, of the D'harawal Elders are represented through the image of a daisy (see Figure 26.1). This figure indicates that there were four overarching themes: Aboriginal *Ways of Doing*, *Barriers* to ICT engagement, *Incentive and Training* for ICTs, and *Anxiety and Trauma* directly and indirectly resulting from ICT engagement and related to government policies and practices.

Before presenting each overarching theme (and the resulting subthemes), it is important to note that whilst there are some varied experiences using internet services, there was a shared reluctance to engage with the internet from all members who participated. At times, though, this was represented through amusing anecdotes as the Elders were forced to deal with emerging technologies during their working lives:

She [Manager] came around to my desk one day and she said, "Why didn't you attend my meeting?" Her office was around the corner from where I was and I just looked at her bewildered and said, "What meeting?" She said, "I sent you an email", "Oh, did you?" I looked at her and I said, "What's an email?" [She said] "Well, the agency's got email and we emailed everybody that we've got email". You work that one out. I said, "Oh yes" and again I asked, "what's an email?" So she got in, "Look it's …" hand movements are frenetic, "You know?" Nearly everybody who teaches anybody computers has frenetic hand movements. I just sat there and watched. She says,

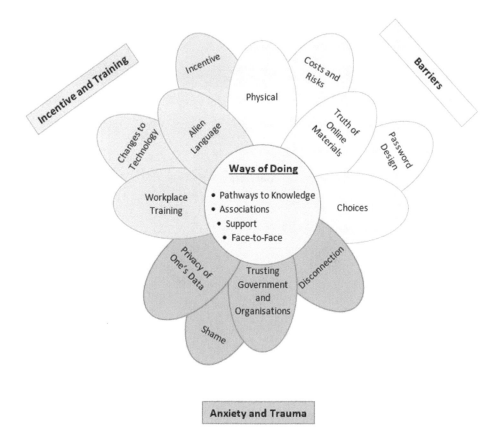

*Figure 26.1*    All themes and subthemes from D'harawal Elders displaying as a daisy—the core theme
Aboriginal Ways of Doing is positive with three negative themes as the petals.

"Here's the meeting and you didn't answer, why didn't you attend?" I said, "Well it
should be obvious to you by now that I don't know what you're talking about".

(Wirridjirridbin)

Despite the good, and at times cheeky humour, the Elders showed a clear reluctance to
engage internet services, particularly in regards to accessing government online services
(e.g. Medicare, myGov, Australian Taxation Office), as opposed to non-compulsory services (e.g. shopping, social media) (See Figure 26.2).

## Barriers

*Barriers* was accepted by the Circle to name the varied negative reasons underpinning why
Elders choose not to engage with online services. The topics included discussions about
physical (age-related) barriers, choices, costs and risks, password design, and truth of
online materials.

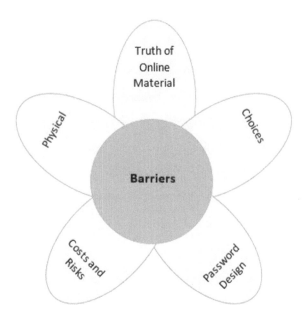

*Figure 26.2* Barriers theme and subthemes.

## Physical

The physical barriers were age related, concerning issues such as: impaired sight, reduced hearing, and generally not being physically able to perform tasks. Wirridjirridbin commented on health issues impacting their memory and ability to undertake tasks, sharing they "become older and progressively more forgetful. Sometimes with the arthritis that comes with age, less physically capable" (Wirridjirridbin).

Elders clearly expressed how age, and physical decline in both motor and mental skills may be hindering their access and use of internet services.

## Choices

The lack of one's right to choose how (and whether) to access online services was a prominent theme for Elders. For example, Garaway and Raven regretted office closures and amalgamations, and the resulting decline of face-to-face services. From this, a sense of trauma emerged as Elders were no longer given the choice to engage with employees, real people, directly.

Bookerrikin shared how, although they did not want to buck the system, they deplored the fact that non-users who on longer have the ability to choose, were beginning to be treated unfairly, resulting in a sense of shame, inadequacy, and uselessness.

> We're getting to the point where we're getting too old to be told and we don't want to buck the system, but if they're not even going to take into account the fact that some people aren't comfortable, without making them feel like they're lepers or whatever,

I mean it does my head in. It makes me feel inadequate. I'm useless. I can't do what I'm expected to be able to do.

(Bookerrikin)

Removal of choice regarding how one accesses these services, shows a distinct lack of regard and respect for these Elders.

## Costs and risks

Whilst the government claims that the cost to access online services is relatively free, Garaway discusses how accessing online services, especially those deemed free, such as at Centrelink offices and local libraries, actually entail numerous other costs like time, transport, and parking. A further aspect of cost, raised by Raven, was based not upon the financial but on emotional costs and risks associated with the security and privacy of the data.

Now, I think a couple of weeks ago, it was on TV [a news report] that there was a fake myGov page out there. It hooked a lot of people. Looked exactly the same. But there was one difference. There was a paragraph [where] people needed to update their information. And all those people got slammed. What about these cyber-people out there that can just come and suck out that information and you're thinking everything's fine. So, that's a big thing because if you lose money, especially when you're on a pension, that knocks you completely out of the sink.

(Raven)

Cost as a barrier extends not only beyond the initial outlay of hardware, software, and internet access, but also includes consumables, maintenance, training, and the risk (and associated trauma) of being hit with fraudulent activities.

## *Password design*

For many years, online users have been required to create unique passwords to access sites, and now are increasingly informed to change them at regular intervals. For some of the Elders, this was also a significant concern.

… all those other numbers that are required and every system has its own length and combination. There's no consistency, so why bother and what I mean by that is simple, do I bother to remember all these system requirements and numbers. Sitting down, not being a mathematical brain who sees beauty in numbers, which I don't. I see no reason at all for me, all those requirements, none of which I had any involvement in the making thereof and no control over.

(Wirridjirridbin)

The majority of online services require the creation of multiple passwords over time, often with differing syntax rules. Whilst this is meant to provide security, ensuring one's information is safe, the complexity of these requirements can be traumatic for the Elders who may already be struggling with memory issues.

## Truth of online materials

Trust in online organisations may be seen as a given, but Lollipop discussed how the truth of available information on the internet is not always apparent.

> There is a lot of false information on the internet. I also have another rule is when I'm doing research, I must have three confirmations of what I'm doing. I spent hours and hours you know searching through the internet and then I started to get a bit annoyed with it for some reason or other there was too much falseness on it. And it was too much speculation and people were without having any basis of research or even just common sense.
>
> (Lollipop)

Wirridjirridbin was also appalled at the lack of care regarding truth and verifiable facts to online content, as unsubstantiated opinions often led to further conflicts (at times within the community).

> [Name] shows me some of stuff that goes down on social media and I am truly appalled, because that's no longer about truth or verifiable fact. Or, taking a position and providing the evidence or reason for it, it's just statement or opinion.
>
> (Wirridjirridbin)

## Barriers conclusion

The barriers identified by the Elders covered a range of subthemes, including physical difficulties, lack of choices, costs, risks, the complexity of password design, and the truth and trustworthiness of online material. What is often seen as advances in technology (e.g., more compact hardware such as mobile phones), as the efficiency of business models that result in the inability to choose to speak to human employees who may be more flexible to the Elders needs (and abilities), and as the hidden costs of accessing internet services either directly or indirectly (e.g., travel, parking, and time required to access internet at free venues), all reveal that certain privileges for the majority of the population are not shared by the Elders. When coupled with a lack of trust of certain online content and increased difficulties in negotiating the very protections (e.g., passwords) against fraudulent activities, one may understand why Elders are not embracing internet technologies as freely as most (See Figure 26.3).

## Anxiety and trauma

For the Elders, emerging anxiety and trauma quickly became evident, especially when considering the intrusiveness and increasing necessity of only being able to access services through online portals. From this theme, topics ranged from: shame, (mis)trust of government and professional organisations, disconnection, and privacy of one's material.

## Shame

According to Bookerrikin, Raven, and Garraway, anxiety, shame, and fear are at the root of older Aboriginal community members not adopting online service access. Shame, a term

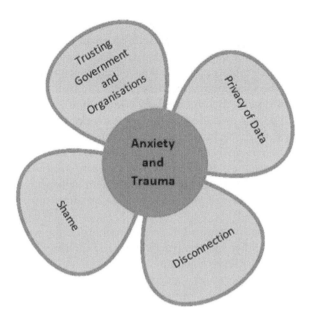

*Figure 26.3* Elders—Anxiety and Trauma theme and subthemes.

used by many in Aboriginal communities, differs from the dominant Western interpretation as it comes more due to attention or circumstances, rather than an act by oneself or another. For Aboriginal peoples, shame often refers to the loss of face within a relationship (that can often extend to the whole community), and it runs deep, stemming from the grief and loss across generations. Shame can be greatly exacerbated by continual restrictive negative policies and language used by those in authority which continually places blame on Aboriginal peoples (e.g., deficit discourses) (Fforde et al., 2013). For example, Raven speaks on behalf of Elders they knew who thought they were at fault for not being able to keep up with the changes in these new technologies.

> "I feel shamed. No, no. I don't want to do it". It's not that they don't want to do it, they just can't do it. That's another reason why, that they feel themselves, it's a burden that they need to address, but they can't which is hard. It's small things like that that make a big difference. We look at it as though, what's the issue? But it's a great issue to them. They won't probably say it to you because they think they're at fault for not being able to keep up with technology.
>
> (Raven)

Improving engagement will not occur unless the narrative of deficit is changed and policy instead begins to focus directly on the needs of Elders.

### Trusting government and organisations

The Elders seemed to castigate those in power, suggesting that a lack of care in the language of law and policy development is an endemic example of its disregard of Aboriginal peoples and communities, and particularly Elders. From this, a level of mistrust was apparent, particularly when considering organisations' abilities to adapt to different circumstances. For example, Wirridjirridbin spoke of a recent failure of electronic systems for banks: "with the banks, when the electronic tablets go down which did happen not so long ago and people had to go in the banks because their computers failed. The banks were totally incapable of handing people their property, their money" (Wirridjirridbin).

This mistrust could be seen as evidence for more systemic and intergenerational traumas. For example, Raven shared the powerful story of their grandmother's experience, who warned their family to remain vigilant when dealing with official organisations. Raven was speaking of their grandmother, who had been taken from her family. This provided a unique context linking Aboriginal historical trauma with generational mistrust of official organisations, as for Raven this still resonated as a lesson on trust today.

> ... I mean, they've gone through a lot. My grandmother, she was taken one of the things I remember about her she was teaching us, and the church come up. The place that she was taken to was run by the nuns. She said, "Don't mention that to me. Your beliefs and truths you carry around with you all day, it's all in here [your heart]. Don't have someone tell you something out of a book that they don't understand about anyway". So, that was a bit wise.
>
> (Raven)

Within Raven's voice, we hear of the duplicity within the actions of religious authorities (nuns), who in representing their organisation (religion), caused considerable harm (e.g., Stolen Generations, cultural genocide) despite the organisation's claims of compassion, love, and trust. For Raven, this duplicity is still evident today in government organisational claims about free internet access that can allegedly better serve the needs of Elders.

### Disconnection

Connectedness and relationships are cornerstone values of Aboriginal culture, and Wirridjirridbin, in particular, saw how internet technologies could negatively impact such relationships.

> Those little one-sentence conversations were going on from people two desks away from each other. Where they could just lean back and say, "Hey did you hear about ..." and I also consider that electronic communication is convenient and sometimes as useful as it can be, it's also very damaging to human relationships, because you don't actually have a relationship with the person you're communicating with.
>
> (Wirridjirridbin)

Whilst the Elders rejoiced that Aboriginal youth are embracing these technologies, this joy is tempered by perceptions of restrictions to youth's creativity by limited verbal interactions and cookie-cutter forms of creativity.

> I would argue, coming from a culture that's jumped on board like the whizz kids I see in Aboriginal society today, it's just amazing. Their ability to actually communicate verbally, ideas and stuff and the degree of verbal impetuousness and their inability

to have exploratory conversations is diminishing rapidly. I think it's doomsday stuff in terms of creativity that I think, it's very limiting to actually, the organic nature or creativity, not the mechanical cut-and-paste form of creativity.

(Wirridjirridbin)

Connection to culture and community are imperative for the Elders collaborating in this research. Loss of connection to each other through the ubiquitous use of online services, websites, and apps is viewed as a major concern.

### Privacy of one's data

Support and improved use of online services by citizens (particularly government websites) is usually impacted by the level of trust they have with the organisations themselves. Users need to be confident in the security of the data they share, that it will not be misused, or used against their interests, or be obtained by others (Walter, 2018). For Garaway, this was of particular concern:

… I noticed a drop in my interest rates—see I've got some small investments and I noticed some drops in my interest rates. So, I checked through it all and printed pages out and the next day the telephone rings. So, I answered it and it was the bank manager and I said, "Oh that's funny. I was just about to come down and see you", and she said, "What for?" I told her about the interest rates. She says, "I've already fixed them up for you". I said, "How come?" and she said, "Oh we saw on the computer that you'd been looking at the interest rates and all that", and I thought, how dicky is that? So they're spying on me.

(Garaway)

Past experiences with those in authority have left Elders apprehensive of being spied upon and of having to share their personal, and guarded information.

### Anxiety and trauma conclusion

The theme of Anxiety and Trauma delved deeply into the lived experiences of these Elders. They bravely discussed issues such as shame and their fears for the future generations, especially as old wounds were opened as the Elders courageously shared how the intrusiveness and [mis]trust of authority, especially government and religious organisations, impacted their perceptions of ICTs and online services (See Figure 26.4). Lived experiences of historical mistreatment and traumas saw the Elders perceive duplicity within the actions of those in authority or those with power. They saw these as critical lessons resonating with a need to become vigilant about messages of improving their well-being today. Security is reciprocal. Elders stated the importance of being confident their information is secure, that it cannot be misused against their interests, or obtained by others without consent.

### Incentive and training

Elders discussed training requirements to use ICTs which occurred primarily within their former workplaces. Whilst most undertook various levels of training, so as to complete required tasks, since retiring, their incentives (and ability) to upskill had been limited. For

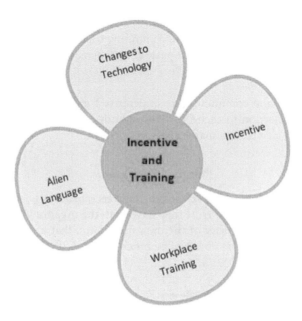

*Figure 26.4* Elders—Incentive and Training theme and subthemes.

those who did not receive adequate workplace training, training from other sources has been a difficult experience.

### Changes to technology

The rapid speed of change was discussed by all Elders, as were difficulties in keeping up to date with the changes through training.

Bookerrikin shared the extent of their fear of using the new technologies. They spoke about the favoured new technologies, smartphones, which many view as preferable to computers, due to their portability. For Bookerrikin, though, their fear extended to smartphones: "I've gone through five phones. I can't do it. I'm terrified of technology. I'm still without an email, still without a smartphone" (Bookerrikin).

Raven laments how learning a skill with new technologies is only the beginning; they also discussed how rapidly the technologies update and change, causing issues: "They changed the computer process so much that when you finally do get something right, bang, they change it" (Raven).

The constant updates of smartphones and computers, and their applications and software, may be often celebrated by the general population, but for the Elders, these updates instead became a significant concern as they struggled to keep up with the ongoing technological 'advances'.

### Workplace training

As already noted, Wirridjirridbin remembers their early training with a manager with frenetic hand movements and uninspiring training and teaching techniques. Unfortunately, while eventually being able to successfully complete required tasks, the training did not instil joy or a desire to update those skills once the Elders retired.

> I knew people across a number of agencies and they all could tell variants of the same story. You'd have a training session, you'd sit in a room with 30 people in front of keyboards, one guy up the front with a screen, boring as, excuse the expression, batshit. Had not clearly any skill at education, communications and education teaching. They'd run this session and you'd be sitting there trying to follow these frenetic [hand movements]. Now half of the class were filled with people who were technically capable of this. The other half of the class were ignoramuses like myself, the people who were struggling, right. So as long as the class was conducted, that was it and that was computer training in the public service.
>
> (Wirridjirridbin)

Bookerrikin also shared their training experience. Whilst not in the workplace, the training is no less harrowing, especially as they also face the frenetic hand movements: "My grandson's the same 'You do this [hands darting]'. 'Hang on. Stop. Rewind. Go back. I want to …', 'Step one, turn the button on the top left hand corner'. 'Whatever'. He's 'You don't…'" (Bookerrikin).

Garaway found the changing look of forms became difficult. Struggling to complete tasks at work, having learned to complete the older forms by rote, changes have since caused anxiety: "… with the [organisation] forms I learnt them pretty good, but when my wife died and I had to do it for myself, the forms had changed so much I had a big problem doing that" (Garaway).

What is obvious from this theme is that despite some access to technology training, this training to them was not engaging and sustainable enough to instil or inspire confidence for them to learn and update skills.

### Incentive

Wirridjirridbin sees no use, or incentive for accessing online services. Although doing their best to keep up with IT training at work, it evoked little interest, as evidenced by their lack of activity after retirement.

> My only incentive to use computers was because of the nature of the work I did and what I thought was its importance that created change or whatever, so I struggled with it when I retired and didn't have the work need. I don't want to deal with [computers], I don't need them, at this phase in my life I have no need for it. I'm uncomfortable with it.
>
> (Wirridjirridbin)

### Alien language

Wirridjirridbin deplored how a foreign language (jargon) was imposed on all who were required to access and utilise online services, stating that their inability to understand the language was a contributing factor to their choice to no longer go online.

The other problem with the computer world, it instantaneously introduced a completely foreign language without a dictionary and without linguistic tuition. People would just talk in language and when the web came, which was a later addition there was this further expansion of the vocabulary which nobody ever taught. So for a person who's not linguistically competent, I don't pick up languages I have a disadvantage, so I have a disinclination to be responsive.

(Wirridjirridbin)

The complex terminology used within technology and related to the internet is difficult for the Elders to negotiate and adapt to.

### Incentive and training conclusion

Many of the Elders shared how they received some form of training using ICTs at their prior workplaces. Several mentioned how, although they became proficient performing these tasks, their little interest in using ICTs and going online continued into their retirement. This disinclination was exacerbated by the introduction of an alien language, especially linguistic training was minimal language.

### Ways of doing

Moving away from the negative perceptions of internet technologies and services, the final theme instead focused on the strengths of being Aboriginal, and in this instance, the strength of being D'harawal. Dodson (2003, p. 42) urges us to remember, "Our peoples have left us deep roots, which empowered us to endure the violence of oppression. They are the roots of survival, but not of constriction. They are the roots from which all growth is possible". Within this theme, Elders shared how they used their strengths, their Aboriginal ways of doing (Martin, 2003) and learning, and abilities to adapt and grow against oppressive odds, to navigate the onslaught of online services (See Figure 26.5).

### Pathways to knowledge

Many Elders discussed how supportive the Aboriginal sharing of knowledge method is, ensuring learning is a positive experience for the learner, and therefore a learning experience that is not embarrassing, or denigrating of their skills or level of knowledge.

Wirridjirridbin spoke of the differences between perceptions of knowledge sharing: discussing the dominant individualistic Western belief of knowledge ownership compared to the inclusive form of Aboriginal knowledge sharing.

... you were given access to the knowledge or the pathways to find that knowledge if you were worthy. It's a clever system because you only got what you were capable of dealing with and handling. [Now] you can go into that library and literally look up any book or reference you need to, you desire to, or your enquiring mind thinks it may be there or useful for whatever purpose. Our libraries culturally were held by people. That person has an ability to make a judgement as to whether you can

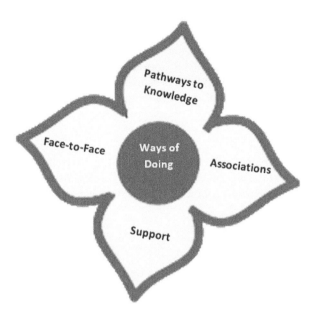

*Figure 26.5* Elders—the Aboriginal Ways of Doing theme and subthemes.

handle that knowledge or whether you won't abuse it, or you're a risk, or whatever. So our knowledge is not about information, it's more about a process of finding and acquiring, okay.

(Wirridjirridbin)

Aboriginal knowledge is an earned responsibility, earned at a pace which suits each individual; comprehension of lore occurs at different stages for different people. Today, with the internet, anyone is able to access any information, whether they deserve to know or are responsible enough to know how to use the knowledge properly.

### Associations

Relationships and the importance of connectedness were shared and named by Lollipop as associations, and they particularly spoke to the relationships between plants and their connections to neighbouring plants. The Aboriginal concept of relationships is that all living and non-living entities are connected; therefore, the lesson taken from this yarn may also apply to how technology training development can be improved by acknowledging the importance of associations.

Mum used to take me out in when she was able to. She used to take me out into the bush, and she would show me a particular plant, made me smell it. And then she would take me to another one, which was the same kind of plant that I've smelled before it didn't smell the same and she said, "Why is it different?" Eventually I learned that plant was growing with a certain group of other plants. That the other one wasn't. And so that started me off, finding associations. And that's what I'm doing. When the plants grow with certain other plants and this is most of our medicine plants, their medicines are much stronger if they're growing in one lot of association than with other associations. And the Aboriginal people knew that. So it makes a difference where they grow. They're like humans. You get a mob of cranky people living in one area, and a lot of nice people living in another area they need others to help them.

(Lollipop)

I, Ros Sawtell, as the principal researcher, took from this yarn that the sharing of stronger associations can support those weaker associations. This led into discussions by each of the Elders on how initial and current computer training has been and is provided by family and friends with skills.

### Support

Support within the kinship networks is predicated upon respect, making it an extremely important value for Aboriginal peoples. With this in mind, Raven warned how lacking support and being pushy often causes the learner to cease trying: "… if we actually keep on going with them and say, 'Come on, you've got to learn it', it has the adverse effect. 'No, it's too complicated for me', and things like that" (Raven).

In contrast, Garaway shared their experience of how an inclusive, supportive environment has positive results in teaching skills: "My elder daughter taught me a hell of a lot throughout my career. They're absolutely good at it without embarrassing you or anything like that" (Garaway).

There are no recriminations of: " 'Oh you should know that'. Nothing" (Garaway).

The Western focus of top-down teaching may be seen as an anathema to the Aboriginal Ways of Doing; therefore, supportive teaching environments have the greatest chance of succeeding.

### Face-to-face

Lollipop was one who spoke of how culturally appropriate and important it is to meet face to face when sharing knowledge and dealing with people. Part of this is the need to make eye contact to better understand another person:

I prefer face to face because I can read the person and with computers you can't do that. If they're uncomfortable, they move around a lot, you know, trying to get a comfortable place. It's not necessarily the chair, they are uncomfortable. Yeh, and so you can read people so much better than you can read a computer.

(Lollipop)

Relationships, a cornerstone of Aboriginal culture, are required to build trust, and for several Elders, face-to-face connection is also required when dealing with people, which stands in contrast to often automated and impersonal online services.

## *Ways of Doing conclusion*

Aboriginal Ways of Doing emerged as the last theme and provided a strong contrast to the negativity and barriers faced by Elders when accessing online services. Ways of Doing provided space where the Elders' voices could explain their strengths, ways of learning, and abilities to adapt and grow and to potentially navigate the onslaught of the ubiquitous roll-outs of online services.

## Conclusion

With the priority to get everyone accessing online services, the Australian government, like its counterparts in business, need to become aware of the responsibilities and stewardship it holds over Elders' access to information and their lives. Government, policy, technology, and training developers should change their narratives and perceptions and learn from what the Elders have shared. From the Elders' voices, we can see the need for the provision of supportive teaching environments. Teaching environments that are underpinned with respect and targeted teaching formats suited to individual Elders, where they can feel positive about learning to use these new technologies, need to be implemented if technology teaching programmes are to be successful. To improve levels of engagement, it is essential that the government ensure developing legitimate options targeted to Elders, and not just declare automatic benefits to some undefined sense of well-being. Listening to what these Elders have shared, as opposed to only listening to what current, often younger, users and developers think, is required to improve engagement.

Respect for Elders and their world views is paramount; therefore, providing a choice of service provision is critical, especially for marginalised peoples who do not have equal access to the internet and other associated, compulsory services.

The Elders felt that while the barriers perceived by the Australian government (cost, access, and skills) are legitimate issues, they are not the only reasons for the limited adoption of online services. Expanding upon those perceptions, Elders bravely shared distressing stories to provide context for their choices. Due to historical and contemporary deficit discourses, the Elders now perceive duplicity within the actions of those in authority, and so are more vigilant today by not only questioning government messages, such as automatic benefits to their well-being, but also resisting the 'services' the government offers.

Despite this, the Elders created a positive space in their yarns (*Ways of Doing*), where their voices sought to honour their connections and relationships, where they affirmed the resilience of their culture. They gave tribute to their shared strengths, resistance, survival, and ability to adapt and grow, enabling them to face the onslaught of online services (and other colonial forces).

Policymakers and training developers must be mindful that Elders are not a homogeneous group, and that one service or training opportunity will not fit all. The gifts of the Elders' yarns show the importance for those in authority to acknowledge the perceptions, relevance, and fears of others outside of the Western privileged lens. Therefore, it is incumbent on people in authority to hear the ideas put forward by Elders within communities, to understand their needs, so that technology training opportunities will better target the Elders' individual needs and requirements.

## Members of the Knowledge Holders Circle

### *Frances Bodkin*

Aunty Frances Bodkin belongs to the Bidigal clan of the D'harawal Nation of south-west Sydney. Her grandfather Albert Perry was the grandson of Albert of the Georges River, who was in turn descended from Ellen Anderson, a very strong D'harawal woman. She is a member of the D'harawal Traditional Descendants and Knowledge Holders Circle.

### *Gavin Andrews*

Uncle Gavin Andrews is a direct descendant of Young Bundle (c. 1770s–1845) of the Nattaimattagal clan of the D'harawal Nation of south-west Sydney, New South Wales. He recently retired after a long career in the public and Aboriginal community sectors. He is a member of the D'harawal Traditional Descendants and Knowledge Holders Circle.

### *John Foster*

Uncle John Foster shares his cultural knowledge within his community. He is a member of the D'harawal Traditional Descendants and Knowledge Holders Circle.

### *Karen Adams*

Aunty Karen Adams works tirelessly within her community as a cultural consultant. She is a member of the D'harawal Traditional Descendants and Knowledge Holders Circle.

### *Ross Evans*

Uncle Ross Evans is a D'harawal man born in Paddington Sydney, in 1955, one of seven children. Uncle Ross works with NSW Police as a community liaison officer teaching Aboriginal kids about the importance of culture. He is a member of the D'harawal Traditional Descendants and Knowledge Holders Circle.

## References

Atkinson, J. (2002). *Trauma trails, recreating song lines: The transgenerational effects of trauma in Indigenous Australia*. Spinifex Press.

Australian Human Rights Commission. (2018). *Human Rights and Technology Issues Paper.* https://humanrights.gov.au/our-work/rights-and-freedoms/publications/human-rights-and-technology-issues-paper-2018

Behrendt, L. (2001). Genocide: the distance between law and life. *Aboriginal History, 25,* 132–147. https://doi.org/10.22459/AH.25.2011.08

Bond, C. J., & Singh, D. (2020). More than a refresh required for closing the gap of Indigenous health inequality. *Medical Journal of Australia, 212*(5), 198–199. https://doi.org/10.5694/mja2.50498

Borg, K., & Smith, L. (2018). Digital inclusion and online behaviour: Five typologies of Australian internet users. *Behaviour & Information Technology, 37*(4), 367–380. https://doi.org/10.1080/0144929X.2018.1436593

Digital Transformation Agency. (2018). *Digital transformation strategy 2018–2025.* www.dta.gov.au/digital-transformation-strategy/digital-transformation-strategy-2018-2025

Dodson, M. (2003). The ending in the beginning: re(de)finding Aboriginality. In M. Grossman (Ed.), *Blacklines: Contemporary critical writing by Indigenous Australians* (pp. 25–42). Melbourne University Press.

Eady, M., & Woodcock, S. (2010). Understanding the need: Using collaboratively created draft guiding principles to direct online synchronous learning in Indigenous communities. *International Journal for Educational Integrity, 6*(2), 24–40. https://doi.org/10.21913/IJEI.v6i2.701

Fforde, C., Bamblett, L., Lovett, R., Gorringe, S., & Fogarty, B. (2013). Discourse, deficit and identity: Aboriginality, the race paradigm and the language of representation in contemporary Australia. *Media International Australia, 149*(1). https://doi.org/10.1177/1329878X1314900117

Laumer, S., Maier, C., Eckhardt, A., & Weitzel, T. (2016). User personality and resistance to mandatory information systems in organizations: A theoretical model and empirical test of dispositional resistance to change. *Journal of Information Technology, 31*(1), 67–82. https://doi.org/10.1057/jit.2015.17

Martin, K. M. B. (2003). Ways of knowing, being and doing: A theoretical framework and methods for Indigenous and Indigenist re-search. *Journal of Australian Studies, 27*(76), 203–214.

Pascoe, B. (2018, January). The imperial mind: How Europeans stole the world. *Griffith REVIEW, 60*, 234–243. https://doi.org/10.3316/informit.586167400847176

Rigney, L. I. (2017). Aboriginal community development and digital inclusion: Hope, haves and have-nots. In C. Kickett-Tucker, D. Bessarab, J. Coffin, & M. Wright (Eds.), *Mia Mia Aboriginal community development: Fostering cultural security* (pp. 186–198). Cambridge University Press.

Rogers, E. M. (2003). *Diffusion of innovations* (5th ed.). Free Press.

Tuck, E., & McKenzie, M. (2105). *Place in research theory, methodology, and methods*. Routledge.

United Nations. (2020). *E-government Survey 2020: Digital Government in the Decade of Action for Sustainable Development*. Department of Economic and Social Affairs. https://publicadministration.un.org/en/Research/UN-e-Government-Surveys

Walter, M. (2018). The voice of indigenous data: Beyond the markers of disadvantage. In J. Schultz, & S. Phillips (Eds.), *Griffith REVIEW, 60*, 256–263. https://doi.org/10.3316/ielapa.586241932732209

Wright, M., & Kickett-Tucker, C. (2017). Djinangingy kaartdijin Seeing and understanding our ways of working In C. Kickett-Tucker, D. Bessarab, J. Coffin, & M. Wright (Eds.), *Mia Mia Aboriginal community development: Fostering cultural security* (pp. 169–185). Cambridge University Press.

# 27

# DIGITAL FUTURES

## Health-seeking on social media

*Bronwyn Carlson*

### Introduction

The incredible popularisation of digital technologies such as social media platforms over the last couple of decades has sparked the interest of a whole range of health researchers and scholars from adjacent fields. Two central questions have been: what are the health implications of social media technologies, and what opportunities does social media afford for improving the health of its users? This expansive body of research has identified a huge variety of health effects for social media on its users. On the one hand, use of social media has been correlated with increased risk of mental health and suicide; and 'heavy' social media use, in particular, is often correlated with a range of deleterious physical, mental and social health outcomes. On the other hand, scholars have identified a range of potential health benefits of social media—including its ability to rapidly spread public health information; to connect users with potential help-sources; to allow users to maintain supportive connections with friends and family; and to foster the emergence of what Newman and colleagues (2011) describe as 'online health communities'. Overall, health scholars remain largely optimistic about the potential public health benefits that social media might afford.

Meanwhile, a wealth of recent research (see Carlson & Berglund, 2021; Carlson & Frazer, 2021; Duarte, 2017; Farrell, 2017; Goodman et al., 2019) has explored the social media practices of Indigenous peoples,[1] unpacking the ways in which these technologies have helped facilitate the production of powerful and supportive connections between individuals and groups. This work has documented the many benefits of social media, including the capacity to practice culture and share knowledges across vast distances; the opportunities it affords in amplifying otherwise marginalised voices and agitating for social change; and most importantly for this chapter, the production and maintenance of distributed networks of concern, care and support. A small body of work has begun to document the potential health benefits social media can bring about for Indigenous people across this continent (see Carlson, Frazer, & Farrelly, 2020; Frazer, Carlson, & Farrelly, 2022; Henson et al., 2022), particularly in connecting people with formal health services, delivering social media users credible health-related knowledges, and building informal

DOI: 10.4324/9781003271802-31

networks of support. In short, there has been hope that social media might be able to help address health needs of Aboriginal and Torres Strait Islander people.

This chapter seeks to further develop insights into the health implications of social media for Aboriginal and Torres Strait Islander users by paying attention to the forces that shape health-seeking practices—seeking help for issues related to health and well-being. Here, I conceptualise online health-seeking behaviours in the broadest sense, to include every-thing from practices in which people explicitly ask for help for their physical and mental health, to much more everyday, mundane and even ambiguous calls for help—such as disguised requests for personal, emotional and relational support.

## Indigenous people and health-seeking

Prolific research over the last few decades has documented persistent health discrepancies between Indigenous peoples and settlers across the whole spectrum of health, including disproportionate rates of mental distress and ill health (see Australian Bureau of Statistics (ABS, 2019)), youth suicide ideation and actualisation (Gooda & Dudgeon, 2014; Zubrick et al., 2004), and chronic disease and early death (see Garvey, 2008). Research has also documented clearly the considerably lower rates of formal help-seeking for health among Indigenous people. While much of this work has implicitly or otherwise framed the issue as one in which Indigenous people are somehow 'failing' to take good care of themselves, more critical work has interrogated the broader cultural, political and historical forces mediating health relations. This more nuanced work (see Carlson et al., 2020; Carlson & Frazer, 2022; Farrelly, 2008; Shand et al., 2013) has examined why Indigenous people do not access health services, even when they are available, and the reasons that formal care sources may not be addressing the needs of Indigenous people. These scholars also explore 'Australia' as a settler-colonial structure to help make sense of poor health outcomes for Indigenous peoples. In short, it is apparent that for Indigenous people, there are many more barriers to accessing formal sources of healthcare (Carlson et al., 2020; Isaacs et al., 2010; McBain-Rigg & Veitch, 2011).

Broadly, this work has highlighted three main ways health outcomes are mediated by settler power relations. First, Indigenous people do not have complete trust in formal healthcare services, and for good reason. Intergenerational trauma related to past policies of child removal and assimilation, and ongoing institutionalised racial discrimination impact powerfully on help-seeking behaviours (Dudgeon et al., 2014; Garvey, 2008; Zubrick et al., 2004). Carlson and Frazer (2020a, p. 89) argue that, in both the historical and the con-temporary context, "[mainstream health services] constitute one of the main mechanisms through which the logic of settler colonialism can be reproduced and effected". Taylor and Thompson (2011) found that for Indigenous people, the historical legacy of these racist practices has fostered what they call 'historical mistrust' of mainstream health services.

Second, research has documented persistent racism in contemporary healthcare settings. Herring (2013, p. 109) writes, "although not all mainstream service providers are overtly racist, negative encounters occur with such frequency, that apprehension by Aboriginal people is warranted and should be recognised as such". This often constitutes 'direct' forms of racism (though some contest the notion that racism against oneself and one's social group can be distinguished as 'direct' or 'indirect'). Work by Aboriginal scholar Yin Paradies and colleague Joan Cunningham (2009) found that 22 per cent of Aboriginal people have experienced racism while accessing health services, and even higher rates while accessing other forms of social services. On the other hand, there are widespread 'indirect' forms of racism, such as the 'difference blindness' and 'cultural incompetence' (Herring et al., 2013) of many health practitioners; what McBain-Rigg and Veitch (2011, p. 72) describe as "an ethos where practitioners treat 'all patients the same' regardless of age, gender, ethnicity or religious belief". These diverse forms of racism mean formal sources of help are often not experienced as safe for Indigenous people (Sjoberg & McDermott, 2016).

Finally, there have been criticisms of the dominant Western biomedical health paradigm mobilised in mainstream health services (Garvey, 2008; Hefler et al., 2019; Sherwood, 2013). Vicary and Westerman (2004) argue that there is a distinct and troubling lack of understanding around how Indigenous people themselves conceptualise health (also see Sjoberg & McDermott, 2016). This is particularly significant for mental health models and approaches to suicide prevention (Taylor & Thompson, 2011), which appear to diverge considerably across peoples and cultures. Westerman (2010, p. 214) argues that low engagement of health services by Indigenous people, particularly youth, is partially a result of this monocultural approach of most health services, described as "the failure of mental health services and clinicians to embrace Aboriginal conceptualisations of health and wellbeing". In doing so, the dominant health discourse across this continent assumes that Indigenous peoples' views of health are invalid and in need of modernising. In response, there have been concerted and growing efforts to better recognise the heterogeneous understandings of health of Indigenous peoples. In particular there has been a push to better accommodate Indigenous people's more 'relational' and 'holistic' conceptions of health, including the "strength and centrality of Aboriginal family and kinship" (Dudgeon et al., 2014, p. 75).

Much of the critical literature on public health explores the impact that existing relations between Indigenous subjects and settler health professionals have on health outcomes. For the reasons above, Aboriginal scholar Juanita Sherwood (2013, p. 30) explicitly describes colonisation as a social determinant of health, arguing that "the fate of health status is not entirely a choice but the product of many historical-political-social determinants that are often not elaborated within the discourse of medicine". It is clear that in seeking to address any disparities in health outcomes, we must also address these deeply ingrained 'cultural barriers' (McBain-Rigg & Veitch, 2011) to Indigenous healthcare.

Considering the social, political and cultural context in which healthcare across this continent is situated for Indigenous people, it is perhaps not surprising that research has indicated that Indigenous help-seeking is typically more informal than that practised by settlers (Farrelly, 2008; Rickwood et al., 2007), with responsibility for help-giving typically falling to family, friends and other social networks (Bishop al., 2012; Isaacs et al., 2010; Carlson & Frazer, 2020a; Carlson, Frazer, & Farrelly, 2020).

## *Possibilities of social media health-seeking*

In the context of these persisting failures to effectively address disparities in health outcomes for many marginalised and considered hard-to-reach populations—including Indigenous peoples, youth, elderly people and LGBTQIA+ people—recent research has looked towards the opportunities provided by digital technologies such as social media (Lin & Kishore, 2021). Through facilitating connections between billions of users, institutions and knowledges, Carlson and Frazer (2020a, p. 89) write, "social media has become one of the primary pathways through which new, more distributed networks of care might be achieved".

To date, social media research on health-seeking has yielded some promising findings. Social media provides a highly accessible and near instant source of health-related information, connecting users to 'informal' sources of help (including friends, family and other online networks) and more 'formal' sources of help, such as social media pages of mainstream health services. In this way, research has found that many people feel empowered when help-seeking online; that is, the personalised connections made possible on social media can foster a sense of agency over the health of users (Lupton, 2019) and help them feel more confident in accessing information and talking about sensitive topics (Gera et al., 2020). People often use social media effectively to meet their needs across a range of health-related domains, including seeking support for weight loss (Ballantine & Stephenson, 2011; Newman et al., 2011), managing chronic health issues such as diabetes (De Angelis et al., 2018), and handling stressful life experiences (Blight et al., 2015; Chang et al., 2018; Frison & Eggermont, 2015). Moreover, social media also allows users to solicit more relational, effective and emotional forms of support from others. Thus, the online help-seeking practices of users vary significantly, allowing users great autonomy over the help they can solicit, the information they divulge, and the connections they rely upon (Buehler, 2017).

## Indigenous online health-seeking

Health and social researchers have begun exploring the opportunities social media provides for Indigenous health-seeking, particularly considering the preference towards more 'informal forms of support'. While Walker and colleagues' (2019) recent comprehensive literature review returned just five academic articles on the topic, by and large they found this work was promising. It demonstrated that on the whole, social media offers "a space for providing social support, sharing health-promoting messages, and increasing awareness and self-efficacy of Aboriginal people in governing their own health" (Walker et al., 2019, pp. 4–5).

Health researchers, practitioners and institutions have been particularly interested in the opportunities social media provides in distributing formal health-promotion information. Tracking the annual Twitter event #IHMayDay, which aims to bring attention to Indigenous health issues, Sweet and colleagues (2015, p. 636) suggest that social media such as Twitter provide "powerful platforms for learning, exchange, advocacy and dialogue about the social and emotional well-being and mental health of Aboriginal and Torres Strait Islander peoples". In the context of health information relating to tobacco use among Indigenous users, Hefler and colleagues (2019, p. 714) similarly found that "Facebook is used by Aboriginal and Torres Strait Islander people as a supportive online environment, which increased real-world social capital". McPhail-Bell and colleagues (2017) note that most research has focused on how social media can be used to change the health behaviours of individual Indigenous users—what they describe as a one-directional model of information dissemination—and instead advocate an approach to online health promotion that is more dialogical, reciprocal and strengths-based.

A second, smaller strand of research has drawn on critical social theories to explore the more 'organic' health-seeking and health-giving practices of Indigenous social media users. Carlson and colleagues (2015) found that networks of friends, family and kin regularly, and often effectively, intervened in mental health crisis situations, recognising moments in which people in their network were at risk of self-harm. Alongside formal health networks, these more 'natural' networks worked to sustain the health of their online connections, mobilising an already existing spectrum of help-giving practices ranging from emotional support to emergency health interventions. Alternatively, looking at the health-seeking practices of Indigenous social media users, Carlson and colleagues (2020) documented five main categories of health-seeking practice: soliciting information and support; direct messaging; joining health-seeking collectives; sharing joyful and inspiring content; and searching for formal sources of help. "While far from being a panacea to existing health disparities", they conclude, "social media does provide unique opportunities and vital resources for many Indigenous help-seekers and help-givers in times of need" (Carlson, Frazer, & Farrelly, 2020, p. 523). This recent work, as Carlson and Frazer (2020a, p. 98) write, shows that "social media can provide pathways to care outside of settler institutions—outside the often-assimilatory forces of the settler state".

Overall, while still modest in scope, the existing work on Indigenous health-seeking on social media has been unequivocally positive, pointing towards potential pathways around existing barriers to health support for Indigenous people (Shand et al., 2013). As Hefler and co-authors (2019, p. 707) argue, for Indigenous people, "social media have the potential to encourage social support and enact an agenda of self-determination and empowerment which aligns with Indigenous notions of health".

## Barriers to online health-seeking

Outside this specific burgeoning literature, however, research on settler populations, both across this continent and elsewhere, has found that there are still myriad barriers to health-seeking in online environments—that is, existing barriers are often reproduced online, and entirely new ones can arise. Social media are not in any way 'neutral' spaces, somehow free from the broader forces that lead to differential health outcomes across different populations in the first place. Instead, unequal power relations, exclusionary social norms, and practices of marginalisation exist online, too, and these often work to mediate the help-seeking and help-giving practices of social media users.

In this vein, Chang and colleagues (2018, p. 9), for instance, found that decisions to respond or not to calls for help "are layered, complex and based on historical relationships". Likewise, Buehler (2017) found that interactions on Facebook, including seeking support through user networks, are informed and shaped by social norms of behaviour. There is a code of conduct online which works to determine which kinds of posts and interactions are appropriate online. In particular, soliciting emotional support can be sometimes seen as inappropriate (i.e. 'oversharing'), contravening implicit norms of online interaction, or popular ideas of 'proper conduct'.

In developing well-grounded understandings of the potential health benefits of social media for Indigenous people, this critical caveat must be taken seriously. It is clear that the benefits, barriers and dangers of using social media for help-seeking are differentially distributed across social groups. While indeed often offering Indigenous people a platform through which they can exercise political and cultural agency, where they can forge powerful connections to other users, institutions, knowledges and practices, and where the unequal power relations of settler colonialism can be resisted and rejected, social media does not escape entirely the logic of settler colonialism. Indeed, it can be a colonising tool, too, in which settler dominance is extended (Matamaros-Fernandez, 2017; Carlson & Frazer, 2021; Carlson & Day, 2022). In seeking help online, Indigenous people must navigate the complex, intersecting planes on which racism, misogyny and homophobia often proliferates

(Carlson, 2019; Bargallie, 2020; Carlson & Day, 2022); they must carefully manage their online interactions under what Ward and Williams (2016) describe as the 'digital panopticon', and what Carlson and Frazer (2020b, p. 1) describe as the latent 'settler gaze'. Therefore, despite their agency as individuals, we must also understand Indigenous social media users as already entangled in broader social, cultural and political systems which work to shape their health-seeking practices.

## Materials and methods

This chapter is the product of a larger research project that has sought to both empirically and critically explore the help-seeking and help-giving behaviours by Indigenous people. This research project has centred around unpacking how Indigenous peoples' unique and diverse notions of well-being dynamically interact with their ways of knowing, doing and being (Martin, 2008; Moreton-Robinson & Walter, 2009: Westerman, 2021) and with a specific consideration of information and technology contexts (Carlson & Frazer, 2022).

I draw on in-depth semi-structured interviews conducted with 41 Indigenous social media users across five communities, including the Illawarra (New South Wales (NSW)), Dubbo (NSW), Brewarrina (NSW), Darwin (Northern Territory (NT)), and Cairns (Queensland). Participants were aged from 19 to 60 years old. Of the 41 participants, 20 identified as women, 16 as men and a further five people identified as non-heterosexual. The interviews focused on the lived experiences of participants as they navigated social media, particularly Facebook, and we sought to untangle the factors that shape, mediate and mitigate their decisions to draw on the connections formed through social media in times of need. Transcripts were analysed using a form of grounded analysis coupled with Indigenist research approaches developed by Indigenous scholars such as Rigney (1999), Nakata (2007), and Tuhiwai-Smith (2012), which encourage researchers to prioritise Indigenous knowledges, practices and ontologies. This approach allowed themes to emerge from the stories of participants, rather than being determined by the researchers at the outset.

## Results

While the vast majority of people I spoke to described using social media for both seeking and receiving help, many also expressed hesitation, ambivalence and resistance about doing so. Many participants explained they were often wary of discussing and disclosing on Facebook issues relating to physical, social and emotional well-being. Through the process of data analysis, I identified four main factors that seem to mediate and mitigate the health-seeking practices of participants: first, social media etiquette and 'proper' online behaviour; second, the tension between help-seeking and so-called attention-seeking behaviours; third, the (mis)trust of social media technologies and the networks they facilitate; and finally, the superficial quality of many social media interactions.

### *Social media etiquette*

A significant portion of participant interviews focused on unpacking the factors that shape whether they choose to seek or provide help through social media. Much of this discussion tended to centre around what was considered 'proper' online behaviour. This question has also been a key concern for social scientists. Since its emergence over a decade ago, researchers have explored the ways in which social media is a platform for the performance of identities. Central to this discussion has been the problematic distinction between 'authentic' and 'inauthentic' performances of the self. While more recent research has moved past this distinction, instead of drawing attention to the processes through which authenticity is constructed, empirical research continues to show that users themselves make nuanced judgements about the authenticity of the expressions of those in their networks. In health-related research, this discussion has tended to centre on identifying differences between help-seeking behaviours and so-called attention-seeking behaviours.

Newman and colleagues (2011, p. 341), for instance, identified a tension in building/maintaining networks between "impression management and sharing information related to a health concern". Buehler (2017) found that interactions on Facebook, including seeking support through users' networks, are informed and shaped by social norms of behaviour. They explore "the delicate dance of impression management that users perform while attempting to achieve their support-receiving goals" (Buehler, 2017, p. 8). Buehler (2017, p. 1) argues that people seeking emotional support on Facebook must balance "their needs for emotional comfort with norms for appropriate behaviour". In this way, online norms, particularly around emotional disclosure, can be a barrier to seeking help. It seems not all forms of social support are effectively sought through Facebook. In particular, seeking emotional support is sometimes seen as inappropriate (i.e. 'oversharing')—contravening implicit norms of online interaction, or popular ideas of 'proper conduct'. Buehler (2017, p. 2) deduces that "verly emotional content is perceived as less appropriate for public sharing".

Two main themes emerged that centred around this question of 'appropriate' forms of health-seeking. The first concerned a broader consideration of social media etiquette. One participant discussed this quite explicitly:

D5: I think it's funny because on social media there's kind of now new rules of social etiquette forming as well. I mean they've kinda been forming for a while, but you see it around what types of Facebook posts or what types of tweets are kind of acceptable. And I found kind of just from not any sort of formal research, but you look at the types of posts about people trying to reach out, and they're kind of, 'this should be private' [...] I think it's just like the etiquette of making these things public, especially on something like Facebook. But you know where I see it generally is in family members who, you know, come from a community and so on, who probably give less shits about sort of the social etiquette of social media. So, for example [laughs], a cousin of mine will just like ask me like straight up on Facebook, like 'who's got 20 dollars, need fuel for my fuckin' car' [laughs]. As well as like requests for any family members to babysit their kids, that kind of thing. But she's also had a lot of struggles with mental health issues and stuff and she's never been afraid to write posts about that either, and reach out through Facebook.

Here, this participant describes a range of help-seeking practices, including some relating to health, and explains that there are complex norms around which are considered 'acceptable'. When participants were asked whether they would prefer to health-seek via social media or in person by phone or face to face, the majority indicated that it would depend on what exactly they were seeking help for. Some participants described Indigenous people as being typically 'private' with their personal lives:

B7: I don't know [if I'd seek help online]. It depends on what you're talking about. With Aboriginal people, they might not [...] Some might talk on there, some might not.

B6: Yeah, Aboriginal people are like, they're pretty quiet and pretty private with their lives.

B7: When it comes to health and that, yeah. Facebook and that, some do put some stuff on there about their health,

B6: But yeah, I don't. I don't broadcast nothing about my personal life on Facebook

For many participants, then, there was a sense that social media wasn't the 'proper place' to express particular thoughts, feelings and needs.

D8: I rarely put up statuses because as opposed to the bad side of it, I don't really feel that Facebook is a good place to vent really personal stuff.

For some participants, this notion of etiquette was culturally inflected, and social media was a place in which different cultural values, norms and mores come into contact and, in some cases, tension:

C1: Especially for them young ones that just don't know certain things. There are ways to behave in our community. And like, social media might have, like Facebook for instance, might have their code of conduct or, you know, their standards of, you know, behaviour and stuff. But there's also *our* stuff. And Facebook can't protect our stuff, our cultural sensitivities, you know? (original emphasis)

C7: I think that younger generation, they use it other than what it is meant to be for, you know. They've got the hook up, the smearing, they're fighting with other kids, and doing stuff like that [...] That's a really bad thing for us, you know. You hear someone's passed away and, you know them young ones are posting about someone saying before their family has had a chance to sit down and break the news together. Stuff like that, that's happening. I don't know. It's just taking a lot away from our culture. But you know, if they can get help and whatever than that is a good thing too.

### *Help-seeking versus attention-seeking*

The second major theme participants articulated around 'proper' online behaviour concerned perceptions of help-seeking versus attention-seeking behaviour as expressed in online posts. Considering whether they would use social media to ask for help for anything, many participants described a tension between attention-seeking and help-seeking practices, which mediated their responses to people in their networks who appeared in need of help:

> B1: But some people will say that for attention too. So, you don't know if it's true or not.

> Interviewer: How do you tell the difference, do you think, between someone who needs help and someone who's just looking for attention?

> B1: Someone who keeps putting up the same old thing over and over again. Like, they say they're gonna do it, but they don't, but they keep going on about it. But then again, you never know. They might need help too.

Likewise, a young person working in an Indigenous community centre in regional NSW described it as the difference between 'crying wolf' and 'the real thing':

> W4: There's a fine line with that, because there is the cry wolf thing, and then there's the real thing. A life's a life until it's gone, and so I try not to be too ignorant instead of going 'Fucking suck it up, would you?' I try to sort of understand it.

A health advocate explained that they also see a lot of these often ambiguous and 'indirect' calls for help on social media:

> D4: There was a term coined years ago called 'vague-booking', where people were posting really vague things, but it's only around attention-seeking. In the context of the work that I do, people *are* seeking attention, so you've gotta kind of validate that. But at what level? (original emphasis)

In an interview with two young people, they described seeing a friend displaying exactly these kinds of 'vague-booking' behaviours, an academic term coined to describe strategic ambiguity used on Facebook to both communicate and conceal sensitive affective content (Child & Starcher, 2016). This mutual friend would post images and text that ostensibly expressed happiness, but would intentionally leave in evidence of injuries they had sustained from a violent partner:

> D3: Yeah, there was one girl that I know, she's been posting lately a lot about, like, photos of her. She's got a black eye. And she keeps, like, putting up for attention, I think, like, for support and stuff. She's like, she's doing it in the wrong way. She's writing song lyrics in her posts, like with her photos of her black eye. And it's weird, but I think she's trying to get attention to get, like, support and stuff.

> D2: Right, okay, so it kind of looks like she's—

> D3: Happy and like, posing up. Like subtly trying to show it [...]

> D2: But I think she does need, like, support and stuff. And she wants that attention. Of course, yeah. But a lot of people have been giving her support. I gave her support.

This tension between supposedly 'genuine' help-seeking and 'inauthentic' attention-seeking mediated the help-seeking practices of some of the participants. A young person from the Northern Territory explained that, working through their own Sorry Business and grief, they used to put up posts each year commemorating the loss of some of their siblings, but have recently stopped doing so:

> D1: I felt like I had to share that. So, I would. I've stopped that now, in the last couple of years [because] I felt guilty. Because I felt like it was attention-seeking. And I didn't know if it was the right platform for it or not.

Similarly, a young person from the NSW South Coast explained that they now avoid discussing online when they have had a bad day and want some support:

> W6: I don't even like doing it because I get no response, and it comes off as sad and desperate and pathetic.

## *Trust in social media*

Scholars in the social sciences, particularly the digital humanities, have recently turned their attention to issues of 'trust' in online communities, technologies and infrastructures (Carlson, 2020; Carlson & Frazer, 2020a; Maddison & Nakata, 2020). Trust, as Cook (2005, p. 6) argues, "is at the very heart of the problem of social order and is essential to the conduct of everyday life". It is central to all relations that matter—including those sustained through social media technologies. Drawing on insights from settler-colonial studies, for instance, Carlson and Frazer (2020a, p. 90) unpack the political dynamics of trust in Indigenous help-seeking. They concluded that "in the absence of material access and social trust of formal help sources, these Indigenous users rely heavily on the often-powerful connections facilitated through social media" (Carlson & Frazer, 2020a, p. 90).

It appears that trust and its absence can powerfully mediate people's online health-seeking practices. While Carlson and Frazer's (2020a) recent work shows social media allows some Indigenous users to produce trustworthy networks of care in the absence of trust in settler institutions, this is evidently not without qualification. Some participants discussed the reliability and accuracy of advice and information to be gained from social media, noting a lack of understanding and misinformation often resulted in informal help sources giving less-than-helpful advice—albeit usually well intentioned. Two participants from regional NSW described how social media can facilitate the spread of potentially harmful misinformation:

> D5: The online social media support is getting better and better amongst peer groups [...] I've seen a lot of misinformation around mental health and mental illness online and in social media groups and in memes and that kind of thing as well. So, there's the positive and negative side to it [...] I think even back then, the understanding around mental health and mental health issues was quite minimal. So, some family and stuff were just like 'Oh, go for a walk'. Which is sweet, I mean, they didn't know, but I think most of us now are aware of like how to respond to these types of things. Well

I'd hope so. But most of the time it was just 'Hey, I love you, try and stay safe'. That kind of thing, rather than any sort of trained responses or things like that.

D6: When you talk about suicide and stuff like that, people can give an opinion, and if that person's actually distressed, sometimes it can be the wrong thing [...] Not a healthy thing.

One participant noted that the intention or motivation of others on social media needed to be taken into consideration when evaluating the trustworthiness of the information and advice they might give others:

D5: I think maybe sort of the negative side to that is there's people maybe engaging in the mental health sector using social media to sort of elevate themselves more so than to support.

Other participants believed that social media was not a safe place to discuss sensitive personal matters, such as would be happening in their health-seeking from formal help sources such as health organisations, for example:

W1: Don't need social media for it. I would just make a phone call or go to a [...] like I use Barnardo's a lot, the Aboriginal playgroup. But other than that, I don't. I'll just make a phone call. I won't use social media for it because someone could see it, or someone could hack into things. It's just not safe enough. If it's personal enough, you wouldn't advertise it in the first place [...] If I need help in urgent situations or things like that, I'd prefer to talk. But yeah, because it's social media, obviously other people can sort of [...] there's people on there you don't want to know your business. Things like that. So, I'd make a phone call or send a text message, private text message, not even use Messenger.

### *Superficiality of social media*

While much has been made of the powerful affordances of social media platforms in forging connections between people across vast distances, there is also a critical discussion about the *quality* of these connections. The crucial question is: what exactly is the *substance* of social media networks? Recent work has conceptualised social media relations as defined by discursive, ideological, emotional and affective qualities—an assemblage of connections that are different in kind (Byron, 2020; Carlson & Frazer, 2021; Frazer et al., 2022). More difficult to conceptualise, however, is the importance of materiality in social media relations. While scholars have moved past reproducing reductive notions of social media as 'disembodied', exactly *how* social media is 'embodied' is still up for debate.

Participants in this study articulated an awareness of the difference that social media makes in health-seeking relations. When they were asked if social media makes them 'feel supported' in any way, many participants made clear distinctions between their online and offline relations:

D2: I don't know [if it makes me feel supported]. I mean, not really. I mean, unless I'm talking to someone. Social media allows me to talk to my friends if I need help, or my family, if I need someone to talk to. But I don't really feel supported. Not really. I mean, I still talk to people, but it's not really the same. [To another interviewee] Do you feel supported?

D3: Uh, not really. Facebook's like everybody and I don't kind of want to put like, my business on Facebook. So, I'd rather like, ring someone and talk to them instead of like, putting it on Facebook.

Interviewer: And does being on Facebook make you feel personally supported in any way?

D2: No [laughs]. Not at all. I mean it's nice when people comment, but unless they actually physically do something, it doesn't, you know, words could be [...] you know 'I'm here for you' or whatever. But unless they actually do reach out then to me, it seems like, I don't know, they didn't really mean it. Or, I don't know. I don't know how to explain it. Actions speak louder than words to me.

D1: Yeah, yeah, I just feel like this online support is superficial in a way. Yeah, like my closest friends I know who like, who I would be able to talk to in person, they, their comments on Facebook I know are genuine. Like, I know if I put up a post and, you know, and say 'thinking of you' or something, I like, I know they're genuine. But then there would be, you know, like, uh what's it called, the like, counting from people that I don't know. Like, why does that matter?

Overall, there was a sense that the relations formed online were qualitatively different from those maintained offline, and this had consequences for the health-seeking and health-giving practices of these users. As the above accounts demonstrate, this was often talked about through the language of 'superficiality'. It could be argued that the level of superficiality that is characteristic of mainstream social media is not readily acceptable in Indigenous networks because there is a responsibility to actually do something if you are able, and that Indigenous people will typically do that rather than just offer superficial platitudes. One participant explained that the quality of offline relations is more appropriate for communicating about health-related issues, and that their beliefs about this are likely founded in how they've been brought up:

B2: I've grown up a certain way that I just won't do it. If I want to talk to somebody about something, I'll tell them face to face. Do it professionally. But again, that's probably because of my age group. We were taught to communicate, you know?

Another participant described accessing an online health service, noting that when the chat bot appeared, they were hesitant to use it:

D2: I think [I was apprehensive] because when I'm talking to someone, I like that connection also. Like face-to-face stuff [...] Because I work in the social service sector as well, like working with Indigenous folk. Even just a phone call to talk to Centrelink brings up a lot of anxieties and stuff. People prefer to go in and pay, face-to-face because I think, with our style of communication, it's a whole sort of body language and all that stuff as well.

## Discussion

To realise the potential health benefits of social media for Indigenous people, already existing help-seeking behaviours need to be better understood. This includes paying close attention to the powerful forces already shaping and determining people's decision to seek help or not—what O'Sullivan (2015) has described as the 'political determinants' of health. Rather than focusing on neoliberal notions of individual agency, we must also understand health as "the product of many historical-political-social determinants that are often not elaborated within the discourse of medicine", as Sherwood suggests (2013, p. 30).

To start working towards this end, this research aimed to identify some of the forces that work to mediate and mitigate the online health-seeking practices of Indigenous social media users. The above findings show that Indigenous people are using social media to connect with one another, support each other, produce caring networks and sustain healthy lives, families and communities (see Carlson & Frazer, 2020b). In terms of barriers to online health-seeking, we identified four main themes that centred around ideas of 'appropriate' forms of health-seeking, and the 'quality' of online relations. These themes provide useful direction for health researchers and practitioners, and health communication targeting Indigenous people in general.

Indigenous social media users are navigating a complex web of values, norms and beliefs that shape what is considered 'proper' online behaviour. In deciding whether to seek help online, they must negotiate multiple intersecting fields of etiquette—the emerging social media etiquette, the values held by their people and community, and their own personal beliefs.

Tensions between whether a behaviour may be perceived as help-seeking or so-called attention-seeking actively mediates both health-seeking and help-giving practices online. The participants in this study appear to be acutely aware that their online expressions of grief, sadness and low spirits could be interpreted as attention-seeking behaviours just as easily as they could be interpreted as help-seeking. This awareness clearly shaped both their responses to people in their networks as well their own help-seeking behaviours. It was understood that seeking attention was not 'acceptable' online behaviour, and even genuine requests for support that could be interpreted as attention-seeking should be avoided. Encouragingly, however, the accounts above also display an awareness that attention-seeking can actually be a form of help-seeking—it can be a way of asking for help, without directly asking for it. Indeed, how can one ask for help without seeking another's attention?

In terms of (mis)trust in social media, it is likely that some Indigenous social media users would be reluctant to make public certain information due to past experiences with government departments, not wanting to draw attention to themselves and incur some sort of intervention from these government departments or attract racial abuse. Such conscious decision-making speaks to an Indigenous-specific social media etiquette that may be already unofficially enacted.

These participant accounts draw attention to the importance of trust, both its presence and its absence, in deciding whether to draw on the networks formed on social media to seek and provide help for health-related issues. While on the one hand, social media opens opportunities for these users to take control of their health, connect with health knowledges, and work to sustain the health of oneself and one's peers, it can equally connect them with harmful knowledges. These participants articulate a healthy suspicion of health-related actors and information online.

The superficial quality of social media interactions also determines the nature and extent of health-seeking online. While social media certainly allows people to connect with friends, family and other sources of help, as a participant above explained, "it's not really the same". Exactly *how* 'it's not the same' is still a question that scholars are grappling with. However, for these participants, it is the lived experience that matters. The materiality and relationality of online health-seeking *feels* different. It doesn't fulfil the criteria required to make them feel truly supported by others. And so, despite being connected to dozens or hundreds of friends, family and acquaintances, many of the participants in this study still prefer the more familiar and, for them, more comfortable experience of seeking help directly from their friends while in their immediate physical presence.

## Acknowledgements

I would like to acknowledge the contribution of the Aboriginal and Torres Strait Islander participants who gave their time and stories for this project. I would also like to acknowledge the Australian Research Council for funding the project, through the Discovery Indigenous programme INI60100049.

## Ethics Approval

This research has ethics approval from the Macquarie University Human Research Ethics Committee, ID: 5201700667.

## Note

1   A note on terminology: There is no universally agreed-upon terminology for referring to the many diverse groups who comprise the Aboriginal and Torres Strait Islander peoples of Australia. In this chapter, I primarily use the term 'Indigenous' to refer to all peoples and groups whose ancestors predate colonisation and who identify as such; 'Aboriginal and/or Torres Strait Islander' is also used where appropriate.

## References

Australian Bureau of Statistics. (2019). 4714.0 National Aboriginal and Torres Strait Islander Social Survey 2014–15. www.abs.gov.au/ausstats/abs@.nsf/mf/4714.0

Ballantine, P. W., & Stephenson, R. J. (2011). 'Help me, I'm fat!': Social support in online weight loss networks. *Journal of Consumer Behaviour, 10*(6), 332–337.

Bargallie, D. (2020). *Unmasking the racial contract: Indigenous voices on racism in the Australian Public Service.* Aboriginal Studies Press.

Bishop, B. J., Vicary, D. A., Mitchell, J. R., & Pearson, G. (2012). Aboriginal concepts of place and country and their meaning in mental health. *The Australian Community Psychologist, 24*(2), 26–42.

Blight, M. G., Jagiello, K., & Ruppel, E. K. (2015). 'Same stuff different day': A mixed method study of support seeking on Facebook. *Computers in Human Behavior, 53*, 366–373.

Buehler, E. M. (2017). 'You shouldn't use Facebook for that': Navigating norm violations while seeking emotional support on Facebook. *Social Media + Society, 3*(3), 1–11.

Byron, P. (2020). *Digital media, friendship and cultures of care.* Routledge.

Carlson, B. (2019). Disrupting the master narrative: Indigenous people and tweeting colonial history. *Griffith Review, 64*, 224–234.

Carlson, B. (2020). Indigenous killjoys: Negotiating the labyrinth of dis/mis trust. In T. Moeke-Pickering, A. Pegoraro, & S. Cote-Meek, S. (Eds.), *Critical reflections and politics on advancing women in the academy* (pp. 105–123). IGI Global.

Carlson, B., & Berglund, J. (2021). *Indigenous peoples rise up: The global ascendency of social media activism*. Rutgers University Press.

Carlson, B., & Day, M. (2022). Colonial violence on dating apps. In H. Arden, A. Briers, N. & Carah (Eds.), *Conflict in my outlook*, (pp. 72–74). University of Queensland Press.

Carlson, B., Farrelly, T., Frazer, R. & Borthwick, F. (2015). Mediating tragedy: Facebook, Aboriginal peoples and suicide. *Australasian Journal of Information Systems, 19*, 1–15.

Carlson, B., & Frazer, R. (2020a). The politics of (dis)trust in Indigenous help-seeking. In S. Maddison & S. Nakata (Eds.), *Questioning Indigenous-settler relations: Interdisciplinary perspectives* (pp. 87–106). Springer.

Carlson, B. & Frazer, R. (2020b). 'They got filters': Indigenous social media, the settler gaze and a politics of hope. *Social Media + Society, 6*(2), 1–11.

Carlson, B., & Frazer, R. (2021). *Indigenous digital life: The practice and politics of being Indigenous on social media*. Palgrave Macmillan.

Carlson, B. & Frazer, R. (2022). 'Looking out for mob: Help-seeking and giving online'. Macquarie University, Sydney. https://researchers.mq.edu.au/en/publications/looking-out-for-mob-on-social-media-help-seeking-and-giving-onlin

Carlson, B., Frazer, R., & Farrelly, T. (2021). 'That makes all the difference': Aboriginal and Torres Strait Islander health-seeking on social media. *Health Promotion Journal of Australia, 32*(3), 523–531. https://doi.org/10.1002/hpja.366

Chang, P. F., Whitlock, J., & Bazarova, N. N. (2018). 'To respond or not to respond, that is the question': The decision-making process of providing social support to distressed posters on Facebook. *Social Media + Society, 4*(1), 1–11.

Child, J. T., & Starcher, S. C. (2016). Fuzzy Facebook privacy boundaries: Exploring mediated lurking, vague-booking, and Facebook privacy management. *Computers in Human Behavior, 54*, 483–490.

Cook, K. S. (2005). Networks, norms, and trust: The social psychology of social capital 2004 Cooley Mead Award address. *Social Psychology Quarterly, 68*(1), 4–14.

De Angelis, G., Wells, G. A., Davies, B., King, J., Shallwani, S. M., McEwan, J., ... & Brosseau, L. (2018). The use of social media among health professionals to facilitate chronic disease self-management with their patients: A systematic review. *Digital Health, 4*, 2055207618771416.

Duarte, M. (2017). Connected activism: Indigenous uses of social media for shaping political change. *Australasian Journal of Information Systems, 21*, 1–12.

Dudgeon, P., Milroy, H., & Walker, R. (2014). *Working together: Aboriginal and Torres Strait Islander mental health and wellbeing principles and practice*. Telethon Kids Institute, Kulunga Aboriginal Research Development Unit, Department of the Prime Minister and Cabinet (Australia).

Farrell, A. (2017). Archiving the Aboriginal rainbow: Building an Aboriginal LGBTIQ portal. *Australasian Journal of Information Systems, 21*, 1–14. https://doi.org/10.3127/ajis.v21i0.1589

Farrelly, T. (2008). The Aboriginal suicide and self-harm help-seeking quandary. *Aboriginal and Islander Health Worker Journal, 32*(1), 11–15.

Frazer, R., Carlson, B., & Farrelly, T. (2022). Indigenous articulations of social media and digital assemblages of care. *Digital Geography and Society, 3*, 100038.

Frison, E., & Eggermont, S. (2015). The impact of daily stress on adolescents' depressed mood: The role of social support seeking through Facebook. *Computers in Human Behavior, 44*, 315–325.

Garvey, D. (2008). Review of the social and emotional wellbeing of Indigenous Australian peoples. *Australian Indigenous HealthInfoNet*. www.healthinfonet.ecu.edu.au/other-health-conditions/mental-health/reviews/our-review

Gera, P., Thomas, N., & Neal, T. (2020, July). Hesitation while posting: A cross-sectional survey of sensitive topics and opinion sharing on social media. In *International Conference on Social Media and Society* (pp. 134–140). Social Media & Society.

Gooda, M., & Dudgeon, P. (2014). *The Elders' report into preventing Indigenous self-harm and youth suicide*. Analysis and Policy Observatory. https://apo.org.au/node/40060

Goodman, A., Snyder, M., Wilson, K., & Whitford, J. (2019). Healthy spaces: Exploring urban Indigenous youth perspectives of social support and health using photovoice. *Health & Place, 56*(March 2019), 34–42. https://doi.org/10.1016/j.healthplace.2019.01.004

Hefler, M., Kerrigan, V., Henryks, J., Freeman, B., & Thomas, D. P. (2019). Social media and health information sharing among Australian Indigenous people. *Health Promotion International, 34*(4), 706–715.

Henson, C., Rambaldini, B., Carlson, B., Wadolowski, M., Vale, C., & Gwynne, K. (2022). A new path to address health disparities: How older Aboriginal & Torres Strait Islander women use social media to enhance community health (Protocol). *Digital Health, 8,* 20552076221084469.

Herring, S., Spangaro, J., Lauw, M., & McNamara, L. (2013). The intersection of trauma, racism, and cultural competence in effective work with Aboriginal people: Waiting for trust. *Australian Social Work, 66*(1), 104–117.

Isaacs, A. N., Pyett, P., Oakley-Browne, M. A., Gruis, H., & Waples-Crowe, P. (2010). Barriers and facilitators to the utilization of adult mental health services by Australia's Indigenous people: seeking a way forward. *International Journal of Mental Health Nursing, 19*(2), 75–82.

Lin, X., & Kishore, R. (2021). Social media-enabled healthcare: A conceptual model of social media affordances, online social support, and health behaviors and outcomes. *Technological Forecasting and Social Change, 166,* 120574.

Lupton, D. (2019). 'I'd like to think you could trust the government, but I don't really think we can': Australian women's attitudes to and experiences of My Health Record. *Digital Health, 5,* 8.

Maddison, S., & Nakata, S. (2020). *Questioning Indigenous-settler relations.* Springer Singapore.

Martin, K. (2008). *Please knock before you enter: Aboriginal regulation of outsiders and the implications for researchers.* Post Pressed.

Matamoros-Fernández, A. (2017). Platformed racism: The mediation and circulation of an Australian race-based controversy on Twitter, Facebook and YouTube. *Information, Communication & Society, 20*(6), 930–946.

McBain-Rigg, K. E., & Veitch, C. (2011). Cultural barriers to health care for Aboriginal and Torres Strait Islanders in Mount Isa. *Australian Journal of Rural Health, 19*(2), 70–74.

McPhail-Bell, K., Appo, N., Haymes, A., Bond, C., Brough, M., & Fredericks, B. (2017). Deadly choices empowering Indigenous Australians through social networking sites. *Health Promotion International, 33*(5), 770–780.

Moreton-Robinson, A., & Walter, M. (2009). Indigenous methodologies in social research. In M. Walter (Ed.), *Social research methods* (2nd ed.). 1–18. Oxford University Press.

Nakata, M. (2007). *Disciplining the savages: Savaging the disciplines.* Aboriginal Studies Press.

Newman, M. W., Lauterbach, D., Munson, S. A., Resnick, P., & Morris, M. E. (2011). 'It's not that I don't have problems, I'm just not putting them on Facebook': Challenges and opportunities in using online social networks for health. In *Proceedings of the ACM 2011 Conference on Computer Supported Cooperative Work*, March 2011 (pp.341–350). Association for Computing Machinery.

O'Sullivan, D. (2015). *Indigenous health: Power, politics and citizenship.* Australian Scholarly Publishing.

Paradies, Y., & Cunningham, J. (2009). Experiences of racism among urban Indigenous Australians: Findings from the DRUID study. *Ethnic and Studies, 32*(3), 548–573.

Rickwood, D., Deane, F., & Wilson, C. (2007). When and how do young people seek professional help for mental health problems? *Medical Journal of Australia, 187*(7), 35–39.

Rigney, L. I. (1999). Internalization of an Indigenous anticolonial cultural critique of research methodologies: A guide to Indigenist research methodology and its principles. *Wicazo Sa Review, 14*(2), 109–121.

Shand, F. L., Ridani, R., Tighe, J., & Christensen, H. (2013). The effectiveness of a suicide prevention app for indigenous Australian youths: Study protocol for a randomized controlled trial. *Trials, 14*(1), 1–7.

Sherwood, J. (2013). Colonisation—it's bad for your health: The context of Aboriginal health. *Contemporary Nurse, 46*(1), 28–40.

Sjoberg, D., & McDermott, D. (2016). The deconstruction exercise: An assessment tool for enhancing critical thinking in cultural safety education. *International Journal of Critical Indigenous Studies, 9*(1), 28–48.

Sweet, M., Geia, L., Dudgeon, P., & McCallum, K. (2015). # IHMayDay: tweeting for empowerment and social and emotional wellbeing. *Australasian Psychiatry, 23*(6), 636–640.

Taylor, K. P. & Thompson, S. C. (2011). Closing the (service) gap: Exploring partnerships between Aboriginal and mainstream health services. *Australian Health Review, 35*(3), 297–308.

Tuhiwai-Smith, L. (2012). *Decolonizing methodologies: Research and Indigenous peoples.* Zed Books.

Vicary, D., & Westerman, T. (2004). That's just the way he is': Some implications of Aboriginal mental health beliefs. *Australian e-Journal for the Advancement of Mental Health, 3*(3), 103–112.

Walker, T., Palermo, C., & Klassen, K. (2019). Considering the impact of social media on contemporary improvement of Australian Aboriginal health: Scoping review. *JMIR Public Health and Surveillance, 5*(1), e11573.

Ward, R., & Williams, L. (2016). Initial views from the Digital Panopticon: Reconstructing penal outcomes in the 1790s. *Law and History Review, 34*(4), 893–928.

Westerman, T. (2010). Engaging Australian Aboriginal youth in mental health services. *Australian Psychologist, 45*(3), 212–222.

Westerman, T. (2021). Culture-bound syndromes in Aboriginal Australian populations. *Clinical Psychologist, 25*(1), 19–35.

Zubrick, S. R., Lawrence, D. M., Silburn, S. R., Blair, E., Milroy, H., Wilkes, T., Eades, S., D'Antoine, H., Read, A., Ishiguchi, P., & Doyle, S. (2004). *The Western Australian Aboriginal Child Health Survey: The Health of Aboriginal Children and Young People.* Telethon Institute for Child Health Research. www.telethonkids.org.au/our-research/aboriginal-health/waachs/

# 28
# INDIGENOUS STUDIES AND THE FUTURE OF KNOWLEDGE FORMATION IN HIGHER EDUCATION

*Tristan Kennedy*

## Introduction

Indigenous Studies is an established discipline within the broader field of humanities, arts and social sciences (HASS). Despite being structurally located most often within the bounds of the HASS discipline, Indigenous Studies requires a post-disciplinary approach which critically interrogates the interface of Indigenous and Western knowledges (Nakata, 2007). It is a highly innovative site for critical engagement with history and creative imagining of the future outside of the bounds of traditional institutional frames. Indigenous researchers examine contemporary and historical impacts of settler colonialism on Indigenous peoples and propose solutions to the question of marginalisation and oppression of Indigenous communities in Australia and across the globe. Housed within higher education institutions, Indigenous Studies researchers are fully engaged in the process of knowledge formation (Connell, 2019), that is, the creation of "an expanding, many-sided, and above all *shared*, body of knowledge" (Connell, 2019, p. 12)—*the* core activity of higher education institutions. As innovative researchers and thinkers, Indigenous academics are at the forefront of the creation of new knowledges based on diverse Indigenous epistemologies and ontologies. However, the substantive contributions to knowledge offered in Indigenous Studies departments are always at risk of being overlooked by those whose conception of Indigenous peoples' presence in higher education institutions is to provide pastoral care for Indigenous students and cultural advice to colleagues (O'Sullivan, 2019). It is difficult not to see this oversight as a form of settler-colonial epistemic violence (Moreton-Robinson, 2014) based on historical assumptions that position Indigenous knowledges as unscientific and non-verifiable cultural knowledge.

On the knowledge created in higher education institutions, Connell (2019, p. 28) suggests:

> It is not just one researcher, one project, or one finding that represents the state of knowledge. Rather it is a growing mass of findings produced by a whole workforce

of researchers, and especially the way the findings are linked up, as fields of knowledge unfold and influence each other. The collective labour of research brings a social reality—the knowledge formation as a whole—into existence, through historical time.

If it is not just one researcher but a whole workforce of researchers who are charged with bringing about a social reality, we cannot then overlook the presence of Indigenous researchers and knowledge holders in our higher education institutions. There are two clear benefits for a reconfiguration of the current position of Indigenous research in higher education. First, adding diverse perspectives to the pursuit of knowledge can only add to the resultant knowledges. Indeed, the combination of Western and Indigenous ontologies and epistemologies in the pursuit of knowledge formation is methodologically prudent. Second, following a social justice approach to education and knowledge creation, the inclusion of Indigenous voices and perspectives in this knowledge formation will drive scholarly examinations of the challenges faced by Indigenous peoples in Australia and through colonised lands across the globe. Through equal contribution and openness to non-Western ways of thinking and being, research may imagine new and innovative answers to future questions (Locke et al., 2021).

The production and dissemination of knowledge among Indigenous peoples is, unsurprisingly, a core facet of Indigenous society and culture. Kaurna Elder Uncle Lewis O'Brien reminds us, "We [Kaurna] ran conferences and gained from each other's expertise and that's how we lasted 60,000 years. It's not on whims and fancies and aimless wandering" (O'Brien & Watson, 2014, p. 454). This continued pursuit of knowledge and knowledge sharing is reflected in the growth of Indigenous Studies research in Australia and across the globe. In Australia, until 2020, the Forum for Indigenous Research Excellence (FIRE) consisted of hundreds of Indigenous researchers and allies who worked collaboratively to advance Indigenous Studies research both at home and internationally. The Native American and Indigenous Studies Association (NAISA) has an international membership that congregates annually to share advances in Indigenous-led research. The Centre for Global Indigenous Futures at Macquarie University, the latest incarnation of FIRE, consists of a rapidly expanding membership of Indigenous and allied researchers. The breadth and diversity of Indigenous Studies was recently recognised within the Australian and New Zealand Standard Research Classifications (ANZSRC) system with a suite of Field of Research codes that reflect the specific interests of an interdisciplinary scholarly field. This, in part, is an increasing recognition of the world-leading research being conducted by and with Indigenous researchers across institutions and disciplines.

Despite their contributions to scholarship across the world, Indigenous peoples' presence on university campuses is still often misunderstood. There remains evidence of a conflation of the roles of Indigenous Studies departments or schools with Indigenous Support Units (ISUs) or cultural centres. This chapter suggests that the dismissal of Indigenous researchers as cultural advisers or support staff is not a result of a simple misunderstanding. Rather, it reflects the settler colonial "logic of elimination" (Wolfe, 2006) which continues to delegitimise Indigenous peoples' presence in the Western academy. Indigenous knowledges are thus relegated to cultural, non-scientific knowledge, and Indigenous scholars are stripped of their legitimacy as qualified scholars capable of world-leading research. While the impacts of this are detrimental to Indigenous peoples and communities, this chapter further suggests that a concerted departure from settler colonial approaches to knowledge formation will yield immense benefit for Indigenous and non-Indigenous people and society.

## Indigenous Support Units

In 1973, the Aboriginal Task Force (ATF) was established at the South Australian Institute of Technology, now the University of South Australia. The task force was formed during a wave of Indigenous political activism that followed the 1967 referendum. The initial role of the ATF was to provide training and qualifications to Indigenous people who might otherwise not gain entry to higher education, many of whom were already making unrecognised contributions in community. The ATF was later to become the David Unaipon College of Indigenous Education and Research at the University of South Australia (Anderson, 2015). It was the first of its kind and the forerunner to contemporary ISUs (Trudgett, 2009) which operate across most Australian universities.

The introduction of ISUs was a response to the fundamental disadvantages faced by Indigenous students within Western institutions. Professor MaryAnn Bin-Sallik, who worked as a counsellor at the ATF, described the problems facing Indigenous students as: "the failure of the secondary school system to equip [Indigenous students] with the higher education prerequisites; the situation of being the only Indigenous student in an otherwise white colonial environment; and a curriculum still embedded in theories of scientific racism" (Bin-Sallik, 2003, p. 22).

Settler colonialism undergirds the assumption that Indigenous peoples are ill-suited to education generally. Since Lachlan Macquarie established the first school for Indigenous students in the early nineteenth century, the education system has been plagued with theories about Indigenous physical and cultural inferiority. These theories have been justified by reference to racialised scientific discourse which positions Indigenous peoples are premodern and uncivilised. Classrooms thus became the sites of "repeated attempts to 'civilise' of the Aboriginal population away from their tribal customs" (Beresford, 2012, p. 85). Approaches to Indigenous education in Australia have gone through several policy shifts that reflected settler colonialism in various forms. Early educational policy was closely tied to Christianity and focused on training Indigenous peoples for lives as domestic servants and labourers (Patrick & Moodie, 2016). Approaches to Indigenous education then shifted to reflect assimilation, integration and self-determination policies throughout the twentieth century. While this shift in thinking was seen as progress by some, participation and completion rates of Indigenous peoples in all levels of education remained low. The continued failure of the education system is a result of a refusal to critically interrogate the impacts settler colonialism which persist today.

As Bin-Sallik (2003, p. 22) pointed out, Indigenous Australian participation in higher education was almost unheard of 50 years ago; In the early 1970s, only 18 Indigenous people were known to be enrolled in higher education. With so few students on campus, it was common for Indigenous students to feel isolated and alone when facing institutional racism and marginalisation. ISUs responded to this challenge and as a result much has changed in 50 years. ISUs are increasingly commonplace in Australian higher education institutions. In 2022, most universities in Australia have either a dedicated ISU or an Indigenous Studies school or department. In many cases, the emergence of Indigenous Studies departments occurred through the teaching activities of staff within ISUs. For instance, at Macquarie University in New South Wales, the Department of Indigenous Studies today sits within the Faculty of Arts as a department focused on Indigenous Studies as a discrete discipline. Previously, the department's teaching, research and community engagement activities were combined with Indigenous student support activities under the name Warawara. As universities recognised a need to deliver some Indigenous content in disciplines like education, health and medicine, ISUs were called on to provide this content. The invitation extended to Indigenous staff to provide this cultural content was far from a recognition of Indigenous Studies as a discipline and more a desire to tick the cultural competency box for non-Indigenous staff and students.

The combined roles of ISUs and Indigenous Studies departments may appear, though, as a logical solution to the challenges to Indigenous participation in higher education. As Bin-Sallik (2003, p. 22) recognised, there was a need to address the systemic barriers that prevent Indigenous peoples from accessing higher education, highlighting the "determination of Indigenous people to safeguard their students from being 'whitewashed' in these institutions by ensuring provisions were in place for a culturally safe environment". Addressing these barriers required both a pragmatic approach to address attraction and retention as well as a scholarly critique of settler colonial institutions. Much of the research that emerged during the period from the 1970s until the early 2000s highlighted the institutional power dynamic which existed and helped establish the discipline of Indigenous Studies in Australia. It also saw a dramatic increase in accessibility of higher education for Indigenous students. ISUs continue to pursue the increased participation of Indigenous students and staff at Australian higher education institutions. As acknowledged by the *Behrendt Report* (Behrendt et al., 2012) and the more recent *Indigenous Strategy Third Annual Report* from Universities Australia (2021), ISUs provide an invaluable site for the crucial connection between Indigenous staff and students, the institution and the wider Indigenous community.

In 1964, the Aboriginal Research Centre at Monash University was the first Centre for Indigenous research in Australia (Monash University, 2022), although it took until 1977 to appoint its first full-time Indigenous director, Professor Colin Burke. Indigenous Studies departments and Indigenous scholars since have continued to build the field of Indigenous Studies across Australia. A uniquely interdisciplinary field, Indigenous Studies departments' research and teaching activities generally reflect what Nakata and colleagues (2012, p. 127) refer to as an "examination of the complex layers of meaning that now circumscribe what it means to be Indigenous and how Indigenous contemporary social conditions and concerns can be understood". Departments such as this also often retain strong links to schools of education and health, continuing to co-teach pre-service teaching and nursing courses reflecting the history of Indigenous participation in higher education as focused on areas important to community such as education, health and welfare (Worby et al., 2016).

From ISUs, Indigenous Studies departments were born. ISUs were the entry point into an academy whose very existence is premised on the subjugation of Indigenous epistemologies. Today, ISUs are a valuable site for 'growing our own', that is, fostering future Indigenous scholars' pathways into academia. However, an emphasis on the separation of ISUs and Indigenous Studies departments is needed if both are to succeed in their specific roles. While Indigenous academics are housed, or assumed to be housed, within ISUs, the marginalisation of Indigenous knowledges and scholarship by the wider Western academy will continue. No longer can Indigenous academics continue to be considered present only to provide cultural advice and pastoral care rather than be leaders in the process of knowledge formation.

## Ticking the box

The conflation of Indigenous Studies and ISUs by a Western academy continues to delegitimise Indigenous knowledges and scholarship. Indigenous scholars are often presumed to be present to provide cultural advice to 'mainstream' researchers and pastoral care to Indigenous students. According to Asmar and Page, Indigenous staff routinely receive requests to 'advise' on the research activity of non-Indigenous colleagues across the university; to provide additional tutorial assistance to Indigenous students; and to provide colleagues with cultural advice on their approaches to 'indigenising' their curriculum (2009 p. 392). Indigenous academics are also often asked to participate in inordinate numbers of community engagement activities as Indigenous representatives (Page & Asmar, 2008). This is particularly troubling for Indigenous academics who work away from Country and reflects a colonial homogenisation of Indigenous culture and identity (Locke et al., 2022, p. 11). These requests may include membership of university committees or being listed on research proposals to give 'legitimacy' to non-Indigenous peoples' investigations into Indigenous lives and culture. The effect of this positioning of Indigenous scholars as outside of the knowledge formation activity of the institution reflects the persistent settler colonial narrative which devalues Indigenous knowledges.

When Indigenous knowledges and perspectives are invited to knowledge formation activities such as conferences, they are still treated as different. In 2021, Professor Bronwyn Carlson tweeted her response to requests to review Indigenous papers for an upcoming conference. She finished the tweet with #moveoverwehere and a declaration that if conference papers are going to be listed in the Indigenous stream, then the papers need to be authored by Indigenous scholars.

> I have been asked to consider abstracts for a discipline specific conference coming up. I received the abstracts—If it is the 'Indigenous stream' then the presenters need to be Indigenous. @IndigStudiesMQ @IndigFutures @IllAcademix #MoveOverWeHere.
> (@BronwynCarlson, Jun 7, 2021)

Carlson's tweet sheds light on two common experiences of Indigenous academics in higher education. Firstly, Indigenous academics are asked to provide cultural adjudication on all manner of activities. Most academics, generally, feel pressure to offer services to the wider community that fall under the categories of administrative or service work. These services take the form of peer review, membership of numerous internal and external committees and advisory boards, and feedback on non-Indigenous academics' research and teaching activities for little or no direct reward (Melin et al., 2014). Indigenous academics are often asked, on top of these activities, to provide cultural advice, acknowledgements and welcomes to Country for non-Indigenous colleagues. Many of these activities simply do not fit current institutional workload models.

Secondly, Carlson's tweet is a response to a request by conference organisers who were seeking an Indigenous academic's expertise in judging the merit of conference papers to be presented in a specific Indigenous stream by presenters who were non-Indigenous. It is difficult not to imagine that this demonstrates a clear box-ticking exercise. This highlights the positioning of Indigenous academics' roles as peripheral and for the provision of cultural clarification and endorsement rather than participation in the dissemination of scholarship. Such misalignment of Indigenous academics' roles within institutions is informed by settler colonial narratives of Indigenous knowledges and clearly a symptom of the conflation of ISUs and Indigenous Studies departments.

I have been asked to review entire ethics applications for non-Indigenous researchers (outside of my duties as a member of an ethics committee). I am asked this despite the existence of extensive resources such as the Guidelines for Ethical Research in Australian Indigenous Studies (GERAIS), the Australian Institute for Aboriginal and Torres Strait Islander Studies (AIATSIS) Code of Ethics (AIATSIS, 2022), and institutional cultural centres and community representatives. All these resources would inform non-Indigenous researchers that the best, and perhaps only ethical way forward is to adhere to the tenet of Indigenous-led research, which is: research with, for, and about Indigenous people *must* involve Indigenous researchers as part of the research leadership team and with "genuine decision-making responsibility" (AIATSIS, 2022, p. 17). Asking Indigenous people to cast an eye over ethics applications or to vet papers submitted to an Indigenous conference stream, is far from genuine decision-making responsibility.

> I regret writing my last employers 1ts Reconciliation Action Plan, it never goes as intended and gives them a shield to hide behind.
>
> (@[anonymous], Jun 30, 2021)

Reconciliation Action Plans (RAPs) are being more frequently implemented in higher education institutions. These are celebrated by institutions that want to advertise their commitment to increasing Indigenous engagement and participation in the workforce. RAPs are administered and approved through a process managed by Reconciliation Australia (2022). Important to remember is that the terminology shift toward 'reconciliation' came in the aftermath of the Hawke government's failure to develop a treaty prior to the Australian bicentenary in 1988 (Burridge, 2009). It was seen as a lighter, less risky alternative by states such as Western Australia whose economy was heavily tied to mining resources (Burridge, 2009). As debates about the character of true reconciliation continue, for Indigenous peoples the "hard issues of treaty, self-determination, and first nations rights, still remain at the crux of the dispute" (Burridge, 2007, p. 75). Despite the desire to tackle the 'hard issues', Indigenous employees such as '@anonymous' above, still feel that institutional and corporate RAPs are 'shields to hide behind' rather than indicative of real commitment.

Institutions can implement a RAP at one of four levels of engagement (reflect, innovate, stretch or elevate) depending on their track record and existing strategies (Reconciliation Australia, 2022). However, Indigenous academics often bear the burden and are asked to participate in lengthy 'strategy' meetings to design and implement RAPs. This adds to the workload for Indigenous academics who give up their time to educate non-Indigenous people on the correct way to implement changes to a system that is fundamentally flawed. RAPs should not be the responsibility of Indigenous people. The expected outcome of reconciliation movements is that non-Indigenous people will recognise and atone for injustices from which they continue to benefit, not for Indigenous people to take time out of their lives to placate feelings of white guilt:

> @CATSINaM @ProfLJP talking about Universities Australia strategy. 1 issue is achieving workforce parity so that this strategy can be fulfilled without burning out few Indigenous staff—so true that white fellas have to step up too!
>
> (@Leoniecox444Cox, Sept 17, 2018).

The expectation that Indigenous academics are available to provide additional support and service activities stems from participation by Indigenous peoples in higher education through the entry point of ISUs. It is also a reflection of the large amount of additional support and community engagement work Indigenous academics have taken on historically (Page & Asmar, 2008). These centres, like the Aboriginal Task Force, which were aimed at improving institutional outcomes vis-à-vis Indigenous student attraction, retention and graduation, were the entry point for Indigenous academics previously unwelcome in the faculties. They are seen as the only legitimate site for Indigenous peoples' contributions to the Western academy. The additional workload around student and community support, to which Page and Asmar refer as "beneath the teaching iceberg" (2008, p. 109), becomes, in the minds of other faculty members, the taken-for-granted role of Indigenous Studies academics.

These continued expectations are informed by what Tuhiwai Smith refers to as "colonising knowledge" (2012), and contribute greatly to an increased workload for Indigenous academics. As Staniland et al. noted of Māori academics' experiences,

> Non-Māori colleagues and management staff believed Māori staff were ultimately responsible for improving Māori experiences in business schools. [Including] activities to enhance Māori representation, improve Māori student engagement and completion rates, and enhance the attractiveness of Māori content.
>
> (2019, p. 10)

Asmar and Page (2009, p. 387) similarly observed of Australian higher education institutions that, "when a non-Indigenous academic is told to Indigenize her curriculum, it is to Indigenous colleagues that she inevitably turns for advice". These expectations placed on Indigenous scholars both add to their workload and reify colonial messages about the role of Indigenous perspectives in a Western institution.

## Colonising knowledge

There is an inherent conflict between Indigenous and non-Indigenous scholarship located at the heart of Western thinking. The conflict is so central to Western thought that in many ways, it can be conceptualised as the driving force behind Western scientific endeavour. Torres Strait Islander Scholar Martin Nakata reflected on the discomfort and disconnect that he witnessed as a Torres Strait Islander student attending a Western school. The "cultural interface" (2007) is what Nakata called the site at which Western and Indigenous knowledges collided, where ontological and epistemological ruptures were made visible. For Nakata, the visibility of these ruptures was profound for Indigenous students, whose world views were not reflected in the curricula, the language and the culture of Western education institutions.

As articulated by Tuhiwai Smith (2012, p. 117), "whilst imperialism is often thought of as a system which drew everything back into the centre, it was also a system which distributed materials and ideas outwards". Thus, the evidence of imperialism in Western textbooks, in the British Museum and in nationalist discourse demonstrates a conquering, an exploration and exploitation of Indigenous peoples' lives, bodies, material possessions, culture and lands. As we can still see, museums across the globe maintain and display collections of 'cultural artefacts' stolen from Indigenous peoples. Their presence is often attributed to some benevolent white philanthropist. However, imperialism, as Tuhiwai

Smith points out, also involved the spreading of ideology. The imperial journeys of the late eighteenth century were preceded by the Enlightenment where Western civilisations were said to have burst forth into the modern world. Scientific rationalisation of the world was seen as the noblest of humanistic endeavours. Central to the exploratory journeys which 'discovered' Australia and New Zealand was the spread of empire and episteme.

The spread of empire through academia was motivated by the acquisition of Indigenous knowledges and cultures. "Western knowledge and science are beneficiaries of the colonization of Indigenous peoples" (Smith, 2012, p. 118). Higher education institutions, the core site of knowledge formation within a Western framework, were provided with the knowledge from imperial 'discoveries' in order to establish and build the suite of disciplines. In addition, the acquired knowledges (including the method of acquisition) were deployed by Western scholars and policymakers alike to reify the position of Indigenous civilisations as inferior, thereby justifying this theft of land and culture.

Research in the Western academy was about solidifying Western dominance on unceded Indigenous lands. As Tuhiwai Smith (2012, p. 119) notes:

> 'Discoveries' about and from the 'new' world expanded and challenged ideas the West held about itself. The production of knowledge, new knowledge and transformed 'old' knowledge, ideas about the nature of knowledge and the validity of specific forms of knowledge, became as much commodities of colonial exploitation as other natural resources.

The commodification of knowledge and knowing by Western institutions fuelled the persistent oppression of Indigenous peoples. Social scientists in various disciplines explored Indigenous peoples and cultures supposed to be remnants of a 'dying race' (Sheridan, 1988). Indeed, this predetermination was based on an assumed "conflict between primitivism and modernity" (Kelm, 2005, p. 372). In every way, non-Indigenous researchers in medicine, anthropology and education all positioned themselves as superior to and far more civilised than Indigenous peoples and knowledges. Such research and scholarship that posited Indigenous peoples as uncivilised and subhuman took on a taken-for-granted value in colonial society and undergirded the legitimisation of colonial policies and practices of assimilation and genocide.

While the suite of disciplines has been deployed at one stage or another to uphold colonial practices, "anthropologists are often the academics popularly perceived by the indigenous world as the epitome of all that is bad with academics" (Smith, 2012, p. 131). Indeed, the observation and measurement of Indigenous peoples by various anthropologists since the late eighteenth century can be linked to the foundations of 'scientific' knowledge that inform the settler colonial narrative to this day. Anthropology appears to be the discipline with, simultaneously, the most to lose and the most to gain from the participation of Indigenous peoples in its ranks. While there may be a risk of destabilising the entire discipline by turning the tables on the traditional East/West, Us/Them, civilised/uncivilised paradigm, it is imperative that anthropology and related disciplines come to terms with the truth of history.

## The future of Indigenous knowledge formation

Indigenous scholars are putting runs on the board through teaching and research outputs. This doesn't mean, however, there has been a dramatic shift in the colonial mindset engrained in the academy. Connell (2019, p. 35) asks some pertinent questions concerning the underlying issue of diversity (or lack of) in the knowledge formation workforce: "What if that workforce is highly unrepresentative; what if knowledge institutions work in an exclusionary way; what if the knowledge economy embeds privilege and exploitation on a global scale?"

Indigenous peoples are still under-represented in higher education both as students and academic staff. A Universities Australia report in March 2021 highlighted that the shortfall is still significant. Indigenous academic staff employed in either teaching or research in 2019 represented less than 1 per cent of all academic staff at universities across Australia. According to the report, a further 1,189 Indigenous academic staff would need to be employed to reach population parity (Universities Australia, 2021). Indigenous peoples have made considerable advances in higher education institutions to date. Through the dissemination of peer-reviewed academic journals dedicated to showcasing Indigenous content, conferences organised to forge collaborative networks among Indigenous scholars worldwide, and alliances being established in local university settings, Indigenous scholars have carved out space in the academy to contribute to the process of knowledge formation. This has been achieved in addition to the added work that comes from the persistent assumptions about Indigenous academics' singular role to provide cultural advice and pastoral care for Indigenous students.

## Conclusion

The problem with inviting Indigenous perspectives into higher education research remains the marginalisation of Indigenous knowledges and scholars by colonial systems designed to oppress Indigenous peoples. Indigenous knowledges are seen as incongruent with Western ways of conducting rational scientific enquiry. However, proposing a way forward, Knopf (2015, p. 183) states:

> Western and Indigenous perspectives must not be seen as entrenched oppositions but as polar points of a contact field where both knowledge systems face each other from various positions within the field, depending on the discipline and aspect, degree of openness of the discipline, and the history of their contact.

The addition of an array of diverse Indigenous perspectives in the process of scientific enquiry, properly understood and implemented, can add immense value to the design, conduct and outcomes of research in higher education. Indigenous scholars must be invited to participate and lead, not as cultural advisers or student support workers (though these roles retain their importance), but as valued and equal researchers concerned with scholarly and rigorous processes of knowledge formation.

As I write this chapter in early 2022, Australia's Eastern seaboard is struggling to stay above water. A 'once in 500-year' flooding event has destroyed towns and left an undetermined clean-up bill. The social and economic impacts of this disaster are immense. Two years earlier, in 2020, some of the same areas were contemplating the clean-up after a major bushfire that reduced houses and lives to ash. In June 2022, the Australia Productivity Commission provided data which suggested only four of 17 priority areas in the Closing the Gap initiative were on track (Australian Government, 2022a). Little progress can be seen when more than 500 Indigenous peoples have died in custody since the handing down of the 1991 *Royal Commission into Aboriginal Deaths in Custody* report, a report indicating that the government has failed to address the recommendations. (Australian Government, 2022b). The issues that we are facing today and into the future are diverse and will impact everybody. They are social, economic, cultural and spiritual. Australia, like other colonised countries, has an immense knowledge base at the ready. However, to deploy Indigenous peoples' intricate and sophisticated knowledges of this country and of society, of economics and environmental management, higher education institutions need to understand the settler colonial ideologies that still undergird decision-making processes within their halls. Indigenous Studies is making, and will continue to make, an immense contribution to what Drucker posited as a 'knowledge society' (1993). As Connell (2019, p. 48) outlines, "the hegemonic curriculum is orderly, closed, and full of answered questions". The future of democratic institutions is a future where Indigenous knowledges enjoy equal value and relevance as we grapple with the challenges and unanswered questions of our time.

Despite the momentous gains made by Indigenous students and scholars in the last 50 years, the experiences of higher education for Indigenous academics in this country continue to reflect the Western academy's tainted relationship with Indigenous peoples. Assumptions about Indigenous peoples' roles as cultural advisers and pastoral care workers on campus continue to delegitimise Indigenous scholarship and Indigenous Studies as a discipline. Furthermore, the barriers and assumptions faced by Indigenous Studies scholars serve only to reify the Western academy as a tool of colonisation. One of the entry points for Indigenous peoples was through the precedent set by the Aboriginal Task Force in South Australia. Indigenous students and knowledge holders who gained entry in the early days, have paved the way for not only a proud Indigenous presence on campus but the inclusion, at many Australian institutions, of Indigenous Studies as a discipline.

## References

Anderson, S. (2015). Aboriginal task force: Australia's first national program dedicated to transitioning Aboriginal and Torres Strait Islander people into university education. *Australian Aboriginal Studies, 2*, 24–32. http://search.informit.org/doi/abs/10.3316/INFORMIT.747074479576341

Asmar, C., & Page, S. (2009). Sources of satisfaction and stress among Indigenous academic teachers: Findings from a national Australian study. *Asia Pacific Journal of Education, 29*(3), 387–401. https://doi.org/10.1080/02188790903097505

Australian Government. (2022a). *Productivity Commission: Closing the Gap Information Repository.* www.pc.gov.au/closing-the-gap-data/dashboard

Australian Government. (2022b). *Australian Institute of Criminology: Deaths in Custody in Australia.* www.aic.gov.au/statistics/deaths-custody-australia

Australian Institute for Aboriginal and Torres Strait Islander Studies (AIATSIS). (2022). AIATSIS Code of Ethics for Aboriginal and Torres Strait Islander Research. https://aiatsis.gov.au/sites/defa ult/files/2020-10/aiatsis-code-ethics.pdf

Behrendt, L. Y., Larkin, S., Griew, R., & Kelly, P. (2012). *Review of higher education access and outcomes for Aboriginal and Torres Strait Islander people.* Department of Industry, Innovation, Science, Research and Tertiary Education.

Beresford, Q. (2012). 'Chapter 3—Separate and equal: An outline of Aboriginal education 1900–1996'. In Q. Beresford, G. Partington, & G. Gower (Eds.), *Reform and resistance in Aboriginal education* (pp. 85–119). University of Western Australia Publishing.

Bin-Sallik, M. (2003). Cultural safety: Let's name it! *Australian Journal of Indigenous Education, 32*, 21–28. http://search.informit.org/doi/abs/10.3316/INFORMIT.174480124475805

Burridge, N. (2007). Meanings and perspectives of reconciliation in the Australian socio-political context. *International Journal of Diversity in Organisations, Communities and Nations, 6*(5), 69–78.

Burridge, N. (2009). Perspectives on reconciliation and indigenous rights. *Cosmopolitan Civil Societies: An Interdisciplinary Journal, 1*(2), 111–128. https://doi.org/10.3316/informit.144640513912869

Connell, R. (2019). *The good university: What universities actually do and why it's time for radical change.* Bloomsbury.

Drucker, P. F. (1993). The rise of the knowledge society. *Wilson Quarterly, 17*(2), 52–72.

Kelm, M. E. (2005). Diagnosing the discursive Indian: Medicine, gender, and the 'dying race'. *Ethnohistory, 52*(2), 371–406. https://doi.org/10.1215/00141801-52-2-371

Knopf, K. (2015). The turn toward the Indigenous: Knowledge systems and practices in the academy. *Amerikastudien / American Studies, 60*(2/3), 179–200.

Locke, M. L., Trudgett, M., & Page, S. (2021). Indigenous early career researchers: Creating pearls in the academy. *Australian Educational Researcher, 50*(2), 237–253. https://doi.org/10.1007/s13384-021-00485-1

Locke, M. L., Trudgett, M., & Page, S. (2022). Building and strengthening Indigenous early career researcher trajectories. *Higher Education Research & Development, 42*(1, 156–170. https://doi.org/10.1080/07294360.2022.2048637

Melin, M., Astvik, W., & Bernhard-Oettel, C. (2014). New work demands in higher education. A study of the relationship between excessive workload, coping strategies and subsequent health among academic staff. *Quality in Higher Education, 20*(3), 290–308. https://doi.org/10.1080/13538322.2014.979547

Monash University. (2022). History of the Monash Indigenous Studies Centre. *Monash Indigenous Studies Centre.* www.monash.edu/arts/monash-indigenous-studies/about/history-of-the-monash-indigenous-studies-centre

Moreton-Robinson, A. (2014). Race matters: The "Aborigine" as a white possession. In R. Warrior (Ed.), *The world of indigenous North America* (pp. 467–483). Routledge.

Nakata, M. (2007). The cultural interface. *The Australian Journal of Indigenous Education, 36*(1), 7–14.

Nakata, M., Nakata, V., Keech, S., & Bolt, R. (2012). Decolonial goals and pedagogies for Indigenous Studies. *Decolonization: Indigeneity, Education & Society, 1*(1).

O'Brien, L., & Watson, I. (2014). In conversation with Uncle Lewis: Bushfires, weather-makers, collective management. *AlterNative: An International Journal of Indigenous Peoples, 10*(5), 450–461. https://doi.org/10.1177/117718011401000502

O'Sullivan, S. (2019). Employability and First Nations' Peoples: Aspirations, agency and commitments. In J. Higgs, G. Crisp, & W. Letts (Eds.), *Education for employability* (Vol. 1). (pp. 143–152). Brill.

Page, S., & Asmar, C. (2008). Beneath the teaching iceberg: Exposing the hidden support dimensions of Indigenous academic work. *Australian Journal of Indigenous Education, 37*(S1), 109–117.

Patrick, R., & Moodie, N. (2016). Indigenous education policy discourses in Australia: Rethinking the 'problem'. In T. Barkatsas & A. Bertram (Eds.), *Global learning in the 21st century* (pp. 165–184). Sense Publishers.

Reconciliation Australia. (2022). *Reconciliation Australia.* www.reconciliation.org.au/

Sheridan, S. (1988). 'Wives and mothers like ourselves, poor remnants of a dying race': Aborigines in colonial women's writing. *Kunapipi, 10*(1). https://ro.uow.edu.au/kunapipi/vol10/iss1/9

Smith, L. T. (2012). *Decolonizing methodologies: Research and Indigenous peoples.* Zed Books.

Staniland, N. A., Harris, C., & Pringle, J. K. (2019). Indigenous and boundaryless careers: Cultural boundaries in the careers of Māori academics. *International Journal of Human Resource Management, 32*(16), 3527–3546. https://doi.org/10.1080/09585192.2019.1651377

Trudgett, M. (2009). Build it and they will come: Building the capacity of Indigenous units in universities to provide better support for Indigenous Australian postgraduate students. *Australian Journal of Indigenous Education, 38*(1), 9–18. https://doi.org/10.1375/S1326011100000545

Universities Australia. (2021). *Indigenous Strategy Third Annual Report.* www.universitiesaustralia.edu.au/policy-submissions/diversity-equity/indigenous-higher-education/

Wolfe, P. (2006). Settler colonialism and the elimination of the native. *Journal of Genocide Research, 8*(4), 387–409. https://doi.org/10.1080/14623520601056240

Worby, G., Kennedy, T., & Tur, S. U. (2016). *The long campaign: The Duguid Memorial Lectures, 1994–2014.* Wakefield Press.

# 29

# DIGITAL INDIGENOUS ORAL KNOWLEDGE

*Ash Markstone, Meryn Murray and Emma Johnstone*

*We acknowledge and pay respects to our ancestors and to all First Nations Elders past and present, who have fought to create the path we now walk, who have protected their Country, and to whose custodianship and guidance we are indebted. We spoke and wrote this chapter into being while on the unceded lands of the Dharawal peoples.*

*Before beginning to read this chapter, we encourage you to be aware of and open to the not-exactly-linear path that we have taken in preparing it. To look to the future as an Indigenous person is to first look to the past.*

## Introduction

First Nations people in Australia are known to be a part of the oldest continuing cultures in the world. We have lived here for tens of thousands of years, and have survived invasion, genocide and ongoing occupation. The strength and ability to do so, derives from our Indigenous epistemological, ontological and axiological frameworks. While Western world views seek to capture us in a position born of primitivist ideologies, as artefacts confined to the past and therefore not a part of any future visions, Indigenous peoples have always looked forward. Indigenous epistemologies show us the value and necessity of sharing what we know with the next generation, to ensure that our future is one that is built from experience and supported with the power of countless generations before us.

For this chapter, we seek to subvert and challenge a Western understanding of 'doing' research and of participating in higher education, and instead offer a way forward that is built on Indigenous epistemological understandings and is a continuation of Indigenous knowledge practices. We argue that a digital oral research and writing practice is a form of Indigenous knowledge sharing, reimagined for a future world.

When first considering ideas for a chapter in this book, we came to an agreement that we wanted to attempt to do something that aligned with the principles of Indigenous futurisms, that is, something that challenged and reimagined what the future could be. We began with the questions 'what does the future look like for Indigenous Australia?' and 'what role

DOI: 10.4324/9781003271802-33

does digital technology have in this future?' We then asked, 'what if we applied lessons learned through Indigenous epistemologies and ontologies to academic work, and matched it with the digital technology available to us, to create a future where our own engagement in education and research production is itself aligned with an Indigenous way of doing things?' What if we used Indigenous ways of sharing knowledge, specifically oral knowledge sharing, to do research, but in a way that incorporated digital technology? For us specifically in this context, this meant undertaking an experiment in what an academic book chapter 'needs' to be and how it can be created.

Each of us three authors came to these discussions from a different place of knowledge and experience, but still united through close ties of relationality and responsibility. As sisters, we are bound together through family, community, culture and kinship. As an academic, a student and a teacher, we each sought to use this process as an act itself of disrupting normative ways of producing and consuming knowledge. Through this process, we attempted to challenge ourselves as well as institutions, systems and structures, to learn a new way forward, one that is not new at all, but rather an act of rediscovery.

Those conversations became a plan of action. We saw that an Indigenous way of sharing knowledge through oral knowledge practices could be applied and enacted with the use of digital technologies. We could use digital technology to record the audio of ourselves having these discussions, transcribe it and use it to form this chapter. We would then use the process itself as a starting place, and through it consider the broader applications and implications, as they became clear to us.

Could we create for ourselves a future where we are able to be not just Indigenous women researching and working in education, but Indigenous women researching and working in education in a way that is structured through Indigenous ways of knowing? Could digital technology help us bring about this future? Could this recovery of our ancestral practices be an act of challenging colonial legacies and also be a way for us to overcome barriers we have faced in our own lived experience of existing within institutions formed through invasion and occupation? Through writing this chapter, we quickly began to see the many connections between our own understandings of Indigenous knowledge systems, and the different ways creating this future for ourselves could be beneficial, and if others were to do the same, perhaps transformative. In this way, and through these conversations with each other, this chapter soon became a case study and an experiment for ourselves, a learning ground, a place of self-reflection and a process of looking back to look forward.

We know, of course, that recording interviews and having them transcribed is already an established methodology within Western research, specifically around data collection (Mahuika, 2019). Indigenous researchers and others have been using this approach for some time, particularly in the revitalisation of Australian Indigenous languages (Smith et al., 2018). While there has been investigation into the use of speech recognition and transcription software, this has mostly been done with a focus on its uses for children with disabilities (Perelmutter et al., 2017). As a group of authors including those with neurodivergence, we were interested also in the potential future applications of digital technologies and Indigenous knowledge to support our own paths in academia. Very little information can be found specifically about the use of digital technologies for adult neurodiverse women, and research into neurodiversity in women is itself incredibly limited (Spiel et al., 2022). This aligns with experiences reported by neurodiverse women, who as adults have struggled to find resources or information to support their own needs (Henry & Jones,

2011). All of these things considered, we felt that there was room to explore alternative approaches to sharing and indeed producing knowledge in a digital Indigenous way.

### Laying the groundwork: our process

We began with recording our first initial conversations about the questions that arose for each of us in response to the themes outlined in the call for chapters. We then took time to reflect individually on whether this was something we thought we could write about. We decided to try and incorporate some blocks of audio transcription throughout the chapter and indicate when it was being used by italicising it, noting who is speaking.

*We are talking very broadly at the moment about Indigenous knowledge production and challenging those ideas around how we actually produce research or writing content. And what if we applied Indigenous knowledge production ideas, which is oral, oral story sharing and oral knowledge sharing and tried to incorporate that into how we do things now today? So, for example, what if instead of going home and doing, you know, a literature review and typing up notes and then like writing that out into paragraphs and things. What if we started at the point of: we've all got years of experience, lots of reading and knowledge of stuff from our daily lives and work lives and academic lives. What if we just met and discussed what we thought about this whole thing and recorded it and then transcribed it, and put it into a Word document?*

(Ash Markstone)

We did this as the act of speaking allowed for us to process the idea itself. When we consider using our voice, to speak out loud our ideas and experiences, we are in a way speaking to the realm of possibility. We talk about our ideas, not just to articulate them or communicate them but to create them. To consider the future, we speak about it, and through speaking it, we can bring that future into being.

*What we're doing is almost like experimenting with different ways of approaching knowledge sharing, and then we're going to essentially write a chapter around why we're doing it this way, and then we're going to discuss like what the benefits of it have been and then align that with the research that we've then also been doing in the background.*

(Ash Markstone)

Through our oral knowledge-sharing process, we formed the following arguments: engaging in Indigenous futurisms is a way of challenging the systems and institutions of colonisation and instead imagining a way to re-engage with Indigenous practices. The role of oral language and narrative in early childhood development and education is already well established. Indigenous knowledge is powerful and valuable, and one way this knowledge is transferred is through oral knowledge sharing, a practice we have done since time immemorial. We argue that academia is a place that has not historically been supportive of Indigenous people and neurodiverse people. We argue that a digital oral research and writing practice (i.e. using audio recording and digital transcription software) is essentially a form of Indigenous knowledge sharing, reimagined for a future world. Using digital technology as a tool to support education has been shown to be helpful for disability access.

We argue that digital Indigenous knowledge sharing can be a valuable tool to support education and research production and increase access to academia for both neurotypical and neurodiverse Indigenous people. Therefore, using digital Indigenous knowledge practices is a way to challenge existing power structures and hierarchies and create a new future where institutions and systems are transformed into places of justice, and accessibility.

## Oral histories and Indigenous knowledge

Indigenous oral histories have been largely devalued by those in Western academia. They have been framed as 'mythology and folklore', thus stripping Indigenous peoples of our right to define and record our own histories and identities. Mahuika (2019, p. 17) argues that the renaming of Indigenous oral histories to 'oral traditions' is part of the colonising process, whereby "the native oral past was stripped of history and repositioned as the unreliable ramblings of superstitious savages". The contentions and politics of naming and the role of language in reflecting unequal relationships of power has been discussed at length by Indigenous academics (Carlson et al., 2014). The term 'traditional' as a description of Indigenous knowledge has often led to it being misconstrued as belonging only to the past (Nakata et al., 2005) despite the fact that Indigenous knowledge is undoubtedly current and continuing, as Indigenous people are ourselves current and continuing. The positioning of it as belonging only to the past is itself an act of epistemic violence. It is an act that seeks to control the knowledge created both about and by Indigenous peoples. It seeks to silence, or devalue, or stop the production itself, of knowledge that does not align with the ideologies of the colonial power paradigm. Within the academy, this attempt to erase and devalue Indigenous knowledge has been described as white patriarchal epistemic violence (Moreton-Robinson, 2011a, p. 428).

The dismissal of Indigenous oral histories is one of the ways in which colonial regimes are able to relegate the Indigenous precolonial world to the realm of 'prehistory', which allows them to neatly ignore the existence of a proud civilisation that predates their colonies.

*Part of the problem with studying Indigenous history is because oral histories are considered unreliable by Western academia. So precolonial Indigenous history is called 'prehistory', like there's nothing happening there that counts. It's before what counts as history, rather than being included under the heading of ancient history. Because these Indigenous civilisations, and it's not just Australian Indigenous people but all over the world, in the Americas and throughout the Pacific, these Indigenous civilisations, they existed at the same time and are often older than Greece, Rome, Egypt, and yet they are called prehistory.*

(Emma Johnstone)

Deconstructing this paradigm illustrates that there is a deficit in understanding of the fact that Indigenous oral histories are not just histories that are read aloud but are their own form of historical record with different rules and structures. This is part of the problem that Western academics face when attempting to record Indigenous oral histories. Oral history within Western academia is often conceptualised as recorded interviews and eye-witness accounts of historical events, whereas Indigenous oral histories go much deeper than this and are created and shared in a completely different way.

Indigenous knowledge is often dismissed as unreliable by Western academics who fail to comprehend or to appreciate Indigenous knowledge production (Semali & Kinchole, 2002). Within the academy and its many institutions, there are those who are still ignorant of Indigenous knowledges, and therefore much of our knowledge systems are deemed unreliable and invalid. Western ignorance of Indigenous knowledge holds profound consequences for everyone. The relationship between the assumed superiority of Western knowledge production and the way this affects Indigenous representation has been interrogated by Moreton-Robinson (2011b, p. 78), who argues that the "hegemony of Western whiteness continues to shape the future of the rest of the world". Colonial attitudes towards Indigenous peoples have led to the dismissal of Indigenous peoples' knowledge about the history of their own societies and the countries in which they live. But the reality is that Indigenous histories have been passed down for generations with an extraordinary level of accuracy. There is a growing amount of scientific evidence which confirms events and information from the supposedly 'unreliable' oral histories of Indigenous peoples.

*As someone who is studying history and ancient history, what I want to see is greater respect for Indigenous history, but for Indigenous history told by Indigenous people. I want to study Indigenous history, not just all the ways that Indigenous people have been treated under white settlement. There are oral histories from Indigenous peoples from before white people got here. Why can't I learn about those?*

(Emma Johnstone)

The longevity and accuracy of Indigenous oral knowledge has been repeatedly shown. An engraved bird track was found in the Keep River region of the Northern Territory, carved with such distinctive detail that archaeologists were able to match it to the Geryornis, an emu-like bird that went extinct about 50,000 years ago (Ouzman et al., 2002). However, the engraving itself is only a few thousand years old. This indicates that the Indigenous people[1] of the Keep River region retained knowledge about this extinct bird and then passed it down through generations, over thousands of years, and to such a level of accuracy that it was able to be reproduced with an incredible amount of detail. In a 2016 study, stories were collected from 21 different places along the Australian coastline which described the effects of the postglacial sea-level rise that occurred more than 7,000 years ago (Nunn & Reid, 2016). The researchers found that each of these stories, despite coming from communities thousands of kilometres apart, all contained the same facts. The oral histories from these communities were able to describe details from an event 7,000 years ago, leading the researchers to argue that the narrative culture of Indigenous people in Australia is both unique and exceptional (Nunn & Reid, 2016).

The nature of Indigenous oral histories is fundamentally different to Western histories, causing Western academics to struggle to understand or recognise the ways in which accuracy is maintained. For example, certain roles within kinship systems include the specific obligation and responsibility of making sure that particular stories are both learned and recounted in the proper way. It is not one person passing along a story to one other, but instead a communal effort to ensure accuracy. It is a requirement of a story to be remembered and discussed between different family lines, creating a cross-generational mechanism for maintaining accuracy across multiple retellings. Indigenous oral histories maintain their accuracy across multiple generations and over thousands of years. They provide a level of detail that often defies belief by some but is repeatedly confirmed by scientific analysis. An example of Western science providing proof that Indigenous knowledge is accurate can be seen in the Indigenous histories of volcanic eruptions which formed three crater lakes in Queensland over 10,000 years ago. These histories describe the region as being covered in eucalypt scrub rather than the current rainforest. These accounts were confirmed by an analysis of fossilised pollen found within the crater lakes (Krenshaw, 1970). Once again, we see that Indigenous histories have been accurately passed down for thousands of years in an "unparalleled human record of events dating back to the Pleistocene era" (Rainforest Conservation Society of Queensland, 1986, p. 41).

What else might we know about the history of this country and its people if more Indigenous histories were afforded the same amount of respect as their Western counterparts? By remaining bound to a Western epistemological framework, society will continue to erase the value of Indigenous oral histories and silence Indigenous voices. If we challenge the discourse that positions Indigenous knowledge systems as primitive and our histories as mythologies, we can instead have them understood in terms of accurate and valuable historical accounts. Indigenous oral histories are not artefacts confined to the past. They are powerful ways of producing, preserving and consuming knowledge.

## Indigenous oral pedagogies in schools

During the discussion around the intersection of oral language in Indigenous knowledge production and the role of oral language in modern classrooms, two clear themes emerged when exploring these concepts within the context of Indigenous Futurism: Indigenous oral methods as pedagogy and the use of technology to facilitate story-sharing, learning and community into the future.

Aboriginal and Torres Strait Islander history, culture and perspectives are embedded to a degree into curriculum content across all Australian schools (ACARA, 2020), but the execution of this is varied and the research into the quality and success of current approaches is limited. There is an emerging argument that we need to move away from Indigenised content and towards Indigenous processes of knowledge transmission and creation (Yunkaporta, 2009). Research suggests that while there is no single 'Indigenous learning style', there is a link between culture and ways of thinking and learning, and some recurrent learning preferences which occur frequently enough in Indigenous learners to warrant attention from educators (Hughes & More, 1997).

The use of oral methods of instruction in First Nations groups across the world have been well documented (Augustine, 2008). While educators need to be careful not to generalise approaches from international research to Indigenous Australian contexts, and still need to acknowledge the diversity within and between Australian First Nations groups, the role of discourse in the classroom is a powerful one. Being intentional in the use of oral strategies, and reimagining these with the support of technology in the modern classroom could support Indigenous learners. Christine Halse and Aunty Mavis Robinson speak about the role of socialisation, collaboration and questioning techniques when designing pedagogical approaches for Aboriginal children. While they point out some differences between Aboriginal knowledge transmission and Western education systems, they posit that these types of oral strategies are also "equally effective for other students' (Halse & Robinson, 1999, p. 213). The role of language in all children's learning and development has been long acknowledged (Vygotsky, 1962), and the high impact of classroom discussion on learner outcomes is well established in contemporary research (Hattie, 2009).

Yarning is an Indigenous practice (Bessarab & Ng'andu, 2010). It is a way of communicating while building respectful relationships and has been used by Indigenous peoples for thousands of years as a way both to learn from and to learn as a collective group (Walker et al., 2014). Yarning also works to preserve and pass on cultural knowledge (Geia et al., 2013). In schools, the use of tarning, in consultation with local communities to ensure contextual appropriateness, can facilitate powerful classroom discussion in a culturally responsive way. Teachers can work with communities and draw upon English as an Additional Language or Dialect (EALD) pedagogical research as it applies to Aboriginal English, Kriols, and bi-dialectal approaches, to use yarning and other oral pedagogies for the deliberate planning of oral interaction during lessons. Yarning circles are already used in literacy centres with some positive results (Mills et al., 2013). They also are increasingly used to build positive classroom communities:

> *I've seen teachers embracing the Yarning Circle as part of their morning routine. We teach them [the students] why it's a circle. You know, there is no beginning and end, we all face each other. This is because here in this space we are all equal. When yarning protocols are explained properly you would probably be surprised just how well children respond and respect these sessions.*
>
> (Meryn Murray)

It is unsurprising, then, that yarning circles have also been used as an effective tool in engagement and well-being programmes to foster positive relationships. Such approaches have been successfully paired with digital technologies, such as the 'Be Deadly Online' programme which uses yarning circles in its online lesson plans, with participants reflecting "this is about community taking control, not whitefellas coming in and imposing a view" (eSafety Commissioner, 2016, 00:00:40). This is a clear example of how using digital-based oral Indigenous knowledge is a way to challenge Western normative epistemologies and create new possibilities for the future classroom. Research by Yunkaporta (2009) examined these and other pedagogical approaches being used by schools in Western NSW. The research sought to find overlaps in teaching and learning styles at the cultural interface and develop a pedagogy which was supportive of Aboriginal people. This research informed a framework that became known as The 8 Ways. Amongst these 8 Ways was the concept of Story Sharing. The Baakindji, Ngiyampaa, Yuwaalaraay, Gamilaraay, Wiradjuri, Wangkumarra and other nations of Western NSW, who own the knowledge this framework was adapted from, approach learning through narrative and connect through the stories shared.

The nature of story sharing as knowledge transmission, relationship-responsive practice and community building continues to evolve in schools as they engage in different ways suited to their unique learners and contexts and respond to the demands of an ever-changing, globalised world. Story sharing through online platforms is another example of digital technology facilitating Indigenous knowledge.

> *...the teachers are using apps where you can set a task and just like they can film themselves, they can record themselves. There's, you know, they can read aloud and use functions to follow the words, and they can do collaborative tasks as well. So, one child can record and then another child can add on their idea. So, there are apps*

*for that. But I think something that is really exciting that is emerging is a concept of shared stories across schools [...] and communities [...] there are websites where we can upload videos of children sharing ideas, singing songs, celebrations that they might have had, to kind of build up local communities and maybe like work towards a joint understanding of what our community is [...] I think we were looking at this last time we spoke about new meanings for Indigeneity that are not necessarily tied to living on ancestral land, which is what we're seeing with the next generation. So that you might have a group of children who are growing up on a land they have no ancestral ties to, but these are our future Elders, our future leaders. I think it is important that they have a means to communicate and collaborate and build identity [...] What will that look like as it evolves over the years? I think those online platforms will potentially play a big part in that because you might only have five or six Indigenous children at one school, but they can still find shared meaning and shared understanding with a larger group of people across broader spaces through technology.*

(Meryn Murray)

One such website, Storylines (2018) is a community-led initiative where Aboriginal people and groups can share stories of identity, culture, history and success in education. Students, teachers, schools and community groups can 'find my mob' or create a new community group to upload videos and articles sharing their stories. This is another clear example of using an Indigenous knowledge transmission practice, specifically oral story sharing, in an innovative way to challenge the Western colonial system to support self-determination and create new ideas of collective identity. Storylines is a free resource provided by the Burraga Foundation, which fittingly is dedicated to Joe Anderson, also known as King Burraga, one of the first Aboriginal men to use film technology to demand recognition for his people. He was filmed on Country in 1933 delivering a message to Australian people challenging colonialism, a message that enacted Indigenous epistemologies through digital technology (Burraga Foundation, 2016). Storylines is just one example of how digital technology and Indigenous knowledge can be used to bring about Australian Indigenous futures. Digital Indigenous knowledge can also be used to increase community control of intellectual and cultural property and improve accurate Indigenous representation by "literally delivering the voice of that community" (O'Sullivan, 2013, p. 140).

The 8 Ways approach also emphasises the importance of a non-linear model for this discourse. Gibson (1993, as cited in Yunkaporta, 2009) suggests that Aboriginal people are not constrained by the serial and sequential nature of linear thinking. In fact, Western pedagogy's focus on linear perspectives may be a key factor in marginalising Aboriginal people (Wheaton, 2000, as cited in Yunkaporta, 2009). Sometimes when planning for classroom discourse, teachers may try to follow a more structured or narrowed form of class discussion, which can be challenging as teachers struggle to over-manage participation of students and guide them towards a common outcome or objective. This was voiced by a research participant in an interview with Yunkaporta (2009, p. 118):

Aboriginal knowledge doesn't work like that [...] we see the whole concept at the beginning but don't have to understand it at that point, just as long as we can see the shape of it. [...] [I]n the mainstream people have that need to see and understand immediately, a greedy, quick and shallow approach to knowledge [...] [W]

431

ith Aboriginal knowledge it has to come in stages, bringing in the focus gradually at points where a person is ready to understand and make connections.

Non-linear methods of oral knowledge transmission were increasingly seen during the 'remote learning' period experienced by schools during the Covid-19 pandemic. Throughout 2020–2022, teachers engaged students across a variety of online platforms to support both continuity of learning and continuity of belonging. Teachers encouraged students to use audio-visual tools such as voice recording and video conferencing for collaboration and group work. Schools used pre-recorded lessons to celebrate Reconciliation Week and National Aboriginal and Islander Day of Celebration Week, and organisations such as the NSW Aboriginal Education Consultancy Group (AECG, 2021) shifted practice to deliver 'online camps' where Indigenous students could communicate with others and overcome restrictions and cultural isolation, engage in hands-on interactive learning experiences online across various subjects, and meet inspiring Aboriginal role models. In higher education, a similar shift to digital technologies during Covid-19 saw "new opportunities for collaboration, support giving, and community building" (Carlson et al., 2021, p. 1). These provide further examples of digital Indigenous knowledge practices.

Indigenous people continue to resist colonial processes, which seek their silence and erasure. We continue to fight for self-determination and to take back ownership over our education. The non-linear, relationship-responsive, narrative-centred approach found in Aboriginal pedagogical models paired with the endless possibilities of technology creates a dynamic flexibility which could inform powerful instructional practice in future schools. The use of Indigenous ways of knowing can create a classroom culture where rich collaborative discourse allows students to build ideas, identity, story and community. Much like the process we have employed to create this chapter, these powerful conversations and thought processes could be recorded, transcribed and used for assessment and reporting purposes while allowing children to focus on learning in ways which they find most efficient, authentic and natural. Perhaps even one day we may see teachers themselves released from the structure and confines of written Western expectations when planning, recording, evaluating and reporting, and instead given the freedom to focus on the core business of quality teaching.

## Indigenous knowledges, neurodiversity and access to academia

Considering the accuracy and value of oral knowledge sharing, we came to consider other implications and applications for this type of research production, not just from an Indigenous perspective, but at the intersection of Indigenous, neurodivergent and gendered experiences of academia. Through this digital Indigenous knowledge-sharing process, we found that there was the potential for using oral knowledge sharing to engage not only with our ancestral practices for the purpose of challenging normative institutional practices as Indigenous people but also to overcome barriers experienced as neurodiverse people within academia as well.

Western academia has historically been the domain of white men and is often hostile to other pedagogical methods and approaches to learning. Knowledge itself has been manipulated and used to reinforce elitism, hierarchies and power structures (Gillberg, 2020). This power structure excludes the perspective of both Indigenous and neurodiverse peoples by valuing the knowledge produced only within a very limited framework and rejecting or discrediting all other forms of knowledge production. Indigenous methods of knowledge production can be more accessible to neurodiverse people, who struggle to perform within the rigid confines of Western academia. Although research into attention deficit hyperactivity disorder (ADHD) has been conducted, many argue that it has retained a narrow focus on male experiences (Babinski et al., 2011). While there is a growing interest in the way ADHD and autism affect the lives and work of academics, there is a further scarcity of information about these conditions within the Indigenous community specifically.

*Reflecting on my own experiences as a neurodiverse Indigenous woman, I have often found that the higher education system is not set up to be either welcoming or easy to navigate. Due to the nature of Western academia, both students and professional academics often struggle to conform to the expectations of the institution.*

(Emma Johnstone)

The way that Western academia is structured leads to a focus on competition and solitary study. Knowledge produced by collaboration and based in social realities is often not valued for the sole reason that it is not produced fast enough (Gillberg, 2020). This is in direct conflict with Indigenous methods of knowledge production, which emphasise collaboration over competition.

*As a neurodiverse university student, I find attempting to write research papers to be a painstaking task and it's not due to my lack of knowledge on the subject, but because of the physical act of needing to write this knowledge down in a way which conforms with strict university standards. But then when we have been having yarns about the subject, I have no trouble speaking in depth about the subject.*

(Emma Johnstone)

This difficulty in capturing thoughts is not an unusual issue for people with ADHD. People with ADHD often describe having non-linear thought patterns, which results in great difficulty in organising information, particularly in an academic context (Dwyer, 2000). When interviewing a group of female university students with ADHD, Dwyer found that a common difficulty they experienced was their struggle with simply writing their thoughts down (Dwyer, 2000). Assistive technologies such as speech-recognition and transcription software, which were originally designed for people with physical disabilities, have been increasingly adopted for use by students with learning disabilities (Higgins & Raskind, 1995). Other people with learning differences, such as those with ADHD or autism, have also been shown to benefit from these kinds of assistive technologies (Quinlan, 2004). By using voice recognition and transcription technologies, people are more effectively able to communicate their ideas without becoming stuck on the aspects of writing which they find difficult (Higgins & Raskind, 1995). Research has shown that students with ADHD or learning difficulties are often unable to effectively or accurately display their academic knowledge. Essays written by students with ADHD or learning difficulties using speech-recognition software are both longer and of higher quality than those written by hand or typed on a computer (Lewandowski et al., 2016).

We argue that a digital Indigenous knowledge practice could be a valuable assistive tool to support education and research participation, for both neurotypical and neurodiverse Indigenous people. Simply speaking aloud is not what makes this form of knowledge creation and sharing effective; rather, it is the environment that is created when undertaking this discussion, an environment that is more focused on the sharing of ideas and information than on the structure in which this knowledge is presented. In this environment, there is no right or wrong way to speak or a need to structure arguments according to specific Western guidelines, and there is no competition between participants. This lack of formality and the embracing of different viewpoints makes Indigenous methods of knowledge production and sharing far more welcoming to neurodiverse people who struggle to conform to the rigid expectations of higher education systems. Many neurodiverse academics are increasingly calling for a movement towards more collaborative forms of research (Rosqvist et al., 2019).

Increasing access to academia for communities of people who have traditionally been excluded from it, is vital work. Without actively seeking to transform these institutions into places that are accessible by all peoples, the voices of marginalised communities will remain silenced. In this way, digital Indigenous knowledge practices can disrupt and challenge the existing power structures and hierarchies and create a new future where academic institutions and systems are transformed into places of justice, and accessibility.

### Challenging current ways and building a vision for the future

Indigenous standpoint theory provides a framework from which to challenge and critique colonial knowledge (Dudgeon, 2020). This framework is necessary as knowledge created through colonial processes is not a practice found only in the past. Indeed, colonisation is an ongoing process that remains active in Australia (Moreton-Robinson, 2011b).

As colonisation remains active, so too does Indigenous resistance (Carlson & Berglund, 2021). This ongoing colonial status can be seen within academia, where Indigenous peoples are still positioned as objects of study. Our knowledge is considered as something to be 'known' rather than Indigenous people being 'knowers' in our own right (Moreton-Robinson, 2004). The hierarchy which positions Western epistemologies and ontologies as superior is maintained through the silencing of Indigenous voices (Kennedy, 2021). Removing the silence and amplifying these voices, our voices, is an act of resistance. Creating new futures, or enacting futurisms for ourselves is an act of both historical reflection and an ongoing resistance to colonial institutions. It is the process of looking to the past to see how colonisation has impacted us as individuals and as communities, followed by the defiant act of resistance through recovering and privileging Indigenous practices and making space in contemporary and future worlds for Indigenous peoples.

Throughout this chapter, we have sought to consider the future by reflecting on our past. We have challenged Western normative understandings of Indigenous histories and research and instead offered a way forward that is built on Indigenous epistemologies. We have argued that using digital technology for an oral research and writing practice is simply a continuation of long-standing Indigenous oral knowledge practices, reimagined for a future world. In schools, the non-linear, relationship-responsive, narrative-centred pedagogical approach of Indigenous oral knowledge transmission and production practices provides endless possibilities when paired with dynamic and innovative technology. Furthermore, digital Indigenous knowledge practices can increase access to academia for both neurotypical and neurodiverse Indigenous people, who have historically been excluded from Western institutions. In this way, digital Indigenous knowledge practices can disrupt and challenge existing power structures and hierarchies and create a new future where institutions and systems are transformed into places of justice, and accessibility.

## Note

1 Disappointingly, the paper detailing the study of this engraving does not name the Indigenous peoples on whose lands the engraving is located. Without knowing the exact location of the engraving, it is difficult to say with certainty which Indigenous peoples have produced and maintained this powerful knowledge. However, from our own investigations, it is likely that this engraving is on the lands of the Miriuwung and Gajerrong peoples. In 2008, the Miriuwung and Gajerrong peoples published the 'Miriuwung-Gajerrong Cultural Planning Framework', which details their desire to be included in any research that takes place on their lands. They ask that research be done in a culturally appropriate way, and that their intellectual and cultural property be retained.

## References

Augustine, S. J. (2008). Oral histories and oral traditions. In R. Hulan & R. Eigenbrod (Eds.), *Aboriginal oral traditions: Theory, practice, ethics* (pp. 2–3). Fernwood Publishing.

Australian Curriculum, Assessment and Reporting Authority. (2020). *Review of the Australian Curriculum F–10*. www.australiancurriculum.edu.au/media/7137/ccp_atsi_histories_and_cultur es_cons ultation.pdf.

Babinski, D., Pelham, W., Molina, B., Waschbusch, D., Gnagy, E., Yu, J., Sibley, M., & Biswas, A. (2011). Women with childhood ADHD: Comparisons by diagnostic group and gender. *Journal of Psychopathology and Behavioral Assessment, 33*(4), 420–429. https://doi.org/10.1007/s10 862-011-9247-4

Bessarab, D., & Ng'andu, B. (2010). Yarning about yarning as a legitimate method in Indigenous research. *International Journal of Critical Indigenous Studies, 3*(1), 37–50. https://doi.org/ 10.5204/ijcis.v3i1.57

Burraga Foundation. (2016). *The Burrraga story* [Video]. www.burraga.org/about.

Carlson, B., & Berglund, J. (Eds.). (2021). *Indigenous peoples rise up: The global ascendency of social media activism*. Rutgers University Press.

Carlson, B., Berglund, J., Harris, M., & Poata-Smith, E. T. A. (2014). Four scholars speak to navigating the complexities of naming in Indigenous Studies. *Journal of Indigenous Education, 43*(1), 58–72. https://doi.org/10.1017/jie.2014.8

Carlson, B., Kennedy, T., Day, M., & Bakic, T. (2021). Introducing the COVID-19 Special Issue: Indigenous academics' resilience during the coronavirus pandemic. *Journal of Global Indigeneity, 5*(1). www.journalofglobalindigeneity.com/article/19427-introducing-the-covid-19-special-issue-indigenous-academics-resilience-during-the-coronavirus- pandemic

Dudgeon, P. (2020). Decolonising psychology: Self-determination and social and emotional well–being. In B. Hokowhitu, A. Moreton-Robinson, L. Tuhiwai-Smith, C. Anderson, & S. Larkin (Eds.), *Routledge handbook of critical Indigenous studies* (pp. 100–114). Routledge.

Dwyer, S. C. (2000). Overcoming obstacles to education: The experience of women university students diagnosed with attention-deficit/hyperactivity disorder. *Canadian Journal of Higher Education, 30*(1), 123–148. https://doi.org/10.47678/cjhe.v30i1.183348

eSafety Commissioner. (2016). *A Yarrabah perspective* [Video]. eSafety. www.esafety.gov.au/educat ors/classroom-resources/be-deadly-online.

Geia, L. K., Hayes, B., & Usher, K. (2013). Yarning/Aboriginal storytelling: Towards an understanding of an Indigenous perspective and its implications for research practice. *Contemporary Nurse, 46*(1), 13–17. https://doi.org/10.5172/conu.2013.46.1.13

Gibson, S. (1993). Culture and learning: A divisive link. *Aboriginal Child at School: A National Journal for Teachers of Aborigines and Torres Strait Islanders, 21*(3), 43–51.

Gillberg, C. (2020). The significance of crashing past gatekeepers of knowledge: Towards full participation of disabled scholars in ableist academic structures. In N. Brown, & J. Leigh (Eds.), *Ableism in academia: Theorising experiences of disabilities and chronic illness in higher education* (pp. 11–30). UCL Press. https://doi.org/10.2307/j.ctv13xprjr.7

Halse, C., & Robinson, M. (1999). Towards and appropriate pedagogy for Aboriginal children. In R. Craven (Ed.), *Teaching Aboriginal Studies* (pp. 199–213). Allen & Unwin.

Hattie, J. (2009). *Visible learning: A synthesis of over 800 meta-analyses relating to achievement.* Routledge. https://doi.org/10.4324/9780203887332

Henry, E., & Jones, S. H. (2011). Experiences of older adult women diagnosed with attention deficit hyperactivity disorder. *Journal of Women & Ageing, 23*(3), 245–262. https://doi.org/10.1080/08952841.2011.589285

Higgins, E., & Raskind, M. (1995). Compensatory effectiveness of speech recognition on the written composition performance of postsecondary students with learning disabilities. *Learning Disability Quarterly, 18*(2) 159–174. https://doi.org/10.2307/1511202

Hughes, P., & More, A. J. (1997, 4 December). Aboriginal ways of learning and learning styles [Paper Presentation]. 1997 Annual Conference of the Australian Association for Research in Education, Brisbane, QLD, Australia. www.aare.edu.au/data/publications/1997/hughp518.pdf.

Kennedy, T. (2021). United front: indigenous peoples' resistance in the online metal scene. In B. Carlson, & J. Berglund (Eds.), *Indigenous peoples rise up: The global ascendency of social media activism* (pp. 185–195). Rutgers University Press. https://doi.org/10.36019/9781978808812-013

Krenshaw, A. (1970). A pollen diagram from Lake Euramoo, North-East Queensland, Australia. *New Phytologist, 69*(3), 785–805. https://doi.org/10.1111/j.1469-8137.1970.tb02463.x

Lewandowski, L., Wood, W., & Miller, L. A. (2016) Technological applications for individuals with learning disabilities and ADHD. In J. Luiselli & A. Fischer (Eds.), *Computer-Assisted and web-based innovations in psychology, special education, and health* (pp. 61–93). Academic Press

Mahuika, N. (2019). *Rethinking oral history and tradition: An Indigenous perspective.* Oxford University Press. https://doi.org/10.1093/oso/9780190681685.001.0001

Mills, K. A., Sunderland, N., & Davis-Warra, J. (2013). Yarning circles in the literacy classroom. *The Reading Teacher, 67*(4), 285–289. https://doi.org/10.1002/trtr.1195

Moreton-Robinson, A. (2004). Whiteness, epistemology and Indigenous representation. In A. Moreton-Robinson (Ed.), *Whitening race: Essays in social and cultural criticism* (pp. 75–88). Aboriginal Studies Press.

Moreton-Robinson, A. (2011a). The white man's burden. *Australian Feminist Studies, 26*(70), 413–431. https://doi.org/10.1080/08164649.2011.621175

Moreton-Robinson, A. (2011b). Virtuous racial states: The possessive logic of patriarchal white sovereignty and the United Nations Declaration on the Rights of Indigenous Peoples. *Griffith Law Review, 20*(3), 641–658. https://doi.org/10.1080/10383441.2011.10854714

Nakata, M., Byrne, A., Nakata, V., & Gardiner, G. (2005). Indigenous knowledge, the library and information service sector, and protocols. *Australian Academic & Research Libraries, 36*(2), 7–21. https://doi.org/10.1080/00048623.2005.10721244

NSW Aboriginal Education Consultative Groups. (2021). *NSW AECG Annual Report 2021.* www.aecg.nsw.edu.au/wp-content/uploads/2022/07/Final_AECG_AR2021_no_financialsindd_web.pdf

Nunn, P., & Reid, N. (2016). Aboriginal memories of inundation of the Australian Coast dating from more than 7000 years ago. *Australian Geographer, 47*(1), 11–47. https://doi.org/10.1080/00049182.2015.1077539

O'Sullivan, S. (2013). Reversing the gaze: Considering Indigenous perspectives on museums, cultural representation and the equivocal digital remnant. In L. Ormond-Parker, A. Corn, C. Fforde, K. Obata, & S. O'Sullivan (Eds.), *Information technology and Indigenous communities* (pp. 139–150). AIATSIS Research Publications.

Ouzman, S., Tacon, P., Mulvaney, K., & Vulgar, R. (2002). Extraordinary engraved bird track from North Australia: Extinct fauna, dreaming being and/or aesthetic masterpiece? *Cambridge Archaeological Journal, 12*(1), 103–112. https://doi.org/10.1017/s0959774302000057

Perelmutter, B., McGregor, K., & Gordon, K. (2017). Assistive technology interventions for adolescents and adults with learning disabilities: An evidence-based systematic review and meta-analysis. *Computers & Education, 114*, 139–163. https://doi.org/10.1016/j.compedu.2017.06.005

Quinlan, T. (2004). Speech recognition technology and students with writing difficulties: Improving fluency. *Journal of Educational Psychology, 96*(2), 337–346. https://doi.org/10.1037/0022-0663.96.2.337

Rainforest Conservation Society of Queensland. (1986). *Tropical rainforests of North Queensland: Their conservation significance; Report to the Australian Heritage Commission*. Special Heritage Publication Series, no. 3. Australian Government Publishing Service.

Rosqvist, H. B., Kourti, M., Jackson-Perry, D., Brownlow, C., Fletcher, K., Bendelman, D., & O'Dell, L. (2019). Doing it differently: Emancipatory autism studies with a neurodiverse academic space. *Disability & Society, 34*(7–8), 1082–1101. https://doi.org/10.1080/09687599.2019.1603102

Semali, L. M., & Kincheloe, J. L. (2002). *What is Indigenous knowledge? Voices from the academy*. Routledge.

Smith, H., Giaco, J., & McLean, B. (2018). A community development approach using free online tools for language revival in Australia. *Journal of Multilingual and Multicultural Development, 39*(6), 491–510. https://doi.org/10.1080/01434632.2017.1393429

Spiel, K., Hornecker, E., Williams, R. M., & Good, J. (2022, 29 April–5 May). ADHD and technology research—investigated by neurodivergent readers. [Proceedings Article]. CHI Conference on Human Factors in Computing Systems (CHI '22), New Orleans, USA. https://doi.org/10.1145/3491102.3517592

Storylines. (2018). *Storylines*. https://storylines.com.au/

Vygotsky, L. (1962). *Thought and language*. MIT Press. https://doi.org/10.1037/11193-000

Walker, M., Fredericks, B., Mills, K., & Anderson, D. (2014,). 'Yarning' as a method for community-based health research with Indigenous women: The Indigenous Women's Wellness Research Program. *Health Care for Women International, 35*(10), 1216–1226. https://doi.org/10.1080/07399332.2013.815754

Wheaton, C. (2000). An Aboriginal pedagogical model: Recovering an Aboriginal pedagogy from the Woodlands Cree. In R. Neil (Ed.), *Voice of the drum: Indigenous education and culture* (pp. 151–166). Kingfisher Publications.

Yunkaporta, T. (2009). *Aboriginal pedagogies at the cultural interface* [Unpublished doctoral dissertation]. James Cook University.

# 30
# REFLECTIONS ON INDIGENOUS LGBTIQ+ COMMUNITIES ONLINE

*Andrew Farrell*

## Introduction

Queer Indigenous knowledge produced by queer Indigenous peoples is a transformative act of self-determination. It is transformative in the sense that it troubles and complicates the way we may know Indigenous peoples in a way that is more expansive and inclusive of complex identities and experience. This chapter challenges stereotypes that position Aboriginal and Torres Strait Islander peoples as incompatible with modern technologies and contends with the ways that Aboriginal and Torres Strait Islander peoples continue to resist settler-colonial gendered, sexed, and sexual categories online. This chapter follows outgoing thoughts and reflections on the embedding of Indigenous queer standpoints through my PhD thesis titled 'Indigenous LGBTIQ+ Community Online', which was awarded in 2022. Prioritising Indigenous LGBTIQ+ peoples, my thesis illuminates the Sovereign Erotics (Driskill, 2004) of Aboriginal and Torres Strait Islander queer peoples in response to the settler-colonial project (O'Sullivan, 2021), connecting them to the globalising resurgence of Indigenous peoples as we recover our cultures, expressions, bodies, and relationalities (Simpson, 2017).

## Jerrinja

Indigenous queer critique, produced by those I respectfully refer to as 'queer mob', contextualises and defines my positionality as a queer-identifying Aboriginal person. I am a Wodi Wodi person—a coastal, saltwater person from the Shoalhaven region located in southern NSW. My matrilineal heritage connects to Wodi Wodi, Wandandian, and Dharawal Country for tens of thousands of years. I was born and grew up in a former Aboriginal mission and reserve which is now called Jerrinja Aboriginal Community, located at the mouth of the Crookhaven River.

This community thrives today. It is a community like many other Indigenous communities in that it is always under siege. It has a history of endemic institutionalisation; waves of historical policies of Protection, Dispossession, and Assimilation; and diaspora like many other communities. It is also under ongoing occupation characterised by infringements on

DOI: 10.4324/9781003271802-34

our sovereignty to the land and sea. It is a Country which draws significant populations of tourists each year and is heavily occupied by a military presence. It is also shaped by a determined Aboriginal community whose resistance to historical and ongoing forms of occupation is a source of pride. Notable achievements include the handing over of the Roseby Park Reserve to the community in 1978, and protests and negotiations against (not with) the military in which we achieved further access to our lands and contributed to the receding of historical plans for military facilities on the northern end of what is now referred to as Jervis Bay (Farrell, 2020; Jerrinja, et al., 1988). All over our unceded lands, there is an ongoing cultural, social, and political struggle at play, and at every juncture we have meet it with an unwavering spirit. The degree of occupation I describe is often associated with a community elsewhere, but it is here on our doorsteps disguised as a tourist destination.

Settler-colonial occupation extends to the gendered and sexual politics of identity that plagues all Indigenous communities. As one of the earlier regions of settler-colonial occupations, my Country has endured occupation to a great extent. Settler occupation was endured by my people prior to and during our quarantining in 1900 when the mission was established. I recall being told about the ways that my grandmother and great grandmother experienced the impunity of administrative overseers from the government and church. My matrilineal forebears were forced into the domestic sphere, expected to carry the sterile expectations of birthing away from our shared cultural birthing practices, and to under-take the sole responsibility to children and housekeeping, surviving through rations. They were met with unachievable expectations to live in the ways of Western women without the associated privileges promised by assimilation (Ellinghaus, 2003). The rest of the community also faced colonial expectations of gender and sexuality; however, the re-humanising settler-colonial tool of gender was especially targeted towards live givers—those recast as sisters, mothers, aunts, and grandmothers (see Cruickshank & Grimshaw, 2019). We continue to face eliminatory processes which have adapted, and the legacy of those histories remain in different ways. It has carried into more recent generations, overlaid and intrusive as we continue to strive to live according to our sovereign ways while constrained by pressures of the state and society at large. Knowing and being subjected to the legacy of these forces as a queer Wodi Wodi person, it has been a compelling motivation to participate in the boundary work of anti-colonial research.

I identify as queer. Queer identity, which I sometimes take for granted, is an identity that has taken several decades to articulate. Over the past few years, my work has included autobiographical autoethnographic data which describes the intersections of my Indigenous queer identity as it has and continues to evolve (Farrell, 2016). I agree with the words of E. J. Milera, a Ngarrindjeri and a Narrunga sexual health worker and advocate, in response to a question relating to authenticity. Milera was asked to form a hierarchy of "which comes first? Gay or Aboriginal?" His response was "I don't think there's anything that really distinguishes them" (Hobson et al., 1993). Such is true for me and for many others where queer and Indigenous identity is indistinguishable (Monaghan, 2015). For many queer mob, our identification often begins with knowing ourselves as Indigenous peoples first and our perceptions of sexuality and gender evolve hereafter. The opposite can also be true. Experiences of Aboriginality across settler-colonial spaces are intersubjective, where those who later find out about their Indigeneity are also valid Indigenous experiences (Carlson, 2016). I just happen to be born into my circumstances.

## Research

To sum up a few years of undergrad study, I came up through the University of Wollongong in visual arts. There, I extended my Creative Arts degree to include a major in Indigenous Studies. I graduated with a Creative Arts/Arts double degree and continued as an honours student and eventually into a PhD in Indigenous Studies. These years were formative years for me as a young queer navigating the local queer scene in Wollongong where I still live, on Country.

Through my undergraduate years, I noticed hegemonic inscriptions produced when applying Westernised binary gender and heterosexuality towards Indigenous societies. While facing these challenges, I also saw the potential of critical research in Indigenous Studies to play an important role in extrapolating, identifying, and including our heterogeneous conceptions of gender, sex, and sexuality beyond the settler-colonial imaginary. A strength of Indigenous Studies is its ability to transmit the diverse subject positions of Indigenous people, and the multidisciplinary character of Indigenous Studies is why I love it.

An important event for my development in all of this was the Cultured Queer/Queering Culture conference led by Professor Bronwyn Carlson, where I had my first forum to speak to what I was then exploring in my work (see Farrell, 2015). I was amongst great thinkers in Indigenous queer academic research including Wiradjuri scholar Professor Sandy O'Sullivan and Cree scholar Dr Alex Wilson among others. This was an intimidating event, but my anxiety was quelled by the desire to make some moves to create meaningful steps in research.

Experiences in the academy are often diametrical to my lived realities, particularly of queerness as an Aboriginal person living in the contemporary world. Quite dramatically, where I am currently employed erodes those perceptions. I work in the Department of Indigenous Studies at Macquarie University. As colleagues, we openly challenge oppressive and exclusionary settler-colonial mechanisms through our own work as well as collaborations and connections that centre Indigenous scholars globally who contribute to the relational modes of justice in the academic space. This is perfectly illustrated by the Centre for Global Indigenous Futures and its in-house journal, the *Journal of Global Indigeneity*

On another front, it has always been difficult to go against engrained norms that reduce Aboriginal and Torres Strait Islander diversities. Violence is often produced through shame, denial, and violent backlash which comes from all sides of community—and replicates itself in colonial structures such as the academy (Dudgeon et al., 2015). There is an inherent risk when criticism extends beyond the common position amongst mob[1] against the colony, to see Indigenous peoples as only experiencing the world from a place of oppression. As we see Indigenous people in more complex ways, we must confront the nuances of interpersonal power systems as a strategic method of solidarity (Hill, 1993; Monaghan, 2015).

My work is undertaken with an investment in the territorialising and self-determination of academic research that produces knowledge about Aboriginal and Torres Strait Islander LGBTIQ+ peoples. In our department, we address this through research and teaching in our course offerings—ABST2035: Indigenous Queer Studies and ABST3035: Indigenous Queer Theory and Practice. As we should know, academic institutions are built on unceded Indigenous Country and they have a responsibility to Indigenous communities in many ways. This includes a reckoning in terms of challenging reductive and prescriptively colonial, heterosexual, and cis-normative Indigenous research. We do this on the unceded lands of the Wallumattagal people of the Dharug Nation on which Macquarie University stands.

## Settler-Colonial Cis-heteropatriarchy

I prescribe to Indigenous queer knowledges and critique which point to prevailing discourses on settler-colonial cis-heteropatriarchy as hierarchies which dominate settler-colonial societies. These containers and hierarchies are challenged by Indigenous-led research which asserts an Indigenous Sovereign Erotics that Driskill (2004, p. 51) defines as an "erotic wholeness healed and/or healing from the trauma that First Nations people continue to survive". When I speak to the Sovereign Erotic in the context of Aboriginal and Torres Strait Islander people, it is similarly applied to our communities, and not singularly fixed on the notion of Indigiqueer (Whitehead, 2017) experiences of settler-colonial gender, sex, and sexual regimes. My focus is queer, but I am cognisant of the work that needs to extend out into our communities to signal its importance to all mob and our relationship with non-Indigenous peoples. As Driskill (2004, p. 52) continues, "Our relationship with the erotic impacts our larger communities, just as our communities impact our sense of the erotic. The Sovereign Erotic relates our bodies [back] to our nations, traditions, and histories".

## Digital midden

A journey into sovereign erotics as a PhD thesis incurs both potential and limitation. Like most students, my capacity to produce a feasible and transformative thesis was reined in and reformed for the better. For me, first and foremost, the project had to centre queer mob in ways that did not perpetuate bad habits of extractive research (Sullivan, 2020). How I achieved that was through a retrospective and ongoing analysis of mainstream discourses on Indigenous LGBTIQ+ identities through online articles, posts, video content, memes and so forth. Beyond digital texts as evidence, it was also important to flag achievements in the recent past where queer mob employed digital mediums in their early iterations to share critical information in the fight against racism, transphobia, and homophobia. There are generations of queer Indigenous people who deserve respect through citations which value their contributions to queer mob activism (see Farrell, 2021a). We mourn mob lost through racism, stigma, shame, violence, and death at the height of the HIV/AIDS epidemic but also since first contact with the colonisers. Flowing on to today, Bundjalung queer scholar Arlie Alizzi argues that Indigenous queers are experiencing an ongoing "crisis of recognition" (Alizzi, 2015a, p. 2). Moving beyond the position of subject, Indigenous peoples challenge what O'Sullivan (2022) writes about as 'symbolic annihilation' as a mode of representational justice which underpins my approach to digital scholarship. Against erasure, we author ourselves in knowledge economies and attain higher levels of agency that enable engagement and participation, particularly in the online space. This is evidenced by the many ways that Indigenous queer mob use representational practices online as a tool of visibility.

As a chronically online person, my focus on digital technologies as a site of research was natural for me. Alongside my thesis I created a digital archive blog project, currently known as the Aboriginal and Torres Strait Islander Rainbow Archive.[2] I was inspired by marginalised queer responses to discourses of recognition underpinned by the perception that there is no knowledge produced on Aboriginal and Torres Strait Islander LGBTIQ+

peoples. It positions queer mob as knowers through curating a space to display their knowledge. Collecting and displaying mainstream representations, I also contend with the harmful and violent representations which impact our mob, positioning my work as a curator and gatekeeper of a project which culminates in a reductive image of queer mob. Underpinned by a politics of care, this project intends to invest in our complexities using the affordances of digital technology.

This blog has served a purpose across academic and non-academic spaces to highlight the kinds of agency evident in our communities. Bringing ancient practices into the future, I constructed the blog using the metaphor and practice of a midden, a digital midden. The idea was informed by Leesa Watego, who argues that blog projects are significant in developing and maintaining cultural specificity where she described blogging as an example of a midden (Watego, 2015). Middens are fossilised deposits of food waste that tell a story of how food cultures have developed throughout history. Middens are familiar to me as my people were sea foragers who created middens out of seashells and seafood waste. These sites over millennia form layers of history that, when unearthed, function to inform and reinscribe elements of past cultural practices into contemporary discourse. Watego argues that blogs, as middens, collect ideas which ultimately shape our understanding of Indigenous cultures in the past and into the future.

The blog was also informed by the website made by the community activist group Queers for Reconciliation, which is one of the first, if not the first, websites devoted to Indigenous LGBTIQ+ political activism. Born out of Mardi Gras, Queers for Reconciliation became an allied activist group of Indigenous and non-Indigenous queers in Sydney which transformed in response to the Wik decision, a landmark legal claim to traditional lands in northern Queensland 1996 (Gai, 1997). The website was used to display the group's rationale and political aims, to document sites of political interests, and to promote and disseminate important materials centring queer mob (Farrell, 2021a). Through glaringly loud rainbow text, the home page reads, "THIS SITE was developed to promote Queers for Reconciliation's participation in Mardi Gras and will continue to be online as a contribution towards Reconciliation". The site is a time capsule of Indigenous digital participation with clear political agency, for example, through petitions. The site reproduces media articles, health reports, biographies, and transcribed speeches. What this group has created is a valuable representation that may be considered a digital "re-storying", the retelling of stories that interrupt dominant histories which "listen to other stories [...] transform our collective futures [...] [and] contribute to movements for social justice" (Driskill, 2016, p. 3). Queers for Reconciliation demonstrated necessary changes and innovation in activist approaches as technology emerged as a social tool in the mid to late 1990s. The website set the tone for future generations of online projects by demonstrating how technology can be useful in assisting and sustaining the remembrance of LGBTIQ+ Aboriginal and Torres Strait Islander peoples so that, as Tim Bishop (2014, para. 1) argues, "people do not forget parts of history that we have experienced or are gone along with our memories and the yarns shared with us".

On the shoulders of activist communities, alongside Queers for Reconciliation, I also want to acknowledge the decades of justice work of queer mob in health work, sex work, and the important but under-recognised roles of community. Here I want to flag my respect for the achievements of queer mob including the important Anwenhekene Gay and Trans conferences and the Gays and Lesbians Aboriginal Alliance who, similarly to Queers for Reconciliation, contributed important voices amongst the discourses on identity, race, gender, and sexuality in their article 'Peopling the Empty Mirror: The Prospects of Lesbian and Gay Aboriginal History' (1993). This text is my bedrock of critical scholarly work. Without it, where would I be?

These activist groups are a part of the historical legacy of anti-colonial activism, as explored in my chapter 'The Rise of Black Rainbow: Queering and Indigenizing Digital Media Strategies, Resistance, and Change' (in *Indigenous People Rise Up: The Global Acendency of Social Media Activism*) (Farrell, 2021a). Black Rainbow[3] is an Aboriginal and Torres Strait Islander LGBTIQ+ non-profit community and activist group that formed through social media. I have been involved with Black Rainbow for near a decade in the capacity of board member, to which I leverage any academic privileges. The incremental achievements we are forming in Black Rainbow include long-term reach and connection to queer mob, research, resource development, celebration and mourning, and a focus on tangible outcomes for mob in all that we do. In an interconnected world, Black Rainbow continues to cultivate queer mob agency in ways that are nationally recognisable, but most importantly, accessible. A thesis on community, and academic work, is no good if there are no accessible forms of reciprocity.

## Digital relationships and assemblage

From Carlson's work on social media, we know that the uptake of social media platforms is at a higher rate for Indigenous users than their non-Indigenous counterparts (Carlson, 2013; 2018; 2021; Rice et al., 2016). Social media is so wonderfully and concerningly entrenched in our lives. As a student who is also a subject, much of my personal and professional lives overlap, and I experience social media as an insider who is also tasked with what is sometimes considered "outsider" work–research. In my daily life, I have observed and experienced the myriad of uses of social media sites as host to the distinct ways that queer mob form relationships with each other, their family, friends, and networks. In 'Feeling Seen: Aboriginal and Torres Strait Islander LGBTIQ+ Peoples, (In)Visibility, and Social-Media Assemblages' (Farrell, 2021b), I explored these connections through assemblage theory (Deleuze & Guattari, 1988; Carlson & Frazer, 2018) to analyse how social arrangements engage with Aboriginal and Torres Strait Islander LGBTIQ+ peoples. These arrangements produced a range of complex lines of assemblages which highlight a myriad of social, cultural, and political configurations.

Social media displays formative relationships which are fluid, conditional, and ultimately unstable. Carlson and Frazer (2018) discuss forms of social unity and disunity between Indigenous and non-Indigenous peoples online drawing on Assemblage Theory. They use assemblages to describe the ways in which social media generates and sustains moments that make, remake, and tether moments of social unity that contribute to anti-colonial political activity. These fluid social boundaries, momentary unities, and shifting alliances are dependent on the discursive, social, cultural, and political themes present in the content shared and discussed online, and these often resonate with prevailing and dominant attitudes offline (Carlson & Frazer, 2018; Farrell, 2021b). My observations of Indigenous queer social media posts support the argument by Carlson and Frazer that the overtly anti-colonial standpoints that Indigenous peoples produce online are often an unwelcome and uncomfortable interruption to dominant settler-colonial discourses both online and offline. When met with identities situated beyond settler-colonial norms of gender, sex, and sexuality, reactionary discontent is apparent.

## Zaro

This can be seen in the posts of Torres Strait Islander and Aboriginal actor and social media influencer Ian Zaro (see Instagram @ian.zaro). Zaro polarises audiences both Indigenous and non-Indigenous, queer and non-queer. His career innovates representational practices on social media by making everyday expressions of queer Indigenous identity widely accessible (Farrell, 2021b). Zaro is a typical social media influencer as he incorporates his everyday life into his content, from platforms such as Dubsmash into the current landscape where TikTok reigns. Zaro's Facebook page performs a flow between traditional media celebrity and meme icon in a marketable and savvy way, with fans spanning his content from social media into his televisual work in the Aboriginal and Torres Strait Islander sketch show, *Black Comedy*.[4]

Zaro often centres his identity online as a proud Torres Strait and Aboriginal gay man through tongue-in-cheek comedy content. This presentation is often met with hostility which fixates on ideas of race, culture, identity, gender, and sexuality. Zaro posted a picture of himself in a white robe and wig on Good Friday. The caption read, "Not sure if this look is black Jesus or bootleg Beyoncé", which drew a polarised response. Zaro responded to the negative comments, saying: "I'm not out here to please everyone. If you don't like it move on [...] Eating a big juicy fucking steak today [...] you know where the block and delete button is". This is in response to comments such as: "you weren't meant for this world ... start respecting your culture [...] die soon". Through the comment section, conflations of Torres Strait and Aboriginal culture with that of Christianity and Catholicism were rampant (Farrell, 2021b). Those familiar with Australian history from an Indigenous perspective understand that these interpersonal experiences are connected to a settler-colonial legacy where norms borne out of religious doctrine continue to be used as a tool of suppression and oppression. Zaro's resilient presence and response against hateful community assemblages of hate speak to the many ways Indigenous people navigate settler colonialism where we see audiences align themselves around discourses of religion and identity—spanning a dichotomy of love/support and reactionary violence. In this case, assemblages of hate target race and queer Indigeneity, simultaneously drawing attention to the complex intersections of hate where aggressive online behaviour is not simply a case of online violence at the hand of Indigenous victims and non-Indigenous perpetrators (Farrell, 2021b). In reference to Torres Strait Islander scholar Martin Nakata (2007, p. 199), these interactions can "shape how we speak of ourselves and of each other, how we understand one another, the ongoing relations between us, and how we describe and represent our lived realities". Queer mob are situated in an online terrain where settler-colonial ideologies around gender, sex, and sexuality continue to do the work of the colony and where even those we see as a part of our own communities can participate in the policing of Indigenous bodies. At the social media interface, these moments are vital in determining our relationships with the world and to each other as Indigenous peoples. These issues must be called out and overcome.

## Love

Conceptions of love were a pleasure to include across the various publications that resulted in my thesis. Love is complicated. I did not explore the sexy side of love in my work. Instead, I am interested in the platonic forms of love online where associations facilitate everyday survival. Again, citing Carlson (2019, p. 14), "It is clear that, for many Indigenous [social media] users, these spaces of potential love, intimacy and joy" are also circumscribed by broader structural processes of homophobia, racism, and misogyny, as seen with Zaro. The colonial policing of gender and sexuality online does more than just get in the way of love; it targets and attempts to diminish it (Carlson, 2019; Carlson & Day, 2021; 2022; Day & Carlson, 2022).

My research shows that queer mob communities are heavily invested in harm reduction. Nobody is ever truly safe online, but Indigenous queer communities have formed community groups in the attempt to collectivise and moderate content in groups catered to queer mob, their friends, and allies. These groups foster safer spaces by prioritising safety for Indigenous gender and sexual diverse peoples (Farrell, 2016; 2020). They serve as forums to connect and collectivise beyond the limitations of mobilisation offline. For example, through these groups, I have been able to connect with people across communities, meeting queer mob nationally and internationally. I have had the opportunity to attended legacy events such as the Anwernekenhe conference in Alice Springs in 2015. At that conference I saw how online care and love was put into practice offline. There, love was expressed through passionate calls for structural change in the health/well-being and human rights sectors where many continue local and national activism for queer mob rights. When put into perspective, I recognise the ways that these impassioned calls were seldom heard. As Indigenous mob, we are often forced to repeat ourselves over generations..

Their calls, and the ongoing relationships that extend into digital technologies are central to bringing queer mob perspectives into conversations on Indigenous relational futures. The intergenerational transmission of their activism is now facilitated where those who have thrived and survived support younger generations through social media leadership. In this way, love and pride is about more than just belonging. It is heavily entrenched in creating fulfilling lives, meeting injustices in the colony, and becoming legible in critical discourses of Indigenous survivance today.

While the community does the important groundwork and provides leadership in research, non-Indigenous researchers have a responsibility to challenge settler colonialism from their positions of power and oppression. When mob highlight settler-colonialism, racism, white supremacy, homophobia, transphobia, and queerphobia, we do so through an Indigenous standpoint. How I see non-Indigenous people, white and non-white, participating in those conversations is to challenge them from my own positionalities within whiteness, gender, class, and so on. One way to be an ally to our work is to cite us, cite us beyond a passing sentence to identify the issue and engage with our work. You can include us in the theoretical and analytic depth of what you are doing and position us as experts and knowers, not simply as those who experience these issues. Our agency can be complemented by reading us and citing us well.

## Conclusion

My research demonstrates the complex relationships queer mob have with settler colonies as well as non-queer Aboriginal and Torres Strait Islander peoples. I have signposted the many ways that these relationships, as explored online, are poisoned by settler-colonial harms such as racism, queerphobia, misogyny, and toxic masculinity (Day & Carlson, 2022; Carlson, 2019; Simpson, 2017). As such, this research is not likely to receive immediate validation as it poses quite a few challenges to mainstream discourses. Like many in a similar position, I may spend a lifetime waiting for that validation. I hate to revise a Rupaul talking point, but it is true that for queer mob, we get to make our own families. Our strength is where we find each other and share in critical dialogues of healing and belonging. My research and my finished thesis is the structure around which family has evolved for me. It has instilled a profound sense of respect I have for the distinct and diverse experiences that exist beyond my purview. You can also imagine my dismay as I am no longer a student, being passed and conferred as Dr Andy Farrell in October of 2022. Being a university student has been a central identifier for me for approximately 15 years. But let's be honest. I did it all with a mind to removing the non-gendered title of 'Mr' and replacing it with 'Dr'

## Notes

1  'Mob' is a colloquial term used by Aboriginal and Torres Strait Islander peoples to refer to them-selves as part of the collective—'us mob' or 'mob only' means no settlers.
2  See https://indigblackgold.wordpress.com
3  See https://blackrainbow.org.au
4  See https://iview.abc.net.au/show/black-comedy

## References

Bishop, T. (2014). First Peoples entries in the Sydney Mardi Gras parade. www.timbishop.com.au/inte ractive-history-first-peoples-entries-sydney-mardi-gras-parade/

Carlson, B. (2013). The 'new frontier': Emergent Indigenous identities and social media. In M. Harris, M. Nakata, & B. Carlson (Eds.), *The politics of identity: Emerging Indigeneity* (pp. 147–168). University of Technology Sydney E-Press.

Carlson, B. (2016). *Politics of identity: Who counts as Aboriginal today?* Aboriginal Studies Press.

Carlson, B. (2019). 'Love and hate at the Cultural Interface: Indigenous Australians and dating apps'. Special Issue: Indigenous Sociology: Contemporary Theoretical Perspectives, *Journal of Sociology*, pp. 1–18.

Carlson, B., & Day, M. (2021). Love, hate and sovereign bodies: The exigencies of online dating. In A. Powell, A. Flynn, & L. Sugiura (Eds.), *The Palgrave handbook on gender, violence and tech-nology* (pp. 181–201). Palgrave Macmillan.

Carlson, B., & Day, M. (2022). 'Colonial violence on dating apps'. In H. Arden, A. Briers, N. & Carah (Eds.), *Conflict in my outlook* (pp. 72–74). University of Queensland Press.

Carlson, B., & Frazer, R. (2018). *Social media mob: Being Indigenous online.* Macquarie University. https://researchers.mq.edu.au/en/publications/social-media-mob-being-indigenous-online

Carlson, B., & Frazer, R. (2021). *Indigenous digital life: The practice and politics of being indigenous on social media.* Palgrave Macmillan.

Cruickshank, J., & Grimshaw, P. (2019). *White women, Aboriginal missions and Australian settler governments: Maternal contradictions.* Brill.

Day, M., & Carlson, B. (2022). Predators & perpetrators: White settler violence online. In D. Callander, P. Farvid, A. Baradaran, & T. Vance (Eds.) *(Un)Desiring whiteness: (Un)Doing sexual racism* (pp. 1–30). Oxford University Press.

Deleuze, G., & Guattari, F (1988). *A thousand plateaus: Capitalism and schizophrenia.* Bloomsbury.

Driskill, Q. (2004). Stolen from our bodies: First Nations two-spirits/queers and the journey to a sov-ereign erotic. *Studies in American Indian Literatures,* 16(2), 50–64.

Driskill, Q. (2016). *Asegi stories: Cherokee queer and two-spirit memory.* University of Arizona Press.

Dudgeon, P., Bonson, D., Cox, A., Georgatos, G., & Rouhani, L. (2015). *Sexuality & Gender Diverse Populations Roundtable Report.* The Healing Foundation. Canberra.

Ellinghaus, K. (2003). Absorbing the 'Aboriginal problem': Controlling interracial marriage in Australia in the late 19th and early 20th century. *Aboriginal History,* 27, 183–207.

Farrell, A. (2015). Can you see me? Queer margins in Aboriginal communities. *Journal of Global Indigeneity, 1*(1). https://ro.uow.edu.au/jgi/vol1/iss1/3/

Farrell, A. (2016). Lipstick clapsticks: A yarn and a Kiki with an Aboriginal drag queen. *AlterNative: An International Journal of Indigenous Peoples, 12*(5), 574–585.

Farrell, A. (2020, June). Queer and Aboriginal in a regional setting: Identity and place. *Archer Magazine*. https://archermagazine.com.au/2020/06/queer-andaboriginal-identity-and-place/

Farrell, A. (2021b). The rise of Black Rainbow: Queering and Indigenizing digital media strategies, resistance, and change. In B. Carlson & J. Berglund (Eds.), *Indigenous peoples rise up: The global ascendency of social media activism* (pp. 140–156). Rutgers University Press.

Farrell. A. (2021a). Feeling seen: Aboriginal and Torres Strait Islander LGBTIQ+ peoples, (in)visibility, and social-media assemblages. *Genealogy, 5*(2), 57–68.

Gal, D. (1997). An Overview of the Wik decision. *University of New South Wales Law Journal, 20*(2), 488–491.

Gays and Lesbians Aboriginal Alliance. (1993). Peopling the empty mirror: The prospects for lesbian and gay Aboriginal history. In R. Aldrich (Ed.), *Gay perspectives II: More essays in Australian gay culture* (pp. 1–62). Department of Economic History, University of Sydney.

Hill Collins, P. (1993). Toward a new vision: Race, class, and gender as categories of analysis and connection. *Race, Sex & Class, 1*(1), 25–45.

Hobson, J., Wafer, J., & Walcott, P. (1993). *Queers of the desert: E.J. Milera (1992–95)*. www.indigoz.com.au/qotd/milera.html

Jerrinja Local Aboriginal Land Council, Wreck Bay Aboriginal Community Council. (Prod. & Dir.) (1988). *We come from the land* [Video file]. YouTube. https://youtu.be/4zNJLySOcCI

Monaghan, O. (2015). Dual imperatives: decolonising the queer and queering the decolonial. In D. Hodge (Ed.), *Colouring the rainbow: Blak queer and trans perspectives: Life stories and essays by Indigenous people of Australia* (pp. 195–207). Wakefield Press.

Nakata, M. N. (2007). *Disciplining the savages, savaging the disciplines*. Aboriginal Studies Press.

O'Sullivan, S. (2021). The colonial project of gender (and everything else). *Genealogy, 5*(3), 67–76.

O'Sullivan, S. (2022). Challenging the colonialities of symbolic annihilation. *Southerly, 79*(3), 16–22. https://doi.org/10.3316/informit.586802496270810

Rice, E., Haynes, E., Royce, P., & Thompson, S. C. (2016). Social media and digital technology use among Indigenous young people in Australia: A literature review. *International Journal for Equity in Health, 15*(81).

Simpson, L. B. (2017). *As we have always done: Indigenous freedom through radical resistance*. University of Minnesota Press.

Sullivan, C. (2020). Who holds the key? Negotiating gatekeepers, community politics, and the 'right' to research in Indigenous spaces. *Geographical Research, 58*(4), 344–354.

Watego, L. (2015). Even the activist's gotta eat: taking ownership, building platforms, *Journal of Global Indigeneity, 1*(2). https://ro.uow.edu.au/jgi/vol1/iss2/7

Whitehead, J. (2017). *Full-metal Indigiqueer*. Talonbooks

# INDEX

People can see the world as the room that they're in, or the street that they live on, or the town or city that they're in. Or, they can be aware—all the time—that we are all on a planet that's spinning on its own axis and orbiting the sun. So while we are all in our rooms, we are also ultimately part of a much much bigger structure, something bigger than all of us. We choose to see our place in the universe.

*Niamh Shaw, STEM communicator, scientist, engineer, writer and performer*
*(Space Specials: Dream big or how to launch a career into space, 15 Dec 2020)*

LIQUIFER    Living Beyond Earth
Architecture for
Extreme Environments

PARK BOOKS

# LIQUIFER

Mars

Moon

Orbit

Earth Land
Earth Ocean

# Residing Among the Stars

Prologue by
Brent Sherwood

Our past and future both reside among the stars.

Every atom in our bodies heavier than hydrogen—oxygen, carbon, nitrogen, phosphorus, sulphur and trace elements—was made in supernovae explosions more than five billion years ago.

We inhabit but an instant of time, a mere blink in the age of the universe. Our solar system is about one-third as old as the cosmos. Anatomically modern humans have roamed the Earth for less than 0.005 percent of its age, just 200,000 years. And human civilization—artefacts, writing, agriculture, technology, architecture and urbanism—has existed for only 5 percent of that brief time.

In just the last 200 years, a blip of the blink, humankind invented powered machinery, tamed electricity and fission, developed semiconductors and created the digital world. In so doing, we also reproduced to over eight billion people, consumed a third of our planet's forests, and overran the carrying capacity of the only biosphere we have. We are directly causing the planet's sixth large-scale extinction event. While the Earth is vast, an incomprehensible $6 \times 10^{21}$ metric tons, our onion-skin-thin biosphere is not. The zone in which complex life can survive is quite limited and vulnerable, a fact that becomes more evident and inescapable every year. To coexist with the plummeting biodiversity remaining on Spaceship Earth, let alone to continue expanding indefinitely, we must return to space.

Only there will we find limitless energy, inexhaustible material resources and the opportunity to make new habitats so that human civilization and Earth life can have an unlimited future.

This existential opportunity should motivate all of us to open and settle the vast domain of space.

But living and thriving in space will be extremely different from what we know, because space is an extreme environment, everywhere. On the Moon, among the asteroids, on Mars, in free-space orbital habitats and eventually crossing interstellar distances, all the future places we could call home are soberingly and frustratingly hazardous and alien, and we must manufacture every aspect of our surroundings just to survive.

This is what Space Architecture is all about: "the theory and practice of designing and building inhabited environments for use in outer space". Space Architecture's built environments must be tailored for the diverse harsh conditions found in terrestrial analogue extreme environments, in Earth orbit, on the Moon, asteroids, Mars and in deep space.

What began as a visionary urge shared by a few curious, future-oriented designers in the late 20th century has become a new professional field of thought and endeavour. Increasingly, Space Architecture appears relevant to our predicament on this limited Earth by offering practical, incremental solutions. The outward-looking solutions aim to tame the harsh domain of space to enable a long tomorrow; the inward-looking solutions aim to transfer lessons from space flight directly back to Earth today, informing a lighter touch on our unique, irreplaceable home.

This book chronicles the journey of an intrepid team of explorers. LIQUIFER comprises a flexible team of designers who are committed to advancing human space flight by designing what it could be, while also making it quintessentially humanistic and promoting our noblest goals: safety, practicality, comfort, productivity, frugality, ingenuity and inspiration. LIQUIFER has, for decades, pioneered the special role of Space Architecture within large aerospace teams, using their ingenuity and humanistic system design principles to earn a seat at the table alongside government agencies and industry leaders.

*Living Beyond Earth: Architecture for Extreme Environments* contains mind-expanding designs for some of the extreme environments of outer space where gravity becomes a parameter, life support systems must work continuously and reliably, and transformable and lightweight designs make solutions possible. Throughout LIQUIFER's approach, nature and humanity remain fundamental.

Along this journey, you will be invited to contemplate deeply challenging questions that percolate at the core of the new field of Space Architecture: What is it about space that seems to pull us outward inexorably? Maybe it's the infinite view. On Earth our horizon is limited by topography and atmospheric haze, while beneath the sea, light scattering and attenuation close us in. But in space we can see forever, all the way back to the origin of the universe. How could this not compel us to explore and expand?
What motivates Space Architects? The allure of designing places for human activity in novel conditions, where even gravity and breath cannot be taken for granted, is so fundamental to the act of architecture that it has become a siren song for many. Architects love hard design problems, which are puzzles of form, material and building. What greater challenge could there be than taming space to make an infinite future for humanity?

What by nature do we require? The rigours of space separate wants from needs. What is atavistic—so intrinsic to human nature and social behaviour that it cannot be changed? Which needs aren't actually needs at all, but merely habits from living on Earth? What if Lunar or Mars partial gravity isn't physiologically tolerable forever? We will need to learn what our deep needs are and accommodate them wherever we find ourselves. Finally, "designer biology" is advancing rapidly; will space humans even be the same as us?

How will we adapt to inconceivably big numbers? Space is truly vast. Travel distances are measured in millions of kilometres and months of time. Even the speed of light becomes noticeable: from Earth, 1.3 seconds to the Moon and nine minutes to the stable Sun-Earth Lagrange Points. Real-time conversations will be impossible between dispersed space habitats. How will we make the transition from our finite Earth to infinite space that still imposes finite constraints? Eventual space urbanism will be different from today's megacities. "Towns" will be modest in scale and months or years apart, as they used to be on Earth.

Can human behaviour evolve? We want to believe that civilization can make the social animal more responsible but history's evidence is not heartening. Will the privation we experience in space cause us to learn new ways of being or will we just extend old habits with us everywhere we go? Can luxury be compatible with draconian efficiency and extreme physical conservation? Increasingly, architecture has enabled social density but arguably it has not really improved human behaviour. Will things be different in space? Will harsh conditions drive spiritual growth?

What about architecture is essential to human community? In space we will learn how technology and community size relate to remote self-sufficiency. Can we learn to consume without appropriating or even use without consuming? Who determines acceptable risk in reaching out a great distance and who gets to go? Utopian and dystopian futures are in tension throughout speculative fiction and in today's world. Will expanding into space be ennobling or oppressive?

This book touches the deep questions that Space Architects engage, argue about and hold in mind as they work. Immersed in LIQUIFER's forward-thinking Space Architecture projects, your imagination will ultimately leave you pondering what types of society we will build in space.

Mars

Moon

Orbit

Earth Land
Earth Ocean

# Living Beyond Earth

Introduction by
LIQUIFER

An interstellar traveller aiming to land on Earth's surface will first encounter a dense, spherical skin of satellites. Approaching Earth through the floating infrastructural haze of the exosphere, the size and shape of one of these satellites will make it stand out. Large panels catching sunlight cover a series of modules and a docking spaceship. It is a space station, home to a handful of humans, orbiting at a distance of 400 kilometres from the planetary surface where each and every other living human resides, along with millions more species.

The International Space Station (ISS) is a technological biosphere in which we explore what it takes to make a new home beyond our planet, now joined in Earth's orbit by China's Tiangong. Constructing such specialised architecture for the extreme environment of space is an endeavour with few parallels in either its complexity or the ingenuity required for success. Its architects are tasked with fulfilling the basic needs of human survival and, at the same time, allowing a small community to live in harmony, far from the familiar, terrestrial environment with which we have co-evolved. This is the challenge LIQUIFER has been engaging for the last 20 years.

This book is built upon the insight gained from this living laboratory and looks towards the far greater settlements we will build, much further from home. Our work at LIQUIFER spans the space-Earth continuum, learning from the constraints imposed by outer space to provide for humans on Earth, in addition to those few who are venturing beyond. From our perspective Earth is one part of space and space is all around us.

## The space–Earth continuum

Our endeavours share one goal, whether delivering humankind beyond the universe's unknown frontiers or finding strategies for more sustainable living on Earth: to support life and to advance knowledge through the combined efforts of science, technology and architecture. Human beings share the same physical needs whether they are astronauts living on a space station or the inhabitants of a house on Earth. Shelter, water, food and oxygen are the essentials for survival. In extreme environments, where the conditions are unforgiving, humans are driven to manage these resources with utmost care.

Architecture goes beyond the provision of essentials for human survival. Manufacturing a technological biosphere for living beyond Earth also requires the design of a quality living environment and a space for thriving social systems. Extreme environments demand invention, adaptation and dedication from those who design them and those who live in them.

## Collaboration as a mindset

The expansion of human presence beyond Earth's horizon is driven by collective imagination, which has already mobilised global networks of resources and ingenuity. The collaborative efforts of teams with diverse sets of knowledge and skills enable the complex solutions required for human space exploration. By setting our practice's default attitude to Space Architecture as firmly transdisciplinary, we ensure diverse perspectives and approaches guide the future outcomes of life in outer space.

LIQUIFER has evolved with direction from its core team of Barbara Imhof, Waltraut Hoheneder and René Waclavicek. Beginning in 2003 with expertise in architecture, design, space applications and economics, the team has since expanded to include systems designers, material scientists, aeronautical engineers and engineering technicians. Our work is predominantly collaborative and routinely part of an international consortium made up of leading industries and academia. These partnerships are financed by the European Union, European Space Agency (ESA), Austrian Research Promotion Agency (FFG), and the Austrian Science Fund (FWF). As a micro-enterprise embedded in cutting-edge science and technology developments for human spaceflight, we develop concepts, scenarios, prototypes, systems and products for future living and working on Earth and in space.

## The history of a name

In the late 1990s, the Australian geologist Nick Hoffman established the "White Mars" hypothesis. He challenged the common assumption that the valley networks on the Martian surface were formed by water, suggesting they could have been shaped by other media. The White Mars hypothesis posited that carbon dioxide flows determined Martian surface features, generating liquifers, not aquifers. In the early noughties, this theory was disproved but it can still encourage thinking beyond the paradigm of Earth. The name LIQUIFER holds this ambition to broaden the range of perspectives, to challenge conventions and investigate the full range of alternative solutions.

## A journey through space

*LIQUIFER Living Beyond Earth: Architecture for Extreme Environments* maps a journey from outer space to our own planet. Our projects are contextualised in the profoundly diverse environments found along the way. LIQUIFER's architectural design concepts, feasibility studies and technological developments confront scarcity issues that challenge life on Mars, the Moon, in Orbit and on Earth.

Woven through this planetary backdrop, a series of texts elaborate the parameters that drive design for outer space, including the utilisation of in-situ resources, the integration of life-support systems, and the requirement to respond to diverse gravitational conditions.

There are multiple routes to navigate this book. For multi-directional travel, the key concepts and projects are connected through a series of wormholes, which can transport you, for example, to the Moon → p. 85 or Mars → p. 47. For a location-based, condition-specific reading of our work, one must ascend or descend through the structure of the book. For a chronological understanding, a timeline → p. 209 documenting our full portfolio is available at the back of the book.

LIQUIFER's work is framed by essays from acclaimed Space Architects Brent Sherwood and Christina Ciardullo. Looking at our work with their own experience, both authors expand on what it takes to be a Space Architect and what it means to envisage how humans may live in outer space in the future. To begin the book, we introduce our team with a series of conversations revealing personal views, ambitions and visions for the future of human life here and beyond Earth.

Join us in our journey from outer space: we will land on the windblown surfaces of Mars, in the silent craters of the Moon, and float through the microgravity of orbital stations, before returning to our home planet.

17

Deep Space

Mars

Moon

Orbit

Earth Land
Earth Ocean

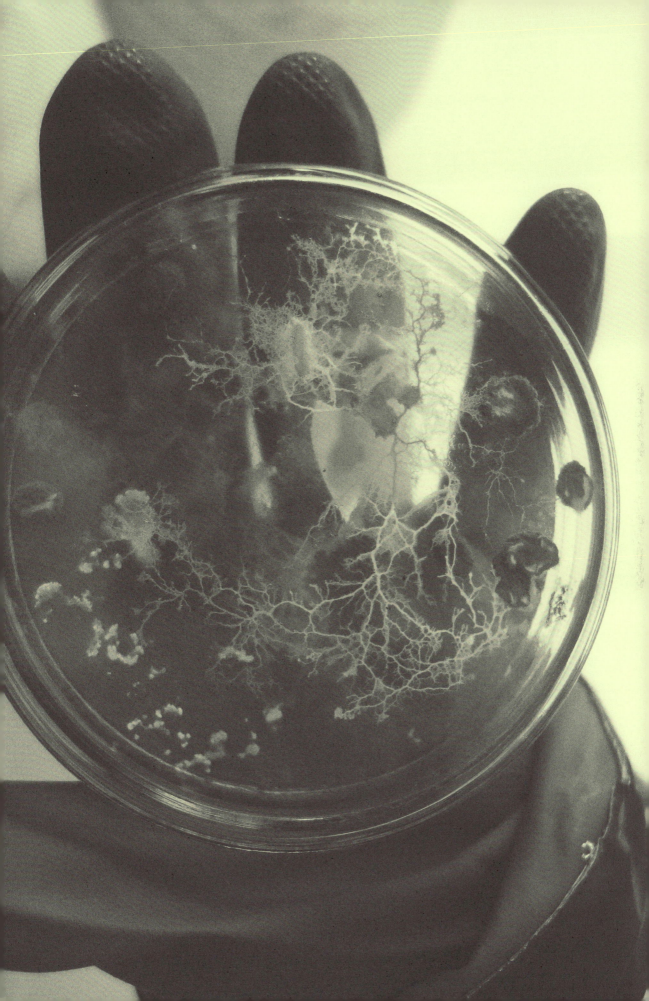

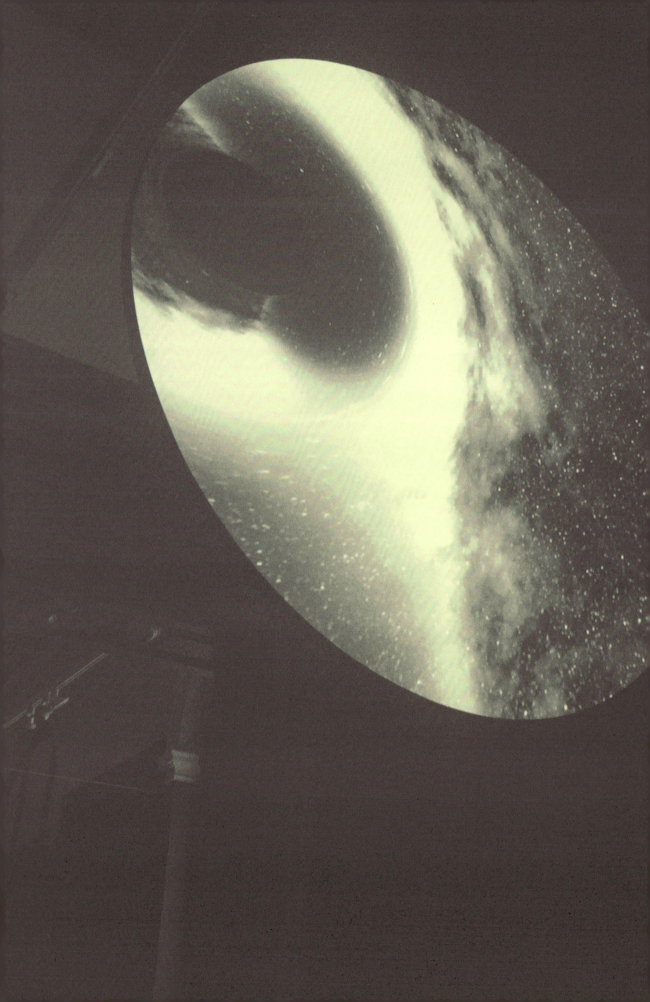

## Travelling through
## the Extraterrestrial

Space Architects are asked one question repeatedly: why put all your effort into outer space when there are so many things to be fixed on Earth? The simple reality is that many people dream of space. As Eva Diáz wrote, outer space is "the place wherein reside fantasies of rebirth, of reinvention, of escape from historical determinations of class, race, and gender inequality, and of aspirations for just societies beyond the protection of the Earth's atmosphere."[1]

We at LIQUIFER each decided to be part of the mission to shape these other worlds. Connected by our passion for outer space, the team pursues a familiar dream, motivated by the complex challenges that arise throughout this extreme environment. Our work is realised due to the variety of opinions, values and voices we bring to the table. In the following series of conversations, we speculate, dream and discuss past, present and future engagements with space. Just like sharing opinions over lunch in our Vienna office, these conversations felt like the most natural way to present the team, our exchange of ideas and how the practice has formed. The conversations invite the reader to reflect on the individual viewpoints of the team, what motivates us to explore outer space, the possibilities in future human spaceflight, the perspective of the architect in outer space, the impact of policy on our work and how knowledge developed for space returns to Earth.

Mars

Moon

Orbit

Earth Land
Earth Ocean

Susmita Mohanty    Asking why humans go to space is a bit like asking why people desire to climb the Himalayas—because it is there. It is often human nature to seek out the unknown or find a way to get to the unreachable.

Bob Davenport    After 50 years in this business, I think the real motivation to go to space is simply that we want to do it. We want to be present as human beings in outer space. We want to do the exploration ourselves, whatever that exploration is. We are motivated by challenges. And I think that these extreme environments provide many people with super challenges.

Chris Gilbert    Agreed. In other words, it's a measure of our achievements.

Stephen Ransom    My interest developed during the time I was designing complex planetary surface habitats and vehicles and launch systems to fulfil international requirements. It also opened up the need for extensive historical research to understand the problems engineers faced in previous space programmes and the solutions they found to fulfil particular applications. Both stressed the need to build teams to combine their experience and expertise.

Mars

René Waclavicek    For me, the unknown sparks curiosity and establishes my drive and motivation. There are still so many unanswered questions. Are we the only intelligent lifeform in the universe? Has there ever been life on Mars? Will we establish a base on the Moon? As children we ask questions to get a better understanding of our world. Venturing into space with robots and humans replaces old questions with new ones. By advancing into space, our horizon expands.

Moon

Orbit

Earth Land
Earth Ocean

Waltraut Hoheneder    I agree, asking questions is inherent to human life. Human space flight is part of basic research on the fundamentals of human existence—on medical, psychological and environmental issues that are necessary to sustain and promote human life. It is about understanding the prerequisites of human life to not only survive but thrive, even under extreme conditions.

**Barbara Imhof** I think the question of why we explore also needs to be framed in a suitable manner. We can use narratives for our motivation that talk about our questions and the answers we have already found. The narrative of the Space Race in the 1960s inspired a whole generation, produced countless scientific publications and many innovations in material science and computer technology. The activities around this race also found a memorable place in our global culture. With narratives we can contextualise our motivation and allow it to be remembered.

**Susmita Mohanty** We are increasingly confronted with a narrative that Earth might become uninhabitable for humans.

**Waltraut Hoheneder** I deeply question the scenario that human space exploration is important because Earth might not be inhabitable anymore. Who would leave the planet and what about the others? This is not a vision I share, rather I think that we will combine all our efforts into restoring the environment on Earth.

**Daniel Schubert** I always say to my students we are already astronauts living on a foreign planet. Earth is a testbed for ecological living and we can transfer that knowledge to the Moon or Mars. By creating biospheres and closed-loop systems we will learn how to leave this planet alone.

**Monika Brandić Lipińska** I would like to do something that would allow us to avoid the question of why we should go to space when we have to solve the problems on Earth. It would be great to maintain the narrative that space exploration really helps Earth because Earth is also one of the planets in space. It's not that because we have to solve problems on Earth, we shouldn't think about space. Instead, thinking about Earth and thinking about outer space need to be understood as the same line of thought.

**René Waclavicek** The narrative is that everything is interconnected. Earth is part of space and space is all around us.

## Life in Deep Space

When we think about the future, we have the tendency to consider it a blank page. Ramia Mazé challenges this thinking in a 2017 essay entitled 'Design and the Future: Temporal Politics of "Making a Difference"', writing: "The future is by no means empty, it will be occupied by built environments, infrastructures, and things that we have designed, it will bear the consequences of our history, structures, policies, and life-styles, which we daily reproduce by habit or with intent and design."[2]
The material futures for life in Deep Space however appear more blank, leaving room for different approaches to the challenge of sustaining life in such extreme environments.

**Daniel Schubert** There is an interesting development within exoplanet research that's going on right now. Virtually every day they are finding a new "Earth" somewhere in the Milky Way. Technologies will continue to advance. It is likely that they will find another civilization outside the solar system.

**Monika Brandić Lipińska** Our thinking about the future of space exploration might drastically change after we find life. It's hard to predict how much impact it will have on our life here, the insight that we're not the only ones. How would this impact our central beliefs? What would it mean for religion?

**Susmita Mohanty** Humans are always looking for carbon-based life forms. In Avi Loeb's recent book, he says we need to look for industrial signatures.[3] Currently, we are obsessed with this whole carbon-based economy, but we need to broaden our search. Let's say, in the past, a certain planet might have had an industrial civilization. So, are there any remnants of that technological past?

**Monika Brandić Lipińska** That reminds me of a conversation with Jill Tarter, co-founder of the SETI Institute,[4] and the American journalist Krista Tippett on what kind of life is going to be found first: will it be biological or technology-based life?[5] There are so many ideas of how to find technology. We are only looking for life as we know it, carbon-based life, and there may be so many other life forms that we cannot even imagine out there. We are looking at everything from our own perspective. The perspective may completely change in 1,000 years.

René Waclavicek        There may be lifeforms based on elements other than carbon. However, due to its structural properties, the number of possible combinations carbon can build is by far greater than the number of chemical compounds of all other elements combined. So, it doesn't seem far-fetched to assume that a significant number of alien lifeforms out there might be made-up of carbon-based chemical compounds. When we look at how long life on Earth was dominated by microbes before a civilisation developed that could leave traces of technological development, we can assume that most traces of life we may find out there are microbial. Of course, we shouldn't limit our search to microbes. Since 1984 the SETI Institute has been searching for signals from extraterrestrial intelligence. This research is pursued regardless of chemical composition. Of course, we can also search for remnants of civilisations but in a galactic timescale they might vanish very fast.  They may therefore be even harder to find than active civilisations emitting detectable signals.

Waltraut Hoheneder        In work we are inclined to speak about settlements and not colonisation in order to think about bases on the Moon and on Mars from a non-violent perspective. A lot of our projects deal with very careful use of local resources. We have a duty of care for these resources and to any kind of extraterrestrial lifeform we might encounter. We cannot afford to make the same mistakes we made on Earth, so we ensure our approach differs from the extractivist principles that currently guide many economies on Earth.

Susmita Mohanty        Just imagine we go to Mars and find native extremophiles and tell them: "Hey, look, we discovered you! Next, we shall document you. Take you to Earth,

Mars

Moon

Orbit

Earth Land
Earth Ocean

26

maybe. Even own you. Monetise the hell out of you." And make a fool of ourselves, all over again, as we did on our home planet. We are very good at that sort of thing.

Barbara Imhof    What I find quite interesting is that we are currently looking at habitable planets, which are very far away in a distant solar system, light years away. When we talk about space exploration nowadays, we mostly talk about dimensions and kilometres; let's say, we need to travel 400 million kilometres to get to Mars or 350,000 kilometres to the Moon. But we have no grasp of light years and we are very far away from being able to travel that far and that fast. In the end, I think humans will always be stuck around Earth, unless we actually start to build generation spaceships. Then we could venture out and go further. When humans are able to do this, there will be a population that leaves Earth and probably never comes back.

Susmita Mohanty    I'd like to sign up for a hibernation experiment. I'd like to hibernate my way to a faraway galaxy. It'd be nice to leave and go on a long voyage to an unknown place with a bunch of like-minded friends. We could start experimenting by sleeping our way to our next-door neighbour Mars. For that, the voyagers would have to be induced into hibernation using drugs and put inside small individual soft-shell pods—like the ones you find in the Clarke-Kubrick science-fiction film. The pods would be darkened and cooled to keep the bodies of the space voyagers at a low temperature for most of the 180-day journey from Earth to Mars.[6]

René Waclavicek    Konstantin Tsiolkovsky wrote that "Earth is the cradle of humanity, but one cannot live in a cradle forever."[7] If Earth is our cradle, the Solar System is our nursery. Human Mars exploration is a necessary stepping stone in learning how to step out of our cradle and learn to walk as an interplanetary and—maybe one day—an interstellar species.

Susmita Mohanty    To me, the prospect of interplanetary travel is like intercontinental travel. It is a matter of overcoming distances through advances in science and technology, as well as the necessary adaptation of human physiology, sociology and psychology for these new journeys.

Monika Brandić Lipińska    If I were born on Mars or somewhere else, I would need a spacesuit to go to Earth, to visit my ancestral origin. Due to growing up in these different environments, a specific architecture might be necessary, like a hotel for people coming from other planets.

Barbara Imhof    That reminds me of '3001', the science-fiction book by Arthur C. Clarke.[8] The protagonist cannot return to Earth completely because his physiology wouldn't allow him to be exposed to terrestrial gravity. A friend takes the space elevator into the Earth's Orbit to visit him in microgravity where he hovers in Orbit.

René Waclavicek    We are witnessing a process similar to when life on Earth left the oceans. Living organisms advanced into regions not inhabitable at that time, preparing the ground for what is an integral part of our biosphere today. Life adapted to new environmental conditions, instead of trying to turn land into ocean.

Waltraut Hoheneder    Technological and living systems will merge. They are merging already in many applications. Technological parts are implanted in living organisms as part of medical treatment: artificial joints, metal plates, tissues—some of them of other organic origin. In the future, technological and biological systems might merge to an extent that their origins are hardly traceable. Advances in artificial intelligence, deep learning and directed evolution may generate life forms, agents and actors, where the distinction between artificial and natural, between technological and biological, become irrelevant.

Susmita Mohanty    If we can start replacing joints and organs with new ones, reverse or prevent osteoporosis, correct age-related diseases propagated through genes and so on, we can certainly extend human lifespans. Maybe in the future we can live for 120 years, 150 years or longer? I think medical advances will allow that. How, then, are we going to accommodate the ever-increasing ageing population?

Barbara Imhof          I read a book by Richard Morgan called *Altered Carbon*, it is about the brain and body being separated yet contained in one physical element.[9] In Morgan's scenario, the brain—or what constitutes us as a thinking species—can be stored as a collection of data in a so-called stack. The body is added to the physical presence as a suit or sleeve. Together, this results in a human being who can potentially live forever, since everything can either be stored as a stack or uploaded into any sleeve. In this world people don't travel with their bodies. They just send their mind as digital information at light speed to their destination, where it is uploaded to another sleeve. Such a scenario is interesting for space exploration because it could enable our species to travel immense distances and act independently in those far-off environments. The field of "Artificial Life" is aiming in a similar direction already. In the deep future, the scenario described above could perhaps be a reality in one way or another. Human space exploration might be able to overcome great distances and time through methods of compacting the self.

Mars

## Space Architecture

Buckminster Fuller's famous quote "We are all astronauts" not only frames Earth as a spaceship but also suggests that all architects are Space Architects.[10]

Moon

Orbit

Earth Land
Earth Ocean

Monika Brandić Lipińska          We currently separate the architecture on the Moon or Mars, or asteroids and so on, from architecture on Earth. Further in the future, architecture on Earth will also be considered space architecture.

Daniel Schubert          Some science-fiction movies might begin to look like documentaries.

28

Chris Gilbert      We have been fed a diet of science-fiction stories and future scenarios for so long that we are taking it for granted that we will live on the Moon and on Mars. It is so easy to create convincing science fiction-based films, with luxurious spaceships appearing to fly at many times the speed of light, but we don't really spend enough time trying to understand or analyse what it will take to achieve these future scenarios. So it is becoming easier to promote visions of settlements in space without giving due consideration to the technological hurdles that must be overcome.

Daniel Schubert      To build a habitat on Mars or the Moon, I think there will be five main functions that every human habitat needs to fulfil. The first function is "In-Situ Resource Utilisation": → p. 106 utilising the resources that can be found there (water, oxygen, fuel, energy, consumables). The second function is "Recycling": in order to establish a closed-loop system in which all the precious resources that have been generated by resource utilisation will be recycled, together with the goods that are transported from Earth. There will be physical and chemical systems, biological systems, recycling of air, water and non-bio-consumables such as plastics and metal, and so on. The third function is "Build and Repair": if something breaks within a habitat, you have to go and repair it, you have to be able to produce spare parts on your own, → p. 102 and, if you have one habitat nucleus, you might want to build a new habitat somewhere else. This function will enable you to reproduce the complete habitat. And since it is a small system—an ecosystem, a biosphere, an ecosphere, or whatever you want to call it—with a lot of players such as humans, machines, animals, plants, you need to "Balance and Control" it, which is the fourth function. You have to be careful that something is not overshooting that could destabilise the whole ecosystem or eventually the whole society. This is something we have not done here on Earth. We are just starting by shifting from fossil energy to renewable energy, for example.

In a very small habitat system, you have to balance and control because the buffers are very small. You see imbalances immediately and they might have devastating effects. That's why you have to keep an eye on them. Lastly, the fifth function is "Resilience and Wellbeing". There will be humans who live in those early habitats. They need to survive and be healthy. It does not make sense to build a big structure, and then nobody wants to live there, or goes there and unfortunately dies after two years. So, apart from system resilience, human factors play an important role which includes telemedicine or medicine in general. I consider those five key functions mandatory for a future habitat on the Moon and Mars. And if you miss out on one, you will fail.

Monika Brandić Lipińska      I think, quite soon, all these visionary ideas for space architecture such as In-Situ Resource Utilisation, → p. 106 will be applied, pushed further by current research and development in experimental architecture. Using the local resources on the Moon and on Mars yields a lot of potential for extracting water and other resources and using 3D printing technologies → p. 90 to construct safe habitats for humans to live in.

René Waclavicek      Some major technical challenges need to be mastered. Developing an autonomous robotic construction process is one, finding solutions for radiation protection is another. These will strongly depend on the funding of research in Lunar exploration.

Stephen Ransom      Long-duration human and robotic exploration of the Moon and Mars will require mobility, in-situ resources and radiation protection. For the Moon and Mars, mobile pressurised manned habitats and laboratories with refuelling capabilities, which have propellants derived from local surface minerals and atmospheric gases, will be needed. New forms of surface manoeuvrability, such as small single-wheeled vehicles, could offer other types of exploration or construction opportunities. These could be operated as clusters where planets have relatively dense

29

atmospheres (e.g. Mars and Titan). Balloons, dirigible airships, fixed-wing aircraft, helicopters, autogyros or even flapping-wing ornithopters might find applications on sites remote from the landing area.

Barbara Imhof     Humans are living beings whose functionality and physiology require gravity. That is our evolutionary development. Our bodies require us to build space stations that rotate and there-fore create artificial gravity. There we could live almost as we do on Earth. These wheel-shaped space stations were first conceived by Konstantin Tsiolkovsky before further development by Herman Potočnik, detail-ing by Wernher von Braun and finally scenic realisations by von Braun and Walt Disney. *2001: A Space Odyssey* by Stanley Kubrick and Arthur C. Clarke is a wonderful illustra-tion of such a construction and I think this is also the future of the long-term hab-itation for many people beyond the Earth's horizon, without causing too much damage or disruption to their health.[11] Of course, this also requires appropriate radiation protection.

René Waclavicek     There may be a time in which the Earth's Orbit has transformed into a living zone, extending the Earth's boundary. I can imagine that there could be an infrastructure ring around the Earth (in Orbit) that is inhabited by many of us and is a self-sufficient ecosphere partly in zero gravity and partly in artificial gravity. It would be a belt of orbital platforms that serve as the extension of our cradle and at the same time as a starting point, a har-bour to access further destinations through shuttle services to the Moon, Mars and asteroids.

Waltraut Hoheneder     A big issue with living in space will be how to compensate for the radical reduction in the number and variety of stimuli that humans are usu-ally exposed to in terrestrial environments. Human life is characterised by rhythms that build on change, alternating periods of extroversion and introversion, of meet-ing and retreating, of going out and coming home. A lively travel activity between space

Mars

Moon

Orbit

Earth Land
Earth Ocean

and Earth might be feasible within low Earth orbit $^{\rightarrow\,p.\,113}$ but how would this work when venturing into deep space?

Daniel Schubert    My motivation when working in space is the creation of closed-loop systems, eco-spheres, biospheres. What I want to see is that we will have some sort of closed-loop habitat on the Moon and that we know so much about habitats and biospheres that we understand how to live independent from resupply.

René Waclavicek    Yes, the Moon $^{\rightarrow\,p.\,85}$ will teach us how to establish permanent outposts under similar conditions. The Moon is the testbed for Mars. Some say that the first Mars $^{\rightarrow\,p.\,47}$ astronaut is already born. Today we are searching for ways to take necessary parts of our biosphere with us in our spacecraft. We are working on solutions to become independent from Earth to try to survive in the hostile environment of outer space.

Waltraut Hoheneder    We have been working on projects that envision self-organising building systems, which may eventually be able to take full care of the needs of their inhabitants. Human space flight might sooner or later be able to get very close to this vision, creating supportive and reliable habitats that host space travellers, to create habitats with adaptable life support systems $^{\rightarrow\,p.\,135}$ aligned with the travellers' needs. The habitats could have their own identities and thrive on their own, in the same way that living organisms do on Earth. Microbes could be the main lifeform supporting these habitable systems. With their self-regulating capacities, microbes might be indispensable for the smooth operation of any infrastructure whether on the Moon, Mars or Earth, $^{\rightarrow\,p.\,141}$ and especially during deep-space missions.

## Space Policies

The governments of major world powers and their outlook on space exploration continue to be the greatest factor affecting funding opportunities for space development. However, the growth of commercial NewSpace $^{\rightarrow\,p.\,212}$ companies will impact how space is experienced and who is able to experience it. Importantly, and realistically, whether humans will one day find themselves on the surface of Mars, orbiting the Moon or on a journey deeper into space will also depend upon unfolding events on Earth—be they the result of political, economical or environmental change.

Bob Davenport    Tourism is the big thing at the moment. It will likely be the driver for commercial interest. I expect it is going to take off in the near future, in which case I think we might soon see the first hotel in space.

Chris Gilbert    Yes, we can, I think, fairly safely predict the growth of commercial spaceflight in low Earth orbit and perhaps suborbital. Probably, if you can bring the cost down quickly, there are sufficient people willing to pay for a flight in space. That might help commercial spaceflight in the long term by stimulating demand for full space flights. The problem with encouraging commercial activities in space is the constant pressure to produce short-term returns on the investment. This leads, for example, to Earth-centric space already being seriously contaminated with debris.

Susmita Mohanty    In the 21st Century, the space race is no longer between nations but between private companies.

Bob Davenport    I would like to see a positive commercialisation of the low Earth orbit environment and not just commercialisation, but also the continued implementation of basic research, so that the International Space Station concept continues or comparable new facilities are built.

Monika Brandić Lipińska   Now we have people living on the ISS but they are not citizens of ISS. Whenever we go to the Moon, it will just be people from Earth going for a mission to the Moon. But when will there be a shift that means people will identify with the Moon or Mars? When will they try to establish their own time zones? Will they be able to begin from scratch?

René Waclavicek   How do we propose living together in a society in outer space? How large is that population?

Daniel Schubert   In the far future of 100 years plus, we might have space settlements, perhaps several thousand people on Mars, and then there might be a time when the Martians will say we want to be independent. Perhaps there will even be a war—who knows? Possibly in the next 500 years, there will be a Martian Independence War. And people on the Moon might also claim independence.

René Waclavicek   When I think of 100 years in the future, I have to look back 100 years to be able to imagine the options. Back then, we were speculating about space travel in a very fantastical way. The mobility age had just begun and with it came the dawn of our understanding and production of today's technologies. We were, so to speak, at a turning point of culture: experiencing the Suffragette movement in Europe, the slow (and continued) demise of colonialism, a shift from monarchies to democracies and other marked changes in political power.

Waltraut Hoheneder   It might be possible that people on Mars do not aspire towards independence. Autonomous living will be part of their everyday life. By then independence might not be even considered desirable, knowing that living systems generally depend on each other.

Susmita Mohanty   We need to introspect how human presence should be responsibly developed in outer space.

René Waclavicek   We should refer to the peaceful uses as stated within the Outer Space Treaty of 1967 in the future for

Mars

Moon

Orbit

Earth Land
Earth Ocean

establishing a society and defining common practices.[12] Specific Lunar cultural practices will form in settlements, first, as we see with the International Space Station, even if Lunar bases are distant from each other.

Monika Brandić Lipińska    We once had a team project on Lunar settlement development and we could approach it any way we wanted.[13] So, we started to think of what we want to do, the time frame, where and what the settlement would be about. Then our discussions shifted from thinking about the space habitat and space settlement into the fact that we don't really have guidelines for how to develop Lunar settlements. With the United Nations Sustainability Goals in our mind, we developed 15 Lunar Sustainability Goals. We made our project based on UN goals but you cannot really map them directly onto space projects, so we developed a series of goals relevant to the environment and concerns of human settlement in space. We developed goals such as: open access, peaceful purposes, international cooperation, education and outreach, heritage protection, health and safety, transportation, zero waste, space debris mitigation, sustainable ISRU → p. 106 and so on.

Chris Gilbert    I wish that the spacefaring nations take more steps to make space travel sustainable, especially in near-Earth orbits, → p. 113 by passing effective legislation requiring satellite operators to remove existing debris when launching new satellites. Currently, new satellite constellations are being launched with inadequate accountability for long-term debris problems they may cause in the future.

Barbara Imhof    In-Situ Resource Utilisation → p. 106 is an important topic, to find resources locally within close proximity to extra-terrestrial settlements. When the infrastructure grows, resources further away from the base can be targeted. That is what humans did on Earth. If our future is a series of joint ventures between governmental, taxpayer-paid missions, and commercial stakeholders, then the question is: to whom do the resources belong? In the Outer Space Treaty there is a paragraph that says: "Outer space is not subject to national appropriation by claim of sovereignty, by means of use or occupation, or by any other means."[14] The Artemis Accords, which [at the time of print] were recently signed by 24 countries and one territory, excludes this paragraph when they claim "extraction of space resources does not inherently constitute national appropriation."[15] The legal aspect of space exploration needs to be defined in the coming years and we need to set a course for how we want to share and distribute resources.

René Waclavicek    Let's take Antarctica as an example. There are 1000 people overwintering but in summer the population increases to around 8000 researchers and 35000 tourists. That could be a valid scenario for the first settlements on the Moon as well. Although Antarctica is not a state and the governing rules depend on the bases' nationalities, there is a certain way of coexistence established amongst the researchers who overwinter. It is probably defined through personal bonds that form a specific culture from living in extreme environments. I assume that people in distress are supported by the closest bases regardless of nationality. I have heard that scientific findings are interchanged by scientists through personal communication rather than through their supporting agencies. The tourists belong to another group in that they enter the continent mainly or only via the Antarctic Peninsula and they are kept separate from the researchers to a large extent. However, all human activity is governed by the Antarctic Treaty of 1959 and connected to the Protocol on Environmental Protection to the Antarctic Treaty, which was established in 1991.[16]

Monika Brandić Lipińska    So Lunar or Martian bases could potentially work in a similar way to those in Antarctica where research and development is mainly funded by governments. Maybe it could also rely on money from public-private partnerships that would be given to research and science.

Daniel Schubert      In that sense, you could even see Antarctica as an analogue, not only as a testing ground but perhaps also for how to best settle on Mars. In the beginning there were expeditions; then there was the race for who would reach the South Pole first. Then in the early years of the last century, there were more and more small stations, occupied only for a couple of months, which in time became permanently inhabited.

Susmita Mohanty      We can start by treating the Moon as our eighth continent for purposes of legal and policy deliberation. Antarctica, our seventh continent, could serve as a precedent to ensure we do not destroy a shared resource despite vested interests and pressure to monetise. If we refuse to act, we will wreck the Moon, much the same way we have wrecked low Earth orbit with millions of human-made debris objects due to the absence of farsighted laws.

René Waclavicek      So, hundreds of years in the future, there might be an advanced society where environmental protection laws are established and where community and capital are hopefully more justly distributed.

Waltraut Hoheneder      Maybe the concept of capital and ownership will have been abandoned by then, not only because of the immense top-down administrative efforts involved but also with the overwhelming establishment of self-organising, open-source infrastructure. Then self-regulatory, robotic infrastructure, enhanced by living systems, will constitute the permanent settlements as independent legal identities. Humans—or whatever they might be called by then—might share a nomadic lifestyle and refrain from settling down.

Mars

Moon

Orbit

Earth Land
Earth Ocean

## Space Technologies for Earth

Due to climate change, the number of extreme environments on Earth is increasing. As a consequence, the challenges terrestrial architects face will become much more closely aligned with those of Space Architects.

Chris Gilbert  I think there will be increased requirements that institutional space budgets should be spent on projects with viable benefits to terrestrial problems.

Susmita Mohanty  There are studies that show that the Earth, as a planet, can only sustain about 2 billion people with the consumption patterns we see in the US. Many people consume way more than they need or way more than what they are willing to neutralise. I think that is the difference: we humans have completely lost a sense of balance and scale.

Waltraut Hoheneder  Human space exploration requires long-term thinking, which is not necessarily characteristic of our common interpretation of evolution as being driven by reactive patterns that allow adaptation to changing environments. Global terrestrial challenges nowadays require long-term approaches as well, since it became obvious with the development of the atomic bomb and human-driven climate change that humans hold the potential to destroy the environment upon which they depend.

Bob Davenport  Human space exploration and aspirations to mitigate terrestrial climate change focus on the same goal: to ensure liveable conditions for humans, by studying the underlying principles of healthy biospheres, and to apply the findings to support and generate them on multiple scales. Our motivations on Earth are comparable.

Waltraut Hoheneder  I agree, human space flight is a testbed for exploring the nature of circularity that enables self-sustaining systems in smaller biospheres. These can generate insights that support the shift towards circular economies on planet Earth.

René Waclavicek  New greenhouse concepts → p. 146 necessary for a closed-loop life support system → p. 135 for a permanent presence in space can help make terrestrial food production much more efficient, environmentally friendly and less ground-consuming.

Waltraut Hoheneder  Humankind has developed technologies that happen to correspond to human or animal systems: they consume organic matter and oxygen, and generate carbon dioxide. In production processes here on Earth, → p. 141 we largely lack technologies that complement such processes, that enable circularity by generating oxygen and consuming carbon dioxide like that of photosynthesis in natural systems. Establishing artificial biospheres in outer space will require careful attention to balancing systems and the development of biotechnological innovations in order to close cycles which may supply important insights for a paradigm shift on Earth.

Daniel Schubert  Mars or the Moon, these are our testbeds, and we can transfer the knowledge back to Earth. We should be able to be really self-sustaining. Once we understand how to do this then it doesn't matter where we live anymore—we could live on the Moon or on Mars or somewhere else in space, maybe near Jupiter, wherever. It doesn't matter because we would be a self-sustaining society living in our own closed-loop environment. We would be completely independent from terrestrial resources. We should aim, in the habitats we live in now, to limit or minimise our ecological footprint towards zero. We should already live today as if we were on a foreign planet.

Susmita Mohanty  According to The Millennium Charter [a 2002 mission statement that articulated the fundamental principles of space architecture], "Space Architecture is the theory and practice of designing and building inhabited environments in outer space."[17,18] → p. 40 Many considerations familiar to Space Architects—productivity, privacy, assembly, aesthetics, identity, sensations, views, mood, safety, utilities and adaptive use, to name just a few—are increasingly relevant to the design of habitable environments in dense cities.[19] Living both in space and in dense cities brings into sharp focus considerations such as sustainability, material recycling and regenerative life support → p. 166

Monika Brandić Lipińska     I think we should make it clear to the public and to people who are not necessarily interested in space exploration that the goal of being self-sustaining is essential to human space exploration. Valuable inputs are coming directly from space research that are applicable to Earth, which means space exploration helps the Earth.

Barbara Imhof          The goal, then, should be to build cities like spaceships, completely self-sustaining. And when we have mastered this, we will be able to build technological biospheres anywhere in the universe. We can build spaceships as cities.

Mars

Moon

Orbit

Earth Land
Earth Ocean

In space we recognise our limits. We put ourselves in a situation where those limits are hard. We only have so much water, so much mass, so much volume and we need to work within these constraints. That mindset is essential for designing for Earth as well.

*Christina Ciardullo, Founder + Principal Architect SEArch+,*
*Researcher Yale Center for Ecosystems + Architecture*
*(Radio Orange Space Specials: Reciprocities: the Earth–space continuum, 13 May 2021)*

I very much believe that architects need to design the whole process. They can't just be concerned about designing a fixed, finished product because the product, as we all know, is never finished... we have to design the whole process, how the building is going to go up, how it's going to come down. We have to design the construction of it and the deconstruction of it. And, that's all part of the design.

*A. Scott Howe, Senior Systems Engineer and Space Architect,*
*NASA's Jet Propulsion Laboratory*
*(Radio Orange Space Specials: MOBITAT – Transformers, 13 Nov 2007)*

# Designing for Outer Space:
# An Extreme Environment

The thickness of the welded aluminium pressure shell of the International Space Station (ISS) measures only 4.8 mm. Standing off from the pressure shell, additional, thin material layers complete the protective shield against micrometeoroids and orbital debris while providing thermal insulation for the humans and machines that populate its interior. These surprisingly thin layers that make up the habitable modules' hull constitute the protection barriers between astronauts and the vacuum environment of low Earth orbit.→ p. 113

Outer space is considered to be the most extreme environment so far identified as a place that humans could inhabit. Designing for such extreme environments teaches us how to deal with the complex scarcity issues in a resource-constrained world.[1] With its successful history of providing a habitat for numerous astronauts and cosmonauts in outer space the ISS represents an archetype of space design, of which certain elements will continue to be referenced in future habitat designs.  In redesigning the favourable conditions of Earth in outer space, Space Architecture studies and designs living and working environments for the survival of humans in the extreme.[2] These environments can and will support crews, bases, settlements, towns and cities in orbital microgravity → p. 113 and in partial gravity on the Moon,→ p. 85  Mars → p. 47 and beyond. In order to protect human life, decades of research has tested living at the extreme for extended periods of time.

Working Method
and Approach

All architectures planned for orbit and other planetary surfaces are dependent on extensive, multidisciplinary collaboration between engineers, astronauts, scientists and architects.[3] A human space exploration project is an international, intercultural and interdisciplinary effort generating working methods that require sensitivity and multifaceted

curiosity extending beyond architecture. To imagine, conceive, design and contribute to building human-tended bases in orbit or on planetary surfaces is, even within the most stringent constraints, an exciting remit for architects. The LIQUIFER team of Space Architects and systems engineering consultants reconfigures according to the requirements of each contracted project, working mainly within multidisciplinary European research projects or as a subcontractor for European Space Agency (ESA) contracts.

Engineers often perceive architectural design to be aesthetically driven, rather than recognising it as closer to systems engineering in practice.[4] In outer space, engineering requirements frequently prevail over architectural design. The work of Space Architects is a constant negotiation between human-centred design and the structural, mechanical and material requirements of extreme environments, with the aim of enabling safe and comfortable habitability in extreme thermal and pressure conditions, while fulfilling transportation requirements.[5]

In the extreme space environment, humans are continuously dependent on a suitably protective habitat. LIQUIFER works on the development of habitation modules and bases, and their related construction methods, mission designs and human factors. Designing for outer space encompasses interrelationships between technology, engineering, space and humans. Therefore, architects must incorporate all possible relationships into their designs: human–human, human–space, human–machine and machine–space.[6] These complex interactions are significant design drivers for human performance and comfort. Mission success is dependent on the integration of humans and technologies on board or in base. Space Architects facilitate this success when they design beyond the mere point of survival towards an environment where astronauts can thrive.

## Environmental
## Influences on Design

In outer space we are faced with a number of environmental factors that significantly differ from habitable locations on Earth, these include: partial or microgravity → p. 131 (depending on planetary size or orbital speed), temperature extremes (dependent on distance and exposure to the Sun), pressure differences (dependent on presence and thickness of an atmosphere), micrometeoroid hazard (when atmosphere is thin or lacking) and exposure to high levels of radiation (without the protection of a magnetic shield). These distinct environmental conditions affect design and material choices and demand a new perspective from architects.

The impact of all of these environmental conditions have led to engineering and architectural standards that accommodate human physiology and psychology as best as possible. Interiors in which humans can survive are the result of a meticulous plan of all aspects of the environment. Onboard life support systems → p. 135 regulate temperature and pressure to create a familiar Earth-like atmosphere. Additionally, design solutions are impacted by factors we are usually protected from on Earth such as a requirement to guard against micrometeoroid strikes. The design of architecture for microgravity → p. 131 radically differs from the design of architecture for Earth or other planetary surfaces. No surface is differentiated—resulting in no true ceiling, floor or walls—but each can be equally accessed and occupied. The rules of terrestrial architecture no longer apply, meaning architects must consider interior space from a new bodily perspective.

## Design Strategies
## for Resource Efficiency

In the extreme environments of outer space, resources and habitable space are restricted as a direct result of the limited capacity of rockets. In the past transportation costs from Earth into low Earth orbit amounted to tens of thousands of US dollars per kilogram of payload. Although recent commercial launch infrastructure has substantially reduced costs, resupply and material choices still run with an "every kilo counts" mentality. In addition, dynamic launch loads must be considered within the design of any component sent to space, which requires lightweight but very robust material and construction solutions. Material choices for human spaceflight must comply with a range of safety requirements, where toxicity, flammability and outgassing (the release of gases by a material) are of major concern.[7]

So far orbital architecture has acted as a testbed but, with each varied extreme environment encountered in outer space, a new set of parameters need to be taken into account that affect transport, construction and habitability. Spacecraft and space station design have different spatial parameters in comparison to stationary architectures planned for the surface of the Moon or Mars. Orbital architecture is generally modular and fully prefabricated, its size is largely determined by the size of the transport vehicle payload shroud, the part of the spacecraft that shield's the storage hold. In the International Habitation Module (I-Hab), the habit module of ESA's forthcom-

I-Hab → p. 118

ing Lunar Gateway space station, the total liveable space for four astronauts is restricted to less than 50 m³. Highly limited spaces result in design strategies that encompass multi-functional, transformable → p. 80 systems involving foldable furniture and room segments or deployable habitat envelope structures. → p. 52 In future, as larger rockets with greater volume and loading capacity become available, it is likely that transport, habitable space and resources will become less restrictive.

The vast distances that must be overcome to reach the planned destinations of long-duration spaceflight directly affect the feasibility of supplying and resupplying materials. Whilst the Moon, our closest neighbour, can be reached within a few days, a journey to Mars will take months. Therefore, the potential to use local resources during space missions has become an urgent area of research.

In-Situ Resource Utilisation, the use of locally available material and energy, sets the parameters for Lunar or Martian surface settlements. Regolith, the surface material of the Moon → p. 85 and Mars, → p. 47 is proposed as a multi-use material to be processed to create infrastructure such as roads for transportation as well as radiation shielding for habitable spaces. Local accessibility of water and energy is key for future long-term missions. Feasibility studies and prototype research is building on autonomous preparatory processes so that humans will find fully operable infrastructure when they arrive on Mars or the Moon.

## Closing Loops:
## Questions of Sustainability

The same sustainable development objectives of creating safer, healthier and more circular economies in the built environment on Earth are shared with the development of closed-loop habitation systems for space.[8] Recycling is a mandatory factor when designing for extreme environments and outer space. When parts break or malfunction, they are considered for future use through upcycling or downcycling. A long-term goal when designing for space is to reuse spacecraft material as feedstock for additive manufacturing processes in order to produce new items in-situ on the Moon and Mars.

Onboard the ISS, oxygen and potable water are largely recovered. Advances in recovery systems which ensure 100 percent circularity has been the goal of many human spaceflight R&D projects. Greenhouses have been allocated an essential role in long-term human missions for local food production. The EDEN-ISS prototype explored plant growth in extreme environments within a shipping container-sized greenhouse that was stationed in Antarctica

EDEN-ISS → p. 146

for a number of years. Upscaling food culture systems is considered paramount for the successful establishment of bases on the Moon and Mars.

## The Space
## Architect's Agenda

Human-inhabited modules in outer space are a primary example of design and architecture in extremely hostile environments. Buildings and the cosmos have always existed in relation to one another;[9] buildings *in* the cosmos will be relational to their very particular surroundings. Beyond scientists and engineers developing machines to stabilise basic environmental conditions for the survival of humans, the role of the Space Architect in the collaborative network is to deal with the basic ergonomic and psychological requirements of humans in these extreme conditions.

When LIQUIFER approaches a design project or feasibility study, we are striving to develop novel, supportive, resource-efficient approaches for long-duration spaceflight. Beyond making a habitable environment tolerable, we approach design with one eye on the development of an intelligent, comfortable environment that cares for its inhabitants, while protecting resources towards a closed-loop ecosystem.

Mars

**44**

Moon

Orbit

Earth Land
Earth Ocean

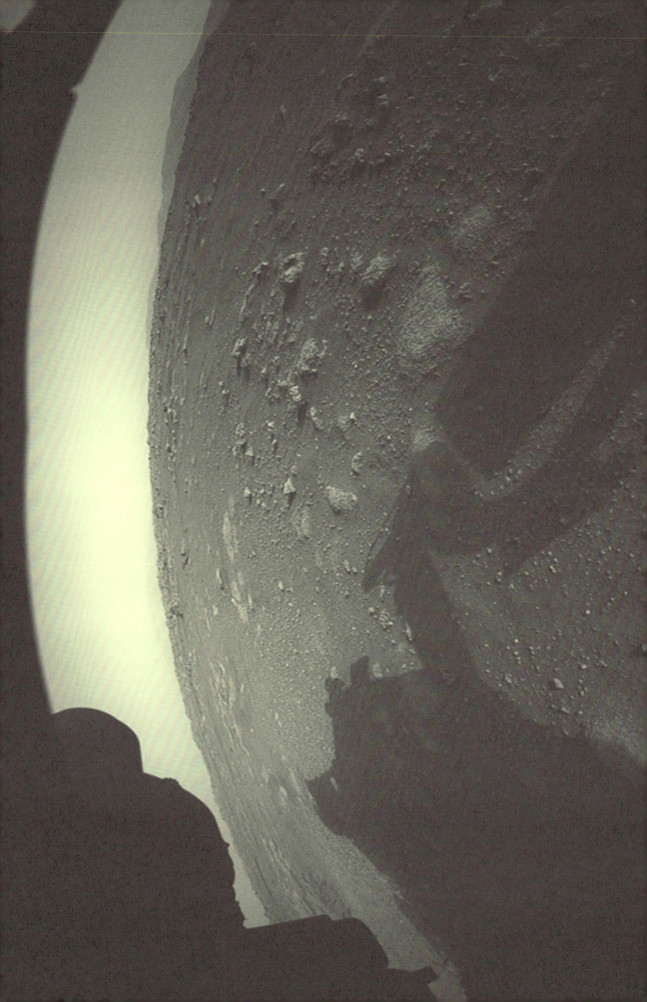

# Mars

## General characteristics

Mars is the fourth planet in the solar system characterised by a rocky crust and an iron-rich core like Mercury, Venus and Earth. The Red Planet derived its historic epithet from the large swathes of iron-rich dust driven over the planetary surface by extreme winds, producing the characteristic reddish hue we can see from Earth. The rocky formations, boulders and sediments that make up its surface have been shaped by historic volcanic activities, asteroid impacts, winds and the presumed presence of liquid surface water billions of years ago. Low gravity and lack of mobile plate tectonics resulted in the emergence of Olympus Mons, the tallest volcanic mountain in the solar system, standing at 21 km. At the same time, Martian topography is characterised by the largest canyon of the solar system, the Valles Marineris, a gigantic equatorial valley system, more than 4000 km long and up to 10 km deep.[1]

## Atmosphere and magnetosphere

Mars is within the habitable zone, a zone defined by the distance from a star that allows the formation of liquid surface water under suitable atmospheric conditions.[2] 20 percent of the ancient Martian surface is thought to have been covered by ocean; at this time the atmosphere was believed to be thicker and the Martian climate warmer and wetter than it is today. It is likely that the interior of the planet progressively cooled to a point when the global magnetic field vanished, an effect that is associated with its small size.[3] Without a global magnetic field, Mars lost its shield against solar winds and over time, most of its atmosphere was stripped away by solar particle bombardment. The thinning of the atmosphere led to Mars' current state as a frozen planet, hostile to life. The orbit of Mars around the Sun is more elliptical than that of Earth, which leads to notably higher temperatures in the southern hemisphere during summer.[4] Resulting thermal imbalances are thought to cause extreme weather events like the giant dust storms that frequently engulf huge regions or even the entire planet.[5]

## Space exploration

The utilisation of local resources→ P. 106 is considered essential for long-term human presence on Mars. Water is accessible at the polar ice caps and by extraction from hydrated minerals.[6] In addition, there is increasing evidence that large amounts of ancient water may exist below the surface of the planet, specifically at the bottom of Valles Marineris.[7]

Solar energy is not expected to be the main source of energy on Mars due to its distance from the Sun as well as the hazard of large-scale, week-long dust storms. Currently, alternative energy sources are being researched. As carbon dioxide makes up almost 95 percent of the Martian atmosphere, biofuel could be produced with microbes that can consume, convert and upgrade carbon dioxide and water. This "biotechnology-enabled in-situ resource utilisation strategy" could produce 2,3-butanediol, a rocket propellant.[8]

Martian regolith contains vital nutrients for raising crops in Martian soil but high levels of toxic perchlorate compounds present in the soil could make produce unsafe for human consumption.[9] The composition of Martian regolith is considered viable for building purposes. Silicon dioxide, one of the most abundant compounds within this regolith,[10] will allow the production of glass-like building materials.[11]

| | Mars | Earth |
|---|---|---|
| Mean Surface Gravity | 3.71 m/s² | 9.80 m/s² |
| Equatorial Diameter | 6792 km | 12756 km |
| Equatorial Circumference | 21297 km | 40030 km |
| Surface Pressure | 6.36 mb | 1014 mb |
| Length of Day | 24.6 hours | 24 hours |
| Length of Year | 687 days | 365 days |
| Temperature Extremes | −153°C to +20°C | −89°C to +57°C |

LIQUIFER Projects for Mars

49—
77

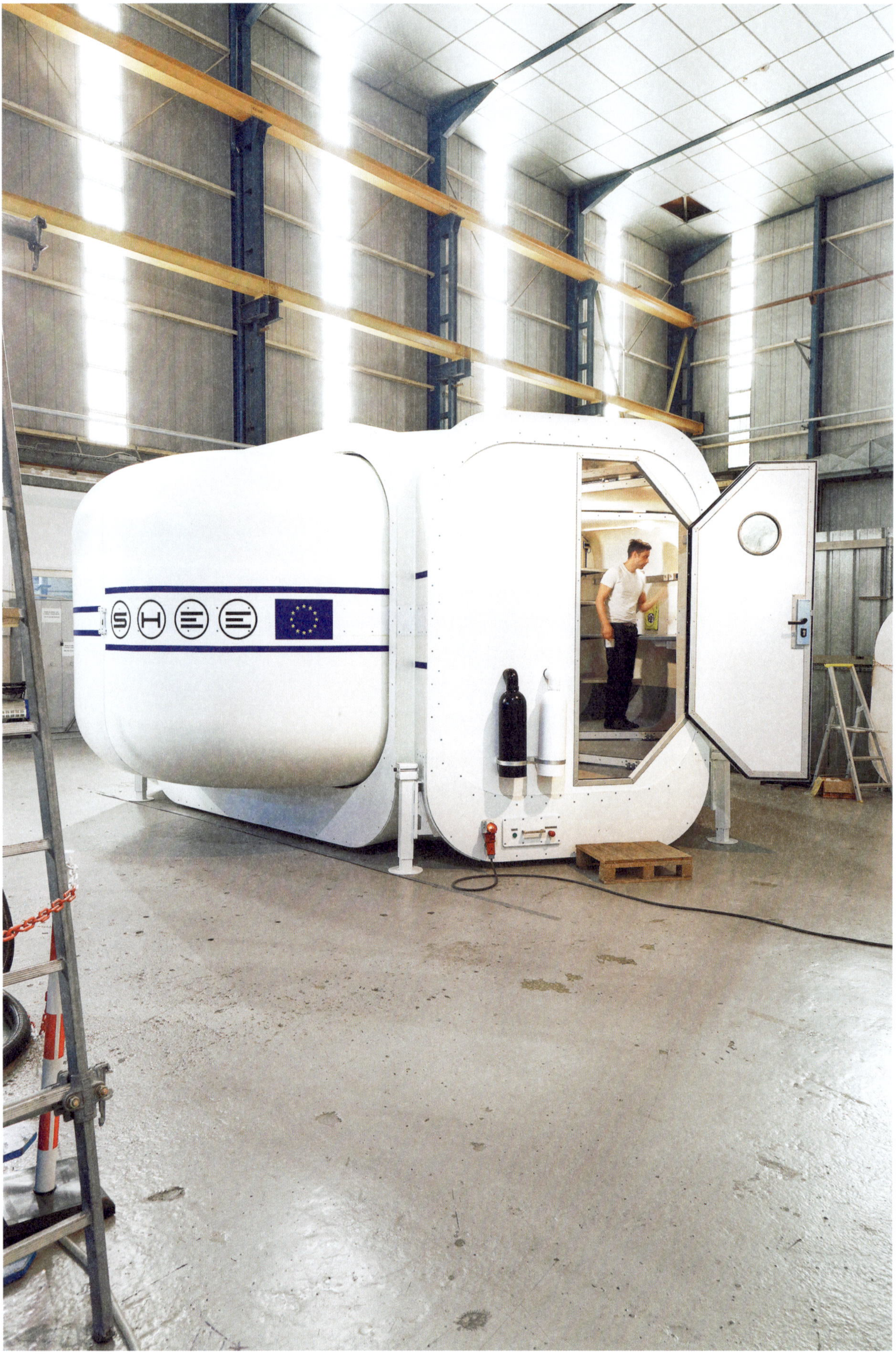
SHEE

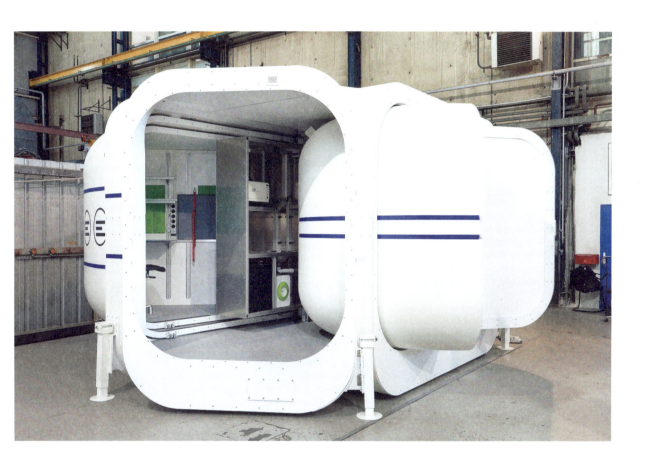

SHEE is an autonomously deployable habitat testbed
for human habitation in extreme environments.

SHEE    (Self-deployable Habitat for Extreme Environments) is a habitable module designed for a planetary surface outpost. It was manufactured as a testbed for analogue simulations on Earth. The main objective of the project was to effectively integrate architecture and robotics in order to reduce volume during transportation and allow automated deployment of the fully outfitted unit before the astronauts' arrival. Two folded SHEE modules fit back-to-back into the cylindrical payload shroud of a rocket taking up only half the space of the fully deployed modules. Unique among analogue habitats, the SHEE design also fully complies with the requirements of standard transportation on Earth; in its folded configuration a single SHEE module does not exceed the dimensions of a high cube shipping container. The module was developed to be combined in a larger base configuration via docking ports and can be alternatively outfitted as habitats, laboratories, greenhouses, storage or medical units. The SHEE concept is also applicable in extreme terrestrial conditions as fully equipped medical or administrative emergency units for disaster mitigation.

The fabricated SHEE version was configured as a habitat for a crew of two and a mission duration of two weeks. Within an extremely confined space, the interior configuration consists of a central area and meeting space as well as four separate compartments within the deployable segments that facilitate retreat on long-duration missions.

LIQUIFER was in charge of the module design and transformability of the envelope as well as the concept, manufacturing and integration of interior furnishing. The transformable interior configurations enable the integration of the collapsible hull shells for transport and allow multifunctional usage during operation. As technical coordinator LIQUIFER was responsible for the integration of all systems.

T    2013 – 2015

P    European Union – Seventh Framework Programme for Research and Technological Development (EU-FP7), in the frame of space

C    Consortium partners – International Space University, France; LIQUIFER Systems Group, Austria; Space Applications Services, Belgium; Institute of Technology, University of Tartu, Estonia; COMEX, France; Sobriety, Czech Republic; Space Innovations, Czech Republic

L    The SHEE mock-up has been presented as part of exhibitions in Cologne, Strasbourg and Vienna and serves as a demonstration and test facility at the campus of the International Space University in Strasbourg.

1    Central meeting area with galley, foldable table and environmental control and monitoring system
2    Crew cabin
3    Office workspace
4    Wet lab and hygiene cabin
5    Hatch
6    EVA suitports
7    Workbench
8    Storage

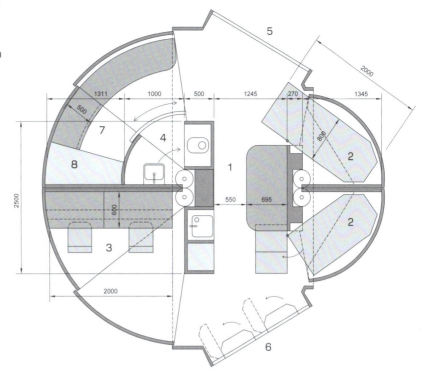

The SHEE module consists of a self-supporting central structure and four deployable compartments that are made from fibreglass foamcore shells with aluminium rims as reinforcement.

For transportation purposes the volume of the deployed configuration can be halved.

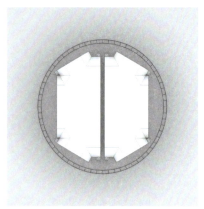

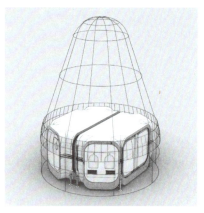

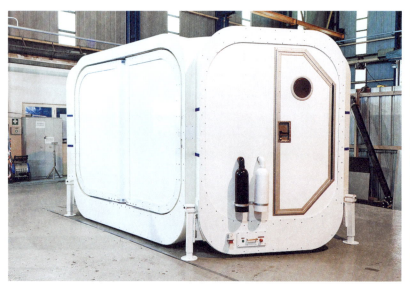

In its packed configuration two SHEE modules can be transported back-to-back in the payload shroud of a heavy lift launcher, and it complies with standard transport regulations on Earth.

Transformable interior furnishings can be compacted for the transport configuration and individually adapted when the module is in operation.

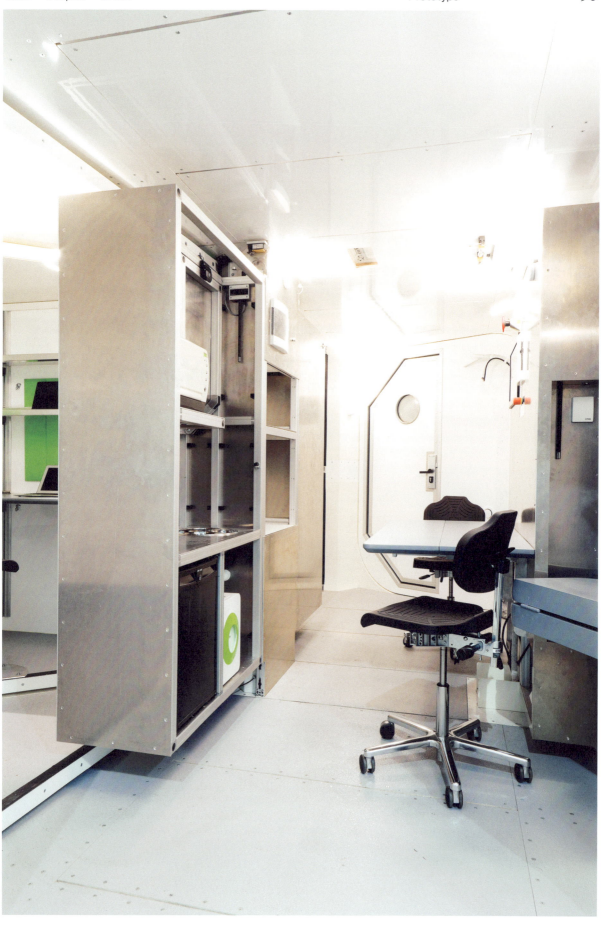

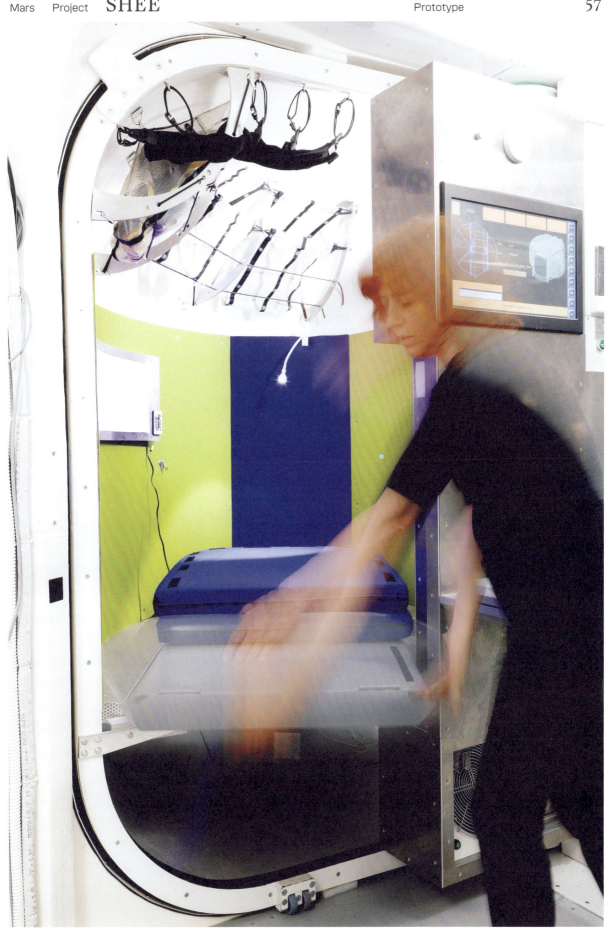

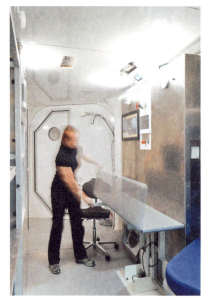

The centre of the habitat is the communal space where the crew prepares and eats their meals or conducts meetings, while easily monitoring the habitat subsystems.

A shelf system on both sides of the central space, retractable curtains and translucent folding walls provide visual screening for private activities in the deployable compartments.

In its folded configuration, the SHEE module can be transported to the simulation site on a flatbed truck. It is fully functional immediately after unloading and deployment.

SHEE was part of the Mars simulation campaign of the Moonwalk project at Rio Tinto in Spain where it served as local mission control centre with a suitport and laboratory.

T       2013 – 2016

P       European Union – Seventh
        Framework Programme for
        Research and Technological
        Development (EU-FP7), in the
        frame of space

C       Consortium partners – DFKI
        Robotics Innovation Center,
        Germany; COMEX, France;
        EADS UK, UK; LIQUIFER
        Systems Group, Austria;
        Space Applications Services,
        Belgium; NTNU Centre for
        Interdisciplinary Research
        in Space, Norway; INTA
        Instituto Nacional de Técnica
        Aeroespacial, Spain

L       Rio Tinto, Spain

Moonwalk    developed scenarios and
technologies for human-robot cooperation
during planetary surface missions and tested
the performance of the astronaut-robot team
at two analogue sites on Earth. Simulation
astronauts (simonauts) were supported by a
small mobile assistant robot during Extravehicular Activities (EVA). The robotic rover was
configured to autonomously follow the astronaut and support a variety of activities such as
exploring terrain inaccessible to the astronaut
or providing equipment for measuring and
sampling activities. In addition the astronaut
could actively direct the rover via control-
by-gestures to perform desired activities. To
simulate several exploration scenarios, → p. 175
the Moonwalk systems and technologies were
tested at the acknowledged Mars → p. 126 analogue
site at Rio Tinto, Spain. A second simulation
→ p. 188 was conducted underwater, → p. 183 offshore of Marseilles, to simulate Lunar gravity.

   LIQUIFER designed a range of mission
scenarios and developed corresponding
mission procedures for astronaut-rover and
astronaut-astronaut collaboration. To support
selected mission scenarios, the team designed
an exchangeable payload system for the rover
chassis and several astronaut tools. The design
included casings for measuring instruments,
sample storage and tool fittings on the rover,
as well as expandable and collapsible tools
for the astronaut that reflect the restrictions
of movement and visibility when wearing
a heavy and bulky EVA suit during operation.
In addition, LIQUIFER was responsible for
the communication and dissemination of the
project Moonwalk.

Focussing on sampling and scouting activities, the Mars simulations in Rio Tinto compared astronaut-astronaut scenarios with astronaut-rover scenarios.

For each simulated mission scenario, SHEE provided the suitport interface for the simonaut's access to the heavy simulation spacesuit.

The rover is either controlled by gestures or follows
the astronaut. It carries an exchangeable payload box,
sampling tools and a Raman spectrometer for the
identification of bio-geological signatures.

With the help of the assistant rover, difficult terrain
could be accessed and explored.

A set of manual sampling tools were designed to
facilitate easy single-handed use by an astronaut. The
Foldable Pick-up Claw and the Pantograph Sampling
Tool were brought by the rover to the sampling site.

The head of the extendable Pantograph Sampling
Tool combines the function of a shovel with a sealable
sampling container. It can be released with a simple
mechanism when repositioned on the payload box.

LavaHive    is a modular Martian habitat
design that applied the concept of "lava-
casting", a 3D printing technology conceived
by engineers from the European Space Agency
(ESA) and the German Aerospace Center
(DLR). In this concept, habitat hulls are made
from regolith, the natural surface material on
Mars, to protect against radiation and micro-
meteorites. LavaHive is an example of in-situ
resource utilisation → p. 106 (ISRU), where materials and energy necessary for manufacturing
and construction are sourced directly from the
building site. In addition to the use of natural
Martian resources, the project proposes the
reuse of flight infrastructure for construction,
so that after the entry vehicle has landed the
back-shell would become part of recyclable
onsite resources. LavaHive was conceived as
a multifunctional facility consisting of a main
habitation unit, airlock module, maintenance
workshop, docking ports, laboratory and
greenhouse.

LIQUIFER was responsible for the overall
design of the Martian base. The team also
developed the interior design, the visualisation
of the project and provided a 3D printed architectural model.

LavaHive was the first ISRU-focused project
undertaken by LIQUIFER. It influenced the
project RegoLight → p. 90 in developing scenarios and designs for solar-sintered shelters
on the Moon.

T    2015

P    Third Prize in the NASA
     3D-Printed Habitat Challenge
     Competition, 2015 World
     Maker Faire New York, USA

C    Consortium partners –
     European Space Agency &
     European Astronaut Centre,
     Germany; LIQUIFER Systems
     Group, Austria

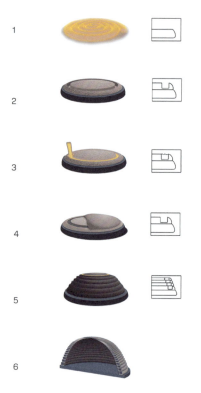

1
2
3
4
5
6

1    Molten regolith foundation
2    Sintered regolith channel
3    Channels filled with
     molten regolith
4    Next regolith layer
5    Repeat on upper layers
6    Remove loose regolith

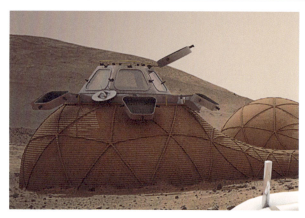

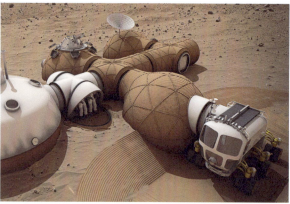

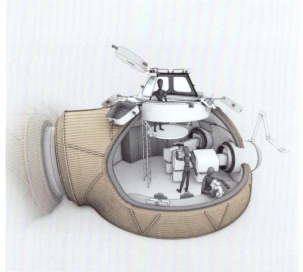

LavaHive is a multifunctional outpost proposal for
the Martian surface. The concept builds on recycled
spacecraft materials and 'lava-casting', a novel
construction technique utilising in-situ regolith.

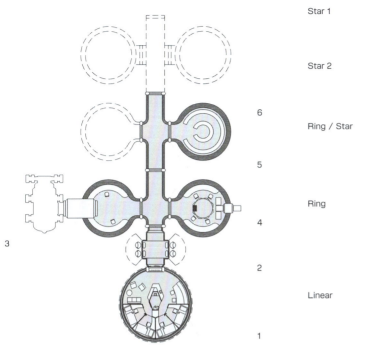

6
5
4
2
3
1

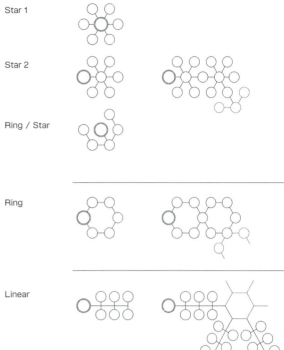

Star 1

Star 2

Ring / Star

Ring

Linear

1   Habitat
2   Node: airlock and suitports
3   Maintenance workshop,
    docking ports and pressurised vehicles
4   Laboratory: cupola,
    sample experiments and glove box
5   Security hatch
6   Greenhouse

Possible LavaHive
configurations.

Floor plan of the habitat with the communal dining
and living area, four individual crew quarters and the
hygiene station in the centre.

FASTER    (the Forward Acquisition of Soil and Terrain for Exploration Rover) was the development of an alternative method of collecting planetary surface information from an unknown terrain during robotic exploration missions. Due to the relative sparsity of data about the Martian surface, the risk of restricted or lost manoeuvrability is a major challenge for robotic surface exploration. The rover may be impeded by a stretch of soft sand or other unforeseen obstacles.

To allow the rover to travel at higher speeds, the consortium developed methods for efficient in-situ testing of soil and terrain properties. The FASTER system employs and advances the concept of two cooperating rovers. It combines the features of a small all-terrain scout rover which can quickly and efficiently test the trafficability of terrain and a lightweight sensor tool attached to the front of the large ExoMars mother rover.

LIQUIFER was responsible for the coordination of the system requirements and interfaces, in addition to the development of sensor tools that fit to the chassis of the mother rover. Two concepts were designed: the "Wheeled Bevameter" and the "Pathbeater". The Wheeled Bevameter concept was built as a mockup and tested at the premises of Airbus in Stevenage, UK. In addition LIQUIFER contributed to the project communication, and visualisation including a video documentary of the project. The robotic mission scenarios of FASTER provided valuable insights for the Moonwalk project's human-robot cooperation scenarios.

T    2011 – 2014

P    European Union – Seventh Framework Programme for Research and Technological Development (EU-FP7), in the frame of space

C    Consortium partners – DFKI Robotics Innovation Centre, Germany; University of Surrey, UK; Astrium, France; Space Applications Services, Belgium; LIQUIFER Systems Group, Austria; Astri Polska, Poland

Indoor FASTER Simulation Testbed trialled at the Airbus Mars Yard in Stevenage, UK.

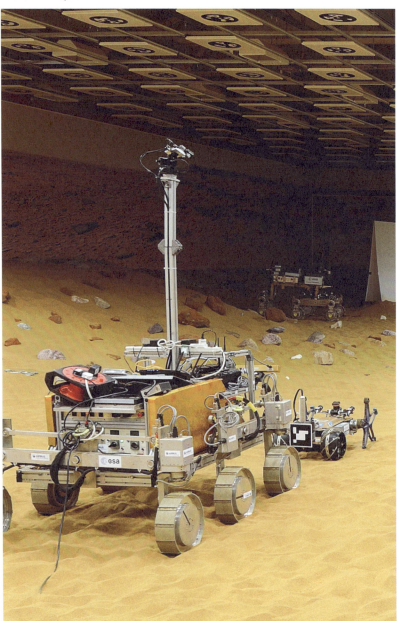

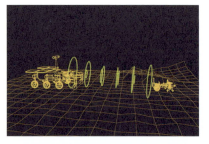

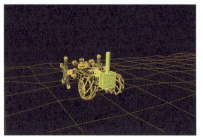

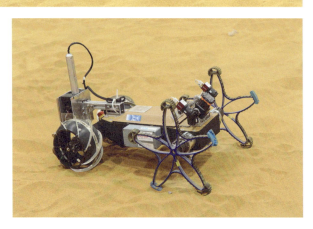

FASTER involves two cooperating robotic rovers.
A small scout rover explores the soil and terrain
properties to support the larger ESA ExoMars rover
to traverse safely.

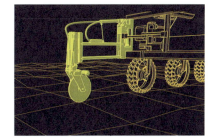

The mother rover is equipped with the Wheeled Bevameter, a soil sensor tool attached to the front of the rover. It analyses on-site bearing strength, shear strength and wheel slippage.

If we digitise the process of constructing or deconstructing a building, we need to consider the possibility of parts that move themselves into position. That simple piece not only takes care of its own geometry, but it takes care of its own movement as well, this is a very important aspect in the design.

*A. Scott Howe, Senior Systems Engineer and Space Architect,*
*NASA's Jet Propulsion Laboratory*
*(Radio Orange Space Specials: MOBITAT – Transformers, 13 Nov 2007)*

We'll have to think about pieces that can be put together easily using robotic means, moving things x, y, z in space, rotating, and so forth. That is a part of our design process.

*A. Scott Howe, Senior Systems Engineer and Space Architect,*
*NASA's Jet Propulsion Laboratory*
*(Radio Orange Space Specials: MOBITAT – Transformers, 13 Nov 2007)*

# The Pursuit
# of Adaptability

Transformability is the pursuit of adaptable design solutions, based on a 'less is more' approach. Its objectives are threefold: space-saving, multifunctionality, and the ability to create temporary spaces. LIQUIFER has implemented transformability into its designs as a means to multiply the potential of interior architectural elements, thus hacking the common limitations of available working and habitable space in elements such as habitats, vehicles and facilities.

## Logics of transformability for design

There are a number of different, overlapping logics of transformation in design, which each demonstrate ways to save space. In all cases, transformable architecture addresses inherent limitations in both interior volume and missions' budgets.

Some solutions primarily aim to reduce the volume of an element while it is being transported, prior to its use. Architecture designed for space missions is either dependent on once-in-a-lifetime deployment or can be designed to allow it to be repeatedly deployed and collapsed, resulting in adaptable, responsive and flexible solutions. Architecture for outer space is often designed to have structural elements that autonomously deploy.

Other solutions aim to save space while in use or between uses. Changing the layout of an interior space without affecting the size of the volume is a common design choice in fixed volumes such as the International Space Station (ISS) or the planned Gateway I-Hab platform. The limitations of interior volumes in the extreme environment of space challenge the architect to optimise the habitable space in a way to allow for alternative uses through the design of adaptable and multifunctional interior spaces.

LIQUIFER has designed multifunctional environments as a response to logistical constraints, such as the need to reuse spaces for diverse activities, and to provide psychological benefits, including maximising astronauts' privacy.

## Designing transformability for transportation

The SHEE [→ p. 52] habitat was designed as a deployable structure to increase the amount of modules that could be transported within a rocket payload shroud. The habitat doubles in volume from its stored configuration to full deployment, with full interior outfitting contained within at all times. The design concept of the SHEE is based on a sequential deployment of rigid shell segments that are stabilised by pressurised sealing. For the purposes of on-Earth transportation, and repeated deployment and relocation, the habitat complies with the dimensions of a high-cube shipping container. When compacted for transportation, interior furniture is partly folded to accommodate the collapsible shell segments within the core structure. Collapsible furnishings also enable multifunctional usage of the interior space during operation. All sensitive, complex systems such as the life support systems [→ p. 135] are fixed and pre-installed in the non-deployable core.

## Designing transformability for multiple uses of space

Dual- or triple-use areas can enhance the use and differentiation of space for astronauts. The habitat design for the RAMA [→ p. 98] mobile research laboratory was defined by the need for a pressurised rover which serves astronauts as a mobile habitat, refuge, workshop and research laboratory for advanced mission applications on the Moon [→ p. 85] and Mars [→ p. 47]. The design concept incorporates multiple interior configurations that allow astronauts to perform daily tasks and work in the highly confined interior space of a vehicle. Seats attached to robotic arms are designed for smooth transformations from driver seat to work stool to meeting chair to lounge chair. The central meeting table can merge with the ground floor to cover access to the sleeping area and storm shelter below.

## Designing transformability for privacy

Privacy is not just a personal, individual need but also a need that is shared among teams and groups.[1] Private areas in space stations are limited and primarily designed for the purpose of sleeping. Often crew quarters additionally function as a retreat from shared social spaces. Deployable crew quarters in the Gateway I-Hab [→ p. 118] were designed to retract with a telescopic mechanism during the day enabling the space to be used for other activities. The Deployable Getaway [→ p. 124] is an example of a collapsible, soft architecture that provides temporary crew quarters for astronauts during crew exchange periods at the ISS.

Mars

**Moon**

**82**

Orbit

Earth Land
Earth Ocean

### General characteristics

The Moon is the sole natural satellite of planet Earth. According to the Giant Impact theory, the Moon formed when Earth collided with a Mars-sized celestial body.[1] When it formed, the Moon was much closer to Earth and currently spirals away by a few centimetres every year.[2] The Moon's rotation is synchronised so that the same side of the Moon is always facing Earth. Surface gravitation→ p. 131 on the Moon is equal to one-sixth of the gravitation on Earth. Due to its substantial size in relation to Earth, the Moon moderates the Earth's wobble on its axis.[3] Its gravitational pull stabilises the Earth's climate and causes the ocean's tidal movements.

The surface of the Moon is characterised by impact craters, some of them hundreds of kilometres in diameter, generated by collisions with asteroids, comets and meteoroids. The solid rocky crust is covered by regolith, a shattered material which includes fragments of local bedrock, meteoroid debris and solar particles. Micrometeoroid impacts continue to erode the Lunar landscape. More than 3 billion years ago the dark zones of the Moon we see from Earth formed: the colour stems from rising magma, a dark iron-rich basaltic material. The lighter-coloured highlands are older and characterised by a heavily cratered terrain of anorthositic rock.

### Atmosphere and magnetosphere

The atmosphere of the Moon is negligible, commonly referred to as an exosphere or a vacuum. The Moon's lack of atmosphere and magnetosphere leaves the Lunar surface unprotected against micrometeoroid bombardment, solar particle events and cosmic radiation. Lunar regolith is sharp-edged and electrically charged, and therefore highly abrasive and clings to other materials. Lunar dust is lifted from the surface by electrostatic levitation creating the 'horizontal glow' that was described by the Apollo astronauts.[4] Without the moderating effects of an atmosphere, temperature differences are extreme.

### Space Exploration

Returning to the Moon is a primary goal in the re-establishment of long-duration human presence in space. The Lunar South pole is considered a feasible location for the first crewed outpost, as it has continuous access to solar energy and permanently shadowed regions with water ice deposits. Other regions away from the poles need to cope with the extensive period of darkness of a Lunar night, which lasts equivalent to 14 days on Earth. Water is also expected to be harvested from Lunar regolith via additional energy sources. Such sources are required for large-scale resource harvesting and mining operations. Apart from the planned application of nuclear fission technology,[5] the harvesting of Helium-3, deposited by Solar winds, is envisioned as a clean source of energy for nuclear fusion technology.[6]

Lunar regolith is considered the main in-situ building material → p. 106 for the construction of large shelters for protection against solar winds, cosmic radiation and micrometeoroids. Experiments in 2022 demonstrated that, despite stressful conditions for growing plants, it is possible to grow food crops in Lunar regolith.[7]

| | Moon | Earth |
|---|---|---|
| Mean Surface Gravity | $1.62 \, m/s^2$ | $9.80 \, m/s^2$ |
| Equatorial Diameter | 3 474.8 km | 12 756 km |
| Equatorial Circumference | 10 917 km | 40 030 km |
| Surface Pressure | $3 \times 10^{-15}$ bar | 1.014 bar |
| Length of Day | 655.7 hours | 24 hours |
| Temperature Extremes | $-250°C$ to $+127°C$ | $-89°C$ to $+57°C$ |

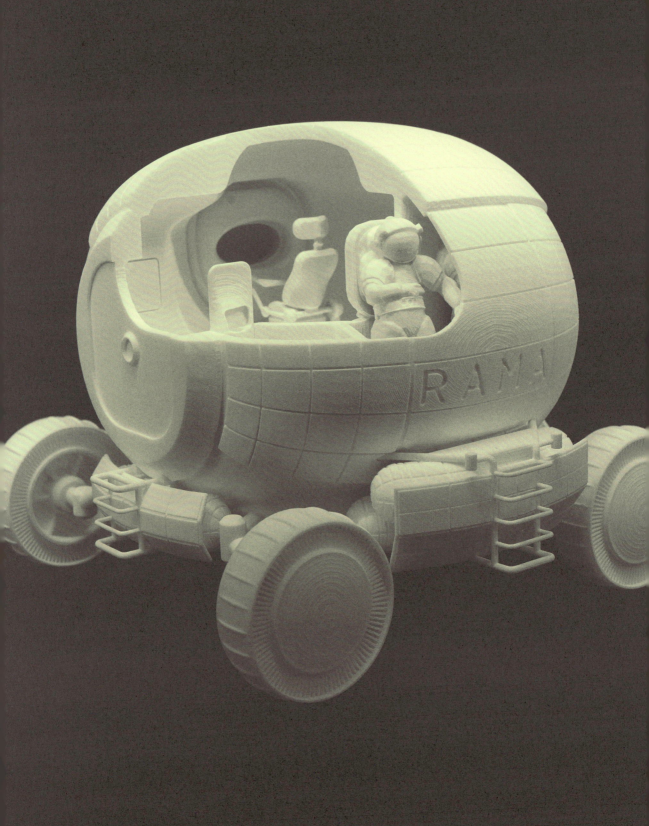

Mars

LIQUIFER Projects for the Moon

**87—
103**

Orbit

Earth Land
Earth Ocean

RAMA is a mobile research laboratory for future
human space missions on the Moon.

T    2015 – 2018

P    European Union – Horizon
     2020 (EU-H2020) project,
     topic of 3D printing /
     advancement of TRL

C    Consortium partners – German
     Aerospace Centre (DLR),
     Germany; Space Applications
     Services, Belgium; LIQUIFER
     Systems Group, Austria;
     COMEX, France; Bollinger
     Grohmann Schneider, Austria

RegoLight    investigated utilising two abundantly available resources on the Moon, regolith and sunlight, for the automated fabrication of solid building elements. Regolith is the shattered material that naturally covers the Lunar surface and unobstructed sunlight is accessible during Lunar daytime, due to the absence of a Lunar atmosphere. RegoLight enhanced the additive layer manufacturing (ALM) technique of solar sintering Lunar regolith for in-situ building purposes → p. 106 and advanced the Technology Readiness Level (TRL) from a TRL3 to TRL5. For testing purposes, a Lunar soil simulant was used which mimicked the characteristics of Lunar regolith. Sintering of Lunar regolith simulant was demonstrated in alternative set-ups using a movable printing table or a mobile printing head. In addition, solar sintering was demonstrated inside a vacuum chamber. The project produced finite element models and conducted mechanical property tests which fuelled architectural scenarios.

LIQUIFER was responsible for scenario development and contributed exemplary designs for a Lunar base. The scenarios and designs primarily address infrastructure elements for micrometeoroid shielding, radiation shielding and dust mitigation which included habitats, levelled terrains and launchpads. LIQUIFER explored the potential of 3D printing to fabricate interlocking building elements that would enable construction without requiring binding material to be supplied from Earth. As part of an iterative design process, LIQUIFER investigated multiple building element geometries for a wide range of applications. In addition, the team organised all outreach and dissemination activities.

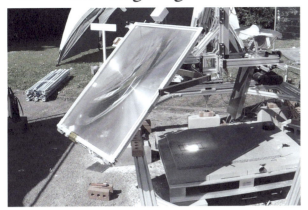

Solar 3D printer with a mobile, lightweight Fresnel lens. Sunlight is concentrated through the moveable lens to heat Lunar regolith simulant on the table below.

Preliminary test results for solar sintering of Lunar regolith simulant with the use of the Mobile Printing Head System.

Solar sintering does not require any additional binder but creates solid parts by heating granular material to the point at which its particles bond.

Sintered samples in test geometries

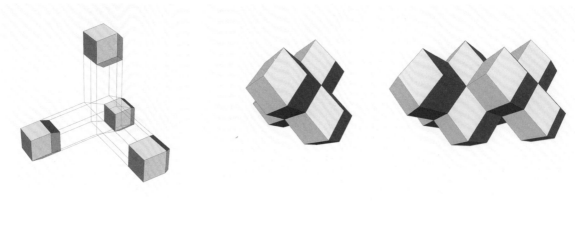

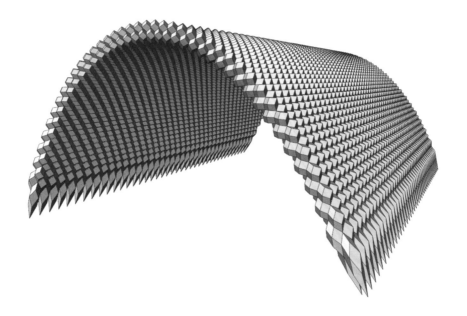

The concept of interlocking building elements has been extensively researched to avoid the use of any mortar during construction. After the form finding process, the rhombic dodecahedron was chosen as the basic geometry element.

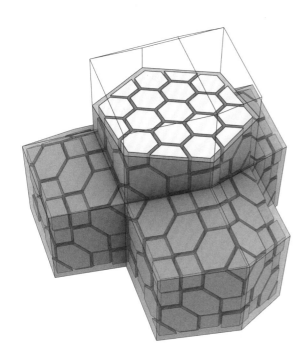

The infill of the building elements is a cell structure of printed chambers enclosing loose material.

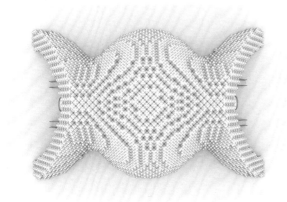

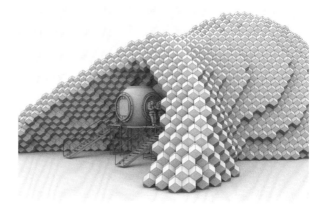

We started using the rhombic dodecahedron as a simple voxel to form various vault structures.

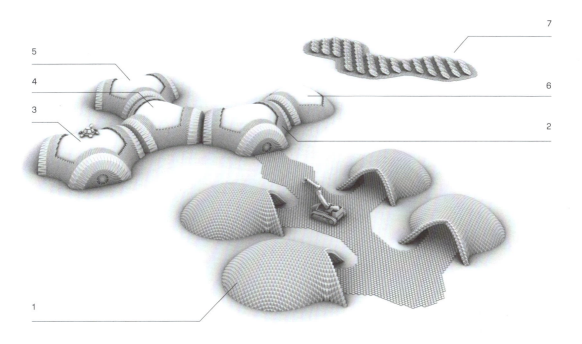

1    Hangars
2    Maintenance
3    Laboratory
4    Habitat
5    Greenhouse
6    Powerplant
7    Solar Array

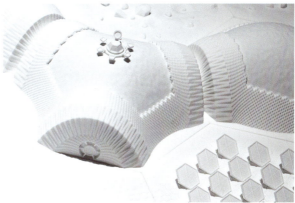

The Lunar south pole with its continuous access to solar light is envisaged as a promising site for a Lunar base.

Solar sintered building blocks are assembled to create self-supporting structures that provide shelter against deadly solar radiation and micrometeoroids.

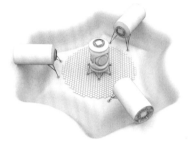

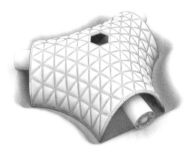

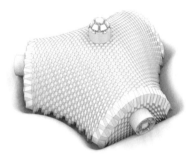

Dome Chamber
Pressurized Module Configuration

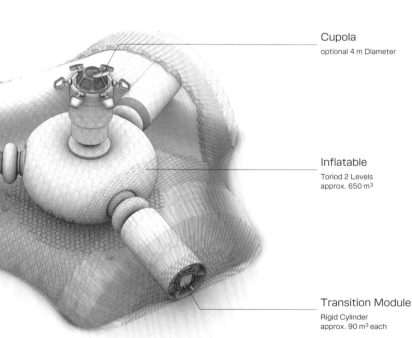

Cupola
optional 4 m Diameter

Inflatable
Toriod 2 Levels
approx. 650 m³

Transition Module
Rigid Cylinder
approx. 90 m³ each

The facility is composed of dome like protection shelters
covering different types of pressurised modules. Each
dome is made of 2-3 metre-thick walls composed of
individually shaped building blocks.

T    2007 – 2009

P    European Space Agency
     project, under subcontract to
     Thales Alenia Space, as part of
     Surface Architecture Studies

RAMA    (Rover for Advanced Mission Applications), a mobile research laboratory for the Moon and Mars, was designed in line with the scientific and operational requirements defined in the European Space Agency (ESA) Surface Architecture Study. The pressurised vehicle is configured to serve two astronauts as a habitat, refuge and laboratory during a 30-day journey on the Lunar or Martian surface. Fundamental issues such as habitability, human-machine interface, safety, dust mitigation, interplanetary contamination and radiation protection are factored into the design of RAMA. The acronym RAMA does not only define the purpose of the vehicle but is also a reference to Sir Arthur C. Clark's science-fiction work *Rendezvous with Rama*.

LIQUIFER was responsible for the concept design including engineering, a technology roadmap and the laboratory's associated costs. The vehicle size was defined by anticipated restrictions of the payload shroud. Transformable elements → p. 80 are key features in the RAMA design: wheels fold below the vehicle cabin during transportation in the rocket. In the interior all required functions, such as the cockpit, laboratory workspace, galley, hygiene cabin, storage and suitports, are integrated along a central void that is continuously transformed by the alternating positions of two robotic chairs. The ergonomically adaptable chairs enable multifunctional use and can be individually reconfigured to personalise the highly confined interior space. The integrated life support system (LSS) → p.135 is positioned below the floor around the central sleeping compartment, which also serves as a storm shelter that protects against elevated radiation levels. A layer of the circular door of the storm shelter can be lifted and transformed into a dining or meeting table.

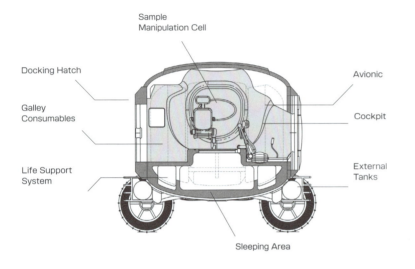

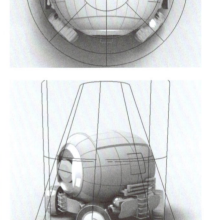

Sample
Manipulation Cell

Docking Hatch

Galley
Consumables

Life Support
System

Avionic

Cockpit

External
Tanks

Sleeping Area

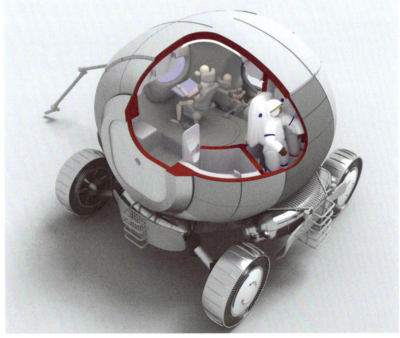

The interior configuration of the mobile research
laboratory RAMA can be continually adapted with
alternating positions of two robotic chairs.

The wheels of the rover can be
folded in order to comply with the
spatial limitation of the payload
shroud in the rocket.

Smartie    (Smart Resource Management based on Internet of Things to support off-Earth manufacturing of Lunar infrastructures), an ESA-funded feasibility study led by LIQUIFER, investigated how to assure self-sustainable long-duration missions on the Moon. This off-Earth manufacturing architecture is based on a combination of additive manufacturing (AM) technologies and the creation of an autonomous Internet of Manufacturing Things (IoMT).

Operational bottlenecks can be identified in autonomous IoMT technology, allowing in-situ resource utilisation → p. 106 and recycling processes to be optimised to efficiently maintain Lunar infrastructure. Additive manufacturing infrastructure on the Lunar surface would be connected to a data cloud as part of a wider Lunar satellite network, like those envisioned in ESA's Moonlight and NASA's LunaNet. In the initial phase, a mirror cloud would be established on Earth to resupply the Lunar base. The long-term goal is to establish a large, autonomous and sustainable Lunar base.

LIQUIFER led the feasibility study and was responsible for establishing the user requirements and Smartie architecture. LIQUIFER supported use cases for smart data management that incorporated AM technology and recycling processes. The project was communicated with an animation and visuals.

T    2021

P    European Space Agency project, under the ESA Open Space Innovation Platform

C    Consortium partners – LIQUIFER Systems Group, Austria; OHB System AG, Germany; Spartan Space c/o BC ESPACE ENTREPRISES, France; Azimut Space GmbH, Germany; Zühlke Engineering GmBH, Austria

One of the most important aspects of growing our capability in operations and settlement in these remote places is how we can build what we need from what we find where we go.

*Brent Sherwood, Senior Vice President for Advanced Development Programs, Blue Origin*
*(Radio Orange Space Specials:*
*Could we prevent people from going to the Moon or Mars? 15 Aug 2006)*

The extraction of resources is going to be a lot about sifting out rare grains in the regolith that contain valuable minerals. We have to get really good at excavating the regolith, transporting it, processing it and sorting it to enrich those rare components that are valuable. The technologies from mineral processing in terrestrial mining are going to be extremely important to extract valuable resources from the Moon, Mars and asteroids.

*Kevin Cannon, Planetary Geologist, Colorado School of Mines*
*(Radio Orange Space Specials: Habitats on Moon and Mars*
*built from local material, 14 May 2022)*

# The New Vernacular
# in Outer Space

A new vernacular architecture emerges from In-Situ Resource Utilisation (ISRU), the approach of utilising local resources and developing innovative technologies for the creation of habitable places in the extremes of outer space. ISRU is a fundamental strategy for long-duration spaceflight, which uses locally available materials for the construction and operation of infrastructure on planetary surfaces. The use of local materials in architecture is not a new strategy but one recurrent in traditions of vernacular architecture where materials and resources from the location impact the form, implementation of technologies and outcome of the built environment. These local architectures, inherently related to their landscapes, are built to meet specific needs whilst factoring in the local economy.

Economically, dependency on the resupply of materials and machines from Earth is not viable due to extortionate costs when launching rockets from Earth into low Earth orbit or beyond. Although commercial launch infrastructure has reduced costs substantially in recent years, launch costs remain a major limiting factor for the expansion of space exploration and planned commercial activities.[1] Furthermore, it is simply not feasible to transport the immense mass of material required to build a Lunar settlement from Earth to the Moon. Reducing costs is built into the concept of ISRU as materials from the Lunar or Martian surfaces are extracted, processed, manufactured and used on site, thereby ensuring sustained operations on location.

As Lunar and Martian inhabitants will mainly live indoors, the primary way to meet their needs will be through the provision of shelter, the generation of energy, water, oxygen and food. To pilot this set-up, the Moon will be used as a test site for future settlements on Mars.[2] Although Mars is richer in resources, the Moon will be utilised to develop autonomous off-Earth manufacturing and construction technologies required for sustainable future settlements. These technologies must reliably function by the time humans go to Mars, where continuous resupply is not feasible and autonomy will be considered a prerequisite. ISRU is enabled by robotics, artificial intelligence, networked systems, and additive manufacturing technologies such as 3D printing.[3] These technologies could enable autonomous operations such as the excavation, transportation, sorting and processing of surface material for the construction of shelters and the extraction and processing of water ice deposits to generate clean liquid water for human consumption or to produce propellants for transportation. ISRU will be a multistage process, meaning a material, equipment and energy continuum will first be put in place that relies on elements from Earth in combination with locally available resources. By the time settlements are in place, the goal is to rely extensively on what is available on the Lunar doorstep.

The primary building and construction material for Lunar and Martian settlements is regolith: a sand-like, loose surface material resulting from billions of years of impacts on rocky planets.[4] Although its composition varies throughout our Solar System, its abundance, as well as its shielding properties make it the material of choice for the future construction of massive shelters which can protect against harmful radiation and micrometeoroids.

RegoLight → p. 90

The development of the RegoLight solar sintering process aimed to increase technological readiness for off-Earth manufacturing purposes on the Moon. This process relies on solar energy, regolith and automated 3D printers to melt the surface of regolith particles in order to generate a solid building mass. RegoLight utilised this technology to form interlocking building elements, as sintered regolith exhibits significant resistance to compressive stresses.

Beyond the forms of building elements, mining and processing techniques of regolith, maintenance of machinery and in-situ energy generation are key for autonomous fabrication on the Moon. Following the technological advances of RegoLight, the Paving the Road project demonstrated how a large laser beam could be used to produce interlocking paving elements to create roads. Roads are the first step in the development of Lunar settlements as they will allow for easy trafficability and dust mitigation on the Lunar surface.

Beyond settlement construction technologies and in-situ materials, an autonomous Internet of Manufacturing Things (IoMT) that enables independence from Earth was proposed in Smartie. Once settlements are under

Smartie → p. 102

construction, the IoMT network would support a sustainable Lunar base through careful resource management and maintenance forecasting, applying ISRU principles to produce an efficient logistics plan. The network would repair and develop extra on-site infrastructure with a combination of resources from Earth and the Moon. As Lunar bases evolve, ISRU will recycle waste materials from the base to manufacture products needed for the development, maintenance and operation of the base.

By accommodating the values imposed by an ISRU approach, its defining principles can be applied to infrastructure on Earth, such as developing 3D printing technologies for low-cost housing and sourcing local materials for building and construction. The investment of time in scientific developments, technological advancements and closed-loop systems for low-waste-living in space environments will lead to applicable closed-loop systems for the built environment on Earth.

Given the environment on the Moon and Mars ISRU is a major challenge. When we look at Earth, we see we don't have much robotic construction, or ISRU construction here, even though a lot of the challenges that we see elsewhere on the other planetary bodies don't exist here. We have no worries about radiation, about oxygen, about resources, water, and yet our construction is still weighted towards manual labour with assistive technologies. That's sort of a sign that this is really, really hard to do, and it'll be an order of magnitude harder on a planetary body other than Earth.

*Haym Benaroya, Professor of Mechanical & Aerospace Engineering,*
*Rutgers University, (Radio Orange Space Specials:*
*Habitats on Moon and Mars built from local material, 14 May 2022)*

When creating a space in space, you need privacy where people can retreat. You need windows where they can look out at the heavens, a place where it is possible to see the Earth as a globe, as an entity, because that seems to be something that the astronauts really like doing.

*Nick Kanas, M.D., Professor Emeritus of Psychiatry*
*at the University of California, San Francisco*
*(Radio Orange Space Specials: Space Psychology and Psychiatry, 16 Jun 2009)*

Mars

Moon

**Orbit**

**110**

Earth Land
Earth Ocean

General characteristics

Atmosphere and
magnetosphere

Space Exploration

Planets orbit around a sun and moon's orbit around planets. Orbits are possible if there is a balance between gravitational and centrifugal forces. Artificial satellites or space stations are placed in orbits with an adequate initial impulse to keep them orbiting. Thousands of artificial satellites orbit Earth in low Earth orbit (LEO)—a region approximately 160 km to 2000 km above sea level—with many more scheduled to be launched. Space stations, satellites and rockets launched from Earth comprise the active LEO infrastructure, which is increasingly threatened by potential collisions with space debris, including an accumulation of inactive satellites, remnants from rocket stages or natural meteoroid debris. Space exploration beyond LEO involves orbits around the Moon, Mars or other planetary bodies of the Solar System and beyond.

Objects in LEO are exposed to the very upper layers of the Earth's atmosphere which causes a slight atmospheric drag. The ambient pressure is extremely low. The International Space Station (ISS) orbits Earth every 90 minutes, at a distance of approximately 400 km and an orbital speed of 7.66 km/sec. At 400 km above sea level, the gravitation of Earth is compensated by the centrifugal forces at the orbital speed of the space station, resulting in a state of microgravity.

The ISS orbits at an altitude where astronauts are still shielded from harmful radiation due to the presence of Earth's global magnetic field. The high-speed subatomic particles emitted by the Sun are largely trapped in Earth's magnetosphere and held within the two Van Allen Belts. Space Stations orbiting around the Moon, as planned with Gateway, → p. 106 a multi-purpose outpost and staging point for future deep space exploration, are challenged with providing sufficient radiation protection for astronauts.

Temperatures in outer space could theoretically reach absolute zero between celestial bodies (0° Kelvin or −273°C). In addition to dramatic temperature ranges in a vacuum, no sound can be transmitted. All objects in this space are exposed to acute dehydration, a consideration affecting the survival of any lifeform within seconds.

The sun is the main energy resource in LEO and provides sufficient power to operate the ISS. In deep space, solar energy needs to be supplemented by additional energy sources. Increasingly, it is envisioned that mineral-rich asteroids will be harvested to provide rare materials such as nickel, iridium, palladium, platinum, titanium and gold. In the long term, the European Space Agency aims to recycle space debris in LEO for orbital space manufacturing.[1]

| | Gateway (Moon orbit) | ISS (Earth orbit) |
|---|---|---|
| Gravity (m/s²) | microgravity | microgravity |
| Orbit Period | 7 days | 90 mins |
| Altitude Range | 1500–70 000 km | 280–460 km |
| Mission Periods | 30 – 90 days | c. 180 days |
| Interior Temperature Range | 4 – 27 °C | 18 – 23 °C |
| Exterior Temperature Extremes | −130°C to +120°C | −160°C to +120°C |
| Internal Pressurised Volume | 125 m³ | 1 000 m³ |

Deep Space

Mars

Moon

LIQUIFER Projects for Orbit **115—127**

Earth Land
Earth Ocean

Visualisation of the future Gateway orbiting the Moon.

<u>I-Hab</u>    is part of the Gateway Lunar Orbital Platform, a space station dedicated to supporting missions beyond low Earth orbit, including future missions to the Moon and Mars. Gateway is a collaboration between the European Space Agency (ESA), NASA, Japan Aerospace Exploration Agency (JAXA) and the Canadian Space Agency (CSA), targeted for completion in 2028.

Stringent design parameters were derived from the launch capacities of rockets, spatial requirements for life support systems, <sup>→ p. 135</sup> and the necessary support for a wide variety of activities for a crew of four during the proposed 30-day mission duration. Virtual architectural models allow designers to explore different spatial configurations and make iterative design developments in order to maximise the use of the module, which has an internal volume of 48 m³. A physical mockup was built at a 1:1 scale to provide a full-body immersive experience of the multi-purpose central volume, as well as the attached science workspace, galley and deployable crew quarters.

LIQUIFER was involved in the architectural design development and the configuration of the 1:1 mockup. Two teams were assigned in parallel by ESA to complete the design concept phase; one headed by Thales Alenia Space Italy (TAS-I) in Turin and the other led by Airbus Defence and Space in Bremen. LIQUIFER initially supported Airbus in architectural design development and in a later phase Thales Alenia Space Italy.  The design presented here shows the early design phase for Airbus.

T    2018 – ongoing

P    European Space Agency under a subcontract to Airbus Bremen (2018-2019) and Thales Alenia Space (2020-ongoing)

C    Consortium partners – (2018-2019) Airbus, Bremen, Germany; Airbus, Friedrichshafen, Germany; Thales Alenia Space TAS-I, Italy; Sener, Spain; QinetiQ, Spain; Space Applications Services, Belgium; Airbus Crisa, Spain, LIQUIFER, Austria. (2020-ongoing) Thales Alenia Space TAS-I, Italy; LIQUIFER, Austria; Spartan Space, France

L    Near-Rectilinear Halo Orbit (NRHO) from 2028 onwards

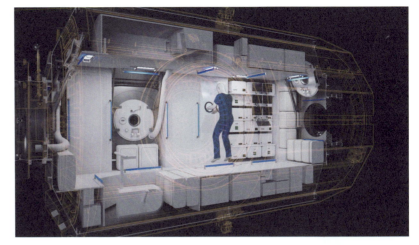

Science Control

Galley

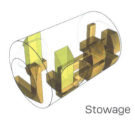

Stowage

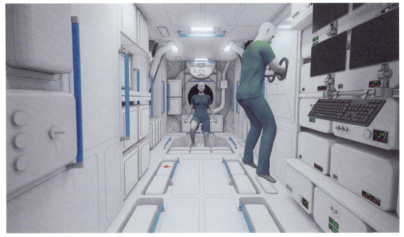

Toilet

Crew Quaters

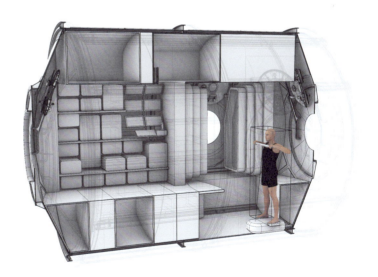

The layout represents the early I-Hab concept design
by LIQUIFER for Airbus. It was built as full-size
mock-up at the Airbus premises in Bremen, Germany.

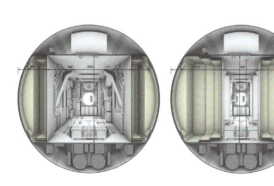

In microgravity all surfaces can accomodate functions, increasing the usability of a confined space. Deployable crew quarters in the I-Hab design provide additional space for alternative use.

1:1 Mock-Up of I-Hab for the first phase of the concept design study located at AIRBUS premises in Bremen, Germany.

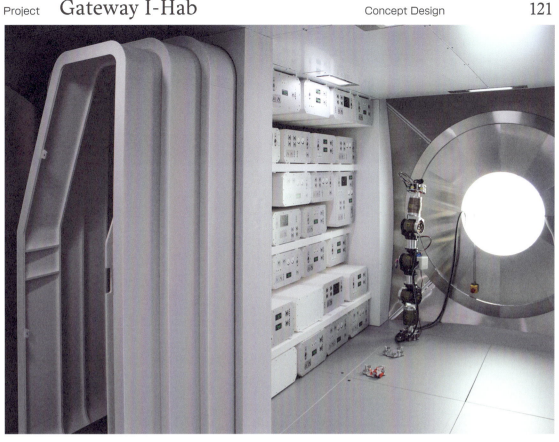

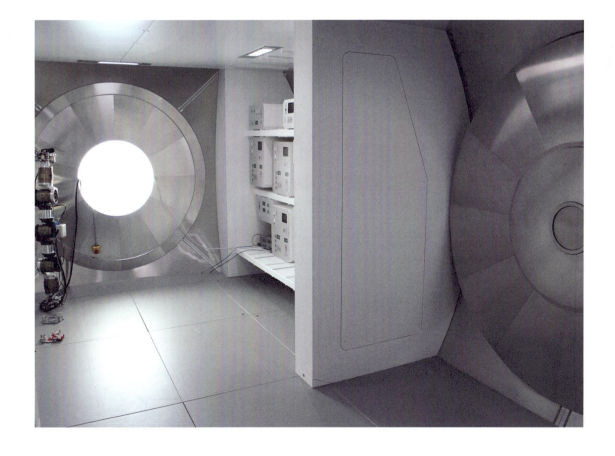

The Deployable Getaway provides a temporary
private retreat for working, relaxing and sleeping
on orbital space stations.

The     Deployable Getaway    is a collapsible
crew quarter <sup>→ p. 80</sup> for use in microgravity <sup>→ p. 131</sup>
orbital stations such as the International Space
Station (ISS). It provides flexible setups for
longer duration missions and intends to improve
habitability for crew exchange periods. In contrast to the permanently integrated cabins, the
Getaway can be positioned at any location on
the space station to establish a private space
suited to the individual preferences of the astronaut. It is conceived to provide a temporary
retreat for relaxation, reflection and power naps
that can lead to better health and safety for
astronauts whose work demands consistent
high performance.

A Deployable Getaway for office environments
on Earth was developed simultaneously. Both
designs have folding geometries in response
to space limitations. But each requires substantially different ergonomic approaches for deployment, accessibility and body support. While the
space Getaway is designed to be handled in
microgravity, where it will be weightless, the
terrestrial solution is designed to evenly distribute its weight. For the design of the space-based
Deployable Getaway, the folding panels had to
be sufficiently thick to meet the acoustic requirements for space stations. Space station hardware
must isolate sounds to mitigate the risk of
excessive noise travelling through the station
but thicker, sound-dampening panels created
challenges for the origami-like folds that allow
the Getaway to collapse when not in use.

T    2007 – 2009

P    LIQUIFER in-house project
     co-funded by the Austrian
     Aeronautics and Space
     Agency of the Austrian
     Research Promotion Agency
     as part of the 5th call of the
     Austrian Space Applications
     Programme

Folding sequence of the crewquarter
cabin on the ISS.

The    ISS – Sleep Kit    is a sleeping bag developed for microgravity and for use on the ISS. It is an advanced version of the design originally produced for the Deployable Getaway →p. 124 crew quarter. LIQUIFER conducted a design study with the goal of testing an alternative sleeping bag for microgravity, working closely with astronaut Gerhard Thiele. The ISS – Sleep Kit supports the neutral posture that a body tends to assume in microgravity while being attached to a structural element, an indispensable feature that prevents uncontrolled floating during sleep. In addition, individual temperature regulation is facilitated through a removable breast cover, as well as ventilation slots at the back and the feet. As back pain may occur due to a lack of weight on the spinal system, the sleeping bag includes access pockets to the lower back area for self-massage. LIQUIFER manufactured an ISS – Sleep Kit prototype with flight-certified Nomex-based textiles. It can be complemented with a lightweight silk lining and a hood to generate the familiar and calming sensation of using a cushion, which is otherwise not required in a microgravity environment. →p. 131

T    2010 – 2012

P    LIQUIFER in-house project co-funded by the Austrian Aeronautics and Space Agency of the Austrian Research Promotion Agency as part of the 7th call of the Austrian Space Applications Programme

C    Consultants: Gerhard Thiele, astronaut; Ulrich Kübler, Airbus Defence and Space

S    Sponsors: IBENA; Velcro GmbH; 3M; Eduard Kupfer; Sanders GmbH & Co. KG; Michael Schultes experimonde

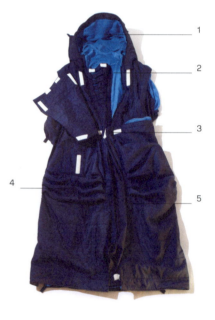

1    100% silk hood inlay attached to Nomex exterior with velcro.

2    100% silk sleeping bag inlay attached to Nomex exterior with velcro.

3    Velcro closure for inverted pleat.

4    Exterior sleeping bag made from Nomex. Expanded area at knees accommodates neutral body position.

5    Inverted pleat added to allow for more movement possibilities.

Mars

Moon

Orbit

Earth Land
Earth Ocean

In a gravity rich
environment our natural state is a state of rest, and we have to actively move ourselves, we have to actively initiate movement to reach for a cup, to get out of a chair, to move across a room. In a microgravity environment our natural state is motion, as such we have to actively steady ourselves to create our static state; and, we have to actively secure objects in order to keep them in a resting position. So, we are completely flipping our relationship with our environment and objects in those two different situations.

*Sue Fairburn, Design Researcher,*
*the Wilson School of Design / Principal, Fibre Design Inc.*
*(Radio Orange Space Specials: Designing from the Unfamiliar, 14 March 2015)*

# When the Natural State is Motion

When watching filmed records of astronauts floating in space, it quickly becomes clear that standard architectural parameters must drastically change when designing for microgravity environments. Because microgravity allows no reference to ground or ceiling, all surfaces and directions are equally accessible. The Space Architect responds to the potential of omnidirectional use by making every surface accommodating and useful at the same time. The design configurations accommodate mission-critical payload, life support systems, hygiene stations, sleeping quarters, and sufficient space for working, exercising, meeting and eating. Solutions respond to both lack of space and the extended possibilities enabled by microgravity.

The natural state for objects and humans in microgravity is motion; a cup will not stay on a table when placed there, nor will water stay in a cup. The securing and storing of things are key design drivers for microgravity spaces, as these things are otherwise moved by the slightest exterior forces. Materials, objects and humans are always in motion, unless secured. Securing solutions are achieved with the use of velcro, clips, duct tape, elastic bungees and magnets. Hygiene kits are velcroed to the wall, food and water are stored in pouches, and cutlery sticks to meal trays with magnets. In the case of loss, an on-Earth stowage team keeps a database of all objects onboard, including trash, and can direct astronauts to the location of an object.[1] Humans, like objects, must be attached to interior elements to remain in one place. In order to secure astronauts when sleeping, their sleeping bags are attached to the sides of their cabin or to any structure within a habitat module. When seated, astronauts stabilise themselves with restraints to achieve their desired position.

Movement through the interior of the International Space Station (ISS) relies on the use of the arms, not the legs, illustrating the physiological adaptations that occur in Orbit as the body adopts strategies other than those determined by gravity. Pulling themselves through laboratories, sleeping quarters, stowage modules or into the cupola, astronauts use handrails or stationary elements to propel themselves forward, to push themselves away or to become steady in space. Opposite to our usual resting state on Earth, microgravity is defined by motion. During a 30-minute tour of the ISS given by previous crew commander Sunita Williams, viewers are introduced to Node, the NASA sleeping quarters, where four of six sleeping cabins are arranged like compass points in the round of the node.[2] Viewers are invited into an individual sleep station, the most personalised area for each astronaut on the ISS. The soft interior (unlike the typically hardware lined modules) stores personal belongings such as notebooks, clothes, photographs and memorabilia in a number of pockets and velcro-secured bags, or attaches them to the "walls" of the booths with elastic.

Although astronauts have the pleasure of effortless movement through space with minor bodily impulses, some sensations cannot be felt in microgravity. Astronauts cannot experience the sensation of lying down. In microgravity, the naturally assumed posture during sleep feels like sitting and can be done in any direction, challenging the orientation of astronauts. Design decisions help to reorient astronauts in a place where up and down, left and right can quickly change with simple bodily movements, by setting a uniform direction for lighting, writing on the walls and computer monitors.[3] Design can create sensations that remind astronauts of life on Earth in order to enhance well-being. LIQUIFER designed the ISS Sleep Kit, → p. 126 a sleeping bag for microgravity, in response to reported experiences of interrupted sleep patterns by astronauts. The Sleep Kit reflects the neutral body posture assumed in microgravity and provides features for easy covering and uncovering. It also incorporates a silk-lined hood to imitate the sensation of a cushion. LIQUIFER applied a similar approach to a previous sleeping bag design as part of the Deployable Getaway, → p. 124 a collapsible crew quarter cabin for the ISS, which included alternative cushion designs. Design solutions for microgravity may mimic habits from Earth, to create "home comforts" through the memory of a sensation.

Exercise equipment for astronauts is important to mitigate the effects of microgravity such as loss of bone density and muscle mass. The bike, treadmill and weightlifting machine are installed in a way so no force is put onto the spaceship structure when astronauts are exercising. Each piece of the exercise equipment is adapted to microgravity. For instance, the bike does not require a seat and, instead, feet are clipped into pedals and a body harness is worn to secure the astronaut. Similarly the treadmill is redesigned with elastic straps which astronauts must wear over the shoulders and around the waist to keep their feet in contact with the running belt. Familiar designs are often adapted for the microgravity environment. In the I-Hab → p. 118 design, the highly restricted space in the module made it necessary to create more space for daily activities, such as exercise, which was resolved through the design of retractable crew quarters.

Watching astronauts navigate through the interior of the space station, it becomes obvious that the logics that guide design on Earth often do not apply here. Architects are challenged to respond with smart solutions that support and potentially "re-ground" astronauts in an otherwise foreign environment.

We are right at the edge of our technology's ability to meet the challenges of outer space. Just keeping people alive in this environment is very, very hard. Once we have solved the fundamental problems over the next 50 years—life support, space radiation, mitigating the deconditioning of reduced gravity, and the psychological challenges—those very hard problems will cease to dominate. Then, as space settlements grow, much older, more familiar human issues will begin to take over. Eventually we will regard life support equipment and variable gravity and radiation shielding as facts of life for which we have routine, predictable solutions. Older challenges of how people interact and how people can be productive and fulfilled in their environment will drive how we design and build places for private, group, and public living and industry that enable space communities and culture and cities. The more traditional issues will take over again.

*Brent Sherwood, Senior Vice President*
*for Advanced Development Programs, Blue Origin*
*(Radio Orange Space Specials: Could we prevent people*
*from going to the Moon or Mars? 15 Aug 2006)*

# When you arrive

in microgravity you do not have the same
references anymore, it is not the same space
anymore as it is when you train on the ground,
it is crowded with stuff and it is totally
different. It is a totally different volume, it is
huge and you realise you live in a volume not
in an area (plane).

*Claudie Haignere, former French Astronaut and Politician*
*(The Human Perspective, Volume: Getting There, Being There, 2010, v25)*

Mars

Moon

Orbit

Earth Land
Earth Ocean

# Replicating
# Terrestrial Systems

Natural life-supporting systems on Earth continue to exist largely unnoticed, revealed only when they are impacted to the point where environments fail to sustain life. Abnormalities such as a colour change in contaminated water or breathing difficulties as a result of air pollution may warn living beings of the potential toxicity of their environments via sensory cues.[1] Nuclear disasters, the aftermath of oil spills and forest fires may threaten living systems in the long term by compromising vital conditions of survival. Human survival is dependent on the life-supporting environmental conditions we are accustomed to on Earth; a continuous supply of uncontaminated air, water and food, and protection from harmful external impacts.

To sustain human life outside the Earth's atmosphere, natural systems from Earth need to be replicated. Living in outer space requires the creation of an artificial biosphere in its most minimal terms. Having sustained the life of more than 250 astronauts and cosmonauts for almost 25 years, the International Space Station (ISS) remains a prominent example of human presence—and survival—in outer space. Its interior hosts a complex, technological Environmental Control and Life Support System (ECLSS) that mimics familiar, life-sustaining factors such as the convection of breathable air, the recovery of water and the removal of noxious gases, trace contaminants and particulate matter from the air. The pressurised habitat modules are operated under standard terrestrial air pressure, with fans to circulate the interior air and keep a moderate temperature of around 20°C. Oxygen is generated and recovered on board by splitting oxygen from water via electrolysis, powered by solar panels. The remaining hydrogen is used in the Sabatier reaction to turn $CO_2$ into water and methane.[2] Water is recovered from urine, wastewater and humidity. As a safe-guarding measure against potential system failure, the system includes redundant backup systems such as pressurised oxygen tanks.

Ensuring contingency in these distant environments is essential as components may not be resupplied or manufactured in time. Remedial maintenance of a life support system (LSS) is undertaken when parts fail, malfunction or break; these can be impacted by technological failures, microbial growth or environmental changes. Both ground control and crew members continuously monitor the data provided by the ECLSS. To alert astronauts to changes in their environment the levels of oxygen, partial oxygen pressure, $CO_2$, radiation, fungal and bacterial growth, volatile organic compounds, humidity, temperature and noise are continuously monitored. NASA astronauts are provided with a Malfunction Procedure Manual to direct them in the circumstance of any predicted system failure.[3] Although not posing an immediate threat to the crew, slight air leakage on the space station is an ongoing issue and requires the search and sealing of microcracks formed due to material fatigue or the load stress of docking and undocking manoeuvres.

When outside of their spacecraft or space station an astronaut relies on a Portable Life Support System (PLSS) which is integrated into each individual spacesuit. These personal biospheres provide a pressurised environment for astronauts to breathe, urinate, hydrate and maintain a stable temperature. Different suits are designed to address different environmental contexts: Extra-Vehicular Activity (EVA), Intra-Vehicular Activity (IVA), microgravity → p. 131 or surface environments. Like the ECLSS on the International Space Station, the PLSS relies on a number of components to support the life of the astronaut. The suit itself is composed of many material layers, each with different functions for the protection or support of the wearer. Tubes that circulate water are woven into a garment to sustain suitable temperature levels inside the suit.[4] Hardware is attached to different parts of the suit. The LSS contained within the backpack of the suit holds and distributes oxygen,

and filters out carbon dioxide. Space suit sensors track multiple parameters such as $CO_2$, oxygen, humidity, respiration, skin temperature, heart rate and blood oxygen levels. For a few hours, the EVA spacesuit is a wearable space habitat.

Long-term missions into deep space will require self-sufficiency involving LSS that mimic the fully circular conditions on Earth. Space habitats will be designed to fully recycle their waste products into water, oxygen, food and other substances. There have been a number of biosphere testbeds in preparation for outer space habitation such as: the Soviet BIOS-3 (1972-1984), Biosphere 2 in Arizona, USA (1990s) and the NASA Lunar-Mars Life Support Test Project (LMLSTP)[5] (1995 and 1997).[6] Each of them provided valuable insights regarding the limits and challenges of the design and engineering of closed ecosystems. LMLSTP, a retrofit of an existing 6 m long vacuum chamber based in the Johnson Space Center, housed astronauts for development and testing → p. 175 of LSS equipment.[7] One of the main takeaways from the retrofit was to develop and design internal configurations → p. 40 together with architects to incorporate human factors. Crew members' well-being and performance are directly influenced by decisions on lighting, colour, configuration and function; all of which are impacted by the arrangement of interior LSSs. Countermeasures against elevated noise levels produced by equipment or other team members are considered critical for crew performance and comfort. Developing a closed-loop system suitable for human habitation also relies on architects factoring in the well-being and performance of astronauts in design.

Reliable bioregenerative LSS, involving microbes and plant-based life are considered key for the success of long-term human missions in outer space. Biogenerative life support systems have been investigated in ESA's MELiSSA programme (Micro-Ecological Life Support System Alternative) for more

than 30 years and are increasingly trialled in terrestrial architecture in order
to address urban sustainability and
resource management. The Living
Architecture project

Living Architecture → p. 166

prototyped a selectively programmable
bioreactor capable of water purification
and generation of low-voltage electricity,
oxygen and biomass, as well as the
recovery of valuable substances such as
phosphate, as a result of microbial
activity. EDEN-ISS,

Eden – ISS → p. 146

a greenhouse and ground demonstration
facility of plant cultivation technologies
for safe food production in space, is
another example of a bioregenerative
LSS component. Both of these architectural scenarios incorporate living systems,
one of them designed to be embedded
in the structure of a building and the
other to be established in the extreme
environments of outer space. Future LSS,
incorporating both physiochemical and
bioregenerative systems, must act as an
all-encompassing system capable of recycling waste back into usable resources.

Mars

Moon

Orbit

**138**
**Earth Land**
Earth Ocean

# Earth

### General characteristics

The abundance of surface water on Earth differentiates it from other planets in our solar system. More than 70 percent of the planetary surface of Earth is covered by oceans and large stretches of land are covered by vegetation. The topological features of the terrain above and below sea level are impacted by active tectonic movements, volcanic activity, erosion and the presence of biological systems.

The Earth's biosphere, the zone where life exists, constitutes a thin layer at the planetary surface, reaching from the ocean floor to several kilometres into the atmosphere. All life forms that feed on organic matter derive their energy from photosynthesising organisms capable of transforming inorganic matter into biomass by using sunlight as a source of energy. Human activity and an increasing global population have significantly affected the planet's biosphere. Today agriculture occupies half of the world's habitable land and its impacts are threatening the biosphere integrity.[1]

### Atmosphere and magnetosphere

Earth orbits the Sun at a distance that allows the formation and persistence of liquid surface water, a prerequisite for life. Life on Earth is protected by the presence of a global magnetic field which is generated by the convective flow of molten iron-rich matter within the Earth's core. This global magnetosphere shields the planet against solar wind by deflecting and trapping solar particles in the Van Allen Belts, two torus-shaped belts around Earth, and thereby prevents the erosion of the climate-moderating atmosphere. Earth's original atmosphere contained large proportions of methane, ammonia and water vapour but no free oxygen.[2] The current presence of 21 percent oxygen is associated with the emergence of photosynthesising organisms that generate atmospheric oxygen as a by-product of their metabolism.

The atmosphere of Earth is defined in layers.[3] The lowest layer, the troposphere, extends from the Earth's surface to an average altitude of 12 km and contains nearly all atmospheric water vapour. It is characterised by rotational turbulence and dynamic weather phenomena that are influenced by temperature, humidity, surface topography and the Earth's axial rotation. The stratosphere sits above the troposphere extending to approximately 50 km in altitude. It holds the ozone layer, a protective layer which absorbs harmful UV radiation from the Sun. From 50 km to 85 km above sea level the mesosphere still contains sufficient gas to cause frictional heating of meteoroids, associated with the visual phenomena of shooting stars. The Kármán Line is the defined border between Earth and space, drawn at 100 kilometres above sea level.

### Space exploration

Some deserts, polar regions or high-altitude regions show similarities with the environmental conditions of other planetary surfaces and have been acknowledged as analogue sites for space mission simulations → p. 175 to test and improve infrastructure and procedures.

Many notable technologies developed for space have been successfully transferred to large-scale applications on Earth and technologies developed on Earth provide solutions for space applications. Certain research fields such as biomimetics provide solutions for varied applications in outer space and on Earth by transferring principles from biological role models into technological solutions. Raising awareness of these shared benefits for both Earth and outer space supports ongoing investment for R&D in space exploration.

### Earth

| | |
|---|---|
| Mean Surface Gravity | $9.80 \text{ m/s}^2$ |
| Equatorial Diameter | 12756 km |
| Equatorial Circumference | 40030 km |
| Surface Pressure | 1.014 bar |
| Length of Year | 365 days |
| Length of Day | 24 hours |
| Temperature Range | −89°C to +57°C |

Mars

Moon

Orbit

LIQUIFER  Projects on  Earth's Land
Earth Ocean

**143—
173**

In October 2017 the Eden – ISS Mobile Test Facility
left from Bremen, Germany. Loaded onto the cargo
ship, the Golden Karoo, in Hamburg it was shipped
to Cape Town, South Africa.

The ship S.A. Agulhas II delivered the Eden – ISS facility to the Antarctic continent where it was unloaded at the sea ice edge on 3 January 2018.

Once transported to the mission site, 400 m from the Neumayer-Station III, the two containers were connected on a stationary platform.

Eden–ISS    demonstrated on-Earth plant cultivation technologies for safe food production onboard the International Space Station (ISS) and for future human space exploration vehicles and planetary outposts. To advance innovative food cultivation technologies in closed-loop systems as an integral part of future space systems, the Mobile Test Facility (MTF) was conceived and installed in the extreme environment of Antarctica. The integral technologies of the project included: an advanced nutrient delivery system; high-performance LED lighting; a bio-detection and decontamination system; imaging systems for monitoring plant health; and robust thermal, power and air management systems.

During the Eden–ISS analogue mission, the MTF was deployed and tested in close proximity to the Neumayer III Antarctic station, operated by the Alfred Wegener Institute. In-situ, the MTF provided 270 kg of fresh, edible produce for the crew during the 2018 Antarctic winter. It continued to serve as an analogue environment for testing plant cultivation under extreme environmental and logistical conditions in Antarctica until 2021. Current plans suggest that the facility will be transferred to the Astronaut Centre of the European Space Agency.

LIQUIFER designed and outfitted the interior of the service section of the Eden–ISS facility. Coordinating the system requirements and the interfaces, the team also co-designed the space mission application of the greenhouse as a deployable greenhouse for the Moon and Mars. LIQUIFER was also responsible for project communication and dissemination activities.

T    2015 – 2019

P    European Union – Horizon 2020 (EU-H2020) project, topic of space exploration & life support

C    Consortium partners – German Aerospace Centre (DLR), Bremen, Germany; LIQUIFER Systems Group, Austria; National Research Council, Italy; University of Guelph, Canada; Alfred Wegener Institute for Polar and Marine Research, Germany; Enginsoft, Italy; Airbus Defence and Space, Germany; Thales Alenia Space, Italy; Aero Sekur, Italy; Wageningen University and Research, The Netherlands; Heliospectra, Sweden; Limerick Institute of Technology, Ireland; Telespazio, Italy

EDEN-ISS during the polar night which began at the end of May and ended in July. Outside temperatures dropped below -42 °C.

Such low temperatures created challenges for the greenhouse system and the DLR scientist, Paul Zabel, tasked with maintaining it and harvesting the plants.

All acquired data and imagery related to plant growth and systems operation were transmitted to the Mission Control Centre at DLR in Bremen for remote oversight.

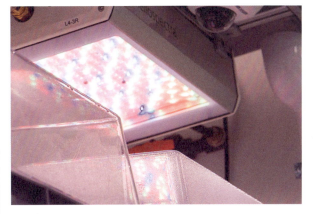

Prior to the test campaign in Antarctica, the Eden – ISS systems were assembled, integrated and tested at DLR premises in Bremen.

The plant cultivation racks were fitted with a highly reliable illumination system which can be adapted to the specific light requirements of the selected crops.

The aeroponic irrigation technique uses a mist environment within the light protected root zone of the plant growth trays.

Early plant growth was supported by 3D-printed structures. Over 20 plant varieties were cultivated including lettuce, cucumber, radishes, dwarf tomatoes and strawberries.

The Mobile Test Facility was preinstalled at the premises of DLR Bremen. It consists of two main sections: the greenhouse and the service section.

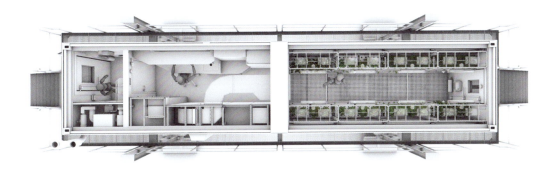

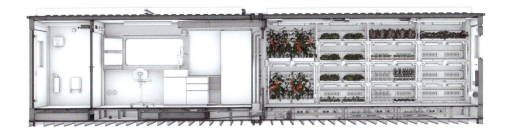

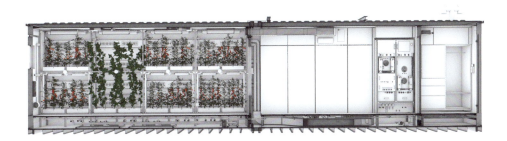

The service section houses all supply and control
systems, a laboratory and the RUCOLA System,
an experiment for plant growth on board the
International Space Station (ISS).

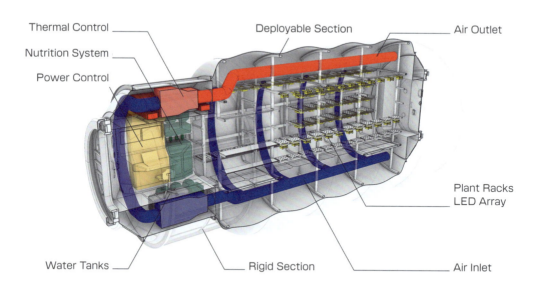

Thermal Control

Nutrition System

Power Control

Deployable Section

Air Outlet

Plant Racks
LED Array

Water Tanks

Rigid Section

Air Inlet

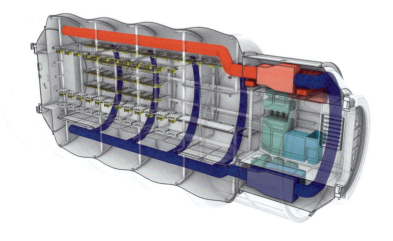

The project EDEN-ISS provided key findings regarding systems performance, crop yield, crew acceptance, and contamination for the design of a future greenhouse on the Moon or Mars.

Bio-regenerative Life Support System are a high priority requirement to meet the physical and psychological challenges of long-duration human space exploration.

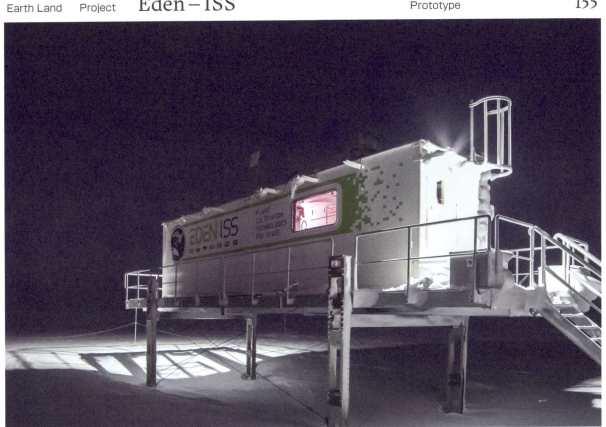

Closed-loop systems that consider the complementary nature of resource exchange within the metabolic processes of biological systems redefine waste as a valuable resource.

GrAB    was an artistic research project that investigated growth patterns and dynamics in nature and applied them to architecture with the goal of creating a new living architecture. An interdisciplinary team from the fields of architecture, biology, art, mechatronics and robotics collaborated in the project. Selected biological processes were explored in depth to identify principles of growth and translate them into exemplary architectural visions. The project nurtured visions that merge alternative building techniques with biology and technology to increase the sustainability and resilience of urban architecture in the future. Principles from biology such as self-organisation, adaptivity and circularity were transferred into artistic concepts. Mobile 3D printing technologies were developed further and employed to produce these differentiated and adaptive structures.

With the support of the host institution, the University of Applied Arts Vienna, LIQUIFER conceived the project with architect Petra Gruber, led the research group and were co-principal investigators of GrAB. The team organised a three-year series of workshops and symposia, disseminating the findings in the book *Built to Grow* and an exhibition at the Angewandte Interdisciplinary Lab (AIL).

T    2013 – 2016

P    Research project funded by the Austrian Science Fund (FWF) as part of PEEK 2012

C    Collaborating institutions – University of Applied Arts, Vienna, Austria; Biomimetics & Mechanical Engineering Group, University of Bath, UK; Botanical Garden & Plant Biomechanics Group, University of Freiburg, Germany; Multi Actor Systems Department, Delft University of Technology, The Netherlands; Ethiopian Institute of Architecture, Building Construction and City Development, Addis Ababa University, Ethiopia; transarch office for biomimetics and transdisciplinary architecture, Austria

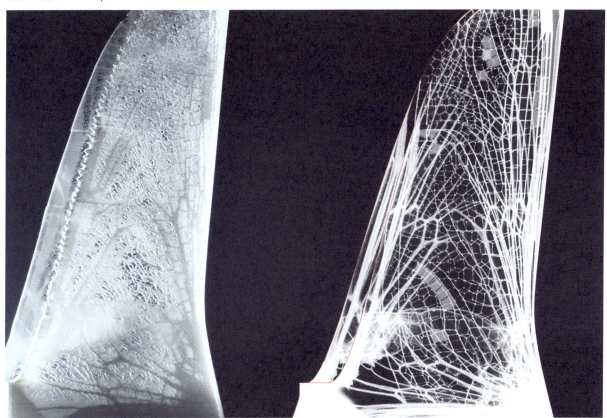

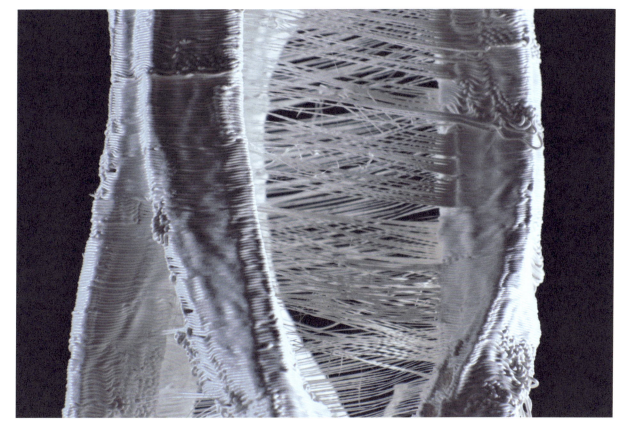

3D printing is an effective technology to mimic
differentiations inherent to natural structures.

Mobile wire printers provide flexibility in transport and deployment. They can work interactively with the existing environment and react to previous building processes.

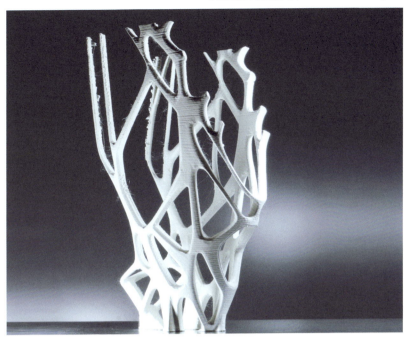

Additive manufacturing is complemented by subtractive methods that apply dissolving agents to the previously printed structure.

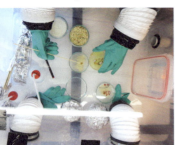

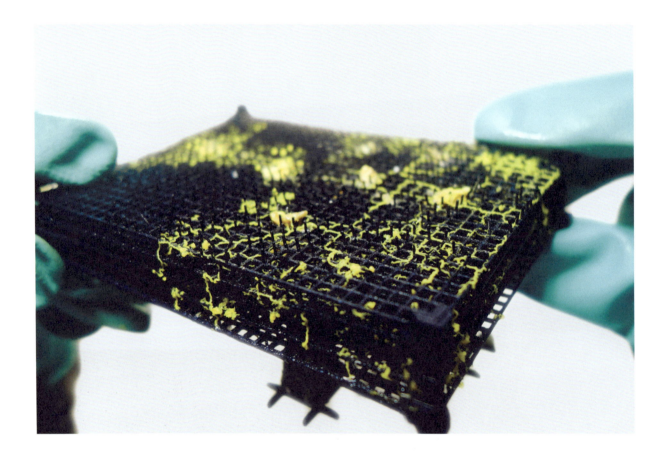

The explorative growth of slime mould within 3D printed structures was integrated into the architectural design process as a method of co-design.

Hands-on experiments are a highly effective way to gain valuable insights into the dynamics and vulnerabilities of living systems.

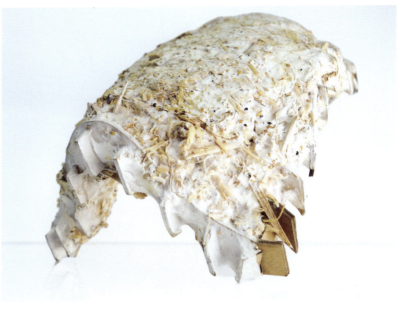

A range of biodegradable support structures were explored to generate shapes of higher complexity than the orthogonal mycelium brick.

Photosynthesizing microorganisms grow within
a transparent tubular system when exposed
to adequate lighting. Fish are incorporated to
add to system robustness.

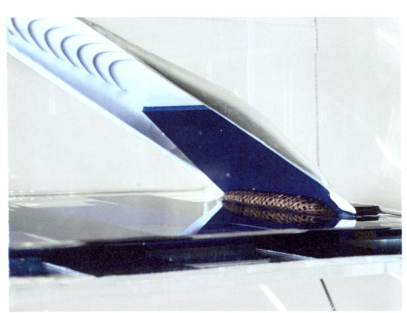

In correspondence to the cellular expansion growth
principle, the characteristics of hydrogels (increasing
in volume through water uptake) was used for the
actuation of kinetic structures.

Employing biological processes within a Living
Architecture will reduce the ecological impact
of the built environment through the establishment
of closed-loop systems.

Living Architecture    provided the proof-of-concept for a next-generation, selectively programmable bioreactor technology that is envisioned as an integral component of human dwellings in the future, capable of complementing or replacing existing building services. At its core, the Living Architecture system processes waste streams in situ within a set of modular bioreactor building blocks that can be stacked to form a freestanding partition wall. The system merges three complementary technologies: the Microbial Fuel Cell (MFC) that purifies wastewater and produces electricity, the Photobioreactor (PBR) that generates oxygen and supplies nutrients for the Synthetic Microbial Consortia (SMC) that recovers valuable substances from the waste streams. With its circular approach, the Living Architecture technologies represent a step towards urban sustainability and responsible resource management.

   As part of the Living Architecture team, LIQUIFER was responsible for scenario development and elaborated use cases for new and existing buildings, with customised solutions for different building types. The concepts were complemented by solar energy harvesting and vertical farming infrastructure. An immersive animation showcased the integrated systems within a multifunctional highrise building. As part of the building block design, LIQUIFER designed and built a brick prototype and produced a wide range of ceramic bioreactor membranes to selectively control the interaction across bioreactor chambers.

T    2016 – 2019

P    European Union – Horizon 2020 (EU-H2020) research project, FET-Open

C    Consortium partners – School of Architecture, Planning and Landscape & Institute for Sustainability, Newcastle University, UK; Unconventional Computing Centre, Department of Computer Science, Faculty of Environment and Technology, University of the West of England, UK; BioEnergy Centre, UK; Bristol Robotics Lab, UK; The Biological Research Centre, Department of Environmental Biology, Spanish National Research Council (CSIC), Spain; LIQUIFER Systems Group, Austria; EXPLORA BIOTECH, Italy; Centre for Integrative Biology, University of Trento, Italy

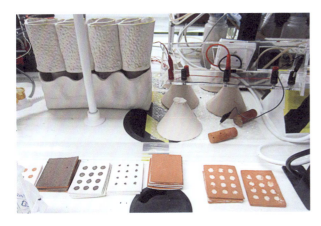

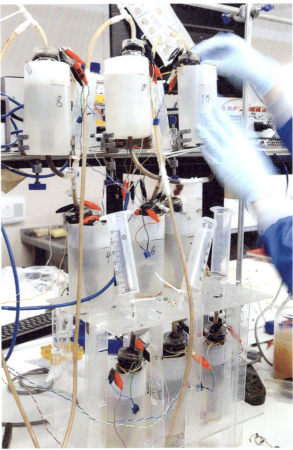

Ceramic membranes, an integral component of the bioreactor, were investigated through material, shape and surface variations.

Preliminary test set-ups explored the performance of alternative ceramic membranes with a focus on energy output or selective permeability.

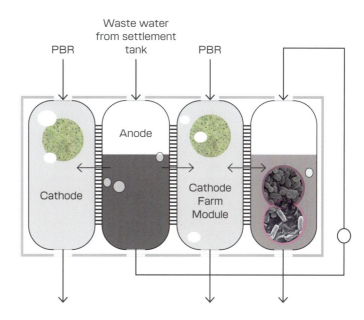

The activities of living organisms complement each other in the Living Architecture brick where three technologies are merged. In the Microbial Fuel Cell (MFC) technology microbes act as catalysts for electrochemical reactions within the anode and cathode system to purify wastewater and generate an electric current.

The photosynthesizing microbes used in the photobioreactor (PBR) technology are fed into the cathode chamber. A Farm Module is simultaneously part of the third technology using synthetic microbial consortia for the recovery of phosphate in the Labour Module.

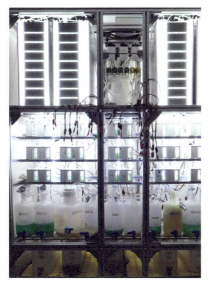

The proof-of-concept was demonstrated under laboratory conditions with a series of 3D printed four-chamber bricks.

1    Hydraulic plug-in connectors
2    Combined photobioreactor,
     cathode and farm chamber
3    Removable glass window
4    Overflow systems
5    Cylindric ceramic membrane
6    Exchangeable cylindric anode
     or labour chamber

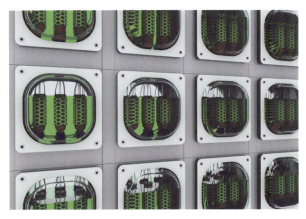

The LIQUIFER brick concept used cylindric anode
and labour chambers immersed in a single volume that
serves as photobioreactor, cathode and farm module.

The soft green glow of the bioreactor wall makes the
metabolic processes visible within the building.

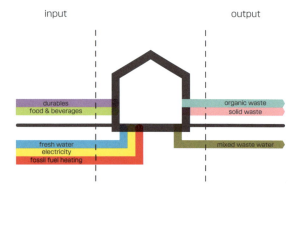

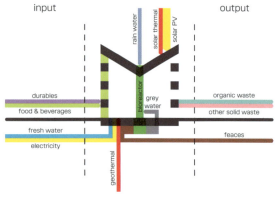

In combination with other renewable technologies, the Living Architecture system has the potential to drastically reduce the existing supply dependencies of the built environment.

Architectural scenarios explored the application of diverse and decentralised resource management for sustainable urban living.

The integration of bioreactor walls within a
multifunctional highrise building was showcased in
an immersive animation.

Mars

Moon

Orbit

Earth Land
Earth Ocean

# Mission Preparation: Simulating Future Explorations

After 110 days, four volunteer students exited the Lunar Palace 1, a bio-regenerative life support facility built to simulate a Lunar base at Beihang University, Beijing. The isolation experiment was the third stage of a 370-day simulation, which aimed to enable the coexistence of humans, animals, plants and microorganisms in an almost closed-loop environment.[1] Lunar Palace 1 was a successful example of a simulation capable of supporting biological chains for an extended duration in a closed environment Lunar base. The approximately 160 m² architecture, integrating the Bio-regenerative Life Support System (BLSS), → p. 135  was composed of three cabins, two of which were solely dedicated to the planting and harvesting of grain, vegetables and fruit.[2] The survival, and ultimate thriving, of individual organisms was dependent on the survival of the others: oxygen generated by plants became breathing air for the volunteers; carbon dioxide from the volunteers was utilised in the photosynthesis of plants; scraps from harvested grain, vegetables and fruit fed mealworms; other byproducts were treated before being used to fertilise plants. The Lunar-like environment was developed to test the design and operation of the BLSS as well as the physiological, social and psychological effects of long-term, closed-quarters isolation on volunteers.[3] As with most mission simulations, Lunar Palace 1 trained multiple skills including complex scenarios (planting, processing and harvesting food), understanding operations (abiding by the needs of the BLSS) and understanding the mission in relation to other crew members (working together to keep the BLSS functioning).

Simulations are a prerequisite phase for all planned missions to space. With limited actual experience in a space environment and the characteristic difficulties it offers, extensive preparation is necessary to minimise potential risks. Earth-based simulations provide researchers with an environment to observe, test and analyse their developments before they are utilised in actual space missions.[4] They can be approached as integrated space mission scenarios, as in the case of Lunar Palace 1, or they may investigate specific research questions in the fields of physics, geology, sociology, psychology or others. Like a rehearsal on a 1:1 scale, simulations follow mission-specific procedures, act out these guidelines, evaluate test setups, find solutions to problems and generate new knowledge. As each simulation is part of an iterative process, the findings fuel scientific, technological, design and procedural improvements. Results from simulations can help to train and test for future simulations and space missions.

Lunar Palace 1 took place in a highly controlled, artificial environment, similar to those developed by governmental space agencies and private enterprises for astronaut training. In addition, natural space analogues are frequently used to perform complex mission scenarios under conditions similar to the proposed space environment. Some extreme environments on Earth are recognised space analogue sites as they represent certain characteristics of the Lunar, Martian or orbital environments relevant to the objective of the simulation. Among others, this includes Arctic locations such as the Haughton impact crater on Devon Island, Canada, which is used to approximate the Martian environment due to its geology and frozen, desert-like landscape. The Atacama Desert, Chile and Rio Tinto, Spain are used as Mars mission analogue sites due to their extremely dry terrains, their pronounced mineral content and the types of microbial ecosystems able to survive in their extreme environments.[5] Underwater environments such as the Aquarius underwater analogue in Florida are used to simulate different gravity levels when performing various EVA scenarios.

All mission simulations have an objective. Some simulations have broad objectives, such as the project Moonwalk, which aimed to enhance European capabilities for future human space exploration, especially surface Extra-Vehicular Activity (EVA) for the Moon and Mars.[6] For

others, there are more specific objectives, as in FASTER, which aimed to develop technologies allowing rovers to safely and efficiently traverse other-planetary terrain.[7] As a less complex simulation with fewer variables, it was possible to test FASTER inside the Airbus DS Mars Yard Facility in Stevenage, England, a purpose-built enclosed site. This type of testing is cheaper and more common than integrated mission simulations such as Moonwalk, which test multiple elements at once. Moonwalk required two space analogue sites: Rio Tinto, Spain and subsea Marseille, France, plus a mission control connected to both

Moonwalk → p. 188

FASTER → p. 74

sites, which was located near Brussels, Belgium. This simulation took place over two weeks, where an astronaut and assistant rover collaborated as partners in mapping, surveying and sampling activities. It tested technical components developed by the seven Moonwalk partners, such as the small assistant robot, the EVA simulation spacesuit, and the EVA information system, in addition to a mission control centre, a biomonitoring system and a set of manual tools for EVA.[8] A series of mission scenarios were designed to test these novel technologies and tools, incorporating procedures similar to those that astronauts use on the International Space Station (ISS). Like a storyboard for a film, mission scenarios sketch the proposed sequence of scenes for each scenario. The "actors" (astronaut and rover) were then able to rehearse a series of actions inside the relevant environment and given timeframes. In repeating these tasks, concepts and technologies that the team had developed could be analysed and evaluated. Scenarios included scouting a site, collecting soil samples, exploring a cave, exploring challenging terrain and exploring a steep slope. The simulation replicated conditions that would be encountered in the Martian environment, including time delay in communicating with Earth-based teams.

In addition to these physical spaces, virtual reality technologies are being utilised to create  simulation "locations." As technology advances, Space Architects can simulate and test their designs with astronauts before constructing a physical prototype. In the case of

I-Hab → p. 118

I-Hab interior design development (a part of the future Lunar Orbital Space Station Gateway), LIQUIFER had the opportunity to interact and receive feedback from ESA astronauts that prime contractor Thales Alenia Space Italy (TAS-I) invited to explore the rendered 48 m³ configuration of the proposed interior layout. In order to design suitable, feasible habitats, simulations are an essential component in preparing for the challenges proposed by future space missions.

By practising simulations, astronauts learn not only what to do during their mission by heart but also rehearse for being in outer space —working and acting as if they are already at their mission destination off-Earth. This familiarising of the strange helps them feel more comfortable when being in actual harsh environments, where errors can have deadly consequences.

*Joseph Popper, artist and designer*
*(Radio Orange Space Specials: Exploring the Peripheries of Outer Space, 18 Oct 2020)*

A simulator is basically the same structure as the real vehicle used in spaceflight in Russian programs because you need to test the hardware. The main difference is the real vehicle flies. We built several samples of vehicles based on the same drawing. Using one of these mock-ups, we basically tried to break it. Usually, after all these tests it became the simulator.

*Sergei Krikalev, Soviet and Russian mechanical engineer and former cosmonaut*
*(Radio Orange Space Specials: Long duration stays on space stations, 19 Aug 2008)*

Simulations allow us to spot the unknown—those elements you couldn't predict and issues that you didn't foresee. You learn from them and optimise them as they allow you to address these sticking points. You need to progressively prepare on Earth so that when the time to do it comes, you are ready. That's the main thing.

*Diego Urbina, Team Leader, Future Projects and Exploration, Space Applications Services*
*(Radio Orange Space Specials: Simulations:*
*space exploration preparations on Earth, 19 Jul 2016)*

In chamber studies you cannot simulate risks to life and health. These two factors, which are common dangers of spaceflight, exist in Antarctica. The point is, no analogue can be perfect for space-flight, so we need to distribute the experience in various analogues like submarines, oil platforms, Antarctica and arctic winter.

*Vadim Gushin, Psychologist for Russian Cosmonauts*
*(Radio Orange Space Specials: Psychology in Space, 28 Dec 2010)*

Mars

Moon

Orbit

Earth Land
**Earth Ocean**
180

General characteristics

Hydrosphere

Space exploration

Liquid water is essential to life. It is a universal solvent and transport medium of energy and matter on multiple scales. Within oceans, water streams and in the bodies of living organisms water transmits nutrients and waste and regulates both temperature and internal cellular pressure.

Underwater, light and sound travel and disperse differently than they do in air. In water, sound waves propagate much faster than in air.[1] Its reflection and absorption of light depend on surface characteristics and the particles present in the water. Water scatters light and absorbs various wavelengths differently, orange/red light can penetrate less deep than blue light, making deep, clear ocean water appear blue. Marine life is supported by solar radiation, which warms the oceanic surface, and supplies energy to photosynthetic microorganisms and phytoplankton which live in the well-lit surface waters of the euphotic zone.[2] Water can shield organisms from harmful cosmic radiation, a characteristic that promoted the evolution of early lifeforms on Earth.

The hydrosphere is the total mass of water on planet Earth including that in a liquid, gaseous and frozen state. Freshwater accounts for a very small share of the global water volume, whilst more than 97 percent is accounted for by saline water.[3] Large volumes of fluids, atmospheric gases and oceanic water are important factors for global heat storage and redistribution. The hydrologic cycle is the redistribution of water by evaporation, condensation, precipitation, transpiration and run-off. Oceanic water circulates globally because of density differences directly related to variations in temperatures and salinity. While surface currents in oceans are affected by planetary rotation and wind, deep oceanic water currents are determined by deep sea and coastal topography. Massive vertical movements of ocean water happen in specific deep convection areas close to the poles where water sinks with increasing density and upwells in equatorial regions.[4] Ocean surface topography maps the highs and lows of the ocean surface affected by weather phenomena and the Moon's gravitational pull on Earth. Seabed topography maps depth contours, oceanic plateaus, plains and basins, subsea volcanoes, banks, ridges and trenches.

Underwater environments are used as testbeds for space exploration missions to simulate → p. 175 reduced gravity → p. 131 environments. Simulation suits are designed to provide variable levels of buoyancy when simulating operations for reduced gravity or microgravity. Simulations are undertaken either in laboratory settings such as the Neutral Buoyancy Laboratory at the Johnson Space Centre or in large bodies of water, often oceans. In simulated microgravity, astronauts learn to no longer rely on their weight, but to move and reposition via propulsive or pulling forces. Underwater training can only approximate the experience of reduced gravity because the movement through water produces considerable drag compared to movement in a vacuum or air. [5] Underwater environments are also used to simulate extended periods of isolation. The operational similarities and living conditions in submarines can be compared to life in space habitats, in terms of the lack of space, lack of resources and extreme pressure differences between the interior and exterior of the vessel.

Underwater

| | |
|---|---|
| Gravity | simulation by buoyancy variation |
| Average Salinity | ~35 g/L |
| Euphotic Zone range | from surface up to 200 m (clear water) |
| Pressure increase with depth | 1 bar / 10 m |
| Speed of Sound | approx. 1500 (water) 340(air) m.s$^{-1}$ |
| Surface Temperature Range | −2 to +35°C |

Deep Space

Mars

Moon

Orbit

Earth Land
LIQUIFER  Projects  in  Earth's Ocean

**185—
195**

<u>Moonwalk</u>    developed scenarios and technolo-
gies for human-robot cooperation at planetary
surface missions and tested the performance of
an astronaut-robot team at two analogue sites
on Earth, in Rio Tinto, Spain →p. 64 and Marseille,
France. Simulation astronauts (simonauts) were
supported by a small mobile assistant robot
during extravehicular activities (EVA). To simulate partial gravity conditions on the Moon,
the astronaut-robot team was tested in underwater environments in Marseilles, at first in a
controllable testing pool and subsequently
in a natural subsea environment.

Underwater simulations entail additional
requirements for hardware operability and safety
standards, when compared to on-ground simulations →p. 64. The rover, spacesuits and tools
designed have to be adapted to a level of buoyancy that simulates partial gravity. Divers' equipment is integrated into the spacesuit to sustain
extended periods underwater. For safety reasons,
each simonaut is accompanied and surveilled by
security divers. In natural subsea environments,
the additional requirements of an adequately
equipped ship and its crew substantially impact
simulation costs. Visibility in a natural subsea
environment can be reduced as a result of natural
turbulence related to weathering and currents.

Apart from the development of mission
scenarios, the LIQUIFER team designed an
exchangeable payload system for the rover
chassis and several astronaut tools. The design
included casings for measuring instruments,
sample storage and tool fittings on the rover,
as well as expandable and collapsible tools for
the astronaut that reflect the restrictions of
movement and visibility when wearing a heavy
and bulky EVA suit. LIQUIFER were also responsible for the communication and dissemination
of the project.

T    2013 – 2016

P    European Union – Seventh
     Framework Programme for
     Research and Technological
     Development (EU-FP7), in the
     frame of space

C    Consortium partners – DFKI
     Robotics Innovation Center,
     Germany; COMEX, France;
     EADS UK, UK; LIQUIFER
     Systems Group, Austria;
     Space Applications Services,
     Belgium; NTNU Centre for
     Interdisciplinary Research
     in Space, Norway; INTA
     Instituto Nacional de Técnica
     Aeroespacial, Spain

L    Marseilles, France

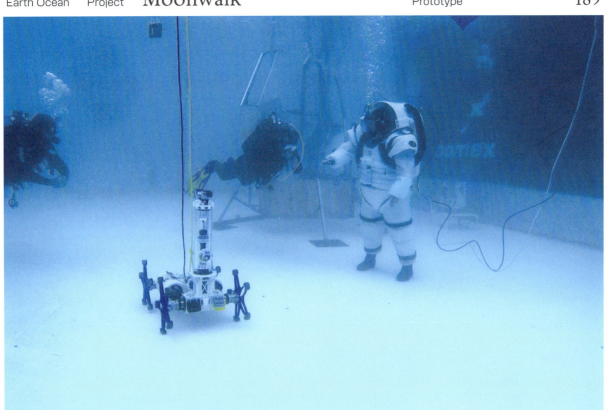

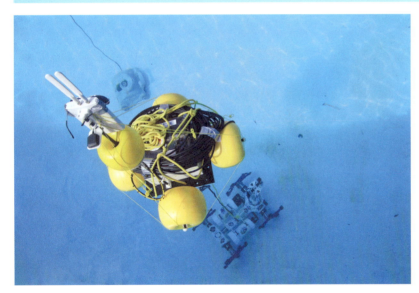

The underwater environment allows the testing of space exploration scenarios under simulated low-gravity conditions.

Pool tests at the COMEX premises in Marseille preceded the simulations in natural underwater environment, both involved a lander mock-up fragment equipped with a suitport, two simulation spacesuits and a robotic rover.

A simonaut accesses the Gandolfi 2 EVA simulation spacesuit through the suitport of the lander mockup and descends to the simulated Lunar surface.

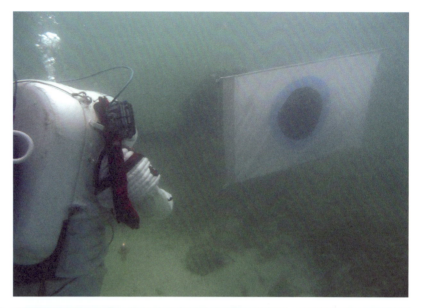

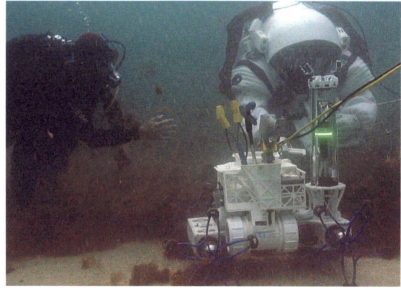

The next generation of space explorers contributed their ideas in the Moonwalk childrens' competition. The winning entry for the Moon flag design was honoured during the subsea simulation.

Simulations in natural subsea environments involve up to five security divers and several sea-going vessels.

In accordance with the Mars simulations carried out in Rio Tinto, Spain, the underwater simulations studied and compared the performance of an astronaut-robot team with an astronaut-astronaut team.

The properties of the simulation spacesuits, the robotic rover and the sampling tools, were adapted for underwater applications to simulate Lunar gravity conditions.

The    Medusa    project explores the feasibility
of inflatable habitats for use on planetary
surfaces such as the Moon or Mars. The simulation →p. 64 concept involves a fully submerged
habitat module that is anchored to the seafloor.
It consists of a rigid core element that contains
life support systems →p. 135, EVA infrastructure
for entrance and exit from below and the
surrounding torus-shaped living space.
Internal vehicular activity (IVA) and EVA can
be tested and validated within and outside
the Medusa habitat. The segmented habitat
hull was conceived as a membrane cushion
structure which can perform various functions.
Transparent structural segments serve as
windows or as algae pods for producing nutrition supplements. For space applications,
all hull membrane segments would be filled
with water to provide radiation shielding
for the crew. For the underwater simulation,
LIQUIFER explored different testing possibil
ities. The hull segments could be filled with
water around an inflated interior space or, in
an alternative configuration, partial gravity can
be simulated within a water-filled interior
space surrounded by inflated hull segments.

   LIQUIFER designed the Medusa deployable
habitat in cooperation with subsea engineers
from French engineering firm COMEX as well
as developing the bioreactor concept with
artist, biologist and space systems researcher
Angelo Vermeulen.

T     2012

P     Concept design for a com-
      petition entry to the Jacques
      Rougerie Foundation

C     Collaborating partners –
      COMEX, France; LIQUIFER
      Systems Group, Austria,
      Delft University of Technology,
      The Netherlands

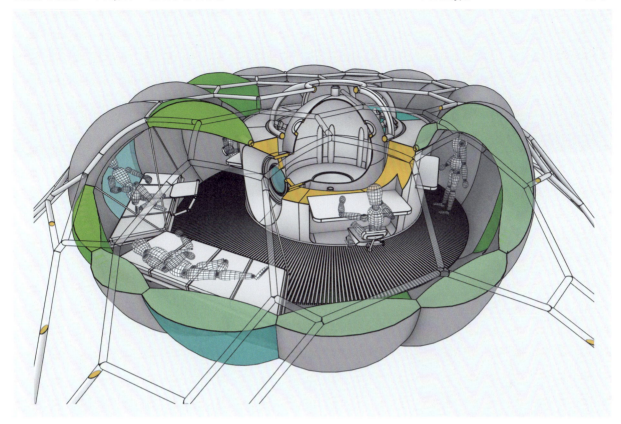

Working and living happens in the open space
that surrounds a rigid core element acting as the entry
point of the habitat.

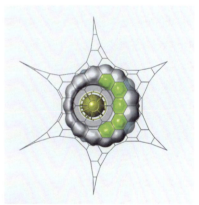

Underwater simulation for an outpost
on the Martian surface.

The 1st Antarctic Biennale began in Ushuaia, Argentina, the southernmost city of our planet. During landings at scientific bases and historic and natural sites in the Antarctic Peninsula artists made temporary, site-specific and ecologically compatible installations and performances.

The following conversation is made up of selected interview segments from the podcast mini-series Antarctic Biennale by Barbara Imhof.

T     March 2017

P     Biennale commissioned and curated by artist Alexander Ponomarev, and curated by Nadim Samman

A     Artists – Alexander Ponomarev, Russia; Abdullah al Saadi, UAE; Alexis Anastasio, Brazil; Andrey Kuzkin, Russia; Gustav Düsing, Germany; Joaquin Fargas, Argentina; Julian Charrière, France/Switzerland; Juliana Cerqueira Leite, Brazil; Julius von Bismarck, Germany; Paul Rosero Contreras, Ecuador; Sho Hasegawa, Japan; Tomas Saraceno, Argentina/Germany; Zhang Enli, China; Yto Barrada, Morocco/France; Eulalia Valldosera, Spain; Shama Rahman, Bangladesh/UK; Yasuaki Igarashi, Japan; Lou Sheppard, Canada

I     Interdisciplinary Partners – Alexander Sekatskii, Russia; Barbara Imhof, Austria; Jean de Pomereu, France; Listen Schultz, Sweden; Carlo Rizzo, Italy/UK; Wakana Kono, Japan; Sergey Pisarev, Russia; Susmita Mohanty, Indian; Hector Monslave, Argentina; Adrian Dannatt, UK; Miguel Petchkovsky, Angola/Portugal; Liz Barry, USA; Nicholas Shapiro, USA

Moon

Orbit

**198**
Earth Land
Earth Ocean

Adrian Dannatt                    Never before have I taken a journey in my life of 12 hours or 24 hours with no change in the landscape around, where nothing changes that I'm looking at.

Dehlia Hannah                    I've had an obsession about coming here for at least the last few years, ever since I've been doing my post-doctoral research on climate change aesthetics. I actually had a dream to get aboard a scientific mission to Antarctica.

Nadim Samman                    Antarctica is a place that is communicated as being central to our understanding of planetary systems, such as climate change, or the geophysical sciences. It's a place that everyone is told about, a place that everyone is expected to care about, a place that grabs the imagination that seems both otherworldly and intensely connected to everything else on this planet. Antarctica is so central to many of our contemporary narratives. And yet, most people will never go. We choose to go here in order to find a way to communicate, perhaps an undiscovered aspect of Antarctica's cultural potential. We do that with artists and philosophers and thinkers in the hope that they may find a way to interpret Antarctica anew.

Juliana Cerqueira Leite                    Just observing the forms that the ice makes and the icebergs that we've gone by, and these glaciers coming down mountains that are just the accumulation of snow. To me there's this process of sedimentation, of compression, of collapse, that is repeated in these shapes that we keep seeing, which I don't think is a normal thing to see. I've been finding it's very much a kind of visual signature of this environment.

Jean de Pomereau                    What we found out is that even what we thought was the most remote and the most detached of places is actually deeply relevant, it is all interdependent. And, what's more, there is a great pleasure to be drawn from that. It's both a place which delights and brings strong emotions of wonder, and at the same time, frightens us in its ability to echo across the world and across climatic issues.

This expedition to the islands of Tonga in the South Pacific was part of the transdisciplinary research project Deep Sea Minding, which proposed the creation of structures that could serve the needs and desires of both humans and marine creatures.

    The following conversation is made up of selected interview segments from the podcast mini-series *Deep Sea Minding* by Barbara Imhof.

T    Summer 2018

P    Summer 2018, expedition commissioned by TBA21–Academy, conceived by the Danish artist group SUPERFLEX

C    Collaborators — SUPERFLEX (Jakob Fenger, Bjørnstjerne Christiansen and Rasmus Nielsen); Francesca Thyssen-Bornemisza & Markus Reymann, TBA21-Academy; Dayne Buddo, Alligator Head Foundation; Ricardo Gomes, KWY.studio; Barbara Imhof, LIQUIFER Systems Group; Alex Jordan, Max Planck Institute Department of Collective Behaviour; Jun Kamei, AMPHIBIO; Maureen Penjueli, Pacific Network on Globalization; Johan Schneévoigt, cinematographer and cameraman

Mars

Moon

Orbit

Earth Land
Earth Ocean

200

Rasmus Nielsen      The project is called Deep Sea Minding. That sounds a little bit like deep sea mining, which is a new mining adventure that is about to take off, where giant machines will start digging into the oceans, for various minerals and metals, because we are supposedly running out of them on land. There is a lot of concern about drilling on the seabed, we know that mining will be or has been disastrous in some parts of the world. So we thought, it would be nice to think of the deep sea as something else that is not a "gold hunt" for minerals, metals and things like that, but rather a "gold hunt" for ideas. So basically, try and imagine that you could learn something from the deep sea, that might influence life on land.

Francesca Thyssen-Bornemisza   Deep Sea Minding suggests dealing with the ocean, in its volume. We tend to look at the ocean as a surface.

Maureen Penjueli      The gravity of the significance of the ocean to life itself is quite significant.

Markus Reymann      When you try to think *from* the ocean, which is a very hard exercise, then you understand that everything is constantly changing. Everything is constantly in movement, everything is constantly in flux. And every action has a reaction and it's pretty visible.

Alex Jordan      I would love to erase or blur that line between the surface world and the deep. Not physically but in terms of intellectual engagement and to have people think about these very questions. What does that world require? What is good in that world?

Bjørnstjerne Christiansen      We wanted to explore the infrastructural relations between above and below, and how humans and sea organisms can interact and live together.

Jakob Fenger      Maybe one solution is to actually do a coexistence of some sort. More people have been to the Moon than to the deepest part of the ocean, it is really an unknown territory.

Ricardo Gomes      Any structure under the water has to allow water to flow through it and also to provide small and large spaces for different species, and their different types of behaviour. So fish may want to interact with the structure at a quantum playing level but most of the time when fish use structures, they do so to hide from predators. Whereas coral or algae will need space that is protected. The initial process was research in terms of what type of structures do fish or other marine life inhabit, or what type of structure do they create for themselves, which is actually quite rare. There's only very few species that actively interact with structures underwater that have been built.

Dayne Buddo      We find that we have to intervene, on an ecological basis, to make sure that we actually are doing the right things to enhance the environment and not degrade the environment by our actions. You can design structures that will actually enhance the marine environment and ecosystem resilience.

## The Space–Earth Continuum

Epilogue
by Christina Ciardullo

Surrounded by a vast sea of darkness, there it is: that pale blue dot carrying everything that ever lived.[1] Just the right distance, just the right temperature, just the right mix of chemicals, at just the right time, to sustain life as we know it. For a very brief moment in the epic scale of space and time, we see evidence of something changing, something breathing, something metabolising, something regulating an atmosphere:[2] for a very brief moment, we exist.

There was a change the moment we saw the Earth from space. That distant view put in perspective just how lucky we are, collectively. It provoked a global evolution of consciousness that decades later can be recognised as a catalyst for some of our most recent environmental movements. And now, for perhaps the first time in more recent industrial and extractive history, there is mass mobilisation towards reconciling the needs of humans with that of our home planet. When we see the Earth from space, we become aware of how critically we are interdependent with our environment. It is the site of the evolution of our bodies. Our physical attributes, our attitudes, our fears and hopes are all a result of an evolutionary dialogue with our environment over hundreds of thousands of years. The way we build is also a reaction to the environment: the climate determines our standards, preconceptions, cultures, histories, geographies, climates, tools and materials. That unlikely chemical mix in time and space, somehow created the conditions for the very particular ways in which we live and create our built environments.

In the past half century heroic efforts have created *Enclosures* (spaceships) to preserve ourselves away from Earth. We have created *Architecture* for outer space. In outer space, architecture will act as a surrogate for our entire planet. A bubble of air and material will be the basis of a *Building,* substituting all the chemical and biological interactions that sustain us on Earth. Rather than conceive of spaceships and habitats as we do buildings on Earth, design for space allows us to remove our assumptions about what we think we know and instead work from a place where natural and social sciences meet design. This new perspective on architecture is not meant for space habitats alone. Now, as we contemplate new space stations and Lunar and Martian settlements, the UN predicts that 68 percent of the world's population will be living in cities. As it stands, maintaining the status quo within building and construction impacts the human condition in today's "developed" world: the majority of people spend 87 percent of their time *inside* buildings,[3] buildings which account for 35 percent of the global energy use and 38 percent of global carbon emissions.[4] On Earth we are still faced with immense scales of material extraction, global manufacturing chains, and energy production which contribute to global climate change and pollution. As the figures prove, the production of buildings is one of the biggest contributors to this fraught reality due to current, outdated approaches to material use, construction and design.

With a number of colleagues we determined that "any experience in creating and demonstrating a human environment that operates within limited means and resources at scale will have immense promise to return knowledge and provide feedback for buildings on Earth."[5] It is clear that there remains such dissonance between the way we propose to build

on the Moon, Mars or further into our universe and the abandon with which we construct "modern" buildings on Earth. We must recognise and begin to act as though materials, energy, physical space, and resources are limited. To do so we must understand that the problems of the built environment in any location are both systemic and interconnected:

Physical Space
Meeting the demands of affordable housing for a rising population is predicted to double the amount of constructed floorspace by 2060. In more "developed" countries the amount of living space per person has doubled due to ageing populations, more people living alone and increases in standards of living. Building more means using more land, more materials, more energy, and more resources. Many have advocated for a shift in consciousness in relation to expectations of space and spaces. In this scenario, individual footprints would be reduced by living in smaller spaces and adapting spaces for multifunctionality or time-sharing.

Astronauts have so far lived in tight quarters, and as long as journeys are brief we can tolerate living small. But, as we design for longer and farther stays off Earth we must balance size and resource use with psychological and social health. It is not about living ascetically but about living well and fully within limited means: a task the designs you see from LIQUIFER have deftly mastered in spades.→ p. 52, 122 Designing for smaller and smarter spaces is not only key to our future on Earth, it is the essential role of the architect in space.

## Resources

Nothing is closer to the human body than water, air, and food, which, after they circulate through our metabolism, flow through building inlets, outlets and civic infrastructure. Yet, nothing is so far removed from us in modern cities. Water is sourced and energetically pumped from faraway, contested lands before being treated in concealed centralised locations, distanced by their public invisibility. We ventilate our waste gases through mechanical systems while remaining dependent on air regenerated from the most dense forests of our planet, which shrink every year. Food, often grown at the expense of native biodiverse lands, is transported across the globe. As a globally interconnected planet, the essential elements of human survival all suffer from a human-made distribution problem where scarcity in some areas is the result of abundance in others.

Water, air and food are in scarce supply in extreme environments. In fact, all that we have will need to be brought with us, grown and then regenerated. A *Building* rather than a *Planet* will be responsible for the flow and processing of these resources. → p. 144, 164 It is possible to sustain ourselves directly in the spaces where those resources are consumed, at the scale of the habitat, the home, the building, and the city.

## Materials

On Earth we often take the availability of steel, concrete, timber, metals and minerals that surround us for granted. All the energy, processing, and transportation that those materials required before they arrived in their "final forms" is easily forgotten. The "embodied energy" of materials has become a critical discussion point for policy makers, especially in relation to their carbon emissions. In turn, the use of non-renewable resources and intensive manufacturing processes is becoming less and less favourable. Similarly, in space we cannot continue to load a launch rocket full of high mass building materials whenever we wish to construct something new. When we descend to the surface of distant planets more frequently we discover similar chemical compositions and materials capable of being roads, bricks, walls, roofs, and furnishings. Ingenuity in local ("in-situ") → p. 106 and low energy material processes move us closer to "living with the land", wherever in the universe that land may be.

Lunar Architecture will look different because it is defined by local materials available on the planetary surface and it will be made differently because of the basic tools we have to work with once there. Like longlasting, low-carbon, vernacular Earth architecture, reliant only on dirt and sunlight, Lunar architecture will combine these well-practised techniques with innovative technologies to sustain future populations on the Moon. → p. 90

## Energy

Over half of the energy used in the building sector lights, heats, cools, and ventilates buildings. Dense, high, urban environments create even more need for light, cooling, and ventilation. Passive design, which reduces the need for additional heating or cooling by working with the local climate, is not a new practice. In fact it is older than new — it is ancient — and derived from the relationship between the climate and the body. Perhaps a building's most essential function is in the creation of a boundary that changes the environment "inside" from the one

206

"outside". Perhaps nothing is more extreme than this boundary in outer space where the pressure difference between life and vacuum could not be clearer.

Turning to the energy of metabolism in their work, LIQUIFER reminds us to capitalise on the synergistic functional systems that we need to live, by combining systems which remediate air and water and produce food, with those that are a source of energy. → p. 164 These methods of working with the interior environment give a new perspective on working seamlessly with nature rather than subduing it by the brute force of machinery.

Given the intensity of these *Architectural* problems on Earth and their relationship to design for outer space, one might ask why even involve the aerospace engineers in questions of habitation for space? This is an issue clearly within the domain of the built environment experts. Traditionally pedagogical and cultural differences between architecture, engineering, and the sciences have kept these problem spaces and their innovations separate. These silos have done little for such complex and interconnected problems. Rather, the common motivations of each discipline provide guiding principles that demonstrate the potential for the co-development of systems essential to sustainable practice and innovation. Such principles can be applied to building on Earth and in space. The intellectual problem space of *Architecture* is systems-based, and we will need integrated efforts across disciplines to inform truly sustainable practice.

Perhaps in this synthetic and interdisciplinary effort, architects, engineers, and scientists will come back to working with the essential tools of life – energy and materials – with a renewed perspective. And, perhaps, this will allow us to welcome a new relationship with our planet. A relationship that reinforces our stewardship of it, our curiosity about it, and our wonder for the miracle of our existence. Armed with renewed love for our home and origins, brandished with a new perspective on the relationship between our bodies and our environment, and with lessons learned from the failures of planetary exploitation, we can more confidently take the first steps to explore alien worlds. Until the next steps in our evolution, we will go out into space not as human beings alone but from spacesuit to spaceship to space city: as a total interconnected and interdependent environment, a total *Architecture*.

# Timeline of work



2004

2004

2005–2006

Sep 2005–Mar 2006

2006–2007

Jun–Jul 2006

2007

2007

2007

2007–2009

Nov 2007–Feb 2009

March 2008 – April 2009

2010

2010–2012

2010–2013

Nov 2011–Nov 2014

2012

Jan 2013–Dec 2015

May 2013–Feb 2016

Oct 2013–Jan 2015

# Timeline of work



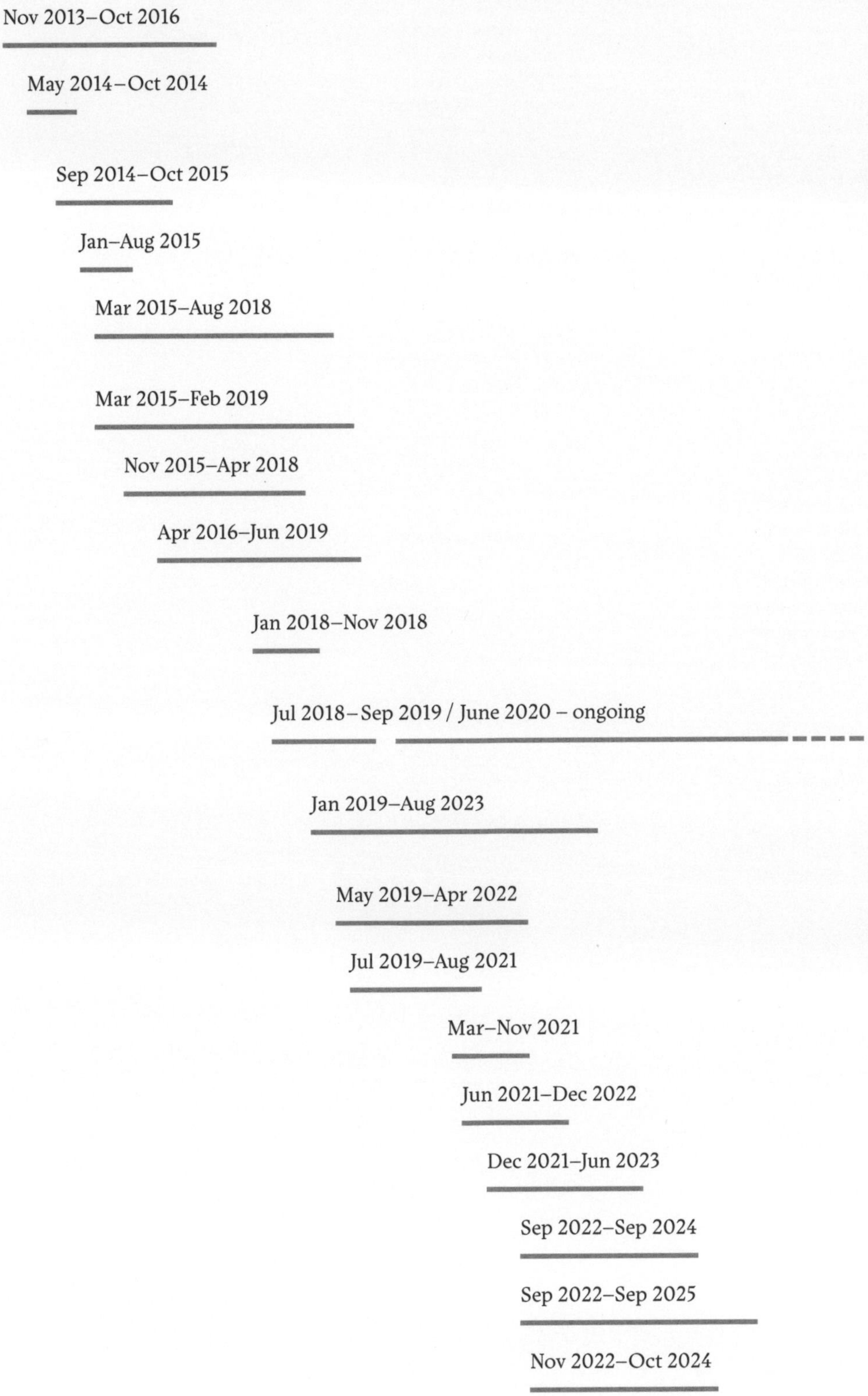
Nov 2013–Oct 2016
May 2014–Oct 2014
Sep 2014–Oct 2015
Jan–Aug 2015
Mar 2015–Aug 2018
Mar 2015–Feb 2019
Nov 2015–Apr 2018
Apr 2016–Jun 2019
Jan 2018–Nov 2018
Jul 2018–Sep 2019 / June 2020 – ongoing
Jan 2019–Aug 2023
May 2019–Apr 2022
Jul 2019–Aug 2021
Mar–Nov 2021
Jun 2021–Dec 2022
Dec 2021–Jun 2023
Sep 2022–Sep 2024
Sep 2022–Sep 2025
Nov 2022–Oct 2024

General

Project

| | | | | |
|---|---|---|---|---|
| AIAA | American Institute of Aeronautics and Astronautics | | FASTER | The Forward Acquisition of Soil and Terrain for Exploration Rover |
| A(L)M | Additive (Layer) Manufacturing | | GrAB | Growing As Building |
| CSA | Chinese Space Agency | | LIAR | Living Architecture |
| ECLSS | Environmental Control Life Support System/s | | SHEE | Self–deployable Habitat for Extreme Environments |
| ESA | European Space Agency | | Smartie | Smart Resource Management based on Internet of Things to support off–Earth manufacturing of Lunar infrastructures |
| EVA | Extravehicular Activity/s | | | |
| HVAC | Heating, Ventilation, and Air Conditioning | | | |
| ISS | International Space Station | | RAMA | Rover for Advanced Mission Applications |
| ISRU | In Situ Resource Utilisation | | | |
| IVA | Intravehicular Activity/s | | | |
| LEO | Low Earth orbit | | | |
| LSS | Life Support System/s | | | |
| MTF | Mobile Test Facility | | | |
| NASA | National Aeronautics and Space Administration | | | |
| NewSpace | Commercial, entrepreneurial, and private space launch and exploration companies and activities | | | |
| PLSS | Portable Life Support System | | | |
| SETI | Search for Extraterrestrial Intelligence | | | |
| TAS-I | Thales Alenia Space Italy | | | |
| TRL | Technology Readiness Level | | | |

## Travelling through the Extraterrestrial
p. 22–36

1 Díaz, E. (2018) We are all Aliens. *E-Flux.* 81. Available at: https://www.e-flux.com/journal/91/197883/we-are-all-aliens/ [Last accessed: 20 Jul 2022].

2 Mazé, R. (2017) 'Design and the Future: Temporal Politics of 'Making a Difference''. In: *Design Anthropological Futures.* R. C. Smith, K. T. Vangkilde, M. G. Kjaersgaard et al. (Eds.) London & New York: Routledge.

3 Loeb, A. (2021) *Extraterrestrial: The First Sign of Intelligent Life Beyond Earth.* Boston, MA: Mariner Books.

4 SETI is an acronym for 'Search for Extraterrestrial Intelligence'.

5 Tarter, J. & Tippett, K. (2020) Jill Tarter: It takes a Cosmos to make a Human. *On Being with Krista Tippett.* First Broadcast: 27 Feb 2020. Available at: https://onbeing.org/programs/jill-tarter-it-takes-a-cosmos-to-make-a-human/ [Last Accessed 20 Jul 2022].

6 Emmett, A. (2017) Hibernation for Space Voyages. *Air Space Magazine.* Available at: https://www.airspacemag.com/space/hibernation-for-space-voyages-180962394/ [Last accessed: 22 Jul 2022].

7 Tsiolkovsky, K. E. (1911) Letter written by K. E. Tsiolkovskiy to B. N. Vorob'yev, 19 Aug 1911.

8 Clarke, A. C. (1997) *3001: The Final Odyssey.* New York: Ballantine Books.

9 Morgan, R. (2002) *Altered Carbon.* London: The Ballantine Book Publishing Group.

10 Fuller, R. B. (1969). *Operating manual for spaceship earth.* New York: Simon and Schuster.

11 Kubrick, S., & Clarke, A. C. (1968). *2001: A space odyssey.* United States: Metro-Goldwyn-Mayer Corp.

12 Treaty on Principles Governing the Activities of States in the Exploration and Use of Outer Space, including the Moon and Other Celestial Bodies (Outer Space Treaty), opened for signature Jan. 27, 1967 18 UST 2410; 610 UNTS 205; 6 ILM 386 (1967).

13 Bauer, C. Bausmeyer, J., Claros, P. M. et al. (2019) Sustainable Moon. *ISU Team Project Report.* Illkirch-Graffenstaden (France) : International Space University.

14 Treaty on Principles Governing the Activities of States in the Exploration and Use of Outer Space, including the Moon and Other Celestial Bodies (Outer Space Treaty), opened for signature Jan. 27, 1967 18 UST 2410; 610 UNTS 205; 6 ILM 386 (1967).

15 The Artemis Accords: Principles for Cooperation in the Civil Exploration and Use of the Moon, Mars, Comets, and Asteroids (2020), https://www.nasa.gov/specials/artemis-accords/img/Artemis-Accords-signed-13Oct2020.pdf [https:// perma.cc/9RM7-EFAE].[Last accessed 26 Jan 2023].

16 The Antarctic Treaty, 402 U.N.T.S. 71, entered into force June 23, 1961. Protocol on Environmental Protection to the Environmental Treaty entered into force 1991

17 The Millenium Charter was authored collectively at a Space Architecture workshop organised by the AIAA DETC Aerospace Architecture Subcommittee in October 2002 at the World Space Congress in Houston.

18 (2002) *The Millenium Charter. Fundamental Principles of Space Architecture.* AIAA DETC Aerospace Architecture Subcommittee Space Architecture Workshop. Houston, Texas, USA: 12 October 2002. Available at: https://spacearchitect.org/wp-content/uploads/2020/06/The-Millennium-Charter.pdf [Last Accessed: 20 Jul 2022].

19 Bannova, O., Clar, R. & Sherwood B. (2008) "The Architecture of Space: Tools for Development In the 21st Century." in *Proc. of the International Astronautical Conference.* Glasgow, Scotland, 29 Sept – 3 Oct 2008.

## Designing for Outer Space: An Extreme Environment
p. 40–43

1 Armstrong, R. (2016) *Star Ark: A Living, Self-Sustaining Spaceship.* Springer: New York, NY: 300.

2 Space Architecture Technical Committee (2020) SATC Charter. *Space Architect.* Available from: http://spacearchitect.org/wp-content/uploads/2020/06/SATC-Charter.pdf. [Last accessed 6 Jun 2023].

3 These collaborations are not limited to individuals from these disciplines, however are often dominated by them.

4 Cohen, M. (2022). Innovation and Tradition in Human Spaceflight Architecture. Keynote Address, University of Lisbon Faculty of Architecture.

5 Ciardullo, C. Pailes-Friedman, R., Morris, M. et al. (2022) Bringing it Home: Finding Synergies Between Earth and Space Construction and Design. *51st International Conference on Environmental Systems ICES-2022-336 Proceedings.* St. Paul, Minnesota, 10–14 July 2022.

6 Häuplik-Meusburger, S. Bishop, S. L & Wise, J. A. (2022) Habitability and the Golden Rule of Space Architecture. *51st International Conference on Environmental Systems ICES-2022-336 Proceedings.* St. Paul, Minnesota, 10–14 July 2022.

7 Finckenor, M. M. (2018) Aerospace Materials and Applications. NASA. Available from: https://ntrs.nasa.gov/citations/20160013391 [Last Accessed: 20 Jul 2022].

8 Ciardullo, C. Pailes-Friedman, R., Morris, M. et al. (2022) Bringing it Home: Finding Synergies Between Earth and Space Construction and Design. *51st International Conference on Environmental Systems ICES-2022-336 Proceedings.* St. Paul, Minnesota, 10–14 July 2022.

9 Buchli, V. (2013) *An Anthropology of Architecture.* Routledge: London & New York.

## The Pursuit of Adaptability
p. 80–81

1 Häuplik-Meusburger, S. Bishop, S. L & Wise, J. A. (2022) Habitability and the Golden Rule of Space Architecture. *51st International Conference on Environmental Systems ICES- 2022-336 Proceedings.* St. Paul, Minnesota, 10–14 July 2022.

## The New Vernacular in Outer Space
p. 106–107

1 Jones, H. W. (2018) 'The Recent Large Reduction in Space Launch Cost.' *48th International Conference on Environmental Systems Proceedings.* Albuquerque, New Mexico, 8–12 July 2018.

2 Benaroya, H, Cannon, K. & Imhof, B. (2022) *Habitats on Moon and Mars built from local material.* Space Specials with Barbara Imhof and guests Haym Benaroya & Kevin Cannon. Radio Orange. First Broadcast: 17.05.2022, Available at: https://cba.fro.at/557370. [Last Accessed 6 Jul 2023].

3 Moses, R. W. & Bushnell, D. M. (2016) *Frontier In-Situ Resource Utilization for Enabling Sustained Human Presence on Mars.* USA: NASA. Available at: https://ntrs.nasa.gov/citations/20160005963. [Last Accessed: 22 Jul 2022].

4 Benaroya, H, Cannon, K. & Imhof, B. (2022) *Habitats on Moon and Mars built from local material.* Space Specials with Barbara Imhof and guests Haym Benaroya & Kevin Cannon. Radio Orange. First Broadcast: 17.05.2022, Available at: https://cba.fro.at/557370. [Last Accessed: 22 Jul 2022].

## When the Natural State is Motion
p. 131–132

1 Meggs, L. (2017) From Tools to Trash: Marshall's Payload Stowage Team Tracks It. *NASA.* Available from: https://www.nasa.gov/mission_pages/station/research/payload_stowage [Last Accessed: 17 Jan 2023].

2 NASA. (2012, Nov 19) Departing Space Station Commander Provides Tour of Orbital Laboratory. [Video file.]. *YouTube.* https://www.youtube.com/watch?v=doN4t5NKW-k. [Last Accessed: 17 Jan 2023].

3 Atkinson, N. (2021) Since There's no Up or Down in Space, How do our Brains Deal With This? *Universe Today.* Available from: https://www.universetoday.com/149559/since-theres-no-up-or-down-in-space-how-do-our-brains-deal-with-this/ [Last Accessed: 17 Jan 2023].

## Replicating Terrestrial Systems
p. 135–137

1 The timeframe at which moderate concentration levels of toxins or pathogens reveal their impacts may only become clear over long periods of time.

2 ESA (2019) New life support system cleans air during full-house Space Station. *ESA.* Available at: https://www.esa.int/Science_Exploration/Human_and_Robotic_Exploration/New_life_support_system_cleans_air_during_full-house_Space_Station [Last Accessed: 26 Jan 2023].

3 Generic, R. J. (2008) Mission Operations Directorate. *Operations Division: National Aeronautics and Space Administration: Lyndon B. Johnson Space Center Houston, Texas.* Available at: https://nasa.gov/centers/johnson/pdf/359891main_125_MAL_G_J_2_E1.pdf [Last Accessed: 5 Sep 2022].

4 NASA (2019) Spacewalk Spacesuit Basics. *NASA.* Available at: https://www.nasa.gov/feature/spacewalk-spacesuit-basics [Last Accessed: 26 July 2022].

5 Renamed the Life Support Systems Integration Facility (LSSIF), see citation below.

6 Connolly, J. H. (2002) 'Architecture'. In: Lane, H. W., Sauer, R. L., Feeback, D. L., eds. *Isolation: NASA Experiments in Closed-Environment Living: Advanced Human Life Support Enclosed System Final Report.* San Diego: Univelt, Incorporated. pp. 131-139.

7 *Ibid.*

## Mission Preparation: Simulating Future Explorations
p. 175–177

1 Zhang, J. (2021) LUNAR PALACE 1 based space food and nutrition research. In Proceedings: 43rd COSPAR Scientific Assembly. 28 January – 4 February.; Space.com Staff (2018) Lunar Palace 1: China's One-Year Mock Moon Mission in Pictures. *Space.* Available at: https://www.space.com/40610-china-mock-moon-mission-Lunar-palace-1-photos.html [Last accessed: 26 Jan 2023].

2 Mingzhu, L. (2020) Lunar Palace 1: To the Moon and Beyond. *Beihang University.* Available at: https://ev.buaa.edu.cn/info/1103/2695.htm [Last accessed: 26 Jan 2023].

3 Hao, Z., Zhu, Y., Feng, S. & Meng, C. (2019) Effects of long term isolation on the emotion change of "Lunar Palace 365" crewmembers. *Science Bulletin.* 64(13). DOI:10.1016/j.scib.2019.05.019.

4 Popper, J. & Imhof, B. (2018) The Joy of Sets presents Capricorn Two: A Mars Mission Simulation. *69th International Astronautical Congress (IAC) Proceedings,* Bremen, Germany, 1-5 October 2018.

5 Amils, R., Fernández-Remolar, D., & The Ipbsl Team (2014). Río tinto: a geochemical and mineralogical terrestrial analogue of Mars. *Life (Basel, Switzerland), 4*(3), 511–534. https://doi.org/10.3390/life4030511.

6 Imhof, B., Hogle, M., Davenport, B. et al. (2017) Project Moonwalk: lessons learnt from testing human robot collaboration scenarios in a Lunar and Martian simulation. *68th International Astronautical Congress (IAC) Proceedings*, Adelaide, Australia, 25–29 September 2017.

7 Allouis, E., Marc, R. Gancet, J. et al. (2017) FP7 FASTER project – Demonstration of Multiplatform Operation for Safer Planetary Traverses. 14th Symposium on Advanced Space Technologies in Robotics and Automation Proceedings, Leiden, The Netherlands, 20–22 June 2017.

8 Executive Study: Moonwalk, Moonwalk Consortium (2016) Executive Study: Moonwalk. Available at: https://liquifer.com/moonwalk-executive-summary-october-2016/ [Last Accessed: 19 Jun 2023].

## The Space–Earth Continuum
p. 204–207

1   Sagan, C. (1994) Pale Blue Dot:Pale Blue Dot: A Vision of the Human Future in Space. New York: Random House.

2   Lovelock, J. (1979) *Gaia: A New Look at Life on Earth.* Oxford: Oxford University Press.

3   Klepeis, N. E., et al. (2001) The National Human Activity Pattern Survey (NHAPS): A Resource for Assessing Exposure to Environmental Pollutants. *Journal of Exposure Science & Environmental Epidemiology.* 11(3): 231–52, https://doi.org/10.1038/sj.jea.7500165.

4   United Nations Environment Programme. (2022) *2022 Global Status Report for Buildings and Construction: Towards Zero-emission, Efficient and Resilient Buildings and Construction Sector.* United Nations Environment Program. Available at: https://globalabc.org/sites/default/files/2022-11/FULL%20REPORT_2022%20Buildings-GSR_1.pdf. [Last Accessed: 4 Apr 2023].

5   Ciardullo, C. Pailes-Friedman, R., Morris, M. et al. (2022) Bringing it Home: Finding Synergies Between Earth and Space Construction and Design. 51st International Conference on Environmental Systems ICES-2022-336. 10-14.07.2022, St. Paul, Minnesota.

CAVEAT
*Sources:*

–   The quotes that appear throughout this volume have been taken from Barbara Imhof's Space Specials, a podcast series that she has hosted since 2006. This is also true for the excerpts included in the Antarctic and Pacific Island Expeditions. All of these episodes are stored on the Cultural Broadcasting Archive website, which can be accessed here: https://cba.fro.at/podcast/space-specials.

## Mars
p. 47

1   NASA Content Administrator (2008) Valles Marineris: The Grand Canyon of Mars. *NASA.* Available at: https://www.nasa.gov/multimedia/imagegallery/image_feature_83.html. [Last Accessed: 27 Feb 2023].

2   De La Torre L. B. (2022) What is the Habitable Zone? *NASA Exoplanet Exploration: Planets Beyond our Solar System.* Available at: https://exoplanets.nasa.gov/resources/2255/what-is-the-habitable-zone/. [Last Accessed: 27 Feb 2023].

3   Wall, M. (2021) Mars was always too small to hold onto its oceans, rivers and lakes. *Space.* Available at: https://www.space.com/mars-too-small-ocean-rivers-lakes. [Last Accessed: 27 Feb 2023].

4   Cooper, K. (2022) Massive Mars dust storms triggered by heat imbalances, scientists find. *Space.* Available at: https://www.space.com/mars-climate-dust-storms-heat-imbalance. [Last Accessed: 27 Feb 2023].

5   *Ibid.*

6   Wernicke, L. J., & Jakosky, B. M. (2021). Martian hydrated minerals: A significant water sink. *Journal of Geophysical Research*: Planets, 126.

7   Wernicke, L. J., & Jakosky, B. M. (2021). Martian hydrated minerals: A significant water sink. *Journal of Geophysical Research*: Planets, 126., NASA Content Administrator (2008) Valles Marineris: The Grand Canyon of Mars. *NASA.* Available at: https://www.nasa.gov/multimedia/imagegallery/image_feature_83.html. [Last Accessed: 27 Feb 2023].

8   Maderer, J. (2021) Making Martian Rocket BioFuel on Mars. *Georgia Tech College of Engineering.* Available at: https://coe.gatech.edu/news/2021/10/making-martian-rocket-biofuel-mars. [Last Accessed: 27 Feb 2023]., Kruyer, N. S. Realff, M. J., Sun, W. et al. (2021) Designing the bioproduction of Martian rocket propellant via a biotechnology-enabled in situ resource utilization strategy. *Nature Communications.* 12:6166. https://doi.org/10.1038/s41467-021-26393-7.

9   David. L. (2013) Toxic Mars: Astronauts Must Deal with Perchlorate on the Red Planet. *Space.* Available at: https://www.space.com/21554-mars-toxic-perchlorate-chemicals.html. [Last Accessed: 27 Feb 2023].

10  Economou, T. et. al. (1997) The Chemical Composition of Martian Rocks and Soil: Preliminary Analyses. Available at: https://mars.nasa.gov/MPF/science/lpsc98/1711.pdf. [Last Accessed: 27 Feb 2023].

11  Schleppi, J. Gibbons, J. Groetsch, A. et al. (2018) Manufacture of glass and mirrors from Lunar regolith simulant. *Journal of Material Science.* 54:3726–3747. https://doi.org/10.1007/s10853-018-3101-y.

*Mars Table Sources:*

–   Williams, D. (2021) Planetary Factsheet Mars. *NASA Solar System Exploration.* Available at: https://nssdc.gsfc.nasa.gov/planetary/factsheet/marsfact.html. [Last Accessed: 27 Feb 2023].

–   Barnett, A. (2022) Mars by the Numbers. *NASA Solar System Exploration..* Available at: https://solarsystem.nasa.gov/planets/mars/by-the-numbers/. [Last Accessed: 27 Feb 2023].

–   Davis. P. (2021) Mars In Depth. *NASA Solar System Exploration.* Available at: https://solarsystem.nasa.gov/planets/mars/in-depth/. [Last Accessed: 27 Feb 2023].

–   Turner, J., Anderson, P., Lachlan-Cope, T. et al. (2009). Record low surface air temperature at Vostok station, Antarctica. *Journal of Geophysical Research.* 114:D24. doi:10.1029/2009JD012104

–   El Fadli, K. I., Cerveny, R. S. Burt. C. C. et al. (2013) World Meteorological Organization Assessment of the Purported World Record 58°C Temperature Extreme at El Azizia, Libya (13 September 1922). *Bulletin of the American Meteorological Society.* 94:2. https://doi.org/10.1175/BAMS-D-12-00093.1.

## The Moon
p. 85

[1] Plain, C. (2020) NASA finds evidence two early planets collided to form Moon. *NASA.* Available at: https://www.nasa.gov/feature/nasa-finds-evidence-two-early-planets-collided-to-form-moon [Last Accessed: 27 Feb 2023].

[2] Mathewson, S. (2018) Days on Earth Are Getting Longer, Thanks to the Moon. *Space.* Available at: https://www.space.com/40802-earth-days-longer-moon-movement.html. [Last Accessed: 27 Feb 2023].

[3] Davis, P. (2022) Earth's Moon Overview. *NASA Solar System Exploration.* Available at: https://solarsystem.nasa.gov/moons/earths-moon/overview/. [Last Accessed: 27 Feb 2023].

[4] Mathewson, S. (2017) 'Levitating' Moon Dust Explained in New NASA Study. *Space.* Available at: https://www.space.com/35240-moon-dust-levitates-nasa-study.html. [Last accessed: 27 Feb 2023].

[5] Harbaugh, J. (2022) Fission Surface Power, Technology Demonstration Missions. *NASA.* Available at: https://www.nasa.gov/mission_pages/tdm/fission-surface-power/index.html [Last Accessed: 27 Feb 2023].

[6] ESA (2019) Helium-3 mining on the Lunar surface. *ESA.* Available at: https://www.esa.int/Enabling_Support/Preparing_for_the_Future/Space_for_Earth/Energy/Helium-3_mining_on_the_Lunar_surface [Last Accessed: 27 Feb 2023].

[7] Strickland, A. (2022) Plants have been grown in Lunar soil for the 1st time ever. *CNN.* Available at: https://edition.cnn.com/2022/05/12/world/plants-Lunar-soil-scn/index.html [Last Accessed: 27 Feb 2023].

*Moon Table Sources:*

– Williams, D. (2021) Planetary Factsheet Moon. *NASA.* Available at: https://nssdc.gsfc.nasa.gov/planetary/factsheet/moonfact.html. [Last Accessed: 27 Feb 2023].

– Barnett, A. (2022) Earth's Moon by the Numbers. *NASA.* Available at: https://solarsystem.nasa.gov/moons/earths-moon/by-the-numbers/. [Last Accessed: 27 Feb 2023].

– Hille, K. (2020) LUNAR RECONNAISSANCE ORBITER: Temperature Variation on the Moon. *NASA.* Available at: https://Lunar.gsfc.nasa.gov/images/lithos/LROlitho7temperaturevariation27May2014.pdf. [Last Accessed: 27 Feb 2023].

– Davis, P. (2022) Earth's Moon In Depth. *NASA Solar System Exploration.* Available at: https://solarsystem.nasa.gov/moons/earths-moon/in-depth/. [Last Accessed: 27 Feb 2023].

– Turner, J., Anderson, P., Lachlan-Cope, T. et al. (2009). Record low surface air temperature at Vostok station, Antarctica. *Journal of Geophysical Research.* 114:D24. https://doi.org/10.1029/2009JD012104.

– El Fadli, K. I., Cerveny, R. S. Burt. C. C. et al. (2013) World Meteorological Organization Assessment of the Purported World Record 58°C Temperature Extreme at El Azizia, Libya (13 September 1922). *Bulletin of the American Meteorological Society.* 94:2. https://doi.org/10.1175/BAMS-D-12-00093.1.

## Orbit
p. 113

[1] J. (2022) Recycling in space: Wannabe or Reality? *European Space Agency.* Available at: https://blogs.esa.int/cleanspace/2022/01/10/recycling-in-space-wannabe-or-reality/. [Last Accessed: 27 Feb 2023].

*Orbital Table Sources:*

– Mars, K. (2022) Gateway. *NASA.* Available at: https://www.nasa.gov/gateway. [Last Accessed: 27 Feb 2023].

– ESA (2018) Reaching the Space Station Infographic. *ESA.* Available at: https://www.esa.int/ESA_Multimedia/Images/2018/06/Reaching_the_Space_Station_infographic. [Last Accessed: 27 Feb 2023].

– Gerstenmaier, W. & Crusan, J. (2018) CisLunar and Gateway Overview. *NASA.* Available at: https://www.nasa.gov/sites/default/files/atoms/files/cisLunar-update-gerstenmaier-crusan-v5a_tagged_0.pdf. [Last Accessed: 27 Feb 2023].

– Frost, R. (2017) What are the highest and lowest points in the orbit of the ISS? *Forbes.* Available at: https://www.forbes.com/sites/quora/2017/03/15/what-are-the-highest-and-lowest-points-in-the-orbit-of-the-iss/?sh=583709a74053. [Last Accessed: 27 Feb 2023].

– NASA (2020) Astronauts answer student questions. *NASA Johnson.* Available at: https://www.nasa.gov/centers/johnson/pdf/569954main_astronaut%20_FAQ.pdf. [Last Accessed: 27 Feb 2023].

– Adamek, C. (2019) Gateway System Requirements. *NASA.* Available at: https://ntrs.nasa.gov/api/citations/20190029153/downloads/20190029153.pdf. [Last Accessed: 27 Feb 2023].

– ESA with Oldenburg, K. (2021) Temperatures on the Space Station. Available at: https://www.esa.int/ESA_Multimedia/Images/2021/08/Temperatures_on_the_Space_Station. [Last Accessed: 27 Feb 2023].

– Hille, K. (2014) Lunar Reconnaissance Orbiter. *NASA.* Available at: https://Lunar.gsfc.nasa.gov/images/lithos/LROlitho7temperaturevariation-27May2014.pdf. [Last Accessed: 27 Feb 2023].

– Brown, M. (2022) NASA Lunar Gateway: Launch Window, Specs and Orbit of the Moon's Space Station. *Inverse.* Available at: https://www.inverse.com/innovation/nasa-Lunar-gateway-codex. [Last Accessed: 27 Feb 2023].

## Earth
p. 141

[1] Richie, H. (2019) Half of the world's habitable land is used for agriculture. *Our World in Data*. Available at: https://ourworldin-data.org/global-land-for-agriculture. [Last Accessed: 1 Mar 2023].

[2] Hayes, J.M. (2016) Evolution of the Atmosphere. *Britannica*. Available at: https://www.britannica.com/topic/evolution-of-the-atmosphere-1703862 [Last accessed 10 Jan 2023].

[3] Buis, A. (2019) Earth's Atmosphere: A Multi-layered Cake. NASA *Global Climate Change*. Available at: https://climate.nasa.gov/news/2919/earths-atmosphere-a-multi-layered-cake/ [Last accessed 10 Jan 2023].

*Earth Table Sources:*

– Williams, D. (2021) Earth Factsheet. *NASA*. Available at: https://nssdc.gsfc.nasa.gov/planetary/factsheet/earthfact.html. [Last accessed 10 Jan 2023].

– Barnett, A. (2022) Earth By the Numbers. *NASA*. Available at: https://solarsystem.nasa.gov/planets/earth/by-the-numbers/. [Last accessed 10 Jan 2023].

– Turner, J., Anderson, P., Lachlan-Cope, T. et al. (2009). Record low surface air temperature at Vostok station, Antarctica. *Journal of Geophysical Research*. 114:D24. https://doi.org/10.1029/2009JD012104

– El Fadli, K. I., Cerveny, R. S. Burt. C. C. et al. (2013) World Meteorological Organization Assessment of the Purported World Record 58°C Temperature Extreme at El Azizia, Libya (13 September 1922). *Bulletin of the American Meteorological Society*. 94:2. https://doi.org/10.1175/BAMS-D-12-00093.1.

## Underwater
p. 183

[1] National Ocean Service (2002) Sound waves propagate faster than in air. *National Oceanic and Atmospheric Administration*. Available at: https://oceanexplorer.noaa.gov/explorations/sound01/background/acoustics/acoustics.html [Last Accessed: 4 Apr 2023].

[2] Mondal, A. & Banerjee, S. (2022) Effect of productivity and seasonal variation on phytoplankton intermittency in a microscale ecological study using closure approach. Sci Rep 12:5939. https://doi.org/10.1038/s41598-022-09420-5.

[3] National Ocean Service (2010) Where is all of Earth's water? *National Oceanic and Atmospheric Administration*. Available at: https://oceanservice.noaa.gov/facts/wherewater.html. [Last Accessed: 4 Apr 2023].

[4] National Ocean Service (2010) Thermohaline Circulation. *National Oceanic and Atmospheric Administration*. Available at: https://oceanservice.noaa.gov/education/tutorial_currents/05conveyor1.html. [Last Accessed: 4 Apr 2023].

[5] ESA (2019) Learning to live with the laws of motion. ESA. Available at: https://www.esa.int/Science_Exploration/Human_and_Robotic_Exploration/Astronauts/Learning_to_live_with_the_laws_of_motion. [Last Accessed: 4 Apr 2023].

*Underwater Table Sources:*

– USGS (2022) Why is the Ocean Salty? *U.S. Department of the Interior*. Available at: https://www.usgs.gov/faqs/why-ocean-salty. [Last accessed 10 Jan 2023].

– Allaby (1994) Euphotic Zone. *European Environmental Agency*. Available at: https://www.eea.europa.eu/help/glossary/eea-glossary/euphotic-zone. [Last accessed 10 Jan 2023].

– National Ocean Service (2021) How does pressure change with ocean depth? *National Oceanic and Atmospheric Administration*. Available at: https://oceanservice.noaa.gov/facts/pressure.html. [Last accessed 10 Jan 2023].

– Wikipedia (2022) Underwater Acoustics. *Wikipedia*. Available at: https://en.wikipedia.org/wiki/Underwater_acoustics. [Last accessed 10 Jan 2023].

– Levy, R. (2022) Sea Surface Temperature. NASA *Earth Observatory*. Available at: https://earthobservatory.nasa.gov/global-maps/MYD28M. [Last accessed 10 Jan 2023].

## LIQUIFER

is a microenterprise with a base in Vienna, Austria, and another in Bremen, Germany. LIQUIFER is committed to collaborative work with international partners from a wide array of disciplines. A small core team with the support of associated experts make it possible that LIQUIFER plays a valuable role in the field of human space exploration.

## LIQUIFER  Core Team

Barbara Imhof  trained as an architect under Wolf D. Prix of Coop Himmelb(l)au. She holds a PhD from the University of Technology Vienna and a Masters in Space Studies from the International Space University. She is a Space Architect, design researcher, and educator. Following her Masters at ISU Barbara interned at NASA Johnson Space Centre, supporting the design of a large simulator for a human mission to Mars as part of Project BIOPLEX. Her work focuses on designing for extreme environments and space. With these she combines two main work paths: one follows designing systems, mission elements and habitats for living beyond the Earth's atmosphere and the other path translates biological role models into the design of architecture. She enjoys working across disciplines and in the past 20 years has collaborated with a wide selection of well-known artists, most notably during her time on the research vessel for the 1st Antarctic Biennale in 2017 and then in 2018 as part of the SUPERFLEX Deep Sea Minding project run by TBA21 Academy. She has an extensive record of teaching (space) design and architecture at universities worldwide most recently as Adjunct Faculty at ISU and as a Project Lead on a number of FWF funded projects at "die Angewandte". Additionally, Barbara has been producing the Space Specials podcast for more than 10 years.

Waltraut Hoheneder  holds a diploma in architecture from the Academy of Applied Arts in Vienna, studio Wolf D. Prix and a diploma in commercial sciences from the Vienna University of Economics and Business. She worked in the fields of market research, product and architectural design before becoming a design

architect in large-scale projects at Coop Himmelb(l)au until 2003. Together with Barbara Imhof she established LIQUIFER Systems Group as a private company in 2005 after the foundation of LIQUIFER as an association by Barbara Imhof, Susmita Mohanty and Norbert Frischauf in 2003. Waltraut is a senior designer at LIQUIFER Systems Group as well as  a co-manager Within this role she focuses on the development of transformable systems and the integration of regenerative infrastructure in building systems. Her recent engagement in research on microbial systems is driven by the huge potential to provide sustainable solutions for contemporary challenges on Earth by implementing these systems into our built environment. Parallel to her work at LIQUIFER she taught within architectural design programmes at the Vienna University of Technology until 2018.

René Waclavicek  originally studied architecture at TU Wien. He is a building construction engineer with extensive experience in architecture and design. In addition to his engineering expertise, he was trained as a mason and carpenter. After joining LIQUIFER in 2005, René continued to work on a number of terrestrial construction projects, including the new construction of the Landesberufsschule, Graz with Michael Walraff.  His skills are applied in interdisciplinary research as well as in architecture and design, especially in the application of parametric methods and the development of geometries. More recently he has been working with 3D printing technologies to be developed for the Lunar and Martian surface. René was made partner at LIQUIFER in 2019 and has been instrumental in design and visualisation of LIQUIFER's portfolio.

## LIQUIFER Co-Founder

Susmita Mohanty  trained as an electrical engineer at Gujarat University, Ahmedabad, before completing two Masters degrees, the first in Industrial Design from the National Institute of Design and the second in Space studies from the International Space University in Strasbourg. Her studies finished with a PhD on Integrated High-Fidelity Planetary Mission

Simulators from Chalmers University of Technology, Göteborg, Sweden. Susmita is the only space entrepreneur in the world to have co-founded space companies on three different continents: EARTH2ORBIT, Bangalore (2009-2021), LIQUIFER, Vienna (2003-ongoing) and MOONFRONT, San Francisco (2001-07). Prior to becoming an entrepreneur, she worked for the International Space Station Program at Boeing in California and did a short stint at NASA Johnson. In 2021, she launched India's first dedicated space think tank Spaceport SARABHAI. In 2019, Susmita was selected as one of BBC's 100 Women laureates crafting a female-led future. In 2017, she was featured on the cover of Fortune Magazine. She is a member of the World Economic Forum Global Future Council for Space Technologies.

## LIQUIFER Consultants

Stephen Ransom  gained a BSc honours degree in Aeronautical Engineering at the University of Salford, England. He began his career in the British aerospace industry in 1961. Following work in the UK, Stephen joined ERNO Raumfahrttechnik in Bremen on the Spacelab programme as a systems engineer for the Spacelab Pallet. After a brief return to the aircraft industry with work at Vereinigte Flugtechnische Werke and MBB's Special Projects Division he rejoined the space division of EADS in 1983 in their advanced projects office in Bremen. His work dealt with future spacecraft and planetary exploration including the International Space Station Columbus programme. During this time he undertook studies on robotic missions to the Moon and Mars, space habitats, EURECA utilisation, an unmanned in-orbit recoverable vehicle, and planetary aerobots. He subsequently established himself as an aerospace consultant in 2005 and became an affiliated consultant to LIQUIFER Systems Group. In addition, he has given lectures on space programmes, the history of the development of aerospace technology to the German Aerospace Society and Universities.

Bob Davenport  gained a BSc in Physics and an MSc in Materials Science from the University of Leeds. He was a space systems engineer with

40+ years of experience in the development and testing of manned space systems, interface definitions, operations scenarios and payload integration for the European module Columbus on the International Space Station (ISS). Bob began his career with Hawker Siddeley Dynamics in Stevenage, U.K., before joining ERNO Raumfahrttechnik, Bremen, Germany (now Airbus Defence and Space) as systems engineer on the Spacelab project. Concurrently with his Airbus activities, Bob was active as a scientific assistant in the Department of Geosciences, University of Bremen, researching the global carbon cycle using remote sensing. Bob joined LIQUIFER as an internal consultant in 2013 and has since worked on several EU/ESA funded projects such as Moonwalk, TRAILER, URBAN, Eden-ISS, Smartie, I-Hab and Paving The Road.

Chris Gilbert initially trained as an engineer at the University of Leicester and began his professional career as a design engineer at Hawker Siddeley Dynamics (now Airbus Defence and Space) in Stevenage, Hertfordshire, working on launch vehicles and satellites. Following completion of a Master of Business Administration degree at Cranfield School of Business he took up a position as system engineer at ERNO Raumfahrttechnik GmbH (now Airbus Defence and Space) in Bremen, Germany, working on the Spacelab programme. He subsequently developed new responsibilities in marketing, business development and strategy, with particular focus on space exploration and space policy. From 2011 – 2012 he attended the George Washington University's Space Policy Institute in Washington, DC, as a visiting scholar, studying issues of international cooperation in space exploration. Since being associated with LIQUIFER Chris has been involved in a number of projects, providing advice and guidance on management and strategic aspects.

Daniel Schubert studied at the Technical University of Berlin and has an engineering diploma in industrial engineering with an emphasis on aerospace and production techniques. In 2011, he initiated the EDEN group at the DLR Institute of Space Systems for technology investigations

on Bio-regenerative Life Support Systems and since served as the team leader of this group. His research expertise is set on habitat interface analysis and plant accommodation and dynamic plant production planning. Throughout many projects for ESA, EU, Bundesministerium für Bildung und Forschung (BMBF), Wirtschaftsförderung Bremen (WfB), Dr. Schubert proved his management- and team leading skills. Outstanding is the Eden – ISS project. He led this project with 15 international partners (incl. LIQUIFER), including the organisation of the deployment mission of the greenhouse system at the Antarctic research station Neumayer III in 2017/18. Daniel's relationship with LIQUIFER started with habitat design studies in 2011 and over the past 10 years has incorporated numerous outreach activities, proposal writing, and engineering expertise.

Monika Lipinska holds a Masters in Architecture from Lund University and a Masters in Space Studies from the International Space University. The focal point of her research during these degrees was on developing architectural and biotechnological solutions for building habitable environments which support human performance and wellbeing in space. During her studies, she worked in architectural offices in Tokyo, Copenhagen, and San Francisco. Currently (2023) she is pursuing her PhD at the Hub for Biotechnology in the Built Environment at Newcastle University in collaboration with NASA Ames Research Centre, where she researches biofabrication strategies for building inhabitable structures on the Moon and Mars. Monika is a co-founder of Bio-Futures for Transplanetary Habitats, a research platform that aims to explore and enable research on transplanetary habitats through an emphasis on biosocial and biotechnological relations. Monika came to LIQUIFER at the beginning of her Space Architecture journey, as a summer intern in 2017. During her continuing studies she gradually began doing research and design work with LIQUIFER before becoming an internal consultant in 2020.

Prologue

Brent Sherwood is a space architect with over 35 years of professional experience in the space industry. He is Senior Vice President, Space Systems Development, for Blue Origin. SSD develops in-space systems for Earth orbital, cislunar, and lunar business. Brent was at the NASA Jet Propulsion Laboratory for 14 years, leading concept and proposal methods and planetary mission formulation. Prior, he was at Boeing for 17 years, leading human exploration concept engineering, space station module manufacturing engineering and commercial space program development. Brent has advanced degrees in architecture (Yale) and aerospace engineering (University of Maryland). He is the 2020 recipient of the American Society of Civil Engineers Columbia Medal and an Associate Fellow of the American Institute of Aeronautics and Astronautics. He edited the book *Out of This World: The New Field of Space Architecture* and has published over 50 papers on the exploration, development and settlement of space.

Epilogue

Christina Ciardullo is an Architect, co-founder of the award-winning space architecture firm SEArch+ and PhD Researcher at the Yale Center for Ecosystems and Architecture. With undergraduate degrees in astronomy and philosophy, and a Masters of Architecture from Columbia University, Christina bridges a career between practice and research at the intersection of the natural sciences and the built environment. She has worked in design positions at New York City Planning, NASA's Habitability Design Center, Ennead Architects, Foster+Partners and LAVA. Supported by a NASA Consortium Grant, she was the 2015/2016 Carnegie Mellon University Anna Kalla Fellow and the 2016 Buckminster Fuller Institute Fellow. In her work with Yale CEA, Christina has collaborated with the United Nations Environment Program on thought leadership in urban agriculture and the embodied and operational carbon of building materials. Committed to work in space that supports sustainable development on Earth, she lectures and publishes on the relationship between energy and resource-efficient practice in space and earth.

## Editorial Team

Jennifer Cunningham holds a Masters in Material Culture and Design Anthropology from University College London. She works as a researcher, writer and editor within the fields of architecture and design. Her work has been included in Copenhagen Design Biennale, Oslo Architecture Triennale and London Design Festival. Jennifer is pursuing a PhD in Digital Media and Architecture at the University of Lisbon, and is a researching editor with the Future Observatory at the Design Museum in London where she undertakes research and commissions work supporting the UK's response to the climate crisis. Jennifer worked as an associate at LIQUIFER to develop the concept, undertake editorial management and co-author Living Beyond Earth: Architecture for Extreme Environments.

Matthew Ponsford studied Philosophy at University College London. He is a London-based journalist and editor who has written for MIT Technology Review, New Scientist, National Geographic, Thomson Reuters, CNN, The Guardian, Financial Times Weekend, BBC, Deutsche Welle and Wired UK. He is co-leader of The Manuals, a global research project on ecosystem restoration, which has hosted participatory design events at the Tate Modern, The Barbican Centre and Royal Botanic Gardens, Kew. Matt worked on LIQUIFER Living Beyond Earth: Architecture for Extreme Environments as a copyeditor.

A number of the projects highlighted in this book would not have been possible without support from the European Union. The following sentences recognise their support, and provide details of the funding.

SHEE: The project has received funding from the European Union's Seventh Framework Programme for research, technological development and demonstration under grant agreement no. 312747.

Moonwalk: The project has received funding from the European Union's Seventh Framework Programme for research, technological development and demonstration under grant agreement no. 607346.

Faster: The project has received funding from the European Union's Seventh Framework Programme for research, technological development and demonstration under grant agreement no. 284419.

RegoLight: This project was funded by Horizon 2020 Research and Innovation Programme, Grant agreement ID: 686202.

Eden ISS: This project was funded by Horizon 2020 Research and Innovation Programme, Grant agreement no. 636501.

Living Architecture: The project has received funding from the European Union's Horizon 2020 Research and Innovation Programme under Grant Agreement no 686585.

Unless otherwise stated below, all photographs are credited to Bruno Stubenrauch and all visualisations are credited to LIQUIFER. Images listed below are copyright to their owner and ordered by page number.

Acknowledgements

LIQUIFER are thankful to everyone who has worked with the team over the years. Valentin Eder, a co-managing director and designer was crucial to the development of the practice from 2011–2014. Petra Gruber was a pivotal co-lead in the GRaB project. We also want to thank (in alphabetical order): Olisa Agulue, Anna Balint, Darren Berlein, Irmgard Derschmidt, Norbert Frischauf, Sandra Häuplik-Meusburger, Kjell Herrmann, Molly Hogle-Stiefel, Melanie Klähn, Barbara Kolb, Sonia Leimer, Ewa Lenart, Paul Mayr, Damjan Minovski, Kürsad Özdemir, Georg Pamperl, Wolfgang Prohaska, Lutz Richter, Anne-Marlene Ruede, Nina Soltani, Anna Stürzenbecher, Angelo Vermeulen and Kaspar Vogel. With his permission LIQUIFER has used 3D models from Swiss artist Max Grüter for their visualisations. We are extremely grateful to those without whom this book wouldn't have been possible: the team at PARK Books who supported our vision, friends who gave feedback early in the development of the book, Matthew Ponsford for his deft editing skills and of course to designers Nik Thoenen and Hannah Sakai.

In memoriam of Bob Davenport.

Concept:
  Jennifer Cunningham & LIQUIFER
Authors:
  Jennifer Cunningham, Waltraut Hoheneder, Barbara Imhof, René Waclavicek, Brent Sherwood and Christina Ciardullo
Copy editing:
  Matthew Ponsford
Proofreading:
  Jennifer Cunningham, Waltraut Hoheneder and Barbara Imhof

Design:
  Nik Thoenen, Hannah Sakai
Image processing:
  Pascal Petignat, Nik Thoenen
Paper:
  Lahnur, Multicolor Mirabell, Lona Art
Typefaces:
  MicroNova, Lexik
Printing and binding:
  Gugler GmbH

© 2023 LIQUIFER and Park Books AG, Zurich

Park Books
Niederdorfstrasse 54
8001 Zurich
Switzerland
www.park-books.com

Park Books is being supported by the Federal Office of Culture with a general subsidy for the years 2021–2024.

ISBN 978-3-03860-345-0

Federal Ministry
Republic of Austria
Arts, Culture,
Civil Service and Sport